D1453140

THE LOGIC OF
RELIABLE INQUIRY

LOGIC AND COMPUTATION IN PHILOSOPHY

Series Editors: Wilfried Sieg (Editor-in-Chief), Clark Glymour, and Teddy Seidenfeld

This series will offer research monographs, collections of essays, and rigorous textbooks on the foundations of cognitive science emphasizing broadly conceptual studies, rather than empirical investigations. The series will contain works of the highest standards that apply theoretical analyses in logic, computation theory, probability, and philosophy to issues in the study of cognition. The books in the series will address questions that cross disciplinary lines and will interest students and researchers in logic, mathematics, computer science, statistics, and philosophy.

Mathematics and Mind
Edited by Alexander George

The Logic of Reliable Inquiry
Kevin T. Kelly

THE LOGIC OF
RELIABLE INQUIRY

KEVIN T. KELLY

New York   Oxford
OXFORD UNIVERSITY PRESS
1996

Magale Library
Southern Arkansas University
Magnolia, Arkansas
DISCARD

Oxford University Press

Oxford New York
Athens Auckland Bangkok Bombay
Calcutta Cape Town Dar es Salaam Delhi
Florence Hong Kong Istanbul Karachi
Kuala Lumpur Madras Madrid Melbourne
Mexico City Nairobi Paris Singapore
Taipei Tokyo Toronto

and associated companies in
Berlin Ibadan

Copyright © 1996 by Kevin T. Kelly

Published by Oxford University Press, Inc.,
198 Madison Avenue, New York, New York 10016

Oxford is a registered trademark of Oxford University Press

All rights reserved. No part of this publication may be reproduced,
stored in a retrieval system, or transmitted, in any form or by any means,
electronic, mechanical, photocopying, recording, or otherwise,
without the prior permission of Oxford University Press.

Library of Congress Cataloging-in-Publication Data

Kelly, Kevin T.
The logic of reliable inquiry / Kevin T. Kelly.
p.   cm.—(Logic and computation in philosophy)
Includes bibliographical references and index.
ISBN 0-19-509195-7
1. Research—Methodology. 2. Research—Evaluation. 3. Logic,
Symbolic and mathematical. 4. Cognitive learning theory.
I. Title. II. Series.
Q180.55.M4K45 1996
121—dc20   95-17166

Illustrations in text are
by Kevin T. Kelly

1 3 5 7 9 8 6 4 2

Printed in the United States of America
on acid-free paper

To Clark Glymour: teacher, friend, and colleague

Preface

There are many proposed aims for scientific inquiry: to confirm or to falsify hypotheses, to explain or to predict events, to maximize expected utilities, or to find hypotheses that are simple or that cohere with our other beliefs in some logical or probabilistic sense. This book is devoted to a different proposal: that the scientist's background assumptions should logically entail that his method will eventually arrive at the truth. I refer to this methodological property as *logical reliability*.

Interest in logical reliability does not originate with me. It arises from an interdisciplinary body of material dating from the early 1960s called *formal learning theory*. Unlike standard statistics, which draws its strength from the theory of probability, formal learning theory draws its insights from the theory of computability. This difference in theoretical background leads to a distinct perspective on a variety of methodological issues. Accordingly, this book should interest philosophers, scientists, statisticians, cognitive scientists, or anyone interested in the aims of science and inductive reasoning. It should also interest mathematicians, logicians, and computer theorists as an alternative application of standard results and constructions.

I had at least three goals in mind when I undertook this project. The first was to bring learning theory to a wider audience. In keeping with this aim, the first four chapters involve a great deal of philosophical background and motivational considerations. Thereafter, the book is organized by topic rather than by order of difficulty, so the reader will find that each chapter is fairly easy at first and builds to more substantial results toward the end. Finally, the text is peppered with cartoons throughout, both to ease the mind over tricky constructions and to make philosophical points as quickly and easily as possible.

My second goal was to develop and to explore a systematic framework in which various standard learning-theoretic results could be seen as special cases of simpler and more general considerations. In chapters 4 through 12, I show how simple topological and recursion-theoretic complexity concepts can account for what is common to the standard settings. This general point of view also raises new questions, such as whether learning-theoretic diagonalization can always establish that an inductive problem is unsolvable (chapter 5).

My third goal was to clarify the relationship between the resulting framework and other standard issues in the philosophy of science, such as probability, causation, and relativism. These topics are developed in chapters 13 through 15.

I did not aim to produce a comprehensive summary of the learning-theoretic literature. (*Systems That Learn*, by D. Osherson, M. Stob, and S. Weinstein (1986) is a fine survey.) Instead of reviewing the extensive results on such standard topics as recursive function identification and language learnability, I have provided just enough discussion to show how they relate to the topics I have elected to present.

The book has exercises and might be considered as a text in various departments, including computer science, philosophy, and cognitive science. I managed to cover the first eight chapters in a philosophy seminar involving students who had not yet seen the equivalent of Rogers (1987) or Cutland (1986). With such a background, more could be expected.

I have been assisted by able colleagues and students at every turn. The material in chapter 12 was done partly in collaboration with Clark Glymour, without whose support and encouragement the project would never have been completed. Many of the results were obtained in close collaboration with Cory Juhl and Oliver Schulte. Oliver Schulte also read the draft and provided valuable corrections to the text. Cory Juhl has used the book in a graduate seminar at the University of Texas, Austin. Much of chapter 13 results from lively discussions with Teddy Seidenfeld. Wilfried Sieg steered me to the application of the Keisler *n*-sandwich theorem in chapter 12. Chapter 8 was written in response to a seminar question by Terence Spies. Dana Scott provided me with a crucial reference that contributed to the main result of that chapter. Chapter 14 benefited from discussions with Richard Scheines and Peter Spirtes, our resident experts on causality. Some of Richard's suggestions showed up as improvements in the definition of actual causation presented there, and Peter provided useful comments on the final draft of the chapter. Many definitions and results are natural generalizations of work by Osherson, Stob, and Weinstein. I am indebted for support in the winter of 1989 from Risø Research Center and Roskilde University Center in Denmark while I was working on the material in chapter 15 and to Stig Andur Pedersen, who encouraged the project from the beginning and read an earlier draft of the manuscript. Vincent Hendricks kindly provided corrections on the final draft. Finally, I appreciate the tender support of my wife, Noriko Nagata.

Pittsburgh, Pennsylvania   K.T.K.
June 1993

Contents

THE LOGIC OF
RELIABLE INQUIRY

1

Introduction

Inquiry begins with ignorance and aims to replace it with true belief. Scientific method is supposed to be our best means for effecting this change. But success is not supposed to be a matter of mere luck or accident. A reliable method is in some sense guaranteed to converge to the truth, given the scientist's assumptions. Guarantees come in various grades. The subject of this book is *logical reliability*, which requires that the method converge to the truth in *each* possible circumstance consistent with the background assumptions of the scientist. In other words, logical reliability demands that the scientist's background assumptions logically entail that the method will in some sense converge to the truth.

The logical reliabilist perspective on scientific method has enjoyed a long history. In the *Meno*, Plato seems to assume that inquiry must be logically guaranteed to terminate with certainty that its answer is correct. Similar requirements were common among ancient skeptics such as Sextus Empiricus. This very strict version of logical reliabilism is still evident in the work of Descartes, Hume, and Kant, over two thousand years later. Subsequently, it was proposed by C. S. Peirce that inquiry might converge to the truth without providing a clear sign that it has done so. This liberalized proposal was developed in the context of the frequentist interpretation of probability by H. Reichenbach.[1] The connection between reliable convergence and modern techniques in mathematical logic and computability theory was introduced by Reichenbach's student H. Putnam, who recognized the strong analogy between a machine taking inputs and a scientist reading data and applied it to a critique of R. Carnap's probabilistic theory of confirmation.[2] The connection between

---

[1] Kelly (1991).
[2] Putnam (1963, 1965).

induction and computability was developed independently by E. M. Gold, who applied it to the analysis to the problem of child language acquisition, where the "scientist" is the child and the "hypothesis" is a mental structure encoding syntactic competence.[3] Because of this application, the computational, reliabilist perspective on methodology is now known under the somewhat misleading rubric of *formal learning theory*.[4] Interest in the theory spread from linguistics to the study of learning machines in artificial intelligence and has now become a recognized branch of computer science. Formal learning theory is the direct inspiration for what follows.

The logical reliabilist conceives of inductive problems the way a computer scientist conceives of computational problems. A solution to a computational problem (an algorithm) is supposed to be guaranteed by its mathematical structure to output a correct answer on every possible input. This logical perspective stands in sharp contrast with the received view among inductive methodologists, who are often more interested in whether belief is justified by evidence, or whether beliefs fit together in a pleasantly coherent way, or whether evidence can force everyone to agree, whether or not what is agreed upon is true. Logical reliabilism simply demands of inductive methods what is routinely required of algorithms.

There seems to be an obvious and fatal flaw in this approach. The most elementary point in the philosophy of science is that *inductive* inference is not *deductive*. Long-division algorithms can be formally guaranteed to output correct answers, but that is because long division is a deductive task. Induction, on the other hand, admits of no such guaranteed, algorithmic solution. But this is a false dichotomy. The division algorithm is logically guaranteed to converge to the right answer with *certainty* (i.e., it outputs the correct answer and then *halts*, thereby signaling that the output is correct). But a method may be logically guaranteed to stabilize to the truth without ever giving a sign that it has found the truth. Then the user is logically guaranteed to have the truth eventually, but may never be certain that the method has found it. So an inductive method can be logically guaranteed to converge to the truth without yielding mathematical certainty of the sort provided by the division algorithm. As we successively weaken the standard of convergence, more and more inductive problems will come to be solvable by methods logically guaranteed to converge to the truth. Thus, we can classify inductive problems into precise layers of difficulty, corresponding to the senses of convergence by which they are solvable and we can do so without going beyond the standard analytical framework of mathematical logic. In particular, we may do so without invoking probabilities, confirmation, or any other notion of properly inductive justified belief.

This book is devoted to the logic of reliable inquiry in the sense just described. Just as in the theory of computability, we can ask successively more general methodological questions such as: whether there exists a reliable method

---

[3] Gold (1965, 1967).

[4] For a survey, cf. Osherson et al. (1986).

for a given problem on given assumptions; whether there exist minimal assumptions on which a given problem is solvable; whether a given problem has a reliable solution that is optimal in terms of convergence time; whether there exist complete architectures for reliable hypothesis assessment and discovery, in the sense that a method constructed according to the architecture will be reliable if any method is; whether reliable discovery implies the possibility of reliable prediction, and so forth. All of these questions will be answered in later chapters, many of them in chapter 4.

Strictly speaking, this book is about logical reliability, not knowledge, justification, probability, or confirmation. But since epistemology is in large part a response to skepticism and skeptics have associated inductive justification with logically reliable methods, our discussion will have some bearing on epistemological discussions. For example, it has become fashionable to argue that normative epistemology must either somehow be an Archimedian point from which we may judge the inductive practices of other cultures, or it must collapse into mere historical and sociological reporting on the activities of science.[5] The sort of methodology just outlined breaks the back of this dilemma. It is neither historical nor sociological, but logical. Nonetheless, it does not criticize inductive practice absolutely, but only relative to the assumptions the scientist brings to inquiry. Such a logic of inquiry puts us in a position to criticize mismatches between assumptions, methods, and the aim of finding the truth, without putting us in a position to criticize any of these parameters in isolation from the others.

A central issue in epistemology and the philosophy of science is *underdetermination*. Underdetermination occurs, roughly, when the same data may arise regardless which of two competing hypotheses is correct. This is just a special way to argue that no logically reliable inductive method exists relative to the scientist's background assumptions. But as we have seen, there are many different grades of reliability corresponding to different notions of convergence. I propose to define underdetermination as the impossibility of reliability (in a given sense) relative to the assumptions at hand. Thus, each sense of reliability corresponds to a notion of underdetermination, so that the more stringent the conception of success demanded, the more underdetermined questions there will be. We may then hope to map out the structure of degrees of underdetermination in a systematic manner. It turns out that there are infinite hierarchies of underdetermination in this sense, in which simple set-theoretic operations can be used to build problems of ever greater underdetermination. These hierarchies will be presented in chapter 4. This imposes some discipline on methodological debates, for a method that converges only in the limit may be defended from criticism if the hypothesis in question is underdetermined in the short run. To compare short-run solutions to easy problems with limiting solutions to hard problems is to compare apples and oranges.

Computationally bounded inductive rationality has been drawing increased attention among epistemologists. Traditional methodological analysis has

---

[5] Rorty (1979): 275–276.

centered on quixotic "ideal agents" who have divine cognitive powers, but who nonetheless bump into walls in the dark just like the rest of us. This idealization is harmless only so long as what is good for ideal agents is good for their more benighted brethren. It will be seen, however, that rules that seem harmless and inevitable for ideal agents are in fact disastrous for computationally bounded agents. A prime example is the simple requirement that a hypothesis be dropped as soon as it is inconsistent with the data, a rule endorsed by almost all ideal methodologies. It turns out that there are problems for which computable methods can be consistent in this sense, and some computable method is a reliable solution, but no computable, consistent method is a reliable solution (chapter 7). Such disasters suggest that computational methodology should be developed from scratch, rather than as an incidental afterthought to an ideal analysis. The strong analogy between logical reliability and computability yields a clear account of the difference between ideal and computable inquiry. In chapter 7 it will be shown how ideal and computational limitations on the agent can be seamlessly interwoven from top to bottom in a logical reliabilist characterization of the scope of computable inductive inference.

For each notion of bounded cognitive power there is the task of providing a structural characterization of the sorts of inductive questions that a computationally bounded agent of a given sort can be guaranteed to converge to the truth about. Such characterizations might well be called *transcendental deductions*, since they provide necessary and sufficient structural conditions for reliable inductive inference from experience. I will examine characterizations of hypothesis assessment, discovery, and prediction for ideal hypothesis assessment methods (chapter 4), for computable assessment methods (chapter 7), for finite-state assessment methods (chapter 8), for ideal discovery methods (chapter 9), for computable discovery methods (chapter 10), and for ideal and computable prediction methods (chapter 11). These characterizations are the unifying core of the text. They reveal strong analogies between ideal and computational agents, as well as sharp limitations on the inductive power of the latter. The characterizations are given in terms of the complexity of the relation of truth or correctness relative to the background assumptions of the scientist. It turns out that in the computationally bounded case, the relevant concepts of complexity automatically embody the constraints required for ideal agents with no cognitive restrictions. The difference between the two is exactly the difference between Borel complexity and arithmetical complexity, a standard topic in mathematical logic.

Definite theories of the world do not have to yield computable predictions, in the sense that some computer exists that returns the prediction for time t when provided with t as input. A natural question for computable methodology is how computable a hypothesis must be if it is to be possible for a computable method to reliably converge to the truth about it. A series of answers to these questions (corresponding to different notions of convergence) will be provided (chapter 7). The most interesting of them shows how a computable method can refute a hypothesis with certainty on any possible, infinite data stream even when the predictions made by the hypothesis are in a precise sense infinitely uncomputable. These results draw upon standard relations between implicit and explicit definability in arithmetic. Such results illustrate the fact that the philosophy of science has lagged behind mathematical logic in its conception of what a logical approach to scientific methodology might be. A logical, scientific methodology is not necessarily confined to the study of simple methods pieced together out of elementary, logical relations such as refutation by or entailment of the data. It is a logical perspective on all possible methods; a perspective that should draw upon the best and the deepest insights that logicians and computability theorists have been able to discern. This book should be understood as just an elementary step in that direction.

It has been popular since Kant to insist that the logic of science concerns rules for testing or for justifying belief in particular hypotheses, while the process of finding hypotheses to test or to justify is a matter of empirical psychology or sociology.[6] On the logical reliabilist view, however, discovery and assessment are simply two different problems that may or may not have reliable solutions. The hoary dictum that there is no logic of discovery is rejected in favor of a unified, logical account of discovery and assessment in which what is justified (relative to the aim of finding the truth) is the choice of a particular method (whether for discovery or for assessment). This point of view raises various questions: Is there a general architecture for turning reliable hypothesis tests into reliable discovery procedures? Is assessment possible when discovery is? And how can discovery be harder for computable agents than for ideal agents? These questions will be investigated in chapters 9 and 10.

Pragmatists tend to assimilate the aim of finding the truth to the aim of predicting the future. If we ignore the constraints of computability, this reduction is valid, since once a true, predictive theory is found, it can be used to truly predict the future. But when we take computational constraints seriously, we can exhibit inductive problems in which it is possible for a computer to stabilize to a theory that makes correct, computable predictions even when it is not possible for a computer to eventually always get the next prediction right. The moral is that the aim of finding the truth cannot be assimilated to that of prediction in the computational case. This result will be derived in chapter 11.

A major objective of science is to infer causes. Aristotle thought that necessary connections can be inferred reliably from observational data. Bacon held the more guarded view that they can be inferred from experimental data. Hume was skeptical even about that. It is therefore interesting to see what the logical reliabilist perspective has to say about the connection between experimentation and causal inference, a topic developed in chapter 14.

One of the greatest concerns in the philosophy of science over the last three decades has been the idealistic thesis that truth and evidence are *theory-laden*. This thesis is sometimes thought to undermine the reliabilist perspective in favor of some sort of purely descriptive sociological investigation of actual scientific

---

[6] Kant (1950), Popper (1968), Carnap (1950), Hempel (1965), and Laudan (1980).

practice. I disagree. What is required is a reliabilist analysis that takes the possibility of such dependencies into account, so that even though data and truth depend to some (unknown) extent upon our own beliefs and concepts, one may still speak of methods guaranteed to arrive at the (relative) truth by means of (theory-laden) data. This approach will be investigated in a preliminary way in chapter 15.

Almost all contemporary, epistemological discussion assumes some recourse to the theory of probability. A remarkable feature of logical reliability is that it provides a nonprobabilistic perspective on scientific inquiry. Since probability is the usual way of looking at induction, it is natural to consider how the two approaches differ. We will see in chapter 13 that probabilistic reliability is a much more lenient standard of success than is logical reliability. In fact, countenancing a zero probability of failure collapses the logical hierarchy of underdetermination down to a tractable level, making every inductive problem for which the measure is defined solvable in the limit.[7] This seems to indicate the superiority of probability over logic as a metatheory for reliability.

I address this concern in chapter 13. In order to emphasize the difference between logical and probabilistic reliability, a simple example is given in which updating by Bayesian conditionalization can fail to converge to the truth in the limit on each member of an uncountable set of possible data streams, even though updating in this manner is guaranteed to succeed with unit probability and even though trivial methods are logically guaranteed to succeed.

To further underscore the differences between the probabilistic and learning theoretic approaches, it is shown that there is a hypothesis that a computer can refute with certainty but that *no* Bayesian updater definable in arithmetic can even gradually decide. Hence, Bayesian recommendations can be an impediment to the reliability of even highly idealized, uncomputable agents.

Then I consider the important question of what it is about probability that gives rise to Bayesian convergence. Tracing through a few standard convergence results, we find that a crucial premise is countable additivity, an axiom that is often defended on grounds of technical expedience. But the axiom is false on a standard interpretation of probability (frequentism), and it is also rejected by some prominent members of the competing school (personalism). The reason for its rejection by some personalists is that it forces a "bias" into probabilities over countable partitions. I will argue that it is exactly this questionable, enforced bias (of the near future over the limit of inquiry) that makes countable additivity such a potent weapon against underdetermination and skepticism. To make the case, I present a simple inductive problem that is solvable with probability 1 assuming countable additivity but that is not solvable with probability 1 by any possible method (conditionalization or otherwise) with respect to some finitely but not countable additive measure. These results illustrate the deep epistemological significance of countable additivity and also

---

[7] Assuming countable additivity.

show that when this allegedly technical assumption is dropped, the negative arguments of logical reliabilism may be of interest to the probabilist.

As a postscript to the probabilistic discussion, the reader is asked to envision what the philosophy of mathematics would look like if measure 1 convergence theorems based on countable additivity were invoked in questions about computability and provability. The answer is that the infinite hierarchy of uncomputability and unprovability that has become standard fare in proof theory and the philosophy of mathematics would collapse just the way the hierarchy of underdetermination collapses when the same theorems are routinely invoked in empirical contexts. This poses the question why such negative results should be of interest to the philosophy of mathematics but not to the philosophy of science.

The book is organized according to the following outline:

   I. Philosophical perspective (chapter 2)
  II. The logic of hypothesis assessment
      A. Ideal (chapters 3, 4, 5)
      B. Turing computable (chapters 6, 7)
      C. Finite state, complexity bounded (chapter 8)
 III. The logic of discovery
      A. Ideal (chapter 9)
      B. Computable (chapter 10)
  IV. The logic of prediction (chapter 11)
   V. Applications and generalizations
      A. Logic (chapter 12)
      B. Probability (chapter 13)
      C. Experiment and causation (chapter 14)
      D. Relativism (chapter 15)

Chapter 2 presents with pictures and intuitive descriptions the basic formal elements of the logical reliabilist account of method. Chapter 3 develops the basic apparatus of skeptical arguments against the possibility of a reliable method. These arguments are personified by inductive demons, who present data in as confusing a manner as is possible, consistent with the background assumptions of the scientist being fooled. Chapter 4 presents a topological framework in which to characterize necessary and sufficient conditions for the existence of reliable methods guaranteed to converge to the truth in different ways. It also settles questions about the existence or nonexistence of optimally reliable and optimally fast inductive methods. In a sense, chapter 4 is the central chapter of the book. All subsequent chapters draw upon the basic analysis developed in detail there. Chapter 5 relates the demonic arguments of skepticism to reducibility arguments in descriptive set theory and also shows how methodological results can depend upon the foundations of set theory. Chapter 6 develops a formal analogy between uncomputability arguments and skeptical arguments against inductive reliability. Chapter 7 revisits the questions of chapter 4 for the case of computable methods, illustrating once again the strong analogy between computation and induction. Chapter 8 extends the analysis of chapter 7 to more restricted models of computability, including primitive recursion and finite-state automata.

Chapter 9 introduces the logic of discovery, in which the task is to produce a true theory directly from the data and background knowledge. Chapter 10 extends the analysis of chapter 9 to the computable case. Chapter 11 characterizes ideal and effective prediction (in the sense that eventually the next prediction is always right) and shows that computable prediction may not be possible when computable discovery of a computable, predictive theory is.

The remaining chapters generalize or apply what has come before. Chapter 12 examines the special application in which theories are stated in a first-order language, so that we can consider relations between first-order model theory and the purely topological and recursion-theoretic arguments of the preceding chapters. Chapter 13 compares the logical reliabilist perspective with the more standard, probabilistic one, with emphasis on the role of countable additivity in statistical convergence theorems. Chapter 14 discusses what happens when the scientist is permitted to manipulate his environment, rather than merely to observe it. Chapter 15 entertains the possibility that data is "theory-laden" and that the truth can change as a function of what the method conjectures. Chapter 16 summarizes what has come before in a conversation between a learning theorist and a more traditional philosopher of science.

There are a few chapters in which nontrivial logical or mathematical concepts are used without introduction, but these are not essential for understanding what comes later and may be skipped on a first reading. Chapter 5 assumes some passing familiarity with the axioms of Zermelo-Fraenkel set theory. Chapter 12 assumes some familiarity with the basic concepts of model theory. The rest of the chapters are self-contained, though of course some mathematical sophistication will be of use throughout.

I include proofs in the text, rather than banishing them to "technical" appendices. Many of the arguments involve explicit constructions of reliable inductive methods or of demonic strategies for feeding misleading data to a method to make it diverge from the truth. These constructions are an essential component of an intuitive understanding of the subject and should not be skipped.

The exercises encourage the reader to think through the arguments and concepts presented in the text and suggest related or more general applications. The reader who attempts them will come away with a much stronger feel for the subject. Starred exercises tend to be difficult or suggest broader issues.

2

Reliable Inquiry

1. Background Assumptions

The scientist starts out with some assumptions. Officially speaking, learning theory is not in the business of challenging these assumptions, though it might very well play a role in such a challenge should it turn out that assumptions nobody wants to grant are required for reliable inquiry. The scientist inquires because his assumptions are incomplete. We will employ a standard device and represent the scientist's background assumptions as the set $\mathcal{K}$ of all possible ways the world could be that would make them true (*Fig. 2.1*). This is essentially what a probabilist does when he chooses a sample space. So far as the scientist is concerned, the actual world is in $\mathcal{K}$. If his assumptions are true, it really is.

2. Methods and Data Streams

The scientist does not interact with his world directly, but only through a data stream. By this I mean nothing more or less than that if the data stream had been the same and the world different, the scientist would have done the same things. I will assume that more and more interaction with the world leads to more and more data so that the scientist continually receives some *infinite data stream* in the limit.[1] The scientist sees only some finite initial segment of this data stream at any given time.

I assume that there is some countable collection H of hypotheses the scientist may propose or investigate and that hypotheses are discrete, finite

---

[1] By "infinite sequence" I shall always mean an ω-sequence or a total function defined on the natural numbers.

possible worlds

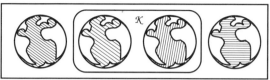

Figure 2.1

objects. Hypotheses might be sentences in some language, but they might also be computer programs, as when a physicist or a psychologist produces a computer model of a system under study. The program itself makes no claim, but it can still be thought of as being correct or incorrect insofar as it duplicates the behavior of the modeled system.

Scientists produce actions and conjectures in light of the data they have scanned so far and in light of any hypothesis they are are assigned to investigate (*Fig. 2.2*). *Actions* may be any acts by the scientist (other than producing conjectures) that may be relevant to the data he will receive in the future. For example, an action may be the implementation of an experimental setup, such as filling a test tube and heating it.

The *conjectures* produced by scientists differ depending on the different types of problems they face. The sort of situation considered paradigmatic by philosophers and by some statisticians is one in which the scientist is handed some hypothesis *h* and is enjoined to test it against the data. A *test* method takes a hypothesis and some finite data sequence as inputs and conjectures a 1 or a 0, indicating *true* and *false* or *accept* and *reject*, respectively. Some methodologists insist that science is a matter of assigning numbers in the [0, 1] interval to given hypotheses on the basis of data. Such a method is referred to as an *inductive logic* or a *confirmation theory* by philosophers and as an *update rule* by Bayesian statisticians. I will refer collectively to all methods that take a hypothesis and data as input and that output a number in the [0, 1] interval (possibly only 0 or 1) as *assessment methods* (*Fig. 2.3*).

In another sort of situation, the scientist is given data and is enjoined to produce a hypothesis (*Fig. 2.4*). Statisticians refer to methods of this type as

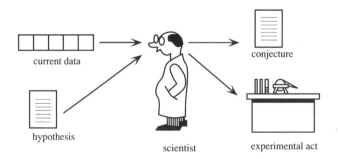

Figure 2.2

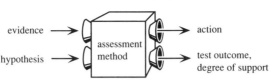

Figure 2.3

estimators. Computer scientists call them *learners* or *identification procedures.* Philosophers speak of *logics of discovery.* I adopt the general term *hypothesis generator* to range over all such methods.

In the philosophy of science, the slogan is still sometimes heard that there is no logic of discovery. By this, philosophers mean either that discovery is not subject to logical analysis the way test or confirmation is or that it is impossible to give explicit rules for discovery. The perspective adopted in this book is quite different. Regarding the first point, one may conceive of assessment as binary discovery (h vs. $\neg h$), so that there may be a difference in degree of complication between the two cases, but no difference relevant to the applicability of logical analysis. Regarding the second point, it will be shown that discovery can be demonstrably easier than assessment, at least so far as finding a correct answer is concerned.

Finally, a scientist may be given some data and may then be asked to guess what some future datum will be (*Fig. 2.5*). Methods of this sort are referred to as *extrapolators* or *predictors.* I will employ the latter term to range over all such methods.

So in general, a *method* is a total function that maps finite sequences of data (and perhaps a given hypothesis) to pairs consisting of actions and conjectures of the relevant type. The careful distinctions between discovery, assessment, and prediction may seem pedantic, but it turns out that none of these problems is generally interreducible to the other for computable agents, so we must not conflate them.

Methods may also be distinguished by their cognitive powers. For example, a method can be easily computable, computable with difficulty, uncomputable, or very uncomputable. We will pay special attention to the extent to which these various restrictions compromise inductive reliability.

Yet another way in which methods are distinguished is by their satisfaction of various philosophical recommendations. For example, a method is a *conditionalizer* just in case its conjectures are always the result of conditioning some joint probability measure on the available evidence. Also, we say that a generator is *consistent* just in case its current hypothesis is never refuted by the

Figure 2.4

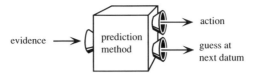

Figure 2.5

available data and the background assumptions. We will examine the effects (particularly the debilitating effects) on reliability of following such recommendations.

In what remains of this chapter, I focus on hypothesis assessors to avoid tedious repetition of similar but distinct definitions. Discovery and prediction will be treated in their own right in chapters 9 to 11.

3. Data Protocols

The *data protocol* is simply the world's disposition to associate data with the actions of the scientist (*Fig. 2.6*). We have assumed that the scientist produces his acts and conjectures in light of the current data. A moment's reflection reveals that this could happen in a variety of ways. Most generally, the data could depend on the whole method employed by the scientist, as when a devious but deranged patient covertly studies the textbooks of whatever psychotherapist he is assigned to so he can get himself released by giving the right answers to the therapist's questions.

In the more usual case, the data protocol is assumed to depend only on what the scientist actually does. This still admits the odd possibility that the scientist's future acts could influence the current data, as in cosmology, when temporal loops are entertained. But in nearly all other applications, it is assumed that the data protocol is *historical*, so that only past acts of the scientist are relevant to what is observed (*Fig. 2.7*). In fact, scientists often proceed in a manner that they hope will sever the influence of history on the current datum (e.g., by washing their test tubes thoroughly and starting the experiment all over again in an isolated setting). Then the data protocol is said to be *immediate*.

When the data protocol is historical, we can represent it as a process that

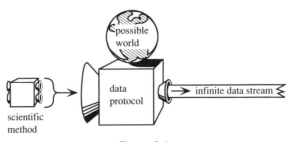

Figure 2.6

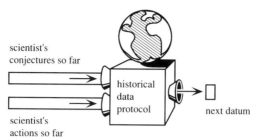

Figure 2.7

produces the current datum in light of the scientist's past conjectures and actions.

The scientist and the data protocol then interact in a loop in the following manner. The scientist starts out by producing a blind conjecture and act in the face of no evidence. Then the protocol and world produce a datum in response to the scientist's act. In general, the scientist bases his *n*th action and conjecture on the total data produced by the protocol by stage $n-1$, and the protocol produces its *n*th datum on the basis of the acts performed by the scientist up to stage $n-1$ (*Fig. 2.8*).

Another class of restrictions on the data protocol concerns the types of acts the evidence received by the scientist depends on. When the data protocol does not depend on the scientist at all, it is said to be *passive* or to represent passive observation on the part of the scientist (*Fig. 2.9*).

Passive data protocols are indicative of situations like that of the observational astronomer, who can only sit and watch the stars move wherever they please, though even in such cases the scientist must aggressively set up his telescopes and computers to record phenomena that otherwise would surely be missed.

When the data stream depends on conjectures as well as acts, it is said to be *theory-laden*. As the name suggests, Theory-ladenness arises from the idealistic proposal that the scientist's current ideas about nature ineluctably shape or color the data he collects to test them (*Fig. 2.10*).

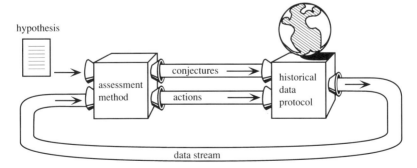

Figure 2.8

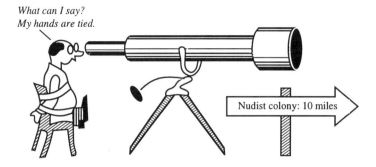

Figure 2.9

Chapters 1 through 13 will assume that the data protocol is passive. Issues that arise from nontrivial experimentation will be introduced in chapter 14. Chapter 15 addresses some issues raised by theory-ladenness.

In any event, I do not assume that the data produced by a data protocol are true, correct, reliable, or even linguistically well formed. The data may all be false. They may all be meaningless. But that doesn't mean they are not useful. For example, data that are always false, or that are true at even times and false at odd times are just as useful as data that are always true. What matters is how much the scientist's knowledge $\mathcal{K}$ entails about how the data stream is generated.

4. Truth and Global Underdetermination

I have spoken so far of the scientist's interest in finding the truth. Truth depends on the hypothesis and the state of the world, but since the scientist's actions affect the data, among other things, it also depends on the scientist's method. Thus, we will consider *truth* to be a fixed relation between possible worlds, scientific methods, and hypotheses (*Fig. 2.11*).

Since classical times, it has been realized that when truth depends on an "underlying" reality rather than on the data stream generated through the

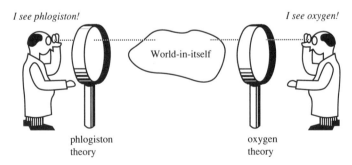

Figure 2.10

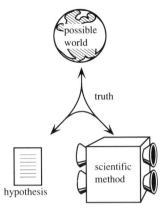

Figure 2.11

scientist's interaction with that reality, the data can in principle be the same for eternity whether or not the hypothesis in question is true (*Fig. 2.12*). In other words, there can be two possible worlds assigning opposite truth values to a given hypothesis such that the same data arises for eternity regardless which world is actual. When this situation obtains, we say that the hypothesis is *globally underdetermined* relative to the scientist's assumptions $\mathcal{K}$ and the scientist's method. I speak of global underdetermination because the data streams produced by the respective worlds are identical for eternity, so that even an ideal agent who could see the infinite future all at once could not reliably determine whether or not the hypothesis is true. When global underdetermination obtains regardless of the scientist's actions, we say that the underdetermination is *absolute*.

Example 2.1   Dreamers, demons, and evil scientists

The oldest sort of argument for global underdetermination plays on our own assumptions about how sense perception works. Sense perception involves physical signals from the sense organs to the brain. But it is fully consistent with these assumptions that some outside influence can break into the system

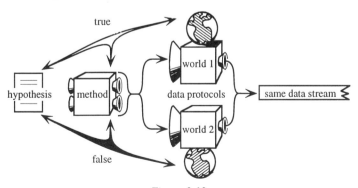

Figure 2.12

Figure 2.13

and feed spurious signals to the brain. Classical skeptics put the matter in terms of dreaming and illusion.[2] Medieval authors put it in terms of God's power to make human meat and blood look like ordinary bread and wine.[3] Descartes put the matter in terms of a malicious demon who aims to fool us. For our age, the argument is updated by an appeal to the medical and information processing technology of the future (*Fig. 2.13*):

> Here is a science fiction possibility discussed by philosophers: imagine that a human being ... has been subjected to an operation by an evil scientist. The person's brain ... has been removed from the body and placed in a vat of nutrients which keeps the brain alive. The nerve endings have been connected to a super-scientific computer which causes the person whose brain it is to have the illusion that everything is perfectly normal. There seem to be people, objects, the sky, etc; but really all the person ... is experiencing is the result of electronic impulses travelling from the computer to the nerve endings.[4]

Example 2.2   Models of general relativity

A standard issue in the philosophy of physics is the problem of determining the global metrical or topological structure of the universe. Strong assumptions about the nature of the protocol by which a cosmologist records measurements are granted without complaint. Demons that make us see rulers and clocks that are not there are flatly ignored. But this perfect understanding of the data protocol does not preclude global underdetermination. Such underdetermination can arise, for example, in a relativistic universe in which galaxies recede from one another at nearly the speed of light. In such cases, each observer may have access to light from only a small region of the universe. This region can

[2] Plato (1931): 482.
[3] John Buridan, *Questions on Aristotle's Metaphysics*, Book II, Question 1 in Hyman and Walsh (1982).
[4] Putnam (1990): 6.

be explanded to a full model of the general theory of relativity in topologically diverse ways.[5]

Example 2.3   The propensity interpretation of probability

Probability is subject to a variety of interpretations. According to the *propensity* interpretation, probability is a feature of the world that can be correctly described by attaching numbers to events. On this view, the statement $P(S) = 0$ is a hypothesis about the world that may or may not be correct. According to propensity theorists, S may happen even though its propensity is 0, and S may fail to happen when its propensity is 1. Indeed, an infinite sequence of probabilistically independent events $S_1, S_2, \ldots$ can occur even when each of them has propensity 0.[6] Thus, the propensity hypothesis $P(S) = r$ is globally underdetermined.

Example 2.4   Theoretical entities

Physics explains observable events by means of unobservable or *theoretical entities*. Since these things cannot be seen, the data can presumably be the same for eternity whether or not they exist.

5.   The Philosophy of Global Underdetermination

We have considered some prima facie examples of global underdetermination, but philosophers have debated whether global underdetermination is possible, even in principle. *Semantic realists* accept the examples at face value and concede that global underdetermination is possible in principle.[7] The contradictory position is argued by *empiricists*. In ordinary language, empiricism is usually taken to be the idea that scientific arguments should appeal to evidence. In that sense, everyone is an empiricist. In philosophical discussions, however, empiricism is a nontrivial thesis about meaning rather than about method. According to the empiricist, a hypothesis is meaningful only insofar as it is either *analytic* (true by meaning or convention) or *synthetic* (it *reduces* in some sense to a claim about the data stream). Since analytic hypotheses are necessarily true and synthetic hypotheses do not go beyond the data stream, no meaningful hypothesis can be globally underdetermined on the empiricist view. Either there is a way to detect whether there is really a bottle on the

---

[5] Glymour (1977), Malament (1977).

[6] For example, Levi (1983).

[7] A semantic realist is always free, however, to dispute whether a concrete case truly is a case of global underdetermination. There may be subtle and unnoticed structure in a given inductive problem that is missed by a coarse analysis in which it is concluded that the truth of the hypothesis in question is globally underdetermined.

table, or talk about real bottles over and above our ways of detecting them is gibberish.[8]

There are different versions of empiricism corresponding to different views about what counts as data and about what the relation of reduction to the data should be. *Phenomenalists* insist that all meaningful concepts be explicitly definable in terms of sensory predicates. *Operationists* teach that scientific concepts be definable in terms of concrete laboratory procedures and their outcomes. *Pragmatists* hold that meaningful hypotheses reduce to their practical consequences. C. S. Peirce held that practical consequences are just true predictions, since such predictions can always be useful. W. James took a more liberal view, so that if belief in success inspires confidence leading to success, the belief in success is true. *Logical positivists* began as phenomenalists and successively retreated to the view that the cognitive significance of a hypothesis can be assessed only relative to the theory in which it occurs and to auxiliary assumptions with which it is proposed.[9]

Empiricism also takes on different names depending on the area of application. *Phenomenalists* attempt to reduce physical discourse to discourse about sense data. *Behaviorists* attempt to reduce mental discourse to discourse about overt behavior. *Physicalists* attempt to reduce mental discourse to physical discourse. *Finitists* wish to reduce the theory of the real numbers to facts about the natural numbers. The language of probability has been blessed with not one but two reductive programs, *frequentism* and *personalism*. Frequentism reduces probabilistic hypotheses to limits of observed relative frequencies, and personalism involves a double reduction: probability to degree of belief and degree of belief to behavioral dispositions regarding the acceptance or rejection of bets.

Example 2.5   Frequentism

R. Von Mises[10] was determined to provide an empiricist reduction of probability. On his view, probability is defined as the limiting relative frequency of occurrence of some observation o in the actual data stream ε. Let $F_\varepsilon(o, n) =$ the number of occurrences of o in ε up to and including stage n. Define the *relative*

---

[8] For example: "If, on the other hand, the putative proposition is of such a character that the assumption of its truth, or falsehood, is consistent with any assumption whatsoever concerning the nature of his future experience, then, as far as he is concerned, it is, if not a tautology, a mere pseudoproposition. The sentence expressing it may be emotionally significant to him; but it is not literally significant" (Ayer 1958: 35).

The antiskeptical power of empiricism has been evident to its proponents from the beginning. For example, Berkeley wrote: "If the principles which I here endeavour to propagate are admitted for true, the consequences which, I think, evidently flow from thence are, that *Atheism and Scepticism will be utterly destroyed*, many intricate points made plain, great difficulties solved, several useless parts of science retrenched, speculation referred to practice, and men reduced from paradoxes to common sense" (Berkeley 1965: 133, my emphasis).

[9] Carnap (1966), chs. 24, 26.

[10] Von Mises (1981).

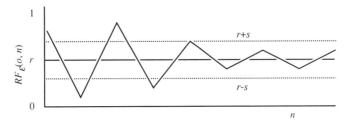

Figure 2.14

frequency of o in ε at stage n as $RF_\varepsilon(o, n) = F_\varepsilon(o, n)/n$. Finally, define the *limiting relative frequency* of o in ε as follows (*Fig. 2.14*):

$$LRF_\varepsilon(o) = r \Leftrightarrow \textit{for each } s > 0 \textit{ there is an } n \textit{ such that for each } m \geq n,$$
$$|RF_\varepsilon(o, m) - r| < s.^{11}$$

Von Mises' reduction of probabilistic language can be expressed as follows, where α is the scientist's assessment method and $\varepsilon(w, \alpha)$ is the data stream generated by world w in response to the acts performed by α:

$$P(o) = r \textit{ is true in world } w \textit{ with respect to method } \alpha \Leftrightarrow LRF_{\varepsilon(w, \alpha)}(o) = r.$$

The proposal completely eliminates global underdetermination, since o can have at most one limiting relative frequency in a given data stream.

Example 2.6   Personalism

The personalist approach to probability theory may be viewed as a two-staged reductionist program. First, there is an *idealist* reduction of probability to the mental notions of belief and utility. Then there is a *behaviorist* reduction of belief and utility to overt decision-making (e.g., betting) behavior. The first reduction is easy. Let h be a hypothesis. Then the statement $P(h) = r$ is reduced to "agent X believes h to degree r," a statement in which no more probabilistic language remains. The behaviorist reduces the mental concept of belief along the lines suggested by the familiar challenge "put up or shut up!" The idea is that X's degree of belief in h is his *fair betting quotient q* for h, where q is a real number between 0 and 1, inclusive. The quotient q is fair for h according to X if X is indifferent between a bet for h in which he contributes $100q\%$ of the stake and a bet against h in which he contributes $100(1 - q)\%$ of the stake. This is supposedly something that can be checked by challenging X to a bet and watching whether he accepts it or rejects it, so the concept of degree of belief is reduced to betting behavior.

This account, like frequentism, eliminates the global underdetermination of probability statements. In order to discover whether the probability of an atom

---

[11] Von Mises also imposed a *randomness* requirement (cf. section 3.4).

splitting is equal to r, we ask whose opinions are in question (perhaps the writer of the physics text), and then we proceed to propose a sequence of bets to this person X until we narrow in on his fair betting quotient. In this way we discover the truth about the probability for X that the atom will split, assuming that X's belief remains fixed while we seek it.[12]

There are complications in the story, however. For example, the bettor may have values at stake other than the official stake of the bet. Thus, we must exchange dollars for some notion of *utility* that reflects all of X's interests. It turns out that one can provide a reduction of utility jointly with the reduction of belief, all in terms of X's preference ordering over acts.[13]

It remains to answer why X's fair betting quotients over various hypotheses should satisfy the axioms of the probability calculus. The spirit of the answer is that otherwise X's preferences over acts will have a self-defeating character. For example, if X prefers act a to act b, but also prefers b to a, then we can pump money from X by trading him a for b plus some money and then trading him b for a plus some money, etc. The actual working out of this proposal is not quite so tidy, as not all of the assumptions required to prove that the probability axioms must be satisfied are as natural as this one.[14]

W. V. O. Quine's *holism* differs from traditional empiricism by dropping the requirement that hypotheses be individually reduced to their empirical consequences.

> The totality of our so-called knowledge or beliefs ... is a man-made fabric which impinges on experience only along the edges.... A conflict with experience at the periphery occasions readjustments in the interior of the field. *Truth values have to be redistributed* over some of our statements. Reevaluation of some statements entails reevaluation of others, because of their logical interconnections—the logical laws being in turn simply certain further statements of the system, certain further elements of the field.[15]

This position undercuts global underdetermination by making truth inside the web a matter of free choice by the scientist among material, logical, and methodological principles.

The discussion so far is summarized in the following diagram. Let us now focus on the semantic realist side. Once global underdetermination is conceded, there arises an epistemological question, namely, whether belief in globally

---

[12] Personalists who are embarrassed by the ease of doing physics on this picture are inclined to reintroduce propensities, so that X has personal degrees of belief over various possible propensities that the atom will split. On this hybrid view, the unreduced propensities remain globally underdetermined, but X's degrees of belief are not. For example, Levi (1983). A hybrid personalist-frequentist view is recommended in Howson and Urbach (1990). For further discussion of this proposal, cf. section 13.7.

[13] Savage (1972).

[14] Cf. Fishburn (1983).

[15] Quine (1951), my emphasis.

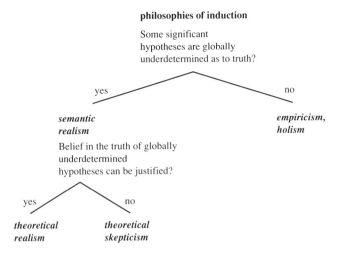

philosophies of induction

Some significant
hypotheses are globally
underdetermined as to truth?

yes   no

semantic   *empiricism,*
realism   *holism*

Belief in the truth of globally
underdetermined
hypotheses can be justified?

yes   no

theoretical   *theoretical*
realism   *skepticism*

Figure 2.15

underdetermined hypotheses can be *justified*. The *theoretical realist* says that it can be, and the *theoretical skeptic* answers in the negative (*Fig. 2.15*).[16]

The theoretical skeptic refuses to engage in the empiricist's reductionistic reconstrual of language. If the hypothesis says there exist particles that do not interact with ordinary matter in any way, then he takes it naively at its word and concludes that it is globally underdetermined. Since the data may be the same forever, no matter whether the hypothesis is true or false, then every empirical method that bases its conjectures only on the data will fail to discern the truth value of the hypothesis in some world producing that data stream. In other words, logical reliability (in the sense of chapter 1) is impossible to achieve. In contrast, the theoretical realist insists that belief can be justified even in such cases. So one way of looking at the difference between the theoretical skeptic and the theoretical realist is that the former ties the notion of epistemic justification to logical reliability and the latter does not.

Let's consider some options open to the theoretical skeptic. Even though the truth of a hypothesis is globally underdetermined, other virtues of the hypothesis may not be. For example, a hypothesis is *empirically adequate* just in case it makes no false prediction about what will occur in the data stream for eternity (*Fig. 2.16*). Empirical adequacy cannot be globally underdetermined since it depends only on the data stream.

Instrumentalists hold that we can be justified in believing that a hypothesis is empirically adequate, but that belief in the globally underdetermined truth

---

[16] What I call theoretical realism and theoretical skepticism are often referred to simply as *realism* and *skpticism*, respectively, but this quickly leads to fruitless equivocations and confusions, as the literature in the subject so often complains.

Figure 2.16

of a hypothesis is not justified.[17] The instrumentalist's position sidesteps global underdetermination by proposing a globally determined goal for inquiry rather than by arguing that truth itself is globally determined. For example, a cognitive scientist who produces an architecture of cognition might begin by saying that it is a true theory of the mind. In light of a host of alternative theories making identical predictions, she may retreat to the position that her proposal is just an empirically adequate model or simulation of overt human behavior.

Empirical adequacy is not the only relation the instrumentalist might propose as a replacement for truth. Global underdetermination is impossible whenever the aim of the scientist is represented by a relation between the hypothesis and the data stream. For example, we might demand in addition that the theory correctly predict everything in the data stream and that it be simple, or computable as well. We might also permit it to make some number of false predictions. Any such notion of correctness is a relation between the hypothesis and the data stream. I will refer to all such hypothesis virtues generically as *empirical* relations. When truth is not globally underdetermined with respect to the scientist's background assumptions and the hypotheses he is concerned with, then truth itself is an empirical relation.

6. The Philosophy of Local Underdetermination

Consider the philosophical ornithologist who is deeply concerned whether all ravens are black. The trouble with this question is that whenever the ornithologist decides it is safe to conclude that all ravens are black, the very next raven could refute him (*Fig. 2.17*).

More generally, *local underdetermination* arises whenever there is an infinite data stream possible for all the scientist knows, such that each initial segment of this data stream could arise regardless whether the hypothesis is true or false (*Fig. 2.18*). Then on this data stream, there is no finite time at which he can tell whether the hypothesis is true or false, even if a demigod who can see the entire future at once could do so. Whereas global underdetermination can thwart even a deity who can see the entire future at once, local underdetermination is sufficient to fool a scientist whose perspective on the data stream is bounded.

[17] For example: "Science aims to give us theories which are empirically adequate and acceptance of a theory involves as belief only that it is empirically adequate. This is the statement of the anti-realist position I advocate" (Van Fraassen 1980: 12).

Figure 2.17

Instrumentalism and the various versions of empiricism have one important feature in common: they are cures for global underdetermination that leave local underdetermination unscathed. The empiricist reduces globally underdetermined theoretical claims to empirical generalizations, but these generalizations are still locally underdetermined. The instrumentalist's notion of empirical adequacy is not merely consistency with the current data; it is consistency with all data that will ever arise. To conclude on the basis of the current data that a hypothesis is empirically adequate goes beyond the current data, so empirical adequacy can be locally underdetermined. The truth of a particular hypothesis in Quine's vibrating web of belief may be a matter of taste, but whether or not a rearrangement of the web will maintain the fit of the whole against the changing situation of future experience is a question that goes beyond past experience. So the future efficacy of alterations in the web is locally underdetermined.

The threat of local underdetermination elicits the same sorts of responses as the global case. First of all, there are those who would deny on semantic grounds that local underdetermination arises. For example, L. J. Savage proposed that local underdetermination does not arise because universal generalizations in science are really intended only to cover finitely many cases, so that they really aren't locally underdetermined at all.

> Evidently, my attitude toward universals tends to be reductionist. I would analyze them away as elliptical and, often more or less deliberately, ambiguous statements of a variety of finite conjunctions.[18]

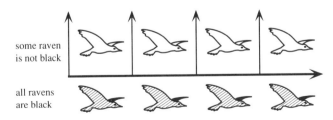

Figure 2.18

[18] Savage (1967).

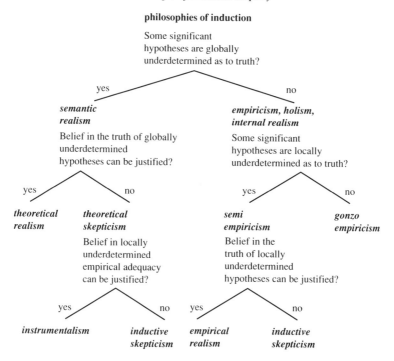

Figure 2.19

I refer to this remarkable position as *gonzo-empiricism*. Gonzo-empiricism defeats local underdetermination just the way theoretical empiricism conquers global underdetermination, but it has been been as popular. Most empiricists have conceded, to the contrary, that the universal quantifiers in inductive generalizations of natural science really do refer to all places and times. I call this position *semi-empiricism* because it concedes the possibility of local underdetermination while denying that global underdetermination is possible.

If we follow the majority in rejecting gonzo-empiricism then we face a new question, namely, whether locally underdetermined beliefs can be justified. As one might guess, philosophers are divided on this issue as well. *Instrumentalists* think that belief in empirical adequacy is justified, since they are at pains to contrast this case with belief in globally underdetermined truth. Many empiricists agree that belief in empirical generalizations can be justified by appeals to confirmation or inductive logic. I refer to these empiricists as *empirical realists*,[19] to emphasize the analogy between their position and that of the theoretical realists. Opposed to the instrumentalists and the empirical realists we have the *inductive skeptics (Fig. 2.19)*.

---

[19] This is another neologism. Philosophical discussions tend to run empirical realism and theoretical realism together under the heading of scientific realism. For my purposes, however, it is important to distinguish positions pertaining to different levels of underdetermination.

Like the theoretical skeptic, the inductive skeptic ties inductive justification to logical reliability. This comes out very clearly in classical and medieval sources. For example, Sextus Empiricus presents the following statement of inductive skepticism:

> [The dogmatists] claim that the universal is established from the particulars by means of induction. If this is so, they will effect it by reviewing either all the particulars or only some of them. But if they review only some, their induction will be unreliable, since it is possible that some of the particulars omitted in the induction may contradict the universal. If, on the other hand, their review is to include all the particulars, theirs will be an impossible task, because particulars are infinite and indefinite. Thus it turns out, I think, that induction, viewed from both ways, rests on a shaky foundation.[20]

Eleven hundred years after Sextus, John Buridan put the issue in this perfectly straightforward manner:

> Second, it is proved that [scientific principles] are fallacious, for experiences only have the force of establishing a universal principle by way of induction from many cases; and a universal proposition never follows from an induction unless the induction includes every singular of that universal, which is impossible. Indeed, consider that whenever you have touched fire, you have sensed it to be hot, and so through experience you judge this fire which you have never touched to be hot, and so on. At length you judge every fire to be hot. Let us assume, therefore, that from the will of God, whenever you have sensed iron, you have sensed it to be hot. It is sure that by the same reasoning you would judge the iron which you see and which in fact is cold, to be hot, and all iron to be hot. And in that case there would be false judgments, however much you would then have as much experience of iron as you now in fact have of fire.[21]

In either case, a recipe is given for showing that no matter how much data an inductive method sees in support of a universal hypothesis, the next datum can show that it is wrong. In other words, no possible inductive method that bases its conclusions on the available data can arrive at the truth value of an empirical generalization on every possible data stream. It is immediately inferred that belief is not justified.

The arguments of inductive skeptics tacitly assume a particular standard of success, namely, that the method in question eventually halt with the correct answer on every possible data stream consistent with background assumptions (*Fig. 2.20*). Such a method may be said to *decide* the hypothesis in question *with certainty* given the background assumptions $\mathcal{K}$. Decision with certainty requires that the data and the background assumptions eventually entail either that the hypothesis is correct or that it is incorrect, which corresponds to the

[20] Sextus (1985): 105.
[21] *Questions on Aristotle's Metaphysics*, Book II, Question 1, in Hyman and Walsh (1982). It should be noted that the quoted passage is not Buridan's opinion, but the statement of a position to which he later responds by appeal to an a priori principle of uniformity of nature.

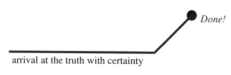

arrival at the truth with certainty

Figure 2.20

extreme demand placed on inquiry by Plato and by his rationalist posterity, up through the seventeenth century.

But decision with certainty is not the only sense in which a method can be logically guaranteed to arrive at the truth given $\mathcal{K}$. For example, K. Popper observed that even if we cannot conclusively verify universal generalizations, we can hope to *refute* them *with certainty* in the sense that for each possible data stream admitted by our background assumptions, if it makes the hypothesis false, our method eventually outputs 0 and stops, but if it makes the hypothesis true, the method never outputs 0.

> These marvelously imaginative and bold conjectures or "anticipations" of ours are carefully and soberly controlled by systematic tests. Once put forward, none of our "anticipations" are dogmatically upheld. Our method of research is not to defend them, in order to prove how right we were. On the contrary, we try to overthrow them. Using all the weapons of our logical, mathematical, and technical armoury, we try to prove that our anticipations were false—in order to put forward, in their stead, new unjustified and unjustifiable anticipations, new "rash and premature prejudices," as Bacon derisively called them.[22]

Popper's position is sometimes referred to as *deductivism*, since the relation of refutation is a logical relation. Popper's deductivism is a way to sidestep the above skeptical arguments without abandoning the skeptic's insistence on a clear, logical connection between following a method and arriving at the truth. The difference is that Popper's notion of success is weaker than the skeptic's, insofar as a successful method must eventually yield certainty only when the hypothesis in question is false, whereas the classical skeptics and the Platonists demanded eventual certainty no matter what.

Dually, an existential hypothesis can be *verified with certainty*, but not refuted, in the sense that for each data stream admitted by our background assumptions, our method outputs 1 and quits if the hypothesis is correct, and never outputs 1 otherwise. Again, verification (i.e., entailment by the data) is a logical relation.

Each of these notions can be thought of as an attenuated but nontrivial definition of methodological success. But weakening decision with certainty to verification or refutation with certainty does not suffice to handle all cases of local underdetermination. Recall Von Mises's frequentist theory of probability. Von Mises was determined to make probability subject to empirical investigation, but unfortunately, the theory makes every probability statement consistent with every finite data sequence. Thus, probability statements cannot be either

[22] Popper (1968): 279.

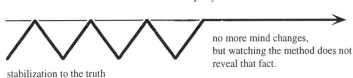

no more mind changes,
but watching the method does not
reveal that fact.

stabilization to the truth

Figure 2.21

refuted or verified with certainty. By these standards of success, Von Mises's reductionist program was a failure.

But more attenuation is possible. One might propose that science should *stabilize* to the truth *in the limit*, in the sense that for each data stream admitted by our background assumptions, the method eventually arrives at the truth and sticks with it, though the user may never know when this has happened since the method may vacillate any number of times prior to convergence (*Fig. 2.21*). William James endorsed this option as one of the cornerstones of his pragmatist epistemology:

> We may talk of the *empiricist* and the *absolutist* way of believing the truth. The absolutists in this matter say that we not only can attain to knowing truth, but we can know when we have attained to knowing it; while the empiricists think that although we may attain it, we cannot infallibly know when. To *know* is one thing and to know for certain *that* we know is another.[23]

It is a more subtle matter whether limiting frequency hypotheses can be assessed in this sense. In fact, we will see that they cannot be, which suggests still more weakening in the notion of success.

H. Reichenbach proposed that science should *approach* the truth in the limit, perhaps never arriving there and never knowing that it has stabilized to within a given degree of approximation of the truth (*Fig. 2.22*). He showed (trivially) that it is possible to gradually approach the true limiting relative frequency in this sense, given that it exists.

As it turns out, each of these logical notions of convergent success is a partial answer to the problem of local underdetermination. Each time we weaken the notion of convergence, more questions come within the scope of reliable inquiry, but many more questions remain beyond it.[24] What concerns the learning theorist, or more generally, the logic of reliable inquiry, is exactly where these lines fall for classes of scientists with different cognitive capacities.

As we have seen, the notion of underdetermination has been the principal driving force behind much of the history of speculation about scientific method. Skepticism, realism, empiricism (phenomenalism, pragmatism, positivism, operationism, behaviorism, frequentism, etc.), instrumentalism, and virtually all the epistemological -isms can be conceived as various attitudes toward belief in the face of underdetermination. Despite this fact, there has been

---

[23] James (1948): 95–6.
[24] The sense of *more* is not cardinality, but *complexity*, in a sense that will be developed in detail in chapters 4 and 7.

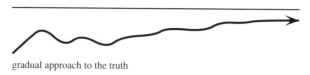

gradual approach to the truth

Figure 2.22

little principled discussion of what underdetermination is. For some it is equal bearing of evidence. For others it is consistency with the total data. For still others it is consistency with the current data or the problem of induction. My proposal is:

Underdetermination = *the impossibility of logically reliable inquiry.*

For each notion of convergent success, and for each kind of problem (discovery vs. assessment) there will be a notion of underdetermination that corresponds to the impossibility of that sort of reliable inquiry. On this view, the logic of underdetermination is just the logic of reliable inquiry.

While this approach to methodology is skeptical in flavor, it is not the barren and trivial skepticism in which all inquiry is futile. It is more analogous to the theory of computability, in which some problems are solvable in a given sense and others are not, so that there is a complex and interesting pattern of positive and negative results for each standard of success. It invites us to distinguish the cases in which our assumptions imply that our methods are headed for the truth from those in which our assumptions imply no such thing, or in which we cannot think of credible assumptions that would. The skeptic's position is anchored in the demand that inductive method bear some clear, logical connection with finding the truth. In that sense, the methodological results in the following chapters may be considered skeptical. But our liberalization of the classical skeptic's strict criterion of convergence and our refusal to question the scientist's initial assumptions mean that there will be positive as well as negative results, depending on how weakly we construe convergence and on how much advance knowledge the scientist claims to have.

7. Scientific Realism, Probability, and Subjunctives

The empiricists, the instrumentalists, and the skeptics all agree that belief cannot be justified in the face of underdetermination. Skeptics conclude from arguments for underdetermination that belief is not justified, empiricists argue that underdetermination is impossible, and instrumentalists lower their sights to investigate globally determined hypothesis virtues. If underdetermination is the impossibility of reliability, as suggested in the preceding section, then each of these positions is broadly motivated by reliabilist considerations. The scientific realist, alone, severs the tie between logical reliability and justified belief.[25] His challenge is therefore to explain how belief can be justified by data in the face of underdetermination, contrary to the assumption of each of his opponents.

In a sense, this challenge is trivial to meet, for if an act is justified insofar as it furthers one's interests, then it suffices to show that inductive practice serves other interests than finding the truth. For example, it can impose consensus when consensus is required for action, as in the formulation and enforcement of government policy. It can also instill a sense of security, or slake our natural sense of curiosity with answers that appeal to our subjective senses of explanation, or maintain a global coherence between our beliefs and the current evidence. But the skeptic is hardly ignorant of the fact that people can think of lots of reasons to embrace underdetermined dogmas. That is just what scares him! His point is that inquiry is not justified by the specific aim of finding the truth when truth is underdetermined.

Some realists simply refuse to engage the skeptic. They propose that some logical or probabilistic relation between evidence and hypothesis justifies belief in the hypothesis whenever it obtains. When asked why, they either appeal to the other aims (simplicity, explanation, etc.) or they insist that confirmation is a fundamental norm (like *modus ponens* in deductive logic) for which no further justification is possible (else it wouldn't be fundamental).[26] But if he is to engage his opponent, the realist must somehow argue that scientific method can serve the interest of finding the truth when no possible method is logically guaranteed to find it, even in the limit.

Probability theory seems to afford the realist a variety of strategies for making his case. Since the time of Carneides, it has been thought that degrees of belief can be justified when all-out acceptance cannot be. But in itself, the distinction between full-blown belief and intermediate degrees of belief is not ultimately of much use to the realist. Think of two fellows, one who always conjectures the values 1 or 0, indicating full belief or full disbelief, respectively, and another who produces intermediate values between 1 and 0, indicating partial degrees of belief. The skeptic may demand, for example, that the former fellow eventually stabilize to 1 if the hypothesis is true and to 0 otherwise,

---

[25] This sentence is to be understood relative to a given level of underdetermination. The empirical realist, for example, adopts the realist perspective with respect to local underdetermination and the empiricist perspective with respect to global underdetermination.

Also, some who call themselves realists simply deny the *actuality* of underdetermination rather than its possibility. According to them, careful examination of past episodes in the history of science reveals that scientists have always been able to expand the range of possible observations to the extent necessary to overcome the apparent underdetermination of the theories available at the time. If this is taken as evidence that underdetermination is impossible, then I classify the position together with empiricism. If it is conceded that underdetermination is possible and belief is not justified when it obtains, then I classify the position together with skepticism. I am concerned in this section only with the more interesting realism that insists that belief can be justified even when a theory is underdetermined.

[26] Horwich (1991).

regardless of which data stream is seen in the limit (relative to assumptions $\mathcal{K}$). He may similarly demand that the second fellow's intermediate degrees of belief gradually approach 1 if the hypothesis is true and approach 0 otherwise. It turns out that these two demands can be satisfied in exactly the same cases (cf. chapter 4). The moral is that *if probabilities are to make inquiry easier, it is not because probabilistic methods are more powerful, but because probabilistic standards of success are weaker*. This is an elementary point, but it is also a common point of confusion among nonspecialists in probability theory.

So now the scientific realist proposes that the skeptic was too strict in demanding that background assumptions $\mathcal{K}$ logically entail that the method in question will eventually find the truth. It suffices, the realist claims, that the method have a high probability of arriving at the truth. The strong law of large numbers, for example, implies that it is possible to get to the truth in the limit with probability 1 about an unknown propensity. This is remarkable, because a propensity hypothesis is logically consistent with any data stream whatsoever in the limit. The strong law of large numbers requires special restrictions on the form of the underlying probability measure, but when we move to problems that are locally but not globally underdetermined, much more general results can be shown. Some of them will be reviewed in chapter 13. So the realist can say that if the benighted antirealist would only concede a zero probability of error in the limit, inquiry could perfectly well serve the interest of finding the truth in the face of underdetermination. What can an antirealist reply to such a reasonable proposal?

First of all, probabilistic reliability is not a univocal response to the skeptic until the probabilist settles on an interpretation of probability. On the frequentist interpretation, a high probability of success in the short run is actually a kind of logical reliability in the long run (a logically guaranteed limiting relative frequency of success). This is not surprising, since the very point of frequentism is to provide an empirical definition of the concept of probability. The skeptic and empiricist can approve of such a frequentist analysis, since success in this sense implies a kind of logically guaranteed reliability.[27] But by that very fact, the proposal no longer provides the realist with an account of justification of underdetermined belief.

On the personalist's position, probabilistic reliability is a matter of some rational agent's opinion about convergent success, where rationality is a matter of coherence rather than of truth or correctness. But of course the skeptic already knew that people often hold the opinion that they will arrive at the truth eventually. What is wanted is some objective connection between truth and method. If the personalist then proves that every rational agent must be almost sure that he is getting to the truth, then the skeptic will cite the unreasonable strength of the conclusion as a reason for rejecting the proposed norms of rationality.

---

[27] In the next chapter it will be shown, for example, that the existence of an unbiased statistical test (of a highly abstract sort) is equivalent to verifiability or refutability in the limit when probabilities are taken to be limiting relative frequencies.

In contrast to the reductive accounts of the frequentist and the personalist, the propensity theorist simply refuses to say anything more about propensities than that they satisfy the axioms of probability theory. Propensities of events entail only propensities of other events. In particular, they are usually taken to entail nothing about what will actually happen, even in the limit. For all that is said about propensities, they might be quantities of mud placed on various propositions by the Deity, who then makes true whichever maximally consistent set of propositions he pleases. In particular, he might place a large chunk of mud on the success of my method and then actualize a world in which it fails. The question the skeptic should ask is why it is a relevant response to the problem of underdetermination that some method or other has a large pile of celestial mud placed on its success. Metaphors of *more* versus *fewer* possibilities come to mind, but in an infinite space there is nothing to the notion of more possibilities other than some assumed probability measure, and that brings us straight back to the significance of the mud.

Regardless of the interpretation of probability adopted by the realist, the skeptic may also argue that possibilities of error the probability theorist calls negligible really may not seem so negligible from a logical point of view. In chapter 13, I will show how Bayesian updating, which converges to the truth with probability 1, can fail to find the truth (or even to change its arbitrary, initial degree of belief) on an uncountably infinite set of data streams, even when it is possible for a trivial method to succeed on every possible data stream and even when the hypothesis is never assigned an extremal probability unless it is logically refuted. This leads one to wonder how probability licenses us to ignore such large sets of possible errors.

Finally, the skeptic may question the probabilistic assumptions underlying the usual convergence theorems. In chapter 13, I show how the personalistic result mentioned in the preceding paragraph can fail when the probabilistic postulate of *countable additivity* is dropped. This postulate is introduced into the theory of probability for technical expedience and on the weight of its desirable consequences. But the antiskeptical consequences are precisely what is at issue with the skeptic, and technical expedience hardly suffices for so weighty an outcome as the defeat of skepticism. Moreover, the postulate is simply false on the frequentist interpretation of probability and prominent personalists like B. DeFinetti have distanced themselves from the postulate because it enforces a bias of opinion over countable collections of mutually exclusive events. This issue is inherited by those propensity theorists who appeal to personalism to justify the assumption that propensities are probabilities.[28] So probabilistic realism defeats skepticism with a principle that many probabilists either cannot or will not accept.

Probabilities help the realist by providing an allegedly principled basis for dispensing a priori with possibilities that give rise to underdetermination. But probabilities are not the only means to this end. R. Nozick[29] has applied recent

---

[28] For example, Lewis (1981).
[29] Nozick (1981).

logical work[30] on the semantics of subjunctive conditionals to the same end. The basic idea is that Sam's belief in *h* is reliable just in case the following subjunctive conditional holds: if *h* weren't true, Sam wouldn't believe *h*. On this story, the skeptic insists on logical reliability (the consequent holds in each possible world in which the antecedent holds), whereas it suffices that the consequent hold in worlds sufficiently close to the actual world in which the antecedent holds.[31] The methodological power of this view is evident in the example "Sam believes the bottle is on the table." A skeptic might object that Sam should suspend belief because the Cartesian demon might be stimulating his mind into hallucinations. But if the closest possible world to the actual world in which the bottle is not on the table is a world in which no demon (or magician, or mirage, etc.) is around, then Sam would not see a bottle and hence would not believe one to be there, so Sam is reliable after all, entirely in virtue of his performance in just one other possible world besides the actual world.

On this view, reliability becomes a *world-dependent* property of a method. Whereas logical and probabilistic reliability are both *world-independent*, in the sense that a logically or probabilistically reliable method is reliable in each possible world if it is reliable in one (assuming that the scientist's background knowledge remains fixed across possible worlds), Nozick's sort of reliability depends essentially upon which possible world is actual. For example, if the actual world is one in which a magician really has rigged the room in advance and is waiting in the wings, determined to make Sam see a bottle if there is no bottle actually present, then the closest world to the actual world in which the bottle is not present would be one in which Sam is fooled into believing that it is present. Since we are uncertain which world is actual, and since subjunctive reliability depends upon which world is actual, we may (actually) be reliable on Nozick's account without being able to tell from the logical structure of our methods or from our background knowledge that we are reliable. For this reason, some philosophers have tended to equate epistemological reliabilism with *naturalism*, the view that the justification of empirical method must be empirical. Many skeptics, including Hume, have objected that empirical reliability arguments are circular, however.[32]

Skeptics aside, the logical and subjunctive approaches complement one another in their strengths and weaknesses. A logically reliable method can be known a priori to be reliable, given background knowledge that could not have been inferred with logical reliability. A subjunctively reliable method can be reliable without strong background knowledge, but cannot be known a priori to be reliable. If knowledge is something like reliably inferred true belief,[33] then subjunctive reliability may explain where underdetermined background

---

[30] Lewis (1973).

[31] For ease of presentation, I assume Stalnaker's (1968) simplified semantics. Nozick actually assumes a variation of Lewis's slightly more complicated account.

[32] Cf. exercise 9.11.

[33] A logical reliabilist need not be committed to this or to any other thesis about the nature of knowledge, though logical reliabilism is certainly relevant to such an account of knowledge.

knowledge could have come from, since it could not have been inferred with logical reliability from nothing. Logical reliability provides a priori guarantees that our current knowledge (which we may not know to be such) will eventually be extended with more truth.[34]

8. The Logic of Reliable Inquiry

The topic of this book is the logic of reliable inquiry, which examines the prospects for methods logically guaranteed to find the truth eventually. As I use the term, underdetermination arises when there exists no such method, so this book is also about underdetermination. As we have seen, skepticism, empiricism, and realism are all responses to underdetermination, so in that sense, the topic is relevant to a wide range of philosophical interests.

On the other hand, realism disagrees with empiricism and skepticism concerning the relation between justified belief and underdetermination. Since this book is about reliability rather than justification, it does not bear directly on the debate. Nonetheless, it has something to say about justification in light of various assumptions. If empiricists and skeptics are right, justification implies reliability, so this book is accidentally about justified belief. If realists are right, justification is possible when logical reliability is not, so the two are different. But even in that case, to know the extent to which the realist's aim of justification supports or interferes with logical reliability would contribute greatly to proper understanding of the realist position.

Logical reliabilism raises a range of interesting methodological questions. These questions may be ranked by their level of abstraction, as measured by the types of entities they quantify over.

Level 0 corresponds to what computer scientists call *hacking*. Here we consider only concrete questions about what a given method will say about a given hypothesis on a given, finite data sequence. We can agree with the method or we can disagree with it. We can see if scientists of the past agreed in particular cases. We can ask whether a particular conclusion drawn by the method is "justified." These are the sorts of questions that can be investigated by sitting down with a method and trying it on various examples. A great deal of the philosophy of science consists of just this: reactions of joy or disgust to particular runs of a given method. Many papers in artificial intelligence have the same character, except that it is a computer program rather than a philosophical definition that elicits delight or dismay.

Such investigations can tell us something about a method's rhetorical value. If we hate what it says, we will never be persuaded to believe what it says, so it cannot produce true beliefs in us. But running a method on a few input examples says little about its logical reliability, which depends on what the method would have done in the future had the world been different from the

---

[34] Cf. exercise 4.14. It turns out that under various interpretations of proximity among worlds, one still ends up with local underdetermination.

way it is. The hacking approach also makes it tempting to compare apples and oranges. If one method is very reliable and another is not, then we shouldn't complain about the former being harder to use since it does more for the extra bother. But if we just run the two programs on a few examples, it can easily look as though the canned program is faster, and thus "improved."

Level 1 questions quantify over possible inputs—finite data streams and hypotheses—so that we may consider the overall input-output disposition of the method. For example, one may ask whether a given test procedure will ever pass a hypothesis that is refuted by the data, or we may ask how the time required to compute the test increases as a function of the size of the hypothesis and the length of the data.

At level *2*, we quantify over possible worlds. This is the level of reliability analysis for particular methods. The *scope* of a method is the set of all possible worlds in which it succeeds. We may compare the scopes of methods to see if one is more reliable than the other according to a given success criterion. This is the sort of question one asks when one has some pet method in mind or some small range of alternative methods to choose among. Thus we have, for example, Reichenbach's "vindication" of the so-called straight rule of induction.

Questions at *level 3* quantify over possible methods. This is the level of problem solvability analysis, since we are asking whether there exists a method that can succeed on a given inductive problem. Level 3 is also the appropriate level for *optimality analysis*, since optimality is a matter of showing that no other method surpasses the scope or convergence time of a given method.

Finally, at *level 4*, we quantify over entire inductive problems. This is the level of abstraction appropriate for comparing notions of problem solvability, since one criterion is *as easy as* another just in case exactly the same problems are solvable in each of the two senses. Two criteria are equivalent just in case each is as easy as the other. A proof of equivalence among solution criteria exposes principled trade-offs among competing notions of reliability. Like conservation laws in physics, they show us how we really don't get anything for nothing, even when it appears to the philosophical imagination that we do. Another sort of question of this sort concerns the relative difficulty of discovery and assessment or of discovery and prediction. Many philosophers have asserted without proof that discovery is impossible while assessment is non-problematic. Others have proposed that the point of discovery is prediction. These are all level 4 questions.

Another, very important question at level 4 concerns the existence of *complete architecutures* for induction. An inductive architecture is a recipe for building methods. For example, a Bayesian may insist that a method consist of conditioning some joint probability measure. An architecture is complete (for a success criterion) just in case every problem solvable under that criterion is solvable by a method built according to the required recipe.

Still another important project at this level of generalization is to provide a logical or structural *characterization* of the problems solvable according to a given success criterion. Such a theorem provides necessary and sufficient conditions for solvability in the sense required. Immanuel Kant referred to proofs of necessary conditions for knowledge as *transcendental deductions*. If we think of knowledge as reliably inferred true belief, along the lines discussed earlier in this chapter, then learning-theoretic characterization theorems may be thought of as transcendental deductions. Since they provide conditions that are sufficient as well as necessary, they may be thought of as complete transcendental deductions, in the sense of being minimal necessary conditions so far as reliability is concerned. Characterization theorems and complete architectures for induction are one of the principal concerns of this book.

3

The Demons of Passive Observation

1. Introduction

In the preceding chapter, several notions of logical reliability were introduced. It was proposed that degrees of underdetermination be defined as the impossibility of reliability in various different senses. In this chapter, I will categorize some inductive problems by their degrees of underdetermination. Thus, we will be engaged in questions of the third level, which demand that inductive problems be shown unsolvable by all possible methods.

Recall that for all the scientist supposes, the actual world may be any world in $\mathcal{K}$. The hypothesis h under investigation is correct for some of the worlds in $\mathcal{K}$ and incorrect for others. The relation C of *correctness* may be truth, empirical adequacy, predictiveness, or any other relation depending only on the hypothesis, the world, and the method the scientist employs. Each world interacts with the scientist through some data protocol and emits a stream of data, of which the scientist can only scan the initial segment produced up to the current stage of inquiry. When the data protocol is historical, we have a simpler situation in which the scientist's conjectures and experimental acts feed back into the world's experimental protocol to generate more data, and so forth (*Fig. 3.1*).

Until chapter 14, I will assume that truth or correctness is an *empirical* relation, depending only on the hypothesis in question and the actual data stream, and that the scientist is a passive observer, so that the data stream does not depend on what the scientist does. Given these simplifying assumptions, the machinery of worlds and data protocols no longer does any work, since each world determines a unique data stream and truth or correctness depends only on the data stream produced. Hence, worlds can be identified with the unique data streams they produce, so that $\mathcal{K}$ is a set of possible data streams

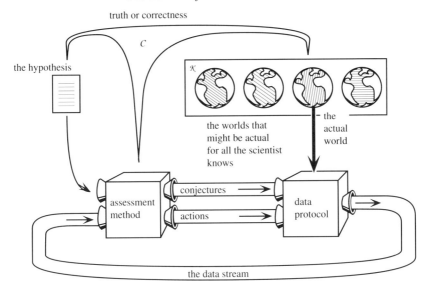

Figure 3.1

and the relation of correctness C holds directly between data streams and hypotheses. We can also ignore the fact that the scientist produces actions, since these actions are irrelevant to correctness and to the data received.

I will assume that the entries in the data stream are natural numbers. These may be thought of as code numbers for other sorts of discrete data. Let ω denote the set of all natural numbers. Let ω^* denote the set of all finite sequences of natural numbers. The set of all infinite data streams is denoted by $\mathcal{N} = \omega^{\omega}$.[1] Define (*Fig. 3.2*):

ε_n = *the datum occurring in position n of ε.*

$\varepsilon|n$ = *the finite, initial segment of ε through position n − 1.*

$n|\varepsilon$ = *the infinite tail of ε starting with position n.*

$lh(e)$ = *the number of positions occurring in finite sequence e.*

$e-$ = *the result of deleting the last entry in e.*

$last(e)$ = *the last item occurring in e.*

$\mathbf{0}$ = the empty sequence

Given the assumption that worlds are interchangeable with data streams, let $\mathcal{K}$ be some subset of $\mathcal{N}$ and let truth or correctness be a relation C between

---

[1] Each element of the infinite cross product of ω with itself is an infinite sequence of natural numbers and hence is a data stream.

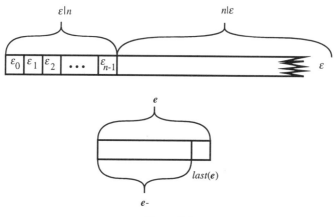

Figure 3.2

data streams and hypotheses. I will also assume that hypotheses are discrete objects coded by natural numbers, so that $H \subseteq \omega$. Thus $C \subseteq \mathcal{N} \times \omega$.

Finally, since I am ignoring the actions recommended by the scientist's assessment method α, I will assume that such a method is an arbitrary, total[2] map from hypotheses and finite data sequences to conjectures (*Fig. 3.3*). *Conjectures* (outputs of the assessment method) will be rational numbers between 0 and 1, together with a special *certainty symbol* '!'.

Now we may consider a traditional inductive problem that is idealized enough to clarify the logic of the approach and yet rich enough to illustrate many different senses of solvability and unsolvability.

Example 3.1 The infinite divisibility of matter

Since classical times, there have been debates concerning the nature of matter. In the seventeenth and eighteenth centuries, this debate took on a renewed urgency. The *corpuscularian* followers of René Descartes believed that matter is continuously extended and hence infinitely divisible. *Atomists* like Newton thought the opposite. Kant held the more measured opinion that the question goes beyond all possible experience:

> For how can we make out by experience ... whether matter is infinitely divisible or consists of simple parts? Such concepts cannot be given in any experience, however extensive, and consequently the falsehood either of the affirmative or the negative proposition cannot be discovered by this touchstone.[3]

The issue has not gone away. It seems that every increase in the power of particle accelerators may lead to a new, submicroscopic universe. Who was right, Descartes, Newton, or Kant?

---

[2] One could also countenance partial maps and require for convergence that the map be defined on each finite initial segment of the data stream. Nothing of interest depends on this choice.

[3] Kant (1950): 88.

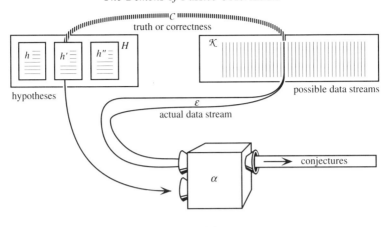

Figure 3.3

Our scientist is a theorist at the IRBP (Institute for Really Big Physics). His attitude toward the infinite divisibility of matter is frankly operational. If no accelerator of any power can split a particle, then he takes it as metaphysical nonsense to say that the particle is divisible, so indivisibility is just indivisibility by some possible accelerator that the IRBP, with its unlimited research budget, could construct. To investigate Kant's question, the theorist is commited to the following experimental procedure.

The lab maintains a list of the particles that have been obtained from previous splits but that have not yet been split themselves. This list is initialized with the original particle p under investigation. At stage n, the lab attempts to split the particle currently at the head of the list. If they succeed, then they remove the split particle from the head of the list and add the new fragments to the tail of the list, write 1 on the data tape, and proceed to stage $n + 1$ without building a larger accelerator. If, however, they fail to split the current particle into any fragments, they report 0. Then they place it at the end of the list; build a new, bigger accelerator; and proceed to stage $n + 1$.

Given no assumptions at all, the reports of the lab may have nothing to do with actual divisions of particles, so that all questions about the divisibility of particles are globally underdetermined: the alleged fragments of particles fed to these accelerators may be artifacts of faulty theory and irrelevant but misleading machinery. To make the issue more interesting, we will grant our theorist some strong theoretical assumptions.

First, we will grant him that the lab accurately reports the result of each attempted cut. It never reports cuts in particles when no such particles or cuts exist, and it always reports cuts that occur. Second, we will grant him that any physically possible cut in a particle given to the lab will eventually be made by his lab. This reflects our theorist's operationist leanings. We will not grant, however, that the very next attempt will succeed if a cut is possible. It may take some time before even the IRBP can secure funding for a sufficiently large accelerator.

Accordingly, if we let h_{inf} denote the hypothesis that particle p is infinitely divisible and let h_{fin} be the hypothesis that p is only finitely divisible, then our assumptions imply that

$C(\varepsilon, h_{inf}) \Leftrightarrow$ *infinitely many 1s occur in ε.*

$C(\varepsilon, h_{fin}) \Leftrightarrow$ *only finitely many 1s occur in ε.*

The scientist can entertain a variety of hypotheses about the fundamental structure of matter. Let h_{simple} be the hypothesis that the particle p is physically indivisible, and let $h_{divisible}$ be the negation of h_{simple}. Then the scientist's assumptions imply that

$C(\varepsilon, h_{simple}) \Leftrightarrow$ *only 0s occur in ε.*

$C(\varepsilon, h_{divisible}) \Leftrightarrow 1$ *occurs somewhere in ε.*

Let $h_{division\ at\ t}$ be the hypothesis that a successful division will occur at t. Then:

$C(\varepsilon, h_{division\ at\ t}) \Leftrightarrow \varepsilon_t = 1.$

$C(\varepsilon, \neg h_{division\ at\ t}) \Leftrightarrow \varepsilon_t = 0.$

Let $h_{LRF(1)=r}$ be the hypothesis that the limiting relative frequency of successful cuts in the experiment under consideration exists and is equal to r.

$C(\varepsilon, h_{LRF(1)=r}) \Leftrightarrow LRF_\varepsilon(1)$ *exists and is equal to r.*

$C(\varepsilon, \neg h_{LRF(1)=r}) \Leftrightarrow LRF_\varepsilon(1)$ *does not exist or exists but is $\neq r$.*

Let H be the set of all these hypotheses. We will assume that the huge accelerators of the IRBP are new and so unprecedented in power that the theorist has to admit that any sequence of 0s and 1s is possible for all he knows or assumes. So $\mathcal{K}$ is just the set 2^ω of all infinite sequences of 0s and 1s.

$\mathcal{K} = 2^\omega.$

Now we have a set of hypotheses H, a set of possible data streams $\mathcal{K}$, and an empirical relation of correctness C, reflecting something of the character of Kant's claim. The question is whether Kant was right, and if so, then in what sense?

2. Decidability with a Deadline

We would certainly like science to be guaranteed to succeed by some fixed time, namely, the time we need the answer by. This corresponds to a trivial notion of *convergence*, where convergence to an answer by stage n of inquiry means simply producing that answer at n. Let b range over possible conjectures. Then define:

$$\alpha \text{ produces } b \text{ at } n \text{ on } h, \varepsilon \Leftrightarrow \alpha(h, \varepsilon|n) = b.$$

This notion of convergence says nothing about being right or wrong. *Success* is a matter of converging to the right conjecture on a given data stream. Traditionally, methodologists have recognized three different notions of contingent success. Verification requires convergence to 1 when and only when the hypothesis is correct. Refutation demands convergence to 0 when and only when the hypothesis is incorrect. Decision requires both. In the present case we have:

$$\alpha \text{ verifies}_C h \text{ at } n \text{ on } \varepsilon \Leftrightarrow [\alpha \text{ produces } 1 \text{ at } n \text{ on } h, \varepsilon \Leftrightarrow C(\varepsilon, h)].$$

$$\alpha \text{ refutes}_C h \text{ at } n \text{ on } \varepsilon \Leftrightarrow [\alpha \text{ produces } 0 \text{ at } n \text{ on } h, \varepsilon \Leftrightarrow \neg C(\varepsilon, h)].$$

$$\alpha \text{ decides}_C h \text{ at } n \text{ on } \varepsilon \Leftrightarrow \alpha \text{ both verifies}_C \text{ and refutes}_C h \text{ by } n \text{ on } \varepsilon.$$

So α can verify h at n on ε by producing anything but 1 (e.g., 0.5) when h is incorrect.

Reliability specifies the range of possible worlds over which the method must succeed. The logical conception of reliability demands success over all possible worlds in $\mathcal{K}$:

$$\alpha \text{ verifies}_C h \text{ at } n \text{ given } \mathcal{K} \Leftrightarrow \text{ for each } \varepsilon \in \mathcal{K}, \alpha \text{ verifies}_C h \text{ at } n \text{ on } \varepsilon$$
$$(Fig. 3.4).$$

$$\alpha \text{ refutes}_C h \text{ at } n \text{ given } \mathcal{K} \Leftrightarrow \text{ for each } \varepsilon \in \mathcal{K}, \alpha \text{ refutes}_C h \text{ at } n \text{ on } \varepsilon$$
$$(Fig. 3.5).$$

$$\alpha \text{ decides}_C h \text{ at } n \text{ given } \mathcal{K} \Leftrightarrow \text{ for all } \varepsilon \in \mathcal{K}, \alpha \text{ decides}_C h \text{ at } n \text{ on } \varepsilon$$
$$(Fig. 3.6).$$

Given definitions of verification, refutation, and decision *at* a given time, we can define verification, refutation, and decision *by* a given time.

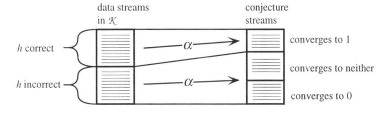

Figure 3.4

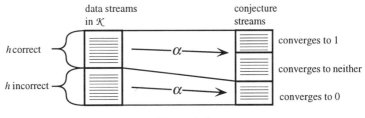

Figure 3.5

$$\alpha \begin{bmatrix} verifies_C \\ refutes_C \\ decides_C \end{bmatrix} h \text{ by } n \text{ given } \mathcal{K} \Leftrightarrow \text{ there is } m \leq n \text{ such that } \alpha \begin{bmatrix} verifies_C \\ refutes_C \\ decides_C \end{bmatrix} h$$

$$\text{at } m \text{ given } \mathcal{K}.$$

There is another sense of guaranteed success. It concerns the *range H* of hypotheses that the method can reliably assess.[4] $\mathcal{K}$ reflects uncertainty about the world under study, whereas H reflects uncertainty about one's next scientific job assignment. Accordingly, we define:

$$\alpha \begin{bmatrix} verifies_C \\ refutes_C \\ decides_C \end{bmatrix} H \text{ by } n \text{ given } \mathcal{K} \Leftrightarrow \text{ for all } h \in H,$$

$$\alpha \begin{bmatrix} verifies_C \\ refutes_C \\ decides_C \end{bmatrix} h \text{ by } n \text{ given } \mathcal{K}.$$

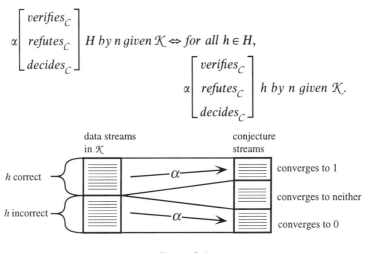

Figure 3.6

[4] Some reliabilist epistemologists seem to confuse these two senses, so that they take a method to be reliable if it *happens* to succeed over a wide range of hypotheses in the actual world. In my view, lucky success over lots of hypotheses does not add up to reliability. It adds up only to lots of lucky success. On my view, a method guaranteed to succeed on a single hypothesis is reliable for that hypothesis even if it fails for every other. I propose that the philosophers in question have confused alleged evidence for reliability with reliability itself. It may be hard to believe that a method could accidentally succeed over a wide range of hypotheses, but what is hard to believe can be true, and here we are defining what reliability *is*, not how we come to believe that a given system is reliable by watching its actual behavior on actual data.

Finally, given a definition of reliability for a particular method, we can immediately ascend to a notion of inductive problem *solvability*. It will be interesting to consider solvability by methods of various different kinds. Let $\mathcal{M}$ be a collection of assessment methods.

$$H \text{ is } \begin{bmatrix} verifiable_C \\ refutable_C \\ decidable_C \end{bmatrix} by \ n \ given \ \mathcal{K} \ by \ a \ method \ in \ \mathcal{M}$$

$$\Leftrightarrow there \ is \ an \ \alpha \in \mathcal{M} \ such \ that \ \alpha \begin{bmatrix} verifies_C \\ refutes_C \\ decides_C \end{bmatrix} H \ by \ n \ given \ \mathcal{K}.$$

When $H = \{h\}$, we will simply speak of the hypothesis h as being verifiable, refutable, or decidable by a given time. When reference to $\mathcal{M}$ is dropped, it should be understood that $\mathcal{M}$ is the set of all possible assessment methods.

Now we may think of a quadruple $(C, \mathcal{K}, \mathcal{M}, H)$ as an *inductive problem* that is either solvable or unsolvable in the sense described. Each notion of problem solvability to be considered may be analyzed into criteria of convergence, success, reliability, and range of application in this manner. A specification of these criteria will be referred to as a *paradigm*. The paradigm just defined is the *bounded sample decision* paradigm.

A basic fact about this paradigm is that verifiability, refutability, and decidability collapse for ideal methods. So henceforth, we need consider only decidability by n unless restrictions on the method class $\mathcal{M}$ are imposed that preclude the following, trivial construction (*Fig. 3.7*).

Proposition 3.2

(a) *The following statements are equivalent*:

 (i) *H is decidable$_C$ by n given $\mathcal{K}$.*

 (ii) *H is verifiable$_C$ by n given $\mathcal{K}$.*

 (iii) *H is refutable$_C$ by n given $\mathcal{K}$.*

(b) *H is decidable$_C$ by n given $\mathcal{K} \Rightarrow H$ is decidable$_C$ by each $n' \geq n$ given $\mathcal{K}$.*

Proof: (b) is immediate. (a) (i) $\Rightarrow$ (ii) & (iii) is immediate. (ii) $\Rightarrow$ (i): Suppose α verifies$_C$ H by n given $\mathcal{K}$. Define α' so that α' produces 1 when α does, and produces 0 otherwise. α' refutes$_C$ H by n given $\mathcal{K}$. (iii) $\Rightarrow$ (i) is similar. ■

The bounded sample decision paradigm is strict, but it is not impossible to meet. The hypothesis $h_{division \ at \ n}$, which states that the particle at hand is split at stage n, is clearly decidable by stage n simply by running the experiment and by looking at what happens at stage n. It is not hard to see that this hypothesis is not decidable by stage $n - 1$ when $\mathcal{K} = 2^\omega$. Suppose that some hypothesis

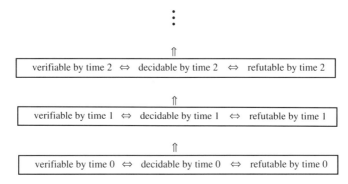

⋮

⇑

| verifiable by time 2 | ⇔ | decidable by time 2 | ⇔ | refutable by time 2 |

⇑

| verifiable by time 1 | ⇔ | decidable by time 1 | ⇔ | refutable by time 1 |

⇑

| verifiable by time 0 | ⇔ | decidable by time 0 | ⇔ | refutable by time 0 |

Figure 3.7

assessor α and some stage n are given. Imagine the scientist as being given a tour of a railroad switching yard, in which each track is an infinite data stream. The engineer of the train is the *inductive demon*, who is fiendishly devoted to fooling the scientist. The scientist makes his guesses, and the demon is free to turn switches in the switching yard wherever and whenever he pleases, so long as the infinite path ultimately taken by the train ends up in $\mathcal{K}$. That is, the only constraint on the demon is that he ultimately produce a data stream consistent with the scientist's background assumptions.

The demon proceeds according to the following, simple strategy (*Fig. 3.8*). He presents the scientist's method α with nothing but 0s up to stage $n - 1$. Method α must conjecture 0 or 1 at stage $n - 1$ in order to succeed by that stage. But if α says 0, the demon presents 1 at stage n and forever after; if α says 1, the demon presents 0 at stage n and forever after. So no matter what α does, it fails on the data stream produced by the demon. But this data stream is in $\mathcal{K}$ because any infinite sequence of 1s and 0s is. Thus α fails to decide$_C$ $h_{division\ at\ n}$ by stage $n - 1$ given $\mathcal{K}$. Since α is arbitrary, no possible assessment method succeeds in the required sense.

This is precisely Hume's argument for inductive skepticism. No matter how many sunrises we have seen up to stage $n - 1$, the sun may or may not rise at

Figure 3.8

stage n. If $\mathcal{K}$ admits both possibilities, the argument is a proof against decidability by stage $n - 1$. The same argument shows that $h_{division\ at\ n}$ is not verifiable or refutable by stage $n - 1$, either. Since n is arbitrary, this argument shows that the relation given in proposition 3.2(b) is optimal, and hence the levels in Figure 3.7 do not collapse. This is the simplest possible demonic argument against all possible scientific methods. As we shall see, the demon's task gets more difficult as the operative notion of convergence is weakened and as the scientist's knowledge is strengthened.

Scientific realists faced with demonic arguments sometimes object that there *is* no demon, as though one must be justified (in the realist's elusive sense!) in believing that a demon exists before such arguments must be heeded. But the real issue is the existence of a logically reliable method for the scientist, and demons are just a mathematical artifice for proving that no such method exists. If the scientist is actually a demonologist interested in whether or not a demon employing some strategy actually exists, then demonic arguments against this scientist would have to invoke metademons that try to fool the scientist about the demons under study.

The argument just presented is driven by the fact that $\mathcal{K}$ contains data streams presenting a fork to the scientist at stage $n - 1$, together with the demand that the scientist arrive at the truth by stage $n - 1$ (*Fig. 3.9*). So it can be overturned either by removing data streams from $\mathcal{K}$ (i.e., by adding background assumptions) or by relieving the stringent demand of convergence by a fixed time.

It is only slightly more complicated to show that $h_{divisible}$, which says that p can be divided, is not verifiable, refutable, or decidable by an arbitrary, fixed time given $\mathcal{K}$. Let's consider the case of verification by stage n. Let α be an arbitrary assessment method. The demon's strategy is to present 0s up to stage $n - 1$, and to wait for α to produce its conjecture at stage n. If the conjecture is 1, then the demon feeds 0s forever after. If the conjecture is anything but 1, the demon feeds 1s forever after (*Fig. 3.10*). In the former case, α produces 1 at n when $h_{divisible}$ is false, and in the latter case, α fails to produce 1 at n when $h_{divisible}$ is true. Either way, α fails to verify or to decide $h_{divisible}$ at stage n. But α and n are arbitrary, so no possible method can verify or decide $h_{divisible}$ by any fixed time. A similar argument works for the case of refutation, except that the demon produces 1 when the scientist produces anything but 0 and produces 0 otherwise. The same argument works for the hypotheses h_{inf}, h_{fin}, and $h_{LRF(1)=r}$, none of which is verifiable, refutable, or decidable by any fixed time.

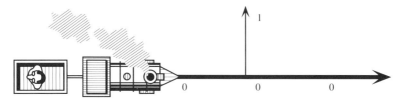

Figure 3.9

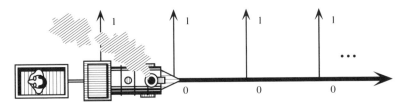

Figure 3.10

Keynes was correct to observe that those of us who are now alive are all dead by some fixed time. But Sextus was equally correct to maintain that by any fixed time we are all unreliable unless we already assume quite a bit. For example, if we assume that if all cuts up to stage n fail, all later cuts fail as well, then $h_{divisible}$ is decidable by stage n.

For those who assume no such thing and who would prefer that inquiry have some logical connection with the truth, it is of interest to investigate weaker senses of convergence that do not demand success by a fixed time, even though it is clear that we would prefer a method guaranteed to succeed in the near future, if such a method were to exist.

3.   Decidability, Verifiability, and Refutability with Certainty

If a method is guaranteed to succeed by a given stage n, then given our assumptions $\mathcal{K}$, the method has the truth at stage n. Thus, the method confers a kind of certainty upon its user at n, given $\mathcal{K}$. This certainty is very desirable when it can be had. Since we can't have certainty about infinite divisibility at some fixed time, perhaps we can have it by *some* time that cannot be specified in advance. Since we no longer know a priori when the method will be sure, it must tell us when it is sure by some sign (*Fig. 3.11*).

Any convention will do. I require that the method write an exclamation mark '!' just prior to announcing its certain conjecture. Nothing prevents a method from producing this mark of certainty several times, so we will take its certain conjecture to be the one immediately following the *first* occurrence of '!'. The others will be ignored, as though the method has finished its job and is merely producing irrelevant noise thereafter. Let $b = 0$ or 1. Then define:

Figure 3.11

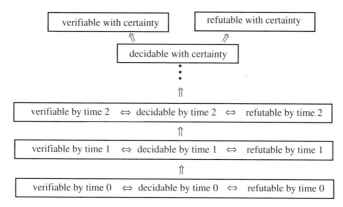

Figure 3.12

α *produces b with certainty on h, $\varepsilon \Leftrightarrow$ there is an n such that*

(a) $\alpha(h, \varepsilon|n) = \text{'!'},$

(b) $\alpha(h, \varepsilon|n + 1) = b,$ *and*

(c) *for each* $m < n$, $\alpha(h, \varepsilon|m) \neq \text{'!'}.$

This concept of convergence induces three notions of success, just as before:

α *verifies$_C$ h with certainty on ε*
$\Leftrightarrow [\alpha$ *produces 1 with certainty on h, $\varepsilon \Leftrightarrow C(\varepsilon, h)]$;*

α *refutes$_C$ h with certainty on ε*
$\Leftrightarrow [\alpha$ *produces 0 with certainty on h, $\varepsilon \Leftrightarrow \neg C(\varepsilon, h)]$;*

α *decides$_C$ h with certainty on ε*
$\Leftrightarrow \alpha$ *verifies$_C$ h with certainty on ε and α refutes$_C$ h with certainty on ε.*

These notions of success give rise to corresponding definitions of reliability, range of applicability, and problem solution just as before. Let $\overline{\mathscr{C}}$ denote the complement of $\mathscr{C}$. Then we have the following basic facts relating these paradigms (*Fig. 3.12*).[5]

Proposition 3.3

(a) *H is verifiable$_C$ with certainty given $\mathscr{K}$*
$\Leftrightarrow$ *H is refutable$_{\overline{C}}$ with certainty given $\mathscr{K}$.*

(b) *H is decidable$_C$ with certainty given $\mathscr{K}$*
$\Leftrightarrow$ *H is both verifiable$_C$ and refutable$_C$ with certainty given $\mathscr{K}$.*

(c) *For each n, if H is decidable$_C$ by time n given $\mathscr{K}$ then H is decidable$_C$ with certainty given $\mathscr{K}$.*

[5] In this case, the result (b) is trivial, but we will see that it fails in more complex paradigms.

Proof: (a) ($\Rightarrow$) Let α_1 verify$_C$ H with certainty given $\mathcal{K}$. Define α_2 to conjecture 0 when α_1 conjectures 1 and to conjecture 1 when α_1 conjectures 0. All other conjectures (including '!') are left unaltered. α_2 refutes H with certainty given $\mathcal{K}$ with respect to $\bar{C}$. ($\Leftarrow$) is similar.

(b) ($\Rightarrow$) Immediate. ($\Leftarrow$) Let α_1 verify$_C$ H with certainty given $\mathcal{K}$, and let α_2 refute$_C$ H with certainty given $\mathcal{K}$. Let method α conjecture 0.5 until either α_1 or α_2 conjectures '!'. Then α conjectures '!', and repeats forever whatever the machine that produced '!' says next.

(c) Suppose α_1 decides$_C$ H at n given $\mathcal{K}$. Define α_2 to mimic α_1 exactly, except at $n-1$, when α_2 produces '!' no matter what. α_2 decides$_C$ H with certainty given $\mathcal{K}$. ∎

We have seen that the hypothesis $h_{divisible}$ is not verifiable, refutable, or decidable by any fixed time given 2^ω. We can also show that $h_{divisible}$ is not decidable with certainty given 2^ω, even when we do not insist on success by a fixed time. Once again, a demonic argument suffices. Let assessment method α be given. The demon's strategy is to present the everywhere 0 sequence (indicating no cuts) until the method produces its first mark of certainty. If the next conjecture is 1, the demon feeds 0 forever after. If the next conjecture is 0, the demon feeds 1 forever after. And if the next conjecture is anything else, it doesn't matter what the demon does, so long as he produces a 0–1 data stream, so we will arbitrarily have him produce all 0s. If α never produces a mark of certainty followed by a 0 or a 1, then α clearly fails to decide $h_{divisible}$ with certainty given $\mathcal{K}$. If α produces '!' followed immediately by 0, then $h_{divisible}$ is true so α is wrong. If α produces '!' followed immediately by 1, then $h_{divisible}$ is false, so α is wrong again (*Fig. 3.13*). So in any case, α fails to succeed on the data stream produced by the demon, which is constructed so as to be in $\mathcal{K}$. Since α is arbitrary, no possible assessment method can decide $h_{divisible}$ with certainty given $\mathcal{K}$.

It follows that h_{simple}, the negation of $h_{divisible}$, is not decidable with certainty given $\mathcal{K}$, either. This is just the problem of universal generalization, and the preceding demonic argument was already familiar to philosophers before the time of Sextus Empiricus. On the other hand, $h_{divisible}$ is verifiable with certainty. The method need only produce conjecture 0 until a successful cut is observed, and then produce '!', 1, 1, ... forever after. Dually, h_{simple} is refutable with certainty. The method just reverses the conjectures of the method for $h_{divisible}$. It follows that $h_{divisible}$ is not refutable with certainty and h_{simple} is not verifiable with certainty. This is an improvement over the situation regarding decidability,

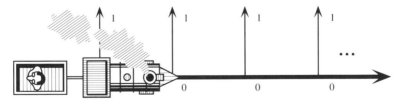

Figure 3.13

verifiability, and refutability by a fixed time, for the same problems are not solvable in those senses. To enhance the scope of reliable inquiry by weakening the skeptic's proposed standard of success (decision with certainty or decision now) is the basic idea behind Popper's falsificationist philosophy of science. Verificationism, the idea that theoremhood can be verified but not refuted with certainty, is the fundamental idea behind the philosophy of mathematical proof.

Let's return to Kant's question about the infinite divisibility of matter. It is readily seen to be neither verifiable nor refutable with certainty. For given an assessment method α, the demon can present α with nothing but successful cuts until α says preceded by '!', at which time the demon provides no more cuts, and α fails to verify infinite divisibility with certainty.

Similarly, the demon can provide only failed cuts until α says 0, after which only successful cuts are announced, so α fails to refute the infinite divisibility hypothesis with certainty. Since α is arbitrary, no possible method can verify or refute infinite divisibility with certainty. Hence, no possible method can decide infinite divisibility with certainty, either. So although verificationism and falsificationism expand the scope of reliable inquiry, they do not save infinite divisibility from Kant's charge of running beyond all possible (local) experience. The situation with limiting relative frequency is even worse. Perhaps we can bring these hypotheses under the purview of logically reliable inquiry by weakening the operative concept of convergence still further.

4. Verification, Refutation, and Decision in the Limit

Certainty demands that a method eventually give a sign that it has arrived at a correct answer. The impossibility of giving such a sign for universal hypotheses is the issue that drives Plato's *Meno* paradox.

> *Meno*: And how will you inquire, Socrates, into that which you do not know? What will you put forth as the subject of inquiry? And if you find what you want, how will you ever know that this is the thing which you did not know?[6]

Meno's underlying assumption is that inquiry is worthless unless it can produce a determinate sign that it has succeeded. But it is possible for a method to be guaranteed to arrive at the truth and to stick with it forever after without ever giving such a sign. Stabilization requires only that inquiry eventually settle down to some fixed assessment value, even though the user of the method may never be sure when stabilization has occurred, since a future reversal is always possible for all he knows (*Fig. 3.14*).

> α *stabilizes to b for h on ε*
> $\Leftrightarrow$ *there is a stage n such that for each later stage $m \geq n$, $\alpha(h, \varepsilon|m) = b$.*

Nonetheless, after the method has stabilized, no such upsets ever occur

---

[6] Plato (1949): 36.

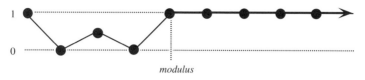

modulus

Figure 3.14

again. We will refer to the earliest time after which all conjectures are the same as the *modulus of convergence*.

$$modulus_\alpha(h, \varepsilon) = the\ least\ n\ such\ that\ for\ all\ m \geq n,\ \alpha(h, \varepsilon|m) = \alpha(h, \varepsilon|n).$$

The convergence criterion of stabilization in the limit gives rise in the usual way to three different concepts of success on a data stream:

$\alpha\ verifies_C\ h\ in\ the\ limit\ on\ \varepsilon \Leftrightarrow [\alpha\ stabilizes\ to\ 1\ on\ h,\ \varepsilon \Leftrightarrow C(\varepsilon, h)].$

$\alpha\ refutes_C\ h\ in\ the\ limit\ on\ \varepsilon \Leftrightarrow [\alpha\ stabilizes\ to\ 0\ on\ h,\ \varepsilon \Leftrightarrow \neg C(\varepsilon, h)].$

$\alpha\ decides_C\ h\ in\ the\ limit\ on\ \varepsilon$
$\quad\Leftrightarrow \alpha\ both\ verifies_C\ and\ refutes_C\ in\ the\ limit\ on\ h,\ \varepsilon.$

The corresponding definitions of reliability, range of applicability, and problem solvability proceed just as before, and need not detain us here.

The idea that inquiry should stabilize to the truth has appealed to philosophers for a long time. Indeed, Plato made it a centerpiece of his theory of knowledge, as presented in the *Meno*.

> While [true opinions] abide with us they are beautiful and fruitful, but they run away out of the human soul, and do not remain long, and therefore they are not of much value until they are fastened by the tie of the cause [reason-why]; and this fastening of them, friend Meno, is recollection, as you and I have agreed to call it. But when they are bound, in the first place, they have the nature of knowledge; and, in the second place, they are abiding. And this is why knowledge is more honorable and excellent than true opinion, because fastened by a chain.[7]

One reading of the passage is that belief formed by a method guaranteed to stabilize to the truth (e.g., Platonic recollection) is eventually stable, and when it stabilizes, so that it does not vacillate in the face of true data, it is knowledge. Reliabilist methodology need not endorse this or any other account of knowledge, but insofar as knowledge is held to be at least stable, true belief formed by a reliable process, the analysis of stabilization to the truth is relevant to the theory of knowledge. The basic logical relations among the limiting assessment paradigms are as follows (*Fig. 3.15*):

[7] Plato (1949): 58–59.

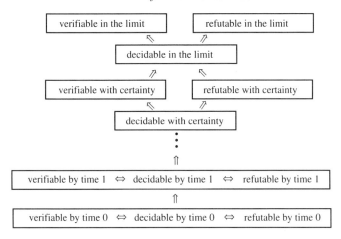

Figure 3.15

Proposition 3.4

(a) *H is verifiable$_C$ in the limit given $\mathcal{K}$*
    ⇔ H is refutable$_{\bar{C}}$ in the limit given $\mathcal{K}$.

(b) *H is decidable$_C$ in the limit given $\mathcal{K}$*
    ⇔ H is both verifiable$_C$ and refutable$_C$ in the limit given $\mathcal{K}$.

(c) *H is decidable$_C$, verifiable$_C$, or refutable$_C$ with certainty given $\mathcal{K}$*
    ⇒ H is decidable$_C$ in the limit given $\mathcal{K}$.

Proof: Let α_1 verify$_C$ *H* in the limit given $\mathcal{K}$. Define $\alpha_2(h, e) = 1 - \alpha_1(h, e)$. α_2 refutes *H* in the limit given $\mathcal{K}$ with respect to $\bar{C}$.

(b) (⇒) Immediate. (⇐) Let α_1 verify$_C$ *H* in the limit given $\mathcal{K}$, and let α_2 verify$_{\bar{C}}$ *H* in the limit given $\mathcal{K}$, by (a). Define method α as follows. α simulates α_1 and α_2 on each initial segment of the current data *e*. If α_1 says something other than 1 more recently than α_2, then α conjectures 0. Otherwise α conjectures 1.

Let $\varepsilon \in \mathcal{K}$, $h \in H$. If $C(\varepsilon, h)$, then α_1 stabilizes to 1 and α_2 does not, so some time after the modulus of convergence of α_1 on ε, α_2 produces a non-1 conjecture, and α produces 1 thereafter. If $\neg C(\varepsilon, h)$, then α_2 stabilizes to 1 and α_1 does not, so by a similar argument α stabilizes to 0.

(c) Let α_1 verify$_C$ *H* with certainty given $\mathcal{K}$. To verify$_C$ *H* in the limit given $\mathcal{K}$, let α conjecture 0 until α_1 produces '!', followed by 1, after which α says 1 no matter what. The decision case follows immediately. A dual construction works for the case of refutation. ∎

Despite the lenience of decidability in the limit, it is not a panacea for local underdetermination. For example, without extra background knowledge, the hypothesis that matter is infinitely divisible is not decidable in the limit. The proof is a limiting generalization of the short-run demonic arguments presented earlier.

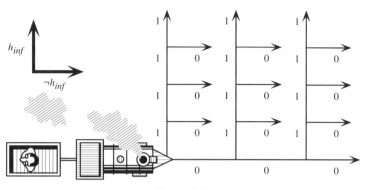

Figure 3.16

Recall the picture of $\mathcal{K}$ as an infinite switchyard through which the inductive demon takes the scientist for a ride. In our problem, $\mathcal{K} = 2^\omega$, so the switchyard is an infinite, binary-branching tree of 1s and 0s (*Fig. 3.16*). The demon starts out by presenting 111 ... until α says 1. If α says 1, the demon switches to all 0s until α says 0. If α then says 0, the demon starts presenting 1s until α says 1. This process continues forever. Either α stabilizes to 1 or to 0 on the data stream provided, or not. Suppose α stabilizes to 1. Then the demon feeds 0s forever after α stabilizes to 1, so h_{inf} is false, and α is wrong. Suppose α stabilizes to 0. Then the demon feeds 1s forever after the modulus of convergence, so h_{inf} is true, and α again fails. But if α does not stabilize to 0 or to 1, α fails again, since α must stabilize to one or the other so long as the data stream contains only 1s and 0s, which it will according to the demon's strategy. So in any event, α fails. Since α is arbitrary, we know that no possible ideal assessment procedure can decide h_{inf} given $\mathcal{K}$ in the limit. This result seems to vindicate Kant's opinion that the question about infinite divisibility goes beyond all possible experience.

On the other hand, h_{inf} is refutable in the limit given $\mathcal{K}$ by a trivial method. Let α_{repeat} simply repeat the last datum it has seen when assessing h_{inf}. If its current datum is a 1, α_{repeat} conjectures 1. If its current datum is 0, α_{repeat} conjectures 0. Let $\varepsilon \in 2^\omega$. Suppose h_{inf} is correct for ε. Then infinitely many 1s occur, so α_{repeat} correctly fails to stabilize to 0. Suppose h_{inf} is incorrect for ε. Then only finitely many 1s occur in ε. After the last 1 is seen, α_{repeat} converges to 0. Thus, the trivial method α_{repeat} refutes h_{inf} in the limit. So in another sense, Kant was wrong. By proposition 4.1, it follows from the fact that h_{inf} is refutable but not decidable in the limit that h_{inf} is not verifiable in the limit. Thus, its negation h_{fin} is verifiable but neither refutable nor decidable in the limit.

There is a tendency for philosophers to suppose that the demon is omnipotent so that the deck is stacked against the scientist. But this is not the case for the *inductive* demons under consideration. Since their outputs are determined locally, just as the scientist's are, the scientist may also be in a position to fool every possible demon. That is just what happens when the scientist uses a logically reliable method. For example, consider the case of verifying h_{fin} in the limit. A would-be demon would have to produce a data

Figure 3.17

stream in $C_{h_{fin}}$ just in case the scientist's conjecture stream does not stabilize to 1. Since the demon only sees the scientist's conjectures as they are produced, he can't tell if the scientist's vacillations will continue forever, or stop. The scientist's successful method of conjecturing the current datum is guaranteed to outwit the demon, since the method converges to 1 if and only if the data stream constructed by the demon does not.

Example 3.5 Cognitive psychology

For many years, cognitive psychologists have been concerned to discover the general computational architecture of the mind. One might object to the implicit assumption that there is such a program to be found. If human behavioral dispositions are actually uncomputable, there is no such program. So it would seem that the first question is whether it is possible, even in the limit, to decide whether or not an arbitrary input-output behavior is computable (*Fig. 3.17*).

J. R. Lucas attempted to give metaphysical arguments based on Gödel's theorem to the effect that human behavior cannot be computable, and recently the physicist R. Penrose has followed suit. A. Newell and H. Simon have responded that the issue is an empirical one: when increasing fragments of human behavior are duplicated by machines, the evidence for the computability of cognition increases.[8] The philosopher H. Dreyfus has answered that individual successes on "microworld" problems will never add up to real intelligence.

[A]n overall pattern has emerged: success with simple mechanical forms of information processing, great expectations, and then failure when confronted with more complicated forms of behavior. Simon's predictions fall into place as just another example of the phenomenon which Bar-Hillel has called the "fallacy of the successful first step." Simon himself, however, has drawn no such sobering conclusions.[9]

[8] Lucas (1961), Penrose (1989), Newell and Simon (1976).
[9] Dreyfus (1979): 129.

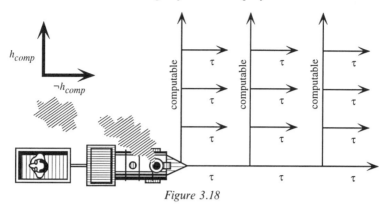

Figure 3.18

The situation is reminiscent of the one concerning the infinite divisibility of matter. Does the question lie beyond all possible experience? In this case, the lab feeds an effective ordering of all possible stimuli to the subject and records the response. To avoid equivocal descriptions of responses, the subject is tied into a Skinner box with only one finger free to press a button (response 0) or to refuse to press it (response 1) within a second. The hypothesis h_{comp} is correct if and only if the response sequence is a computable sequence of 1s and 0s. For all the scientist assumes a priori, any response sequence may arise, so again we let $\mathcal{K} = 2^\omega$.

Let α be an assessment method. The demon has at his disposal an infinite list of all the computable data streams in 2^ω.[10] He also has in hand a fixed, noncomputable data stream $\tau \in 2^\omega$.[11] He feeds α data generated by the first compatable data stream until α eventually produces a non-0 conjecture. He starts presenting τ from the beginning until α says 0. Then he finds the next computable data stream that agrees with the data produced so far and presents it until α makes a non-0 output, and so forth (*Fig. 3.18*). Such a data stream can always be found, since each finite chunk e of data can be recorded in a lookup table by some computer program that computes a data stream extending e.

If α stabilizes neither to 1 nor to 0, then α fails to decide h_{comp} in the limit on the data presented. If α stabilizes to 1, then the uncomputable data stream τ is presented in its entirety (after some finite data sequence has been presented). Thus, the overall data stream presented is uncomputable, so h_{comp} is false and α fails to decide h_{comp} in the limit on the data provided. If α stabilizes to 0, then the data stream presented is computable, so h_{comp} is true and α again fails. So in any case, α fails on the data stream presented. Since α is arbitrary, h_{comp} is not decidable in the limit given 2^ω.

On the other hand, h_{comp} is verifiable in the limit by an ideal method given 2^ω. The ideal method α_{cogsci} maintains a list of all the computable sequences of

---

[10] There are just countably many since there are at most countably many computer programs to compute them.

[11] Examples of uncomputable functions in 2^ω will be given in chapter 6.

1s and 0s. It initializes a pointer to the beginning of this list. Each time the data disagrees with the data stream currently pointed to, the pointer is bumped to the next computable data stream consistent with the data, and the method returns 0. If the data agrees with the sequence the pointer currently points to, the method outputs 1.

If h_{comp} is correct for data stream ε, then the pointer never bumps past some machine in α_{cogsci}'s enumeration, so the method correctly stabilizes to 1. If h_{comp} is incorrect for data stream ε, then ε matches no computable sequence in the list, so the pointer never stops bumping, and infinitely many 0s are output, which is again correct. This *bumping pointer* method is a very general technique for obtaining positive results concerning limiting verifiability, as we shall see in the next chapter.

So computable cognition turns out to be exactly dual to infinite divisibility, so far as ideal inquiry is concerned. The former is verifiable but not refutable in the limit, and the latter is refutable but not verifiable in the limit. Both questions are difficult, but some questions are even harder, as we shall now see.

Example 3.6   Limiting relative frequency again

Let o be a possible datum or outcome. Recall that $F_\varepsilon(o, n) =$ the number of occurrences of o in ε up to and including time n, $RF_\varepsilon(o, n) = F_n(o, n)/n$, and that the limiting relative frequency of o in ε is defined as follows:

$$LRF_\varepsilon(o) = r \Leftrightarrow \text{for each } s > 0 \text{ there is an } n \text{ such that for each } m \geq n,$$
$$|RF_\varepsilon(o, m) - r| < s.$$

Statisticians are often concerned with finding out whether some probability lies within a given range. Accordingly, for each set S of reals between 0 and 1, define:

$$LRF_S(o) = \{\varepsilon: LRF_\varepsilon(0) \in S\}.$$

I will refer to $LRF_S(o)$ as a *frequency hypothesis for o*. Special cases include *point hypotheses* of form $LRF_{\{r\}}(o)$ and *closed interval hypotheses* of form $LRF_{[r, r']}(o)$. There are also *open interval hypotheses* (e.g., $LRF_{(r, r')}(o)$) and more complicated hypotheses in which S is not an interval.

Now we may ask: What sorts of frequency hypotheses may be decided, verified, or refuted in the limit? When no background assumptions are given, the result is rather dismal.

Proposition 3.7

If $\mathcal{K} = 2^\omega$ then no nonempty frequency hypothesis is verifiable in the limit.

Proof: Let $r \in S$. Without loss of generality, we consider the case in which $r > 0$, the case in which $r < 1$ being similar. Let α be an arbitrary assessment method.

Let $q_0, q_1, \ldots, q_n, \ldots$ be an infinite, monotone, increasing sequence of rationals converging to r such that for each i, $0 < q_i < r$. The demon proceeds in stages as follows. At stage 0, the demon's plan is to repeatedly drive the relative frequency of o below q_0 and above q_1. At stage $n + 1$, the demon's plan is to drive the relative frequency of o between q_n and r and then to repeatedly drive the relative frequency of o below q_{n+1} and above q_{n+2} without ever going below q_n or above r. The demon moves from stage n to stage $n + 1$ when the following conditions are met:

(a) α has conjectured at least $n + 1$ non-1s on the data presented so far.
(b) Enough data has been seen to dampen the effect on relative frequency of a single datum so that it is possible for the demon to hold the relative frequency of o above q_n and below r during stage $n + 1$.

Suppose α stabilizes to 1. Then the demon ends up stuck for eternity at some stage $n + 1$, and hence presents a data stream in which the relative frequency of o oscillates forever below q_{n+1} and above q_n, so no limiting relative frequency exists and hence $LRF_S(o)$ is incorrect. So suppose α does not stabilize to 1. Then the demon runs through each stage in the limit, so the relative frequency of o is constrained in ever tighter intervals around r and hence $LRF_S(o)$ is correct (*Fig. 3.19*). So α is wrong in either case. Since α is arbitrary, the result follows.   ∎

Proposition 3.8

If $\mathcal{K} = 2^\omega$ then no nonempty frequency hypothesis is refutable in the limit.

Proof: Let $r \in S$. Without loss of generality, suppose that $r > 0$, the case in which $r < 1$ being similar. Choose ε so that $LRF_\varepsilon(o) = r$. Let α be an arbitrary assessment method. Let q, q' be rationals such that $0 < q < q' < r$. The demon starts by feeding ε to α until α says something other than 0. Then the demon proceeds to drive the relative frequency of o below q and above q', until α once again says 0 and the relative frequency has been driven below q and above q' at least once. When α says 0, the demon continues feeding ε, from where he left off last. If α stabilizes to 0, then the limiting relative frequency of o in the data stream is r since the data stream is just ε with some initial segment tacked on, so $LRF_S(o)$ is correct. If α produces a conjecture other than 0 infinitely often,

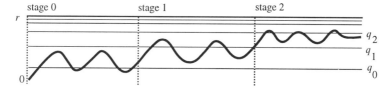

Figure 3.19

then the observed frequency of o vacillates forever outside of the fixed interval from q to q', so no limiting relative frequency exists, and hence $LRF_S(o)$ is false. So α is wrong in either case. Since α is arbitrary, the result follows. ∎

In the standard theory of statistical significance tests, it is usually assumed that the frequency hypothesis in question is to be tested only against other frequency hypotheses, and not against the possibility that the limiting relative frequency does not exist. Accordingly, let $LRF(o)$ denote the set of all data streams in which the limiting relative frequency of outcome o is defined. This time the result is more optimistic.

Proposition 3.9

(a) $LRF_{[r, r']}(o)$ is refutable in the limit given $LRF(o)$.

(b) $LRF_{(r, r')}(o)$ is verifiable in the limit given $LRF(o)$.

Proof: (a) Method α works as follows. α comes equipped with an infinitely repetitive enumeration $q_0, q_1, \ldots, q_n, \ldots$ of the rationals in $[0, 1]$ (i.e., each such rational occurs infinitely often in the enumeration). α starts out with a pointer at q_0. On empty data, α arbitrarily outputs 1 and leaves the pointer at q_0 (*Fig. 3.20*).

Given finite data sequence e, α calculates the relative frequency w of o in e (i.e., $w = RF_e(o, lh(e))$). Let q_i be the rational number pointed to after running α on $e-$. Then α checks whether $w \in [r - q_i, r' + q_i]$. If so, then the pointer is moved one step to the right and α conjectures 1. Otherwise, the pointer is left where it is and α conjectures 0.

Let $\varepsilon \in LRF_{[r, r']}(o)$. Then for some s such that $r \leq s \leq r'$, $LRF_\varepsilon(o) = s$. So for each q_i, there is an n such that $RF_\varepsilon(o, n) \in [r - q_i, r' + q_i]$. So the pointer is bumped infinitely often and α correctly fails to converge to 0. Suppose $\varepsilon \in LRF(o) - LRF_{[r, r']}(o)$. Then since $\varepsilon \in LRF(o)$, there is an $s \notin [r, r']$ such that $LRF_\varepsilon(0) = s$. Without loss of generality consider the case in which $s > r'$. Pick some q_i such that $0 < q_i$ and $q_i + r' < s$.

For some n, we have that for each $m \geq n$, $RF_\varepsilon(o, m) \notin [r - q_i, r' + q_i]$. There is a j past the current pointer position at stage n such that $q_i = q_j$, since the enumeration is infinitely repetitive. Since for each $m \geq n$, $RF_\varepsilon(o, m) \notin$

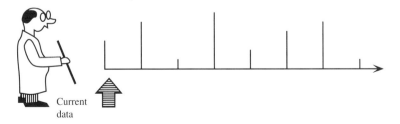

Current
data

Figure 3.20

$[r - q_i, r' + q_i]$, the pointer is never bumped past j, so α converges to 0, as required.

(b) Similar argument, switching 1 for 0 and $[0, 1] - (r, r')$ for $[r, r']$. ∎

Now the question is whether the strategy described could possibly be improved to decide frequency hypotheses in the limit, given that a limiting relative frequency exists. The answer is negative.

Proposition 3.10 (C. Juhl)

(a) *If $0 < r$ or $r' < 1$ then $LRF_{[r,r']}(o)$ is not verifiable in the limit given $LRF(o)$.*

(b) *$LRF_{(r,r')}(o)$ is not refutable in the limit given $LRF(o)$.*

Proof: In light of the preceding two results, it suffices to show that neither hypothesis is decidable in the limit given $LRF(o)$. (a) Without loss of generality, suppose that $r' < 1$. Let $q = 1 - r'$. Let $q_1, q_2, \ldots, q_n, \ldots$ be an infinite descending sequence of nonzero rationals that starts with q and that converges to 0 without ever arriving at 0. The demon starts by feeding data from some data stream ε such that $LRF_\varepsilon(o) = r'$ and such that the relative frequency of o never goes below r'. When α says 1, the demon presents data that drive the relative frequency of o ever closer to $r' + q_1$ without leaving the interval $[r', r' + q_1]$. When α says something other than 1, the demon resumes driving the observed frequency back to r' from above, without leaving the interval $[r', r' + q_1]$. This may not be possible immediately after α says 1, but it will be eventually, once sufficient data have been presented to dampen out the effect on observed relative frequency of a single observation. Therefore, the demon may have to wait some finite time before implementing this plan. The next time α says 1, the cycle repeats, but with q_2 replacing q_1, and so on, forever. If α stabilizes to 1, then the limiting relative frequency of o in the data stream presented lies outside of $[r, r']$, so $LRF_{[r,r']}(o)$ is false and α fails. If α does not stabilize to 1, then either α conjectures 1 infinitely often or not. If α does not conjecture 1 infinitely often, then the demon gets stuck at a given stage and drives the relative frequency to r' so $LRF_{[r,r']}(o)$ is true but α fails to converge to 1. If α does conjecture 1 infinitely often without stabilizing to 1, then the demon goes through infinitely many distinct stages so the limiting relative frequency of o is again r', and $LRF_{[r,r']}(o)$ is once again true (*Fig. 3.21*), so α fails in every case. Since α is arbitrary, no possible assessment method can verify $LRF_{[r,r']}(o)$ in the limit. (b) is similar. ∎

The preceding results permit us to relate limiting verification, refutation, and decision to standards of reliability more frequently encountered in classical statistics. From a sufficiently abstract point of view, a *statistical test* is an assessment method that conjectures 0 or 1 on each finite data sequence, where

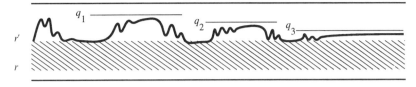

Figure 3.21

1 is read as *acceptance* and 0 is read as *rejection*. In statistical jargon, a *type 1 error* occurs when a true hypothesis is rejected and a *type 2 error* occurs when a false hypothesis is accepted. A standard goal of statistical testing is then to logically guarantee no more than a given limiting relative frequency r_1 of type 1 error, while minimizing the limiting relative frequency r_2 of type 2 error as much as possible given r_1. To minimize the limiting relative frequency of type 2 error is to maximize the limiting relative frequency $1 - r_2$ of rejecting the hypothesis when it is false. Neyman put the matter this way:

> It may often be proved that if we behave according to such a rule, then in the long run we shall reject h when it is true not more, say, than once in a hundred times, and in addition we may have evidence that we shall reject h sufficiently often when it is false.[12]

If such an r_1 exists, then it is said to be the *significance* of the test (with respect to h and $\mathcal{K}$). If such an r_2 exists, then $1 - r_2$ is called the *power* of the test (with respect to h and $\mathcal{K}$). A test is said to be *biased* when its power does not exceed its significance. In such a case, the limiting relative frequency of rejecting the hypothesis when it is false does not exceed the limiting relative frequency of rejecting it when it is true, so that flipping a fair coin to decide rejection would do as well as using the test so far as limiting relative frequencies of error are concerned. For this reason, biased tests are sometimes said to be *less than useless*. It is therefore of interest to examine the conditions under which an *unbiased* test exists.

It turns out that the relationship between unbiased testability and stabilization to the truth in the limit is sensitive to whether the significance level is strictly greater than or merely no less than the limiting relative frequency of type 1 error over all of $\mathcal{K}$. We may call the test *open* in the former case and *closed* in the latter. These ideas yield a learning-theoretic paradigm with a statistical flavor. Define:

$$\alpha(h, \varepsilon) = \tau \Leftrightarrow \forall n, \, \tau_n = \alpha(h, \varepsilon | n).$$

---

[12] Neyman and Pearson (1933): 142.

In other words, $\alpha(h, \varepsilon)$ denotes the infinite conjecture sequence produced by α as more and more of ε is read. Let $\mathscr{C}_h$ denote the set of all data streams for which h is correct. Then define:[13]

> α is an open unbiased test$_C$ for h given $\mathscr{K}$ at significance $r \Leftrightarrow \forall \varepsilon \in \mathscr{K} - \mathscr{C}_h$,
> $LRF_{\alpha(h, \varepsilon)}(0)$ exists and is $\geq r$ and $\forall \varepsilon \in \mathscr{K} \cap C_h$,
> $LRF_{\alpha(h, \varepsilon)}(0)$ exists and is $< r$.

> α is a closed unbiased test$_C$ for h given $\mathscr{K}$ at significance $r \Leftrightarrow \forall \varepsilon \in \mathscr{K} - \mathscr{C}_h$,
> $LRF_{\alpha(h, \varepsilon)}(0)$ exists and is $> r$ and $\forall \varepsilon \in \mathscr{K} \cap C_h$,
> $LRF_{\alpha(h, \varepsilon)}(0)$ exists and is $\leq r$.

> h is open [closed] unbiased testable$_C$ given $\mathscr{K}$
> $\Leftrightarrow$ there is an α and an r such that α is an open [closed, clopen] unbiased test$_C$ for h given $\mathscr{K}$ at significance r.

We may now consider the relationship between unbiased testability and limiting verification and refutation. The result is one of exact equivalence, depending on whether the limiting frequency of type 1 errror is $\leq r$ or $< r$.

Proposition 3.11   (with C. Juhl)

(a) h is open unbiased testable$_C$ given $\mathscr{K}$
$\Leftrightarrow$ h is verifiable$_C$ in the limit given $\mathscr{K}$.

(b) h is closed unbiased testable$_C$ given $\mathscr{K}$
$\Leftrightarrow$ h is refutable$_C$ in the limit given $\mathscr{K}$.

Proof: (a) ($\Rightarrow$) Let α be an open unbiased test$_C$ of h given $\mathscr{K}$ with significance level r. We construct a limiting verifier$_C$ of h given $\mathscr{K}$ that uses the successive conjectures of α. The proof of proposition 3.9(b) yields that $LRF_{[0, r)}(0)$ is verifiable in the limit given $LRF(0)$, say by method β. Let $\gamma = \beta \circ \alpha$. Let $\varepsilon \in C_h \cap \mathscr{K}$. Then $LRF_{\alpha(h, \varepsilon)}(0)$ exists and is $< r$. Let $\alpha(h, \varepsilon)$ denote the infinite sequence of conjectures $\alpha(h, \varepsilon|0)$, $\alpha(h, \varepsilon|1)$, ... Hence, $\alpha(h, \varepsilon) \in LRF_{[0, r)}(0)$, so β stabilizes to 1 on $\alpha(h, \varepsilon)$. So γ stabilizes to 1 on ε. Let $\varepsilon \in \mathscr{K} - C_h$. Then $LRF_{\alpha(h, \varepsilon)}(0)$ exists and is $\geq r$. Hence, $\alpha(h, \varepsilon) \notin LRF_{[0, r)}(0)$, so β does not stabilize to 1 on $\alpha(h, \varepsilon)$. So γ does not stabilize to 1 on ε.

($\Leftarrow$) Suppose that α verifies$_C$ h in the limit given $\mathscr{K}$. We construct an open, unbiased test with significance level 1 that uses the conjectures of α. β maintains a list c of natural numbers initialized to (0). β simulates α on the data as it feeds in and adds n to the end of the list when α has produced exactly n conjectures less than 1. β produces its current conjecture in accordance with

---

[13] The senses of statistical testability defined here are more general than usual in the sense that real tests produce conjectures depending only on the current sample, without reference to the samples taken before. They are more specific in the sense that, statistical tests are supposed to work when the truth of the hypothesis changes spontaneously from test to test, whereas in the paradigm just defined it is assumed that the truth of h is fixed for all time.

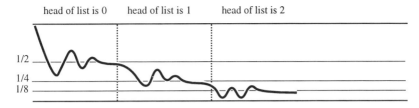

Figure 3.22

the number at the head of the list c. If the number at the head of the list is currently n, then β produces conjectures in $\{0, 1\}$ in such a way as to drive the relative frequency of 1s to $1/2^{n+1}$ without ever allowing the observed frequency to exceed $1/2^n$. This is trivial when $n = 0$. If $n + 1$ occurs next in the list, then when (a) the current frequency of 1 conjectures is between $1/2^n$ and $1/2^{n+1}$ and (b) enough conjectures have been made so that it is possible not to exceed $1/2^{n+1}$ at the next stage, then the first item in c is deleted (*Fig. 3.22*).

Let $\varepsilon \in \mathcal{K} \cap C_h$. Then α stabilizes to 1. So only finitely many numbers are ever added to c, so $LRF_{\beta(h, \varepsilon)}(1) > 0$ and hence $LRF_{\beta(h, \varepsilon)}(0) < 1$. Let $\varepsilon \in \mathcal{K} - C_h$. Then every number is eventually added to c, so for each n, the relative frequency of 1s conjectured by β on ε eventually remains below $1/2^n$ and hence $LRF_{\beta(h, \varepsilon)}(1) = 0$, so $LRF_{\beta(h, \varepsilon)}(0) = 1$. Hence, β is an open unbiased test$_C$ of h given $\mathcal{K}$ with significance level 1. (b) follows by a similar argument. ∎

Frequentists usually add to background knowledge the assumption that the data stream is random.[14] A *place selection* is a total function that picks a position in the data stream beyond position n when provided with a finite initial segment of the data stream of length n. Then if we run the place selection function over the entire data stream, it will eventually pick out some infinite subsequence of the original data stream. A place selection π is said to be a *betting system* for ε just in case the limiting relative frequency of some datum o in the subsequence of ε selected by π is different from the limiting relative frequency of o in ε. Let $\mathcal{PS}$ be a fixed, countable collection of place selections. Let ε be a data stream in which the limiting relative frequency of each datum occurring in ε exists. Then ε is $\mathcal{PS}$-*random* just in case there is no betting system for ε in $\mathcal{PS}$. Since randomness is a property of data streams, it is yet another empirical assumption that is subject to empirical scrutiny (cf. exercise 3.3). If it is assumed as background knowledge, however, then the ($\Rightarrow$) side of the preceding result may not hold, since there is no guarantee that the data stream produced by the demon in the proof is random. The effect of randomness assumptions upon logical reliability is an important issue for further study.

[14] Von Mises (1981).

5. Decision with *n* Mind Changes

Whenever α stabilizes to b for h on ε, α changes its conjecture about h only finitely many times. The number of times α changes its conjecture will be called the number of *mind changes* of α for h on ε, which I denote $mc_\alpha(h, \varepsilon)$. More precisely,

$$mc_\alpha(h, \varepsilon) = |\{n \in \omega\colon \alpha(h, \varepsilon|n) \neq \alpha(h, \varepsilon|n + 1)\}|.$$

Decision in the limit countenances an arbitrary number of mind changes by α. The prospect of surprises in the future is what keeps the scientist's stomach churning. It would be nice if some a priori bound could be placed on the number of mind changes the scientist will encounter. Then if the method happens to use up all of its mind changes, the scientist can quit with certainty.

When mind changes are counted, it turns out to matter what sort of conjecture the method α starts with before seeing any data. In the case of a universal generalization such as "all ravens are black," the scientist can succeed with one mind change starting with 1 by assuming the hypothesis is true until it is refuted. In the case of an existential hypothesis, the scientist can succeed in one mind change starting with 0 until the hypothesis is verified. We may then speak of α deciding h in n mind changes *starting with b*. Recall that **0** denotes the empty data sequence.

(M1) α *decides$_C$ h with n mind changes starting with b on ε* $\Leftrightarrow$

(a) α *decides$_C$ h in the limit on ε and*

(b) $mc_\alpha(h, \varepsilon) \leq n$ *and*

(c) $\alpha(h, \mathbf{0}) = b.$

Defining the associated notions of reliability, applicability, and problem solvability is straightforward and is left to the reader.

The following proposition summarizes the elementary properties of the bounded mind-change paradigm (*Fig. 3.23*).

Proposition 3.12

For $n \geq 0$ and for all r such that $0 < r < 1$,

(a) *H is decidable$_C$ with n mind changes starting with 1 given $\mathcal{K}$*
$\Leftrightarrow$ *H is decidable$_{\overline{C}}$ with n mind changes starting with 0 given $\mathcal{K}$.*

(b) *H is decidable$_C$ with n mind changes starting with r given $\mathcal{K}$*
$\Leftrightarrow$ *H is decidable$_C$ with n mind changes starting with 1 given $\mathcal{K}$ and
H is decidable$_C$ with n mind changes starting with 0 given $\mathcal{K}$.*

(c) *H is decidable$_C$ with n mind changes given $\mathcal{K}$*
$\Leftrightarrow$ *H is decidable$_C$ with n mind changes starting with 1 given $\mathcal{K}$ or
H is decidable$_C$ with n mind changes starting with 0 given $\mathcal{K}$.*

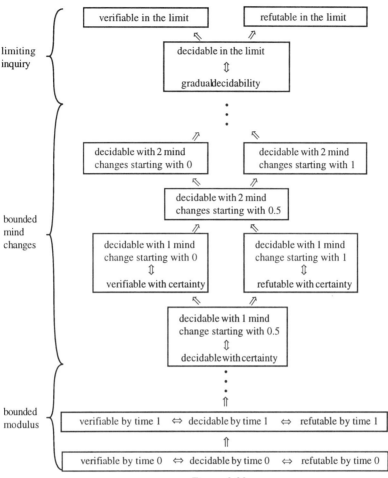

Figure 3.23

(d.1) *H is refutable$_C$ with certainty given $\mathcal{K}$*
⇔ *H is decidable$_C$ with one mind change starting with 1 given $\mathcal{K}$.*

(d.2) *H is verifiable$_C$ with certainty given $\mathcal{K}$*
⇔ *H is decidable$_C$ with one mind change starting with 0 given $\mathcal{K}$.*

(d.3) *H is decidable$_C$ with certainty given $\mathcal{K}$*
⇔ *H is decidable$_C$ with one mind change starting with r given $\mathcal{K}$.*

Proof: Exercise 3.2. ■

For each natural number n and $b \in \{0, 1\}$, there are hypotheses that can be decided with n mind changes starting with b, but that cannot be decided with fewer than n mind changes starting with b. For example, consider the hypothesis "there is exactly one black raven." A scientist can conjecture that this hypothesis is false until a black raven is seen. Then the scientist conjectures that it is true until another black raven is seen. In the worst case, this scientist changes his mind twice, starting with 0. The hypothesis "either there is exactly one black raven or there are exactly three black ravens" requires another mind change. Continuing the sequence in this manner shows that the implications among the mind-change paradigms are all proper.

6.   Gradual Verification, Refutation, and Decision

We have seen that limiting relative frequencies fall beyond the scope of reliable verification or refutation in the limit. This suggests that another weakening of the notion of convergence should be considered. We will say that α approaches b just in case α's conjectures get closer and closer to b, perhaps without ever reaching it.

α *approaches b on h, ε $\Leftrightarrow$ for each rational $s \in (0, 1]$,*
there is a stage n such that for each later
stage $m \geq n$, $|b - \alpha(h, \varepsilon|m)| \leq s$.

I refer to rationals in $(0, 1]$ as *degrees of approximation*. If α approaches b on h, ε, then we may think of α as stabilizing with respect to each degree of approximation s by eventually remaining within s of b. Accordingly, the modulus of convergence for a given degree of approximation is the least time after which the conjectures of α remain always within that degree of b (*Fig. 3.24*).

$modulus_\alpha (h, s, b, \varepsilon) = the\ least\ n\ such\ that\ for\ all\ m \geq n,$
$|b - \alpha(h, \varepsilon|m)| \leq s.$

Success may now be defined as follows:

α *verifies$_C$ h gradually on ε $\Leftrightarrow$ [α approaches 1 on h, ε $\Leftrightarrow$ $C(\varepsilon, h)$].*

α *refutes$_C$ h gradually on ε $\Leftrightarrow$ [α approaches 0 on h, ε $\Leftrightarrow$ $\neg C(\varepsilon, h)$].*

α *decides$_C$ h gradually on ε $\Leftrightarrow$ [α verifies$_C$ and refutes$_C$ h*
gradually on h, ε].

The corresponding definitions of reliability, range of applicability, and problem solvability are again left to the reader.

When we turn to the logical relations among these paradigms, we discover

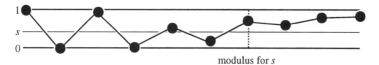

Figure 3.24

that gradual decidability is equivalent to decidability in the limit. Thus, gradual verifiability and refutability do not jointly imply gradual decision in the the limit. In other words, it is not in general possible to construct a gradual decider out of a gradual verifier and a gradual refuter, contrary to the situation in the limiting case! It will be seen that these implications cannot be reversed or strengthened.

Proposition 3.13

(a) *H is verifiable$_C$ gradually given $\mathcal{K}$*
    ⇔ H is refutable$_{\bar{C}}$ gradually given $\mathcal{K}$.

(b) *H is decidable$_C$ gradually given $\mathcal{K}$*
    ⇔ H is decidable$_C$ in the limit given $\mathcal{K}$.

(c) *H is decidable$_C$, verifiable$_C$, or refutable$_C$ in the limit given $\mathcal{K}$*
    ⇒ H is verifiable$_C$ and refutable$_C$ gradually given $\mathcal{K}$.

Proof: (a) As usual. (b) (⇐) trivial, since stabilization to b implies approach to b. (⇒) Let α gradually decide$_C$ H given $\mathcal{K}$. Define:

$$\beta(h, e) = \begin{cases} 1 & \text{if } \alpha(h, e) > 0.5 \\ 0 & \text{otherwise.} \end{cases}$$

β stabilizes to 1 if and only if α approaches 1, and similarly for 0. Thus β decides$_C$ H in the limit given $\mathcal{K}$. (c) It is immediate that verification in the limit implies gradual verification, and similarly for refutation. Suppose α_1 verifies$_C$ H in the limit given $\mathcal{K}$. Let α_2 proceed as follows. α_2 simulates α_1 on each initial segment of the current data e, and counts how many times α_1 makes a conjecture other than 1. Call the count k. Then α_2 conjectures $1/2^k$ (*Fig. 3.25*).

Let $\varepsilon \in \mathcal{K}$, $h \in H$, and suppose $C(\varepsilon, h)$. Then α_1 stabilizes to 1, so α_2 stabilizes to some value $1/2^k$, and hence does not approach 0. If $\neg C(\varepsilon, h)$, then α_1 does

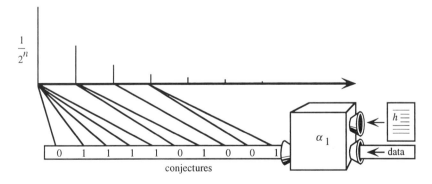

Figure 3.25

not stabilize to 1, and hence emits infinitely many non-1 conjectures, so α_2 approaches 0. Thus, α_2 approaches 0 if and only if $\neg C(\varepsilon, h)$, and hence gradually refutes$_C$ H given $\mathcal{K}$. The implication from refutability in the limit to gradual verifiability may be established in a similar manner.   ∎

We have already seen several examples of hypotheses that are verifiable but not refutable or decidable in the limit. By proposition 3.13(c), such hypotheses are both gradually verifiable and gradually refutable. But by proposition 3.13(b), such hypotheses are not gradually decidable. Thus, 3.13(c) cannot be strengthened. *Figure 3.26* summarizes all the paradigms introduced

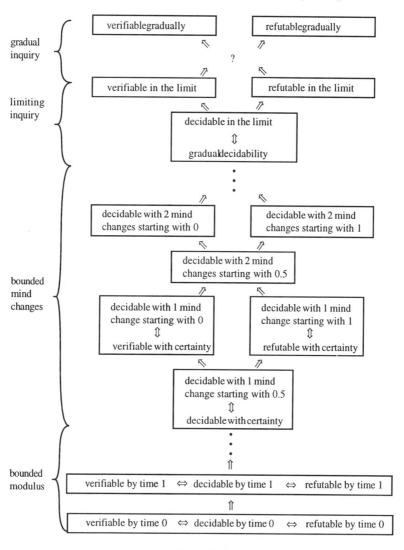

Figure 3.26

so far. The question mark indicates where we might have expected gradual decidability to be, in analogy with the lower levels of the diagram.

Unlike gradual decidability, gradual verification and refutation do increase the scope of reliable inquiry. In particular, limiting relative frequencies are gradually verifiable given 2^ω, as we shall now see. Recall that $LRF_{\{r\}}(o)$ says that the actual limiting relative frequency of o will be r.

Proposition 3.14

(a) $LRF_{\{r\}}(o)$ is verifiable gradually given 2^ω.

(b) $LRF_{\{r\}}(o)$ is not refutable gradually given 2^ω.

Proof: (a) Let $\alpha(e) = 1 - |RF_e(o, lh(e)) - r|$. Method α evidently verifies $LRF_{\{r\}}(o)$ gradually given 2^ω.

(b) Either $r \neq 1$ or $r \neq 0$. Without loss of generality, suppose $r < 1$. Let $q = 1 - r'$. Let $q_1, q_2, \ldots, q_n, \ldots$ be an infinite, descending sequence of nonzero rationals that starts with q and that converges to 0. The demon proceeds as follows. When α produces a conjecture between $1/2^n$ and $1/2^{n+1}$, the demon adopts the plan of bouncing the observed relative frequency on either side of $[r + q_{n+2}, r + q_{n+1}]$ without leaving the interval $[r, r + q_n]$. The plan is not implemented until enough stages have elapsed to dampen the effect on relative frequency of a single datum so the plan can be implemented. The plan is then implemented at least long enough for one bounce to be accomplished and the demon remembers what α does while the plan is in place. Then the demon puts the plan corresponding to α's next conjecture into place, and so forth. If α approaches 0, then the demon drives the observed frequency into smaller and smaller intervals around r, so that $LRF_{\{r\}}(o)$ is true and α is wrong. If α fails to approach 0, then α produces a conjecture greater than $1/2^n$ infinitely often, so the demon makes the data bounce forever to either side of $[r + q_n, r + q_{n+1}]$. Thus no limiting relative frequency exists. ■

So gradual inquiry extends the scope of reliable inquiry to statistical point hypotheses, at least in the one-sided sense of verifiability.

7. Optimal Background Assumptions

One important task of inductive methodology is to optimize inductive methods so that they are reliable given the weakest possible assumptions. This raises the question whether there are such assumptions. Define:

$\mathcal{K}$ *is the optimum assumption for verifying$_C$ H in the limit* $\Leftrightarrow$

(a) *H is verifiable$_C$ in the limit given $\mathcal{K}$ and*

(b) *for all $\mathcal{J}$ such that H is verifiable$_C$ in the limit given $\mathcal{J}$, $\mathcal{J} \subseteq \mathcal{K}$,* and similarly for each of the other standards of success. Of course, whenever H is verifiable$_C$ in the limit given $\mathcal{N}$, $\mathcal{N}$ represents the optimum assumption for the problem, since $\mathcal{N}$ contains all the data streams we are considering in our setting. Are there any other examples of optimum assumptions? In fact there are none. And the situation is even worse than that. Define:

> $\mathcal{K}$ *is optimal for verifying*$_C$ *H in the limit* $\Leftrightarrow$
>
> (a) *H is verifiable*$_C$ *in the limit given* $\mathcal{K}$ *and*
>
> (b) *for all* $\mathcal{J}$ *such that* $\mathcal{K} \subset \mathcal{J}$, *H is not verifiable*$_C$ *in the limit given* $\mathcal{J}$.

The optimum assumption (if it exists) is optimal, but the converse may fail if there are several, distinct, optimal sets of data streams. It will be useful to have a simple way to refer to the set of all data streams on which a given method α succeeds. Accordingly, define:

> $limver_{C,H}(\alpha) = \{\varepsilon: \alpha \text{ } verifies_C \text{ } H \text{ } in \text{ } the \text{ } limit \text{ } on \text{ } \varepsilon\}$.

If $limver_{C,H}(\alpha)$ is the optimum assumption for verifying$_C$ H in the limit, then we say that α is an *optimum* limiting verifier$_C$ for H. If $limver_{C,H}(\alpha)$ is optimal for verifying$_C$ H in the limit, then we say that α is an *optimal* limiting verifier$_C$ for H. Now it turns out that:

Proposition 3.15

> *If H is not verifiable*$_C$ *in the limit given* $\mathcal{N}$ *then*
>
> (a) *no* $\mathcal{K} \subseteq \mathcal{N}$ *is optimal for verifying*$_C$ *H in the limit, and hence*
>
> (b) *no* α *is an optimal limiting verifier*$_C$ *for H.*

Proof: Suppose H is not verifiable$_C$ in the limit given $\mathcal{N}$. Let α be a method and let $\mathcal{K} = limver_{C,H}(\alpha)$. Then $\mathcal{K} \subset \mathcal{N}$. Choose $\varepsilon \in \mathcal{N} - \mathcal{K}$. Define:

$$
\alpha'(h, e) = \begin{cases} 1 & \text{if } e \subset \varepsilon \quad \text{and} \quad \varepsilon \in C_h \\ 0 & \text{if } e \subset \varepsilon \quad \text{and} \quad \varepsilon \notin C_h \\ \alpha'(h, e) & \text{otherwise.} \end{cases}
$$

α' verifies$_C$ H in the limit given $\mathcal{K} \cup \{\varepsilon\}$.   ∎

One can view the situation described in proposition 3.15 either as a disaster (no optimal methods are available) or an an embarrassment of riches, as when a genie offers any (finite) amount of money you please. Any amount asked for could have been larger, but it is hard to call the situation bad, except insofar as a kibbitzer can always chide you for not asking for more. This situation is typical of worst-case methodology and will be seen to arise in many different ways when we consider computable methods. The patching argument of proposition 3.15 also applies to refutation and decision in the limit, and to gradual refutation and verification. It does not apply in the case of verification with certainty, however, as we shall see in the next chapter with the help of some topological concepts.

Exercises

*3.1. Recall Kant's claim that infinite divisibility and composition by simples are contradictories. This isn't so clear. Leibniz's model of the plenum packed an infinity of spheres in a finite space by filling interstices between larger spheres with smaller ones, and so on, until every point in the volume is included in some sphere (*Fig. 3.27*). Assuming that these spheres are simple particles, we have an infinitely divisible finite body that is composed of simples, so the contradiction disappears.

Imagine the IRBP attempting splits at higher and higher energies, and then attempting to split the results at higher and higher energies, etc. Given the theorist's assumption that each possible split is eventually found, a mass is composed of simples just in case this procedure leads in the limit to a history of splits such that each product of fission is either simple itself or leads eventually to a simple particle. In the case of a finite composite of simples, each path in the history of splits terminates in an indivisible particle, but in an infinite composite of simples like Leibniz' plenum, there will be infinite paths of splits. Nonetheless, each fission product is either simple or gives rise to a simple particle later (*Fig. 3.28*).

The denial of composition by simples is not just infinite divisibility, but rather the possession of a fragment or region that contains no simples. This amounts to the existence of a fragment, every subfragment of which is divisible. Such a mass is *somewhere densely divisible*. A somewhere densely divisible mass may either *contain a simple* (i.e., some indivisible fragment is eventually reached) or *be everywhere densely divisible* (i.e., each part is divisible). Nothing prevents a mixture of simples together with densely divisible parts. In fact, J. J. Thomson's *raisin pudding* theory of the atom had just this character, for electrons were envisioned as simple particles floating in an undifferentiated "smear" of positive charge (*Fig. 3.29*).

So perhaps Kant was merely being sloppy when he opposed composition by simples with infinite divisibility, rather than with somewhere dense divisibility. To study such hypotheses, the scientist must modify the experimental design at the IRBP. Instead of merely writing down 1 or 0 to indicate *successful cut* and *failed cut*, respectively, he instructs the lab to assign a new name to each new particle discovered, and to write down at each stage the list $(p_k, (p_{m_1}, \ldots, p_{m_n}))$, where p_k is the particle placed in the accelerator and $p_{m_1}, \ldots, p_{m_n}$ are the n fission products resulting from the split of p_k. If the split fails, the message $(p_k, ())$ is returned. Assume as before that the lab's data is true and that the lab's technique eventually discovers every physically possible split. For

Figure 3.27

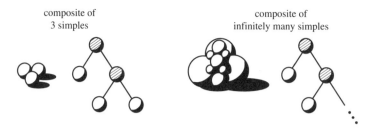

Figure 3.28

each of the following hypotheses, find the strongest sense in which its truth can be reliably determined. This requires showing that the problem is solvable in a given sense and that the demon has a winning strategy if the problem is to be solved in any stronger sense.

- a. *m* is everywhere densely divisible.
- b. *m* is a raisin pudding.
- c. *m* is either a composite of 1 simple or a composite of 3 simples.
- d. *m* is composed of simples.
- e. *m* is a finite composite of simples.

3.2. Prove proposition 3.12.

3.3. In what sense can we reliably investigate $\mathcal{PS}$-randomness given that $\mathcal{PS}$ is countable and the limiting relative frequency of each datum occurring in the data stream exists?

*3.4. Suppose you have a system involving a car on a track subject to unknown forces (*Fig. 3.30*).
Consider the following hypotheses:

h_1: *the position of the car at t is x.*
h_2: *the velocity of the car at t is v.*
h_3: *the acceleration of the car at t is a.*

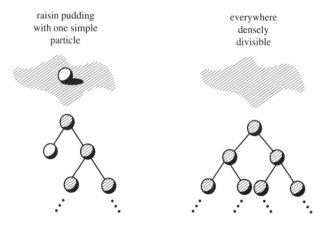

Figure 3.29

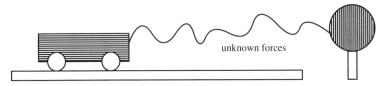

Figure 3.30

h'_1: *the trajectory of the car through time is $f(t)$.*
h'_2: *the velocity of the car through time is $v(t)$.*
h'_3: *the acceleration of the car through time is $a(t)$.*

Consider the following bodies of background knowledge:

$\mathcal{K}_1$: *f is any function from reals to reals.*
$\mathcal{K}_2$: *f is continuous.*
$\mathcal{K}_3$: *f is differentiable.*
$\mathcal{K}_4$: *f is twice differentiable.*

Now consider the following data protocols:

P_1: We can measure time and position exactly and continuously so that by time t we have observed $f\,|\,t = \{(x, y): f(x) = y \text{ and } x \le t\}$.

P_2: We can have the lab repeat the motion exactly at will and set a super camera to record the exact position of the car at a given time. We can only run finitely many trials in a given interval of time, however.

P_3: Like P_2 except that the camera technology is limited so that a given camera can only determine position to within some interval Δx. The lab can improve the camera at will, however, to decrease the interval to any given size greater than 0.

P_4: We must now use a fixed camera that has no guaranteed accuracy. However, we know that if the car is in position x at time t, then an infinite sequence of repeated trials of the experiment will have limiting relative frequencies of measurements at t satisfying a normal distribution with mean x and variance v.

Provide a logical reliabilist analysis of the various inductive problems that result from different choices of hypothesis, background knowledge, and protocol.

4

Topology and Ideal Hypothesis Assessment

1. Introduction

In this chapter, we move from the consideration of particular methods and problems to the characterization of problem solvability over entire paradigms. So while the issues treated in the preceding chapter were all located at level 3 of the taxonomy of questions presented at the end of chapter 2, the questions treated in this chapter belong to level 4. A characterization condition is a necessary and sufficient condition for the existence of a reliable method, given entirely in terms of the structures of $\mathcal{K}$, C, and H. In other words, a characterization theorem isolates exactly the kind of background knowledge necessary and sufficient for scientific reliability, given the interpretation of the hypotheses and the sense of success demanded. To revive Kant's expression, such results may be thought of as *transcendental deductions* for reliable inductive inference, since they show what sort of knowledge is necessary if reliable inductive inference is to be possible.

To state a characterization condition, one must describe the structure of a set of possible data streams without reference to scientists or to reliability. We therefore require some framework in which to state such descriptions. It turns out that topology provides just the right concepts.

2. Basic Topological Concepts

A *topological space* is an ordered pair $\mathfrak{T} = (\mathcal{T}, T)$, such that $\mathcal{T}$ is an arbitrary set, and T is some collection of subsets of $\mathcal{T}$ with the following, simple

74

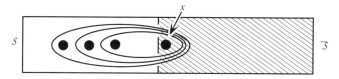

Figure 4.1

properties:

> *T is closed under arbitrary unions,*
>
> *T is closed under finite intersections, and*
>
> $\mathcal{T}, \varnothing \in T.$

The elements of *T* are known as the *open sets* of $\mathfrak{T}$. If $x \in \mathcal{T}$, then $S \subseteq \mathcal{T}$ is a *neighborhood* of *x* just in case $x \in S$ and $S \in T$. Claims about all neighborhoods of some point may be viewed, intuitively, as claims about what happens arbitrarily close to this point. All other topological concepts are defined in terms of the open sets of $\mathfrak{T}$, and hence are all relative to $\mathfrak{T}$, but explicit reference to $\mathfrak{T}$ will be dropped for brevity. A *closed set* is just the complement of an open set. A *clopen set* is both closed and open.

To simplify notation, when one speaks of subsets of $\mathfrak{T}$, one means subsets of $\mathcal{T}$. Of special importance to methodology is the notion of *limit points* of subsets of $\mathfrak{T}$. A limit point of a set *S* is an object $x \in \mathcal{T}$ that is so close to *S* that no open set (neighborhood) around *x* can fail to catch a point of *S* (*Fig. 4.1*).

> *x is a limit point of S $\Leftrightarrow$ for each open O, if $x \in O$ then $O \cap S \neq \varnothing$.*

The *closure* of *S* is the result of adding all the limit points of *S* to *S*. The closure of *S* will be denoted $cl(S)$. The following facts relating closed sets to the closure operation are among the most basic in topology. Since they will also turn out to be fundamental to the study of logical reliability, it is worth reviewing them here.

Proposition 4.1

(a) *S is closed $\Leftrightarrow S = cl(S)$.*

(b) *cl(S) is the least closed superset of S.*

Proof: (a) ($\Rightarrow$) Suppose *S* is closed. Then $\bar{S}$ is open. Suppose for reductio that some limit point *x* of *S* is missing from *S*. Then $\bar{S}$ is an open set containing *x* that is disjoint from *S*, so *x* is not a limit point of *S* (*Fig. 4.2*). Contradiction. Thus $x \in S$.

($\Leftarrow$) Suppose *S* contains all its limit points. Then for each $x \notin S$, *x* is not

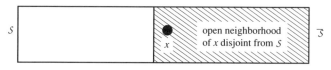

Figure 4.2

a limit point of S. Thus for each $x \notin S$, there is some open set $\mathcal{R}_x$ disjoint from S such that $x \in \mathcal{R}_x$. $\bar{S}$ is identical to the union of all these sets $\mathcal{R}_x$ (*Fig. 4.3*). But since each $\mathcal{R}_x$ is open, so is the union. Thus, $\bar{S}$ is open and hence S is closed.

(b) From (a) it is clear that $cl(S)$ is closed. Suppose for reductio that there exists some closed $\mathcal{R}$ such that $S \subseteq \mathcal{R} \subset cl(S)$. Then some $x \in cl(S)$ is missing from $\mathcal{R}$ and hence is also missing from S. Since x is a limit point of S, there is no open O containing x that fails to contain some element of S. But since $S \subseteq \mathcal{R}$, there is no open O containing x that fails to contain some element of $\mathcal{R}$. Thus x is a limit point of $\mathcal{R}$ as well, so $\mathcal{R}$ is missing one of its own limit points. So by (a), $\mathcal{R}$ is not closed. Contradiction. ∎

An *interior point* of S is a point that is a member of an open subset of S (*Fig. 4.4*). The *interior* of S, denoted $int(S)$, is the set of all interior points of S. The interior of S is dual to the closure of S is the sense that while the latter is the least closed superset of S, the former is the greatest open subset of S.

Proposition 4.2

$int(S)$ is the greatest open set contained in S.

Proof: Each $x \in int(S)$ is contained in an open subset of S. The union of these open subsets is open and is identical to $int(S)$. Suppose there is an open $\mathcal{R}$ such that $int(S) \subset \mathcal{R} \subseteq S$. Then there is some $x \in \mathcal{R} - int(S)$. But since $\mathcal{R}$ is open and $x \in S$, it follows that $x \in int(S)$. Contradiction. ∎

A *boundary point* of S is a point that is a limit point both of S and of $\bar{S}$. The *boundary* of S, denoted $bdry(S)$, is defined as the set of all boundary points of S, which is evidently the same as $cl(S) \cap cl(\bar{S})$.

The boundary of S is the "residue" lying between the best closed

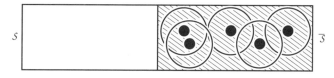

Figure 4.3

Figure 4.4

approximation of S from without and the best open approximation of S from within (*Fig. 4.5*).

Proposition 4.3

$$bdry(S) = cl(S) - int(S).$$

Proof: ($\subseteq$) By definition, $bdry(S) \subseteq cl(S)$. Suppose for reductio that some $x \in bdry(S)$ is also in $int(S)$. Then there is some open subset of S that includes x, so x is not a limit point of $\bar{S}$, and hence is not in $bdry(S)$. Contradiction.

($\supseteq$) Suppose that $x \in cl(S) - int(S)$. Then x is a limit point of S. Suppose for reductio that x is not a limit point of $\bar{S}$. Then for some open $Q \subseteq S$, $x \in Q$. So $x \in int(S)$. Contradiction. Hence, x is a limit point of S, so $x \in bdry(S)$. ∎

It is therefore evident that a set is clopen just in case its boundary is empty; i.e., just in case it can be perfectly approximated both by a closed and by an open set.

S is *dense* in $\mathcal{R}$ just in case $\mathcal{R} \subseteq cl(S)$.[1] Thus, S is arbitrarily close to everything in $\mathcal{R}$ and may be thought of as spread throughout $\mathcal{R}$.

A *basis* for $\mathfrak{T}$ is a collection $\mathcal{B}$ of open sets of $\mathfrak{T}$ such that every open set of $\mathfrak{T}$ is a union of elements of $\mathcal{B}$. It will turn out that the topological concept of basis is closely related to the methodological concept of a finite data sequence.

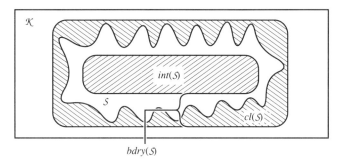

Figure 4.5

---

[1] This definition is nonstandard. The usual definition requires $\mathcal{R} = cl(S)$. But this clearly excludes cases in which $\mathcal{R}$ is not closed. The intuition of being "spread throughout" $\mathcal{R}$ does not require that $\mathcal{R}$ be closed, however. It suggests only that everything in $\mathcal{R}$ be arbitrarily close to something in S, which accords with the condition $\mathcal{R} \subseteq cl(S)$.

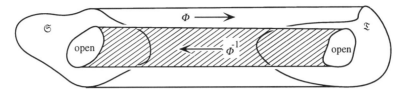

Figure 4.6

Let $\mathfrak{S}$ and $\mathfrak{T}$ be two topological spaces, and let Φ be a function from $\mathfrak{S}$ to $\mathfrak{T}$. Then Φ is *continuous* if and only if for each open subset S of $\mathfrak{T}$, $\Phi^{-1}(S)$ is open in $\mathfrak{S}$ (*Fig. 4.6*).

Topology was originally conceived as a kind of generalized geometry, in which the geometrical equivalence relation of *congruence* (one figure coincides with the other when laid on top of it) is replaced with the topological equivalence relation of *homeomorphism* (continuous, 1–1 deformability of one figure into another). A triangle and a square are homeomorphic in the Euclidean plane because each can be stretched or beaten into the other without cutting, tearing, or gluing. That is, regions that are arbitrarily close in the square remain arbitrarily close in the triangle (*Fig. 4.7*). On the other hand, a square cannot be stretched and beaten into a figure eight without cutting or gluing. Gluing brings into arbitrary proximity regions that were once apart, violating continuity (*Fig. 4.8*).

The apparatus of open sets provides a very general setting for the study of continuity. It is a remarkable fact that this abstract treatment of continuity also captures the local perspective of ideal inductive methods that distinguishes them from perfectly clairvoyant deities who can see the entire future all at once. Just as the conjecture sequence of a scientific method is determined by its conjectures on finite approximations of the infinite data stream, the value of a continuous function at a point in a topological space is determined by its values over open sets around the point. In the next section we examine a standard topological space in which points correspond to infinite data streams, sets of points become empirical hypotheses, elements of a countable basis correspond to finite data sequences, and continuity reflects the bounded perspective of the scientist.

3. The Baire Space

The *Baire space* $\mathfrak{N}$ is a topological space of special relevance to analysis, logic, and the study of inductive inference.[2] The Baire space is usually defined in

Figure 4.7

---

[2] The learning-theoretic relevance of continuity in the Baire space is also discussed in Osherson et al. (1986).

Figure 4.8

terms of a basis for its open sets. Let e be a finite sequence of natural numbers. Think of e as a finite data sequence, where data are encoded as natural numbers. Now consider the set $[e]$ of all infinite data streams in $\mathcal{N}$ that extend e. Thus, $[e] = \{\varepsilon: \varepsilon | lh(e) = e\}$. I refer to $[e]$ as the *fan* with *handle e* (*Fig. 4.9*).

We may think of the fan with handle e as representing the empirical uncertainty of a scientist who has just seen e, but whose background assumptions are vacuous (so that $\mathcal{K} = \mathcal{N}$). For all he knows, the actual data sequence may be any infinite extension of e. Let e, e' be finite data sequences. We say $e \subseteq e'$ just in case e' *extends* e or is identical to e. For any two fans, either one includes the other, or the two are disjoint. That is, $[e'] \subseteq [e] \Leftrightarrow e \subseteq e'$.

If one fan includes the other, then their intersection and union are also fans. Otherwise, the intersection is empty and the union may or may not be a fan (*Fig. 4.10*). The whole space $\mathcal{N}$ is the fan whose handle is the empty sequence **0**. The empty set is not a fan. The intersection of a countable collection of fans is nonempty just in case there is some infinite data stream ε that extends the handles of all fans in the intersection (*Fig. 4.11*). If there is no bound on the lengths of the handles involved, then the intersection is $\varnothing$ or exactly $\{\varepsilon\}$. Otherwise the intersection is either empty or identical to the fan in the intersection with the longest handle.

The Baire space is just the space $\mathfrak{N} = (\mathcal{N}, B)$, where B is the collection of all sets formed by taking an arbitrary union of fans. Recall that ω^* denotes the set of all finite sequences of natural numbers. Then B is defined as follows:

$$\mathcal{P} \in B \Leftrightarrow \text{there is a } G \subseteq \omega^* \text{ such that } \mathcal{P} = \bigcup\{[e]: e \in G\}.$$

To see that $\mathfrak{N}$ is indeed a topological space, observe that $\mathcal{N} = [\mathbf{0}]$ where **0** is the empty data sequence, so the whole space is open since each fan is. $\varnothing$ is also open, since it is the trivial union $\bigcup \varnothing$ of the empty set of fans. Unions of open sets are trivially open since open sets are arbitrary unions of fans. Finally, consider a finite intersection of open sets. We have just seen that a finite

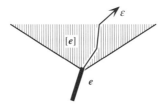

Figure 4.9

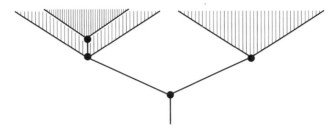

Figure 4.10

intersection of fans is either empty (and hence open) or a fan. Thus a finite intersection of unions of fans is either a union of fans or the empty set, both of which are open.

Since the fans constitute a basis for $\mathfrak{N}$, the open sets of $\mathfrak{N}$ are arbitrary unions of fans. Since there are only countably many distinct fans, all such unions are countable. An open set S may be thought of as a hypothesis verifiable with certainty through observation or, rather, as the set of all data streams for which such a hypothesis is correct. As soon as some handle of some fan in S is seen, the scientist knows that S is correct, since every extension of the handle is a data stream in S. An example of such a hypothesis is "you will eventually see a 1." Once a 1 is seen, it doesn't matter what further data occurs. That is, once a 1 is seen by the scientist, he has entered a fan included in the open set.

The closed sets of $\mathfrak{N}$ are just the complements of open sets. Hence, a closed set corresponds to a hypothesis that can be refuted with certainty by finite observation if it is false. That is, the complement of a closed set is verified when one of its handles is seen in the data, and hence the closed set is refuted. Closed set correspond therefore to universal hypotheses such as "all ravens are black." Once a white raven is observed, the hypothesis is known with certainty to be false, no matter what further evidence is observed. A *clopen* set of $\mathfrak{N}$ is a set that is decidable with certainty.

Limit points in the Baire space also have an important methodological interpretation.

Proposition 4.4

ε *is a limit point of* S *in* $\mathfrak{N}$
    ⇔ *for each n there is an* $\varepsilon' \in S$ *such that* $\varepsilon|n = \varepsilon'|n$.

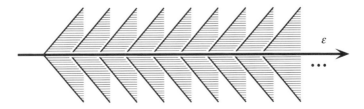

Figure 4.11

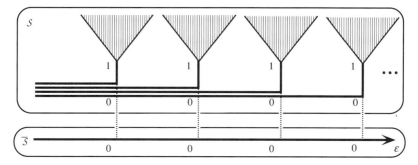

Figure 4.12

Proof: ($\Rightarrow$) Suppose ε is a limit point of S in $\mathfrak{N}$. Then by definition, for each open O, if $\varepsilon \in O$ then $O \cap S \neq \varnothing$. Then for each n, $[\varepsilon|n] \cap S \neq \varnothing$, since $[\varepsilon|n]$ is an open set containing ε. So there is an $\varepsilon' \in S$ such that $\varepsilon' \in [\varepsilon|n]$. Hence, $\varepsilon|n = \varepsilon'|n$. So for each n there is an $\varepsilon' \in S$ such that $\varepsilon|n = \varepsilon'|n$.

($\Leftarrow$) Suppose that for each n there is an $\varepsilon' \in S$ such that $\varepsilon|n = \varepsilon'|n$. Let $O \in B$. Suppose $\varepsilon \in O$. Then since O is a union of fans, there is an n such that $[\varepsilon|n] \subseteq O$. By assumption, there is $\varepsilon' \in S$ such that $\varepsilon'|n = \varepsilon|n$. Hence, $\varepsilon' \in O$. So $O \cap S \neq \varnothing$. Thus ε is a limit point of S in $\mathfrak{N}$. ∎

A limit point of S in $\mathfrak{N}$ may be thought of as a data stream ε with data streams in S veering off infinitely often. *Figure 4.12* depicts the open set $S = \bigcup\{[e]: e$ is a finite string of 0s with a 1 at the end$\}$. S corresponds to the hypothesis that some non-0 will eventually be observed. $\bar{S}$ is a closed set that corresponds to the universal hypothesis that 0 will always be observed. Since each initial segment of the everywhere 0 data stream is an initial segment of a data stream in S, we have by proposition 4.4 that the everywhere 0 sequence is a limit point of S. This is a case in which a limit point of S is missing from S. It is also an instance of the problem of induction, for a demon can present data along ε until the scientist becomes sure that he is in $\bar{S}$, after which the demon is free to veer back into S. In fact, whenever a limit point ε of S is not in S, the same argument can be given, in light of proposition 4.4. Therefore:

> *The problem of induction arises when either the hypothesis or its complement is not closed.*

In other words, the problem of induction arises exactly in the *boundaries* of hypotheses.

In Figure 4.12, I did not overlap ε and the shared initial segments of data streams in S as in *Figure 4.13*. This is because the overlapped versions of such diagrams are dangerously misleading, since they depict *trees*, and tree structure does not uniquely determine the topological structure of the set so depicted. Let $G \subseteq \omega^*$ be a set of finite data sequences. G is a *tree* just in case each initial

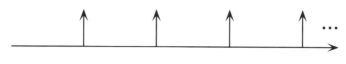

Figure 4.13

segment of a member of *G* is a member of *G*. The *tree generated by S* (denoted *Tree*(*S*)) is defined as the set of all finite, initial segments of elements of *S*. *S* is not always uniquely determined by *Tree*(*S*). For example, let *S* be the set of all data streams in which 1 occurs somewhere. Then *Tree*(*S*) = *Tree*(𝒩). In general, *Tree*(*S*) = *Tree*(𝓡) if and only if *S* is dense in 𝓡. This fact is important to keep in mind when relying on tree diagrams. Since such diagrams are finite, they cannot indicate whether limit points are missing or present, but missing limit points are exactly what local underdetermination and the problem of induction are about.

To fix intuitions, it is useful to consider some simple examples of open and closed sets in the Baire space. ∅ and 𝒩 are both clopen. Each singleton {ε} is closed, since it is the complement of an open set (namely, the union of the fans whose handles are not extended by ε). Each finite union of closed sets is closed, so each finite subset of 𝔑 is closed and each cofinite subset of 𝔑 is open. Since a set cannot be both finite and cofinite, we also have that finite sets are properly closed (i.e., closed but not open) and cofinite sets are properly open (i.e., open but not closed). Closed sets can also be the closures of infinite open sets, as when we add the missing limit point ε to the set *S* in the preceding example.

Say that an open set is *n-uniform* just in case it is a union of fans whose handles are all bounded in length by *n*, and say that an open set is *uniform* just in case it is *n*-uniform for some *n*. Each uniform open set *S* is clopen, since its complement consists of the union of all fans not included in *S* whose handles are of length *n* (*Fig. 4.14*).

Not all clopen sets are uniform. For example, consider the union of all fans with handles of form *n*e*, where *e* is a string of 0s of length *n*. This set is a union of fans whose handles come in every length, but all the handles are distinct at position 1. Evidently, this set is not uniform, since the handles of the fans in the union come in all lengths. That it is open can be seen from the fact that

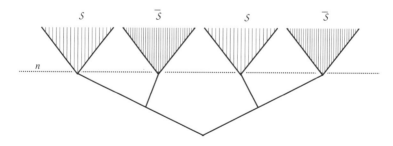

Figure 4.14

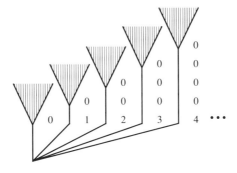

Figure 4.15

the set is a union of fans. That it is also closed can be seen from the fact that it is missing no limit point (*Fig. 4.15*). On the other hand, each clopen set is uniform if the space is finitely branching (cf. exercise 4.14).

4. Restricted Topological Spaces

Let $\mathfrak{T} = (T, T)$ be a topological space, and let $\mathcal{K} \subseteq T$. The *restriction* of $\mathfrak{T}$ to $\mathcal{K}$, denoted $\mathfrak{T}|\mathcal{K}$, is the space that results if we toss out of $\mathfrak{T}$ everything that is not in $\mathcal{K}$ while retaining essentially the same structure. The way to carry this out is to replace T with $T \cap \mathcal{K}$ and to replace T with the set $T|\mathcal{K}$ of all intersections $O \cap \mathcal{K}$ such that $O \in T$. Accordingly, let $\mathfrak{T}|\mathcal{K} = (T \cap \mathcal{K}, T|\mathcal{K})$. The elements of $T|\mathcal{K}$ are said to be $\mathcal{K}$-*open*. Sets of the form $\mathcal{K} - O$, where $O \in T|\mathcal{K}$, are said to be $\mathcal{K}$-*closed*. Sets that are both $\mathcal{K}$-open and $\mathcal{K}$-closed are $\mathcal{K}$-*clopen*. It is not too hard to show that $\mathfrak{T}|\mathcal{K}$ is itself a topological space, so all the results established previously apply to restricted spaces.

In the Baire space, restricting to some set $\mathcal{K}$ of data streams corresponds to adopting background assumptions about how the data will appear in the limit. The topological significance of background knowledge is to make sets simpler given the restriction than they are without it, and that is why local underdetermination depends crucially on what the scientist's background assumptions are.

5. A Characterization of Bounded Sample Decidability

It is now time to characterize the various notions of reliable success in topological terms. To do so, it is useful to let C_h denote the set of all data streams for which h is correct (according to C). We may think of C_h as the *empirical content* of h since C_h includes all the infinite data streams that might arise, given that h is correct (*Fig. 4.16*).

Bounded sample decidability is easy to characterize in terms of fans. Recall that $S \subseteq \mathcal{N}$ is *n-uniform* just in case S is a union of fans whose handles are

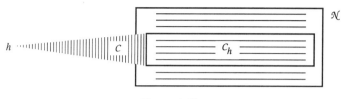

Figure 4.16

all bounded in length by n. Like all the other concepts, this one relativizes to background knowledge $\mathcal{K}$. Then it is simple to see that:

Proposition 4.5

H is decidable$_C$ by time n given $\mathcal{K} \Leftrightarrow$ for each $h \in H$,
$C_h \cap \mathcal{K}$ is $\mathcal{K}$-n-uniform.

Proof: ($\Leftarrow$) Suppose that $C_h \cap \mathcal{K}$ is $\mathcal{K}$-n-uniform. Thus, there is a $G_h \subseteq \omega^*$ such that each $e \in G_h$ is no longer than n and $C_h \cap \mathcal{K}$ is the union of all $[e] \cap \mathcal{K}$ such that $e \in G_h$. Define method α as follows (*Fig. 4.17*):

$$\alpha(h, e) = \begin{cases} 1 & \text{if } e \text{ extends some } e' \in G_h \\ 0 & \text{otherwise.} \end{cases}$$

Let $\varepsilon \in \mathcal{K}$. Suppose $\varepsilon \in C_h$. Then for some $k \leq n$, $\varepsilon|k \in G_h$. Thus by time $k \leq n$, α stabilizes to 1 and hence conjectures 1 at time n. Suppose $\varepsilon \notin C_h$. Then $\varepsilon|n \notin G_h$, so $\alpha(h, \varepsilon|n) = 0$.

($\Rightarrow$) Suppose that for some $h \in H$, $\mathcal{K} \cap C_h$ is not $\mathcal{K}$-n-uniform. Then there are ε, $\varepsilon' \in \mathcal{K}$ such that h is correct for ε but not for ε' and $\varepsilon/n = \varepsilon'/n$. This is just what the demon needs to fool α (*Fig. 4.18*). For the demon merely checks the scientist's conjecture $\alpha(h, \varepsilon|n)$. If the conjecture is 1, the demon continues feeding with ε'. If it is anything else, the demon continues feeding ε. If α doesn't produce 1 or 0 at n, then α fails by default, and if α produces either

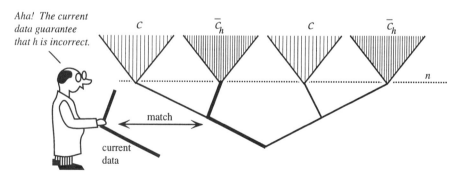

Figure 4.17

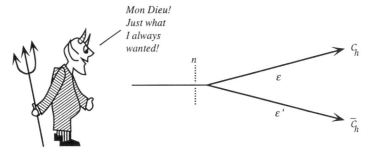

Figure 4.18

1 or 0 at n, then α is wrong. Since α is arbitrary, H is not decidable$_C$ by n given $\mathcal{K}$. ∎

6. Characterizations of Certain Assessement

We have already seen that open and closed sets are like existential and universal hypotheses, respectively. It is therefore to be expected that open sets are verifiable with certainty and closed sets are refutable with certainty. The following proposition also shows that the converse is true: if a hypothesis is verifiable with certainty, it determines an open set and if a hypothesis is refutable with certainty, it determines a closed set.

Proposition 4.6

$$H \text{ is } \begin{bmatrix} verifiable_C \\ refutable_C \\ decidable_C \end{bmatrix} \text{ with certainty given } \mathcal{K}$$

$$\Leftrightarrow \text{for each } h \in H, C_h \cap \mathcal{K} \text{ is } \begin{bmatrix} \mathcal{K}\text{-open} \\ \mathcal{K}\text{-closed} \\ \mathcal{K}\text{-clopen} \end{bmatrix}.$$

Proof: It suffices to show the verifiability case, since the refutation case follows by duality and the decision case follows immediately from the first two in light of proposition 3.3(b). ($\Leftarrow$) Suppose that $C_h \cap \mathcal{K}$ is $\mathcal{K}$-open. Then for some $G_h \subseteq \omega^*$, C_h is the union of all $[e] \cap \mathcal{K}$ such that $e \in G_h$. Let α conjecture 0 until some element of G_h is extended by e, at which time α conjectures the certainty mark '!' and continues producing 1s thereafter (*Fig. 4.19*).

$$\alpha(h, e) = \begin{cases} \text{'!'} & \text{if } e \in G_h \\ 1 & \text{if } e \text{ properly extends some } e' \in G_h \\ 0 & \text{otherwise.} \end{cases}$$

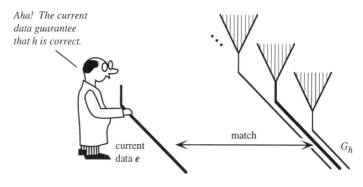

Figure 4.19

Let $\varepsilon \in \mathcal{K}$. Suppose that $\varepsilon \in C_h$. Then for some n, $\varepsilon|n \in G_h$. Thus, α produces 1 with certainty. Suppose $\varepsilon \notin C_h$. Then for no n is $\varepsilon|n$ in G_h. So α never produces 1 with certainty.

($\Rightarrow$) Suppose that for some $h \in H$, $C_h \cap \mathcal{K}$ is not $\mathcal{K}$-open. Thus $\overline{C_h} \cap \mathcal{K}$ is not $\mathcal{K}$-closed. So by proposition 4.1(a), $\overline{C_h}$ has a limit point ε in $\mathcal{K}$ that is not in $\overline{C_h} \cap \mathcal{K}$. But that is just the sort of situation that permits the demon to fool an arbitrary scientist regarding h given $\mathcal{K}$, as we saw in the preceding chapter (*Fig. 4.20*). The demon feeds ε until α produces its mark of certainty '!' followed by a 1. Otherwise he continues feeding ε forever. If α ever produces the mark of certainty followed by 1, then the demon presents a data stream for which h is incorrect$_C$, so α fails. Otherwise, the demon presents ε, for which h is correct, and α fails to produce 1 with certainty. Since α is arbitrary, no possible method can verify h (and hence H) with certainty given $\mathcal{K}$. ∎

The demonic construction in the above proof is just Sextus' ancient argument for inductive skepticism, which we considered in the preceding two chapters. What we have just seen is that the argument arises for *every* hypothesis h such that C_h is not $\mathcal{K}$-open. It is interesting that this argument is an instance of the basic topological fact that each nonclosed set is missing one of its limit points (i.e., proposition 4.1).

I promised at the very end of the preceding chapter to apply topological concepts to the question whether some α that does not verify$_C H$ with certainty given $\mathcal{N}$ could nonetheless be an optimally reliable certain verifier for C, H.

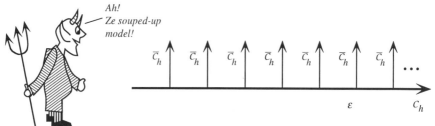

Figure 4.20

Throw away shaded region to make C_h open

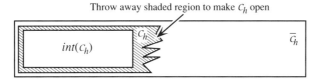

Figure 4.21

Now that we know that $\mathcal{K}$-openness characterizes verifiability with certainty given $\mathcal{K}$, the general resolution of the question is at hand.

Consider a single hypothesis in isolation. We will make use of the fact that the interior of a set is the *best* open approximation of the set from within. Then if we throw out of $\mathcal{N}$ every data stream in C_h that is not in the interior of C_h, we will have converted C_h into an open set in a *minimally destructive manner*, thereby arriving at minimal assumptions under which h is verifiable$_C$ with certainty (*Fig. 4.21*). In keeping with this strategy, define:

$$\mathcal{M}ax(C, h) = \mathcal{N} - (C_h - int(C_h)).$$

$C_h \cap \mathcal{M}ax(C, h)$ is $\mathcal{M}ax(C, h)$-open, since $C_h \cap \mathcal{M}ax(C, h) = int(C_h)$, so by proposition 4.6, there is some method α that verifies$_C$ h with certainty given $\mathcal{M}ax(C, h)$. By the following proposition, this method is optimal in terms of reliability.[3]

Proposition 4.7

*h is verifiable$_C$ with certainty given $\mathcal{M}ax(C, h)$ but not given
any proper superset of $\mathcal{M}ax(C, h)$.*

Proof: Suppose $\mathcal{M}ax(C, h) \subset \mathcal{K}$. Then we may choose $\varepsilon \in (C_h \cap \mathcal{K}) - int(C_h)$. Since $\varepsilon \notin int(C_h)$, and $int(C_h)$ is the union of the set of all fans included in C_h, we have that ε is not an element of any fan included in C_h. Thus, for every n, $[\varepsilon|n]$ contains some element $\tau[n]$ of $\mathcal{N} - C_h$. But then $[\varepsilon|n]$ also contains some element of $\mathcal{M}ax(C, h) - C_h$ since $\overline{C_h} \subseteq \mathcal{M}ax(C, h)$ (*Fig. 4.22*).

Thus, ε is not included in any $\mathcal{K}$-fan included in $C_h \cap \mathcal{K}$, so $C_h \cap \mathcal{K}$ is not $\mathcal{K}$-open. So by proposition 4.6, h is not verifiable$_C$ with certainty given $\mathcal{K}$. ∎

$\mathcal{M}ax(C, h)$ is also *uniquely* optimal, so we have a complete characterization of the optimal assumptions required for verification with certainty of an arbitrary hypothesis.

Proposition 4.8

*If $\mathcal{K} \neq \mathcal{M}ax(C, h)$ and h is verifiable$_C$ with certainty given $\mathcal{K}$, then
h is verifiable$_C$ with certainty given some proper superset of $\mathcal{K}$.*

---

[3] For the refutation and decision with certainty cases, cf. exercise 4.5.

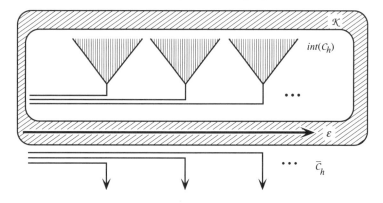

Figure 4.22

Proof: Suppose $\mathcal{K} \neq Max(C, h)$. Then $\mathcal{K} \subset Max(C, h)$ or there is some $\varepsilon \in \mathcal{K} - Max(C, h)$. In the former case, we are done: h is verifiable$_C$ with certainty given $Max(C, h)$, by proposition 4.7. So let $\varepsilon \in \mathcal{K} - Max(C, h)$. Then $\varepsilon \in C_h$ and, as was shown in the preceding proof, $[\varepsilon|n]$ contains some element $\tau[n]$ of $\mathcal{N} - C_h$, for each n. Since h is verifiable$_C$ with certainty given $\mathcal{K}$, we have by proposition 4.6 that ε is contained in some $\mathcal{K}$-fan $[\varepsilon|n'] \subseteq C_h \cap \mathcal{K}$. Let m be the least such n'. So for all $m' \geq m$, $\tau[m'] \notin \mathcal{K}$. Let $\mathcal{K}' = \mathcal{K} \cup \{\tau[m + 1]\}$ (*Fig. 4.23*).

Let α verify$_C$ h with certainty given $\mathcal{K}$, by hypothesis. Now define:

$$\alpha'(h, e) = \begin{cases} 0 & \text{if} \quad e \subset \tau[m + 1] \\ \alpha(h, e) & \text{otherwise.} \end{cases}$$

This verifies$_C$ h with certainty given $\mathcal{K}'$. ∎

7. Characterizations of Limiting Assessment

So far, we have isolated topological characterizations of verifiability, refutability, and decidability with certainty in terms of open, closed, and clopen sets, respectively. Open, closed, and clopen sets may be thought of as especially

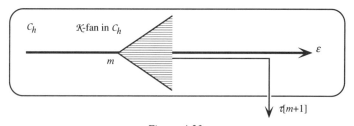

Figure 4.23

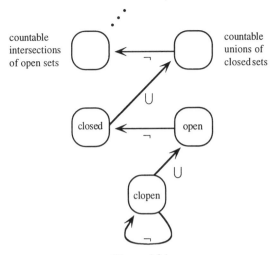

Figure 4.24

simple sets in a topological sense. Since we already know that limiting success is easier to guarantee than success with certainty, it is clear that we must consider weaker notions of topological simplicity if we are to characterize the other notions of reliability introduced in the preceding chapter. Happily, there is a standard scale of such notions, known as the *finite Borel hierarchy*. The Borel hierarchy is a system of mathematical cubbyholes that forms the lowest and most elementary part of the classificatory structure of *descriptive set theory*. The aim of descriptive set theory is to provide a kind of shipshape mathematics, in which there is a place for everything, and everything is put in its place. Each cubbyhole reflects a kind of intrinsic, mathematical complexity of the objects within it. Understanding is obtained by seeing the relative complexities of objects in terms of the cells in the hierarchy. The striking fact is that methodological success can be characterized *exactly* in terms of cubbyholes that are already familiar through other applications in logic, probability theory, and analysis.

To form the finite Borel hierarchy, we start out with the clopen sets. To build more complex sets, we iterate the operations of complementation and countable union (*Fig. 4.24*). The more countable unions and complementations it takes to generate a set, the higher the complexity of the set. That's all there is to it.[4] It is convenient to name the classes according to the following notational scheme due to Addison (1955). The first *Borel class* is just the collection of all clopen sets of the Baire space:

$$S \in \Sigma_0^B \Leftrightarrow S \text{ is clopen.}$$

[4] The full Borel hierarchy does not stop here, for we can form countable unions of sets drawn from each Π_n^B class, which are Borel sets that may reside at no finite level Π_n^B. We will have no use for such sets until chapter 13.

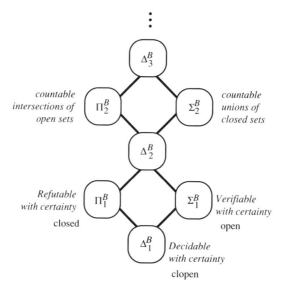

Figure 4.25

The other finite Borel classes are defined by the following induction:

$$S \in \Sigma_{n+1}^B \Leftrightarrow S \text{ is a countable union of complements of } \Sigma_n^B \text{ sets.}[5]$$

The *dual Borel classes* are defined as follows:

$$S \in \Pi_n^B \Leftrightarrow \bar{S} \in \Sigma_n^B.$$

Finally, there are the *ambiguous Borel classes*:

$$S \in \Delta_n^B \Leftrightarrow S \in \Sigma_n^B \cap \Pi_n^B.$$

Thus $\Sigma_0^B = \Pi_0^B = \Delta_0^B =$ the class of clopen sets, the open sets are the Σ_1^B sets (since each open set is a union of fans and hence is a *countable* union of clopen sets), the closed sets are the Π_1^B sets (since they are complements of open sets), and the clopen sets are the Δ_1^B sets (both closed and open). Σ_2^B sets are countable unions of closed sets and Π_2^B sets are countable intersections of open sets. Since every singleton $\{\varepsilon\}$ is closed in $\mathcal{N}$, and hence is the complement of an open set, every countable subset of $\mathcal{N}$ is Σ_2^B, and every complement of a countable set is Π_2^B. It will be shown later that every level in this classificatory structure contains new subsets of $\mathcal{N}$ (*Fig. 4.25*).

---

[5] I.e., $S \in \Sigma_{n+1}^B \Leftrightarrow$ there is a countable $\Gamma \subseteq \Sigma_n^B$ such that $S = \bigcup \{\bar{\mathcal{R}}: \mathcal{R} \in \Gamma\}$.

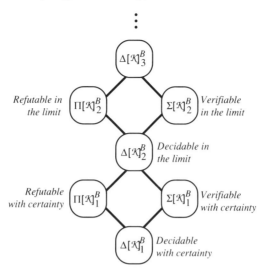

Figure 4.26

Proposition 4.9

For each n, $\Delta_n^B \subset \Sigma_n^B$.

Proof Deferred until chapter 7. ∎

The finite Borel classes can be defined for restrictions of $\mathcal{N}$ to $\mathcal{K}$ just by starting out with $\mathcal{K}$-clopen sets instead of clopen sets and carrying through the induction from there. For $S \subseteq \mathcal{K}$ define:

$S \in \Sigma[\mathcal{K}]_0^B \Leftrightarrow S$ is $\mathcal{K}$-clopen.

$S \in \Sigma[\mathcal{K}]_{n+1}^B \Leftrightarrow S$ is a countable union of complements of $\Sigma[\mathcal{K}]_n^B$ sets.

The dual and ambiguous classes are defined in terms of these as before. When we restrict the hierarchy to $\mathcal{K}$, it may collapse, depending on the character of $\mathcal{K}$. For a trivial example, if $\mathcal{K}$ is a singleton $\{\varepsilon\}$, then each $S \subseteq \mathcal{N}$ is $\Delta[\mathcal{K}]_0^B$, and if $\mathcal{K}$ is countable, then each $S \subseteq \mathcal{N}$ is $\Sigma[\mathcal{K}]_2^B$. Since the levels in the hierarchy will be seen to correspond to levels of local underdetermination by evidence, it is clear that to determine the sorts of assumptions that give rise to such collapse is a matter of the highest methodological importance.

The characterization of limiting reliability may now be stated (*Fig. 4.26*).[6]

---

[6] The following approach is a relativized, noncomputational version of the techniques introduced in Gold (1965) and Putnam (1965). A similar perspective is developed in Kugel (1977).

Proposition 4.10 (Gold 1965, Putnam 1965)

$$H \text{ is } \begin{bmatrix} verifiable_C \\ refutable_C \\ decidable_C \end{bmatrix} \text{ in the limit given } \mathcal{K}$$

$$\Leftrightarrow \text{ for each } h \in H, \, C_h \cap \mathcal{K} \in \begin{bmatrix} \Sigma[\mathcal{K}]_2^B \\ \Pi[\mathcal{K}]_2^B \\ \Delta[\mathcal{K}]_2^B \end{bmatrix}.$$

Proof: It suffices to show the verifiability case. The refutability case follows by duality, and the ambiguous case follows from proposition 3.4(b). ($\Leftarrow$) Suppose that for each $h \in H$, $C_h \cap \mathcal{K} \in \Sigma[\mathcal{K}]_2^B$. So $C_h \cap \mathcal{K}$ is the union of some countable sequence $S[h]_0, S[h]_1, \ldots, S[h]_n, \ldots$ of $\mathcal{K}$-closed sets. Thus, for each i, there is some $G[h]_i \subseteq \omega^*$ such that $\overline{S[h]_i}$ is the union of all $\mathcal{K}$-fans $[e] \cap \mathcal{K}$ such that $e \in G[h]_i$ (*Fig. 4.27*).

When provided with hypothesis h and evidence e, α proceeds as follows. A pointer is initialized to 0. Then α scans e in stages $e|0, e|1, \ldots, e|lh(e)$. The pointer moves forward one step at a given stage if the data refutes the closed set $S[h]_i$ that the pointer points to upon entering that stage, and the pointer stays put otherwise. More precisely:

$$pointer(h, \mathbf{0}) = 0$$

$$pointer(h, e|n + 1) = \begin{cases} pointer(h, e|n) + 1 \\ \quad \text{if } e \text{ extends some member of } G[h]_{pointer(h, e|n)}. \\ pointer(h, e|n) \text{ otherwise.} \end{cases}$$

The method α conjectures 0 when the pointer moves on reading the last datum in e, and conjectures 1 otherwise (*Fig. 4.28*):

$$\alpha(h, \mathbf{0}) = 0$$

$$\alpha(h, e*x) = \begin{cases} 1 & \text{if } pointer(h, e*x) = pointer(h, e) \\ 0 & \text{otherwise.} \end{cases}$$

Now we verify that α works. Let $h \in H$, $\varepsilon \in \mathcal{K}$. Suppose $\varepsilon \in C_h$. Then there is some $\mathcal{K}$-closed set in α's enumeration containing ε. Let $S[h]_i$ be the first such. Since $\varepsilon \notin \overline{S[h]_i}$, there is no n such that $\varepsilon|n \in G[h]_i$, so the pointer can never move past position i. Thus, there is some time after which the pointer stops moving and at this time α stabilizes correctly to 1 on ε. Suppose $\varepsilon \notin C_h$. Then ε is not in any $S[h]_i$. So for each i, $\varepsilon \in \overline{S[h]_i}$. Thus, for each i, there is an $e' \in G[h]_i$ such that $\varepsilon|lh(e') = e'$. It follows that the pointer never stops moving, so α does not stabilize to 1.

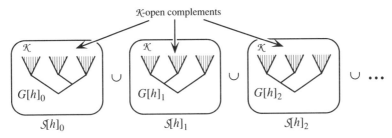

Figure 4.27

($\Rightarrow$) In previous characterizations, we have constructed demons to show that an arbitrary scientist can be fooled if the characterization condition is false. This time it is easier to do something different. We will use the fact that the scientist succeeds to decompose $C_h \cap \mathcal{K}$ into a countable union of $\mathcal{K}$-closed sets, showing directly that $C_h \cap \mathcal{K} \in \Sigma[\mathcal{K}]_2^B$. This technique was originally employed by Gold (1965) and Putnam (1965) in a computational setting, but it also works in the ideal case.

Suppose that some method α verifies H in the limit given $\mathcal{K}$. Then we have for each $h \in H$:

$$\forall \varepsilon \in \mathcal{K}[C(\varepsilon, h) \Leftrightarrow \exists n \, \forall m \geq n, \, \alpha(h, \varepsilon|m) = 1].$$

We can think of this fact as a definition of C_h over the restricted domain $\mathcal{K}$:

$$\forall \varepsilon \in \mathcal{K}, \, \varepsilon \in C_h \cap \mathcal{K} \Leftrightarrow \exists n \, \forall m \geq n \, \alpha(h, \varepsilon|m) = 1.$$

The set $\mathcal{A}_h(m)$ of all $\varepsilon \in \mathcal{K}$ such that $\alpha(h, \varepsilon|m) = 1$ is $\mathcal{K}$-clopen, since we only

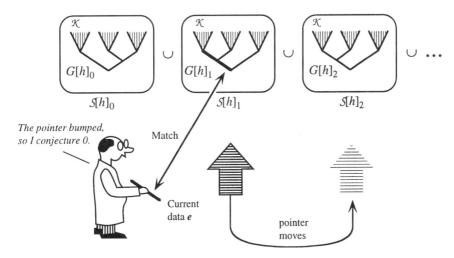

Figure 4.28

have to look at the data up to time m to determine what α will do. Also, for each $\varepsilon \in \mathcal{K}$ we have:

$$(\forall m \geq n \; \alpha(h, \varepsilon|m) = 1) \Leftrightarrow \varepsilon \in (\mathcal{A}_h(n) \cap \mathcal{A}_h(n+1) \cap \mathcal{A}_h(n+2), \ldots).$$

Let $\mathcal{B}_h(n)$ denote this countable intersection. Then we have for each $\varepsilon \in \mathcal{K}$:

$$\varepsilon \in C_h \cap \mathcal{K} \Leftrightarrow \exists n \; \forall m \geq n \; \alpha(h, \varepsilon|m) = 1$$

$$\Leftrightarrow \varepsilon \in (\mathcal{B}_h(0) \cup \mathcal{B}_h(1) \cup \mathcal{B}_h(2) \cup \cdots).$$

Thus $C_h \cap \mathcal{K} \in \Sigma[\mathcal{K}]_2^B$.   ∎

The method α constructed in this proof may be called the *bumping pointer method*. What we have just seen is that it is a *complete architecture* for verification in the limit, in the sense that for any inductive problem $(C, \mathcal{K}, H)$ verifiable in the limit by an ideal agent, the bumping pointer method employing the appropriate decomposition of each C_h into a countable union of $\mathcal{K}$-closed sets verifies $(C, \mathcal{K}, H)$ in the limit.

There is a very direct picture of how topological structure guarantees the bumping pointer method's success. Suppose that $C_h \cap \mathcal{K} \in \Sigma[\mathcal{K}]_2^B$. Then $C_h \cap \mathcal{K}$ is a countable union of $\mathcal{K}$-closed sets. Hence, the complement of $C_h \cap \mathcal{K}$ is a countable intersection of $\mathcal{K}$-open sets. Each $\mathcal{K}$-open set is a union of $\mathcal{K}$-fans. Recall that the intersection of two fans is empty unless one fan is a subset of the other, in which case the intersection is the fan with the longer handle. So a countable intersection of open sets can yield infinitely many paths determined by countable intersections of fans with shared handles, as in the case of ε in *Fig. 4.29*.

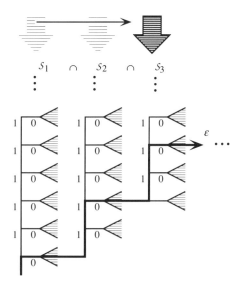

Figure 4.29

When $\varepsilon \notin C_h$, the data stream will "break through" each open set and the pointer will be moved infinitely often, so that the method emits infinitely many 0s. When $\varepsilon \in C_h$, there is some open set that ε never breaks through, so the pointer eventually remains fixed.

Karl Popper[7] has recommended holding onto a theory that has "passed muster" until it is refuted. Proposition 4.10 shows that this is not a very good idea if reliability is at stake. Recall the hypothesis h_{fin} that particle p is only finitely divisible. Popper's method would always stabilize to 1 on this hypothesis and hence would fail to verify it in the limit, since it is consistent with all possible data streams (given the setup described in chapter 3). But the bumping pointer architecture just described is guaranteed to verify$_C$ h_{fin} in the limit. In fact, it will beat Popper's proposal whenever $C_h \cap \mathcal{K} \in \Sigma[\mathcal{K}]_2^B - \Pi[\mathcal{K}]_1^B$. When $C_h \cap \mathcal{K} \in \Delta[\mathcal{K}]_2^B$, then there are two bumping pointer methods α_1, α_2, such that α_1 verifies$_C$ h in the limit given $\mathcal{K}$ and α_2 refutes$_C$ h in the limit given $\mathcal{K}$. When these two methods are assembled together according to the strategy of proposition 3.4(b), we have a method that decides$_C$ h in the limit given $\mathcal{K}$. This method beats Popper's proposal whenever $C_h \cap \mathcal{K} \in \Delta[\mathcal{K}]_2^B - \Pi[\mathcal{K}]_1^B$. Moreover, if the hypothesis is refutable with certainty, as Popper's method requires, the bumping pointer method can be set up so as to be guaranteed to succeed in this sense. The only modification required is to replace the infinite enumeration of $\mathcal{K}$-closed sets with a single $\mathcal{K}$-closed set and to have the method return '!', 0 when this set is refuted. Thus, the bumping pointer architecture can be modified so as to obey Popper's requirement whenever doing so doesn't get in the way of reliability, and to relax it just when it does.

Another application of this result concerns the question of optimal reliability.[8] We have already seen by proposition 3.15 that if h is not verifiable$_C$ in the limit given $\mathcal{N}$ but is verifiable in the limit given $\mathcal{K} \subset \mathcal{N}$, then there is an $\varepsilon \notin \mathcal{K}$ such that h is verifiable$_C$ in the limit given $\mathcal{K} \cup \{\varepsilon\}$. In purely topological terms, this amounts to:

Corollary 4.11

If $\mathcal{P} \notin \Sigma_2^B$ and $\mathcal{P} \in \Sigma[\mathcal{K}]_2^B$ then for some nonempty, finite $S \subseteq \mathcal{N} - \mathcal{P}$, $\mathcal{P} \in \Sigma[\mathcal{K} \cup S]_2^B$. ∎

The question then arises whether the result can be strengthened to show that $\mathcal{K}$ can be weakened by an *infinite* set of possible data streams. In fact, this is

---

[7] Popper (1968).

[8] This issue was visited at the end of the preceding chapter as well as in proposition 4.7.

true, as the following proposition shows.[9] In some cases, it can even be shown that weakening by an uncountably infinite set of data streams is possible.[10]

Proposition 4.12 (with C. Juhl)

If $P \notin \Sigma_2^B$ and $P \in \Sigma[\mathcal{K}]_2^B$ then for some countably infinite $S \subseteq \mathcal{N} - \mathcal{K}$, $P \in \Sigma[\mathcal{K} \cup S]_2^B$.

Proof: Given that $P \notin \Sigma[\mathcal{K}]_2^B$ then $\mathcal{N} - \mathcal{K}$ is infinite, else by proposition 3.15, $P \in \Sigma_2^B$. Then either (I) $(\mathcal{N} - \mathcal{K}) - P$ is infinite or (II) $(\mathcal{N} - \mathcal{K}) \cap P$ is infinite. Let α verify P in the limit given $\mathcal{K}$, as guaranteed by hypothesis and by proposition 4.10. Case (I). Either (A) there is an infinite, closed $S \subseteq (\mathcal{N} - \mathcal{K}) - P$ or (B) there is not. (A) Consider a method that verifies P in the limit given $\mathcal{K} \cup S$ as follows. Let α' conjecture 0 until S is refuted, and agree with α thereafter. If $\varepsilon \in S$ then α' correctly stabilizes to 0. Else, S is eventually refuted with certainty, after which α' agrees with α, which is guaranteed to work given $\mathcal{K}$. (B) Suppose there is no infinite, closed $S \subseteq (\mathcal{N} - \mathcal{K}) - P$. Then in particular, $(\mathcal{N} - \mathcal{K}) - P$ is not closed, and hence has a limit point in $\mathcal{K} \cup P$. Let Γ be a sequence of distinct elements of $(\mathcal{N} - \mathcal{K}) - P$ that converges to some $\varepsilon \in \mathcal{K} \cup P$. Let S be the range of Γ. Since Γ converges to ε, ε is the only limit point of S missing from S and hence (*) $S \cup \{\varepsilon\}$ is closed. Let $b = 1$ if $\varepsilon \in P$ and let $b = 0$ otherwise. Then construct the method α' that conjectures b until ε is refuted, that conjectures 0 until $S \cup \{\varepsilon\}$ is refuted, and that agrees with α thereafter. On data stream ε, α' correctly stabilizes to b. If $\varepsilon' \in S$, then α' correctly stabilizes to 0. If $\varepsilon' \notin S$ and $\varepsilon' \neq \varepsilon$, then eventually the set $S \cup \{\varepsilon\}$ is refuted by (*), and α' correctly agrees with α, which is correct given $\mathcal{K}$. Case (II) is similar. ∎

8. Efficient Data Use

A standard objection to the limiting analysis of inductive methods is that success in the limit is consistent with any crazy behavior in the short run.[11] As far as

---

[9] Proposition 4.12 belongs to what we might describe as *inverted complexity theory*. In standard complexity theory, one starts with a fixed, "tidy" space (e.g., $\mathcal{N}$), and with a given object (e.g., $P \subseteq \mathcal{N}$). The question is then to determine what the complexity (e.g., Borel complexity) of the object is in the fixed space. In propositions 4.12, 4.7, and 4.11, the issue is rather to specify an object P and a fixed complexity (e.g., Σ_2^B), and then to describe the set of all possible background spaces $\mathcal{K} \subseteq \mathcal{N}$ in which the object has the given complexity. This is what distinguishes epistemological applications of topology from standard results in descriptive set theory.

[10] We might ask, further, whether it is possible to expand $\mathcal{K}$ by an uncountable $S \subseteq \mathcal{N} - \mathcal{K}$ when $P \notin \Sigma_2^B$ and $P \in \Sigma[\mathcal{K}]_2^B$. It is possible to do so if $\mathcal{N} - \mathcal{K} - P$ is what is known as a *Suslin set*, for each such set has an uncountable, closed subset (Moschavakis 1980: 79, theorem 2C.2). Let S be this uncountable closed subset. Let α verify P in the limit given $\mathcal{K}$. Let α' conjecture 0 until S is refuted, and agree with α thereafter. Similarly, when $\mathcal{N} - \mathcal{K} \cap P$ is a Suslin set, let α' conjecture 1 until S is refuted and agree with α thereafter.

[11] Salmon (1967): 87.

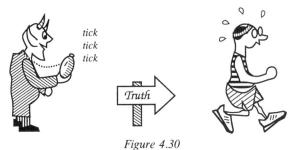

Figure 4.30

convergence is concerned, this is true. But that doesn't mean that any method reliable in the limit is as good as any other, for insanity in the short run may needlessly delay the onset of convergence (*Fig. 4.30*). Recall that

modulus$_\alpha(h, \varepsilon) = $ *the least n such that for all m $\geq$ n, $\alpha(h, \varepsilon|n) = \alpha(h, \varepsilon|m)$.*

To simplify what follows, we will let the modulus function assume value ω when no such *n* exists. Define:

$\beta \leq^H_{\mathcal{K}} \alpha \Leftrightarrow$ *for all $h \in H$, $\varepsilon \in \mathcal{K}$, modulus$_\beta(h, \varepsilon) \leq$ modulus$_\alpha(h, \varepsilon)$.*

$\beta <^H_{\mathcal{K}} \alpha \Leftrightarrow \beta \leq^H_{\mathcal{K}} \alpha$ *but not $\alpha \leq^H_{\mathcal{K}} \beta$.*

In the former case we say that β is *as fast* as α on H given $\mathcal{K}$. In the latter case we say that β is *strictly faster*. β is strictly faster than α on H given $\mathcal{K}$ just in case β stabilizes as soon as α on each hypothesis in H and data stream in $\mathcal{K}$, and properly faster on some hypothesis in H and data stream in $\mathcal{K}$. This is a special case of what decision theorists call *weak dominance*.[12]

It would be nice to have a reliable method that is as fast as every other reliable method on H given $\mathcal{K}$. Let $\mathcal{M}$ be a class of methods. Define:

α *is strongly data-minimal in $\mathcal{M}$ for H, $\mathcal{K}$*
$\Leftrightarrow \alpha \in \mathcal{M}$ *and for each $\beta \in \mathcal{M}$, $\alpha \leq^H_{\mathcal{K}} \beta$.*

In other words, for each method β in $\mathcal{M}$, a strongly data-minimal method α gets to the truth as quickly as β on each data stream. We will be interested in cases in which $\mathcal{M}$ is the set of all solutions to the inductive problem in question. Strongly data-minimal limiting verifiers exist only for very trivial inductive problems. For example, if $C_h = \emptyset$ for each $h \in H$, then the constant method $\alpha(h, e) = 0$ is data-minimal over all limiting-verifiers of H. However, as soon as we have a nontrivial hypothesis (i.e., $C_h \neq \mathcal{K}, \emptyset$} and $\mathcal{K}$ has at least two data streams, we can forget about strongly data-minimal solutions. For suppose

---

[12] One act *weakly dominates* another if its outcome is as good in each possible world state and is better in some possible world state. Here, the possible world states are possible data streams in $\mathcal{K}$ and the outcome of using a method is better insofar as one gets to the truth sooner.

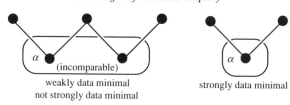

Figure 4.31

$\alpha(j, \mathbf{0}) = 1$. Then since $C_h \neq \mathcal{K}$, there is some $\varepsilon \in \mathcal{K} - C_h$, so α cannot be as fast on ε as the method that returns 0 until the current data e deviates from ε. A similar argument holds if $\alpha(h, \mathbf{0})$ is any other value.

The situation becomes more interesting when we lower our sights to methods that are not weakly dominated by any other method in $\mathcal{M}$ (*Fig. 4.31*):

$$\alpha \text{ is weakly data-minimal}^{13} \text{ in } \mathcal{M} \text{ for } H \Leftrightarrow \alpha \in \mathcal{M} \text{ and for each } \beta \in \mathcal{M},$$
$$\beta \not\prec^H_{\mathcal{K}} \alpha.$$

In other words, there is no method in $\mathcal{M}$ that gets to the truth on each data stream as fast as α and that beats α on some data stream. Weak data minimality is weaker than strong data minimality because it countenances situations in which α gets to the truth sooner than β on some data stream and β also gets to the truth sooner than α on some other data stream. In decision theory, an *admissible* strategy is one that is not weakly dominated by any other strategy. Weak data minimality is a special case of admissibility if weak dominance is understood with respect to convergence time over all possible data streams, and the competing strategies are all in $\mathcal{M}$.

Weakly data-minimal solutions to problems of verifiability in the limit are much easier to find. Recall the hypothesis h_{fin}, which says that only finitely many 1s will occur and define the simple method:

$$\alpha_0(h, e) = \begin{cases} 1 & \text{if } e \text{ ends with } 0 \\ 0 & \text{otherwise.} \end{cases}$$

Proposition 4.13

α_0 is weakly data-minimal among limiting verifiers$_C$ of h_{fin} given 2^ω.

Proof: It is evident that α_0 verifies$_C$ h_{fin} in the limit. Suppose β also verifies$_C$ h_{fin}. Suppose β's modulus is strictly smaller than that of α_0 on some $\varepsilon \in C_h$. Then ε stabilizes to 0 at some n, so the modulus of α_0 is n, and $\varepsilon_{n-1} = 1$. The modulus of β is strictly less than n, say n'. Let $\tau | n - 1 = \varepsilon | n - 1$ and let τ have only 1s thereafter, so that τ stabilizes to 1 with modulus $n - 1$. Then the

---

[13] Cf. Gold (1967) and Osherson et al. (1986).

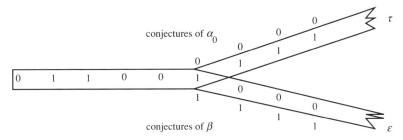

Figure 4.32

modulus of α_0 on τ is $n - 1$, but the modulus of β on τ is at best n, so β is not strictly faster than α_0 (*Fig. 4.32*). So $\beta \not<^H_{\mathcal{K}} \alpha_0$.

Suppose then that β's modulus n is strictly smaller than that of α_0 on some $\varepsilon \in 2^\omega - C_h$. Then β stabilizes to 0 on ε. If α_0 stabilizes to 0 on ε, the argument is as before. If α_0 does not stabilize to 0 on ε, then there is some $k > n$ such that α conjectures 1 on $\varepsilon|k$ after β has stabilized to 0. Thus, $\varepsilon_k = 0$, by the definition of α_0. Extend $\varepsilon|k$ with all 0s thereafter to form τ. The modulus of α_0 is k on τ, but the modulus of β cannot be lower than $k + 1$ since β conjectures 0 on $\tau|k$. So $\beta \not<^H_{\mathcal{K}} \beta$. ∎

This is just one very simple example. Can it be extended to other cases? The surprising answer is that every problem solvable in the limit has a weakly data-minimal solution. I begin with the limiting decidability case, which is simpler, and then proceed to the more interesting case of limiting verifiability.

Proposition 4.14[14]

> *If H is decidable$_C$ in the limit given $\mathcal{K}$ then some weakly data-minimal method decides$_C$ H in the limit given $\mathcal{K}$.*

Proof: By hypothesis, for each $h \in H$, $C_h \cap \mathcal{K} \in \Delta[\mathcal{K}]^B_2$. We define method α as follows. Let h and e be given. There are $\mathcal{K}$-closed sets $S_0, \mathcal{R}_0, S_1, \mathcal{R}_1, \ldots$ such that:

$$C_h \cap \mathcal{K} = S_0 \cup S_1 \cup \cdots \cup S_n \cup \cdots$$
$$\overline{C_h} \cap \mathcal{K} = \mathcal{R}_0 \cup \mathcal{R}_1 \cup \cdots \cup \mathcal{R}_n \cup \cdots.$$

Enumerate the set of all pairs of form $(S_i, 1)$, $(\mathcal{R}_j, 0)$ as $\pi_0, \pi_1, \ldots$. Let α conjecture the Boolean value associated with the first pair whose $\mathcal{K}$-closed set is not refuted by e (*Fig. 4.33*).

It is easily verified along the lines of proposition 4.10 that α decides$_C$ H in the limit given $\mathcal{K}$. Now it is shown that α is data-minimal. For suppose there is a β such that β decides$_C$ H in the limit given $\mathcal{K}$ and for some $h \in H$, $\varepsilon \in \mathcal{K}$, β converges sooner than α does. First, suppose that $\varepsilon \in C_h$. Let $modulus_\beta(h, \varepsilon) = n$.

---

[14] Similar to Gold (1967) and Osherson et al. (1986).

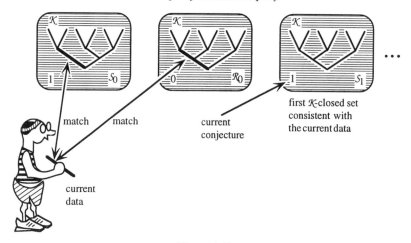

Figure 4.33

For some $m \geq n$, $\alpha(h, \varepsilon|m) = 0$. Hence, α's pointer points to some pair $\pi_k = (\mathcal{R}, 0)$ at stage m. So $\mathcal{R}$ is not refuted by $\varepsilon|m$. Hence, there is an $\varepsilon' \in \mathcal{K} - C_h$ such that ε' extends $\varepsilon|m$. α's pointer is never moved after stage m on ε', so $modulus_\alpha(h, \varepsilon') \leq m$. But $\beta(h, \varepsilon'|m) = 1$, so $modulus_\beta(h, \varepsilon') > m$. A similar argument works when $\varepsilon \notin C_h$. Since β is an arbitrary limiting decider$_C$ of H given $\mathcal{K}$, α is data-minimal among such solutions. ∎

The preceding argument works because whenever α has not yet stabilized to 1 on some $\varepsilon \in \mathcal{K} \cap C_h$, it can be excused because there is some $\tau \in \mathcal{K} - C_h$ that it might have already stabilized to 0 on. It is not obvious that the same sort of argument can be given in the case of limiting verification. For suppose that h is verifiable but not decidable in the limit and that α verifies h in the limit. Then α fails to converge to 0 on infinitely many data streams that make h false. But then there is a method β that also converges to 0 on a data stream ε making h false on which α fails to converge to 0 (i.e., define β to conjecture 0 until the actual data veers off from ε and to pass control to α thereafter). On ε, the modulus of α is infinitely greater than that of β. It therefore seems that it should be possible to speed up any limiting verifier of h. But in fact, we can define α so that any β that converges to 0 when α does not must converge to 1 later than α on some data stream making h true.

Proposition 4.15

(a) *If H is verifiable$_C$ in the limit given $\mathcal{K}$ then some method is weakly data-minimal over limiting verifiers$_C$ of H in the limit given $\mathcal{K}$.*

(b) *The limiting refutation case is similar.*

Proof: (a) Suppose that for each $h \in H$, $C_h \cap \mathcal{K} \in \Sigma[\mathcal{K}]_2^B$. For each $h \in H$, choose $\mathcal{K}$-closed sets $S[h]_i$ such that

$$C_h \cap \mathcal{K} = S[h]_0 \cup S[h]_1 \cup \cdots \cup S[h]_n \cup \cdots$$

and if $C_h \cap \mathcal{K} \neq \varnothing$, then no $S[h]_i = \varnothing$. The function *pointer*(h, e) is set up just as in the proof of proposition 4.10 above. The method α is given as follows. For each h, e, let $\tau_{h,e}$ be an arbitrary, fixed choice of a data stream extending e in $\mathcal{K} - C_h$, if such a data stream exists, and let $\tau_{h,e}$ be undefined otherwise.

$\alpha(h, e)$:

(0) *if $C_h \cap \mathcal{K} = \varnothing$, then conjecture 0*

(1) *else if $e = \mathbf{0}$, then conjecture 1*

(2) *else if there is an $e' \subseteq e$ such that pointer$(h, e') \neq$ pointer(h, e') and $\tau_{h,e'}$ extends e, then conjecture 0*

(3) *else conjecture 1.*

The idea is that $\tau_{h,e}$ is "entertained" by α if the pointer bumps on e, and it continues to be entertained until data deviating from it is seen (*Fig. 4.34*). While some $\tau_{h,e}$ is entertained, α conjectures 0. Otherwise, α conjectures 1. This inductive architecture will be referred to as the *opportunistic architecture*, since it takes advantage of opportunities to stabilize to 0 in order to block the argument that some other method is properly faster.

First it must be shown that α verifies$_C$ H in the limit given $\mathcal{K}$. Let $h \in H$. Let $\varepsilon \in C_h \cap \mathcal{K}$. Then for some i, $\varepsilon \in S[h]_i$. Thus the pointer cannot bump past position i, so the pointer bumps only finitely many times on ε, say on $\varepsilon|n_1$, $\varepsilon|n_2, \ldots, \varepsilon|n_k$. Since $\varepsilon \in C_h \cap \mathcal{K}$, $\varepsilon \neq \tau_{h,\varepsilon|n_1}, \ldots, \tau_{h,\varepsilon|n_k}$. So for some time m, $\varepsilon|m$ is not extended by $\tau_{h,\varepsilon|n_k}$, and hence (2) is never again satisfied after stage m. Moreover, (0) never applies, since for each n, $\varepsilon \in [\varepsilon|n] \cap C_h \cap \mathcal{K}$. So (3) applies forever after m, and α stabilizes correctly to 1 (*Fig. 4.35*).

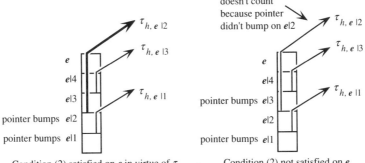

Condition (2) satisfied on e in virtue of $\tau_{h,e|2}$.   Condition (2) not satisfied on e.

Figure 4.34

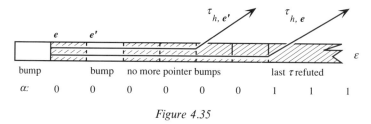

Figure 4.35

Now suppose $\varepsilon \in \mathcal{K} - C_h$. For each i, $\varepsilon \notin S[h]_i$, so the pointer is bumped infinitely often. Moreover, ε itself witnesses the existence of $\tau_{h, \varepsilon|n}$, for each n, so condition (2) is satisfied infinitely often, and infinitely many 0s are conjectured by α on ε (*Fig. 4.36*).

It remains to show that α is weakly data-minimal. Suppose that for some $\varepsilon \in \mathcal{K}$ and for some limiting verifier β of h given $\mathcal{K}$, $n' = modulus_\beta(h, \varepsilon) < modulus_\alpha(h, \varepsilon) = n$. Suppose $\varepsilon \in C_h \cap \mathcal{K}$. Then both β and α stabilize to 1 on ε. So $\alpha(h, \varepsilon|n - 1) = 0$. (0) is not satisfied by $\varepsilon|n - 1$, since $\varepsilon \in C_h \cap \mathcal{K}$. So $\varepsilon|n - 1$ satisfies (2). Then by condition (2), there is some $\tau_{h, \varepsilon|n-1} \in \mathcal{K} - C_h$ that extends $\varepsilon|n - 1$, and by condition (2), $modulus_\alpha(h, \tau_{h, \varepsilon|n-1}) = n - 1$. But since $\beta(h, \varepsilon|n - 1) = 1$, $modulus_\beta(h, \tau_{h, \varepsilon|n-1}) > n - 1$. So β is not strictly faster than α (*Fig. 4.37*).

Now suppose $\varepsilon \in \mathcal{K} - C_h$. Since $n' = modulus_\beta(h, \varepsilon) < modulus_\alpha(h, \varepsilon)$, β stabilizes to 0 and α either stabilizes to 0 later or never stabilizes. Either way, there exists $n \geq n'$ such that $\alpha(h, \varepsilon|n) = 1$. Suppose this happens due to clause (1). In that case, $n' = 0$. Since clause (0) was bypassed, $C_h \cap \mathcal{K} \neq \varnothing$, so $S[h]_0 \neq \varnothing$, by our specification of the enumeration $S[h]_i$. Hence, there exists $\tau \in S[h]_0$ such that the pointer remains forever stuck at 0 on τ, so α stabilizes to 1 on τ with modulus 0. Since β starts out with 0, its modulus on τ can be no less than 1, so β is not strictly faster than α. Suppose, finally, that $\alpha(h, \varepsilon|n) = 1$ in virtue of clause (3). As in the proof of correctness for α, ε itself witnesses that for each k, $\tau_{h, \varepsilon|k}$ exists. Then (2) fails for $\varepsilon|n$ because $pointer(\varepsilon|n - 1) = pointer(\varepsilon|n)$. Let k be the pointer position on $\varepsilon|n$. Then $\varepsilon|n$ is extended by some $\varepsilon' \in S[h]_k \subseteq C_h$. $Modulus_\alpha(h, \varepsilon') = n$, since the pointer remains stuck at k on ε' and hence α stabilizes to 1 on ε at least by n. But since $\beta(h, \varepsilon|n) = 0$, $modulus_\beta(h, \varepsilon') > n$. So again β is not strictly faster than α. ∎

Each opportunistic method is *consistent* in the sense that it stabilizes to 0 immediately when the hypothesis under test is refuted (i.e., when $C_h \cap \mathcal{K} \cap [e] = \varnothing$), and it stabilizes to 1 immediately when the hypothesis under test is

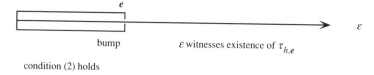

Figure 4.36

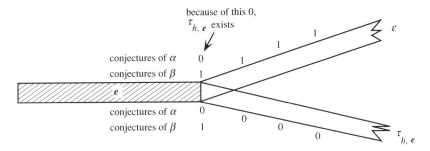

Figure 4.37

entailed by the data (i.e., when $\mathcal{K} \cap [e] \subseteq C_h \cap [e]$). In fact, consistency is necessary for weak data minimality in limiting verification problems (cf. exercise 4.7).

A remarkable feature of the above result is that no limiting decision procedure is strictly faster than an *arbitrary* specification of the opportunistic architecture for the problem in question, even though some other method may stabilize to 0 on more data streams. It is also interesting that such methods can be weakly data-minimal employing a pointer that bumps only one step each time a closed set in the enumeration is refuted. It would seem that a method employing a pointer that advances immediately to the first unrefuted closed set ought to be properly faster, but this is not the case.

9. A Characterization of *n*-Mind-Change Decidability

It is clear that if there is an n such that h is decidable with n mind changes given $\mathcal{K}$ then h is decidable in the limit given $\mathcal{K}$. The converse is false (cf. proposition 4.17 (a)). Since there are problems solvable with fixed numbers of mind changes that are neither verifiable nor refutable with certainty (section 3.5), the complexity of decidability with bounded mind changes is located above refutation and verification with certainty and below decidability in the limit (*Fig. 4.38*).

So we cannot characterize bounded mind change decidability in terms of Borel complexity, as there are no Borel classes left to characterize it. But as it turns out, there is another scale of topological complexity, the *finite difference hierarchy*,[15] that lies precisely in the required position. I will label this hierarchy with the superscript D. Whereas the finite Borel hierarchy builds complexity

---

[15] Cf. Kuratowski (1966). I am indebted to J. Tappenden for this reference, of which I was unaware when I worked out the results in the following two sections of this chapter. I was led to the question by Putnam (1965), which falls somewhat short of the full characterization, though providing such a characterization was not the point of the paper.

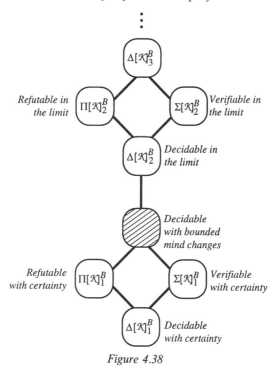

Figure 4.38

by complementation and countable union, the finite difference hierarchy builds complexity by finite intersection and union of alternating sequences of open and closed sets, so that O is simpler than $O \cap P$, which in turn is simpler than $(O \cup P) \cap O'$, and so forth, where O, O' are open and P is closed. Let $S \subseteq \mathcal{K}$. Then we define:

$$S \in \Sigma[\mathcal{K}]_0^D \Leftrightarrow S \text{ is } \mathcal{K}\text{-clopen.}$$

$$S \in \Sigma[\mathcal{K}]_{n+1}^D \Leftrightarrow \text{ for some } \mathcal{R} \in \Sigma[\mathcal{K}]_n^D, \text{ for some } \mathcal{K}\text{-open } O,$$
$$S = \bar{\mathcal{R}} \cap O.$$

$$D_\mathcal{K} = \bigcup_{i \in \omega} \Sigma[\mathcal{K}]_i^D$$

The dual and ambiguous classes are defined in terms of the Σ classes in the usual way. It is now possible to state the characterization.

Proposition 4.16

For each $n \geq 0$, for each r such that $0 < r < 1$,

(a–c) *H is decidable with n mind changes starting with* $\begin{bmatrix} 0 \\ 1 \\ r \end{bmatrix}$ *given* $\mathcal{K}$

$\Leftrightarrow$ *for each* $h \in H,\ C_h \cap \mathcal{K} \in \begin{bmatrix} \Sigma[\mathcal{K}]_n^D \\ \Pi[\mathcal{K}]_n^D \\ \Delta[\mathcal{K}]_n^D \end{bmatrix}.$

(d) *H is decidable with n mind changes given* $\mathcal{K}$
   $\Leftrightarrow \forall h \in H,\ C_h \cap \mathcal{K} \in \Sigma[\mathcal{K}]_n^D \cup \Pi[\mathcal{K}]_n^D.$

Proof: (a) ($\Rightarrow$) Suppose that α decides$_C$ H given $\mathcal{K}$ in n mind changes starting with 0. Let

$$\alpha'(h, e) = \begin{cases} 1 & if\ \alpha(h, e) = 1 \\ 0 & otherwise. \end{cases}$$

α' decides$_C$ H given $\mathcal{K}$ in n mind changes starting with 0, and α' conjectures only 0s and 1s. Let $h \in H$. Define $\varepsilon \in O(\varepsilon, n) \Leftrightarrow \alpha'$ changes its conjecture for h at least n times on ε, and define $\mathcal{P}(\varepsilon, n) \Leftrightarrow \alpha'$ changes its conjecture for h at most n times on ε. $O(\varepsilon, n)$ is $\mathcal{K}$-open and $\mathcal{P}(\varepsilon, n)$ is $\mathcal{K}$-closed. First, consider the case when n is even. Then since α' starts with conjecture 0 and never uses more than n mind changes over $\mathcal{K}$ on h, we have:

$\varepsilon \in C_h \cap \mathcal{K} \Leftrightarrow \alpha'$ *changes its mind some odd number of times*

$\leq n - 1$ *about h on* ε

$\Leftrightarrow (O(\varepsilon, 1)\ \&\ \mathcal{P}(\varepsilon, 1)) \vee (O(\varepsilon, 3)\ \&\ \mathcal{P}(\varepsilon, 3)) \vee \cdots$

$\vee (O(\varepsilon, n - 1)\ \&\ \mathcal{P}(\varepsilon, n - 1))$

$\Leftrightarrow [O(\varepsilon, 1)\ \&\ \mathcal{P}(\varepsilon, 1)] \vee [O(\varepsilon, 1)\ \&\ O(\varepsilon, 3)\ \&\ \mathcal{P}(\varepsilon, 3)]$

$\vee [O(\varepsilon, 1)\ \&\ O(\varepsilon, 3)\ \&\ O(\varepsilon, 5)\ \&\ \mathcal{P}(\varepsilon, 5)] \vee \cdots$

$\vee [O(\varepsilon, 1)\ \&\ O(\varepsilon, 3)\ \&\ O(\varepsilon, 5)\ \&\ \cdots$

$\&\ O(\varepsilon, n - 3)\ \&\ O(\varepsilon, n - 1)\ \&\ \mathcal{P}(\varepsilon, n - 1)]$

$\Leftrightarrow O(\varepsilon, 1)\ \&\ [\mathcal{P}(\varepsilon, 1) \vee [O(\varepsilon, 3)\ \&\ [\mathcal{P}(\varepsilon, 3) \vee \cdots$

$\vee [O(\varepsilon, n - 1)\ \&\ \mathcal{P}(\varepsilon, n - 1)]]]]$ *(by factoring)*.

So $C_h \cap \mathcal{K} \in \Sigma[\mathcal{K}]_n^D$. Now for the case in which n is odd. Since α starts out with conjecture 0 and never uses more than n mind changes over $\mathcal{K}$ on h, we have:

$\varepsilon \in C_h \cap \mathcal{K} \Leftrightarrow \alpha'$ *does not change its mind some even number of times*

$\leq n$ *about h on* ε

$\Leftrightarrow \neg P(\varepsilon, 0) \,\&\, \neg(O(\varepsilon, 2) \,\&\, P(\varepsilon, 2)) \,\&\, \cdots$

$\&\, \neg(O(\varepsilon, n-1) \,\&\, P(\varepsilon, n-1))$

$\Leftrightarrow O(\varepsilon, 1) \,\&\, [P(\varepsilon, 1) \vee O(\varepsilon, 3)] \,\&\, [P(\varepsilon, 3) \vee O(\varepsilon, 5)]$

$\&\, [P(\varepsilon, 5) \vee O(\varepsilon, 7)] \,\&\, \cdots \,\&\, [P(\varepsilon, n-3) \vee O(\varepsilon, n-1)]$

$\Leftrightarrow O(\varepsilon, 1) \,\&\, [P(\varepsilon, 1) \vee O(\varepsilon, 3)] \,\&\, [P(\varepsilon, 1) \vee P(\varepsilon, 3)$

$\vee \, O(\varepsilon, 5)] \,\&\, [P(\varepsilon, 1) \vee P(\varepsilon, 3) \vee P(\varepsilon, 5) \vee O(\varepsilon, 7)]$

$\&\, \cdots \,\&\, [P(\varepsilon, 1) \vee P(\varepsilon, 3) \vee \cdots \vee P(\varepsilon, n-5) \vee \cdots$

$\vee \, P(\varepsilon, n-3) \vee O(\varepsilon, n-1)]$

$\Leftrightarrow O(\varepsilon, 1) \,\&\, [P(\varepsilon, 1) \vee [O(\varepsilon, 3) \,\&\, [P(\varepsilon, 3) \vee \cdots$

$\&\, [P(\varepsilon, n-3) \vee O(\varepsilon, n-1)]]]]$ *(by factoring)*.

So $C_\eta \cap \mathcal{K} \in \Sigma[\mathcal{K}]_n^D$.

($\Leftarrow$) Suppose that for each $h \in H$, $C_h \cap \mathcal{K} \in \Sigma[\mathcal{K}]_n^D$. Then $C_h \cap \mathcal{K}$ may be expressed in the forms

$$O_1 \cap [P_2 \cup [O_3 \cap [P_4 \cup \cdots [P_{n-1} \cup O_n]\ \textit{if n is odd,}$$
$$O_1 \cap [P_2 \cup [O_3 \cap [O_4 \cup \cdots [P_{n-1} \cap O_n]\ \textit{if n is even,}$$

where each O_i is open and each P_i is closed. In either case, define α to conjecture 0 for h until O_1 is verified by the data, after which α says 1 until P_2 is refuted by the data, after which α says 0 until O_3 is verified by the data, after which α says 1 until... α will succeed with at most n mind changes starting with 0.

(b) follows from (a) by duality, and (c) follows from (a) and (b) by proposition 3.12(b). (d) follows from (a), (b), and proposition 3.12(c). ∎

The following proposition is an illustration of proposition 4.16 (*Fig. 4.39*).

Proposition 4.17

Let $\mathcal{K}$ be the set of all data streams that stabilize to some value. Then

(a) $D_{\mathcal{K}} \subset \Delta[\mathcal{K}]_2^B$.

(b) *For each n,* $\Sigma[\mathcal{K}]_n^D \subset \Sigma[\mathcal{K}]_{n+1}^D$.

(c) $D_{\mathcal{K}}$ *is the finitary Boolean closure of* $\Sigma[\mathcal{K}]_1^D$.

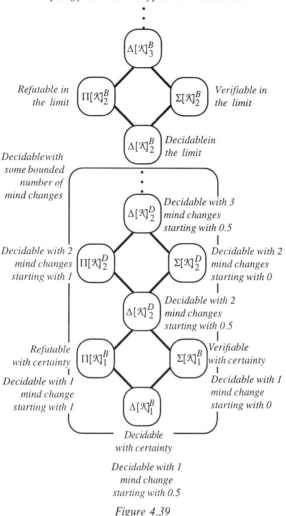

Figure 4.39

Proof: (b) To show that the inclusion is proper, define $\#0(\varepsilon)$ = the number of 0s occurring in ε. Let $H = \omega$ and define C as follows:

$$
C(\varepsilon, h) = \begin{cases} \left(\bigvee_{k=1}^{h/2} \#0(\varepsilon) = 2k \right) \text{ if } h \text{ is even} \\[2ex] \left(\left(\bigvee_{k=1}^{(h-1)/2} \#0(\varepsilon) = 2k \right) \text{ or } \#0(\varepsilon) \geq h+1 \right) \text{ if } h \text{ is odd}. \end{cases}
$$

h is readily seen to be decidable in h mind changes starting with 0. A simple demonic argument shows that h cannot be decided$_C$ with fewer mind changes starting with 0. Now apply proposition 4.16.

(a) Let C be defined as in the proof of (b). Add h^* to H, and define $C(\varepsilon, h^*) \Leftrightarrow C(\varepsilon, \varepsilon_1)$. Let α and n be given. The demon feeds $n + 1$ as the first datum and then forces α to change its mind concerning h^* at least $n + 1$ times, as in (b). By proposition 4.16, $C_{h^*} \cap \mathcal{K}$ is not in any class $\Sigma[\mathcal{K}]_n^D$, so $C_{h^*} \cap \mathcal{K} \notin D_{\mathcal{K}}$. But it is easy to decide$_C$ h^* in the limit. By proposition 4.10, $C_{h^*} \cap \mathcal{K} \in \Delta[\mathcal{K}]_2^B$.

(c) Each finite Boolean combination of open sets may be rewritten in disjunctive normal form. But by the closure of open [closed] sets under finite intersection, each disjunct can be rewritten in one of the following forms: $(O \cap P)$, O, or P, where O is open and P is closed. Each disjunct of form $(O \cap P)$ is settled in two mind changes (say zero until O is verified; then say one until P is refuted). Each O and each P can be handled with one mind change, so the hole disjunction can be handled in some finite number of mind changes. Apply proposition 4.16.   ∎

10. A Demon-Oriented Characterization of *n*-Mind-Change Decidability

The proof of proposition 4.16 makes it more transparent how the scientist can succeed than how the demon can. What eactly does a demon need in order to be sure of fooling an arbitrary scientist n times about h given background assumptions $\mathcal{K}$? Let's consider the case of one mind change. We have seen in the proof of proposition 4.6 that the demon requires only the following pattern of "tracks" somewhere in $\mathcal{K}$ in order to fool at least twice a scientist who starts out conjecturing 0 (*Fig. 4.40*). To fool a scientist who starts out with conjecture 0 at least three times, the demon requires a slightly more complex system of tracks in $\mathcal{K}$ (*Fig. 4.41*).

The demon starts by steaming down the track depicted by the bold arrow. Eventually, the scientist says 1 because all tracks headed to the right make h true. At that point, the demon turns left onto a track for $\overline{C}_h$. He rolls down this track until the scientist says 0, which again must happen, else the scientist produces falsehood forever on this track. At this point, the demon again turns right, forcing the second mind change on pain, once again, of producing infinitely many false conjectures on a data stream in $\mathcal{K}$.

The demon's needs are becoming clear. What he requires is something like an infinite *feather*. The demon always starts out on the *shaft* of the feather, and then shunts back and forth along *barbs*, barbs of barbs, and so forth (*Fig. 4.42*). Each time the demon moves from a barb to a barb of a barb, the truth value of h changes. The *dimension* of the feather (the number of times one can turn

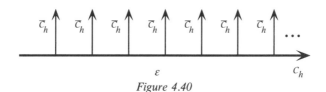

Figure 4.40

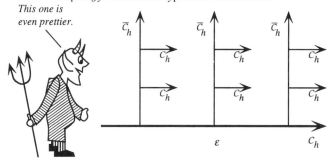

This one is even prettier.

Figure 4.41

direction, traveling out from the shaft) determines how many times the demon can force the scientist to change his mind.

We may define *n*-feathers inductively, as follows. Let $\mathcal{K}, \mathcal{P} \subseteq \mathcal{N}$.

> $\mathcal{K}$ is a 1-*feather* for $\mathcal{P}$ with shaft $\varepsilon \Leftrightarrow \varepsilon \in \mathcal{P} \cap \mathcal{K}$.
>
> $\mathcal{K}$ is an *n* + 1-*feather* for $\mathcal{P}$ with shaft $\varepsilon \Leftrightarrow \varepsilon \in \mathcal{P} \cap \mathcal{K}$ and
>
> $\forall m \; \exists \varepsilon' \in \mathcal{K}$ such that
> $\varepsilon | m = \varepsilon' | m$ and
> $\mathcal{K}$ is an *n*-feather with shaft ε' for $\bar{\mathcal{P}}$.
>
> $\mathcal{K}$ is an *n*-feather for $\mathcal{P} \Leftrightarrow \exists \varepsilon$ such that $\mathcal{K}$ is an *n*-feather for $\mathcal{P}$ with shaft ε.

An *n* + 1 feather for $\mathcal{P}$ is a data stream for $\mathcal{P}$ that has *n*-feathers for $\bar{\mathcal{P}}$ branching off infinitely often (*Fig. 4.43*). An *n* + 1-feather for $\mathcal{P}$ has its shaft in $\mathcal{P}$, whereas an *n*-feather for $\bar{\mathcal{P}}$ has its shaft in $\bar{\mathcal{P}}$. We may now define the *feather dimension* of $\mathcal{K}$ for $\mathcal{P}$.

> $Dim_{\mathcal{P}}(\mathcal{K}) = n \Leftrightarrow \mathcal{K}$ is an *n*-feather for $\mathcal{P}$ and $\mathcal{K}$ is not an *n* + 1-*feather* for $\mathcal{P}$.

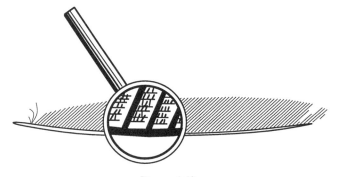

Figure 4.42

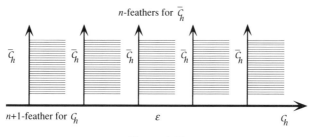

Figure 4.43

The obvious demonic argument yields that if $\mathcal{K}$ is an n-feather for C_h, then no scientist can decide h with n mind changes given $\mathcal{K}$, starting with conjecture 0. It is a bit less obvious that whenever $\mathcal{K}$ is not an n-feather for C_h, h is decidable with at most n mind changes given $\mathcal{K}$, starting with 0.

Proposition 4.18

(a) *H is decidable$_C$ given $\mathcal{K}$ in n mind changes starting with 0*
    $\Leftrightarrow \forall h \in H$, $\mathcal{K}$ is not an $n + 1$-feather for C_h.

(b) *H is decidable$_C$ given $\mathcal{K}$ in n mind changes starting with 1*
    $\Leftrightarrow \forall h \in H$, $\mathcal{K}$ is not an $n + 1$-feather for $\overline{C_h}$.

(c) *H is decidable$_C$ given $\mathcal{K}$ in n mind changes starting with 0.5*
    $\Leftrightarrow \forall h \in H$, $\mathcal{K}$ is not an $n + 1$-feather for C_h or for $\overline{C_h}$.

(d) *H is decidable given $\mathcal{K}$ in n mind changes*
    $\Leftrightarrow \forall h \in H$, $\mathcal{K}$ is not an $n + 1$-feather for C_h or $\mathcal{K}$ is not an $n + 1$-feather for $\overline{C_h}$.

It follows immediately from proposition 4.16 that:

Corollary 4.19

$C_h \cap \mathcal{K} \in \Sigma[\mathcal{K}]_n^D \Leftrightarrow \mathcal{K}$ *is not an $n + 1$-feather for C_h.*

$C_h \cap \mathcal{K} \in \Pi[\mathcal{K}]_n^D \Leftrightarrow \mathcal{K}$ *is not an $n + 1$-feather for $\overline{C_h}$.*

$C_h \cap \mathcal{K} \in \Delta[\mathcal{K}]_n^D \Leftrightarrow \mathcal{K}$ *is not an $n + 1$-feather for C_h and $\mathcal{K}$ is not an*
                                        $n + 1$-feather for $\overline{C_h}$.

$C_h \cap \mathcal{K} \in \Sigma[\mathcal{K}]_n^D \cup \Pi[\mathcal{K}]_n^D \Leftrightarrow \mathcal{K}$ *is not an $n + 1$-feather for C_h or*
                                        $\mathcal{K}$ is not an $n + 1$-feather for $\overline{C_h}$.

Proof: (a) & (b) ($\Rightarrow$) Prove the contrapositive by the obvious demonic argument.

($\Leftarrow$) Argument by induction on n. Base case for (b): Suppose that $\mathcal{K}$ is not a 1-feather for C_h. Then $C_h \cap \mathcal{K} = \varnothing$. Let $\varepsilon \in \mathcal{K}$. Then $\varepsilon \notin C_h$. So the trivial

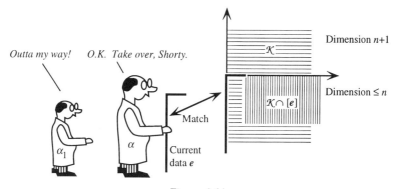

Figure 4.44

method always conjectures 0 no matter what succeeds in 0 mind changes. The base case for (a) is similar.

Now suppose (a) and (b) for each $m \leq n$. Suppose that for each $h \in H$, $\mathcal{K}$ is not an $n + 2$-feather for C_h. Define the method (*Fig. 4.44*):

$$\alpha(h, e) = \begin{cases} 0 & \textit{if } e = 0 \\ 0 & \textit{if } Dim_{C_h}(\mathcal{K} \cap [e]) > n \textit{ and } Dim_{\overline{C_h}}(\mathcal{K} \cap [e]) > n \\ \alpha_1(h, e) & \textit{if } Dim_{\overline{C_h}}(\mathcal{K} \cap [e]) \leq n \\ \alpha_0(h, e) & \textit{otherwise (i.e., if } Dim_{C_h}(\mathcal{K} \cap [e]) \leq n). \end{cases}$$

where α_1 decides h with n mind changes starting with 1 given $\mathcal{K} \cap [e]$ and α_0 decides h with n mind changes starting with 0 given $\mathcal{K} \cap [e]$, as guaranteed by the induction hypothesis when $Dim_{C_h}(\mathcal{K} \cap [e]) \leq n$ or $Dim_{\overline{C_h}}(\mathcal{K} \cap [e]) \leq n$, respectively.

There are just two cases to consider.

    (i) $\forall k \ Dim_{C_h}(\mathcal{K} \cap [\varepsilon|k]) > n$ and $Dim_{\overline{C_h}}(\mathcal{K} \cap [\varepsilon|k]) > n$.

    (ii) $\exists k \ Dim_{C_h}(\mathcal{K} \cap [\varepsilon|k]) \leq n$ or $Dim_{\overline{C_h}}(\mathcal{K} \cap [\varepsilon|k]) \leq n$.

Lemma 4.20

If (i) *then* $\varepsilon \notin C_h$ *and* α *stabilizes correctly to 0 on* h, ε
with no mind changes.

Proof: For suppose that $\varepsilon \in C_h$. Then since for each k, $Dim_{\overline{C_h}}(\mathcal{K} \cap [\varepsilon|k]) > n$, we have that for each k, there is an ε' such that $\mathcal{K} \cap [\varepsilon|k]$ is an $n + 1$ feather for $\overline{C_h}$ with shaft ε' and $\varepsilon'|k = \varepsilon|k$. Hence, $\mathcal{K}$ is an $n + 2$-feather for C_h with shaft ε, contrary to the hypothesis. Now observe that for each k, the second clause of α is satisfied on $\varepsilon|k$, so for each k, $\alpha(h, \varepsilon|k) = 0$. ∎

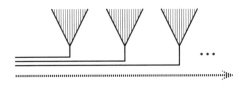

Figure 4.45

Lemma 4.21

If (ii) *then* α *succeeds in* $n + 1$ *mind changes.*

Proof: Let m be the least k such that $Dim_{C_h}(\mathcal{K} \cap [\varepsilon|k]) \leq n$ or $Dim_{\overline{C_h}}(\mathcal{K} \cap [\varepsilon|k]) \leq n$. Suppose that $Dim_{\overline{C_h}}(\mathcal{K} \cap [\varepsilon|k]) \leq n$. Then $\alpha(h, \varepsilon|m') = 0$, for all $m' < m$ and $\alpha(h, \varepsilon|m'') = \alpha_1(\varepsilon|m'')$ for all $m'' \geq m$. Since α_1 decides C_h over $\mathcal{K} \cap [\varepsilon|m]$ in n mind changes starting with 1 and α outputs only 0 prior to invoking α_1, α succeeds in $n + 1$ mind changes starting with 0. In case $Dim_{C_h}(\mathcal{K} \cap [\varepsilon|k]) \leq n$, we have a similar situation, except that α_0 starts with 0, so α succeeds in n mind changes.   ∎

The induction for (b) is similar, except that the method employed starts out with 1s until the submethods α_0 and α_1 are invoked. (c) and (d) may be obtained just as in proposition 4.16(c) and (d).   ∎

By corollary 4.19, the feather perspective and the D-hierarchy perspective coincide exactly. It is revealing to see how the correspondence works by constructing feathers out of intersections and unions of open and closed sets. The D-hierarchy starts at level Σ_1^D with open hypotheses. The open set depicted in (*Fig. 4.45*) clearly yields a 1-feather which affords the demon the chance to fool a scientist who starts with 0 once, and a scientist who starts with 1 twice.

To generate a properly Π_1^D set, we take the complement of the open set to arrive at a closed set, which allows the demon to fool twice a scientist who starts with conjecture 0, and to fool once a scientist who starts with conjecture 1 (*Fig. 4.46*).

To obtain a Σ_2^D set, we add an open set to out closed set. This yields a 2-feather, which affords the demon an opportunity to fool twice a scientist who starts with conjecture 1, and to fool three times a scientist who starts with conjecture 0 (*Fig. 4.47*).

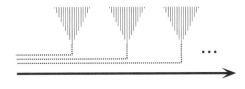

Figure 4.46

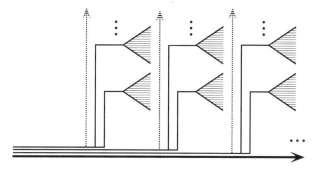

Figure 4.47

Complementing this set yields Π_2^D set and a dual 2-feather (*Fig. 4.48*). Now we are again free to add a dimension by augmenting this set with an open set. By successive complementations and open set additions, we can build a feather of arbitrary finite dimension.

11. Characterization of Gradual Assessment

The following characterization introduces a complete architecture that generalizes the bumping pointer architecture. Noteworthy features of this result are that Σ and Π switch sides regarding verification and refutation and decidability drops a level below $\Delta[\mathcal{K}]_3^B$.

Proposition 4.22

$$H \text{ is } \begin{bmatrix} \text{verifiable}_C \\ \text{refutable}_C \\ \text{decidable}_C \end{bmatrix} \text{ gradually given } \mathcal{K}$$

$$\Leftrightarrow \text{ for each } h \in H, \, C_h \cap \mathcal{K} \in \begin{bmatrix} \Pi[\mathcal{K}]_3^B \\ \Sigma[\mathcal{K}]_3^B \\ \Delta[\mathcal{K}]_2^B \end{bmatrix}.$$

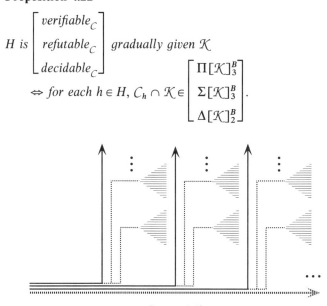

Figure 4.48

Proof: As usual, it suffices to prove the verification case. The refutation case follows by duality, and the decidability case follows from proposition 3.13(b).

($\Leftarrow$) Suppose that for each $h \in H$, $C_h \cap \mathcal{K} \in \Pi[\mathcal{K}]_3^B$. Then $C_h \cap \mathcal{K}$ is the intersection of some countable sequence $S[h]_0, S[h]_1, \ldots, S[h]_n, \ldots$ of $\Sigma[\mathcal{K}]_2^B$ sets. Let G and H' be such that for each i there is an $h_i \in H'$ such that $G_{h_i} = S[h]_i$. Since each G_{h_i} is $\Sigma[\mathcal{K}]_2^B$, we have by proposition 4.10 that there is a method α_h that verifies$_G$ H' in the limit given $\mathcal{K}$. Define method α as follows. On hypothesis $h \in H$ and finite data segment e of length k, α considers the sequence of conjectures $\alpha_h(h_0, e)$, $\alpha_h(h_1, e) \cdots \alpha_h(h_k, e)$ until some conjecture less than 1 is produced. Let $n \le k$ be the number of consecutive 1s occurring in this sequence. α conjectures $1 - 2^{-n}$ (*Fig. 4.49*). Let $h \in H$, $\varepsilon \in \mathcal{K}$. Suppose $\varepsilon \in C_h$. Then for each $h_i \in H'$, $\varepsilon \in G_{h_i}$. Then since α_h verifies$_G$ H' in the limit given $\mathcal{K}$, we have that for each h_i, α_h stabilizes to 1 on ε for h_i. Thus, for each i, there is a time after which α_h has stabilized to 1 for $h_0, \ldots, h_i$. Thereafter, α's conjecture never drops below $1 - 2^{-i}$. Since i is arbitrary, α correctly approaches 1 on ε for h. Suppose $\varepsilon \notin C_h$. Then for some $h_i \in H'$, $\varepsilon \notin G_{h_i}$. Thus, α_h does not stabilize to 1 for h_i on ε, so infinitely often, the conjecture of α for h on ε is no greater than $1 - 2^{-i}$. Thus α correctly fails to approach 1 for h on ε.

($\Rightarrow$) Suppose that α verifies$_C$ H gradually given $\mathcal{K}$. Then for each $h \in H$, we have:

$$\forall \varepsilon \in \mathcal{K}, \quad C(\varepsilon, h) \Leftrightarrow \forall \text{ rational } r > 0 \; \exists n \; \forall m \ge n \; 1 - \alpha(h, \varepsilon | m) < r.$$

The set $\mathcal{A}_h(m, r)$ of all $\varepsilon \in \mathcal{K}$ such that $1 - \alpha(h, \varepsilon | m) < r$ is $\mathcal{K}$-clopen. For all $\varepsilon \in \mathcal{K}$,

$$\forall m \ge n, \; 1 - \alpha(h, \varepsilon | m) < r$$

$$\Leftrightarrow \varepsilon \in (\mathcal{A}_h(n, r) \cap \mathcal{A}_h(n + 1, r) \cap \mathcal{A}_h(n + 2, r) \cap \cdots)$$

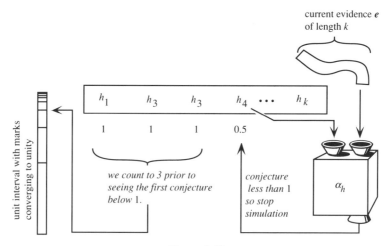

Figure 4.49

Let $\mathcal{B}_h(n, r)$ denote this countable intersection. $\mathcal{B}_h(n, r) \in \Pi[\mathcal{K}]_1^B$. Then for each $\varepsilon \in \mathcal{R}$ we have:

$$\exists n \, \forall m \geq n, \, 1 - \alpha(h, \varepsilon \,|\, m) < r$$

$$\Leftrightarrow \varepsilon \in (\mathcal{B}_h(0, r) \cup \mathcal{B}_h(1, r) \cup \mathcal{B}_h(2, r) \cup \cdots)$$

Let $\mathcal{D}_h(r)$ denote this union. $\mathcal{D}_h(r) \in \Sigma[\mathcal{K}]_2^B$. Let $r_0, r_1, \ldots, r_n, \ldots$ be an enumeration of the rationals greater than 0. Finally, for each $\varepsilon \in \mathcal{R}$ we have:

$$C_h = (\mathcal{D}_h(r_0) \cap \mathcal{D}_h(r_1) \cap \mathcal{D}_h(r_2) \cap \cdots).$$

Thus, $C_h \in \Pi[\mathcal{K}]_3^B$. ∎

The complete assessment architecture introduced in the proof of this theorem may be referred to as the *consecutive ones* architecture, since it counts the consecutive 1s output by a simulated limiting verifier method to produce its conjecture.

12. The Levels of Underdetermination

The results of this chapter are summarized in *Figure 4.50*. Some hypotheses concerning the divisibility of matter are located in their proper places. The dots at the top of the diagram indicate that topological complexity continues upward forever (and then for infinitely many more eternities), even though our intuitions about what would count as limiting success for science pretty well peter out by level 3.

The characterizations bear on some traditional issues of empiricism. Recall that the empiricist draws a line in the sand so that hypotheses that fall on one side are gibberish and hypotheses that fall on the other are scientific. Empiricists have always had trouble deciding where the line should be, however. In his influential article on this subject, C. Hempel proposed the principle that empirical significance or meaningfulness should be closed under finitary Boolean operations.[16] He rejected $\Pi[\mathcal{K}]_1^B$ and $\Sigma[\mathcal{K}]_1^B$ as characterizations of empirical significance because neither class is closed under negation. B. Van Fraassen's (1980) version of instrumentalism countenances belief when there is no global underdetermination, but prohibits belief when there is, without regard to the level of local underdetermination. If a dichotomy has to be drawn, then perhaps it would be better to draw it at $\Delta[\mathcal{K}]_2^B$. This class contains both of the classes entertained by Hempel and is also closed under finitary Boolean operations, as Hempel required. And unlike Van Fraassen's line between local and global underdetermination, $\Delta[\mathcal{K}]_2^B$ characterizes both gradual decidability and decidability in the limit—a natural place for line drawing if lines must be drawn.[17]

---

[16] Hempel (1965): 102.

[17] Kugel (1977) emphasizes the importance of $\Delta[\mathcal{K}]_2^B$ for inductive inference.

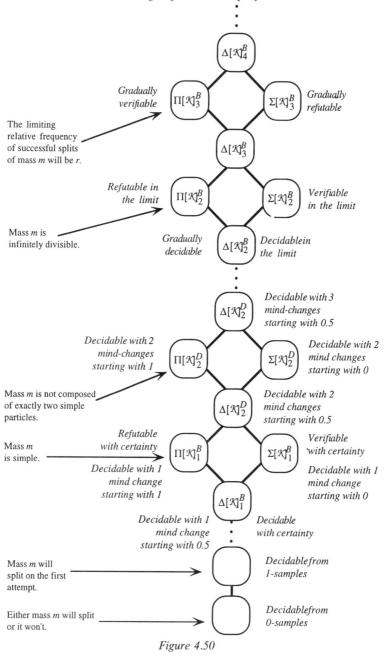

Figure 4.50

Someone could well demand that if we are going to drop the criterion of demarcation from global determination to $\Delta[\mathcal{K}]_2^B$, then we ought to drop it still further, for $\Delta[\mathcal{K}]_2^B$ characterizes success for *ideal* rather than for computational agents. If we do not entertain the fiction that we can scan the entire data stream in an instant, then why should we entertain the fiction that we can decide all formal questions in an instant? This point is well taken, and will be explored in detail in chapter 7.

Exercises

4.1. Prove that the restriction of a topological space is a topological space.

4.2. Verify the closure laws summarized in *Figure 4.51*, for each $n > 0$.

4.3. Let O be open the let P be closed. Verify the following closure laws:

(a) *For each $n > 0$:*   *if $S \in \Pi_n^D$ then*   *if $S \in \Sigma_n^D$ then*
$\bar{S} \in \Sigma_n^D.$ $\bar{S} \in \Pi_n^D;$
$S \cup P \in \Pi_n^D;$ $S \cap O \in \Sigma_n^D;$
$S \cap O \in \Sigma_{n+1}^D:$ $S \cup P \in \Pi_{n+1}^D.$

(b) *For each odd $n > 0$:*   *if $S \in \Pi_n^D$ then*   *if $S \in \Sigma_n^D$ then*
$S \cap P \in \Pi_n^D;$ $S \cup O \in \Sigma_n^D;$
$S \cup O \in \Pi_{n+1}^D:$ $S \cap P \in \Sigma_{n+1}^D.$

(c) *For each even $n > 0$,*   *If $S \in \Pi_n^D$ then*   *If $S \in \Sigma_n^D$ then*
$S \cup O \in \Pi_n^D;$ $S \cap P \in \Sigma_n^D;$
$S \cap P \in \Pi_{n+1}^D:$ $S \cup O \in \Sigma_{n+1}^D.$

4.4. Show that the hypothesis $LRF(o)$ that a real-valued limiting relative frequency for outcome o exists is gradually verifiable. (Hint: a sequence ζ of rationals is a *Cauchy sequence* just in case for each rational $r > 0$ there is an n such that for all $m, m' \geq n$, $|\zeta_m - \zeta_{m'}| < r$. Recall from analysis that a sequence of rationals approaches a real if and only if it is Cauchy. Now design a method that can verify the hypothesis that the sequence of relative frequencies of o in ε is Cauchy.)

4.5. Prove an analogue of proposition 4.7 for refutation and decision with certainty.

	countable union	countable intersection	complement	finite intersection	finite union
Σ_n^B	yes	no	no	yes	yes
Δ_n^B	no	no	yes	yes	yes
Π_n^B	no	yes	no	yes	yes

Figure 4.51

4.6. A collection Θ of subsets of $\mathcal{N}$ is an *ideal* $\Leftrightarrow$

   (i) $\emptyset \in \Theta$,

   (ii) *if* $S \in \Theta$ *and* $\mathcal{P} \subseteq S$ *then* $\mathcal{P} \in \Theta$, *and*

   (iii) *if* $S \in \Theta$ *and* $\mathcal{P} \in \Theta$ *then* $S \cup \mathcal{P} \in \Theta$.

Show that for some h, C, the collection $\Gamma = \{\mathcal{K}: h \text{ is verifiable}_C \text{ in the limit given } \mathcal{K}\}$ is not an ideal. Which of the conditions is Γ guaranteed to satisfy?

4.7. Find a data-minimal architecture for decision with n mind changes.

4.8. Show that each opportunistic limiting verifier is *consistent* in the sense that it stabilizes to 0 as soon as h is refuted by the data relative to $\mathcal{K}$, and it stabilizes to 1 as soon as h is entailed by the data relative to $\mathcal{K}$. (Hint: if $\mathcal{K} \cap [e] \subseteq C_h \cap [e]$, then $\tau_{h,e}$ does not exist, and if $\mathcal{K} \cap C_h \cap [\varepsilon|n] = \emptyset$, then $\tau_{h,\varepsilon|m}$ does not exist if $m \geq n$.) Show that consistency is necessary for weak data minimality among limiting verifiers for a given inductive problem.

4.9. Show that if $\mathcal{P} \in \Sigma[\mathcal{K}]_2^B$ and $S \cap \mathcal{P} = \emptyset$ and $S \in \Delta[\mathcal{K} \cup S]_2^B$, then $\mathcal{P} \in \Sigma[\mathcal{K} \cup S]_2^B$. (Hint: use a limiting decider for S given $\mathcal{K} \cup S$ to determine whether you are in S, and either output 0 or switch to a limiting verifier of $\mathcal{P}$ given $\mathcal{K}$ according to the current conjecture of the decider.) Show by example that the result cannot be improved to the case in which $S \in \Sigma[\mathcal{K} \cup S]_2^B - \Delta[\mathcal{K} \cup S]_2^B$. (Another hint: let $\mathcal{P} = $ the set of all sequences in which infinitely many 1s occur, let $\mathcal{K} = \mathcal{P}$ and let $S = \mathcal{N} - \mathcal{K}$).

4.10. Derive the upper bounds in exercise 3.1 by using the characterization theorems of this chapter. (Hint: construct C_h as a Borel set of the appropriate complexity.)

*4.11. I have assumed that the stages of inquiry are discrete. But we can imagine an inductive method implemented as an electronic device whose input at time t is the intensity of current in an input wire at t and whose conjecture at t is the position of a needle on a meter (scaled from 0 to 1) at t (actually a bit after t to allow the signal to travel through the circuits of the machine). Say that the method stabilizes just in case its value is fixed after some finite time interval. Similar definitions can be given in the bounded mind change and gradual cases. Extend the characterization results of this chapter to continuous methods in the paradigm just described, taking a fan to be the set of all unbounded extensions of a finite segment. Be careful when defining the Borel hierarchy, since open sets will not be countable unions of fans in this setting. What happens to the characterizations if the method is not assumed to be continuous?

*4.12. In the paradigm described in the preceding question, show that the set of all solutions to an ordinary, first-order differential equation is always closed in the corresponding topology. Discuss the methodological significance of this fact.

*4.13 (The epistemology of real analysis). Topologize the real line $\mathfrak{R}$ by taking open intervals with rational endpoints as basic open sets. Think of each real number as a complete "possible world." Then a *data stream* for $r \in \mathfrak{R}$ is a downward nested collection

$\{I_k: k \in \omega\}$ of closed intervals such that $\bigcap\{I_k: k \in \omega\} = \{r\}$. Let $\mathcal{H}, \mathcal{K} \subseteq \mathfrak{R}$. Think of $\mathcal{H}$ as a hypothesis and of $\mathcal{K}$ as background knowledge. An *inductive method* α maps finite sequences of closed intervals into $[0, 1] \cup$ '!'. Define:

$$\alpha \text{ verifies } \mathcal{H} \text{ in the limit given } \mathcal{K} \Leftrightarrow \forall r \in \mathcal{K}, \forall \text{ data stream } \{I_k: k \in \omega\} \text{ for } r,$$
$$r \in \mathcal{H} \Leftrightarrow \exists n \, \forall m \geq n, \alpha(I_m) = 1,$$

and similarly for the other notions of reliability.

(i) Characterize the various notions of reliability in this paradigm.
(ii) Show that only $\varnothing$ and $[0, 1]$ are decidable with certainty given $[0, 1]$.
(iii) Show that each $\mathcal{H}$ is decidable with certainty given $\mathfrak{R} - \text{bdry}(\mathcal{H})$.
(iv) Contrast result (ii) with the fact that nontrivial subsets of 2^ω are decidable with certainty in the usual, Baire-space paradigm. Explain the difference.

*4.14. $\mathcal{K} \subseteq \mathcal{N}$ is compact $\Leftrightarrow$

for each collection Γ of open sets such that $\bigcup\Gamma = \mathcal{K}$, there is a finite $\Gamma' \subseteq \Gamma$ such that $\bigcup\Gamma' = \mathcal{K}$.

(i) Show that if $\mathcal{K}$ is compact, then $\forall \mathcal{H} \subseteq \mathcal{K}$, if $\mathcal{H}$ is $\mathcal{K}$-clopen then $\exists n$ such that $\mathcal{H}$ is n-uniform in $\mathcal{K}$. Rephrase this fact in methodological terms.
(ii) Using (a), show that $\mathcal{N}$ is not compact.
(iii) Show that $2^\omega \subseteq \mathcal{N}$ is compact.
(iv) Show that no properly open subset of 2^ω is compact.

*4.15 (Subjunctive learning theory). Recall the discussion of subjunctive reliability in chapter 2. We can investigate this proposal using techniques developed in chapter 4. Think of $\mathcal{K}$ as the set of possible worlds. A notion of "closeness" of possible worlds is a space $\mathfrak{R} = (\mathcal{K}, K)$, where K is some collection of subsets of $\mathcal{K}$. Let $\mathcal{A}, \mathcal{B} \subseteq \mathcal{N}$. Then define the subjunctive conditional $(\mathcal{A} \mapsto \mathcal{B})_{\mathfrak{R}} \subseteq \mathcal{K}$ as follows:

$\forall \varepsilon \in \mathcal{K}, \varepsilon \in (\mathcal{A} \mapsto \mathcal{B})_{\mathfrak{R}} \Leftrightarrow$ *either*
    (i) $\forall S \in K, S \cap \mathcal{A} = \varnothing$ *or*
    (ii) $\exists S \in K$ *such that* $S \cap \mathcal{A} \neq \varnothing$ *and* $S \cap \mathcal{A} \subseteq \mathcal{B}$.

We may think of $(\mathcal{A} \mapsto \mathcal{B})_{\mathfrak{R}}$ as saying "if $\mathcal{A}$ were the case then $\mathcal{B}$ would be the case."[18] Now define:

$\alpha \text{ verifies}_C \, h \text{ in the limit given } \mathfrak{R} \text{ on } \varepsilon \Leftrightarrow$

(a) $(C_h \mapsto \alpha(h, \_) \text{ stabilizes to } 1)_{\mathfrak{R}}$ *and*
(b) $(\overline{C_h} \mapsto \alpha(h, \_) \text{ does not stabilize to } 1)_{\mathfrak{R}}$.

$\mathcal{LV}_C[h]_{\mathfrak{R}} = \{\varepsilon: \exists \alpha \text{ such that } \alpha \text{ verifies}_C \, h \text{ in the limit given } \mathfrak{R} \text{ on } \varepsilon\}$.

Similar definitions can be given for the other senses of reliability. Let $\mathcal{DC}, \mathcal{VC}$, and $\mathcal{RC}$ correspond to decidability, verifiability, and refutability with certainty, respectively.

---

[18] The definition is due to Lewis (1973). Lewis adds extra constraints on $\mathfrak{R}$.

Recall that $\mathfrak{N}$ is the Baire space $(\mathcal{N}, B)$. Let $\mathfrak{N} + \mathfrak{S}$ be the result of adding all singletons to $\mathfrak{N}$. Let $\mathfrak{D} = (\mathcal{N}, 2^{\mathcal{N}})$ be the discrete topology on $\mathcal{N}$. Let $\mathfrak{T} = (\mathcal{N}, \{\varnothing, \mathcal{N}\})$ be the trivial topology on $\mathcal{N}$. Let $\mathfrak{W} = (\mathcal{N}, \Delta)$, where Δ is the set of all closed balls under the distance function $\rho(\varepsilon, \tau) = \sup_n |\varepsilon_n - \tau_n|$, where the distance is ∞ if the sup does not exist.

(i) Show that $\forall \varepsilon$, h is verifiable$_C$ in the limit given $\mathfrak{T}$ on $\varepsilon \Leftrightarrow h$ is verifiable$_C$ in the limit given $\mathcal{N}$.

(ii) Let $C_h = \{\zeta\}$. Show that h is not verifiable$_C$ with certainty given $\mathfrak{N}$, $\mathfrak{T}$, or $\mathfrak{W}$, on ζ, whereas h is decidable$_C$ with certainty given $\mathfrak{D}$ on ζ. Show that a structure $\mathfrak{K}$ satisfies "h is decidable$_C$ with certainty given $\mathfrak{K}$ on ζ" just in case $\exists n$ such that $\zeta \in (\overline{\{\zeta\}} \mapsto \{\zeta\}$ is refuted by stage $n)_{\mathfrak{K}}$. Do you believe that if a universal hypothesis is actually true then there is some fixed time such that if the hypothesis were false it would be refuted by that time? What does this say about the prospects for Nozick's program (cf. section 2.7) as a response to the problem of local underdetermination? Show that for every $\mathfrak{K}$, $\zeta \in (\overline{\{\zeta\}} \mapsto \exists n$ such that $\{\zeta\}$ is refuted by stage $n)_{\mathfrak{K}}$. Why does the placement of the existential quantifier matter so much? (The former placement is said to be *de re*, or *of things*, while the latter placement is said to be *de dicto*, or *of words*.)

(iii) Show that for each ε, h_{fin} is not refutable in the limit given $\mathfrak{N}$, $\mathfrak{T}$, or $\mathfrak{W}$ on ε.

(iv) Show that:

   (a) $\mathcal{DC}_C[h]_{\mathfrak{N}+\mathfrak{S}} = \mathcal{DC}_C[h]_{\mathfrak{N}} = C_h - bdry(C_h)$.
   (b) $\mathcal{VC}_C[h]_{\mathfrak{N}+\mathfrak{S}} - \mathcal{DC}_C[h]_{\mathfrak{N}+\mathfrak{S}} = bdry(C_h) - C_h$.
   (c) $\mathcal{RC}_C[h]_{\mathfrak{N}+\mathfrak{S}} - \mathcal{DC}_C[h]_{\mathfrak{N}+\mathfrak{S}} = bdry(C_h) - \overline{C_h}$.
   (d) $int(\overline{C_h}) = \varnothing \Rightarrow \mathcal{DC}_C[h]_{\mathfrak{N}+\mathfrak{S}} = C_h$ (i.e., "h is decidable with certainty" is the same proposition as h).

(v) What happens to (b) and (c) in $\mathfrak{N}$?

(vi) Relate results (iv a–c) to the discussion in this chapter in which it was claimed that the problem of induction arises in the boundaries of hypotheses.

(vii) What is the significance of (d) for naturalistic epistemology, the proposal that we should use empirical inquiry to find out if we are or can be reliable?

5

Reducibility and the Game of Science

*White has
the first move,
Monsieur.*

*Why do I always
start out with
only one guy?*

1. Introduction

Many of the negative arguments considered so far have involved demons who attempt to feed misleading evidence to the inductive method α, as though science were an ongoing game between the demon and the scientist, where winning is determined by what happens in the limit. This game-theoretic construal of inquiry is familiar in skeptical arguments from ancient times, and it is the purpose of this chapter to explore it more explicitly than we have done so far. One reason it is interesting to do so is that the theory of infinite games is central to contemporary work in the foundations of mathematics, so that the existence of winning strategies for inductive demons hinges on questions unanswered by set theory.[1] In set theory, infinite games are known to be intimately related to the notion of continuous reducibility among problems and inductive methods turn out to determine continuous reductions. It is therefore natural to consider games and continuous reducibility all at once. The discussion of continuous reducibility in this chapter will help to underscore the analogy between reliable inductive inference on the one hand and ordinary computation on the other, which will be developed in the next chapter.

---

[1] Material presented in this chapter assumes some elementary issues in set theory, but may be skipped without loss of comprehension in the chapters that follow.

2. Ideal Inductive Methods as Continuous Operators on the Baire Space

Consider a hypothesis assessment method α. α takes a hypothesis and a finite data sequence as arguments and returns a rational number in the interval $[0, 1]$. Let ξ be a fixed $1-1$ map from the rational numbers in $[0, 1]$ to the natural numbers. This way, we may think of α as conjecturing natural code numbers for rationals. Then for fixed h, we may think of α as determining a function $\Phi_{\alpha, h} \colon \mathcal{N} \to \mathcal{N}$ from data streams to conjecture streams such that the code number of the nth conjecture of α on h is the nth entry in the infinite conjecture stream that is the value of $\Phi_{\alpha, h}(\varepsilon)$ (*Fig. 5.1*). In other words:

$$\Phi_{\alpha, h}(\varepsilon)_n = \xi(\alpha(h, \varepsilon | n)).$$

A function Φ from $\mathcal{N}$ to $\mathcal{N}$ is called an *operator*. It turns out that the operator $\Phi_{\alpha, h}$ is continuous with respect to the Baire space. Recall that Φ is continuous just in case $\Phi^{-1}(S)$ is open if S is. In the Baire space, this amounts to the requirement that successive conjectures in $\Phi(\varepsilon)$ depend only on finite initial segments of ε, so continuity captures the bounded perspective of the scientist. The following proposition makes the connection precise (*Fig. 5.2*).

Proposition 5.1

> $\Phi \colon \mathcal{N} \to \mathcal{N}$ *is continuous* $\Leftrightarrow \forall \varepsilon, \forall n, \exists e \subseteq \varepsilon$ *such that* $\forall \varepsilon'$ *extending* e, $\Phi(\varepsilon')_n = \Phi(\varepsilon)_n$.

Proof: ($\Leftarrow$) Assume the right-hand side of the fact. Let O be an open subset of $\mathcal{N}$. Then for some $G \subseteq \omega^*$, O is the union of all $[e]$ such that $e \in G$. Let $\mathcal{R}(k, n)$ be the union of all $[e']$ such that for each ε extending e', $\Phi(\varepsilon)_n = k$. $\mathcal{R}(k, n)$ is open since each $[e']$ is (*Fig. 5.3*).

Hence, the finite intersection $\mathcal{R}(e) = \mathcal{R}(e_0, 0) \cap \cdots \cap \mathcal{R}(e_{lh(e)-1}, lh(e))$ is open (*Fig. 5.4*).

The union $\mathcal{R}$ of the $\mathcal{R}(e)$ over all $e \in G$ is therefore open. Let $\varepsilon \in \mathcal{R}$. Then $\varepsilon \in \mathcal{R}(e)$, for some $e \in G$. Thus, $e \subseteq \Phi(\varepsilon)$, by the definition of $\mathcal{R}(e)$, so $\Phi(\varepsilon) \in O$ (*Fig. 5.5*). Thus $\mathcal{R} \subseteq \Phi^{-1}(O)$.

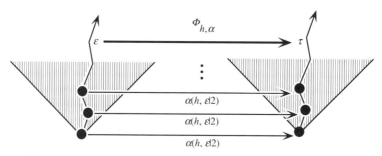

Figure 5.1

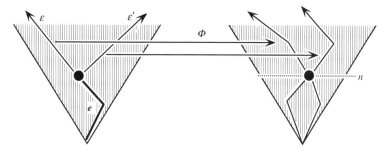

Figure 5.2

Let $\varepsilon \in \Phi^{-1}(O)$, so $\Phi(\varepsilon) \in O$. Since $\Phi(\varepsilon) \in O$, there is some $e \in G$ such that $e \subseteq \Phi(\varepsilon)$. But by hypothesis, for each $n \leq lh(\varepsilon)$ there is an $e' \subseteq \varepsilon$ such that for each ε' extending e' $\Phi(\varepsilon')_n = \Phi(\varepsilon)_n$. Thus, $\varepsilon \in \mathcal{R}(e') \subseteq \mathcal{R}$. So $\Phi^{-1}(O) = \mathcal{R}$, and hence $\Phi^{-1}(O)$ is open.

($\Rightarrow$) Suppose that Φ is continuous. Then for each open set O, $\Phi^{-1}(O)$ is open. Let $\varepsilon \in \mathcal{N}$, $n \in \omega$ be given. Suppose $\Phi(\varepsilon)_n = k$. Let $S(k, n)$ be the set of all infinite sequences ε' such that $\varepsilon'_n = k$. $S(k, n)$ is just the union of all fans $[e]$ such that $lh(e) \geq n$ and $e_n = k$, and hence is open. By the continuity of Φ, $\Phi^{-1}(S(k, n))$ is open. Hence, there is some $G \subseteq \omega^*$ such that $\Phi^{-1}(S(k, n))$ is the union of all $[e'']$ such that $e'' \in G$ (*Fig. 5.6*). Since $\Phi(\varepsilon)_n = k$, some initial segment e^* of ε is in G. But then for each extension ε'' of e^*, $\varepsilon'' \in \Phi^{-1}(S(k, n))$, so $\Phi(\varepsilon'') \in S(k, n)$ and hence $\Phi(\varepsilon'')_n = k$. ∎

Since $\Phi_{\alpha, h}$ clearly satisfies the right-hand side of proposition 5.1, the continuity of $\Phi_{\alpha, h}$ follows immediately. It is not the case, however, that each continuous Φ is identical to some $\Phi_{\alpha, h}$. Continuity leaves open the possibility of waiting for relevant data to arrive. For example, define:

$$\Phi(\varepsilon) = \begin{cases} \tau & \text{if } \varepsilon_{100} = 0 \\ \tau' & \text{otherwise.} \end{cases}$$

τ and τ' are any conjecture streams that differ up to time 100. Φ is continuous, but no α that is forced to produce a conjecture on each finite initial segment of the data can induce Φ. Nevertheless, it turns out that this extra generality

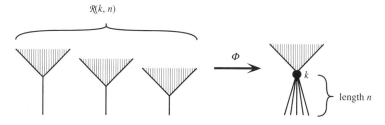

Figure 5.3

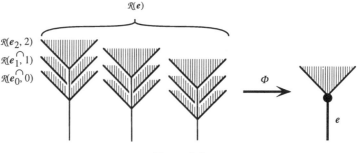

Figure 5.4

doesn't matter for our applications, since we are interested in methods that converge, and convergence is undisturbed if a method stalls by repeating its previous conjecture until some relevant datum arrives in the data stream, as we shall see in the next section.

3. Assessment as Reduction

Many results in topology, descriptive set theory, logic, and the theories of computability and computational complexity are about *reducibility*. The following approach is common to each of these fields. Let G be a collection of operators on $\mathcal{N}$. We may think of G as characterizing all operators corresponding to agents of a given cognitive power. For example, arbitrary operators correspond to the abilities of the Judeo-Christian deities who can see the entire future at a timeless glance. Continuous operators correspond to the abilities of "ideal agents" who cannot see the future but who can intuit all mathematical relations in an instant. Computable operators (cf. chapter 7) correspond to the abilities of a scientist who follows an algorithmic inductive method (or who lets a digital computer do his work for him). Finite state operators (cf. chapter 8) correspond to the abilities of a computer with a fixed memory store. Let $\mathcal{A}, \mathcal{B} \subseteq \mathcal{N}$. Then define (*Fig. 5.7*):

$$\mathcal{A} \leq_G \mathcal{B} \Leftrightarrow \text{ there is a } \Phi \in G \text{ such that for each } \varepsilon \in \mathcal{N}, \varepsilon \in \mathcal{A} \Leftrightarrow \Phi(\varepsilon) \in \mathcal{B}.$$

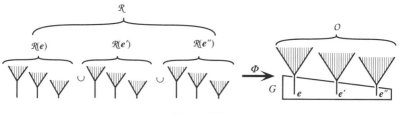

Figure 5.5

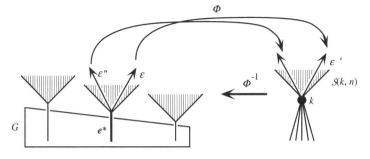

Figure 5.6

When $\mathcal{A} \leq_G \mathcal{B}$, we may say that $\mathcal{A}$ is **G-reducible** to $\mathcal{B}$. **G-equivalence** is defined in the obvious manner:

$$\mathcal{A} \equiv_G \mathcal{B} \Leftrightarrow \mathcal{A} \leq_G \mathcal{B} \text{ and } \mathcal{B} \leq_G \mathcal{A}.$$

We may think of $\mathcal{A} \leq_G \mathcal{B}$ as saying that $\mathcal{A}$ is no harder than $\mathcal{B}$, so far as operators in **G** are concerned. Let **Cnt** denote the continuous operators on $\mathcal{N}$. Then the relation $\leq_{Cnt}$ of continuous reducibility satisfies the following properties.[2]

Proposition 5.2

(a) $\leq_{Cnt}$ *is reflexive and transitive over the subsets of* $\mathcal{N}$, *so* $\equiv_{Cnt}$ *is an equivalence relation over these sets.*

(b) *If* $\mathcal{A} \leq_{Cnt} \mathcal{B}$ *then* $\bar{\mathcal{A}} \leq_{Cnt} \bar{\mathcal{B}}$.

(c) *If* $\mathcal{A} \in \begin{bmatrix} \Sigma_n^B \\ \Pi_n^B \\ \Delta_n^B \end{bmatrix}$ *and* $\mathcal{B} \leq_{Cnt} \mathcal{A}$ *then* $\mathcal{B} \in \begin{bmatrix} \Sigma_n^B \\ \Pi_n^B \\ \Delta_n^B \end{bmatrix}$.

(d) *We may substitute D for B in* (c).

Proof: Exercise 5.1. ■

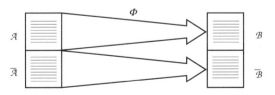

Figure 5.7

[2] Continuous reducibility is called *Wadge reducibility* in the logical literature and is denoted by $\leq_w$ (Moschavakis 1980).

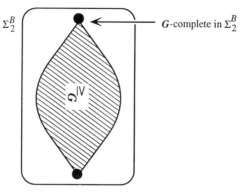

Figure 5.8

Let Θ be a complexity class of subsets of $\mathcal{N}$ (e.g., Σ_n^B). Then a **G**-complete set in Θ is a maximally complex member of Θ (*Fig. 5.8*).

> $\mathcal{A}$ is **G**-complete in $\Theta \Leftrightarrow$ (i) $\mathcal{A} \in \Theta$ and (ii) for each $\mathcal{B} \in \Theta$, $\mathcal{B} \leq_G \mathcal{A}$.

It turns out that if we fix $\mathcal{K} = \mathcal{N}$, then reliability is equivalent to **Cnt**-reducibility to one of the following sets, which correspond to the various notions of convergence. Recall that ξ is a fixed, 1–1 map from the rationals in [0, 1] to the natural numbers.

$S_1 = \{\tau \in \mathcal{N}$: *there is an n such that $\tau_n = 1\}$.*

$S_2 = \{\tau \in \mathcal{N}$: *there is an n such that for all $m \geq n$, $\tau_m = 1\}$.*

$S_2(k) = \{\tau \in \mathcal{N}$: $\tau \in S_2$ *& there are at most k positions i such that*
$\qquad \tau_i \neq \tau_{i+1}\}$.

$S_3 = \{\tau \in \mathcal{N}$: *for each rational $s > 0$ there is an n such that for all*
$\qquad m \geq n$, $1 - \xi^{-1}(\tau_m) \leq s\}$.

The correspondence is made precise in the following proposition.

Proposition 5.3

(a) H is verifiable$_C$ $\begin{bmatrix} \text{with certainty} \\ \text{in the limit} \\ \text{gradually} \end{bmatrix} \Leftrightarrow$ *for each $h \in H$, $C_h \leq_{Cnt} \begin{bmatrix} S_1 \\ S_2 \\ S_3 \end{bmatrix}$.*

(b) H is refutable$_C$ $\begin{bmatrix} \text{with certainty} \\ \text{in the limit} \\ \text{gradually} \end{bmatrix} \Leftrightarrow$ *for each $h \in H$, $\overline{C_h} \leq_{Cnt} \begin{bmatrix} S_1 \\ S_2 \\ S_3 \end{bmatrix}$.*

(c) *H is decidable$_C$* $\begin{bmatrix} with\ certainty \\ in\ the\ limit \end{bmatrix}$

$\Leftrightarrow$ *for each* $h \in H$, $\overline{C_h}$, $C_h \leq_{Cnt} \begin{bmatrix} S_1 \\ S_2 \end{bmatrix}$.

(d) *If* $0 < r < 1$, *then H is decidable$_C$ with n mind changes starting with*

$\begin{bmatrix} 0 \\ 1 \\ r \end{bmatrix} \Leftrightarrow$ *for each* $h \in H$, $\begin{bmatrix} C_h \\ \overline{C_h} \\ C_h, \overline{C_h} \end{bmatrix} \leq_{Cnt} S_2(n)$.

Proof: I present only the certainty case of (a), the other cases being similar. ($\Rightarrow$) Let α decide$_C$ h with 1 mind change starting with 0. $\Phi_{\alpha, h}$ is the required reduction. ($\Leftarrow$) Suppose that for each $h \in H$, $C_h \leq_{Cnt} S_1$. Let continuous Φ_h be such that for each $\varepsilon \in \mathcal{N}$, $\varepsilon \in C_h \Leftrightarrow \Phi_h(\varepsilon) \in S_1$. Define the method α as follows. (Remember that conjectures following the declaration of certainty are irrelevant.)

$$\alpha(h, e) = \begin{cases} 1 & \text{if } e \neq 0 \text{ and } \alpha(h, e-) = \text{'!', else} \\ \text{'!'} & \text{if there is an } n \text{ such that for each } \varepsilon \in [e], \Phi_h(\varepsilon)_n = 1 \\ 0 & \text{otherwise.} \end{cases}$$

Let $\varepsilon \in \mathcal{N}$. Suppose $\varepsilon \in C_h$. Then $\Phi_h(\varepsilon) \in S_1$. So for some n, $\Phi_h(\varepsilon)_n = 1$. So by proposition 5.1, there is some finite $e \subseteq \varepsilon$ such that for each ε' extending e, $\Phi_h(\varepsilon')_n = 1$. Hence, $\alpha(h, e)$ produces a certainty mark '!' followed by 1. Suppose $\varepsilon \notin C_h$. Then by a similar argument, $\alpha(h, e)$ never produces the certainty mark. ∎

Proposition 5.3 shows that the ability of a continuous map to wait is of no consequence when the question concerns reduction to a convergence set, since a method α that is always forced to produce a conjecture at every stage can simply repeat its previous conjecture until the information the continuous map is waiting for appears.

4. Ideal Transcendental Deductions as *Cnt*-Completeness Theorems

We have just seen that a reliable method is a continuous reduction to some convergence set. It also turns out that when $\mathcal{K} = \mathcal{N}$ the characterization theorems of the preceding chapter may be thought of as proofs that the various notions of convergence are complete for their respective Borel complexity classes.

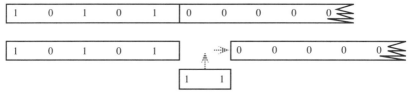

Figure 5.9

Proposition 5.4

$$\begin{bmatrix} S_1 \\ S_2(n) \\ S_2 \\ S_3 \end{bmatrix} \text{ is } \textbf{\textit{Cnt}}\text{-complete in } \begin{bmatrix} \Sigma_1^B \\ \Sigma_n^D \\ \Sigma_2^B \\ \Pi_3^B \end{bmatrix}.$$

Proof of Σ_2^B case: Let C_h be an arbitrary Σ_2^B set. Then by proposition 4.10, some α verifies$_C h$ in the limit given $\mathcal{N}$. So $\Phi_{\alpha, h}$ is a continuous reduction of C_h to S_2. So for each $P \in \Sigma_2^B$, $P \leq_{Cnt} S_2$. Moreover, it is immediate by definition that $S_2 \in \Sigma_2^B$. So S_2 is ***Cnt***-complete in Σ_2^B. The other cases are similar. ∎

The idea behind proposition 5.4 is more general than the particular notions of convergence considered. Say that S is *closed under finite repetition* just in case for each $\varepsilon \in S$, the result of inserting an arbitrary, finite number of xs after each occurrence of x in ε is still in S (*Fig. 5.9*).

It is easy to see that S_1, S_2, $S_2(n)$, and S_3 are all closed under finite repetition. For each convergence set closed under finite repetition, the existence of a reliable method is equivalent to the existence of a continuous reduction, as in proposition 5.3. To extend inquiry to Σ_n^B, all we have to do is to invent a new notion of convergence that yields a convergence set closed under finite repetition that is ***Cnt***-complete in Σ_n^B (cf. exercise 5.4).

5.   Inductive Demons as Continuous Counterreductions

In each of the demonic arguments employed in the preceding chapters, the demon looks at the conjectures produced by the scientist so far and generates the next datum to be fed to the scientist. So we may view the demon explicitly as a map δ from finite sequences of conjectures to data points. In this sense, the demon is a mirror image of the scientist, who maps finite sequences of data points to conjectures (*Fig. 5.10*).

The demon's goal is also a mirror image of the scientist's goal. The scientist's method is supposed to reduce C_h to S, where S is the set of all sequences that converge in the relevant sense. The demon's job is to produce a data stream in

Figure 5.10

C_h if and only if the given conjecture stream is not in S. Just like a scientific method, a demonic strategy δ induces an operator Φ_δ on $\mathcal{N}$. A successful demon therefore witnesses the relation $\bar{S} \leq_{Cnt} C_h$, just as a successful scientific method witnesses the relation $C_h \leq_{Cnt} S$. How does $\bar{S} \leq_{Cnt} C_h$ conflict with $C_h \leq_{Cnt} S$? The answer is that demonic arguments, like characterization theorems, may be viewed as completeness proofs (*Fig. 5.11*).

Proposition 5.5

$$\text{If } C_h \in \begin{bmatrix} \Sigma_1^B \\ \Sigma_n^D \\ \Sigma_2^B \\ \Pi_3^B \end{bmatrix} \text{ and } \begin{bmatrix} \overline{S_1} \\ \overline{S_2(n)} \\ \overline{S_2} \\ \overline{S_3} \end{bmatrix} \leq_{Cnt} C_h,$$

$$\text{then } C_h \text{ is } \textbf{Cnt}\text{-complete in } \begin{bmatrix} \Pi_1^B \\ \Pi_n^D \\ \Pi_2^B \\ \Sigma_3^B \end{bmatrix}.$$

Proof: Immediate consequence of proposition 5.4. ∎

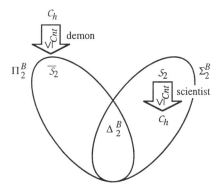

Figure 5.11

For example, $C_{h_{inf}}$ is Π_2^B complete by proposition 5.5 and the demonic argument given in chapter 3. By the Borel hierarchy theorem (proposition 4.9), there is a non-Σ_2^B set $\mathcal{R} \in \Pi_2^B$. So $C_{h_{inf}}$, which is Π_2^B-complete, reduces $\mathcal{R}$. By the contrapositive of proposition 5.2(c), any set that continuously reduces a non-Σ_2^B set is a non-Σ_2^B set, so $C_{h_{inf}}$ is not Σ_2^B. By the characterization theorem for limiting verifiability (proposition 4.10), h is not verifiable$_C$ in the limit. Similar arguments apply in the other cases. So a demonic argument shows not only that C_h is not in the Borel complexity class characterizing inductive success of the required sort, but also that C_h is at least as impossible to solve for ideal agents as the worst problem in the dual complexity class.

The parallelism between the demon and the scientist can be extended to background knowledge. $\mathcal{K}$ tells the scientist what sort of data stream the demon may produce in the limit. Suppose we were to restrict the scientist to producing conjecture streams in some set $\mathcal{D}$, so that $\mathcal{D}$ is the demon's background knowledge about what the scientist will do in the limit. The demon's task would become easier, just the way the scientist's task becomes easier when $\mathcal{K}$ is strengthened. For example, consider what happens when the hypothesis investigated by the scientist is h_{fin}, but the demon knows that the scientist will never say 1 again once he stops conjecturing 1.

6. Science as a Limiting Game

We have seen that a continuous demon suffices to show that an inductive problem is unsolvable and that when the problem is solvable, it is as though the scientist has turned tables on the demon, exploiting the latter's restricted view of the scientist's conjectures. But this raises a question, namely, whether there are inductive problems for which neither the scientist nor the demon has a winning strategy. In other words, is the game of inquiry always *determined*?

The question belongs to the theory of infinite games of perfect information, which has found important applications in logic and set theory.[3] We assume that there are two players, which I will provide with the suggestive names S and D, for the scientist and the demon, respectively. A *strategy* is just a function $\phi: \omega^* \to \omega$ from finite sequences of natural numbers to natural numbers. Let α, δ be strategies for S and for D, respectively. The *play sequence* $P_{\alpha,\delta}$ of α and δ is built up as follows. The strategy α of S is applied to the empty sequence, yielding the first play $\alpha(0) = s_0$. Then the strategy δ of D is applied to the sequence (s_0), yielding the first play by D, namely $\delta((s_0)) = d_0$. In general, the nth play of S is the value of α on all previous plays by δ, and the nth play of D is the value of δ on all previous plays by α. In the limit, the interaction of α and δ generates the infinite play sequence:

$$P_{\alpha,\delta} = (s_0, d_0, s_1, d_1, s_2, d_2, \ldots)$$

[3] For a review, see Moschavakis (1980).

where s_i is the ith play of the scientist α and d_i is the ith play of the demon δ. If $\varepsilon \in \mathcal{N}$, then define

$$P_{\alpha, \varepsilon} = (\alpha(\varepsilon|0), \alpha(\varepsilon|1), \alpha(\varepsilon|2), \ldots) \quad \text{and} \quad P_{\varepsilon, \delta} = (\delta(\varepsilon|0), \delta(\varepsilon|1), \delta(\varepsilon|2), \ldots).$$

In other words, a sequence of numbers may be viewed as a fixed strategy that ignores past plays by the opponent. The subsequence

$$D_{\alpha, \delta} = (d_0, d_1, d_2, \ldots)$$

is the infinite sequence of plays of δ in response to α, and the infinite play sequence

$$S_{\alpha, \delta} = (s_0, s_1, s_2, \ldots)$$

is the infinite sequence of conjectures produced by α in response to δ.

An *infinite game of perfect information* is now just a set $\mathcal{W} \subseteq \mathcal{N}$. Winning is defined with respect to $\mathcal{W}$ in the following way:

α *wins for S against* δ *in* $\mathcal{W} \Leftrightarrow P_{\alpha, \delta} \in \mathcal{W}$

δ *wins for D against* α *in* $\mathcal{W} \Leftrightarrow \alpha$ *does not win for S against* δ *in* $\mathcal{W}$.

Once the players select their respective strategies, one and only one of them is destined to win the game $\mathcal{W}$, by the definition of winning. But we are not interested in mere winning. We are interested in strategies logically guaranteed to win, no matter which strategy the opponent selects.

α *is a winning strategy for S in* $\mathcal{W}$
  $\Leftrightarrow \forall$ *strategy* δ, α *wins for S against* δ *in* $\mathcal{W}$.

δ *is a winning strategy for D in* $\mathcal{W}$
  $\Leftrightarrow \forall$ *strategy* α, δ *wins for D against* α *in* $\mathcal{W}$.

S has a winning strategy in $\mathcal{W}$
  $\Leftrightarrow \exists \alpha$ *such that* α *is a winning strategy for S in* $\mathcal{W}$.

D has a winning strategy in $\mathcal{W}$
  $\Leftrightarrow \exists \alpha$ *such that* δ *is a winning strategy for D in* $\mathcal{W}$.

When either S or D has a winning strategy in $\mathcal{W}$, we say that $\mathcal{W}$ is *determined*. It is not obvious from the definition of determinacy that all games $\mathcal{W}$ are determined. In fact, the answer to this question hinges on debates concerning the foundations of mathematics so that the foundations of inductive methodology and the foundations of mathematics are intertwined.

In standard, Zermelo-Fraenkel set theory[4] with the axiom of choice added (ZFC), there is a powerful positive result for determinacy.

Proposition 5.6   (Martin 1975)

If $\mathcal{W}$ is a Borel set then $\mathcal{W}$ is determined.   ■

As a corollary to this result, whenever C_h is a Borel set, underdetermination (in any of the senses introduced in chapter 3) implies a winning strategy for the demon, because the definition of the winning set in such a game adds just a bit of complexity to the Borel complexity of C_h.

Since conjectures less than 1 can be converted to 0 conjectures, we may assume without loss of generality that scientific strategies for limiting verification produce only 0–1 conjectures. This permits us to dispense with the fussy encoding of rationals into natural numbers. Let ρ be an infinite play sequence and let ρ_D and ρ_S be the demon's and the scientist's plays in ρ, respectively. Since α produces only 0–1 conjectures, $\rho_S \in \mathcal{N}$. Then the game of limiting verification can be defined as follows:

$$\mathcal{L}imver_C(h) = \{\rho: \rho_D \in C_h \Leftrightarrow \rho_S \in S_2\}.$$

It is clear that $\mathcal{L}imver_C(h)$ is Borel if C_h is, and the same is true for the other criteria of success.

Outside of the Borel hierarchy, however, ZFC yields spotty results. Above the Borel hierarchy is the *projective hierarchy*, and the sets in this hierarchy are known as the *projective sets*. The precise definition of the projective hierarchy is not essential for our purposes here. Suffice it to say that they are formed by existential quantification over functions on the natural numbers rather than by existential quantification over natural numbers (i.e., countable union).

Proposition 5.7[5]

There are projective sets whose determinacy is independent of ZFC.   ■

Projective determinacy is the hypothesis that all games based on projective sets are determined. Projective determinacy has been shown to be independent of ZFC, and hence has been entertained as an additional axiom of set theory. Beyond the projective sets, ZFC entails the existence of nondetermined games:

Proposition 5.8   (Gale and Stewart 1953)

ZFC implies the existence of a nondetermined game.   ■

---

[4] Cf. Kunen (1980) for an introduction to ZFC.
[5] Moschovakis (1980): 297.

The Gale-Stewart theorem does not settle our question in the negative, however, since scientific games have a special form and the game produced by the Gale-Stewart construction is not guaranteed to have this form. If we grant the continuum hypothesis, then a nondetermined limiting verification game exists. The *continuum hypothesis* (CH) says that there are no uncountable cardinals between $|\omega|$ and $|2^\omega| = |\mathcal{N}|$. The continuum hypothesis is known to be independent of ZFC (i.e., neither it nor its negation is entailed by ZFC) *if* ZFC is itself consistent.[6] I leave open the question whether a nondetermined limiting verification game exists when the continuum hypothesis is dropped.

Proposition 5.9 (Juhl 1991)

> ZFC + CH *implies that there exists a* C_h *such that* $Limver_C(h)$ *is not determined.*

Proof: Using the axiom of choice, well-order the set of all scientific strategies as $\{\alpha_\mu : \mu < \omega_1\}$ and the set of all demonic strategies as $\{\delta_\mu : \mu < \omega_1\}$, where ω_1 is the first uncountable ordinal. By the continuum hypothesis, each $\mu < \omega_1$ is countable. Now we define an ordinal sequence $\mathcal{A}_\mu$, $\mathcal{B}_\mu$ of sets of data streams such that at each stage $\mu < \omega_1$, $\mathcal{A}_\mu \cap \mathcal{B}_\mu = \varnothing$. We will let $C_h = \bigcup_{\mu < \omega_1} \mathcal{A}_\mu$. The idea is that at each stage $\mu < \omega_1$, we add a data stream to $\mathcal{A}_\mu$ or to $\mathcal{B}_\mu$ that ensures that neither the scientific strategy α_μ nor the demonic strategy δ_μ wins $Limver_C(h)$. The idea is complicated by the fact that we may not be able to find the right sort of data stream to add to ensure that δ_μ loses, but it will turn out in such cases that δ_μ is not a winning strategy anyway.

Stage 0: $\mathcal{A}_0 = \mathcal{B}_0 = \varnothing$.

Stage μ: Let $\mathcal{A} = \bigcup_{\mu' < \mu} \mathcal{A}_{\mu'}$ and $\mathcal{B} = \bigcup_{\mu' < \mu} \mathcal{B}_{\mu'}$.

To ensure that α_μ is not a winning strategy: Find the first δ such that $D_{\alpha_\mu, \delta} \notin \mathcal{A} \cup \mathcal{B}$. Such a δ exists because $\forall \mu' \leq \mu$, μ' is countable and $\mathcal{A} \cup \mathcal{B}$ is therefore countable since at most two items are added at each stage μ' (as will be seen in the construction that follows). If $S_{\alpha_\mu, \delta}$ stabilizes to 1, then set $\mathcal{A}'_\mu = \mathcal{A}$ and set $\mathcal{B}'_\mu = \mathcal{B} \cup \{D_{\alpha_\mu, \delta}\}$. Otherwise, set $\mathcal{A}'_\mu = \mathcal{A} \cup \{D_{\alpha_\mu, \delta}\}$ and set $\mathcal{B}'_\mu = \mathcal{B}$. In other words, we put $D_{\alpha_\mu, \delta}$ wherever it would make α_μ fail.

To ensure that δ_μ is not a winning strategy: Find the first α such that $D_{\alpha, \delta_\mu} \notin \mathcal{A}'_\mu \cup \mathcal{B}'_\mu$, if there is one. If S_{α, δ_μ} stabilizes to 1, then set $\mathcal{A}_\mu = \mathcal{A}'_\mu \cup \{D_{\alpha, \delta_\mu}\}$ and set $\mathcal{B}_\mu = \mathcal{B}'_\mu$. Otherwise, set $\mathcal{A}_\mu = \mathcal{A}'_\mu$ and set $\mathcal{B}_\mu = \mathcal{B}'_\mu \cup \{D_{\alpha_\mu, \delta}\}$. In other words, we put D_{α, δ_μ} wherever it would make δ_μ fail.

Now let $C_h = \bigcup_{\mu < \omega_1} \mathcal{A}_\mu$. It is clear that α_μ fails to be a winning strategy for

[6] Cf. Kunen (1980): 209.

the scientist because it loses against the δ chosen at stage μ. It is also clear that δ_μ fails to be a winning strategy for the demon whenever the α sought at stage μ exists. It remains only to show that δ_μ fails to be a winning strategy for the demon even when the α sought at stage μ does *not* exist. In that case,

(*) $\forall \alpha, D_{\alpha,\delta_\mu} \in \mathcal{A}'_\mu \cup \mathcal{B}'_\mu.$

(*) says that the demon δ_μ responds to all possible scientific strategies with just a countable set of data streams. Since the demon's response is a function only of what the scientist actually plays, the (countable) set of all of δ_μ's responses is

$\mathcal{P} = \{D_{\tau,\delta_\mu} : \tau \in \mathcal{N}\}.$

Recall that S_2 denotes the set of all ω-sequences that stabilize to 1. For reductio, assume that

(**) $\forall \tau, \tau' \in \mathcal{N}, D_{\tau,\delta_\mu} = D_{\tau',\delta_\mu} \Rightarrow [S_{\tau,\delta_\mu} \in S_2 \Leftrightarrow S_{\tau',\delta\mu} \in S_2]$ (*Fig. 5.12*).

(**) implies that if we look at how δ_μ responds to fixed conjecture sequences by the scientist, any two fixed conjecture sequences $\tau, \tau' \in \mathcal{N}$ that lead δ_μ to produce the same data stream either both converge to 1 or both fail to converge to 1. We may therefore define $\overline{S_2}$ as the set of all fixed scientific strategies $\tau \in \mathcal{N}$ against which δ_μ produces a data stream in the countable set $\mathcal{A}'_\mu \cup \mathcal{B}'_\mu$ that is (in light of **) generated only against nonconvergent conjecture sequences. More precisely, define the set of all data streams produced by δ_μ against nonconvergent conjecture streams as follows:

$\mathcal{R} = \{\varepsilon \in \mathcal{P} : \forall \sigma \in \mathcal{N}, D_{\sigma,\delta_\mu} = \varepsilon \Rightarrow \sigma \notin S_2\}.$

Now I claim:

(***) $\tau \notin S_2 \Leftrightarrow D_{\tau,\delta_\mu} \in \mathcal{R}.$

For suppose $D_{\tau,\delta_\mu} \in \mathcal{R}$. By the definition of $\mathcal{R}$, $D_{\tau,\delta_\mu} \in \mathcal{P}$ and $\forall \sigma \in \mathcal{N}, D_{\sigma,\delta_\mu} = D_{\tau,\delta_\mu} \Rightarrow \sigma \notin S_2$. Choosing σ as τ, we obtain $\tau \notin S_2$. Now suppose $D_{\tau,\delta_\mu} \notin \mathcal{R}$. Then by the definition of $\mathcal{R}$, $\exists \sigma \in \mathcal{N}$ such that $D_{\sigma,\delta_\mu} = D_{\tau,\delta_\mu}$ and $\sigma \in S_2$. By (**), $\tau \in S_2$.

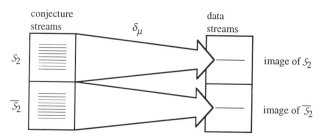

Figure 5.12

By (***), we have:

$$\tau \notin S_2 \Leftrightarrow \exists \varepsilon \in \mathcal{R} \text{ such that } \forall n, \varepsilon_n = D_{\tau \mid n, \delta_\mu}.$$

Since $\mathcal{R}$ is countable and $\{\tau : \varepsilon_n = D_{\tau \mid n, \delta_\mu}\}$ is clopen, $\overline{S_2} \in \Sigma_2^B$, which is absurd since S_2 is complete in Σ_2^B. So we may conclude that (**) is false. Hence:

$$\exists \tau, \tau' \in \mathcal{N} \text{ such that } D_{\tau, \delta_\mu} = D_{\tau', \delta_\mu} \text{ and } S_{\tau, \delta_\mu} \in S_2 \text{ but } S_{\tau', \delta_\mu} \notin S_2.$$

So whether or not $D_{\tau, \delta_\mu} \in C_h$, δ_μ loses against either the fixed strategy τ or the fixed strategy τ'. Hence, $Limver_C(h)$ is undetermined. ∎

Recall that the characterization of n-mind change decidability (proposition 4.18) was proved in terms of a generalized demonic construction ($n + 1$-feathers) whereas no such construction was given for the verification in the limit case (proposition 4.10). It seems very intuitive that there should be such a construction, since the limiting demonic arguments given in particular cases have been based on pictures that look like infinite dimensional feathers (e.g., Fig. 3.16). But even though it appears to be a small step from n-feathers to ω-feathers, no such proof of proposition 4.10 should be expected, and the preceding proposition shows why. Let GD be the claim that a generalized demonic construction for proving proposition 4.10 exists (e.g., ω-feathers). Let LVD denote the claim that all limiting verification games are determined. Now suppose that ZFC entails GD. Then (a) ZFC entails LVD, since GD implies that the demon has a winning strategy whenever the scientist does not. By proposition 5.4, ZFC + CH entails ¬LVD. So by (a), we have that ZFC entails ¬CH. But by the independence of the continuum hypothesis, if ZFC is consistent, then ZFC does not entail ¬CH. Hence, ZFC is inconsistent. We have just shown (by contraposition) that:

Corollary 5.10

If ZFC is consistent, then ZFC does not entail GD. ∎

Since ZFC is the mathematical framework we have tacitly assumed throughout this study, we should not expect to show that the demon has a winning strategy whenever the scientist does not. It may then be wondered why demonic arguments were found in each particular example considered in chapter 3. The answer is that each such example involved a Borel hypothesis, and such hypotheses are covered by proposition 5.6.

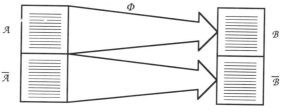

Figure 5.13

Exercises

5.1. Prove proposition 5.2.

5.2. Finish the proof of proposition 5.3.

5.3. Show that for each n, there are no ***Cnt***-incomplete sets in $\Sigma_n^D - \Pi_n^D$ or in $\Pi_n^D - \Sigma_n^D$, and for each $n \leq 3$, there are no ***Cnt***-incomplete sets in $\Sigma_n^B - \Pi_n^B$ or in $\Pi_n^B - \Sigma_n^B$. (Hint: use propositions 5.5 and 5.6.) Extend the latter result to the case in which $n = 4$. (Hint: cf. exercise 5.4.)

5.4. Invent a convergence criterion that is Σ_4^B-complete.

*5.5. This chapter has illustrated how the transcendental deductions and demonic arguments of logical reliabilism correspond to the structures of reduction and completeness, which are familiar to logicians and computability theorists. Recall, however, that the entire discussion assumes that $\mathcal{K} = \mathcal{N}$. When there is background knowledge, the tight relationships between reducibility, methods, and demons break down unless we modify the standard concept of reduction. Recall that when $\mathcal{A} \leq_G \mathcal{B}$, the picture in (*Fig. 5.13*) obtains.

When there is background knowledge, a successful scientist is free to do anything on a data stream violating that knowledge (*Fig. 5.14*):

This could be handled simply by defining reduction modulo a set, so that $\mathcal{A} \leq_G \mathcal{B}$ mod $\mathcal{K}$ if and only if for some $\Phi \in G$, for each $\varepsilon \in \mathcal{K}$, $\varepsilon \in \mathcal{A} \Leftrightarrow \Phi(\varepsilon) \in \mathcal{B}$. So far so good. But that won't help with the demon. While the scientist is free to ignore all sequences outside of $\mathcal{K}$, the demon is required to produce a sequence in $\mathcal{K}$ (*Fig. 5.15*).

What is really going on is that we are interested in reductions and counterreductions between binary partitions. The scientist is supposed to reduce the partition $(\mathcal{A} \cap \mathcal{K}, \bar{\mathcal{A}} \cap \mathcal{K})$ to the partition $(\mathcal{B}, \bar{\mathcal{B}})$, and the demon is supposed to reduce the partition $(\bar{\mathcal{B}}, \mathcal{B})$ to the partition $(\mathcal{A} \cap \mathcal{K}, \bar{\mathcal{A}} \cap \mathcal{K})$. The order of the cells matters. In general, let

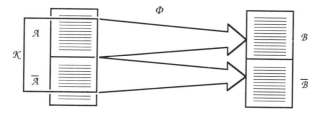

Figure 5.14

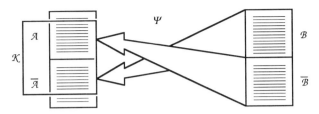

Figure 5.15

$\Pi = S_1, \ldots, S_k, \ldots)$ and let, $\Pi' = (\mathcal{R}_0, \ldots, \mathcal{R}_k, \ldots)$ be sequences of subsets of $\mathcal{N}$ such that for each distinct i, j, $S_i \cap S_j = \varnothing$ and $\mathcal{R}_i \cap \mathcal{R}_j = \varnothing$. Then define:

$$\Pi \leq_G \Pi' \Leftrightarrow \textit{there is a } \Phi \in G \textit{ such that for each } \varepsilon \in \mathcal{N}, \textit{ for each } i \in \omega, \varepsilon \in S_i$$

$$\Leftrightarrow \Phi(\varepsilon) \in \mathcal{R}_i \textit{ (Fig. 5.16)}.$$

This generalized notion of reduction properly handles the background assumptions $\mathcal{K}$. How do the results of this chapter work out when we add nontrivial background knowledge and move to partition reductions? Give an account of empirical verifiability and decidability in the limit given $\mathcal{K}$ in terms of partition reductions.

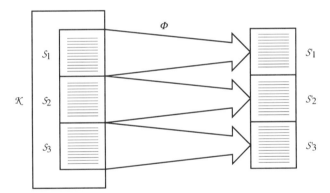

Figure 5.16

6

The Demons of Computability

*I am also very
pleased to meet you!*

1. Introduction

Formal learning theory has been invented and developed to a large extent by experts in the theory of computability. This is no accident. The theory of computability suggests a strong analogy between the situation of a computer working on a purely formal problem and that of an empirical scientist working on a purely empirical problem, and learning theorists have instinctively followed this analogy when thinking about inductive inference. I will argue, in fact, that uncomputability and empirical underdetermination have the same, underlying logical structure, so that it is difficult to dismiss the demons of induction while acknowledging the significance of uncomputability. On the one hand, this analogy counters the tendency in traditional epistemology to study ideal norms for agents free of all computational limitations. On the other hand, it raises questions about the motivation behind the sharp divergence of philosophical attitudes toward formal and empirical inquiry. The purpose of this chapter is to explore the analogy between computability and inductive reliability, both to illustrate the strong ties between computability theory and skeptical methodology and to introduce some computational tools that will be vital to the discussion of computationally bounded inductive inference in chapter 7.

2. Church Meets Hume

The problem of induction begins with the assumption that the human perspective on the universe is spatiotemporally bounded. In traditional epistemology, at most finitely many experimental trials can be observed by a given time. This locality of observation is captured by allowing the scientist

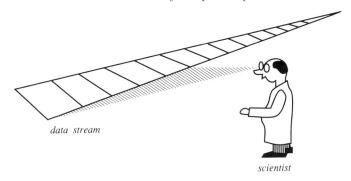

data stream

scientist

Figure 6.1

access only to a finite initial segment of a data stream at a given time (*Fig. 6.1*).

Alan Turing reasoned from a philosophical explication of the limitations of a human following an explicit procedure to a formal model of computability.[1] A *Turing machine* consists of a *read-write head* scanning a potentially infinite *tape*, in the sense that another square of tape is always provided when the machine uses up the tape at hand. The read-write head is like an experimental scientist according to the definition given in chapter 2. The experimental acts available to the read-write head are to move right on the tape, to move left on the tape, or to write something down on the square of tape currently scanned. Its observation at a given stage of inquiry is the symbol written on the tape square scanned at that stage. Finally, its current experimental act is determined entirely by the current datum and its current *state*, of which there are at most finitely many. We may think of these states as the possible configurations of a finite memory store. Just as a scientist sees only a finite, initial segment of his data by any given time, the read-write head sees only a finite chunk of the tape by any given time (*Fig. 6.2*).

Church's thesis is the claim that a Turing machine can do whatever a person (called a *computor*) following an explicit, step-by-step procedure can do. Church's thesis is nontrivial, because Turing computability is a mathematically precise notion, whereas following an explicit procedure is not. Turing's account of the limitations of the human computor provides an informal argument for this thesis. A major limitation figuring into the argument is that a human doing a computation can only see or alter at most a finite number of discrete jottings at once.[2] The human computor is transformed into the Turing read-write head, and his bounded range of observation is transformed into the fact that the read-write head can scan at most one square at a time. So both the classical problem of induction and the modern theory of computability are founded on the idea of a bounded perspective on the infinite.

[1] Turing (1936).
[2] Turing (1936). For a detailed discussion of Turing's analysis of computability and its relevance to Church's thesis, cf. Sieg (1994).

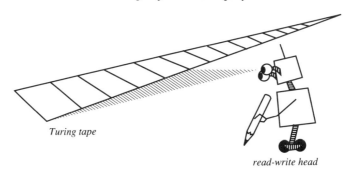

Figure 6.2

The bounded perspective of the read-write head leads to the key computational metaphor of *search*. In fact, search is what distinguishes the *recursive* functions from the *primitive recursive* functions. The latter can always be computed with an a priori bound on how long the read-write head must wait before finding a relevant datum (compare to empirical decidability by time *n*), whereas the recursive functions may require an unbounded search for their computation (compare to empirical decidability with certainty). In search, it is natural to think of the read-write head as primed to wait for some construct to appear on the tape, without ever knowing whether it will appear. Even though the initial input to the Turing machine, together with the machine's program, mathematically determines what patterns will arise, the read-write head doesn't always "know" what it will "see" in the future. It has to generate the sequence of patterns and inspect them, just the way an empirical scientist looks at increasing data about his unknown world. The sequence of patterns seen by the read-write head on a given input may be thought of as a kind of data stream, except that the data concerns a mathematical structure rather than the physical world.

Despite the similarities between the situation of the read-write head and that of an experimental scientist, the theory of computability has pursued a very different course from that adopted by most scientific methodologists. Instead of attaching degrees of belief to various hypotheses about what will eventually appear on the tape, or about what the correct solution to a computational problem might be, the machine is expected to find the correct answer. In other words, the theory of computability is a logical reliabilist arena for the assessment of computer programs. Indeed, the criteria of reliability assumed in the theory of computability are exactly parallel to those applied to inductive methods in the preceding chapters.

3. Programs as Reliable Methods

To speak of a Turing machine as computing outputs from inputs, we have to say what it is to give the machine an input and what it is for the machine to

Figure 6.3

produce an output. It turns out not to matter much which conventions we choose, so long as we stick with them. To input *n*, put the read-write head into its designated start state and then write *n* + 1 1s to the right of the head on an otherwise blank tape (*Fig. 6.3*).

A Turing machine outputs *n* when the read-write head goes into its designated halting state and an uninterrupted sequence of *n* 1s appears to the left of the read-write head on an otherwise blank tape (*Fig. 6.4*).

Just as we could interpret one and the same inductive method as trying to succeed in various different ways (e.g., verification in the limit, decision with certainty), the theory of computability can interpret one and the same Turing machine as converging to an output in correspondingly different ways. Turing machine *M* can be viewed as computing a function ϕ from inputs to outputs, called a *partial recursive function*. If *M* fails to make an output on some input *x*, then ϕ is undefined for *x* and we write $\phi(x)\uparrow$. Otherwise, we write $\phi(x)\downarrow$. If ϕ is total, then ϕ is called a *recursive function*. Let $\mathcal{PR}$ denote the class of all partial recursive functions and let $\mathcal{R}$ denote the set of all (total) recursive functions. A *decision procedure* is a Turing machine that computes the *characteristic function* of some relation on the natural numbers. That is, a decision procedure outputs 1 if a given sequence of numbers is in the relation, and outputs 0 otherwise. A *positive test* is a Turing machine that returns 1 on a given input if and only if the input is in a given set. On objects not

Figure 6.4

in the set, the machine is entitled to produce any output other than 1 and is also free to go into an infinite loop. A relation that has a decision procedure is said to be *recursive*. A relation that has a positive test is said to be *recursively enumerable*, or *r.e.* for short. If a relation's complement is r.e., then the relation is said to be *co-r.e.* Thus, a co-r.e. relation has a *negative test* (just reverse 1s and 0s in the positive test for its complement).

An r.e. relation may be thought of as a formal proposition that can be verified with certainty by a Turing machine, and a co-r.e. relation corresponds to a proposition that is refutable with certainty. A recursive relation can then be thought of as a hypothesis that can be decided with one mind change regardless of first conjecture. Indeed, all of the criteria of inductive success introduced in chapter 3 can be adopted as notions of computational success. Consider a machine that produces an infinite sequence of 1s and 0s in the limit after it is started with an input number n. Then define:

> M is a limiting positive test for S
> $\Leftrightarrow \forall n \in \omega, n \in S \Leftrightarrow$ the output stream of $M[n]$ stabilizes to 1.
>
> M is a limiting negative test for S
> $\Leftrightarrow \forall n \in \omega, n \notin S \Leftrightarrow$ the output stream of $M[n]$ stabilizes to 0.
>
> M is a limiting decision procedure of S
> $\Leftrightarrow M$ is both a limiting positive test and a limiting negative test for S.
>
> S is limiting r.e. $\Leftrightarrow S$ has a limiting positive test.
>
> S is limiting co-r.e. $\Leftrightarrow \bar{S}$ is limiting r.e. [$\Leftrightarrow S$ has a limiting negative test].
>
> S is limiting recursive $\Leftrightarrow S$ has a limiting decision procedure.
>
> S is an n-trial predicate $\Leftrightarrow S$ has a limiting decision procedure that changes its mind at most n times on each input.

The terms *limiting recursive* and *limiting r.e.* are taken from E. Mark Gold.[3] H. Putnam referred to the former as *trial and error predicates*.[4] Putnam also introduced the notion of *n*-trial predicates.[5] The limiting recursive relations are analogous to hypotheses decidable in the limit. The limiting r.e. relations are analogous to hypotheses verifiable in the limit. And *n*-trial predicates are analogous to hypotheses decidable with *n* mind changes. As in the empirical case, we can usefully refine the notion by specifying the first conjecture:

> S is an n-trial predicate starting with 1
> $\Leftrightarrow S$ has a limiting decision procedure that changes its mind at most n times on each input $n \in \omega$, starting with 1.

---

[3] Gold (1965).
[4] Putnam (1965).
[5] Putnam (1965).

One might weaken the demands on the machine further, and require only that it produce a sequence of code numbers for rationals that gradually approaches 1 if and only if $n \in S$.[6] Sets having such machines may be called *gradually r.e.*, and sets having gradual refutation procedures may be called *gradually co-r.e.*, while sets having both may be called *gradually recursive*.

4. The Arithmetical Hierarchy

All these notions of success can be located in a hierarchical setting entirely parallel to the finite Borel hierarchy introduced in chapter 4. Much early work in the theory of computability concerns the *arithmetical* or *Kleene hierarchy*. Where R is a k-ary relation on ω, define:

$R \in \Sigma_0^A \Leftrightarrow R$ *is recursive.*

$R \in \Sigma_{n+1}^A \Leftrightarrow$ *there is some $k + 1$-ary $R' \in \Sigma_n^A$ such that for each $n_1, \ldots,$*
$\qquad n_k \in \omega, R(n_1, \ldots, n_k) \Leftrightarrow \exists n_{k+1}$ *such that*
$\qquad \neg R'(n_1, \ldots, n_k, n_{k+1})$.

As usual, the dual and ambiguous classes are defined in terms of Σ_n^A.

$R \in \Pi_n^A \Leftrightarrow \bar{R} \in \Sigma_n^A$.

$R \in \Delta_n^A \Leftrightarrow R \in \Sigma_n^A \ \& \ R \in \Pi_n^A$.

Just as the Borel hierarchy starts out with clopen sets (sets of data streams decidable by an ideal scientist on the basis of data), the arithmetical hierarchy starts out with recursive sets (sets of numbers decidable by a computer). Just as Σ_1^B sets are the open sets, which are verifiable with certainty by an ideal scientist, Σ_1^A sets are r.e. sets, which are verifiable with certainty by a computer. The correspondence goes all the way up to ω (*Fig. 6.5*).[7] By way of illustration, let's establish the limiting r.e. case.

Proposition 6.1 (Gold 1965, Putnam 1965)

S is limiting r.e. $\Leftrightarrow S \in \Sigma_2^A$.

Proof: ($\Leftarrow$) Suppose that $S \in \Sigma_2^A$. Then S is of the form $\{x: \exists n \ \forall m \ R(x, n, m)\}$, where R is a recursive relation. We construct a machine M that proceeds as follows. Let M_R be a decision procedure for R. On input x, M sequentially outputs $M_R(x, 1, 1), M_R(x, 1, 2), \ldots$ until for some n, $M_R(x, 1, n) = 0$. If a zero is received, then M outputs 0 and then outputs $M_R(x, 2, 1), M_R(x, 2, 2), \ldots$ until

---

[6] This idea is proposed and developed in Hàjek (1978).

[7] Recall that the Borel hierarchy does not stop at ω. The arithmetical hierarchy does stop at ω.

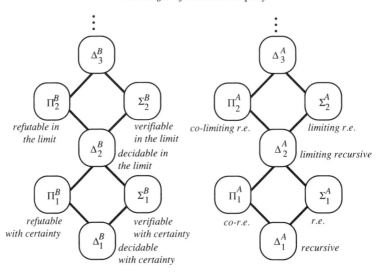

Figure 6.5

another zero is received, and so forth. All of this is effective, so by Church's thesis, it can be implemented as a Turing machine M. It is easy to verify that M is a limiting positive test for S.

($\Rightarrow$) Suppose that S is limiting r.e. Then there is some machine M such that

$$x \in S \Leftrightarrow \exists n \, \forall m > n \text{ the } m\text{th output of } M[x] \text{ is defined and equal to } 1.$$

Since M is assumed to output an infinite sequence, the predicate

the mth output of $M[x]$ is defined and equal to 1

is recursive. Hence, S has form $\exists n \, \forall m \, R[x, n, m]$, where R is recursive. Thus, $S \in \Sigma_2^A$. ∎

This is all parallel to the characterizations of decidability and verifiability in the limit presented in chapter 4. Just as fans provide basic empirical tests that can be built up using quantifiers into ever more subtle empirical hypotheses, recursive relations provide basic formal tests that can be built up using quantifiers into ever more subtle computational problems.

5. Uncomputability and Diagonalization

It might be objected at this point that it is quite appropriate for the theory of computability to insist on reliability because computation is just deduction and deduction can be guaranteed to yield certainty. Inductive inquiry, on the other hand, concerns answers we can never be sure about, and hence demands that we introduce notions of justified belief, evidential support, and probability. The truth is quite otherwise. The whole force of the theory of computability is to show that a bounded agent like the Turing read-write head cannot be guaranteed to arrive at certainty concerning most formal questions. The reason for this limitation is entirely parallel to the reason for inductive skepticism, namely, a bounded perspective on an unbounded data stream. To illustrate this point, let us consider how uncomputability arguments can be recast as classical demonic arguments for the local underdetermination of empirical hypotheses.

It turns out that the easiest problems to prove intractable are those that have a kind of self-referential character based on the effective assignment of code numbers to Turing machines. Assume some such fixed assignment of numbers to Turing machines. Let W_i denote the set of all inputs on which machine M_i halts. W_i is an r.e. set, since we can trivially modify M_i to output 1 whenever M_i halts. Moreover, each r.e. set S is some set W_i, since the machine M_i can be produced by modifying the positive test for S to go into an infinite loop whenever it halts with an output not equal to 1.

The *halting problem* K is defined as follows:

$$K = \{i: i \in W_i\}.$$

That is, the halting problem contains all indices i such that the machine with index i halts when fed its own index i as an input. It is easy to see that K is r.e. A machine can simulate the operation of M_i on input i until M_i is observed to drop into its halting state. At that point, the simulating machine outputs 1. If the halt state is never reached, the simulating machine waits forever. The simulation just constructed is a computable positive test for K. (Notice the close analogy between the strategy of the machine and that of an empirical scientist waiting for some crucial datum to verify an empirical hypothesis.)

We will now see that $\bar{K}$ is not r.e. by means of a simple *diagonal argument*.

Proposition 6.2

$\bar{K} \notin \Sigma_1^A$.

Proof: We can form an infinite table T as follows (*Fig. 6.6*):

$$T(x, y) = \begin{cases} 1 & \text{if } y \in W_x \\ 0 & \text{otherwise.} \end{cases}$$

We can think of an r.e. set S as uniquely represented by a sequence of 0s and 1s, with 1 in position y if $y \in S$ and 0 in position y otherwise. So each row in the table represents the characteristic function of some r.e. set. The important point is this: since we have seen that each r.e. set is some set W_i, each r.e. set is some row in the table.

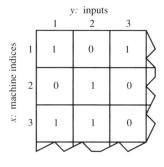

Figure 6.6

Now let us consider whether $\bar{K}$ is represented by some row in the table. If not, then $\bar{K}$ is not r.e. Recall that $K = \{x: x \in W_x\}$. The question whether $i \in W_i$ is answered by looking at table entry $T_{i,i}$. Hence, K is represented by the diagonal sequence of the table. Therefore, $\bar{K}$ is represented by the result of reversing 1s and 0s along the diagonal of the table to form the *counterdiagonal sequence* of the table (*Fig. 6.7*).

But the counterdiagonal sequence differs from each row of the table in at least one place (namely, on the diagonal). Therefore, $\bar{K}$ is represented by no row in the table, and hence is not r.e.   ∎

The sense in which the preceding proof is a diagonal argument is clear. It proceeds by depicting $\bar{K}$ as the counterdiagonal of a table whose rows include the characteristic functions of all r.e. sets.

6.   The Demons of Uncomputability

The diagonal argument rehearsed in the preceding section doesn't look like a demonic argument, since there is no demon who feeds misleading data to the

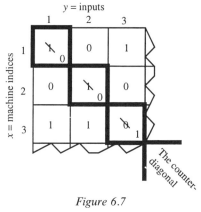

Figure 6.7

Hmm. It must be in an
infinite loop.

But then again, maybe
it's just about to produce
the answer

bang
bang
bang

Figure 6.8

Turing read-write head. Nonetheless, there remains a strongly intuitive feeling that any would-be decision procedure is foiled for inductive reasons: no matter how long the decision procedure waits for machine M_i to halt on input i before concluding that the computation $M_i[i]$ is in an infinite loop, the computation may halt at the very next moment. Anyone who encounters a bug in a slow-running program knows the feeling. One doesn't know whether to turn off the machine and start over (wasting all the time spent up until now if the program was just about ready to make an output) or to continue to wait (which may take forever) (*Fig. 6.8*).

There is one important disanalogy between a computer and an inductive method: the computer receives no infinite data stream and an inductive method does. So whereas an inductive demon can feed misleading data to an inductive method in response to its conjectures thus far, a computational demon cannot. But a computational demon can still watch what machine M_i does through time, waiting, for example, for M_i to declare its certainty by returning 1 on a given input. Moreover, the demon itself can be a computer program, since it is no problem for one computer program to simulate another to see what it does on a given input. The plot thickens when the index provided to M_i in the demon's simulation is the demon's *own* index. Then when M_i is observed to become certain (in the demon's simulation) that the demon's index has a given property, the demon can make an output so that his own program fails to have the property M_i is certain that it has!

In particular, we can use such a demonic argument to show that $\bar{K}$ is not r.e. Suppose that M_i aspires to be a positive test for $\bar{K}$. The demonic program M_{d_i} works like this. On input y, it simply ignores y altogether and proceeds to simulate M_i, step by step, on input d_i (i.e., the demon's own index). The demon continues this simulation until the computation $M_i[d_i]$ returns 1, at which time the demon returns 1 as well. Otherwise, the demon continues to wait for $M_i[d_i]$ to return 1, and hence makes no output on y (*Fig. 6.9*).

Thus we have that $d_i \in W_{d_i} \Leftrightarrow M_i[d_i]$ returns 1, so M_i is not a positive test for $\bar{K}$. Assuming that such a d_i exists for each i, no M_i is a positive test for $\bar{K}$ and hence $\bar{K}$ is not r.e. The index d_i, if it exists, is a "computational disguise" for an inductive demon dedicated to the befuddlement of machine M_i (*Fig. 6.10*).

But it is not a trivial question whether such a demonic index d_i exists for each machine M_i. It seems that we have to know what d_i is before we can write

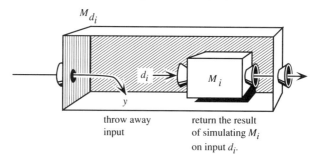

Figure 6.9

down the demonic procedure M_{d_i}, because M_{d_i} feeds d_i to M_i. But we cannot know what d_i is until after we write down the procedure M_{d_i}, since d_i is the code number of that procedure. So the question remains whether the inductive demon can always don a computational disguise d_i appropriate for a given machine M_i.

The self-referential miracle required for the demon's disguise is effected by the *Kleene recursion theorem*. Before proving it, we will need a pair of simple results.

Proposition 6.3   The *s-m-n* theorem

Suppose $\psi(x, y)$ is a partial recursive function. Then there is a total recursive function s such that for each $x, y \in \omega$,

$$\phi_{s(x)}(y) = \psi(x, y).$$

Proof: Let $M[x, y]$ be a program for ψ. To compute $s(a)$, take the program M, stick in input y, and return the code number of the resulting program $M[a, y]$, which now only accepts input y.   ∎

Proposition 6.4   The universal machine theorem

There is a $u \in \omega$ such that for each $i, x \in \omega$, $\phi_u(i, x)$
$= \phi_i(x)$ if $\phi_i(x)$ is defined and is undefined otherwise.

Proof: u is the index of a program that decodes i and that simulates the resulting program on input x, returning whatever output the simulated program yields, if any.   ∎

Now we may proceed to the main result.

Proposition 6.5   The Kleene recursion theorem[8]

For each total recursive f, there is an index i such that $\phi_{f(i)} = \phi_i$.

---

[8] The nice, tabular proof that follows is adapted from Cutland (1986).

Mon frere!
You do not trust me?

Figure 6.10

Proof: Consider a table filled with partial recursive functions so that at position x, y, we have the function $\phi_{\phi_x(y)}$, where we stipulate that $\phi_{\phi_x(y)}$ denotes the everywhere undefined function if $\phi_x(y)$ is undefined. Consider the table's diagonal sequence of functions:

$$D = (\phi_{\phi_0(0)}, \phi_{\phi_1(1)}, \phi_{\phi_2(2)}, \ldots).$$

Since $h(x) = \phi_x(x)$ is partial recursive, there is some i such that $h = \phi_i$, so D is also the ith row in the table (*Fig. 6.11*).

Let f be a total recursive function. Let

$$D^* = (\phi_{f(\phi_0(0))}, \phi_{f(\phi_1(1))}, \phi_{f(\phi_2(2))}, \ldots).$$

Then D^* is a row of the table, since $h'(x) = f(\phi_x(x))$ is computable and hence is some ϕ_k. If ϕ_k is not total, we can choose a total k' that gives rise to the very same row by the following lemma, so that we may assume that ϕ_k is total.

Lemma

If ϕ_k is not total, we may replace k with j so that $\phi_j(x)$ is an index for the everywhere undefined function whenever $\phi_k(x)$ is undefined and $\phi_j(x) = \phi_k(x)$ otherwise, so that the jth row is identical to D^*.

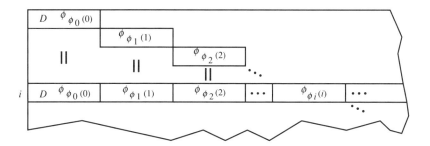

Figure 6.11

Proof of lemma: Define: $\psi(x, y) = \phi_u(\phi_k(x), y)$, where u is the universal index guaranteed by the universal machine theorem (proposition 6.4). $\psi(x, y)$ is partial recursive and amounts to the result of simulating index $\phi_k(x)$ on input y if $\phi_k(x)$ is defined, and is undefined otherwise. So we may apply the *s-m-n* theorem (proposition 6.3) to yield a total recursive s such that $\phi_{s(x)}(y) = \psi(x, y)$. Let j be an index for s.   ■

Returning to the proof of the proposition, observe that $\phi_{f(\phi_k(k))}$, the kth entry of D^*, is on the diagonal because D^* is row k of the table. Since row i is identical to the diagonal sequence D, the kth entry of D is identical to the on-diagonal entry in D^*. Thus

$$\phi_{f(\phi_k(k))} = \phi_{\phi_k(k)}.$$

This is immediate from *Figure 6.12*. But by the lemma, $\phi_k(k)$ is defined since ϕ_k is total. Thus, $\phi_k(k)$ is the index promised in the theorem.   ■

How does this theorem yield the self-referential disguise d_i for the demon's program for fooling M_i? Consider a procedure that on inputs x, y simulates the computation of M_i on input x. When the procedure observes that M_i returns 1 on input x, it returns 0 for x, y. Otherwise, it continues to wait for M_i to return 1 for x. The procedure's behavior is the following partial recursive function:

$$\psi(x, y) = \begin{cases} 0 & \text{if } M_i \text{ returns } 1 \text{ on input } x \\ \uparrow & \text{otherwise.} \end{cases}$$

By proposition 6.3, there is a total recursive s such that for all x, y, $\phi_{s(x)}(y) = \psi(x, y)$. Now apply the recursion theorem to obtain an index d_i such that

$$\phi_{s(d_i)} = \phi_{d_i}.$$

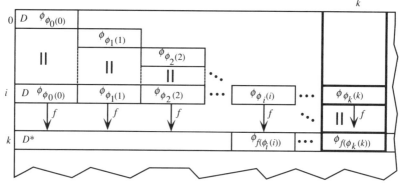

Figure 6.12

The self-referential magic has occurred, for now we have

$$\phi_{d_i}(y) = \begin{cases} 0 & \textit{if } M_i \textit{ returns 1 on input } d_i \\ \uparrow & \textit{otherwise.} \end{cases}$$

One can also use the recursion theorem to prove that a problem is not limiting r.e. in a fashion very similar to the limiting skeptical arguments of chapter 3. Consider the problem $T = \{i: \phi_i \textit{ is total}\}$. Let M_i be a Turing program that would like to be a limiting positive test for T. If M_i fails to produce an infinite sequence of outputs on some input, then it fails to be a limiting positive test in any case, so suppose that M_i always does so. On inputs x, y, the demonic procedure feeds x to M_i and waits until there are at least y stages when the current output is less than 1. Then the demon returns 0. The procedure computes the function:

$$\psi(x, y) = \begin{cases} 0 & \textit{if there are at least y stages when } M_i[x]\textit{'s current output} \\ & \textit{is not 1} \\ \uparrow & \textit{otherwise.} \end{cases}$$

Applying propositions 6.3 and 6.4 just as before yields an index d_i such that

$$\phi_{d_i}(y) = \begin{cases} 0 & \textit{if there are at least y stages when } M_i[d_i]\textit{'s current} \\ & \textit{output is not 1} \\ \uparrow & \textit{otherwise.} \end{cases}$$

This function is total if M_i fails to stabilize to 1 on k and has finite domain otherwise, so M_i is not a limiting positive test for T. Since i is an arbitrary machine that outputs an infinite sequence of outputs for each given input, there is no limiting positive test for T.

The same demonic technique can be used to prove that broad classes of problems are nonrecursive or non-r.e. Let $\mathcal{A} \subseteq \mathcal{PR}$ (recall that $\mathcal{PR}$ is the class of all partial recursive functions). Let $index(\mathcal{A})$ denote the set of all indices for functions in $\mathcal{A}$. That is,

$$index(\mathcal{A}) = \{i: \phi_i \in \mathcal{A}\}.$$

Let $S \subseteq \omega$. S is an *index set* just in case for some $\mathcal{A} \subseteq \mathcal{PR}$, $S = index(\mathcal{A})$. This amounts to the requirement that no partial recursive function has one index in S and another out of S. For example, the halting problem K is not an index set. To see why this is so, we note that every partial recursive function has infinitely many distinct indices (take a program M_i for ϕ and add arbitrarily many do-nothing clauses to M_i). But using the Kleene recursion theorem, we can construct a partial recursive function ϕ_n that halts only on n, so that $n \in K$

but no other index of ϕ_n is in K. The construction is as follows. The following function is partial recursive by Church's thesis:

$$\psi(x, y) = \begin{cases} 0 & \text{if } y = x \\ \uparrow & \text{otherwise.} \end{cases}$$

Then by the *s-m-n* theorem there is a total recursive function *s* such that

$$\phi_{s(x)}(y) = \begin{cases} 0 & \text{if } y = x \\ \uparrow & \text{otherwise.} \end{cases}$$

By the Kleene recursion theorem, there is an *n* such that

$$\phi_n(y) = \begin{cases} 0 & \text{if } y = n \\ \uparrow & \text{otherwise.} \end{cases}$$

On the other hand, the halting problem restricted to a fixed input *n* *is* an index set:

$$K_n = \{x: n \in W_x\}.$$

So is the set $I = \{n: W_n \text{ is infinite}\}$ which contains all indices of functions with infinite domains or the set *T* of all indices of total recursive functions. We can now show by a demonic argument that only trivial index sets are recursive.

Proposition 6.6   Rice's theorem

Let S be an index set. Then S is recursive $\Leftrightarrow$ S = $\varnothing$ or S = ω.

Proof: Suppose that for some $\mathcal{A}$, $S = index(\mathcal{A})$. Suppose, further, that $S \neq \varnothing$ and $S \neq \omega$. The everywhere undefined function $\varnothing$ is either in $\mathcal{A}$ or it is not. Let M_i be an arbitrary Turing machine.

Case 1: Suppose that the everywhere undefined function $\varnothing$ is in $\mathcal{A}$. Then since $S \neq \omega$, there is some $\psi \notin \mathcal{A}$ such that $\psi \neq \varnothing$. Intuitively, the demonic index d_i for M_i watches what M_i does on input d_i and produces output $\psi(y)$ as soon as M_i becomes sure that d_i is in S so that d_i is an index for $\psi \notin \mathcal{A}$ and M_i is wrong. Otherwise, d_i continues to stall forever so that d_i is an index for $\varnothing \in \mathcal{A}$ and M_i is again wrong for failing to recognize that $d_i \in S$. As in the case of the halting problem, we use the Kleene recursion theorem to construct such an index d_i. Define:

$$\delta(x, y) = \begin{cases} \psi(y) & \text{if } M_i[x] \text{ halts with } 1 \\ \mathcal{K} & \text{otherwise.} \end{cases}$$

To compute this function, the demon need simply simulate the computation of

M_i on input x and pass along the result of simulating $\psi(y)$ if $M_i[x]$ returns 1. Applying the s-m-n theorem, we have a total recursive function s such that

$$\phi_{s(x)}(y) = \begin{cases} \psi(y) & \text{if } M_i[x] \text{ halts with 1} \\ \uparrow & \text{otherwise.} \end{cases}$$

By the Kleene recursion theorem, there is a d_i such that

$$\phi_{d_i}(y) = \begin{cases} \psi(y) & \text{if } M_i[d_i] \text{ halts with 1} \\ \uparrow & \text{otherwise.} \end{cases}$$

Thus, we have that $M_i(d_i)$ halts with $1 \Leftrightarrow d_i \notin S$, so M_i is not a decision procedure for S.

Case 2, in which the undefined function $\varnothing$ is *not* in $\mathcal{A}$ proceeds in a similar manner, except that 1 is replaced with 0 in the definition of δ.   ∎

We may also show by a demonic argument that a wide range of index sets are not r.e.

Proposition 6.7   The Rice-Shapiro theorem

$\forall \mathcal{A} \subseteq \mathcal{PR}$, *if index*$(\mathcal{A})$ *is r.e.*
then $\forall \phi \in \mathcal{PR}$, $\phi \in \mathcal{A} \Leftrightarrow \exists$ *finite* $\theta \in \mathcal{A}$ *such that* $\theta \subseteq \phi$.

Proof: Suppose that the consequent of the proposition is false of some $\phi \in \mathcal{PR}$. Let M_i be an arbitrary Turing machine. Case 1: Suppose first that the ($\Rightarrow$) side of the biconditional is false. Then $\phi \in \mathcal{A}$ but for each finite $\theta \subseteq \phi$, $\theta \notin \mathcal{A}$. Then to fool M_i, a demonic index d_i ought to proceed (by watching $M_i(d_i)$) so that d_i is an index for some finite $\theta \subseteq \phi$ if $M_i(d_i)$ halts (i.e., becomes sure that d_i is in S) and so that d_i is an index for ϕ otherwise. This can be arranged as follows:

$$\psi(x, y) = \begin{cases} \phi(y) & \text{if } M_i(x) \uparrow \text{ within } y \text{ steps} \\ \uparrow & \text{otherwise.} \end{cases}$$

This function is computable in light of Church's thesis since we can effectively simulate $M_i(x)$, counting each step as we go until y steps are used and then check whether M_i produces an output by that time. If not, we simulate $\phi(y)$ and pass along the output, if any. If so, we go into an infinite loop. Applying the s-m-n theorem and the recursion theorem in the usual way yields

$$\phi_{d_i}(y) = \begin{cases} \phi(y) & \text{if } M_i(d_i) \uparrow \text{ within } y \text{ steps} \\ \uparrow & \text{otherwise.} \end{cases}$$

Hence, $M_i(d_i) \downarrow \Rightarrow d_i$ is an index for some finite initial segment θ of $\phi \Rightarrow d_i \notin S$, and $M_i(d_i) \uparrow \Rightarrow d_i$ is an index for $\phi \Rightarrow d_i \in S$, so $S \neq W_i$.

In case 2, the ($\Leftarrow$) side of the biconditional is false, so we have that there is a $\phi \in \mathcal{PR} - \mathcal{A}$ and there is a finite $\theta \subseteq \phi$ such that $\theta \in \mathcal{A}$. In this case, we want the demonic index d_i to be for ϕ if $M_i(d_i)$ becomes sure that d_i is in S and to be for θ otherwise. Define:

$$\psi(x, y) = \begin{cases} \phi(y) & \text{if } M_i(x) \downarrow \text{ or } y \in dom(\theta) \\ \uparrow & \text{otherwise.} \end{cases}$$

To compute ψ, first check whether $y \in dom(\theta)$, using a lookup table. Then check whether $M_i(x)$ halts. If so, simulate $\phi(y)$ and return the result. Applying the *s-m-n* and recursion theorems, we obtain d_i such that

$$\phi_{d_i}(y) = \begin{cases} \phi(y) & \text{if } M_i(d_i) \downarrow \text{ or } y \in dom(\theta) \\ \uparrow & \text{otherwise.} \end{cases}$$

Now we again have that $M_i(d_i) \downarrow \Rightarrow d_i$ is an index for $\phi \Rightarrow d_i \notin S$ and $M_i(d_i) \uparrow \Rightarrow d_i$ is an index for $\theta \Rightarrow d_i \in S$, so $S \neq W_i$. ∎

This result was proved by means of a demonic argument, but it has an epistemological flavor in its own right. Suppose we have a fixed, 1–1 encoding of pairs of natural numbers into numbers other than 0. 0 is reserved as a special symbol. Let $\varepsilon \in \mathcal{N}$ be a data stream. We say that ε is *for* ϕ just in case ε lists code numbers for all and only the pairs $(x, \phi(x))$ such that $\phi(x)$ is defined, together, possibly, with some 0s added. The funny business with 0 ensures that there is a data stream for the everywhere undefined function $\emptyset$, which otherwise would have none, since there is no pair in $\emptyset$ to present. Notice that other functions may have gratuitous 0s in their data streams as well, so that seeing a 0 is not a dead giveaway that the data stream will be for $\emptyset$. Let $data(\phi)$ be the set of all data streams for ϕ. If $\mathcal{A} \subseteq \mathcal{PR}$, let $data(\mathcal{A})$ be the union of all $data(\phi)$ such that $\phi \in \mathcal{A}$. Finally, let $h_{\mathcal{A}}$ denote the empirical hypothesis that the data stream will be in $data(\mathcal{A})$, and assume that correctness is truth. Now we have:

Corollary 6.8

(a) If $\mathcal{A} \subseteq \mathcal{PR}$ and $index(\mathcal{A})$ is r.e. then $data(\mathcal{A})$ is $data(\mathcal{PR})$-open.

(b) If $\mathcal{A} \subseteq \mathcal{PR}$ and $index(\mathcal{A})$ is r.e. then $h_{\mathcal{A}}$ is ideally verifiable with certainty given $data(\mathcal{PR})$.

Proof: (a) By the Rice-Shapiro theorem, we have that for each $\phi \in \mathcal{PR}$, $\phi \in \mathcal{A} \Leftrightarrow$ there is a finite $\theta \in \mathcal{A}$ such that $\theta \subseteq \phi$. Then we have for each $\varepsilon \in data(\mathcal{PR})$,

$$\varepsilon \in data(\mathcal{A}) \Leftrightarrow \exists \text{ finite } \theta \in \mathcal{A}, \exists n \in \omega$$
$$[\forall m \in dom(\theta) \ \theta(m) = y \Leftrightarrow \exists k \leq n \ \varepsilon_k \text{ codes } (m, y)].$$

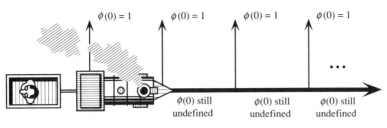

$\phi(0) = 1$ $\phi(0) = 1$ $\phi(0) = 1$ $\phi(0) = 1$

$\phi(0)$ still $\phi(0)$ still $\phi(0)$ still
undefined   undefined   undefined

Figure 6.13

All the quantifiers occurring within the square brackets are bounded, and hence correspond to *finite* unions or intersections. The relation ε_k *codes*(m, y) is clopen in $\mathcal{N}$. Finally, the only remaining quantifiers are existential quantifiers over countable domains (since there are at most countably many finite θ), which correspond to countable unions. (b) follows from (a) and proposition 4.6. ∎

What these corollaries tell us is that demonic arguments against ideal scientists with background knowledge *data*($\mathcal{PR}$) can be used to show that a broad class of purely fromal questions do not admit of computable positive tests. In other words, the failure of index sets violating the Rice-Shapiro condition to be r.e. is an instance of inductive underdetermination. The two phenomena involve exactly the same topological structure. By way of illustration, consider the problem $K_0 = \{x : 0 \in W_x\}$. Let α be a scientific method facing the hypothesis that the data stream is in *data*(K_0). The demon simply feeds α the data stream $0, 0, 0, \ldots$ until α emits the certainty mark '!' followed by 1. Thereafter, the demon feeds *code*$(0, 1)$ forever after (*Fig. 6.13*). If α ever says '!' immediately followed by 1, then the data stream is for the function $\{(0, 1)\}$, which is defined at 0 and hence is not in $\overline{K_0}$. But if the method never becomes sure, the data stream is for the everywhere undefined function, which is in $\overline{K_0}$. This is an instance of Sextus's ancient argument against inductive generalization. But in light of corollary 6.8, it shows a purely computational fact, namely, that $\overline{K_0}$ is not r.e.

7.   Some Disanalogies

The purpose of this chapter has been to illustrate the strong structural and philosophical analogy between standard results in the theory of computability and classical skeptical arguments for local underdetermination, so that degrees of uncomputability may be thought of as levels of underdetermination. The analogy between ideal inquiry and Turing computability is not exact, however. First, the analogy has been illustrated here only for index sets or for closely related sets like $\overline{K}$. Second, the converse of proposition 6.7 fails because it is easy to construct non-r.e. index set problems that generate inductive inference problems that are ideally verifiable with certainty.[9] It also turns out that demonic arguments cease to establish the uncomputability of index sets at level 3 because the data set corresponding to any index set is always $\Delta[data(\mathcal{PR})]^B_3$. This follows simply from the fact that $\mathcal{PR}$ is countable. This is also the best general upper bound available given just background knowledge $data(\mathcal{PR})$.

Proposition 6.9

(a) *For each countable S, $data(\mathcal{A}) \cap data(S) \in \Delta[data(S)]^B_3$.*

(b) *$\exists \mathcal{A} \exists S \subseteq \mathcal{PR}$ such that*
$$data(\mathcal{A}) \cap data(\mathcal{PR}) \notin \Sigma[data(S))]^B_2 \cup \Pi[data(S)]^B_2,$$

Proof: (a) Let $\mathcal{A}, S \subseteq \mathcal{P}$ be given, with S countable. Let $\varepsilon \in \mathcal{N}$. Then we have, for each $\varepsilon \in data(S)$:

$\varepsilon \in data(\mathcal{A})$

$\Leftrightarrow \exists \phi \in \mathcal{A} \cap S$ such that $\forall x, y \in \omega, \phi(x) = y \Leftrightarrow \exists z \, \varepsilon_z$ encodes (x, y)

$\Leftrightarrow \exists \phi \in \mathcal{A} \cap S$ such that $\forall x, y [(\phi(x) = y \, \& \, \exists z$ such that ε_z encodes

$(x, y))$ or $(\phi(x) \neq y \, \& \, \forall z, \varepsilon_z$ does not encode $(x, y))]$

$\Leftrightarrow \exists \forall [\exists \cdots$ or $\forall \cdots]$

$\Leftrightarrow \exists \forall \forall \exists \cdots$

$\Leftrightarrow \exists \forall \exists \cdots$

Since the quantifiers all range over countable sets, they correspond to countable intersections and unions, so $data(\mathcal{A}) \cap data(S) \in \Sigma[data(S)]^B_3$. Also, for each $\varepsilon \in data(S)$,

$\varepsilon \in data(\mathcal{A}) \Leftrightarrow \forall \phi \in S - \mathcal{A},$

$\exists x, y \in \omega$ such that $\phi(x) = y$ and $\forall z \, \varepsilon_z$ does not encode (x, y) or

$\exists x$ such that $\phi(x) \uparrow$ and $\exists z, w$ such that ε_z encodes (x, w).

By regrouping the quantifiers, it follows that

$$data(\mathcal{A}) \cap data(S) \in \Pi[data(S)]^B_3.$$

(b) Let $\mathcal{A}_{even} = \{\phi: \exists n \, \forall$ even $m \geq n, \phi(m) = 0\}$ and let $\mathcal{A}_{odd} = \{\phi: \exists n \, \forall$ odd $m \geq n, \phi(m) = 0\}$. Let $\mathcal{A} = \mathcal{A}_{even} \cap \overline{\mathcal{A}_{odd}}$. Now proceed with a demonic argument along the lines of the one given in the example at the end of section 6 to show that $data(\mathcal{A})$ is neither $\Sigma[data(\mathcal{PR})]^B_2$ nor $\Pi[data(\mathcal{PR})]^B_2$. ∎

---

[9] Cf. exercise 6.6.

Propositions 6.7 and 6.9 leave open an interesting question. Can we always show that an index set is not Σ_2^A by means of an ideal demonic argument? That is:

Question 6.10

If $\mathcal{A} \subseteq \mathcal{PR}$ and $index(\mathcal{A})$ is Σ_2^A then is it the case that
$$data(\mathcal{A}) \cap data(\mathcal{PR}) \text{ is } \Sigma[data(\mathcal{PR})]_2^B?$$
∎

It is easy to show that if we restrict our attention to those Σ_2^A sets that are r.e. unions of co-r.e. index sets, then the answer is affirmative (exercise 6.7). But since a Σ_2^A index set could conceivably be an r.e. union of co-r.e. sets that are not index sets, it is not clear that the answer is affirmative in general.

Exercises

6.1. Prove the analogue of proposition 6.1 for the other notions of computational success introduced in section 6.2.

6.2. Define the *limiting halting problem* as follows:

$$K_{\lim} = \{x: M_x \text{ started on input } x \text{ outputs a sequence that stabilizes to } 1.\}$$

Show that $K_{\lim} \in \Sigma_2^A - \Pi_2^A$, both by means of depicting $\overline{K_{\lim}}$ as the counterdiagonal of a table and by means of a demonic argument using Kleene's recursion theorem.

6.3. Use corollary 6.8(a), together with a demonic argument, to show that $\{i: W_i \text{ is infinite}\}$ is not r.e.

6.4. Use a demonic argument based on Kleene's recursion theorem together with proposition 6.3 and the results of exercise 6.1 to prove that $I = \{i: W_i \text{ is infinite}\}$ is not Π_3^A. Follow the strategy of the arguments presented after proposition 6.4.

6.5. Show the converses of corollary 6.8 are false.

6.6. Complete the proof of proposition 6.9(b).

6.7. Settle question 6.10 in the affirmative in the restricted case of r.e. unions of co-r.e. index sets.

7

Computers in Search of the Truth

1. Ideal Epistemology and Computability

So far, our study of inductive methodology has acceded to the time-honored cult of the *ideal agent*. An ideal agent is a curious sort of deity who is limited in evidence-gathering ability more or less the way we are, but who suffers from no computational limitations whatsoever. An ideal agent can decide all mathematical relations in an instant, but in a dark room he bumps into the walls with the rest of us.

Whatever we are, we are not ideal agents. If cognitive psychologists are right, we are computers. But a methodologist needn't debate the point, since methods should be routinely followable, without appeal to arcane powers of insight that cannot be accessed at will. A. Turing's conception of the Turing machine was intended to explicate just this notion of explicitly directed, method-driven behavior. Accordingly, Turing computability seems a natural constraint to impose on methodological principles.

Ideal epistemologists propose norms for the conduct of ideal scientists. But computational agents cannot do what ideal agents can do. In fact, this is an extreme understatement: there are uncountably many distinct problems solvable by noncomputable agents, but there are at most countably many distinct problems that are solvable by computational agents. If *ought* implies *can*, then we should expect computationally bounded methodology to be different from ideal methodology. In this chapter, we will consider both the differences and the similarities between ideal and computationally bounded methodology, all from a logical reliabilist point of view.

The ideal epistemologist might respond that ideals also bind computable agents, who should strive to satisfy the ideal even though exact compliance is impossible. That is not my opinion, however. If ideals may be utterly indifferent

Figure 7.1

to our frailties, then inductive methodology would be the world's shortest subject; believe the whole truth and nothing but the truth. It is a candid admission of our severely limited perspective on the world that leads us to consider probabilities, inductive logics, and confirmation theories in the first place. To ignore computational boundedness after acknowledging perceptual boundedness makes little sense on the face of it (*Fig. 7.1*), and makes far less sense in light of the strong analogies between computability and ideal inductive inference that were discussed in the preceding chapter.

One solution is to find some hypothetical imperatives that justify approximations to the ideal directly. Maybe one can define degrees of *else*, so that it is clear to all that greater degrees of *else* are more horrible than smaller degrees of *else*. If one can also define degrees of approximation to the ideal that are achievable by bounded agents, then one can say strive harder and you will get more. This solves the problem, but it also seems to jettison the ideal. The degrees of the ideal are not ideal norms, but rather bounded norms achievable by bounded agents. The ideal, itself, ceases to do any work, and we are back to computationally bounded methodology.

A different approach is to hold that an ideal norm is binding in a given case if and only if it is achievable. If it is not achievable, then the violator is forgiven.[1] On this view, a computationally bounded agent is left entirely without

---

[1] "Standards of ideal rationality are not limiting cases of standards of bounded rationality. The standards are ideal in the sense that the capacity to satisfy them is one which an ideally rational agent, in contrast to a human agent, possesses. To advocate a standard of ideal rationality is not to promote realizable actions which approximate the prescriptions of such standards. Rather it is to promote conformity to such standards wherever that is feasible. The standard is an ideal in the sense that often we are incapable of meeting its requirements. In that case, we are urged to devise ways and means of satisfying these requirements in a larger number of cases" (Levi 1990): 214.

guidance in many cases unless unachievable ideals are augmented with achievable norms achievable in those cases.

Ideal methodology is not bad in itself. What a demigod can't do, a computer can't do. If a problem is so hard that gods cannot solve it, to say merely that it is uncomputable is like saying that Everest is a bit of a hill. Another reason for interest in ideal methodology is that it enables us to separate the purely topological (informational) dimensions of a problem from its purely computational dimensions by comparing the degree of underdetermination of a problem for ideal agents with its degree of underdetermination for computationally bounded agents.

Ideal results are fine so long as they are contrasted with and qualified by their computational counterparts. I depart company, however, when ideal results are portrayed as what is essential to methodology while computational considerations are brushed aside as bothersome details of application. As we saw in the preceding chapter, classical skepticism and the modern theory of computability are reflections of the same sorts of limitations and give rise to similar demonic arguments and hierarchies of underdetermination. I will accordingly treat computational boundedness as a full partner with perceptual boundedness, rather than as an accidental afterthought.

2. Computation as Internalized Inductive Inquiry

Some hypotheses lie beyond the scope of limiting, computable inquiry, even though they are decidable with certainty by an ideal agent. Consider, for example, a problem in which the first datum is an encoded clue that gives the problem away to an ideal agent, but that is too hard for a computer to decode. More precisely, let $S \subseteq \omega$, and let $P_S = \{\varepsilon : \varepsilon_0 \in S\}$. Now let C, h be such that $C_h = P_S$. Intuitively, h says that the first observation will be in S, so the members of S are clues that permit an ideal scientist to decide$_C$ h by time 1 (Fig. 7.2).

Now consider the following question. How does the purely computational complexity of S relate to the ability of a computer to decide$_C$ the truth value

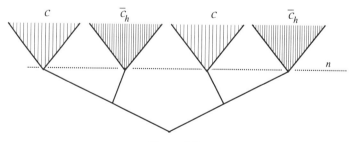

Figure 7.2

of h? If S is recursive, then a computer can succeed with certainty after scanning just the first datum, just like an ideal scientist. The computer uses its computable decision procedure to decide whether the first datum is in or out of S, and conjectures 1 or 0 forever after, accordingly.

Now suppose $S \in \Sigma_1^A - \Pi_1^A$. Then no computable method α can decide h with sample size 1, for otherwise α could be used as a decision procedure for S, contrary to assumption: to determine whether $n \in S$, feed $\alpha(h, \_)$ the sequence $n, 0, 0, 0, \ldots$ until the first '!' is returned and output the subsequent conjecture of α. On the other hand, some computable method α can verify h with certainty. This method simulates a positive test M for S for several steps on ε_1 every time a new datum arrives. α outputs 0 until M halts with 1, and outputs 1 thereafter. α treats membership in S as a kind of *internal* inductive problem that is, in fact, intrinsically harder than the ideal *external* empirical problem of deciding the truth of h. The required mind change is due entirely to the computational difficulty of this internal inductive question, rather than to the Borel complexity of $\mathcal{P}_S$ (*Fig. 7.3*). If $S \in \Pi_1^A$ and $C_h = \mathcal{P}_S$, then by similar reasoning, h can be refuted$_C$ with certainty by a computable scientist.

Suppose next that $S \in \Sigma_2^A - \Pi_2^A$. Then h cannot be decided$_C$ in the limit by a computable scientist. For suppose otherwise. Then we can construct a limiting recursive test M for S using the computable scientist α, as follows. To test $n \in \omega$, M feeds $\alpha(h, \_)$ the sequence $n, 0, 0, 0, \ldots$, which is clearly an effective task. Each time α makes an output, M makes the same output. Since α stabilizes to 1 if h is correct and to 0 otherwise, M stabilizes to 1 if $n \in S$ and to 0 otherwise, and hence is a limiting recursive test for S. But this is impossible by proposition 6.1. On the other hand, some computer can verify h in the limit by once again treating S as an internal inductive inference problem. Since $S \in \Sigma_2^A$, S is limiting r.e., so S has a limiting positive test M, by proposition 6.1. Our effective scientist α just feeds ε_1 to M and then repeats the outputs of M, ignoring all further empirical evidence. Similar points can be made concerning gradual verification and refutation.

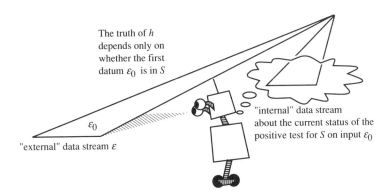

The truth of h depends only on whether the first datum ε_0 is in S

"internal" data stream about the current status of the positive test for S on input ε_0

ε_0

"external" data stream ε

Figure 7.3

3. The Arithmetical Hierarchy over the Baire Space

We have just seen that a very trivial inductive problem in the ideal sense can be arbitrarily hopeless for a computer to solve. The problem is that clues that give away an inductive problem to an ideal agent can generate inductive difficulties for a computer. But our study so far has been restricted to a very particular type of inductive problem in which ideal and computational considerations are kept neatly separate to make the point as clearly as possible. It remains to characterize just how these two kinds of complexity—ideal and computational—interact to determine whether or not an inductive problem is solvable by a computer. Once again, we need a way to describe the computational structure of a hypothesis in a way that makes no reference to computable scientists or to decision.

Recall that the Borel hierarchy provides a natural characterization of the complexity of ideal inductive inference, because it is based on the notion of empirical verifiability. We will now consider the *arithmetical hierarchy of sets of functions*, built on the notion of empirical verifiability by a computer. This hierarchy will provide a natural setting for the characterization of the computational complexity of inductive inference.

Recall that a correctness relation $C(\varepsilon, h)$ is a relation of mixed type, holding between data streams (type 2 objects) and code numbers of hypotheses (type 1 objects). In general, a relation S might have any number of type 1 and type 2 arguments. For example, $S(\varepsilon, \tau, n, k)$ has two type 2 arguments and two type 1 arguments. In general, we say that S is of *type* (k, n) just in case it has k arguments of type 2 and n arguments of type 1. We will define arithmetical complexity all at once for relations of all types (k, n), not out of a misplaced love of generality, but because it makes the inductive definition easier to state. The arithmetical hierarchy defined in the preceding chapter will turn out to be a special case, in which only relations of type $(0, n)$ are considered.

In the case of ordinary computation, the base of the hierarchy is the set of recursive relations of type $(0, n)$. But now our relations have infinite data streams as arguments. How do we interpret a Turing machine as accepting an infinite input? The trick is to provide the machine with an extra input tape for each infinite input stream. But it might be objected that the machine still cannot read the whole infinite sequence written on the tape prior to making an output. That is correct, but it doesn't matter. A decision procedure is still required to output 1 or 0 after a finite amount of time, just as in the case of finite inputs. It follows that the decision procedure must extract whatever information it requires for an answer after scanning only some finite chunk of the infinite input tape carrying ε.[2]

With this picture in mind, we see that our previous definitions of decision procedure, positive test, limiting positive test, and so on all apply to the case of relations of type (k, n), so long as the procedure in question is provided with a separate tape for each infinite input. In particular, a *decision procedure* for a

---

[2] In the theory of computability, this is sometimes referred to as the *use principle*.

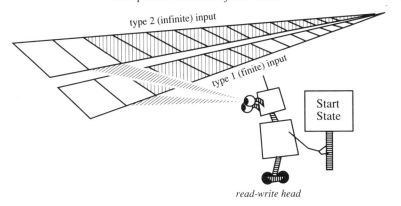

type 2 (infinite) input

type 1 (finite) input

Start State

read-write head

Figure 7.4

relation S of type (k, n) is a Turing machine that when provided with finite arguments in the usual way and with a separate tape for each of the k infinite arguments in the manner just described eventually halts with 1 if S holds of the inputs, and with 0 otherwise. S is said to be *recursive* just in case it has a decision procedure (*Fig. 7.4*).

It is straightforward to extend the arithmetical hierarchy defined in the preceding chapter to relations of mixed type. Let S be a type (k, m) relation. To eliminate tedious repetitions and subscripts, let $\bar{x}$ denote an n-vector of natural numbers and let $\bar{\varepsilon}$ denote a k-vector of data streams, so that we may write $S(\bar{\varepsilon}, \bar{x})$ instead of $S(\varepsilon[1], \dots, \varepsilon[k], x_1, \dots, x_m)$, where each $\varepsilon[i] \in \mathcal{N}$.

$S \in \Sigma_0^A \Leftrightarrow S$ *is recursive.*

$S \in \Sigma_{n+1}^A \Leftrightarrow$ *there is some type $(k, m + 1)$ relation $\mathcal{V} \in \Sigma_n^A$ such that for each $\bar{\varepsilon} \in \mathcal{N}^k$, $\bar{x} \in \omega^m$, $S(\bar{\varepsilon}, \bar{x}) \Leftrightarrow \exists x_{m+1}$ such that $\neg \mathcal{V}(\bar{\varepsilon}, \bar{x}, x_{m+1})$.*

The Π_n^A classes and the ambiguous Δ_n^A classes are defined in terms of Σ_0^A in the usual way.

To illustrate the relationship between this hierarchy and the finite Borel hierarchy, we can extend the latter notion to cover relations of mixed type. Let $\mathfrak{T}_1, \dots, \mathfrak{T}_n$ be topological spaces with countable bases $B_1, \dots, B_n$, respectively. The *product space* $\mathfrak{T}_1 \times \cdots \times \mathfrak{T}_n$ then has the basis $B_1 \times \cdots \times B_n$. Now consider the space $\mathcal{N}^k \times \omega^n$. Each space $\mathcal{N}$ carries the Baire topology, and we will think of ω as having the *discrete topology*, in which each singleton $\{n\}$ is a basic open set. This choice is not arbitrary. Basic open sets correspond in our application to what is directly input to the inductive method at a given stage of inquiry. In the Baire space, finite chunks of data are given and, in hypothesis assessment, we assume that discrete hypotheses are given to be investigated.

Thus, each singleton $\{h\}$ should be basic open.[3] Accordingly, a basic open set in $\mathcal{N}^k \times \omega^n$ is a cross product of k fans and n singletons containing natural numbers. Now the definition of the finite Borel hierarchy can be rephrased so as to mimic the definition of the arithmetical hierarchy. Let S be of type (k, m). Then we have:

$$S \in \Sigma_0^B \Leftrightarrow S \text{ is clopen in } \mathcal{N}^k \times \omega^m.$$

$$S \in \Sigma_{n+1}^B \Leftrightarrow \text{ there is some type } (k, m+1) \text{ relation } \mathcal{V} \in \Sigma_n^B \text{ such that}$$
$$\text{for each } \bar{\varepsilon} \in \mathcal{N}^k, \ \bar{x} \in \omega^m,$$
$$S(\bar{\varepsilon}, \bar{x}) \Leftrightarrow \exists x_{m+1} \text{ such that } \neg \mathcal{V}(\bar{\varepsilon}, \bar{x}, x_{m+1}).$$

The crucial point for our purposes is that this definition of *ideal* complexity differs from the preceding definition of *computational* complexity only in the base case. I will refer to this as the *new sense* of the Borel hierarchy until I show that it agrees with the one defined in chapter 4 over type $(1, 0)$ relations.

The discrete topology on ω causes the structure of the type 1 part of a mixed type relation to wash out of its Borel complexity classification in the following sense:

Proposition 7.1

Let S be of type (k, n). Let $S_{\bar{x}} = \{\bar{\varepsilon}: S(\bar{\varepsilon}, \bar{x})\}$. Then $S \in \Sigma_n^B$ (in the new sense) $\Leftrightarrow$ for each $\bar{x} \in \omega^n$, $S_{\bar{x}} \in \Sigma_n^B$ (in the new sense). ∎

It follows from this fact that the new version of the Borel hierarchy agrees with the old on type $(1, 0)$ relations, so we needn't distinguish the two senses any longer for subsets of $\mathcal{N}$.

Proposition 7.2

Let $S \subseteq \mathcal{N}$. Then S is Σ_n^B in the old sense $\Leftrightarrow$ S is Σ_n^B in the new sense. ∎

In light of proposition 7.2, the arithmetical hierarchy over $\mathcal{N}$ is sometimes referred to as the *effective, finite Borel hierarchy*. It follows from proposition

---

[3] If, on the other hand, hypotheses were parametrized by a real-valued parameter θ, then it might be impossible to give one to a method except by specifying ever narrower intervals around it. In that case, the set of hypotheses would also carry a nontrivial topology in which basic open sets are intervals with rational-valued endpoints. Each singleton containing a hypothesis would then be closed but not open. In such a setting, determining which hypothesis one is supposed to investigate can be as hard as determining the truth of that hypothesis from data, so ideal inquiry becomes more analogous to computable inquiry in this respect.

7.2 and the fact that the base case of the arithmetical hierarchy is at least as stringent as the base case of the Borel hierarchy, that membership in an arithmetical complexity class implies membership in the corresponding Borel complexity class. The example at the beginning of this section makes it clear that all the inclusions are proper (just insert arbitrarily complex subsets of ω in for S in the example). Thus:

Proposition 7.3

For each n, $\Sigma_n^A \subset \Sigma_n^B$. ∎

Proposition 7.1 explains why we could characterize the scope of ideal inquiry in terms of the topological complexities of each C_h, instead of in terms of C as a relation, since the Borel complexity of C is entirely determined by the complexities of each C_h. But when we move to the computable case, the complexity of C can be arbitrarily high even when the computational complexity of each C_h is trivial. For the simplest example, consider $C(\varepsilon, h) \Leftrightarrow h \in X$, where X is some arbitrarily hard to decide subset of ω. Here, correctness does not depend on the data at all, so any particular hypothesis can be decided a priori by a method with a fixed conjecture. Nonetheless, the difficulty of matching the right a priori conjecture with the right hypothesis prevents a single computable method from assessing all hypotheses in ω.

The failure of proposition 7.1 in the computational case means that computable inquiry must be characterized in terms of the arithmetical complexity of the entire correctness relation C, rather than pointwise, in terms of each C_h, as in the ideal case. It also means that both the scientist's background assumptions $\mathcal{K}$ and the range H of hypotheses he might have to assess are relevant to the complexity of his problem. Accordingly, we must relativize arithmetical complexity both to $\mathcal{K}$ and to H.

$$S \in \Sigma[\mathcal{K}, H]_n^A \Leftrightarrow \exists \mathcal{V} \in \Sigma_n^A \text{ such that } \forall \bar{\varepsilon} \in \mathcal{K}^k,\ \bar{x} \in H^n,$$
$$S(\bar{\varepsilon}, \bar{x}) \Leftrightarrow \mathcal{V}(\bar{\varepsilon}, \bar{x}).$$

4. Universal Relations and Hierarchy Theorems

It will be shown in this section that the Borel and arithmetical hierarchies are genuinely hierarchies, in the sense that each complexity class contains hypotheses not contained in any lower complexity class. The proof will be based on a way of assigning indices to all the problems in a given Σ_n^A class by means of a *universal relation* for the class. The idea of a universal relation depends essentially on the notion of encoding finite sequences of numbers and finite sequences of data streams. Let $\langle\ \rangle$ be a 1–1, effective encoding of ω^* into ω, so that $\langle e \rangle$ is a code number for e. We may also encode a finite vector of data streams into a single data stream using the same encoding. Let $\bar{\varepsilon} = (\varepsilon[1], \ldots, \varepsilon[n])$. Define:

$$\langle \bar{\varepsilon} \rangle = (\langle \varepsilon[1]_0, \ldots, \varepsilon[n]_0 \rangle, \langle \varepsilon[1]_1, \ldots, \varepsilon[n]_1 \rangle, \ldots,$$
$$\langle \varepsilon[1]_m, \ldots, \varepsilon[n]_m \rangle, \ldots).$$

In other words, $\langle \bar{\varepsilon} \rangle_m = \langle \varepsilon[1]_m, \ldots, \varepsilon[n]_m \rangle$, for each $m \in \omega$.

The *Turing relation* $\mathcal{T}(i, \langle \bar{\varepsilon} \rangle, \langle \bar{x} \rangle, k)$ is to be understood as saying that machine M_i halts on inputs $\bar{\varepsilon}, \bar{x}$ within k steps of computation.[4] This relation is recursive by Church's thesis since it is a straightforward matter to decode i, $\langle \bar{\varepsilon} \rangle$, and $\langle \bar{x} \rangle$ and to simulate the computation $M_i[\bar{\varepsilon}, \bar{x}]$ for k steps, observing whether the computation halts by that time. Let $\mathcal{U}$ be a type $(1, 2)$ relation. Now define:

$\mathcal{U}$ *is universal for complexity class* $\Theta \Leftrightarrow$

(1) $\mathcal{U} \in \Theta$ *and*

(2) *for each* $S \in \Theta$, *there is an* i *such that for all* $\bar{\varepsilon}, \bar{x}$,
$S(\bar{\varepsilon}, \bar{x}) \Leftrightarrow \mathcal{U}(i, \langle \bar{\varepsilon} \rangle, \langle \bar{x} \rangle).$

In other words, for each $S \in \Theta$, there is an index i such that $S = \{(\bar{\varepsilon}, \bar{x}): \mathcal{U}(i, \langle \bar{\varepsilon} \rangle, \langle \bar{x} \rangle)\}$. The question now is whether there exists a universal relation for each complexity class Σ_n^A. One candidate is defined inductively as follows:

$$\mathcal{U}_1^A(i, \langle \bar{\varepsilon} \rangle, \langle \bar{x} \rangle) \Leftrightarrow \exists k \text{ such that } \mathcal{T}(i, \langle \bar{\varepsilon} \rangle, \langle \bar{x} \rangle, k).$$
$$\mathcal{U}_{n+1}^A(i, \langle \bar{\varepsilon} \rangle, \langle \bar{x} \rangle) \Leftrightarrow \exists k \text{ such that } \neg \mathcal{U}_n^A(i, \langle \bar{\varepsilon} \rangle, \langle \bar{x}, k \rangle).$$

$\mathcal{U}_n^A$ is a type $(1, 2)$ relation. The inductive clause follows the usual mechanism for building complexity in our hierarchies: existential quantification and negation. The trick is that the existential quantifier is added without adding to the arity of the relation at the lower level by means of coding the bound variable k into $\langle \bar{x}, k \rangle$. Since the coding is 1–1, it does not "erase" any extra complexity added by the quantifier. Now we have:

Proposition 7.4   The arithmetical indexing theorem[5]

(a) *For each* $n \geq 1$, $\mathcal{U}_n^A$ *is universal for* Σ_n^A.

(b) *For each* $n \geq 1$, $\overline{\mathcal{U}_n^A}$ *is universal for* Π_n^A.

---

[4] There is no ambiguity about the arities of $\bar{\varepsilon}$ and of $\bar{x}$ because the encoding $\langle \_ \rangle$ is 1–1 from ω^* to ω.

[5] The following two proofs follow Hinman (1978).

Proof: (a) (1) A simple induction establishes that $\mathcal{U}_n^A \in \Sigma_n^A$. (2) We now show that $\mathcal{U}_n^A$ indexes all Σ_n^A relations. *Base*: Suppose $S \in \Sigma_1^A$. Let M_i be a positive test for S. Then for all $\bar{\varepsilon}$, $\bar{x}$, $S(\bar{\varepsilon}, \bar{x}) \Leftrightarrow \exists k$ such that $\mathcal{T}(i, \langle \bar{\varepsilon} \rangle, \langle \bar{x} \rangle, k) \Leftrightarrow \mathcal{U}_1^A(i, \langle \bar{\varepsilon} \rangle, \langle \bar{x} \rangle)$. *Induction*: Suppose the result for all $n' \leq n$. Let $S \in \Sigma_{n+1}^A$. Then for some $G \in \Sigma_n^A$, for all $\bar{\varepsilon}$, $\bar{x}$, $S(\bar{\varepsilon}, \bar{x}) \Leftrightarrow \exists k \, \neg G(\bar{\varepsilon}, \bar{x}, k)$. By the induction hypothesis there is some i such that for all $\bar{\varepsilon}$, $\bar{x}$, k, $G(\bar{\varepsilon}, \bar{x}, k) \Leftrightarrow \mathcal{U}_n^A(i, \langle \bar{\varepsilon} \rangle, \langle \bar{x}, k \rangle)$. Thus $S(\bar{\varepsilon}, \bar{x}) \Leftrightarrow \exists k \, \neg \mathcal{U}_n^A(i, \langle \bar{\varepsilon} \rangle, \langle \bar{x}, k \rangle)$. (b) is similar. ∎

Now it is not hard to see that there is always something new at each level in the hierarchy.

Proposition 7.5 The arithmetical hierarchy theorem

For each n, $\Delta_n^A \subset \Sigma_n^A$.

Proof: The inclusions are immediate. That they are proper is shown as follows. Define the diagonal relation

(a) $\mathcal{D}_n(x) \Leftrightarrow \mathcal{U}_n^A(x, \langle \, \rangle, \langle x \rangle)$,

where $\langle \, \rangle$ in the second argument position denotes the infinite sequence of code numbers for the empty vector $\mathbf{0}$. From the definition of $\mathcal{U}_n^A$ it is evident that $\mathcal{D}_n \in \Sigma_n^A$. Suppose $D_n \in \Delta_n^A$. Hence $\overline{\mathcal{D}_n} \in \Sigma_n^A$. Since $\mathcal{U}_n^A$ is universal for Σ_n^A (proposition 7.4), there is some b such that for all x,

(b) $\overline{\mathcal{D}_n}(x) \Leftrightarrow \mathcal{U}_n^A(b, \langle \, \rangle, \langle x \rangle)$.

So in particular,

(c) $\overline{\mathcal{D}_n}(b) \Leftrightarrow \mathcal{U}_n^A(b, \langle \, \rangle, \langle b \rangle)$.

But by (a),

(d) $\mathcal{D}_n(b) \Leftrightarrow \mathcal{U}_n^A(b, \langle \, \rangle, \langle b \rangle)$.

Thus by (d) and (c),

$$\overline{\mathcal{D}_n}(b) \Leftrightarrow \mathcal{D}_n(b),$$

which is a contradiction. ∎

All the complexity exhibited by $\mathcal{U}_n^A$ is computational, since the diagonalization is based entirely on numeric arguments rather than on infinite data streams. We know that Borel complexity is a lower bound on arithmetical complexity, so it would be very useful to be able to see how to build arbitrary complexity through diagonalization in the Borel hierarchy as well. It is thus useful at this

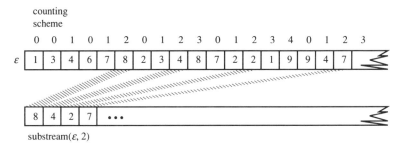

Figure 7.5

point to examine the proof of the analogous result for the finite Borel hierarchy, which was announced without proof as proposition 4.9. The argument is due to K. Kuratowski.[6] Once again, we proceed in two steps, constructing a universal relation for finite Borel classes and then diagonalizing to show that the hierarchy does not collapse.

Since there are already uncountably many open subsets of $\mathcal{N}$ (just think of all the ways of taking countable unions of disjoint fans), we cannot use natural numbers as indices as we did in the computational case. Kuratowski's idea was to use data streams as indices for Borel sets. Let ε be a data stream. Count off positions in ε according to the following fixed and effective pattern: $0; 0, 1; 0, 1, 2; \ldots 0, 1, 2, \ldots, n; \ldots$. Then *substream*$(\varepsilon, n)$ is just the subsequence of ε whose positions are marked with n when we label successive positions in ε according to this fixed counting scheme (*Fig. 7.5*). Clearly, for each ω-sequence Ψ of data streams, there is a unique data stream ε such that for each n, $\Psi_n = substream(\varepsilon, n)$: simply write the ith data stream listed in Ψ_n into the positions labeled i in the standard counting scheme. Now we may define the following candidate for a universal relation for Σ_n^B:

$$\mathcal{U}_1^B(\tau, \varepsilon) \Leftrightarrow \exists i \in \omega \text{ such that } \tau_i = \langle e \rangle \text{ and } \varepsilon \in [e].$$

$$\mathcal{U}_{n+1}^B(\tau, \varepsilon) \Leftrightarrow \exists i \text{ such that } \neg \mathcal{U}_n^B (substream(\tau, i), \varepsilon).$$

Proposition 7.6 Borel indexing theorem

(a) *For each* $n \geq 1$, $\mathcal{U}_n^B$ *is universal for* Σ_n^B.

(b) *For each* $n \geq 1$, $\overline{\mathcal{U}_n^B}$ *is universal for* Π_n^B.

Proof: (a) A simple induction establishes that $\mathcal{U}_n^B \in \Sigma_n^B$. *Base*: Let $G \subseteq \mathcal{N}$ be Σ_1^B. Then for some $G \subseteq \omega^*$, G is the union of all fans $[e]$ such that $e \in G$. Let τ be an enumeration of the code numbers of elements of G. Then $\varepsilon \in G \Leftrightarrow \mathcal{U}_1^B(\tau, \varepsilon)$. *Induction*: Suppose $G \in \Sigma_{n+1}^B$. Then G is a countable union of sets $\neg S_0 \cup \neg S_1 \cup \neg S_2 \cup \ldots$ such that each $S_i \in \Sigma_n^B$. By the induction hypothesis, for each S_i, there is a data stream $\tau[i]$ such that $S_i = \{\varepsilon : \mathcal{U}_n^B(\tau[i], \varepsilon)\}$.

---

[6] Kuratowski (1966): 368–371.

Construct τ so that for each i, $\tau[i] = substream(\tau, i)$. Then $\varepsilon \in G \Leftrightarrow \exists i \; \varepsilon \notin S_i \Leftrightarrow$ $\exists i \; \neg \; \mathcal{U}_n^B(\tau[i], \varepsilon) \Leftrightarrow \exists i \; \neg \; \mathcal{U}_n^B(substream(\tau, i), \varepsilon) \Leftrightarrow \mathcal{U}_{n+1}^B(\tau, \varepsilon)$. (b) is similar. ∎

The Borel hierarchy theorem (proposition 4.9) can now be established by diagonalization on $\mathcal{U}_n^B$, just as in the arithmetical case:

Proposition 7.7 Borel hierarchy theorem

For each n, $\Delta_n^B \subset \Sigma_n^B$. ∎

We now have two powerful techniques for constructing an inductive problem with arbitrarily high ideal or computational complexity when $\mathcal{K} = \mathcal{N}$ and $H = \omega$. Of course, restrictions on $\mathcal{K}$ and H can collapse the hierarchy to some finite level. For example, if $\mathcal{K} = \{\varepsilon\}$, then every subset of $\mathcal{K}$ is $\Delta[\mathcal{K}]_1^B$. The general question of how the hierarchy theorems depend on $\mathcal{K}$ and H is an interesting and important one that lies beyond the scope of this book.[7]

5. Characterization Theorems

The characterizations for the effective case look very much like the characterizations for the ideal case, except that the Borel hierarchy on $\mathcal{N}$ is exchanged for the arithmetical hierarchy on $\mathcal{N}$. As it turns out, very few modifications of the proofs given for the ideal case are necessary. First, all the basic correspondences established for ideal agents in chapter 3 hold in the computable case as well.

Proposition 7.8

(a) *H is verifiable$_C$* $\begin{bmatrix} with\ certainty \\ in\ the\ limit \\ gradually \end{bmatrix}$ *by a Turing machine given $\mathcal{K}$*

$\Leftrightarrow$ *H is refutable$_{\bar{C}}$* $\begin{bmatrix} with\ certainty \\ in\ the\ limit \\ gradually \end{bmatrix}$ *by a Turing machine given $\mathcal{K}$.*

(b) *H is decidable$_C$* $\begin{bmatrix} with\ certainty \\ in\ the\ limit \end{bmatrix}$ *by a Turing machine given $\mathcal{K}$*

$\Leftrightarrow$ *H is both verifiable$_C$ and refutable$_C$ by a Turing machine given $\mathcal{K}$.*

(c) *H is decidable$_C$ with n mind changes starting with 1 by a Turing machine given $\mathcal{K}$ $\Leftrightarrow$ H is decidable$_{\bar{C}}$ with n mind changes starting with 0 by a Turing machine given $\mathcal{K}$.*

---

[7] Some ideas about this issue may be found in Moschavakis (1980).

(d) *For each r such that $0 < r < 1$, H is decidable$_C$ with n mind changes starting with r $\Leftrightarrow$ H is decidable$_C$ with n mind changes starting with 0 by a Turing machine given $\mathcal{K}$ and H is decidable$_C$ with n mind changes starting with 1 by a Turing machine given $\mathcal{K}$.*

∎

Now the characterizations of reliable inquiry by Turing-computable agents may be stated as follows:

Proposition 7.9[8]

(a) *H is* $\begin{bmatrix} verifiable_C \\ refutable_C \\ decidable_C \end{bmatrix}$ *with certainty by a Turing machine given $\mathcal{K}$*

$$\Leftrightarrow C \cap (\mathcal{K} \times H) \in \begin{bmatrix} \Sigma[\mathcal{K}, H]_1^A \\ \Pi[\mathcal{K}, H]_1^A \\ \Delta[\mathcal{K}, H]_1^A \end{bmatrix}.$$

(b) *H is* $\begin{bmatrix} verifiable_C \\ refutable_C \\ decidable_C \end{bmatrix}$ *in the limit by a Turing machine given $\mathcal{K}$*

$$\Leftrightarrow C \cap (\mathcal{K} \times H) \in \begin{bmatrix} \Sigma[\mathcal{K}, H]_2^A \\ \Pi[\mathcal{K}, H]_2^A \\ \Delta[\mathcal{K}, H]_2^A \end{bmatrix}.$$

(c) *H is* $\begin{bmatrix} verifiable_C \\ refutable_C \\ decidable_C \end{bmatrix}$ *gradually by a Turing machine given $\mathcal{K}$*

$$\Leftrightarrow C \cap (\mathcal{K} \times H) \in \begin{bmatrix} \Pi[\mathcal{K}, H]_3^A \\ \Sigma[\mathcal{K}, H]_3^A \\ \Delta[\mathcal{K}, H]_2^A \end{bmatrix}.$$

Proof: By proposition 7.8, we need consider only the verification case of each statement, except for the case of gradual decidability, which follows from (b) along the lines of proposition 3.13(b). It is convenient to treat the ($\Rightarrow$) side of all three statements together. (a) If computable α verifies H with certainty given $\mathcal{K}$, then we have for all $\varepsilon \in \mathcal{K}$, $h \in H$,

$$C(\varepsilon, h) \Leftrightarrow \exists n [\alpha(h, \varepsilon | n) = \text{'!'} \, \& \, \alpha(h, \varepsilon | n + 1) = 1 \quad \text{and}$$
$$\forall m < n, \alpha(h, \varepsilon | m) \neq \text{'!'}].$$

---

[8] (a) and (b) are in Gold (1965).

Since α is total recursive, the relation in square brackets is recursive. Hence,

$$C(\varepsilon, h) \cap (\mathcal{K} \times H) \in \Sigma[\mathcal{K}, H]_1^A.$$

(b) If computable α verifies H in the limit given $\mathcal{K}$, then we have for all $\varepsilon \in \mathcal{K}$, $h \in H$,

$$C(\varepsilon, h) \Leftrightarrow \forall n \, \exists m \geq n \, \alpha(h, \varepsilon|m) = 1.$$

Since $\alpha(h, \varepsilon|m)$ is a recursive relation, we have $C(\varepsilon, h) \cap (\mathcal{K} \times H) \in \Sigma[\mathcal{K}, H]_2^A$.
(c) If computable α verifies H gradually given $\mathcal{K}$, then we have for all $\varepsilon \in \mathcal{K}$, and for all $h \in H$,

$$C(\varepsilon, h) \Leftrightarrow \forall \text{ rational } r > 0 \, \exists n \, \forall m \geq n \, 1 - \alpha(h, \varepsilon|m) < r,$$

so $C(\varepsilon, h) \cap (\mathcal{K} \times H) \in \Pi([\mathcal{K}, H]_3^A$, since the rationals may be effectively encoded 1–1 by natural numbers.

($\Leftarrow$) All we do is to show that the universal architectures introduced in chapter 5 can be implemented on Turing machines whenever C has the corresponding arithmetical complexity. (a) is immediate.

(b) Suppose $C \cap (\mathcal{K} \times H) \in \Sigma[\mathcal{K}, H]_2^A$. Then there is some co-r.e. relation G such that for each $\varepsilon \in \mathcal{N}$, $h \in H$, $C(\varepsilon, h) \Leftrightarrow \exists n \, G(\varepsilon, h, n)$. Let M be a refutation procedure for G. Then we implement an effective version of the bumping pointer architecture using M. Let $h \in H$ be given. On the empty data sequence $\mathbf{0}$, the method α outputs 0. When $e \neq \mathbf{0}$, define:

$$pointer(h, e) = \begin{cases} \text{the least } i \leq lh(e) \\ \quad \text{such that } M[e, h, i] \text{ does not return } 0 \text{ in } lh(e) \text{ steps,} \\ \quad \text{if there is such an } i \\ lh(e) \text{ otherwise.} \end{cases}$$

The pointer is clearly recursive. Now let $\alpha(h, \mathbf{0}) = 1$ and define:

$$\alpha(h, e*x) = \begin{cases} 1 & \text{if } pointer(h, e) = pointer(h, e*x) \\ 0 & \text{otherwise.} \end{cases}$$

On data e, the pointer is moved to the least $i \leq lh(e)$ such that $M[e, h, i]$ does not return 0 in $lh(e)$ steps if there is one and to $lh(e)$ otherwise. Then the pointer is moved to the least $i \leq lh(e)$ such that $M[e*x, h, i]$ does not return 0 in $lh(e)$ steps if there is one, and to $lh(e) + 1$ otherwise. If this position is different from the previous one, α conjectures 0. Otherwise, α conjectures 1 (*Fig. 7.6*).

It is readily seen that this procedure is computable. It is left to the reader to verify that it works.

(c) Suppose $C \cap (\mathcal{K} \times H) \in \Pi[\mathcal{K}, H]_3^A$. Then for some $\Sigma[\mathcal{K}, H]_2^A$ relation G, we have for each $\varepsilon \in \mathcal{K}$, $h \in H$, $C(\varepsilon, h) \Leftrightarrow \forall n \, G(\varepsilon, h, n)$. By an argument similar

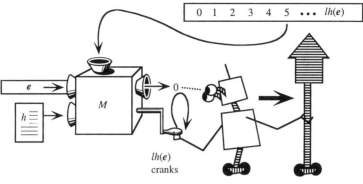

Figure 7.6

to the preceding, we obtain a single machine M that for each fixed n, $M[h, e, n]$ is a limiting verifier for $G(\varepsilon, h, n)$. Since M is total, we can dispense with crank counting. On inputs e, h, our method α simulates M for $n = 0, 1, \ldots, lh(e)$, and then counts how many successive 1s starting from position 0 are in the sequence $M[e, h, 0], M[e, h, 1], \ldots, M[e, h, lh(e)]$. Call this number k. Then α conjectures $1 - 2^{-k}$ (*Fig. 7.7*).

Again, it is clear that this procedure is computable, and the verification of correctness is left to the reader.   ∎

Proposition 7.9 vindicates the promise in chapter 1 that the reliabilist approach to method provides a seamless analogy between computable and ideal methodology. The characterizations listed under proposition 7.9 are almost identical to the ideal characterizations, except that arithmetical complexity requires computable decidability in its base case whereas Borel complexity demands only ideal decidability. Moreover, the complete computable architectures introduced in the proof are but minor variants of the ideal methods seen in the preceding chapter.

The analogy can be carried through for decision with n mind changes as well. First we must introduce an effective version of the finite difference hierarchy, which will be denoted d. The d hierarchy is defined just like

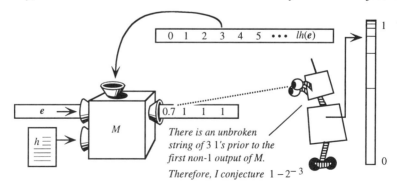

Figure 7.7

the D hierarchy, except that we substitute $\mathcal{K}$-r.e. sets and their complements for $\mathcal{K}$-open sets and $\mathcal{K}$-closed sets, respectively. Now we may state the characterization:

Proposition 7.10

For all r such that $0 < r < 1$, H is decidable$_C$ with n mind changes

starting with $\begin{bmatrix} 0 \\ 1 \\ r \end{bmatrix}$ *by a Turing machine given $\mathcal{K}$*

$$\Leftrightarrow C \cap (\mathcal{K} \times H) \in \begin{bmatrix} \Sigma[\mathcal{K}, H]_n^d \\ \Pi[\mathcal{K}, H]_n^d \\ \Delta[\mathcal{K}, H]_n^d \end{bmatrix}.$$

Proof: Exercise 7.4. ∎

The tools developed so far place us in a good position to compare ideal underdetermination to its computationally bounded counterpart. For example, we now know that each computationally underdetermined problem involves two components: a purely topological component reflective of purely empirical (or "external") underdetermination, together with a purely computational component reflective of formal (or "internal") underdetermination. Different problems partake of different mixtures of these two factors. For example, when $C_h = \mathcal{P}_S$ (i.e., the set of all data streams whose first data points are in S), the topological complexity of C_h is trivial, but the computational complexity of C_h can be arbitrarily high, depending on the nature of S (i.e., $S \in \Delta_1^B - \Sigma_n^A$, where n may be as high as we please). On the other hand, in some problems, virtually all the computational difficulty is topological. This is true of the infinite divisibility hypothesis, which is in $\Pi_2^A - \Sigma_2^B$, so there is no gap at all between the abilities of ideal and computable scientists so far as this problem is concerned. Other problems involve some intermediate mixture of the two factors. We will consider an interesting example of such a problem in section 7 of this chapter.

6. Data-Minimal Computable Methods

Chapter 4 presented the surprising result that every solvable limiting verification problem has a data-minimal solution. A natural question is whether computationally bounded inquiry can boast the same result. One might worry in this regard that the universal architecture for limiting verification tests a co-r.e. subset of C_h for just a bounded number of steps before pausing and asking for the next datum. This business of letting formal analysis pile up on the desk while new data comes in reflects the problem that there is no way to be sure

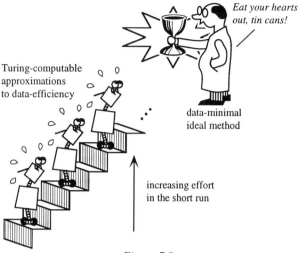

Figure 7.8

in the present that a proof of inconsistency between the data and a given co-r.e. set will never be found by computational means. Perhaps no matter how hard the computer works, there will in principle always be some computational backlog on its desk, so that a more industrious method that does more formal work at each stage converges to the truth sooner. Indeed, this is the case. Recall that $\mathcal{R} = \{\phi: \phi$ is total recursive$\}$ and let $\mathcal{P}_K = \{\varepsilon: \varepsilon_0 \in K\}$, where K is the halting problem (cf. chapter 6). Let $C_h = \mathcal{P}_K$. Then we have:

Proposition 7.11[9]

If $C_h = \mathcal{P}_K$ then $C_h \in \Sigma_1^A$ but no computable α is a weakly data-minimal limiting decider of h.

Proof: $C_h \in \Sigma_1^A$. Let computable α decide$_C$ h in the limit. There is an $\varepsilon \in \mathcal{N}$ such that $modulus_\alpha(\varepsilon) > 1$, else the computable function $\phi(x) = \alpha(h, (x))$ decides K. Suppose $\varepsilon \in \mathcal{P}_K$. Then $\varepsilon_0 \in K$. Define:

$$\beta(h, e) = \begin{cases} 1 & \text{if } e_0 = \varepsilon_0 \\ \alpha(h, e) & \text{otherwise.} \end{cases}$$

Now $modulus_\beta(h, \varepsilon) < modulus_\alpha(h, \varepsilon)$, but for all other data streams, β's modulus remains unchanged if the first datum is not ε_0, and β's modulus is improved if the first datum is ε_0. The case in which $\varepsilon \notin \mathcal{P}_K$ is similar. ∎

When it is impossible to avoid testing co-r.e. sets for consistency with the data, there is some ideal, data-minimal solution and a chain of ever better recursive approximations to data minimality that expend ever greater effort in finding refutation proofs in the short run (*Fig. 7.8*).

---

[9] This result is analogous to proposition 8.2.3.A in Osherson et al. (1986).

At the beginning of this chapter it was proposed that to regulate concrete action among bounded agents an ideal methodological norm should come with an argument to the effect that extra degrees of striving toward the ideal yield extra degrees of some value that exact achievement of the ideal would provide completely. Here we have exactly such a situation. A computable method may not be able to decide logical consistency with the data, but spending more time on the problem in the short run before examining the next datum may lead to a proof of refutation earlier and hence may sometimes lead to earlier convergence to the truth. Such a method must use some runtime bound to succeed at all, and hence can never duplicate the data-minimality of an ideal method; but increasing effort in the short run brings it ever closer to that unreachable ideal, so there is a reward for extra effort expended in the short run.

7. The Empirical Irony of Cognitive Science

A sentence h is *self defeating* when

> h *is true* $\Rightarrow$ h *is false.*

For example:

> *All sentences involving more than three words are false.*

A hypothesis h is *empirically self-defeating in the limit for us* just in case

> h *is true* $\Rightarrow$ h *is not verifiable in the limit by us.*

Are any hypotheses of independent interest empirically self-defeating? It turns out that the cognitivist hypothesis that human behavior is computable provides such an example! Recall that $C_{h_{comp}}$ is the set of all computable data streams in 2^{ω}. We have already seen by a demonic argument that h_{comp} is verifiable$_C$ but not decidable$_C$ in the limit by ideal scientists, so $C_{h_{comp}}$ is in $\Sigma_2^B - \Delta_2^B$. On the computational side, the basic result is:

Proposition 7.12

$C_{h_{comp}} \in \Sigma_3^A - \Pi_3^A.$

Proof: Rogers (1987): 327, theorem XVI. ∎

Hence:

> h_{comp} *is empirically self-defeating in the limit for us.*

For suppose that h_{comp} is true. Then human behavior is computable, and hence our inductive behavior is computable. So by proposition 7.12, we cannot verify$_C$ h_{comp} in the limit. If we are Turing computable, we cannot verify this fact in the limit because we are Turing computable. This result is interesting in its own right, but also because it illustrates a case in which the characterization theorem is useful in obtaining a negative result. A direct, demonic argument is not at all easy to provide in this case, as the reader may check (cf. exercise 7.13). A similar argument can be given if we replace verification in the limit with gradual verification (cf. exercise 7.6).

8. The Computable Assessment of Uncomputable Theories

Imagine an ideal scientist who investigates a complete, deterministic theory of a given system. So complete is this theory that it determines uniquely every future observation. We can imagine an ideal scientist who derives (without effort) successive predictions from the theory and then compares each of them with what is actually observed. In this way, the theory is eventually rejected by the scientist if and only if it misses a prediction.

Now suppose the scientist is a computer. The picture just described of sequentially obtaining new predictions from the theory then presupposes that the theory is computable, in the sense that its prediction for time n is a recursive function of n. We now face an important methodological question: Do the predictions of a theory have to be derivable from the theory by computable means if a computable method is to decide the truth value of the theory in the limit? Or do there exist theories whose predictions cannot be derived by computable means that can nonetheless be decided in the limit or even refuted with certainty by computable inductive methods?

In this discussion we will consider only hypotheses that make determinate predictions about each datum that will appear in the limit. Say that h is *empirically complete$_C$* just in case for some ε, $C_h = \{\varepsilon\}$. That is, there is a unique data stream for which h is correct. When $C_h = \{\varepsilon\}$, we know from the preceding characterization theorems that h is effectively verifiable in the limit just in case $\{\varepsilon\} \in \Sigma_2^A$. So we may think of the arithmetical complexity of $\{\varepsilon\}$ as the *inductive* or *scientific complexity* of h. But the hypothesis h also has a deductive complexity that corresponds to the computational difficulty of formally deriving predictions from h. We take the deductive complexity of h to be the arithmetical complexity of ε, where ε is identified with its graph: $\{(0, \varepsilon(0)), (1, \varepsilon(1)), \ldots\}$. It is easily verified that for any function ε, if ε is in Σ_1^A, then ε is partial recursive. If ε is also total, then ε is total recursive and $\varepsilon \in \Delta_1^A$. Since a data stream is assumed to be total, we have that $\varepsilon \in \Sigma_1^A$ if and only if $\varepsilon \in \Delta_1^A$.

To summarize, the deductive complexity of an empirically complete hypothesis h such that $C_h = \{\varepsilon\}$ is just the arithmetical complexity of ε, whereas the inductive or scientific complexity of h is just the arithmetical complexity of $\{\varepsilon\}$. It is striking that the essential difference between the nature of induction and the nature of deduction can be captured by the difference in arithmetical complexity between ε and $\{\varepsilon\}$! But the subtle difference in notation belies a world of difference between the two kinds of complexity, as will soon be apparent.

Now we may restate our question. How does the deductive complexity of h depend on the scientific complexity of h? In other words, how does the computational complexity of deriving predictions from h depend on the computational complexity of determining the truth value of h from data?

An ideal scientist can decide any empirically complete$_C$ h with one mind change starting with 1. We can see this two ways. First, we already know that each singleton $\{\varepsilon\}$ is Π_1^B, so the result follows from the ideal characterization theorem. More directly, consider an ideal scientist that checks (in an uncomputable manner) successive entries in ε against successive entries in the data stream, and says 1 until some discrepancy is found. On the other hand, a simple demonic argument shows that no ideal scientist can verify such a hypothesis with certainty. Thus we have:

Proposition 7.13

Let $h_C = \{\varepsilon\}$. Then

(a) *h is ideally refutable$_C$ with certainty.*

(b) *h is not ideally verifiable$_C$ with certainty (i.e., $\{\varepsilon\} \in \Pi_1^B - \Sigma_1^B$).* ■

A computable scientist can play the same game, provided that $\varepsilon \in \Sigma_1^A$ (and hence $\varepsilon \in \Delta_1^A$ since ε is total). For then, the computable scientist can compute the next position of ε and check the outcome of this computation against the data, waiting for a discrepancy. From these simple observations, we already know that:

Proposition 7.14

Let $h_C = \{\varepsilon\}$. Then if ε is recursive, then h is refutable$_C$ with certainty by a Turing machine (i.e., $\varepsilon \in \Sigma_1^A \Rightarrow \{\varepsilon\} \in \Pi_1^A$). ■

But in the other direction, we would expect that a highly intractable ε would pose problems for a computable scientist trying to investigate h. For suppose that ε is not recursive. Then there must be infinitely many predictions entailed by the theory $\{\varepsilon\}$ that an arbitrary, computable scientist fails to derive correctly, either by drawing a mistaken prediction that the theory does not actually entail or by failing to derive any prediction at all. For suppose otherwise. Then the procedure that fails to derive only finitely many predictions could be "patched" with a finite lookup table to provide a procedure that computes ε. If there is no background knowledge, then any underived prediction can be wrong for all the scientist knows. This leads one to suspect that h is not effectively refutable with certainty unless ε is computable. It is hard to see how to succeed otherwise, unless there is some miraculous method of rejecting a hypothesis if and only if it is false without deriving its successive predictions and checking them against

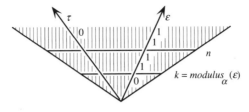

Figure 7.9

the data. As it turns out, the suspicion is correct in the special case in which h predicts only finitely many different kinds of outcomes. In fact, something much stronger is the case:

Proposition 7.15[10]

Let $h_C = \{\varepsilon\}$ and let $rng(\varepsilon)$ be finite. Then if h is verifiable$_C$ in the limit by a Turing machine, then ε is recursive (i.e., if $\{\varepsilon\} \in \Sigma_2^A$ then $\varepsilon \in \Delta_1^A$).

Proof: Suppose $rng(\varepsilon)$ is finite and recursive α verifies$_C h$ in the limit. Let $k = modulus_\alpha(\varepsilon)$. Thus, (*) for each $\tau \in rng(\varepsilon)^\omega$, we have that $\tau = \varepsilon \Leftrightarrow$ for each $m \geq k$, $\alpha(h, \varepsilon|m) = 1$. Think of $rng(\varepsilon)^*$ as an infinite but finitely branching tree in which ε is an infinite path. Each node in the tree may be labeled effectively with the conjecture $\alpha(h, e)$, where e is the unique path to that node from the root of the tree. Imagine that the tree is completely labeled. Then in virtue of (*), ε is the unique infinite path labeled with all 1s after position k. Say that a finite path e such that $lh(e) \leq m$ is *m-dead* just in case each extension of e of length m has a value less than 1 occurring on it between k and m. Then we have:

Lemma 7.16

If $n \geq k$ then for each $m \geq n$, $\varepsilon|n$ is not m-dead (Fig. 7.9).   ∎

Also, we have:

Lemma 7.17

If $n \geq k$ then there is some $m \geq n$ such that for each $e \in rng(\varepsilon)^n$ such that $e \neq \varepsilon|n$, e is m-dead.

Proof: Suppose $n \geq k$. Suppose for reductio that for all $m \geq n$, there is an $e \in rng(\varepsilon)^n$ such that $e \neq \varepsilon|n$ and e is not *m-dead*. Then for each m, there is an extension $e[m]$ of e of length m along which α conjectures only 1s for h. So $S = \{e[m]: m \geq n\}$ is an infinite, finitely branching tree. By König's lemma, S has an infinite path γ labeled entirely with 1s by α after position k. So by (*), $\gamma = \varepsilon$. Thus $e = \gamma|n = \varepsilon|n$, contrary to assumption.   ∎

[10] With Oliver Schulte.

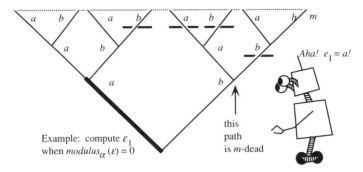

Figure 7.10

The procedure for computing ε is as follows. $M(n)$: Use α to effectively label the tree, from bottom to top, level by level, until for some m, the tree is labeled up to level m, and it is effectively verified (by exhaustion) that there is a unique path e of length n that is not m-dead. (By lemmas 1 and 2, $e = \varepsilon | n$). Return $e_n(=\varepsilon_n)$ (*Fig. 7.10*). ■

So now we know that if an empirically complete hypothesis h is effectively verifiable in the limit, then its predictions are computable, so long as it predicts only finitely many different kinds of events.

On the other hand, there is a hypothesis h predicting only finitely many different sorts of outcomes that can be refuted in the limit by a Turing machine even though its predictions are infinitely impossible to derive by computational means. At first blush, this seems like magic. By assumption, it is hopeless to expect a scientist to recover correctly all the predictions of h by computational means, and since there is no background knowledge, the demon can arrange the data to agree with any mistaken prediction the scientist derives. What could h be like? The answer is given in the following proof.

Proposition 7.18 (Hilbert and Bernays)[11]

There are C, h, ε such that $C_h = \{\varepsilon\}$ and for each n, $C_h \notin \Sigma_n^A$ but h is refutable$_C$ in the limit by a Turing machine (i.e., there is an ε such that for each n, $\varepsilon \notin \Sigma_n^A$ but $\{\varepsilon\} \in \Pi_2^A$).

Proof: Recall the universal relation $\mathcal{U}_n^A$ defined in section 7.4. Consider the characteristic function of $\mathcal{U}_n^A$:

$$v(\langle n, i, \bar{x}\rangle) = \begin{cases} 1 & \text{if } \mathcal{U}_n^A(i, \langle\rangle, \langle\bar{x}\rangle) \\ 0 & \text{otherwise.} \end{cases}$$

Recall from the hierarchy theorem that $\mathcal{D}_n \notin \Delta_n^A$. But v is at least as complex as

[11] Cf. Hinman (1978): 106–107.

$\mathcal{D}_n$ because for each z, $\mathcal{D}_n(z) \Leftrightarrow v(\langle n, i, \langle z \rangle \rangle) = 1$, where i is such that $\mathcal{D}_n(z) \Leftrightarrow \mathcal{U}_n^A(i, \langle \rangle, \langle z \rangle)$, by universality. It remains to show that $\{v\} \in \Pi_2^B$. A simple induction shows that

$\varepsilon = v \Leftrightarrow$

(a) $\forall k \in \omega, \varepsilon_k \leq 1$ *and*

(b) $\forall i \in \omega, \bar{x} \in \omega^*[\varepsilon(\langle 1, i, \bar{x} \rangle) = 1 \Leftrightarrow \exists k \mathcal{T}(i, \langle \rangle, \langle \bar{x} \rangle, k)]$ *and*

(c) $\forall n, i \in \omega, \bar{x} \in \omega^*[\varepsilon(\langle n + 1, i, \bar{x} \rangle) = 1$
$\qquad\qquad \Leftrightarrow \exists k$ *such that* $\varepsilon(\langle n, i, \langle \bar{x}, k \rangle \rangle) = 0]$

Condition (a) says that ε is a characteristic function, condition (b) duplicates condition (1) of the definition of $\mathcal{U}_n^A$, and condition (c) duplicates condition (2) of the definition of $\mathcal{U}_n^A$. Hence, $\{v\} \in \Pi_2^B$. ■

The curious hypothesis introduced in the proof of the proposition can be re-described in a more intuitive manner. Let V denote the set of all code numbers of truths of arithmetic. It turns out[12] that v is computationally equivalent to the problem of deciding V, so the hypothesis that a given black box yields a complete proof system for arithmetic is refutable in the limit by a computable method.

This point is relevant to a celebrated debate about the computational nature of mind. J. R. Lucas (1961) concludes from Gödel's theorem that humans cannot be computers since humans can always "intuit" the truth of the Gödel sentence for a consistent formal system, but each consistent formal system has a Gödel sentence that is true but that is not entailed by the system. In chapter 3, I argued that the real question is empirical, namely, whether human behavior is actually as claimed. The hypothesis involved in proposition 8.4 may be thought of as Lucas's hypothesis that a given human is an enumerator of the complete arithmetical truth. The correct resolution of the empirical issue is that the hypothesis is ideally refutable with certainty and effectively refutable in the limit.

The logical trick behind proposition 7.1 is that recursion on a function variable can simulate arbitrary alterations of numeric quantifiers, thereby building arbitrary arithmetical complexity into a single definition. To see how arbitrary arithmetical complexity can be unwound from the definition of v, consider the case of $v(\langle 4, i, \bar{x} \rangle)$. Each time the recursive clause (c) in the definition of v reduces the argument n by 1, another '$\exists\neg$' is added until the base case is reached, at which point '$\exists$' is added. Driving the negations through the sequence '$\exists\neg, \exists\neg, \exists\neg, \exists$' yields '$\exists\forall\exists\forall$'.

$$v(\langle 4, i, \bar{x} \rangle) = 1 \Leftrightarrow \exists k_1 \neg v(\langle 3, i, \langle \bar{x}, k_1 \rangle \rangle) = 1$$
$$\Leftrightarrow \exists k_1 \neg \exists k_2 \neg v(\langle 2, i, \langle \bar{x}, k_1, k_2 \rangle \rangle) = 1$$
$$\Leftrightarrow \exists k_1 \neg \exists k_2 \neg \exists k_3 \neg v(\langle 1, i, \langle \bar{x}, k_1, k_2, k_3 \rangle \rangle) = 1$$
$$\Leftrightarrow \exists k_1 \neg \exists k_2 \neg \exists k_3 \neg \exists k_4 \mathcal{T}(i, \langle \rangle, \langle \bar{x}, k_1, k_2, k_3 \rangle, k_4)$$
$$\Leftrightarrow \exists k_1 \forall k_2 \exists k_3 \forall k_4 \mathcal{T}(i, \langle \rangle, \langle \bar{x}, k_1, k_2, k_3 \rangle, k_4).$$

[12] Rogers (1987): 318, theorem X.

The distinction between the deductive and the inductive complexity of an empirically complete hypothesis coincides exactly with the logical distinction between explicit and implicit definability in arithmetic. An *explicit definition* of ε is a formula of arithmetic $\Phi(x, y)$ with free variables x and y such that $\Phi(x, y)$ is satisfied in arithmetic if and only if x and y are assigned to numbers n, m such that $\varepsilon(n) = m$. An *implicit definition* of ε is a formula of arithmetic $\Phi(\varepsilon)$ free only in function variable ε such that $\Phi(\varepsilon)$ is satisfied in arithmetic if and only if the variable ε is interpreted by the function ε. It turns out that ε is explicitly definable in arithmetic by a formula with $n - 1$ quantifier alternations starting with $\forall[\exists]$ if and only if $\varepsilon \in \Pi_n^A [\Sigma_n^A]$. It also turns out that ε is implicitly definable in arithmetic by a formula with $n - 1$ quantifier alternations starting with $\forall[\exists]$ if and only if $\{\varepsilon\} \in \Pi_n^A [\Sigma_n^A]$. When $C_h = \{\varepsilon\}$, the arithmetical complexity of $\{\varepsilon\}$ is just what I have called the inductive complexity of h, and the arithmetical complexity of ε is just what I have called the deductive complexity of h.

The original motivation for the study of implicit definability had nothing to do with the relationship between inductive and deductive complexity. It was intended, rather, as a precise analysis of the relative power of two different strategies for defining new concepts in arithmetic, with an eye toward the reduction of suspect notions in higher mathematics to the relatively clearer concept of the "natural" numbers. It is striking that the comparison of explicit and implicit complexity, a subject motivated by investigations into the foundations of mathematics, should have such direct and surprising implications for computable scientific inquiry.

If the range of predictions made by ε is finite, proposition 7.18 cannot be improved to yield a nonarithmetical ε such that $\{\varepsilon\}$ is refutable with certainty by a Turing machine, due to proposition 7.15. But what if the range of predictions made by ε is infinite? It seems odd to suppose that this might increase the power of computable inquiry, since it implies that there are more different sorts of predictions for the machine to worry about. But as a matter of fact, it can help, since there is an infinitely complex ε such that ε is refutable with certainty by a Turing machine. This seems even more magical than the preceding result, for now it is (infinitely) impossible for a machine to derive all predictions from ε, and ε could be wrong anywhere for all we know, but a Turing machine can eventually reject the hypothesis with certainty if and only if it is false! This result shows that the common picture of scientific inquiry, in which the scientist sequentially tests the predictions of a theory against the evidence, falls infinitely short of capturing the full potential of computable science.

Proposition 7.19[13]

There are C, h, ε such that $C_h = \{\varepsilon\}$ and for each n, $C_h \notin \Sigma_n^A$ but h is refutable$_C$ with certainty by a Turing machine (i.e., there is an ε such that for each n, $\varepsilon \notin \Sigma_n^A$ and $\{\varepsilon\} \in \Pi_1^A$).

---

[13] Hinman (1978): 106–107.

Proof: Let v be as in the proof of the preceding proposition. $\{v\} \in \Pi_2^A$, so there is a recursive relation G such that for all ε, $\varepsilon = v \Leftrightarrow \forall x \exists y G$ (ε, x, y). Define:

$$\delta(x) = \langle v(x), \mu y G(v, x, y) \rangle.$$

A Δ_n^A definition for δ would yield a Δ_n^A definition for v, since $v(x)$ can be recovered by decoding $\delta(x)$ and returning the first coordinate. Thus, for each n, $\delta \notin \Delta_n^A$. It remains only to show that $\{\delta\} \in \Pi_1^A$. Let $(\langle x, y \rangle)_1 = x$ and $(\langle x, y \rangle)_2 = y$. Let $(\alpha)_1$ denote the infinite sequence $(\alpha(0)_1, \alpha(1)_1, \alpha(2)_1, \ldots)$. It will now be shown that:

$\varepsilon = \delta \Leftrightarrow$

  (a) $\forall x \, G((\varepsilon)_1, x, (\varepsilon(x))_2)$ &

  (b) $\forall x, y \, [y < (\varepsilon(x))_2 \Rightarrow \neg G((\varepsilon)_1, x, y)]$.

which is a Π_1^A definition for $\{\delta\}$. ($\Rightarrow$) Recall that $\forall x \exists y G(v, x, y)$. Thus G holds if we choose the least such y: $\forall x G(v, x, \mu y(G(v, x, y)))$. But $\mu y(G(v, x, y)) = \delta(x)_2$ and $v = (\varepsilon)_1$, so $\forall x G((\varepsilon)_1, x, (\varepsilon(x))_2)$, which is (a). And (b) follows because $(\delta(x))_2$ is the least y such that $G((\varepsilon)_1, x, y)$. ($\Leftarrow$) Suppose that (a) $\forall x G((\varepsilon)_1, x, (\varepsilon(x))_2)$. Then $\forall x \exists y G((\varepsilon)_1, x, y)$. Thus $(\varepsilon)_1 = v$. Assuming (b), we have that for all x, $(\varepsilon(x))_2$ is the least y such that $G(v, x, y)$. Thus $\varepsilon = \delta$, as required. ∎

The range of data stream δ may be infinite, because the minimization in the second coordinate has no bound. Thus there is no contradiction of our previous result that when $rng(\varepsilon)$ is finite, computable refutation with certainty implies that ε is recursive.

The results of this section provide a complete picture of how complex the deductive complexity of an empirically complete theory can be, given that the theory has some specified inductive complexity (*Fig. 7.11*).

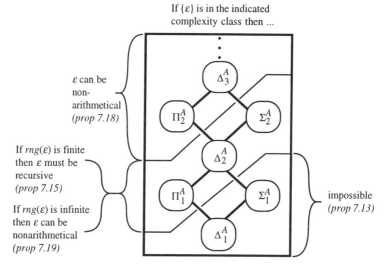

Figure 7.11

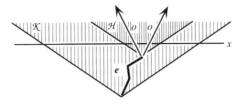

Figure 7.12

So far, we have considered only empirically complete hypotheses. Typically, a scientific theory entails predictions only in light of previous observations e, and even then it may fail to make any prediction for a given time. Define h, $e \vDash_C (n, o) \Leftrightarrow$ for each $\varepsilon \in C_h$ such that ε extends e, $\varepsilon_n = o$ (*Fig. 7.12*). Define $PRED_C(h) = \{(e, n, o): h, e \vDash_C (n, o)\}$. So if $(e, n, o) \in PRED_C(h)$, then h predicts o at n given that e has been observed. Proposition 7.20, which is presented in *Figure 7.13*, summarizes the facts concerning both the empirically complete case and the general case. Each bound given in the table[14] can be shown best by means of an example. In Figure 7.13, assume that $\mathcal{K} = O^\omega$, where $O \subseteq \omega$.

For the proof of proposition 7.20, see exercise 7.12.

9. Ideal Norms and Computational Disasters

In the introduction to this chapter, I emphasized that bounded scientific norms are different from ideal norms. Recommendations that are good for ideal agents can be very bad for computationally bounded ones. A methodological norm is

Proposition 7.20 Given arithmetical bounds on C_h			Best arithmetical bound on $PRED_C(h)$			
			$\mathcal{H}$ is empirically complete		General case	
(cf. exercise 7.12)			O is finite	O is infinite	O is finite	O is infinite
certainty case	a	Δ_1^A	Impossible if $|O| > 1$		Δ_1^A	Π_1^A
	b	Σ_1^A			Π_1^A	Π_1^A
	c	Π_1^A	Δ_1^A	none	Σ_1^A	none
limiting case	d	Δ_2^A	Δ_1^A	none	Π_2^A	none
	e	Σ_2^A	Δ_1^A	none	Π_2^A	none
	f	Π_2^A	none	none	none	none

Figure 7.13

[14] Kelly and Schulte (1995).

*C'est terrible!
They have
thrown ze book at
you, monsieur.*

Figure 7.14

restrictive[15] for a class of agents just in case no agent in the class who obeys the norm can solve a given inductive problem that is solvable by a method of the same kind that violates the norm (*Fig. 7.14*).

Let's consider a concrete example of an ideal norm that is restrictive for computational agents. A standard, ideal requirement for science is that a hypothesis be rejected immediately when it is inconsistent with the available evidence. This requirement has been recommended, for example, by K. Popper.[16] We can think of it as a property of scientists, relative to a given inductive problem:

h is consistent$_C$ with e given $\mathcal{K} \Leftrightarrow \exists \varepsilon \in C_h \cap \mathcal{K} \cap [e]$.

α is consistent for h given $\mathcal{K} \Leftrightarrow (\forall e \in \omega^*, h$ is not consistent$_C$ with e given $\mathcal{K} \Rightarrow \alpha(h, e) = 0)$.

Just a little reflection yields the following:

Proposition 7.21

Consistency is not restrictive for ideal methods in any of the paradigms of hypothesis assessment introduced in chapter 3.   ∎

Indeed, we saw in chapter 4 that consistency is necessary for ideal data-minimality and that each ideally solvable problem is solvable by a data-minimal method. Now let's consider the situation for computable methods. The relation of consistency may be nonrecursive. For example, recall the hypothesis $\mathcal{P}_K = \{\varepsilon: \varepsilon_0 \in K\}$, where K is the halting problem. If $x \notin K$, then (x) is inconsistent with $\mathcal{P}_K$, but no computer can decide whether $x \in K$. This suggests that consistency is restrictive for effective scientists. In fact, something far stronger

---

[15] Osherson, et al. (1986).
[16] Popper (1968).

is true. Say that

> α *is weakly conservative$_C$ for h given $\mathcal{K} \Leftrightarrow \forall \varepsilon \in \mathcal{K}, \varepsilon \in C_h \Rightarrow \alpha$ does not stabilize to 0 on h, ε*

It is immediate that:

Proposition 7.22

$$\text{If } \alpha \begin{bmatrix} verifies_C \\ refutes_C \\ decides_C \end{bmatrix} h \begin{bmatrix} in\ the\ limit \\ gradually \end{bmatrix} given\ \mathcal{K},$$

then α is weakly conservative$_C$ for h given $\mathcal{K}$. ∎

Then we have the following result:

Proposition 7.23

If $C_h = \{\varepsilon\}$ and α is consistent$_C$ for h given $\mathcal{K}$ and α is weakly conservative$_C$ for h given $\mathcal{K}$ and $\alpha \in \Sigma_n^A$, then $\varepsilon \in \Sigma_n^A$.

Proof: Given the conditions of the proposition, we claim:

$$\varepsilon_n = k \Leftrightarrow \exists e \text{ such that } lh(e) \geq n \ \&\ e_n = k \ \&\ \alpha(h, e) \neq 0.$$

($\Rightarrow$) Suppose $\varepsilon_n = k$. Since α is weakly conservative, $\exists m \geq n$ such that $\alpha(h, e) \neq 0$, so let $e = \varepsilon | m$.

($\Leftarrow$) Suppose $\varepsilon_n \neq k$. Since α is consistent, for each e such that $h(e) \geq n$ and $e_n = k$, $\alpha(h, e) = 0$.

Finally, since $\alpha \in \Sigma_n^A$, $\varepsilon \in \Sigma_n^A$. ∎

Now recall the example $C_h = \{\delta\}$ of proposition 7.19. δ is not in any class Σ_n^A, but $\{\delta\} \in \Pi_1^A$. Then we have the following result, which illustrates the difficulties that accompany insistence on consistency, even for highly idealized, arithmetically definable methods.

Corollary 7.24

Let $C_h = \{\delta\}$, as in proposition 7.19. Then h is computably refutable with certainty but no consistent, arithmetically definable α can even gradually refute$_C$ or verify$_C$ h.

Proof: $\{\delta\} \in \Pi_1^A$ so h is computably refutable with certainty. Suppose that α gradually refutes$_C$ or verifies$_C$ h. Then by proposition 7.22, α is weakly conservative$_C$ for h given $\mathcal{K}$. Suppose α is also consistent$_C$ for h given $\mathcal{K}$. Then if $\alpha \in \Sigma_n^A$, so is δ, by proposition 7.23. But for each n, $\delta \notin \Sigma_n^A$. So for each n, $\alpha \notin \Sigma_n^A$. ∎

Hence, insisting that a method notice immediately when data refutes a hypothesis entails a severe restriction on reliability. There is a hypothesis $C_h = \{\delta\}$ that a computable method can refute with certainty that no arithmetically definable method that notices refutation right away can even refute or verify gradually.

Nor can one require that a computable method be *maximally consistent*, in the sense that no method obeys consistency everywhere α does and somewhere else as well. Let α be an arithmetically definable method that verifies$_C$ h in the limit. Thus, α is not consistent. Then there is some e not extended by δ such that $\alpha(h, e) \neq 0$. Let α' be just like α except that $\alpha'(h, e) = 0$. α' is arithmetically definable (α' checks whether the current data is e, and then switches to a program for α if it is not) and α' is more consistent than α. But α' is still not entirely consistent, by corollary 7.24, so α' can be improved in the same way, and so on, forever. This situation is more the rule than the exception when we consider the reliability of computable methods satisfying ideal norms. Such norms are often restrictive and often fail to admit of optimal approximations among the reliable methods.

Intuitively, the problem with demanding consistency is that it requires a method to complete its consistency test before reading the next datum, whereas an arithmetically definable method may only be able to succeed by putting off the consistency test until after more data is read. It should not be supposed that this procrastination means that the consistency problem can be solved effectively in the limit but not in the short run. That would imply that $\delta \in \Sigma_2^A$, but in fact δ is not in any class Σ_n^A. The truth is more subtle. The computable method that refutes $C_h = \{\delta\}$ with certainty actually *uses* future data as an empirical oracle to help it decide whether past data is consistent with the hypothesis, so that not even a limiting, arithmetically definable method could decide whether past data is consistent with the hypothesis, given the past data alone (cf. exercise 7.15). This remarkable phenomenon underscores how formal and empirical problems blend into one another from a learning theoretic perspective.

10.   Computable Inquiry

In this chapter, the difference between ideal and computationally bounded underdetermination in hypothesis assessment problems was characterized. The difference amounts to the difference in the base case between the arithmetical and the finite Borel hierarchies. We have seen that computational agents may treat formal difficulties as internal inductive inference problems solved in parallel with the ongoing external investigation. An important result of this chapter is that our ability to compute predictions from an empirical theory corresponds to its explicit definability in arithmetic, while the ability of a computer to determine the truth of the hypothesis in the limit corresponds to its implicit definability in arithmetic. This correspondence permits us to make use of standard results in mathematical logic to prove the surprising result that theories whose predictions are infinitely impossible for a computer to derive can nonetheless be computably refutable with certainty. Without guidance from classical results in mathematical logic, such a possibility would be hard to imagine, much less to demonstrate.

This chapter extends the strong analogy between empirical and formal inquiry introduced in chapter 6. There are differences to be found between the two cases, and it is interesting to analyze just what they are, but the general picture is one of confluence rather than of sharp dichotomies between the respective logics of formal and empirical inquiry. That is not to say that ideal norms are good for computationally bounded agents, but rather that from the logical reliabilist point of view, inductive methodology for computationally bounded agents involves a smooth interleaving of formal and empirical considerations.

Exercises

7.1. Prove proposition 7.1 and use it to prove proposition 7.2.

7.2. Prove proposition 7.8 and show that the methods constructed in the proof of proposition 7.9 work as claimed.

7.3. Prove proposition 7.10.

7.4. (Putnam 1965) Recall the n-trial predicates defined in section 6.3. Define an effective, finite difference hierarchy for relations over the natural numbers, and characterize the n-trial predicates in terms of the cells of this hierarchy as follows: For each r such that $0 < r < 1$ and for each $n \in \omega$,

$$
S \text{ is an } n\text{-trial predicate starting with } \begin{bmatrix} 0 \\ 1 \\ r \end{bmatrix} \Leftrightarrow S \in \begin{bmatrix} \Sigma_n^d \\ \Pi_n^d \\ \Delta_n^d \end{bmatrix}.
$$

7.5. Prove proposition 7.7 following the strategy of proposition 7.5.

7.6. Show that h_{comp} is gradually empirically self-defeating for us.

7.7. Prove proposition 7.13.

7.8. Prove proposition 7.14.

7.9. Say that a method is *conservative*[17] with respect to C, $\mathcal{K}$, H just in case for each $h \in H$, it refuses to change its conjecture from 1 to 0 unless $C_h \cap \mathcal{K} = \emptyset$. Show that conservatism is restrictive for ideal verification in the limit.

[17] Osherson et al. (1986).

7.10. Prove proposition 7.21.

7.11. To apply the approach of chapter 5 to computable methods, we must introduce the notion of an *assessment* **G**-*reduction* as follows:

$$C \leq_G \mathcal{B} \Leftrightarrow \text{there is a } \Phi \in G \text{ such that for each } \varepsilon \in \mathcal{N}, h \in \omega, C(\varepsilon, h)$$
$$\Leftrightarrow \Phi(h, \varepsilon) \in \mathcal{B}.$$

Let $\Phi: \omega \times \mathcal{N} \to \mathcal{N}$ be an operator. Define:

Φ *is recursive* $\Leftrightarrow$ *there is a partial recursive function* $\phi(h, e, x)$ *such that for all* $\varepsilon \in \mathcal{N}, h, x, y \in \omega, \Phi(h, \varepsilon) = y \Leftrightarrow \text{there exists } e \subseteq \varepsilon \text{ such that } \phi(h, e, x) = y.$

Let **Rec** be the class of all recursive operators. Now prove analogues of propositions 5.3, and 5.4 for recursive assessment reducibility.

*7.12. Prove proposition 7.20 (*Fig. 7.13*).

Hints: (Oliver Schulte) to show that the infinite O, general case of (a) is optimal, let $O = \omega$ and let

$$\varepsilon \in C_h \Leftrightarrow [\varepsilon(\varepsilon(0)) \neq 0 \Rightarrow \phi_{\varepsilon(0)}(\varepsilon(0)) \text{ halts within } \varepsilon(\varepsilon(0)) \text{ steps}].$$

(Oliver Schulte) To show that the finite O, general case of (b) is optimal, let $O = \{0, 1\}$ and define the hypothesis:

$$\varepsilon \in C_h \Leftrightarrow \exists k [(\forall k' < k, \varepsilon(k') = 1) \text{ and } \varepsilon(k) = 0 \text{ and } (\varepsilon(k) + 1 \neq 0 \Rightarrow k \in K)].$$

To show that the finite O, general case of (c) is optimal, let $O = \{0, 1\}$, let S be Π_2^A-complete and let $R \in \Sigma_2^A$ be such that for all n, $n \in S \Leftrightarrow \forall z R(n, z)$. Now define the hypothesis:

$$\varepsilon \in C_h \Leftrightarrow \forall x [x \in \bar{K} \quad or \quad \varepsilon(x) = 0].$$

(Oliver Schulte) To show that the finite O, general case of (d) is optimal, define the hypothesis:

$$\varepsilon \in C_h \Leftrightarrow if \ [\exists n \ (1^n)*0*1 \text{ is extended by } \varepsilon] \text{ then } [\exists n \ \exists m \ (1^n)*0*(1^m)*0 \text{ is extended by } \varepsilon \text{ and } \neg R(n, m)].$$

The upper bound given in the infinite O, general case of (e) can be established as follows: let α verify$_C h$ in the limit. If $(e, n, o) \notin PRED_C(h)$, then α stabilizes to 1 on some infinite extension ε of e such that $\varepsilon_n \neq o$. Use this fact to get a Σ_2^B definition of $\overline{PRED_C(h)}$, from which the result follows. The rest of the proposition follows from elementary logical dependencies in the table or from results similar to those already proved in section 7.8.

*7.13. Take up the challenge of providing a direct demonic argument to show that h_{comp} is not gradually refutable$_C$ in the limit by a Turing machine (cf. proposition 7.12), from which it would follow that $C_{h_{comp}} \notin \Pi_3^A$. What is required is a demon who presents a nonrecursive data stream if and only if the given method α approaches 0. Such a demon exists by proposition 5.6.

7.14. Develop the generalized setting for hypothesis assessment described in footnote 3 and characterize the various senses of success in this setting.

*7.15. Using the implicit definition of the hypothesis $C_h = \{\delta\}$ of proposition 7.19, explain how the obvious method for refuting this hypothesis with certainty uses the information in future data to determine if past data is inconsistent with the hypothesis.

8

So Much Time, Such Little Brains

1. Introduction

In the preceding chapter, we saw that recommendations that make perfect sense for ideal agents can be disastrous for Turing machines, and it was concluded that when computational agents cannot possibly satisfy a methodologist's recommendations, it is the methodologist rather than the agent who is at fault. But this moral might very well be tossed back at me, for Turing computability is itself highly idealized. Turing machines have infinite tapes. Of course, the tape doesn't have to exist all at once. The intention is that whenever the read-write head is about to fall off the end, a paper factory can glue on an extension just in time. When all the forests are used up, we have to start making paper out of the earth itself. When the earth is used up, neighboring planets are made into paper, and then neighboring solar systems, and so forth (*Fig. 8.1*). If there is finitely much matter in the universe, then we simply cannot implement all possible Turing computations.

This ideal character of Turing computation is not a fault in itself. The concept was developed for the purpose of establishing negative facts about the powers of a mathematician following an algorithm. What is not Turing computable is not computable in any more lenient way, so negative results are strengthened rather than weakened by the idealization. But on the positive side, methodological recommendations that make sense for Turing machines may make as little sense for more severely restricted agents as recommendations for ideal agents make for Turing machines. This chapter examines the powers of more constrained sorts of scientists, including finite state automata and primitive recursive functions, with emphasis on the former.

Figure 8.1

2. Finite State Automata

A *deterministic finite state automaton* (*DFA*) is a clockwork device that reads symbols (drawn from *O*) off of an input tape.[1] A DFA is so constituted (with some finite number of discretely toothed gears, say) that when started in a conventional starting state *s*, it reads the first input symbol a_1 and moves to state $\tau(s, a_1)$. Then it reads the next symbol, and so forth. Every time a symbol *a* is read, the machine outputs $o(q)$, where *q* is the state it ends up in after reading the symbol *a*. A DFA may be thought of as a Turing machine whose infinite working tape is truncated at both ends and that reads an input symbol and writes an output symbol at each stage of computation (*Fig. 8.2*).

For a very simple example, imagine a child who cannot find a friend to ride the teeter-totter with her (*Fig. 8.3*). She can either sit on the right side by herself (call this input 0) or sit on the left side by herself (call this input 1). The two states of the system are *right-side down* and *right-side up*. Sitting on the low side causes no change. Sitting on the high side does. The child finds the teeter-totter with the right side down. Suppose we take the system to be in

Figure 8.2

---

[1] The issue of scientific automata came to my attention in a term project by Terence Spies during a seminar on an earlier draft of this text at Carnegie-Mellon in the autumn of 1990.

Figure 8.3

an *accepting state* when, and only when, the left side is down. Then we may view it as accepting the input strings: 1, 01, 001, 011, 0011, . . .

This system is summarized by the *state transition diagram* presented in *Figure 8.4*. System states are represented as circles, the output produced in a given state is written inside the corresponding circle, and $\tau(q, o) = q'$ just in case there is an arrow labeled with o from q to q' in the diagram. In general, a *DFA* is a sequence $M = \langle O, Q, o, \tau, s \rangle$ where

> O is a finite set called the input alphabet (i.e., the observation vocabulary).
>
> Q is a finite set of objects called states.
>
> $o: Q \rightarrow \{1, 0, \#\}$ is called the output assignment.
>
> $\tau: Q \times O \rightarrow Q$ is a total function called the state transition function.
>
> $s \in Q$ is the starting state.

The symbol '$\#$' is a stall conjecture that permits a DFA to decide a hypothesis with n mind changes starting with neither 0 nor 1. Let $q, q' \in Q, o \in O, e \in O^*$. I will use the following conventions:

> $M[q, a] = q' \Leftrightarrow \tau(q, a) = q'$.
>
> $M[q, e] = q' \Leftrightarrow \exists \boldsymbol{q} \in Q^{lh(e)}$ such that
> $\boldsymbol{q}_0 = q$ and
> $M[\boldsymbol{q}_{lh(q)-1}, e_{lh(e)-1}] = q'$ and
> $\forall n < lh(e) - 1, M[\boldsymbol{q}_n, e_n] = \boldsymbol{q}_{n+1}$.
>
> $M[e] = q \Leftrightarrow M[s, e] = q$.
>
> $M[e]$ returns $b \Leftrightarrow o(M[e]) = b$.

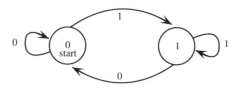

Figure 8.4

It will be useful to refer to the result of redesignating q as the start state of M by the expression M_q. DFAS are usually viewed as *accepting* sets of finite strings. The usual convention is to say that

> M *accepts* $e \Leftrightarrow M[e]$ *returns* 1.
>
> $L_M = \{e \in O^*: M \text{ accepts } e\}.$
>
> M *accepts* $L \Leftrightarrow L = L_M.$

That is, M accepts e if, after reading e, M is in some state that returns 1 and M accepts a set of strings if M accepts each string in the set.

3. Regular Sets

The sets of strings accepted by automata have an elegant structural character-ization due to S. Kleene.[2] Let O be a finite input alphabet. Let $A, B \subseteq O^*$. $AB = \{ee': e \in A \& e' \in B\}$. $A^* =$ the set of all finite concatenations of strings in A. The *regular sets* over O are the least class X closed under the following conditions.

> $\varnothing \in X.$
>
> $\{\mathbf{0}\} \in X.$
>
> $\forall a \in O, \{(a)\} \in X.$
>
> If $A, B \in X$ then $AB \in X$, $A \cup B \in X$, and $A^* \in X$.

Regular sets are often denoted by *regular expressions*, in which the singleton $\{a\}$ is denoted by the constant $\underline{a}$, the empty sequence is denoted by $\underline{\mathbf{0}}$, $\varnothing$ is denoted by $\underline{\varnothing}$, and $\cup$ is denoted by $+$. Thus, $\{\mathbf{0}\}(\{a\} \cup \{b\})^*\{c\}$ is denoted by the more legible formula $\underline{\mathbf{0}}(\underline{a} + \underline{b})^*\underline{c}$.

Proposition 8.1 (S. Kleene)

> $\forall L \subseteq O^*$, L *is regular* $\Leftrightarrow L$ *is accepted by some* DFA.

Proof: Cf. Hopcroft and Ullman (1979): 28–35. ∎

This result provides a simple structural analysis of the sets acceptable by DFAS that makes no reference whatever to computational concepts. Our goal in successive sections will be to obtain parallel characterizations for hypotheses that can be investigated reliably by DFAS in various senses.

---

[2] Kleene (1956).

4. Scientific Automata

Most learning-theoretic analyses involving DFAS use them to model the environment under study rather than the scientist, who is usually assumed to be a Turing machine.[3] But despite their cognitive limitations, DFAS may be viewed as mechanical scientists in their own right. Indeed, DFAS have some attractive properties as scientists. Unlike a Turing machine, a DFA's next conjecture depends only on its current state and the next datum to arrive. Since a DFA has at most finitely many states, it can remember at most some fixed, finite amount of the data seen up to the present, so the model automatically precludes the idealization that a method can perfectly recall its entire history. Also, DFAS take just one step to process each new datum, whereas Turing machines can require any number of steps each time a new datum arrives. Thus, DFAS can process data in real time, rather than lagging progressively behind it. Finally, DFAS cannot implement the powerful but idealized enumeration procedures proposed in the previous chapter for Turing machines.

For ease of exposition, our DFA methods will not take hypotheses as inputs. Thus a DFA will be thought of as dedicated to a particular hypothesis h. Since we have defined DFAS so as to produce a conjecture in $\{0, 1, \#\}$ on each datum, there is no problem in speaking of such a machine as verifying or refuting a hypothesis in the limit, or with n mind changes given $\mathcal{K}$, starting with 0, 1, or neither. On the other hand, our DFAS could not possibly conjecture infinitely many distinct rationals, so if a DFA approaches 1 or 0, it also stabilizes to the same value. Therefore, gradual verification and refutation collapse for DFAS to verification and refutation in the limit, and for that reason they will not be considered separately. We may simply define verification, refutation, and decision with certainty as decision with 1 mind change starting with 0, 1, or $\#$, respectively. This dispenses with the complication of adding states to handle the conjecture of '!' prior to 1 or 0.

5. Scientific Automata and Certainty

Recall that Turing machines can verify with certainty any hypothesis that is a union of fans whose handles constitute an r.e. set. The natural analogue of this condition of DFAS is that $C_h \cap \mathcal{K}$ be open with a *regular* set of handles (*Fig. 8.5*).

Since we are going to be speaking a good deal about open and closed sets determined by regular sets of handles, it is useful to have a clean notation for such sets. Let $G \subseteq O^*$. Then I let $G^{\downarrow}$ denote the open set with handles in G:

$$G^{\downarrow} = \bigcup_{e \in G} [e].$$

$$G^{\uparrow} = \overline{G^{\downarrow}}.$$

---

[3] E.g., Angluin (1981), Angluin (1978) and Gold (1978).

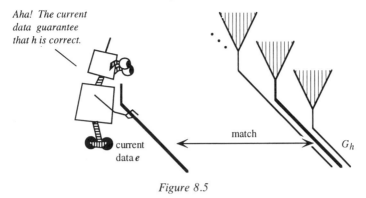

Figure 8.5

$G^{\downarrow}$ may be read *down-G* and $G^{\uparrow}$ may be read *up-G*. Now define:

S is regular-$\mathcal{K}$-open $\Leftrightarrow \exists$ regular set G such that $S \cap \mathcal{K} = G^{\downarrow} \cap \mathcal{K}$.

S is regular-$\mathcal{K}$-closed $\Leftrightarrow \exists$ regular set G such that $S \cap \mathcal{K} = G^{\uparrow} \cap \mathcal{K}$.

S is regular-$\mathcal{K}$-clopen $\Leftrightarrow S$ is regular $\mathcal{K}$-closed and regular $\mathcal{K}$-open.

Then the following is immediate:

Proposition 8.2

(a) *h is verifiable$_C$ with certainty given $\mathcal{K}$ by a* DFA
    $\Leftrightarrow C_h$ *is regular-$\mathcal{K}$-open.*

(b) *h is refutable$_C$ with certainty given $\mathcal{K}$ by a* DFA
    $\Leftrightarrow C_h$ *is regular-$\mathcal{K}$-closed.*

(c) *h is decidable$_C$ with certainty given $\mathcal{K}$ by a* DFA
    $\Leftrightarrow C_h$ *is regular-$\mathcal{K}$-clopen.* ∎

Moreover, none of these cases collapses, as the reader may readily verify (e.g., consider the teeter-totter example).

6. Scientific Automata in the Limit

Things become more interesting when we consider the hypotheses that automata can assess reliably in the limit. The teeter-totter refutes in the limit the infinite divisibility hypothesis h_{inf}, for it eventually becomes stuck in the highlighted circuit involving only its accepting state just in case the data stream stabilizes to 1 (*Fig. 8.6*).

So DFAS can refute in the limit some hypotheses that are properly Π_2^4, and hence can verify in the limit some hypotheses that are properly Σ_2^4. Since a one-state machine returns the same conjecture no matter what, no such machine

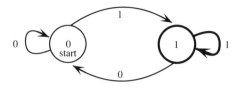

Figure 8.6

verifies h_{inf} in the limit, so the teeter-totter is a *minimal state solution* of the limiting inference problem in question.

For a more interesting example, consider the hypothesis h_{abc} that after some finite time the data converges to an alternating sequence of the form $(abcabcabc...)$. The DFA scientist depicted in *Figure 8.7* verifies h_{abc} in the limit.

This machine stabilizes to 1 on ε just in case, after some time, ε gets caught in the highlighted circuit of three states that return 1. For another sort of example, consider the hypothesis h_{-00} that asserts that after some finite time, 00 is never seen again. That is, $C_{h_{-00}} = \{\varepsilon: \exists n\, \forall m \geq n\, \neg(\varepsilon_m = 0\, \&\, \varepsilon_{m+1} = 0)\}$. h_{-00} is verified in the limit by the machine depicted in *Figure 8.8*. Again, if the hypothesis is true, then the data stream eventually becomes trapped in the highlighted component.

If regular open sets characterize verification with certainty by a DFA and hence are the DFA analogues of r.e. sets of data streams, then what are the DFA analogues of Σ_2^A sets, in terms of which we may characterize what DFAs can verify in the limit? Define:

$\mathcal{P}$ is limiting regular in $\mathcal{K} \Leftrightarrow \exists$ regular sets $L_1, \ldots, L_n, J_1, \ldots, J_n$ such

$$\text{that} \quad \mathcal{P} \cap \mathcal{K} = \left[\bigcup_{i=1}^{n} L_i(J_i\!\uparrow) \right] \cap \mathcal{K}.$$

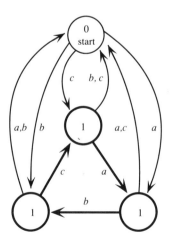

Figure 8.7

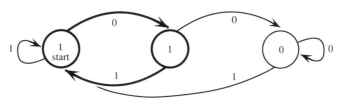

Figure 8.8

It turns out that the limiting regular sets correspond exactly to the hypotheses verifiable in the limit by finite state automata, and hence are the DFA versions of Σ_2^A sets.

Before launching into the proof, let's compare this characterization with those given in the ideal and Turing-computable cases. The comparison is enhanced if we rephrase the earlier results in terms of our new $\uparrow$ notation. The claim under consideration is that DFAS can verify$_C$ in the limit exactly those h such that

$$C_h \cap \mathcal{K} = \left[\bigcup_{i=1}^{n} A_i(B_i^{\uparrow}) \right] \cap \mathcal{K},$$

where for each $i \le n$, A_i, B_i are regular subsets of O^*, and where O is a finite alphabet. Rephrasing proposition 7.9(b) in terms of up-arrows and taking into account the discussion following proposition 7.2, Turing-computable scientists can verify$_C$ in the limit exactly the hypotheses h such that for some j

$$C_h \cap \mathcal{K} = \left[\bigcup_{k \in W_j} W_k^{\uparrow} \right] \cap \mathcal{K},$$

where W_k is interpreted as an r.e. subset of O^* by means of a fixed, effective encoding of finite sequences into natural numbers. Rephrasing proposition 4.10 in terms of up-arrows, we have that ideal scientists can verify in the limit exactly the hypotheses corresponding to sets of the form

$$C_h \cap \mathcal{K} = \left[\bigcup_{k \in R} S_k^{\uparrow} \right] \cap \mathcal{K},$$

where R is an arbitrary, countable subset of ω and each S_k is an arbitrary, countable subset of O^*.

The characterizations differ in the kind of union that may be taken (finite, r.e., or countable, respectively) and in the kind of set that can sit under the up-arrow (regular, r.e., or open, respectively). In the automaton case, there is the further complication that the regular-closed sets under the union may have arbitrary, regular sets concatenated onto the fronts of them. It might be thought that this is an accidental feature of the characterization and that further argument would permit us to drop this factor, so that the characterization

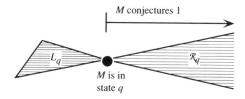

Figure 8.9

would be more nearly parallel to the others. But the tacked-on regular sets are essential: we have already seen that automata can verify properly Σ_2^B sets, and no such set is expressible as a finite union of closed sets, much less as a finite union of regular-closed sets. The tacked-on regular sets compensate for the fact that the union is finite.

Now I proceed to the characterization, which is the main result of this chapter.

Proposition 8.3[4]

(a) h is verifiable$_C$ in the limit given $\mathcal{K}$ by a DFA $\Leftrightarrow C_h$ is limiting regular in $\mathcal{K}$.

(b) h is refutable$_C$ in the limit given $\mathcal{K}$ by a DFA $\Leftrightarrow \overline{C_h}$ is limiting regular in $\mathcal{K}$.

(c) h is decidable$_C$ in the limit given $\mathcal{K}$ by a DFA $\Leftrightarrow C_h$, $\overline{C_h}$ are both limiting regular in $\mathcal{K}$.

Proof: ($\Rightarrow$) Suppose DFA M with states Q verifies$_C$ h in the limit given $\mathcal{K}$. Define:

$$L_q = \{e \in O^*: q \in M[e]\}.$$

$$\mathcal{R}_q = \{\varepsilon \in O^\omega: \forall n, o(M_q[\varepsilon|n]) = 1\} \ (Fig.\ 8.9).$$

Suppose $\varepsilon \in \mathcal{K} \cap C_h$. Then $\exists n \, \forall m \geq n$, $o(M[\varepsilon|m]) = 1$. Let $k = modulus_M(\varepsilon)$. Let $q = M[\varepsilon|k]$. Then $\varepsilon|k \in L_q$. Also, $\forall n \, o(M_q[(k|\varepsilon)|n]) = 1$, so $k|\varepsilon \in \mathcal{R}_q$. Suppose $\varepsilon \in \mathcal{K} - C_h$. Then (*) $\forall n \, \exists m \geq n$ such that $o(M[\varepsilon|m]) \neq 1$. Let $m \in \omega$, $q \in Q$ be given. Suppose $\varepsilon|m \in L_q$. Suppose for reductio that $m|\varepsilon \in \mathcal{R}_q$. Then $\forall k \geq m$, $o(M[\varepsilon|k]) = 1$, contradicting (*). So $\forall q \in Q$, $\varepsilon \notin L_q\mathcal{R}_q$. Thus,

$$C_h \cap \mathcal{K} = \left[\bigcup_{q \in Q} L_q\mathcal{R}_q \right] \cap \mathcal{K}.$$

[4] The proof of this fact draws up techniques of R. McNaughton (1966), who drew in turn on logical work by R. Büchi (1960, 1962). I am indebted to Dana Scott for the reference to Büchi's work.

It remains to show that L_q is regular and that $\mathcal{R}_q$ is regular-closed. Let M^q be just like M except that q is the unique accepting state of M^q. Then $L_q = L_{M^q}$, so L_q is regular.

Let M' be the result of deleting all nonaccepting states from M. Let $d \notin Q$. Let M^* be the result of letting every transition undefined in M' terminate in d (including all transitions originating in d) and designating d as the unique accepting state. Let M_q^* be the result of designating q as the start state of M^* (*Fig. 8.10*). Let $\varepsilon \in \mathcal{R}_q$. Then $\forall n, o(M_q[\varepsilon|n]) = 1$. Hence, $\forall n, M_q^*[\varepsilon|n] \neq d$ so $\forall n, o(M_q^*[\varepsilon|n]) \neq 1$. Let $\varepsilon \notin \mathcal{R}_q$. Therefore, $\exists n$ such that $M_q^*[\varepsilon|n] = d$, so $\exists n$ such that $o(M_q^*[\varepsilon|n]) = 1$. We now have that $\varepsilon \in \overline{\mathcal{R}_q} \Leftrightarrow \exists n\, o([\varepsilon|n]) = 1$, so

$$\mathcal{R}_q = (L_{M_q^*})^\uparrow.$$

Thus, $\mathcal{R}_q$ is regular-closed.

($\Leftarrow$) Suppose $\exists$ regular sets $L_1, \ldots, L_n, J_1, \ldots, J_n$ such that

$$C_h \cap \mathcal{K} = \left[\bigcup_{i=1}^n L_i(J_i^\uparrow) \right] \cap \mathcal{K}.$$

Let machines $M_1, \ldots, M_n$ accept $L_1, \ldots, L_n$, respectively, and let $M_1', \ldots, M_n'$ accept $J_1, \ldots, J_n$, respectively. By the following lemma, it suffices to show that each set of form $L(J^\uparrow)$ is verifiable in the limit by some DFA.

Lemma 8.4

Let $M_1, \ldots, M_n$ verify $\mathcal{P}_1, \ldots, \mathcal{P}_n$ in the limit given $\mathcal{K}$, respectively. Then there is an $M \in$ DFA that verifies $\mathcal{P}_1 \cup \cdots \cup \mathcal{P}_n$ in the limit given $\mathcal{K}$.

Proof of lemma: Let M simulate $M_1, \ldots, M_n$ on ε. M maintains a pointer initialized to M_1. The pointer is bumped to the next machine if the machine pointed to returns some value $\neq 1$ (the "next" machine is M_1 when the pointer currently points to M_n, so that the pointer may be viewed as traveling in a finite circuit). Otherwise, the pointer stays put. M returns a 1 on an input symbol if the pointer stays put when that symbol is read and returns a 0

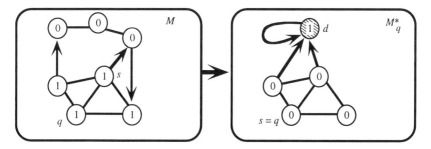

Figure 8.10

otherwise. M is a finite state machine since its state at a time is determined entirely by the vector $(q_1, \ldots, q_n, pointer)$, where q_i is the current state of M_i in the simulation and *pointer* is the current pointer position, and its next state is determined entirely by its current state and the current input. The proof of correctness for M is straightforward (exercise 8.6).   ∎

Returning to the proof of proposition 8.3(a), let L, J be regular. We construct an $M'' \in$ DFA that verifies $L(J^\uparrow)$ in the limit given $\mathcal{K}$. Let M' accept L and let M accept J. Let k be the number of states in M. Now construct $k + 1$ copies $M_1, M_2, \ldots, M_{k+1}$ of M. We construct a finite state *Control* to manage these machines, so that the overall assemblage has only finite memory. For each i from 1 to $k + 1$, *Control* labels machine M_i as *active* or *inactive*. These labels are all initialized to inactive. *Control* also maintains a *pointer* that points to one of the machines M_i. The pointer points initially to M_1. As in the proof of the lemma, when the pointer reaches M_{k+1}, the "next" machine to point to is M_1, so that the pointer may be viewed as going around a finite circuit. Finally, all the machines M', M_i are initialized to their start states. Now *Control* operates as follows (*Fig. 8.11*):

Control:
loop
set $b :=$ read the next datum;
set $M :=$ the first inactive machine;
feed b to M';
if b *puts* M' into an accepting state, activate M;
$\forall i \leq k + 1$, do:
    if M_i is active, and $M_i \neq M$ then feed b to M_i;
    if M_i goes into an accepting state after reading b, then do:
        deactivate M_i;
        initialize M_i to its start state
$\forall i, j \leq k + 1$, do:
if M_i, M_j are active machines in the same state after reading b, de-activate whichever one is not pointed to, or deactivate the first if neither is pointed to.
if the machine currently pointed to is inactive, then
    move the pointer to the next machine;
    return 0;
    go loop
else return 1;
go loop.

Consider vectors of the following form, where q ranges over states of M', q_i ranges over states of M_i, i ranges from 1 to $k + 1$ (representing the pointer's position), and a_i is a Boolean indicator of *activity* for machine M_i:

$$(q, q_1, \ldots, q_{k+1}, i, a_1, \ldots, a_{k+1}).$$

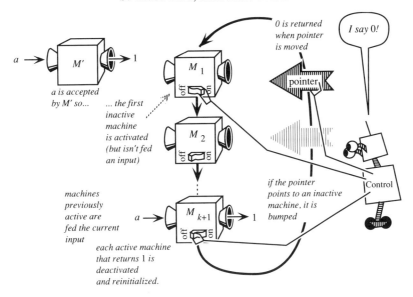

Figure 8.11

There are only finitely many such vectors. Inspection of the program of *Control* reveals that *Control*'s current state vector is a function f of its previous state vector and the current input. Our finite state automaton M is constructed using the possible state vectors of *Control* as states and using f as the transition function. M emits 0 whenever a transition leads to a vector whose pointer position differs from that of the previous state. Thus M emits 1s and 0s on arcs rather than on states (such a machine is called a *Mealy machine*). But it is a standard result of automata theory that such a machine can be turned into a behaviorally equivalent machine that emits 0s and 1s on states rather than on arcs (such a machine is called a *Moore machine*).[5]

Now we verify that *Control*, hooked up to M', $M_1, \ldots, M_{k+1}$ verifies $L(J^{\uparrow})$ in the limit given $\mathcal{K}$. Let $\varepsilon \in L(J^{\uparrow}) \cap \mathcal{K}$. Then there is an m such that $\varepsilon|m \in L$ and $m|\varepsilon \in J^{\uparrow}$. Let m' be the first such m. So M' accepts $\varepsilon|m'$ and for each j, M does not accept $(m'|\varepsilon)|j$. Upon reading $\varepsilon|m'$, *Control* activates some machine M_i. An inactive machine is available, since whenever two copies M_i, M_j of M are in the same state, *Control* deactivates one of them and while M has only k states, there are $k + 1$ copies of M, so at least two are always in the same state. By the definition of m', the activated machine M_i never accepts any initial segment of $m'|\varepsilon$, and hence is never deactivated, so the pointer can never be bumped past M_i in the future. Thus, *Control* emits only finitely many 0s upon reading ε. Since *Control* always emits either 0 or 1, we are done.

On the other side, suppose $\varepsilon \in \mathcal{K} - L(J^{\uparrow})$. Then $\forall m$, if $\varepsilon|m \in L$ then (*) $\exists m' \geq m$ such that $(m|\varepsilon)|m' \in J$. Case 1: there are just finitely many m such that $\varepsilon|m \in L$. Then for each such m, *Control* activates a new machine. But by (*),

---

[5] An easy proof of the equivalence may be found in Hopcroft and Ullman (1979): 44.

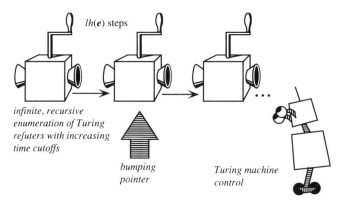

Figure 8.12

each activated machine is eventually inactivated, and after some time no machine is activated, so the pointer bumps forever after and only 0s are conjectured. Case 2: there are infinitely many m such that $\varepsilon|m \in L$. Then by (*), whichever activated machine *Control* points to, this machine eventually goes into an accepting state, causing the pointer to bump and causing *Control* to emit a 0. Thus *Control* conjectures infinitely many 0s, as required.

(b) Follows by duality. (c) Exercise 8.6.   ∎

It is interesting to compare the complete architecure for DFA verification in the limit with the complete architectures for the ideal and Turing-computable cases. The ideal architecture has a deity maintain a pointer over an ideal enumeration of closed sets. In the universal architecture for Turing machines, a Turing-computable control maintains a pointer over a Turing-computable enumeration of indices of Turing machines that refute co-r.e. sets (*Fig. 8.12*). In order to avoid infinite loops, the control meters out steps to the Turing machines in the enumeration.

In the finite state case we have a finite state control that maintains a pointer over a *finite* circuit of *finite state* refuters of regular-closed sets (*Fig. 8.13*).

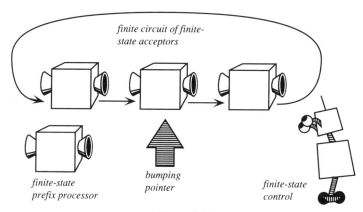

Figure 8.13

Control need not meter out steps to the refuters, since they are finite state automata and therefore cannot go into an infinite loop on a new input. Finally, there is a finite state preprocessor, which handles irregularities in the data stream prior to stabilization. As we have seen, this preprocessor cannot be eliminated without restricting the limiting verification power of DFA scientists.

7. Limiting Regular Expressions

Limiting regular sets may be described by expressions analogous to Kleene's regular expressions. The *limiting regular expressions* are the least collection X such that for each regular expression E and for each $H, H' \in X$:

$$\underline{\varnothing} \in X,$$

$$E^{\uparrow} \in X,$$

$$EH \in X,$$

$$H + H' \in X.$$

As before, + denotes union and concatenation denotes concatenation. The closure rules for regular sets imply that each limiting regular set is describable by a limiting regular expression.[6]

For example, the hypothesis of finite divisibility corresponds to this expression:

$$(\underline{0} + \underline{1})^*(\underline{0}^*\underline{1})^{\uparrow},$$

assuming that unary operators have precedence over binary operators. The expression says that we may see anything for a while, since $(\underline{0} + \underline{1})^* = O^*$, but after some point we see only 0, for the first 1 encountered would follow a finite (possibly empty) sequence of 0s, and hence would be in $(\underline{0}^*\underline{1})$. h_{-00} corresponds to the expression

$$(\underline{0} + \underline{1})^*((\underline{0} + \underline{1})^*\underline{00})^{\uparrow}.$$

This says that we may for a while see anything (the regular part) and after that time we see an infinite sequence in which no pairs of 0s occur (the regular closed part). In general, the hypothesis that finite sequence $e \in O^*$ will eventually disappear forever may be stated as $O^*(O^*\underline{e})^{\uparrow}$.

The proof of proposition 8.3 actually provides an algorithm for producing a DFA from a given limiting regular expression. Let us carry out the construction in a simple example.

---

[6] Cf. exercise 5.

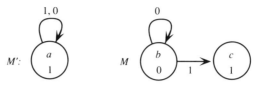

Figure 8.14

Example 8.5 Finite divisibility

$$C_{h_{fin}} = (\underline{0} + \underline{1})^*(\underline{0}^*\underline{1})^\uparrow.$$

Consider the two machines M and M' depicted in *Figure 8.14*. Clearly, M' accepts $(\underline{0} + \underline{1})^*$ and M accepts $(\underline{0}^*\underline{1})$. Following the construction, we end up with the data structure depicted in *Figure 8.15* to be manipulated by *Control*.

The state set of M'' is given by the vectors of form $(q, q_1, q_2, q_3, pointer, a_1, a_2, a_3)$ where the q's represent the respective states of M', M_1, M_2 and M_3, *pointer* gives the position of the pointer (over the set $\{1, 2, 3\}$), and each a_i is a Boolean indicator of the activity status of M_i. There are 192 such vectors. But fortunately, the program of *Control* ensures that only a few of these states can ever be entered from the initial state. First of all, notice that recording the state of M' is gratuitous, since it is always the same. Also, whenever a machine goes into state c, c', or c'', the machine is in an accepting state, and hence is deactivated and restarted in the same cycle, so no state vector involving c, c', or c'' can possibly be visited. But then we may as well drop these states from the vector notation, since all visited vectors will have the initial segment (a, b, b', b''). Also observe that M_3 will never be activated, since it is only

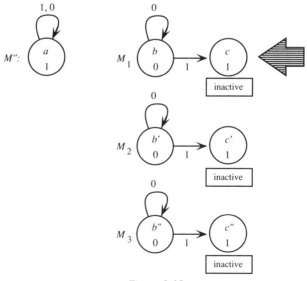

Figure 8.15

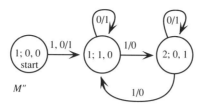

Figure 8.16

activated if the other two machines are active in distinct states, but if one of the machines is in its second state, it is automatically deactivated. So we may restrict our attention to the possible states of the vector (*pointer, a_1, a_2*), of which there are at most 8. The program of *Control* now determines a Mealy machine M'' (*Fig. 8.16*) that outputs 1s and 0s on transitions rather than on states. In the notation a/b, a is the symbol read and b is the symbol output upon that transition.

Let's examine how *Control* gives rise to M''. Consider the initial state $(1; 0, 0)$. Suppose *Control* now sees a 1. M' goes into an accepting state on 1 (since M' is always in an accepting state). *Control* therefore activates the first inactive machine M_1. Since no other machines were previously active, none of them is fed 1. Finally, the pointer now points to an active machine, so it remains where it is and *Control* returns 1. So on reading 1 in the start state *Control* ends up in state $(1; 1, 0)$. *Control* ends up in the same state if a 0 is read in the initial state. Consider the next state, $(1; 1, 0)$. If *Control* reads a 0, then since M' goes into an accepting state upon reading 0, *Control* activates the first inactive machine M_2, and then passes 0 to M_1, which was already active. M_1 was in state b, and stays in state b upon seeing 0. Since b does not return 1, M_1 remains active. But now M_1 and M_2 are both active and in the same state, so one must be deactivated. Since the pointer is at M_1, it receives preference and M_2 is deactivated again. The pointer remains at an active machine, and hence does not move, so *Control* returns 1 and ends up in state $(1; 1, 0)$ again. If *Control* reads a 1, however, then M_2 is activated (since M' is always in an accepting state) and M_1 goes into an accepting state and is deactivated. Since M_1 is deactivated, M_2 is left activated. Since the pointer now lies at an inactive machine, it is moved to the next active machine M_2, so *Control* moves to state $(2; 0, 1)$ and conjectures 0. From here, if a 0 is read, M_1 is activated but M_2 is not deactivated after reading 0, so M_1 is deactivated again and the pointer does not move. Hence, *Control* remains in state $(2; 0, 1)$ and conjectures 1. If a 1 is read, M_1 is activated and M_2 is fed 1, which causes it to accept so it is deactivated, the pointer is moved, and a 1 is emitted, landing *Control* back in state $(1; 1, 0)$ with a conjecture of 0. No other states are accessible from the start state, so we are done.

The start state of M'' merely reads one arbitrary character, and hence may be neglected so far as verifiability in the limit is concerned. That minor simplification yields the Mealy machine depicted in *Figure 8.17*.

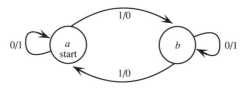

Figure 8.17

The standard construction of Moore machines from Mealy machines[7] directs us to form a new state set by pairing the states of M'' with the output vocabulary of M'' (in this case $\{0, 1\}$) and then to define $M_s((q, a), b) = (q', a')$, where $q' = M''(q, b)$ and a' is the output produced by M'' on the transition in M'' from q to q' on input b. The initial state of M_s is arbitrarily selected from the set of pairs (q, b), where q is the start state of M'', and the output of state (q, b) is defined to be b. Performing this construction, M_s turns out to be the DFA depicted in *Figure 8.18*, which solves the original problem.

8. ω-Expressions

Recall that the finite divisibility hypothesis may be written as $(\underline{0} + \underline{1})*(\underline{0}*\underline{1})^\uparrow$. It is easier to understand the expression

$$(\underline{0} + \underline{1})*\underline{0}^\omega,$$

where $\underline{0}^\omega$ is to be interpreted as the set containing just the data stream in which only 0s occur. In general, if L is a set of finite strings of input symbols (i.e., $L \subseteq O*$), then define:

$$L^\omega = \{\varepsilon \in O^\omega: \forall n, \varepsilon | n \in L^*\}.$$

That is, L^ω is the set of all infinite concatenations of elements drawn from L. Now we may define the ω-analogue of limiting regularity:

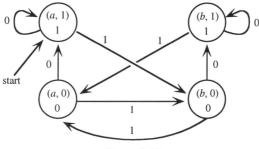

Figure 8.18

[7] Hopcroft and Ullman (1979): 44–45.

$\mathcal{P}$ *is ω-regular in* $\mathcal{K} \Leftrightarrow \exists$ *regular sets* $L_1, \ldots, L_n, J_1, \ldots, J_n$ *such that*

$$C_h \cap \mathcal{K} = \left[\bigcup_{i=1}^{n} L_i(J_i^{\omega}) \right] \cap \mathcal{K}.$$

But some ω-regular sets are not verifiable in the limit even by ideal scientists. For example, the infinite divisibility hypothesis can be written very easily as an ω-regular expression:

$$((\underline{0}^*)\underline{1})^{\omega}.$$

Since finite divisibility is also ω-regular, ω-regularity cannot characterize either verification or refutation in the limit by DFAs. This leads to an interesting question: what sort of DFA reliability (if any) does ω-regularity characterize? The answer is given in the following theorem due to R. McNaughton.[8]

Let $M \in$ DFA, and let Q be the states of M. Let $\varepsilon \in O^{\omega}$. Define:

$$Q_{\varepsilon} = \{q \in Q \colon \textit{for infinitely many } n, M[\varepsilon | n] \textit{ is in } q\}.$$

Let G be a set of sets of states (i.e., $G \subseteq power(Q)$) and let $\mathcal{P} \subseteq O^{\omega}$. Now define:

M ω-accepts ε mod $G \Leftrightarrow Q_{\varepsilon} \in G$.

M ω-accepts $\mathcal{P}$ mod $G \Leftrightarrow [\forall \varepsilon, \varepsilon \in \mathcal{P} \Leftrightarrow M \omega$-accepts ε mod G].

That is, M ω-accepts $\mathcal{P}$ mod G just in case $\varepsilon \in \mathcal{P}$ if and only if the set Q_{ε} of all states visited infinitely often in M on an arbitrary data stream ε is a member of G. Let power (S) denote the power set of S. Now we may state McNaughton's theorem:

Proposition 8.6 (McNaughton 1966)

$\mathcal{P}$ is ω-regular $\Leftrightarrow \exists M \in$ DFA, $\exists G \subseteq power(states(M))$
such that M ω-accepts $\mathcal{P}$ mod G.

Proof: Similar to the proof of proposition 8.3.　　　　　　　　　　　　■

From proposition 8.6, it follows easily that:

Corollary 8.7

All limiting regular sets are ω-regular but not conversely.

---

[8] McNaughton's (1966) work was motivated not by inductive inference but by independent developments in logic and switching theory.

Proof: Suppose $\mathcal{P}$ is limiting regular. By proposition 8.3, let $M \in$ DFA verify $\mathcal{P}$ in the limit. Let Inf_ε be defined as the set of all accepting states visited infinitely often as M reads ε. Define:

$$G = \{Inf_\varepsilon : \varepsilon \in \mathcal{P}\}.$$

Suppose $\varepsilon \in O^\omega \cap \mathcal{P}$. Then M stabilizes to 1 on ε, so $Q_\varepsilon = Inf_\varepsilon \in G$. Now, suppose $\varepsilon \in O^\omega - \mathcal{P}$. Since M does not stabilize to 1 on ε, M must visit rejecting states infinitely often upon reading ε, but there are only finitely many states to visit, so some rejecting state is visited infinitely often. Since $\bigcup G$ contains only accepting states, we have that $Q_\varepsilon \notin G$. The falsity of the converse follows from the fact that infinite divisibility is ω-regular. ∎

9. The Inductive Power of Indeterminism

Let us now suppose that several possible states can possibly follow a given state on a given input, as though the automaton could freely elect one of several transitions on a given input. Then we may modify our earlier notation so that $M[q, b] = \{q_1, \ldots, q_n\}$ just in case M can possibly go into any one of the states $q_1, \ldots, q_n$ upon observing b in state q. As before, we may extend this notation to input strings so that if $e \in O^n$, then

$$q' \in M[q, e] \Leftrightarrow \exists s \in Q^n \text{ such that}$$
$$s_0 = q \text{ and}$$
$$q \in M[s_{n-1}, e_{n-1}] \text{ and}$$
$$\forall i < n - 1, s_{i+1} \in M[s_i, e].$$
$$M[e] = M[s, e].$$

Such machines are called *nondeterministic finite state automata* (NFAS).

NFA M *accepts* a string e just in case some accepting state is in $M[e]$. Then as before, L_M is the set of strings accepted by M. Nondeterminism seems to make life easier for NFAS, since they can accept "by luck." But it is a familiar fact of automata theory that NFAS cannot accept any more languages than DFAS can. The idea is that a DFA with lots of states can deterministically simulate all possible moves within an NFA.[9]

Proposition 8.8

If L is accepted by an NFA then L is accepted by some DFA.

Proof: Let M be an NFA with state set Q. We define a machine $det(M)$ whose state set Q' is the power set of Q. Let $S, R \in Q'$. Then define $det(M)[R, x] = S \Leftrightarrow S = \{q : \exists q' \in R \text{ such that } q \in M[q', x]\}$. The start state of $det(M)$ is $\{s\}$,

---

[9] Hopcroft and Ullman (1979): 26.

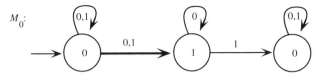

Figure 8.19

where s is the start state of M. A state R of $det(M)$ is accepting if it contains an accepting state of M. It is straightforward to verify that $det(M)$ accepts $e \Leftrightarrow M$ accepts e. ∎

The situation becomes more interesting when we consider an NFA *scientist* who reads an infinite data stream in the limit. Consider the NFA of *Figure 8.19*.

This machine may "freely" choose whether to stay in its start state or to exercise the transition to the second state. Let ε be an infinite data stream. In light of M's freedom, there are two possible conventions concerning what it means for M to process ε.

> NFA M *accepts* ε *continuously in the limit* $\Leftrightarrow \exists \sigma \in Q^\omega$ *such that*
>
> (i) σ_0 *is the start state of M and*
> (ii) $\forall n,\ \sigma_{n+1} \in M[\sigma_n, \varepsilon_n]$ *and*
> (iii) $\exists n'$ *such that* $\forall m > n',\ o(\sigma_m) = 1$.
>
> *(i.e., ε can give rise to an infinite, unbroken path σ of possible transitions in M that eventually passes through only accepting states).*
>
> NFA M *accepts* ε *piecemeal in the limit* $\Leftrightarrow \exists n\ \forall m \geq n\ \exists q \in Q$ *such that* $o(q) = 1$ *and* $q \in M[\varepsilon|m]$. *(i.e., eventually, each finite, initial segment of ε is nondeterministically accepted by M).*
>
> NFA M *verifies$_C$* h *in the limit given* $\mathcal{K}$ *in the piecemeal [continuous] sense* $\Leftrightarrow \forall \varepsilon \in \mathcal{K},\ \varepsilon \in C_h \Leftrightarrow M$ *accepts* ε *piecemeal [continuously] in the limit.*

The distinction between piecemeal and continuous acceptance in the limit makes a big difference for a particular machine. Consider the NFA M_0 depicted in *Figure 8.19*. M_0 accepts 0^ω in the limit in the piecemeal sense, since M_0 nondeterministically accepts all strings of length greater than 0, and hence can nondeterministically accept all finite, initial segments of an arbitrary data stream ε after stage 1. But in the continuous sense, M_0 accepts in the limit the set of all data streams that converge to 0, and hence verifies finite divisibility in the limit. Intuitively, piecemeal acceptance permits M_0 to back up infinitely often across the transition from the first state to the second, whereas continuous acceptance permits this transition to be traversed at most once, making it into a one-way trapdoor.

Are NFAS more powerful as scientists on the one interpretation than they are on the other? Are DFAS less powerful as scientists than NFAS are on either interpretation? Piecemeal indeterminism adds nothing to the limiting verification power of DFAs, for suppose that NFA M accepts S in the limit in the piecemeal sense. By proposition 8.7, there is some DFA M' such that $L_M = L_{M'}$. Hence, M' accepts S in the limit in the usual, deterministic sense.

The continuous interpretation is more interesting. The reader may verify that applying the usual deterministic simulation (proposition 8.8) to the machine M_0 depicted in *Figure 8.19* does not yield a deterministic machine that accepts the same set in the limit in the continuous sense (exercise 8.7). The continuous interpretation of limiting acceptance seems to endow M_0 with a powerful oracle for convergence. For consider the data stream $\varepsilon = (0, 0, 1, 0, \ldots)$ that ends with all 0s. M_0 accepts this data stream in the continuous sense by leaving the start state after the last 1 is observed. If this transition is traversed too soon (i.e., before ε converges to 0), then M_0 is stuck, since the 1 that appears later will send M_0 irrevocably into a rejecting sink from which M_0 cannot escape. So the nondeterministic transition functions as a magic oracle for convergence. A user who could observe the states of the machine would know for *certain* that ε has converged to 0 upon observing that the transition has been triggered, so the transition does something that no possible inductive method could do. It seems that the possession of a neuron with this property should significantly increase a scientist's power. But in fact DFAs can verify in the limit any hypothesis that NFAs can under the continuous interpretation, magic neurons notwithstanding!

Proposition 8.9

The following statements are all equivalent:

(1) h is verifiable$_C$ in the limit given $\mathcal{K}$ in the piecemeal sense by an NFA.

(2) h is verifiable$_C$ in the limit given $\mathcal{K}$ in the continuous sense by an NFA.

(3) h is verifiable$_C$ in the limit given $\mathcal{K}$ by a DFA.

(4) C_h is limiting regular in $\mathcal{K}$.

Proof: (3) $\Leftrightarrow$ (4) is just proposition 8.3. (1) $\Rightarrow$ (3) by proposition 8.8. (3) $\Rightarrow$ (1) and (3) $\Rightarrow$ (2) are immediate. So it suffices to show (1) $\Rightarrow$ (4). Suppose NFA M verifies$_C$ h in the limit given $\mathcal{K}$ in the continuous sense. Define:

$$L_q = \{e \in O^*: q \in M[e]\}.$$

$$\mathcal{R}_q = \{\varepsilon \in O^\omega: \exists \sigma \in Q^\omega,$$

(a) $\sigma_0 = q$ and
(b) $\forall n \; \sigma_{n+1} \in M_q[\sigma_n, \varepsilon_n]$ and
(c) $\forall n \; o(\sigma_n) = 1\}$.

Suppose $\varepsilon \in \mathcal{K} \cap C_h$. Then M accepts ε in the limit in the continuous sense. So $\exists \sigma \in Q^\omega$ such that (i) σ_0 is the start state of M, (ii) $\forall i, \sigma_{i+1} \in M[\sigma_i, \varepsilon_i]$ and (iii) $\exists n \; \forall m \geq n, o(\sigma_m) = 1$. Let k be the least such n. Let $q = \sigma_k$. Then

$q \in M[\varepsilon|k]$,[10] and hence $\varepsilon|k \in L_q$. It also follows that (a) $(k|\sigma)_0 = q$, (b) $\forall n$ $(k|\sigma)_{n+1} \in M_q[(k|\sigma)_n, (k|\varepsilon)_n]$, and (c) $\forall n$, $o((k|\sigma)_n) = 1$, so $k|\varepsilon \in \mathcal{R}_q$. Hence, $\varepsilon = (\varepsilon|k)*(k|\varepsilon) \in L_q\mathcal{R}_q$, where * denotes concatenation for the rest of this proof.

Suppose $\varepsilon \in \mathcal{K} - C_h$. Then (*) M does not accept ε in the limit in the continuous sense. Let $m \in \omega$, $q \in Q$ be given. Suppose $\varepsilon|m \in L_q$. Then $q \in M[\varepsilon|m]$. So $\exists s \in Q^m$ such that $\forall n < m - 1$, $s_{n+1} \in M[s_{n-1}, \varepsilon_{n-1}]$ and $q \in M[s_m, \varepsilon_m]$. Suppose for reductio that $m|\varepsilon \in \mathcal{R}_q$. Then $\exists \sigma \in Q^\omega$ such that (a) $\sigma_0 = q$ and (b) $\forall n, \sigma_{n+1} \in M_q[\sigma_n, (m|\varepsilon)_n]$ and (c) $\forall n, o(\sigma_n) = 1$. Hence, (i) $(s*\sigma)_0$ is the start state of M, (ii) $\forall n, (s*\sigma)_{n+1} \in M[(s*\sigma)_n, \varepsilon_n]$ and (iii) $\forall k \geq m, o((s*\sigma)_k) = 1$. So $(s*\sigma)$ witnesses that M accepts ε in the limit in the continuous sense, contradicting (*). So $m|\varepsilon \notin \mathcal{R}_q$. Hence, $\forall q, \varepsilon \notin L_q\mathcal{R}_q$. Now we have:

$$C_h \cap \mathcal{K} = \left[\bigcup_{q \in Q} L_q\mathcal{R}_q \right] \cap \mathcal{K}.$$

It remains to show that L_q is regular and $\mathcal{R}_q$ is regular closed. Let M^q be just like M except that q is the unique accepting state of M^q. Then $L_q = L_{M^q}$. By proposition 8.8, $det(M^q)$ is a DFA such that $L_q = L_{det(M^q)}$, so L_q is regular.

Let M_q^* be constructed from M by the procedure given in the proof of proposition 8.3. That is, delete all nonaccepting states from M, add a new state d, define all missing transitions to terminate in d (including transitions originating in d), and redesignate q as the initial state. Now let $M_q^\dagger$ be the result of making $\{d\}$ the unique accepting state of $det(M_q^*)$.

Suppose $\varepsilon \in \mathcal{R}_q$. Then $\exists \sigma \in Q^\omega$ such that (a) $\sigma_0 = q$ and (b) $\forall n \ \sigma_n + 1 \in M_q[\sigma_n, \varepsilon_n]$ and (c) $\forall n \ o(\sigma_n) = 1$. So $\forall n, \sigma_{n+1} \in M_q^*[\sigma_n, \varepsilon_n]$, since M_q^* differs from M_q only in transitions to rejecting states. So $\forall n, M_q^*$ accepts $\varepsilon|n$. Thus, $\forall n, \exists q \neq d$ such that $q \in M_q^*[\varepsilon|n]$. Hence, $det(M_q^*)[\varepsilon|n] \neq \{d\}$. So $M_q^\dagger$ does not accept $\varepsilon|n$.

Now suppose $\varepsilon \notin \mathcal{R}_q$. Then $\forall \sigma \in Q^\omega$, if $\sigma_0 = q$ and $\forall n, \sigma_{n+1} \in M_q[\sigma_n, \varepsilon_n]$, then $\exists n$ such that $o(\sigma_n) \neq 1$. Suppose for reductio that (*) $\forall n, \exists \sigma \in Q^\omega$ such that $\sigma_0 = q$ and $\forall k, \sigma_{k+1} \in M_q[\sigma_k, \varepsilon_k]$ and $\forall m \leq n, o(\sigma_m) = 1$. Define:

$$\mathcal{T} = \{\sigma \in Q^\omega: \sigma_0 = q \text{ and } \forall k, \sigma_{k+1} \in M_q[\sigma_k, \varepsilon_k]\}.$$

$$T = \{s \in Q^*: \exists \sigma \in \mathcal{T} \text{ such that } s \subset \sigma \text{ and } \forall i < lh(s), o(s_i) = 1\}.$$

By (*), T is infinite. Since $T \subseteq Q^*$, T is finitely branching, so by König's lemma, there is an infinite path γ in T. So (a) $\gamma_0 = q$ and (b) $\forall n, \gamma_{n+1} \in M_q[\gamma_n, \varepsilon_n]$ and (c) $\forall n, o(\gamma_n) = 1$. Hence, $\varepsilon \in \mathcal{R}_q$, which is a contradiction. So by reductio we have that $\exists n \ \forall \sigma \in Q^\omega$, $(\sigma_0 = q$ and $\forall k, \sigma_{k+1} \in M_q[\sigma_k, \varepsilon_k] \Rightarrow \exists m \leq n$ such that $o(\sigma_m) \neq 1)$. Let j be the least such n. Hence, $\forall s \in Q^{j+1}$, if $s_0 = q$ and $\forall k < j$, $s_{k+1} \in M_q[s_k, \varepsilon_k]$, then $\exists w \leq j$ such that $o(s_w) \neq 1$. Thus, $\forall s \in Q^{j+1}$, if $s_0 = q$ then $\exists w \leq j$ such that $d \in M_q^*[s_w, \varepsilon_w]$. But if $d \in M_q^*[s_w, \varepsilon_w]$, then $\forall r \in Q$, $r \notin M_q^*[s_w, \varepsilon_w]$, by the

---

[10] Recall that since positions in ε are numbered starting with 0, the last entry of $\varepsilon|n + 1$ is ε_n.

construction of M_q^*. Hence, $det(M_q^*)[\varepsilon|w + 1] = \{d\}$, so $M_q^\dagger$ accepts $\varepsilon|w + 1$. We now have that $\varepsilon \notin \mathcal{R}_q \Leftrightarrow \exists n \ M_q^\dagger$ accepts $\varepsilon|n$. So we have

$$\mathcal{R}_q = (L_{M_q^\dagger})^\uparrow.$$

Thus, $\mathcal{R}_q$ is regular-closed.   ∎

10. Primitive Recursion

The *primitive recursive functions*[11] include all of the ordinary functions of integer arithmetic, including addition, multiplication, subtraction, exponentiation, prime factorization, and more. The set $\mathcal{PRIM}$ of all primitive recursive functions is defined as the least set X such that

> X *contains all constant functions* $c_a^n(x_1, \ldots, x_n) = a$.
>
> X *contains all position selection functions* $p_k^n(x_1, \ldots, x_n) = x_k$.
>
> X *contains the successor function* $s(x) = x + 1$.
>
> X *is closed under composition: If* $f(x_1, \ldots, x_n), g(x_1, \ldots, x_k) \in X$ *then* $f(g(x_1, \ldots, x_k), \ldots, g(x_1, \ldots, x_k)) \in X$.
>
> X *is closed under primitive recursion: Let* $\boldsymbol{x}$ *be an n-vector of variables. If* $h(y, z, \boldsymbol{x}) \in X$ *and* $g(\boldsymbol{x}) \in X$ *then the unique function* $f(y, \boldsymbol{x})$ *determined by the following equations is also in* χ:
> $f(0, \boldsymbol{x}) = g(\boldsymbol{x})$ *and*
> $f(y + 1, \boldsymbol{x}) = h(y, f(y, \boldsymbol{x}), \boldsymbol{x})$.

The basic functions are all total and the two operations for building new functions both yield total functions when provided with total functions, so the primitive recursive functions are all total recursive.

A *relation* is primitive recursive just in case its characteristic function is primitive recursive, so all primitive recursive relations are recursive. It is easy to show by diagonalization, however, that not all total recursive functions are primitive recursive. The primitive recursive relations are closed under finitary Boolean operations, and hence under bounded quantification. If f and P are primitive recursive, then so are the following functions:

$$\mu x < k(P(x)) = \begin{cases} the\ least\ x < k\ such\ that\ P(x), if\ there\ is\ one \\ k\ otherwise. \end{cases}$$

$$g(x) = \begin{cases} f(x)\ if\ P(x) \\ h(x)\ otherwise. \end{cases}$$

---

[11] For elementary proofs of all the following claims about primitive recursion, cf. Cutland (1986): 95–99.

Recall the Turing relation from the preceding chapter:

$$\mathcal{T}(i, x, k) \Leftrightarrow \text{the Turing computation } P_i[x] \text{ halts within } k \text{ steps.}$$

In a similar vein, we may define the step-bounded universal function:

$$v(i, x, k) = \begin{cases} \phi_i(x) + 1 & \text{if } \mathcal{T}(i, x, k) \\ 0 & \text{otherwise.} \end{cases}$$

This function simply simulates the computation $P_i(x)$ for k steps, returns 0 if the computation has not halted yet, and adds 1 to the output and passes it along otherwise. Since simulating a given step of a Turing computation for one step is trivial, it should come as no surprise that $\mathcal{T}$ and v are both primitive recursive. Hence, primitive recursion will do anything a Turing machine can do, so long as there is a bound established in advance on when to stop. Turing computability, on the other hand, supports *unbounded* searches that go on and on until they find what they are looking for. In light of the analogy between induction and computation, Turing-decidable predicates correspond to formal hypotheses decidable with certainty and primitive recursive predicates are analogous to formal hypotheses decidable under some a priori time bound.

Are primitive recursive scientists as reliable as Turing-computable scientists? That seems dubious, because not all total recursive functions are primitive recursive. But it turns out that so long as no bound is placed on the time by which convergence to the truth must occur, primitive recursive scientists are just as powerful as Turing-computable scientists. The reason for this is fairly intuitive. A Turing machine is prepared in advance to go to any lengths, including weeks without sleep at the office, to get the job done. A primitive recursive scientist works as hard as anyone during the day, but will do so only if quitting time is clearly specified in advance. Fortunately, convergence to the truth is consistent with this more leisurely lifestyle, so long as tomorrow's work is not postponed for eternity. In fact, that is just how the general, Turing-computable architecture for limiting verification presented in the proof of proposition 7.9(b) works. A quick inspection of its definition shows that it is primitive recursive, since it is defined in terms of primitive recursion and composition over primitive recursive relations.

It is a little more surprising that the same thing is true in the certainty case. After all, the hypotheses that are decidable with certainty are exactly the *recursive* subsets of the Baire space, and didn't I just say at the beginning of this section that not all recursive sets are primitive recursive? The solution is that not all recursive sets of *numbers* are primitive recursive, but all recursive sets of *data streams* are primitive recursive. When a set of numbers must be decided, a primitive recursive agent must know in advance how long to compute on a given input. If unbounded searches are required, the agent cannot know in advance how large the search bound must be. But each finite initial segment of an infinite data stream counts as a distinct input, so a primitive recursive agent can always give itself more time to work on a formal problem by postponing the work until more data is read and then setting the current runtime bound to be the length of the data.

Proposition 8.10 (Gold 1965)

$$H \text{ is } \begin{bmatrix} verifiable_C \\ refutable_C \\ decidable_C \end{bmatrix} \begin{bmatrix} with\ n\ mind\ changes \\ in\ the\ limit \\ gradually \end{bmatrix} given\ \mathcal{K}\ by\ a\ Turing\ machine$$

$$\Leftrightarrow some\ primitive\ recursive\ method\ can\ do\ so.$$

Proof: The verifiability and refutability in the limit cases are handled by the proof of proposition 7.9(b). For the *n*-mind change case and decidability in the limit case, let α decide$_C$ h with n mind changes starting with a and let $\alpha = \phi_i$. Define:

$$f(e) = \begin{cases} max\ y \le lh(e)\ such\ that\ \mathcal{T}(i, e \mid y, lh(e)),\ if\ there\ is\ one \\ lh(e) + 1\ otherwise. \end{cases}$$

$$\beta(e) = \begin{cases} a\ if\ e = 0\ or\ f(e) = lh(e) + 1 \\ v(i, e \mid f(e), lh(e)) - 1\ otherwise. \end{cases}$$

β is primitive recursive in light of preceding remarks. $\beta(e)$ is the conjecture α makes on the longest initial segment of e on which α can produce a conjecture in $lh(e)$ steps if there is such a conjecture and is the initial conjecture a of α otherwise. So β succeeds in n mind changes starting with a if α does.[12] The gradual case is left as an exercise. ∎

11.   The Empirical Irony of Cognitive Science Revisited

Recall that if it is true that we are Turing machines, then it is impossible for us to verify in the limit that we are. What about the cognitive hypothesis that we are primitive recursive devices? Define:

$$C_{h_{prim}} = \{\varepsilon: \varepsilon\ is\ a\ primitive\ recursive\ function\}.$$

This hypothesis is much easier to investigate than the hypothesis that ε is a Turing-computable sequence.

---

[12] β does not handle the verification in the limit or gradual verification cases because it may converge to 1 when α does not by skipping all of α's 0 conjectures.

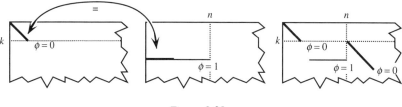

Figure 8.20

Proposition 8.11

$C_{h_{prim}} \in \Sigma_2^A - \Pi_2^B.$

Proof: I leave $C_{h_{prim}} \in \Sigma_2^A$ as exercise 8.10. I will show that $C_{h_{prim}} \notin \Pi_2^B$. For reductio, let ideal scientist α refute$_C$ h_{prim} in the limit. The primitive recursive definitions can be effectively encoded by natural numbers. Let f_i denote the primitive recursive function whose definition receives code number i. Hence, there is a total recursive function g such that for each i, $x \in \omega$, $g(i, x)$ is the value of the ith primitive recursive function on argument x. The function g can be computed simply by decoding the code number i and by simulating the computation directed by that definition on x. We may think of g as determining a table whose ith row is the primitive recursive function f_i.

The demon begins by feeding $g(0, 0) + 1, g(1, 1) + 1, \ldots, g(n, n) + 1, \ldots$ to α until α says 0, which must happen, else α converges to 1 on a sequence that is not primitive recursive (since it differs from each row of the table in at least one place). Let $g(x, y) + 1$ be the datum presented when this happens. Then the demon finds some i such that f_i agrees with what has been presented so far. There exists one, since any finite sequence can be memorized by a primitive recursive program (using a composition of constant functions and place selection functions). Then the demon proceeds to feed the values of f_i, starting from where the current data stops, until α says 1 again, say at stage n. Next, the demon starts presenting $g(x, n + 1) + 1$, $g(x + 1, n + 2) + 1, \ldots, g(x + k, n + k + 1) + 1, \ldots$ until α conjectures 0, and so forth (*Fig. 8.20*). In the limit, a zigzag diagonal sequence is presented that differs from each f_i in at least one place, but α changes its mind infinitely often instead of converging to 0. Contradiction. ∎

Since we have just seen that primitive recursive scientists can verify in the limit whatever effective scientists can, the hypothesis that we are primitive recursive could be verified by us in the limit if it were true. Thus, h_{prim} is not self-defeating in the way h_{comp} is.

h_{prim} is nonetheless a hard hypothesis that could not be decided even in the limit even by an ideal agent with no computational limitations. It doesn't help to propose that the mind is a finite state automaton. Define $C_{h_{DFA}} = \{\varepsilon \in 2^\omega: \varepsilon \text{ is computed by some DFA}\}$. The argument of proposition 8.11 applies directly to the automaton case as well, so we have:

Corollary 8.12

$$C_{h_{DFA}} \in \Sigma_2^A - \Pi_2^B. \qquad\qquad\qquad\qquad\qquad\qquad \blacksquare$$

Exercises

8.1. Prove proposition 8.2.

8.2. Show that each set represented by a limiting regular expression is limiting regular.

8.3. Find a limiting regular expression for C_{aabb}. Sketch three automata and write the limiting regular expressions for them.

8.4. Build a minimal state DFA that verifies the hypothesis $(\underline{010^*\underline{0}})^*(\underline{0010^*\underline{1}})^\dagger$ in the limit given 2^ω.

8.5. Are limiting regular sets closed under finite intersection?

8.6. Finish the proof of lemma 8.4. Also prove proposition 8.3(c).

8.7. Show that applying the construction of proposition 8.8 to $\mathbf{M_0}$ does not yield a DFA that accepts in the limit the same data streams as $\mathbf{M_0}$ does under the continuous interpretation.

8.8. Write an algorithm that turns an automaton into a limiting regular expression for the hypothesis it verifies [refutes, decides] in the limit. Provide an algorithm that turns a limiting regular expression into an automaton that verifies the hypothesis it represents in the limit.

8.9. Find a Σ_2^A set that is not limiting regular. Assume that there exists a nonregular set.

8.10. Prove that $C_{h_{prim}} \in \Sigma_2^A$. (Construct a computable scientist that enumerates and tests all primitive recursive functions.)

8.11. State and prove the gradual cases of proposition 8.10.

*8.12. Suppose we are interested in the computational resources demanded by α to produce its conjecture at each stage of inquiry. Let $\mathcal{K} \subseteq O^\omega$, where O is a finite alphabet. We may define:

α *runs in polynomial time* $\Leftrightarrow \exists i$ such that $\phi_i = \alpha$, $\exists$ *polynomial function p such that* $\forall e \in O^*$, $\mathcal{T}(i, e, p(lh(e)))$.

For example, h_{fin} has a polynomial time limiting verifier, namely the teeter-totter automaton. Show that, unfortunately, *every* limiting decision problem that has a Turing-computable solution has a polynomial time solution. Show the same for the n-mind change and limiting verification cases. What if we define complexity only with respect to weakly data-minimal solutions? How about if we define complexity only relative to a given modulus function? Draw some philosophical morals about what computational complexity means for limiting inference problems.

9

The Logic of Ideal Discovery

1. Introduction

So far, we have focused on hypothesis assessment problems, in which a scientist is assigned some particular hypothesis to investigate. But from the broadest perspective, inquiry poses the problem of coming up with a correct theory of one's subject, and the assessement and rejection of various hypotheses is merely a means toward this goal. Much discussion in the philosophy of science has revolved around the question of how to build discovery procedures out of assessment procedures. For example, many philosophers have advocated an architecture for discovery in which hypotheses are produced or invented in sequence and the first hypothesis to "pass muster" is conjectured until it fails. The philosopher Karl Popper begins his treatise on the logic of scientific discovery with these two paragraphs:

> A scientist, whether theorist or experimenter, puts forward statements, or systems of statements, and tests them step by step. In the field of the empirical sciences, more particularly, he constructs hypotheses, or systems of theories, and tests them against experience by observation and experiment.
>
> I suggest that it is the task of the logic of scientific discovery, or the logic of knowledge, to give a logical analysis of this procedure; that is, to analyze the method of the empirical sciences.[1]

In this passage, Popper describes what he takes to be the actual architecture of scientific discovery and proposes that the logic of discovery analyze its performance. From the logical reliabilist perspective, there is a more important question, namely, whether there is a more reliable way to organize inquiry than

---

[1] Popper (1968): 27.

what Popper takes to be the actual way. In fact there is, and a mathematical characterization of the extent of the improvement will be provided in this chapter. It seems that for all his admonitions against confusing "ought" with "is",[2] Popper is guilty of precisely that error at the very outset of his treatise.

Another tendency in the philosophy of science has been to insist that "there is no logic of dicovery."[3]

> An adequate rule of induction would therefore have to provide, for atomic theory and for every other conceivable case, mechanically applicable criteria determining unambiguously, and without any reliance on the inventiveness or additional scientific knowledge of its user, all those new abstract concepts which need to be created for the formulation of the theory that will account for the given evidence. Clearly, this requirement cannot be satisfied by any set of rules, however ingeniously devised; there can be no general rules of induction in the above sense; the demand for them rests on a confusion of logical and psychological issues. What determines the soundness of a hypothesis is not the way it is arrived at ... but the way it stands up when tested.[4]

Such claims have their appeal. If it were easy to come up with important, new ideas, everyone would have a Nobel prize. But just like any other sort of problem, discovery problems come in degrees of difficulty, ranging from the unsolvable in principle to the computationally trivial. The interesting and objective question is where the line between the solvable and the unsolvable discovery problems falls. The aim of the present chapter is to draw this line from a logical reliabilist point of view.

Another position in the philosophical literature is that although there may be methods of discovery, their study is somehow an inappropriate topic for inductive methodology.

> One must ask what is specifically philosophical about studying the genesis of theories. Simply put, a theory is an artifact, fashioned perhaps by certain tools (e.g., implicit rules of 'search'). The investigation of the mode of manufacture of artifacts (whether clay pots, surgical scalpels, or vitamin pills) is not normally viewed as a philosophical activity.[5]

Somewhat later, the same author insists that the logic of hypothesis *assessment*, in contrast with the logic of hypothesis *generation*, *is* of great philosophical interest. From the viewpoint of the preceding chapters, however, methodological analysis is a matter of reliability relative to background beliefs, and nothing precludes holding discovery methods to the same standard. Indeed, assessment can be viewed as a *special case* of discovery, where what is to be discovered is

---

[2] "[The logic of analysis of scientific knowledge] is concerned not with questions of fact (Kant's *quid facti*) but only with questions of justification or validity (Kant's *quid juris*)" (Popper 1968): 31.
[3] A notable exception is Simon (1973).
[4] Hempel (1965): 6.
[5] Laudan (1980): 182.

whether *h* is correct or incorrect. Both in discovery and in assessment, the question is whether the method employed is guaranteed to arrive at a correct result relative to what is assumed in advance. From this point of view, the presumed sharp distinction between assessment and discovery is spurious.

2. Basic Definitions

A hypothesis assessment method α takes a finite data sequence and a hypothesis as inputs, and outputs an assessment or test value. A *hypothesis generator*, on the other hand, conjectures a hypothesis in response to a finite data sequence (*Fig. 9.1*).

Let γ be a hypothesis generator and let ε be a data stream.

> *γ stabilizes to h on ε*
>   ⟺ *there is a stage n such that for each later stage $m \geq n$, $\gamma(\varepsilon|m) = h$.*

Successful discovery demands that a correct hypothesis be found for each data stream in $\mathcal{K}$. It may seem harsh to require that a correct hypothesis be found when none exists, but if it is desired to exempt α from failure in such circumstances, this can be readily accomplished by choosing $\mathcal{K} \subseteq dom(C)$. Recall that from the most general perspective, $\bar{\mathcal{K}}$ is the set of data streams on which α is exempted from failure, and one good reason for clemency would be that no correct hypothesis exists. Therefore, the exemption need not be written into our definition of success on a given data stream.

> *γ identifies a correct$_C$ hypothesis in the limit on ε*
>   ⟺ *there is an h such that $C(h, \varepsilon)$ and γ stabilizes to h on ε.*
>
> *γ identifies correct$_C$ hypotheses in the limit given $\mathcal{K}$*
>   ⟺ *for each $\varepsilon \in \mathcal{K}$, γ identifies a correct$_C$ hypothesis in the limit on ε.*

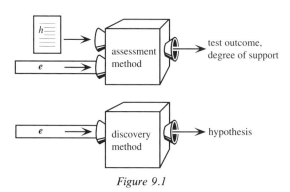

Figure 9.1

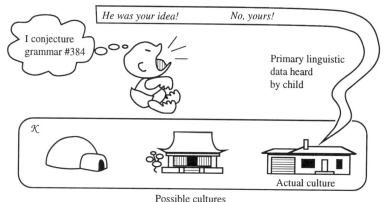

Possible cultures

Figure 9.2

Parallel notions of being correct by stage n, with certainty, or with n mind changes can be defined along the lines of chapter 3. In the certainty case, the first hypothesis to follow the first occurence of '!' is taken to be the hypothesis conjectured with certainty by γ.

We obtain different paradigms for discovery when we specify different concrete correctness relations C. For example, the *language learnability paradigm*[6] is supposed to model the problem of an infant who must converge to a correct grammar for his natural language, no matter what natural language his culture speaks (*Fig. 9.2*).

Since a grammar provides at least a computable positive test for a language, languages are modeled as r.e. sets. The scientist (or child, in this case) is required to converge to a correct r.e. index for a given set over all possible enumerations of the set. This corresponds to the dubiously severe assumption that the child has no knowledge about what kind of sentence will follow another one in his data:

Example 9.1 Language learnability by r.e. index[7]

Correctness: $C_{r.e.}(\varepsilon, i) \Leftrightarrow rng(\varepsilon) = W_i$;

Knowledge: $\mathcal{K} \subseteq \mathcal{K}_{r.e.} = \{\varepsilon: rng(\varepsilon) \text{ is r.e.}\}$.

Many variations on the language learning paradigm have been considered. An obvious variant requires the child to infer a decision procedure for his language, rather than merely a positive test, since nobody seems to get caught in an infinite loop when confronted with gibberish.[8] Let χ_S denote the characteristic function of S. Then define:

---

[6] Gold (1967).
[7] Gold (1967) and Osherson et al. (1986).
[8] Gold (1967).

Example 9.2 Language learnability by recursive index

Correctness: $C_{rec}(\varepsilon, i) \Leftrightarrow \chi_{rng(\varepsilon)} = \phi_i$;

Knowledge: $\mathcal{K} \subseteq \mathcal{K}_{rec} = \{\varepsilon: rng(\varepsilon) \text{ is recursive}\}$.

Another paradigm that has seen a great deal of study by computer scientists is recursive function identification.[9] This corresponds to the problem of automated computer programming, in which, for example, the automated programmer is shown increasing numbers of examples of what the program to be written is supposed to do, and must inductively infer a correct procedure for the task at hand. It also corresponds to the problem facing a scientist who examines a discrete system whose law is known to be some simple, computable function such as a polynomial with rational coefficients. Formally, the problem is to infer the index of some Turing machine that computes exactly the input evidence sequence.

Example 9.3 Recursive function identification

Correctness: $C_{cmp}(\varepsilon, i) \Leftrightarrow \varepsilon = \phi_i$;

Knowledge: $\mathcal{K} \subseteq \mathcal{R}$ (= *the set of all total recursive functions*).

A total program provides a prediction for each observation. It may be easier to find a program that leaves some determinate number of predictions unspecified.

Example 9.4 Incomplete function identification

Correctness: $C_{cmp}^{k}(\varepsilon, i) \Leftrightarrow \phi_i \subseteq \varepsilon \text{ and } |\varepsilon - \phi_i| = k$;

Knowledge: $\mathcal{K} \subseteq \mathcal{R}$.

Each of these correctness relations has a fairly low Borel complexity. Thus in light of the Borel determinacy theorem (proposition 5.6), unsolvability can always be shown by means of a demonic argument in these cases.[10]

Proposition 9.5

(a) $C_{r.e.} \in \Pi_2^B - \Sigma[\mathcal{K}_{r.e.}]_2^B$.

(b) $C_{rec} \in \Pi_2^B - \Sigma[\mathcal{K}_{rec}]_2^B$.

(c) $C_{cmp} \in \Pi_1^B - \Sigma[\mathcal{R}]_1^B$.

(d) $C_{cmp}^{k} \in \Pi_1^B - \Sigma[\mathcal{R}]_1^B$.

---

[9] Gold (1965).
[10] E.g., Angluin (1980) and Osherson et al. (1986).

Proof Exercise 9.1   ■

It was shown in section 7.8 that there is no need to exclude uncomputable hypotheses from learning theoretic analysis, even in the case of computable methods. Recall the arithmetical indexing theorem (proposition 7.4). This theorem yields an indexing for each arithmetical complexity class Σ_b^A. Instead of identifying recursive or r.e. indices, we could require identification in terms of indices for higher complexity classes instead.

3. Assessment as Discovery

Each hypothesis assessment problem can be thought of as a discovery problem in which there are just two hypotheses to consider, "h is correct" and "h is not correct," coded by 1 and 0, respectively. Conversely, when $rng(C) \subseteq \{0, 1\}$, then to identify correct$_C$ hypotheses is just to decide$_C$ hypothesis 1.

The reason discovery is often preferable to the assessment of a single hypothesis is that the catchall hypothesis "h is incorrect" is often very uninformative (*Fig. 9.3*). For example, the hypothesis that every attempted cut of a given particle will succeed is correct only relative to the everywhere 1 data stream, and hence is incorrect for every other data stream but this one. To know that the hypothesis is correct is to know exactly what will happen at every step in the future, but to know that it is incorrect is to know nothing about what will happen at any given stage of inquiry. The general point is that *content* is not the same thing as *complexity*. An empirically complete hypothesis is always Π_1^B, so higher complexity hypotheses are actually *weaker* in terms of excluding possible data streams.

If the hypothesis language is sufficiently expressive, discovery problems can chop $\mathcal{K}$ into more evenly matched chunks of relatively similar informational value (*Fig. 9.4*). Unfortunately, this means that the scientist must in some sense consider many alternative hypotheses; perhaps infinitely many. In the next chapter, we will examine what *consideration* of hypotheses amounts to and how it can make computable inquiry impossible.

4. Conjectures and Refutations

We have just seen that hypothesis assessment may be viewed as a special kind of discovery problem. On the other side, it is natural to ask whether reliable

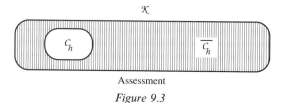

Assessment

Figure 9.3

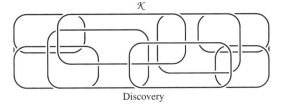

Discovery

Figure 9.4

discovery methods can always be built up out of reliable assessment methods. Popperians and methodologists known as hypothetico-deductivists are wedded to a particular proposal for doing just this. According to them, inquiry should proceed by enumerating hypotheses and by testing them, sequentially, according to some assessment criterion. The hypothesis enumeration may reflect arbitrary psychological urges, or it may be ordered according to boldness, symmetry, simplicity, or whatever formal properties of hypotheses one might prefer. A conjecture is retained until it fails the test, at which time the method proceeds in the enumeration until a new conjecture is found that passes muster (*Fig. 9.5*).

Accordingly, let η be an enumeration of hypotheses, and let α be a hypothesis assessor defined on the hypotheses occurring in η. Define the *enumerate and test* method generated by α, η as follows:

$\gamma_{\alpha, \eta}(e) = $ *the first h in η such that $\alpha(h, e) = 1$.*

γ is an *enumerate and test method* just in case for some α, η, $\gamma = \gamma_{\alpha, h}$. Let $consist_{C, \mathcal{K}}(h, e)$ be a consistency test for the correctness of h in the following sense:

$$consist_{C, \mathcal{K}}(h, e) = \begin{cases} 1 & \text{if } C_h \cap \mathcal{K} \cap [e] \neq \varnothing \\ 0 & \text{otherwise.} \end{cases}$$

For example, Popper's recommended method of "bold conjectures and refutations" has η enumerate some hypothesis space H by descending "audacity"

Figure 9.5

and employs $consist_{C, \mathcal{K}}$ as the operative assessment method. When $\gamma = \gamma_{\alpha, \eta}$, where $\alpha = consist_{C, \mathcal{K}}$, we say that γ is a *conjectures and refutations method*. The question whether this is how inquiry ought to proceed involves at least the following pair of questions:

(1) *Is the conjectures and refutations architecture restrictive (i.e., is there a solvable identification problem that no conjectures and refutations method can solve?)*

(2) *If so, is there a different architecture that is not restrictive?*

It is easy to see that the conjectures and refutations architecture is indeed restrictive as far as identification in the limit is concerned, even for ideal agents. Consider two hypotheses h, h' such that C_h = the set of all binary data streams that stabilize to 1 and $C_{h'}$ = the set of all binary data streams that stabilize to 0, where $\mathcal{K} = C_h \cup C_{h'}$. C_h and $C_{h'}$ each contain a limit point missing from the other. C_h contains the everywhere 1 sequence, each initial segment of which is an initial segment of some data stream that stabilizes to 0, and $C_{h'}$ contains the everywhere 0 sequence, each initial segment of which is an initial segment of some data stream that stabilizes to 1. But no matter how much "creative intuition" is involved in the enumeration η of these two hypotheses, one must precede the other. Suppose h precedes h'. Then if the true data stream is the everywhere 0 sequence, h is incorrect but is refuted by no finite sequence of 0s, so the conjectures and refutations method stabilizes to the incorrect hypothesis h. The case when h' precedes h is similar.

One diagnosis of the diffulty is that the consistency test can use just one mind change starting with 1, so that if it verifies h *in the limit, it also refutes h* with certainty. But neither of the hypotheses in our example is refutable with certainty given $\mathcal{K}$. In fact, both h and h' are decidable in the limit given $\mathcal{K}$ by

$$\alpha(h, e) = \begin{cases} 1 & \textit{if the last entry in e is 1} \\ 0 & \textit{otherwise.} \end{cases}$$

$$\alpha(h', e) = \begin{cases} 1 & \textit{if the last entry in e is 0} \\ 0 & \textit{otherwise.} \end{cases}$$

On the other hand, neither h nor h' is verifiable or refutable with certainty, as may be readily verified by demonic argument. If we let α be the method just defined, then $\gamma_{\alpha, \eta}$ identifies $correct_C$ hypotheses in the limit given $\mathcal{K}$, where $\eta = (h, h')$.

In the preceding example, we saw a problem for which enumerate and test is restrictive if the test employed is logical refutation. It might be objected that logical refutation is a narrow notion of test. But one can readily modify the preceding example so that:

(a) *each hypothesis is verifiable in the limit and*

(b) *some enumerate and test method identifies correct hypotheses in the limit, but*

(c) *no enumerate and test method whose test method is a limiting verifier does so.*

In other words, the following problem can be solved by an enumerate and test method only if the test employed is less reliable than it could have been! This is bad news for the familiar thesis, expressed in the quotation at the beginning of this chapter, that discovery procedures inherit their normative force from the test procedures they employ.

Proposition 9.6

Let $C(\varepsilon, h) \Leftrightarrow$ the odd-numbered subsequence of ε stabilizes to 0, let
$C(\varepsilon, h') \Leftrightarrow$ the even-numbered subsequence of ε stabilizes to 1, and let
$$\mathcal{K} = C_h \cup C_{h'}.$$

Then (a), (b) *and* (c) *hold.*

Proof: (a) Immediate. (c) By the usual, demonic argument, neither h nor h' is decidable$_C$ in the limit given $\mathcal{K}$. Suppose α verifies$_C$ h, h' in the limit given $\mathcal{K}$. Then (*) for some $\varepsilon \in \mathcal{K} - C_h$, α conjectures 1 on ε, h infinitely often (else α decides$_C$ h in the limit given $\mathcal{K}$, which is a contradiction), and similarly for h'. By the symmetry of h, h', we may assume without loss of generality that h precedes h' in η. By (*) there is some $\varepsilon \in \mathcal{K} - C_h$ such that α conjectures infinitely many 1s on ε, h. But each time this happens, $\gamma_{\alpha, \eta}$ incorrectly conjectures h. (b) Let α' be just like α except that when $\alpha(h, e) = \alpha(h', e) = 1$ and α says 0 for h more recently for h' on e, then $\alpha'(h, e) = 0$ and $\alpha(h', e) = 1$. $\gamma_{\alpha', \eta}$ identifies correct$_C$ hypotheses in the limit given $\mathcal{K}$. ∎

We have just seen that the enumerate and test architecture can sometimes turn an unreliable test into a reliable discovery procedure. There is also a general way to turn reliable test procedures into reliable discovery procedures, but it is *not* the enumerate and test architecture recommended by hypothetico-deductivists. Let η enumerate $rng(C)$, and let α be an assessment method. The *bumping pointer method*[11] $\beta_{\alpha, \eta}(e)$ works as follows. Let η' be some result of padding η so that every hypothesis that occurs in η occurs infinitely often in η', but no hypothesis that does not occur in η occurs in η'. The method uses α to test η'_0 on increasing segments of e until it is found that for some $i \leq lh(e)$, $\alpha(\eta'_0, e|i) \neq 1$. Then the pointer is bumped to η'_1, until α returns a value less than 1 for η'_1, and so forth, until all of e is read. The hypothesis the pointer remains at after scanning all of e is conjectured by $\beta_{\alpha, \eta}(e)$ (*Fig. 9.6*).

---

[11] This method and the following argument were introduced in Osherson and Weinstein (1991) in the first-order hypothesis setting.

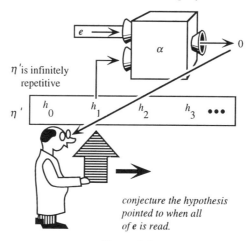

η' is infinitely
repetitive

Figure 9.6

Proposition 9.7

Let $H \subseteq \omega$. If $\mathcal{K} \subseteq \bigcup \{C_h : h \in H\}$ and α verifies$_C$ H in the limit given $\mathcal{K}$, then $\beta_{\alpha, \eta}$ identifies correct$_C$ hypotheses in the limit given $\mathcal{K}$.

Proof: Let $\varepsilon \in \mathcal{K}$. Then for some for some $h \in H$, $\varepsilon \in C_h$. So for some n, we have that $\forall m \geq n$, $\alpha(h, \varepsilon | m) = 1$. Moreover, h occurs in η' (the infinitely repetitive version of η employed by $\beta_{\alpha, \eta}$) infinitely often, and hence at some position $m' \geq n$ in η'. Thus, the pointer cannot move beyond position m'. Now suppose h' occurs at some position m'' prior to m' in η' and $\varepsilon \notin C_{h'}$. Then α returns 0 infinitely often for h' on ε. Thus, the pointer cannot remain at position m'' forever. So the pointer must remain forever at some correct hypothesis, and $\beta_{\alpha, \eta}$ stabilizes to this hypothesis. ∎

5.   A Complete Architecture for Discovery

We have just seen some strategies for converting reliable, uniform assessment procedures into reliable discovery procedures. But none of the architectures considered so far is complete, because discovery can be reliable even when no assessment method can reliably verify all hypotheses in the limit. This may seem paradoxical, since working on an assigned hypothesis seems like a simpler matter than constructing a correct hypothesis de novo. But a few examples quickly reveal otherwise. For a trivial case, if some hypothesis is always correct, then a discovery procedure can succeed by conjecturing this hypothesis in all circumstances, without assessing any other hypothesis. More generally, $\mathcal{K}$ may be covered by some subset of H containing only simple hypotheses, so that hypotheses in H that are too complex to verify in the limit need not be considered.

Figure 9.7

Discovery can be made easier in a yet more general way. A discovery method is free to pretend that correctness is *more stringent* than it really is, where the more stringent correctness relation $\mathcal{D} \subseteq C$ is obtained from the original relation C by making some hypotheses incorrect on data streams on which they were previously deemed by C to be correct. Then the discovery method can employ a reliable assessor α attuned to this imaginary notion of correctness, and whatever α judges correct will be correct, but not conversely (*Fig. 9.7*).

This may again seem paradoxical. How could pretending that fewer hypotheses are correct for various data streams make it easier to find correct hypotheses? The answer is that making a correctness relation more stringent can also make it far less complex, just as planing wood from a rough surface can make it smooth. For example, consider the discovery problem posed by:

Correctness relation: $C(\varepsilon, h) \Leftrightarrow \varepsilon_0 = h$ or h occurs infinitely often in ε.

Knowledge: $\mathcal{K} = \mathcal{N}$.

Hypothesis set: $H = \omega$.

No hypothesis in H is verifiable$_{C_0}$ in the limit. But we can define a more stringent correctness relation $\mathcal{D}(\varepsilon, i) \Leftrightarrow \varepsilon$ begins with i, so that $\mathcal{D} \subseteq C$ and $\mathcal{D} \in \Delta_1^B$. So each hypothesis is decidable with certainty with respect to $\mathcal{D}$, and hence by proposition 9.3, identification in the limit is possible (*Fig. 9.8*).

It is possible to make $\mathcal{D}$ too stringent. The simplest and most stringent notion of correctness makes no hypotheses correct under any circumstances. But of course, such a relation is also a useless guide for what to conjecture. We must insist that in reducing complexity, we retain some correct hypothesis for

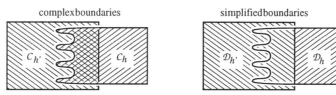

Figure 9.8

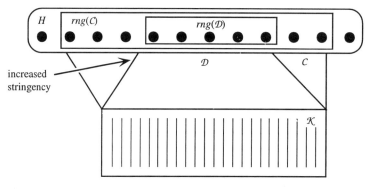

Figure 9.9

each data stream in $\mathcal{K}$ that has a correct hypothesis according to C. That is, we must require that $dom(C) \subseteq dom(\mathcal{D})$. These considerations give rise to a simple, topological characterization of reliable discovery in the limit (*Fig. 9.9*):

Proposition 9.8

Correct$_C$ hypotheses are identifiable in the limit given $\mathcal{K}$
    $\Leftrightarrow$ *there is some $\mathcal{D}$ such that*

(1) $\mathcal{D} \subseteq C$ *and*

(2) $\mathcal{K} \subseteq dom(\mathcal{D})$ *and*

(3) *for each $h \in \omega$, $\mathcal{D}_h \cap \mathcal{K} \in \Sigma[\mathcal{K}]_2^B$.*

Corollary 9.9

The proposition remains true if we add the condition: (4) $\mathcal{D}$ is single valued.

Corollary 9.10

The proposition remains true if we replace $\Sigma[\mathcal{K}]_2^B$ with $\Delta[\mathcal{K}]_2^B$ in (3).

Proof: ($\Rightarrow$) Let γ identify correct$_C$ hypotheses in the limit given $\mathcal{K}$. Then by the definition of identification in the limit we have:

    (i) $\forall \varepsilon \in \mathcal{K}, \exists n, \forall m \geq n, \gamma(\varepsilon|m) = \gamma(\varepsilon|n) \, \& \, C(\varepsilon, \gamma(\varepsilon|m))$.

Next, define $\mathcal{D}$ relative to $\mathcal{K}$ as follows:

    (ii) $\forall \varepsilon \in \mathcal{K}, \forall h \in \omega, \mathcal{D}(\varepsilon, h) \Leftrightarrow \exists n \, \forall m \geq n, \gamma(\varepsilon|m) = h$.

(1), (2), and (3) are immediate from (i) and (ii). For corollary 9.9, observe that $\mathcal{D}$

is single valued, by (ii). For corollary 9.10, define $\alpha(h, e) = 1$ if $\gamma(e) = h$, and 0 otherwise. For each $h \in \omega$, α stabilizes to 0 when h is incorrect$_\mathcal{D}$ and stabilizes to 1 when h is correct$_\mathcal{D}$, so α decides$_\mathcal{D}$ ω in the limit given $\mathcal{K}$.

($\Leftarrow$) Suppose conditions (1–3) are met for some $\mathcal{D} \subseteq C$. Then let α verify$_\mathcal{D}$ ω in the limit given $\mathcal{K}$. Let η be an enumeration of $rng(\mathcal{D})$. Then $\mathcal{K} \subseteq \bigcup \{\mathcal{D}_h : h \in \omega\}$. So by proposition 9.7, $\beta_{\alpha, \eta}$ identifies correct$_\mathcal{D}$ hypotheses in the limit given $\mathcal{K}$. By (1) and (2), $\beta_{\alpha, \eta}$ identifies correct$_C$ hypotheses in the limit given $\mathcal{K}$. In this direction, the corollaries are immediate. ∎

This amounts to a proof that the bumping pointer architecture is complete for identication in the limit. Unlike all the characterizations considered in preceding chapters, this condition forces us to search for low-complexity definitions of subrelations of C, rather than merely to consider the complexity of C. This extra complication may be ignored in special cases in which it is clear that no subrelation $\mathcal{D} \subseteq C$ with the same domain as C can have a lower complexity than C has. Say that C is *disjoint* given $\mathcal{K}$ just in case for each h, $h' \in rng(C)$, $C_h \cap C_{h'} \cap \mathcal{K} = \varnothing$ or $C_h \cap \mathcal{K} = C_{h'} \cap \mathcal{K}$ (*Fig. 9.10*).

For example, $C_{r.e.}$, C_{rec}, and C_{cmp} are all disjoint given $\mathcal{N}$, but C_{cmp}^k is not disjoint given $\mathcal{K}_{cmp}$. Then the following corollaries of proposition 9.8 are immediate.

Corollary 9.11

If C is disjoint given $\mathcal{K}$ then correct$_C$ hypotheses are identifiable in the limit given $\mathcal{K} \Leftrightarrow$

(1) *$\mathcal{K} \subseteq dom(C)$ and*

(2) *for each $h \in rng(C)$, $C_h \cap \mathcal{K} \in \Sigma[\mathcal{K}]_2^B$.*

Corollary 9.12

$\Sigma[\mathcal{K}]_2^B$ in (2) can be replaced with $\Delta[\mathcal{K}]_2^B$. ∎

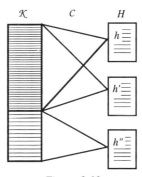

Figure 9.10

In such cases we can prove unsolvability by showing that some hypothesis correct for some data stream in $\mathcal{K}$ is not decidable in the limit. For example, consider the following discovery problem:

$C(\varepsilon, i) \Leftrightarrow i$ *occurs infinitely often in* ε.

$\mathcal{K} = \{\varepsilon$: *exactly one* $i \in \omega$ *occurs infinitely often in* $\varepsilon\}$.

To show that correct$_C$ hypotheses are not identifiable in the limit given $\mathcal{K}$, it suffices to show that no ideal method can decide$_C$ 0 in the limit given $\mathcal{K}$, which follows by a simple demonic argument.

6. Data-Minimal Limiting Discovery

Suppose that correct$_C$ hypotheses are identifiable in the limit given $\mathcal{K}$. Then by proposition 9.8, we know that for some $\mathcal{D} \subseteq C$, $\mathcal{K} \subseteq dom(\mathcal{D})$ and for each $h \in rng(\mathcal{D})$, $\mathcal{D}_h \cap \mathcal{K} \in \Sigma[\mathcal{K}]_2^B$. So for each $h \in rng(\mathcal{D})$, there is a collection of $\mathcal{K}$-closed sets $\{S[h]_i : i \in \omega\}$ such that $\mathcal{D}_h \cap \mathcal{K} = S[h]_0 \cup S[h]_1 \cup \cdots \cup S[h]_n \cup \cdots$. Pick an infinitely repetitive enumeration ξ of all these sets, where each set is labeled with the hypothesis h it corresponds to. On evidence e, search for the first set in ξ not yet refuted by the data and conjecture its associated hypothesis. This architecture is like the hypothetico-deductive architecture in the sense that it employs an enumeration and a refutation test, but unlike the hypothetico-deductive architecture, the refutation test is applied not to *hypotheses*, which may not be refutable with certainty, but to *closed subsets* of hypotheses. This may be referred to as the *quasi enumerate and test architecture*.

Say that $\mathcal{D}$ is a *single valued version* of C just in case $\mathcal{D} \subseteq C$ and for each $h \in rng(C)$, there is a unique $h' \in rng(\mathcal{D})$ such that $\mathcal{D}_{h'} \cap \mathcal{K} = C_h \cap \mathcal{K}$. In other words, $\mathcal{D}$ retains a unique representative of each empirical equivalence class of hypotheses in $rng(C)$. It turns out that if C is disjoint given $\mathcal{K}$, then no matter how we set up the quasi enumerate and test architecture for a single valued version of C, we end up with a data-minimal discovery procedure, assuming that the problem posed by C is solvable at all (*Fig. 9.11*).

Proposition 9.13

Suppose that C is disjoint given $\mathcal{K}$ and that correct$_C$ hypotheses are identifiable in the limit given $\mathcal{K}$. For each single valued version $\mathcal{D}$ of C, each quasi enumerate and test method set up for $\mathcal{D}$ and $\mathcal{K}$ in the manner just described is a data-minimal limiting identifier of correct$_C$ hypotheses given $\mathcal{K}$.

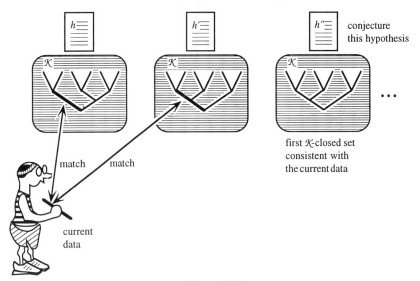

Figure 9.11

Corollary 9.14

$C_{r.e.}$,[12] C_{rec}, and C_{cmp}[13] all have data-minimal limiting identifiers.

Proof: Suppose C is disjoint given $\mathcal{K}$ and that correct$_C$ hypotheses are identifiable in the limit given $\mathcal{K}$. Let $\mathcal{D}$ be a single valued version of C. We may then set up a quasi enumerate and test method γ for $\mathcal{K}$ and for $\mathcal{D}$ as described. It is easy to verify that γ is a limiting identifier for C, $\mathcal{K}$. Suppose, however, that some other method γ^* identifies correct$_C$ hypotheses in the limit given $\mathcal{K}$ and, furthermore, that on some $\varepsilon \in \mathcal{K}$ the modulus of γ^* is strictly less than that of γ. Let γ stabilize to h on ε and let γ^* stabilize to h' on ε. Since C is disjoint given $\mathcal{K}$ and $\varepsilon \in C_h \cap C_{h'} \cap \mathcal{K}$, it follows that $C_h \cap \mathcal{K} = C_{h'} \cap \mathcal{K}$. If the modulus of γ is n on ε, we have that for some $h'' \neq h$, $\gamma(\varepsilon|n-1) = h''$. But then since $\mathcal{D}$ is single valued, $\mathcal{D}_h \cap \mathcal{D}_{h''} \cap \mathcal{K} = \varnothing$. Thus, at stage $n-1$, the pointer of γ is located at some pair (S, h'') where S is a $\mathcal{K}$-closed subset of $\mathcal{D}_{h''}$ that is not refuted by $\varepsilon|n-1$ given $\mathcal{K}$. So for some $\varepsilon' \in S$ such that $\varepsilon'|n-1 = \varepsilon|n-1$, γ stabilizes to h'' on ε *with modulus* $n-1$ (*Fig. 9.12*).

Since γ^* succeeds, γ^* stabilizes on ε' to some h^* such that $C_{h^*} \cap \mathcal{K} = C_{h''} \cap \mathcal{K}$. Thus, $C_{h^*} \cap C_{h'} \cap \mathcal{K} = \varnothing$, so $h^* \neq h'$ (*Fig. 9.13*). Therefore, the modulus of γ^* on ε' is at least n, while the modulus of γ on ε' is at most $n-1$. Thus, γ is data-minimal over all limiting identifiers of correct$_C$ hypotheses given $\mathcal{K}$. ∎

When we drop the assumption that C is disjoint given $\mathcal{K}$, there may be no data-minimal solution for a solvable, limiting discovery problem. So while this

---

[12] Osherson et al. (1986): proposition 8.2.1.
[13] Gold (1965).

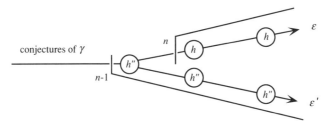

Figure 9.12

situation arises for assessment problems only in the computational case (cf. chapter 4), it arises even for ideal methods in the logic of discovery. In the case of computational assessment, the absence of a data-minimal solution for a problem results from the fact that faster convergence can always be obtained by expending more computational effort in the short run. In the following example, we will see that faster convergence in discovery can be obtained by starting out inquiry with a weaker conjecture.

Proposition 9.15 (C. Juhl)

There are C, $\mathcal{K}$ such that correct$_C$ hypotheses are identifiable in the limit given $\mathcal{K}$, but there is no data-minimal such method.

Proof: Define C, $\mathcal{K}$ as follows (*Fig. 9.14*):

$$C(\varepsilon, i) \Leftrightarrow \text{ for each } n, \varepsilon_n \leq i.$$

$$\mathcal{K} = \{\varepsilon: rng(\varepsilon) \text{ is finite}\}.$$

First it is clear that correct$_C$ hypotheses are identified in the limit given $\mathcal{K}$ by the method $\gamma(e) = max(rng(e))$. Now let γ be an arbitrary limiting identifier of correct$_C$ hypotheses. We will now construct a strictly faster solution. Let $k = \gamma(0)$. Let ε be the data stream consisting of $k + 1$ repeated forever, so $\varepsilon \in \mathcal{K}$. Thus for each $k' \geq k + 1$, $C(\varepsilon, k')$. γ stabilizes to some value $\geq k'$ on ε, and hence

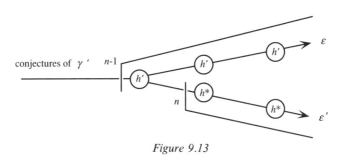

Figure 9.13

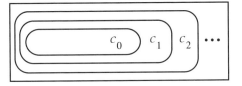

Figure 9.14

produces only finitely many distinct conjectures. Let k'' be the greatest conjecture produced by γ on ε. Now define:

$$\gamma^*(e) = \begin{cases} k'' & \text{if } \gamma(e) \le k'' \\ \gamma(e) & \text{otherwise.} \end{cases}$$

It is clear that γ^* succeeds. Since $\gamma(0) = k$, and γ stabilizes to some value $k' \ge k + 1$, γ changes its mind at least once on ε, but γ^* does not, since γ never produces a conjecture greater than k'' on ε. So γ^* stabilizes sooner than γ does on ε. Let $\varepsilon' \in \mathcal{K}$. If γ stabilizes on ε', then so does γ^*. If γ never produces a conjecture greater than k'' on ε' then γ^* has modulus 0 on ε'. Finally, if γ does produce a conjecture greater than k'' on ε' then γ^* has a modulus identical to that of γ. So γ^* is properly faster than γ. ∎

On the other hand, it is not hard to construct examples in which C is not disjoint given $\mathcal{K}$ but there is nonetheless a data-minimal solution. One such example is the problem C, $\mathcal{K}$ such that $C(\varepsilon, i) \Leftrightarrow i$ occurs at most finitely often in ε and $\mathcal{K} = C_0 \cup C_1$. In this case one data-minimal method is: $\gamma(e) = 0$ if more 1s than 0s occur in e and $\gamma(e) = 1$ otherwise.

7. Discovery with Bounded Mind Changes

We have seen that the bumping pointer architecture can turn limiting verifiers of hypotheses into limiting discovery methods. It is not hard to see that a parallel result holds in the case of identification with one mind change when each $C_h \cap \mathcal{K}$ is $\mathcal{K}$-open. The identifier produces an arbitrary conjecture until some hypothesis is verified with certainty and then produces that hypothesis with certainty.

This happy correspondence between mind changes in assessment and mind changes in discovery breaks down, however, when hypotheses are no longer all open. To see why, let $\mathcal{K}$, C be given as in *Figure 9.15*. Each of h, h', h'' is decidable with at most one mind change given $\mathcal{K}$, since each has at worst a 1-feather in $\mathcal{K}$. But the demon can lead an arbitrary limiting identifier on a path inducing at least two mind changes. The difference between the number of mind changes required to decide each hypothesis and the number of mind changes required to identify correct$_C$ hypotheses can easily be made as great as we please, by extending the picture in the obvious way.

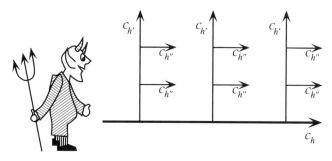

Figure 9.15

The point is that the number of mind changes required for discovery depends not only on the topology of each hypothesis, but also on how the structures of different hypotheses are interleaved together. This interleaved structure is not captured by the complexities of individual hyptheses, but it can be captured exactly if we generalize the notion of n-feathers so as to capture what is going on in the preceding diagram.

$\mathcal{K}$ *is a 0-feather for* C *with spine* $\varepsilon \Leftrightarrow \varepsilon \in \mathcal{K}$.

$\mathcal{K}$ *is an* $n + 1$-*feather for* C *with spine* ε
$\Leftrightarrow \varepsilon \in \mathcal{K}$ &
    $\forall h \, \forall n \, \exists m > n \, \exists \tau$ *such that*
(a) $C(\varepsilon, h) \Rightarrow \neg C(\tau, h)$ &
(b) $\tau | m = \varepsilon | m$ &
(c) $\mathcal{K}$ *is an* n-*feather for* C *with spine* τ.

Proposition 9.16

Correct$_C$ hypotheses are identifiable in n *mind changes starting with* h *given* $\mathcal{K} \Leftrightarrow \forall \varepsilon \in \mathcal{K}$, *if* $\mathcal{K}$ *is an* n-*feather for* C *with spine* ε *then* $C(\varepsilon, h)$.

Proof: Exercise 9.4.   ■

8. A Characterization of Almost Stable Identification in the Limit

Identification in the limit demands that the discovery method γ stabilize to some unique, correct hypothesis. We might also require something weaker, namely, that γ eventually produce only correct hypotheses without necessarily stabilizing to a particular correct hypothesis.

γ *unstably identifies correct$_C$ hypotheses in the limit given* $\mathcal{K}$
    $\Leftrightarrow$ *for each* $\varepsilon \in \mathcal{K}$ *there is an* n *such that for each* $m \geq n$, $C(\varepsilon, \gamma(\varepsilon | m))$.

When it is useful to emphasize this distinction, I will refer to the requirement that the scientist stabilize to a particular hypothesis as *stable identification*. In the case of unstable identification, we can no longer separate convergence from success. What is required is convergence to the state of conjecturing a correct hypothesis, rather than convergence to a particular hypothesis that is correct. This seemingly innocuous difference turns out to make discovery much, much easier than when convergence to a particular hypothesis is required. Between stable and unstable identification is the following notion of success:[14]

> γ *almost stably identifies correct$_C$ hypotheses in the limit given* $\mathcal{K}$
> $\Leftrightarrow$ *for each* $\varepsilon \in \mathcal{K}$, γ *conjectures only finitely many distinct hypotheses on* ε *and there is an n such that for each* $m \geq n$, $C(\varepsilon, \gamma(\varepsilon|m))$.

γ succeeds almost stably just in case γ succeeds unstably and on each infinite data stream in $\mathcal{K}$, γ produces at most finitely many distinct hypotheses, though γ is permitted to oscillate among these distinct hypotheses forever.

It is immediate that stable identification in the limit implies almost stable identification in the limit, which in turn implies unstable identification in the limit. That these implications are proper is witnessed by the following examples, which also shed light on what is new about the weaker standards of success.

$C^1(\varepsilon, i) \Leftrightarrow i$ *occurs infinitely often in* ε.

$\mathcal{K}^1 = 2^\omega$.

$C^2(\varepsilon, i) \Leftrightarrow$ *some* $j \leq i$ *occurs infinitely often in* ε.

$\mathcal{K}^2 = \{\varepsilon:$ *some* i *occurs infinitely often in* $\varepsilon\}$

Proposition 9.17 (C. Juhl)

Correct$_{C^1}$ hypotheses are almost stably but not stably identifiable in the limit given $\mathcal{K}^1$.

Proof: The method

$\gamma(e) =$ *the* $i < 2$ *that occurs most recently in* e

almost stably identifies correct$_{C^1}$ hypotheses given $\mathcal{K}^1$.

Let γ be given. The demon feeds 0s until γ conjectures 0. Then the demon feeds all 1s until γ says 1, after which the demon returns to feeding 0s, and so forth. Let ε be the data stream so produced. $\varepsilon \in \mathcal{K}^1$ since only 0s and 1s occur in ε. γ does not stably identify a correct$_{C^1}$ hypothesis on ε unless γ stabilizes

---

[14] Almost stable identification has been studied in the special case of the recursive function identification paradigm under the rubric of FEX identification (Case and Smith 1982).

to 0 or to 1 on ε. Suppose γ stabilizes to 0. Then ε stabilizes to 1, so γ is wrong. And if γ stabilizes to 1 then ε stabilizes to 0, so γ is again wrong.   ■

Proposition 9.18

Correct$_C{}^2$ hypotheses are unstably but not almost stably identifiable in the limit given $\mathcal{K}^2$.

Proof: The method that succeeds unstably just conjectures the current length of the data: $\gamma(e) = lh(e)$. This method succeeds because some $i \in \omega$ occurs infinitely often and after some time the length of the data remains greater than i.

Suppose for reductio that γ almost stably identifies correct$_C{}^2$ hypotheses given $\mathcal{K}^2$. The demon feeds 111... until γ conjectures some $i_1 \geq 1$. Then the demon feeds 0 followed by $i_1 + 1$ until γ conjectures some $i_2 \geq i_1 + 1$, etc. Suppose γ produces only finitely many distinct conjectures on the data stream ε so presented. Then ε stabilizes to 1 + the maximum number conjectured by γ, so $\varepsilon \in \mathcal{K}^1$, but γ fails to stabilize to a correct hypothesis on ε. So suppose that γ produces infinitely many distinct conjectures on ε. Then γ does not succeed almost stably on ε, but 0 occurs infinitely often in ε, so $\varepsilon \in \mathcal{K}^1$.   ■

These separation results imply that almost stable and unstable identifiability cannot be characterized in terms of $\Sigma[\mathcal{K}]_2^B$ complexity along the lines of proposition 9.8. Is there some other Borel characterization of either standard of success? In the case of almost stable identification, a slightly more complicated condition suffices. The proof involves the construction of a demonstrably complete architecture for almost stable identification.

Let $S \subseteq \omega$ be a finite set of hypotheses. Let h_S denote a new hypothesis not in ω. Let X be the result of adding to ω all hypotheses of form h_S, where S is a finite subset of ω. Let C be an arbitrary correctness relation, and let $\mathcal{K} \subseteq \mathcal{N}$. We extend C to X as follows (*Fig. 9.16*):

$$C'(\varepsilon, h_S) \Leftrightarrow \exists h' \in \omega - S \text{ such that } C(\varepsilon, h').$$

Intuitively, h_S says that *some* hypothesis *not* in S is correct.

In the following proposition, let $C'_\varepsilon = \{h: C'(\varepsilon, h)\}$.

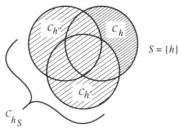

Figure 9.16

Proposition 9.19 (with C. Juhl)

Correct$_C$ hypotheses are almost stably identifiable in the limit given $\mathcal{K}$
  ⇔ there is some $\mathcal{D} \subseteq C$ such that

(1) $\mathcal{K} \subseteq dom(\mathcal{D})$ *and*

(2) *for each $h \in \mathcal{D}'_h \in \Pi[\mathcal{K}]_2^B$ and*

(3) *for each $\varepsilon \in \mathcal{K}$, $\mathcal{D}_\varepsilon$ is finite.*

Let $[h]_{C,\mathcal{K}} = \{h' : C_h \cap \mathcal{K} = C_{h'} \cap \mathcal{K}\}$. That is, $[h]_{C,\mathcal{K}}$ is the empirical equivalence class of hypotheses generated by h (*modulo C, $\mathcal{K}$*). Say that C is *almost disjoint* given $\mathcal{K}$ just in case for each $\varepsilon \in \mathcal{K}$, $\{[h]_{C,\mathcal{K}} : h \in C_\varepsilon\}$ is finite. That is, for each $\varepsilon \in \mathcal{K}$, there are at most finitely many empirical equivalence classes of hypotheses correct for ε. In particular, if C is disjoint given $\mathcal{K}$, then for each $\varepsilon \in \mathcal{K}$, there is at most one equivalence class of hypotheses correct for ε. For example, C_{cmp}^k, defined in section 9.2, is almost disjoint but not disjoint given $\mathcal{N}$. Then we have:

Corollary 9.20

Proposition 9.19 remains true if condition (3) is replaced with the condition (3′) $\mathcal{D}$ is almost disjoint given $\mathcal{K}$.

Corollary 9.21

If $rng(C)$ is finite then correct$_C$ hypotheses are (unstably) identifiable in the limit given $\mathcal{K}$ ⇔ there is some $\mathcal{D} \subseteq C$, such that

(1) $\mathcal{K} \subseteq dom(\mathcal{D})$ *and*

(2) *for each $h \in \omega$, $\mathcal{D}_h \in \Pi[\mathcal{K}]_2^B$.*

Proof of Proposition 9.19: (⇒) Suppose γ succeeds in the almost stable sense. Let $\varepsilon \in \mathcal{K}$. Then γ is eventually always correct on ε and γ produces at most finitely many hypotheses on ε. Any hypothesis conjectured infinitely often must be correct:

(i) $\forall \varepsilon \in \mathcal{K} [(\forall n \, \exists m \geq n \text{ such that } \gamma(\varepsilon|m) = h) \Rightarrow C(\varepsilon, h)]$.

Since only finitely many distinct hypotheses are conjectured and infinitely many conjectures are made, at least one correct hypothesis is conjectured infinitely often:

(ii) $\forall \varepsilon \in \mathcal{K}$, $\exists h \in \omega$ such that $C(\varepsilon, h)$ & $\forall n \, \exists m \geq n$ such that $\gamma(\varepsilon|m) = h$.

Define $\mathcal{D}$ relative to $\mathcal{K}$ as follows:

(iii) $\forall \varepsilon \in \mathcal{K}$, $h \in \omega$, $\mathcal{D}(\varepsilon, h) \Leftrightarrow \forall n \, \exists m \geq n \, \gamma(\varepsilon|m) = h$.

$\mathcal{D} \subseteq \mathcal{C}$ by (i), (iii). (1) follows from (ii) and (iii). (3) follows from (iii) and the fact that at most finitely many hypotheses are conjectured by γ on ε. It remains to derive the complexity bound (2). Let $h \in \omega$. Then the bound holds by (iii). Let $h_S \in X - \omega$, where S is a finite subset of ω. Then for each $\varepsilon \in \mathcal{K}$:

$$\mathcal{D}'(\varepsilon, h_S) \Leftrightarrow \exists h \in \omega - S \text{ such that } \mathcal{D}(\varepsilon, h)$$
$$\Leftrightarrow \exists h \in rng(\mathcal{D}) - S \text{ such that } \forall n \; \exists m \geq n \text{ such that } \gamma(\varepsilon|m) = h$$
$$\Leftrightarrow \forall n \; \exists m \geq n \text{ such that } \gamma(\varepsilon|m) \notin S.$$

The first equivalence is by the definition of the extension of $\mathcal{D}$ to $\mathcal{D}'$, the second equivalence is by (iii), and the ($\Leftarrow$) side of the last equivalence follows from (ii). Thus we have the bound (2).

($\Leftarrow$) Suppose $\mathcal{D} \subseteq \mathcal{C}$ satisfies (1), (2), and (3). Let η be an enumeration of $X - \omega$. By (2), for each $h \in \omega$, $\overline{\mathcal{D}'_h} \in \Sigma[\mathcal{K}]^B_2$. Let α be a limiting verifier$_{\overline{\mathcal{D}'}}$ of ω given $\mathcal{K}$ (by proposition 4.10). Now define the method $\beta'_{\alpha, \eta}$ that generalizes the idea behind the bumping pointer method as follows:

> $\beta'_{\alpha, \eta}(e)$: Follow the standard bumping pointer method $\beta_{\alpha, \eta}$ (cf. section 9.4) to find $\beta_{\alpha, \eta}(e) = h_S$. Let $n = |S|$ and set $p_n = \beta'_{\alpha, \eta}(e) = h_S$. Now let $\eta[n-1]$ be an enumeration of all $h_{S'}$ such that $S' \subseteq S$ and $|S'| = n - 1$. Set $p_{n-1} = \beta_{\alpha, \eta[n-1]}(e)$. Continue this process to find $p_{n-2}, p_{n-3}, \ldots$, until $\beta_{\alpha, \eta[1]}(e) = p_1 = h_{\{h'\}}$ is reached. Conjecture h' (*Fig. 9.17*).

Now we verify that this method works. Let $\varepsilon \in \mathcal{K}$. Note that $\overline{\mathcal{D}'}(\varepsilon, h_S) \Leftrightarrow S$ contains all $h \in \omega$ such that $\mathcal{D}(\varepsilon, h)$. By (3), if any $h \in \omega$ is correct$_{\mathcal{D}}$, then some hypothesis h_S is correct according to $\overline{\mathcal{D}'}$. Then by proposition 9.7, $\beta_{\alpha, \eta}$ eventually stabilizes to a particular hypothesis $p_n = h_{S_n}$ as the data increases.

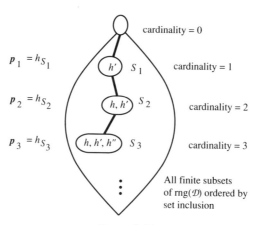

Figure 9.17

Now all hypotheses in ω that are correct for ε according to $\mathcal{D}$ are in S_n. If not every hypothesis in S_n is correct according to $\mathcal{D}$, some subset S_k of S_n contains all and only the hypotheses in ω correct$_\mathcal{D}$ for ε. By a similar argument, p_{n+1} stabilizes to some $h_{S_{n-1}}$ where $|S_{n-1}| = n - 1$ and $\bar{\mathcal{D}}'(\varepsilon, h_{S_{n-1}})$. Continuing this argument inductively, each successive position $p_{n-1}, p_{n-2}, \ldots, p_{k-1}, p_k$ in path p is eventually stabilized, and p_k stabilizes to h_{S_k}. Now, no matter how the chain is completed to $p_1 = h_{\{h'\}}$, h' is correct according to $\mathcal{D}$ (since the chain involves, by construction, only subsets of S_k). Thus h' is correct$_C$, since $\mathcal{D} \subseteq C$. The operation and convergence of the method are depicted in *Figure 9.18*.

Corollary 9.20 is established by eliminating all but one representative from each empirical equivalence class of hypotheses (with respect to $\mathcal{D}, \mathcal{K}$). Corollary 9.21 is immediate from the proposition and from corollary 9.20. ∎

The method constructed in the proof of the preceding proposition illustrates the difference in difficulty between stable and almost stable identification. The idea is that the method never knows when the path it constructs has stabilized as far as it will stabilize in the limit. Therefore, after the path has grown to its full length, the method continues to construct vacillating extensions of this path at each stage. Stable identification does not countenance this eternal vacillation. It requires that some path be stabilized all the way to a singleton. When stable convergence is possible, β' will do so.

In light of corollary 9.21, $\Pi[\mathcal{K}]_2^B$ hypothesis complexity is characteristic of almost stable identification when the set of possible hypotheses is finite. The following example shows that the $\Pi[\mathcal{K}]_2^B$ bound is insufficient for almost stable identification when H is infinite.

Correctness relation: $C^1(\varepsilon, i) \Leftrightarrow i$ *occurs infinitely often in* ε.

Knowledge: $\mathcal{K}^3 = \{\varepsilon:$ *some* $i \in \omega$ *occurs infinitely often in* ε *and at most finitely many* $i \in \omega$ *occur infinitely often in* $\varepsilon\}$.

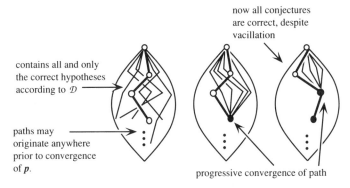

now all conjectures
are correct, despite
vacillation

contains all and only
the correct hypotheses
according to $\mathcal{D}$

paths may
originate anywhere
prior to convergence
of p.

progressive convergence of path

Figure 9.18

Proposition 9.22

Correct$_{C^1}$ hypotheses are not almost stably identifiable given $\mathcal{K}^3$ and C^1, $\mathcal{K}^3$ satisfy (1) and (2) of corollary 9.21, but $rng(C^1)$ is infinite.

Proof: The demon of proposition 9.18 produces a data stream in $\mathcal{K}^3$, so C^1 is not almost stably identifiable given $\mathcal{K}^3$. (1) and (2) are trivially satisfied by C^1, and it is clear that $rng(C^1)$ is infinite.   ∎

Proposition 9.22 justifies the added complexity of the extended hypotheses in proposition 9.19 when there are infinitely many distinct equivalence classes of hypotheses. For a positive example that illustrates the extra generality of the proposition (compared to corollary 9.21), a slight modification of the preceding example suffices.

$$\mathcal{K}^4 = \{\varepsilon\colon \text{some } i \in \omega \text{ occurs infinitely often in } \varepsilon \text{ and at most finitely many}$$
$$i \in \omega \text{ occur in } \varepsilon\}.$$

Proposition 9.23

Correct$_{C^1}$ hypotheses are almost stably identifiable in the limit given $\mathcal{K}^4$.

Proof: A successful method is $\gamma(e) = last(e)$.   ∎

The key difference between $\mathcal{K}^3$ and $\mathcal{K}^4$ is that $\mathcal{K}^3$ allows arbitrarily many occurrences of numbers that occur only finitely often, whereas $\mathcal{K}^4$ does not. So $\mathcal{K}^3$ permits misleading sequences like

$$(1, 1, 0, 2, 2, 2, 0, 3, 3, 3, 3, 0, 4, 4, 4, 4, 4, 0, \ldots)$$

in which 0 occurs infinitely often, but it is always the case that some finitely occurring entry occurs more often in the short run. In $\mathcal{K}^4$ this padding with distinct, finitely occurring items must stop after some time. The same effect is obtained more crudely by the condition in corollary 9.21 that the hypothesis language be essentially finite. When there are only finitely many hypotheses, such padding must stop after finite time, since the demon runs out of new items to pad with.

When we restrict attention to singleton hypotheses, the difference between identification in the limit and almost stable identification in the limit disappears, since each such problem has a stable limiting identifier.

9. Unstable Identification in the Limit

So far, every notion of reliable success considered has succumbed to a transcendental deduction in terms of the relative Borel complexity of C or of some subrelation of C. In the case of almost stable identification, we had to extend C to extra hypotheses to obtain a characterization. But unstable identification defies all such attempts to place a priori complexity bounds on its power. This may be seen most directly if we pursue the usual strategy for establishing a bound. Recall that if some γ stably identifies correct$_C$ hypotheses in the limit given $\mathcal{K}$ then we can define a relation $\mathcal{D} \subseteq C$ with $dom(C) = dom(\mathcal{D})$ as follows:

$$\forall \varepsilon \in \mathcal{K}, \, \mathcal{D}(\varepsilon, h) \Leftrightarrow \exists n \, \forall m \geq n \, \gamma(\varepsilon|m) = h.$$

This definition witnesses that each $\mathcal{D}_h \cap \mathcal{K} \in \Sigma[\mathcal{K}]_2^B$. Now suppose we pursue the same strategy in the case of unstable identification. Then all we have is this:

$$\forall \varepsilon \in \mathcal{K}, \, \mathcal{D}(\varepsilon, h) \Leftrightarrow \exists n \, \forall m \geq n \, C(\varepsilon, \gamma(\varepsilon|m)).$$

The trouble is that this definition of $\mathcal{D}$ is given in terms of C, whose complexity is unknown. In the other success criteria, success implies a global, syntactic constraint on the conjecture stream, whereas no such constraint is implied by unstable convergence. Convergence is defined in terms of correctness, and this is why convergence cannot be used to define correctness.

But we do know something about when this elusive inductive power arises. It does not arise if a correct hypothesis is conjectured infinitely often whenever a correct hypothesis exists, for then the infinite repetition is a syntactic feature we can use to define a relation $\mathcal{D} \subseteq C$ whose complexity is no greater than $\Pi[\mathcal{K}]_2^B$. Indeed, conjecturing members of an empirical equivalence class infinitely often would be a sufficient clue, since some other ideal method could always produce a canonical representative of the equivalence class. So to reap the rewards of instability, the successful method must somehow stabilize to the state of being correct without producing infinitely many empirically equivalent conjectures (as in the proof of proposition 9.18).

10. Gradual Identification

According to a popular conception of inquiry, science may never stabilize to a correct hypothesis or even produce a correct conjecture but can nonetheless be expected to produce ever better *approximations* to a correct view of the world. In order to analyze this proposal, we need some notion of approximate correctness. As a guiding example, suppose that hypotheses are parametrized by binary decimal expansions corresponding to reals in the $[0, 1]$ interval. If s is a finite, binary sequence such that $s|n = \theta|n$, then s *approximates* θ to the nth order. Since hypotheses are now infinite sequences, correctness is a relation $C \subseteq \mathcal{N}^2$.

When a hypothesis is an infinite sequence, an assessment method reads the hypothesis just like a data stream, by looking at finite initial segments. Then verification in the limit can be generalized in a natural manner, where we now let $\mathcal{H} \subseteq \mathcal{N}$. The switch in notation from H to $\mathcal{H}$ reflects the change in type from finite hypotheses to infinite hypotheses.

α verifies$_C$ $\mathcal{H}$ in the limit given $\mathcal{K} \Leftrightarrow \forall \theta \in \mathcal{H}$, $\forall \varepsilon \in \mathcal{K}$, $\exists n \, \forall m \geq n$, $\alpha(\theta|m, \varepsilon|m) = 1$.

The definition of success has become entirely symmetrical in $\mathcal{H}$ and $\mathcal{K}$. Only its intended interpretation tells us that $\mathcal{H}$ is a set of hypotheses and $\mathcal{K}$ a set of data streams. It is an easy exercise to show:[15]

Proposition 9.24

$\mathcal{H}$ is verifiable$_C$ in the limit given $\mathcal{K} \Leftrightarrow C \cap (\mathcal{K} \times \mathcal{H}) \in \Sigma[\mathcal{K}, \mathcal{H}]_2^B$. ∎

In the case of discovery problems, we do not have the awkward feature that the infinite hypothesis θ must be given to the method for eternity. The method must, rather, find better and better approximations to θ as time goes on. I will suppose that a discovery method for infinite hypotheses outputs at each stage some finite sequence intended as an approximation of some correct, infinite sequence θ. Accordingly, a discovery method is now a function γ from finite data sequences to finite, initial segments of hypotheses.

We may now define a notion of gradual identification that is analogous to gradual verification (*Fig. 9.19*).

γ identifies correct$_C$ hypotheses gradually given $\mathcal{K} \Leftrightarrow \forall \varepsilon \in \mathcal{K}$, $\exists \theta$ such that $C(\varepsilon, \theta)$ and $\forall k \, \exists n \, \forall m \geq n$, $\theta|k \subseteq \gamma(\varepsilon|m)$.

This notion of success demands only that there be a correct hypothesis θ such that each degree of approximation is eventually met by γ, even if γ never stops making mistakes. The hypothesis so converged to is nonetheless unique.

Example 9.25   The straight rule of induction

H. Reichenbach held the view that all induction could be reduced to the estimation of probabilities. As a frequentist, he took probabilities to be limiting relative frequencies in the data stream. He proposed to discover limiting relative frequencies by means of the so-called *straight rule of induction*, also known as *induction by enumeration*. The straight rule simply conjectures the observed frequency of outcome o in the current data e.[16]

$\gamma[o](e) = RF_e(o)$.

---

[15] Exercise 7.14.
[16] Reichenbach (1938, 1949, 1956), Salmon (1967).

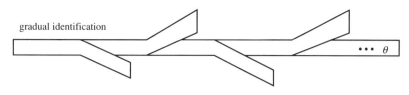

Figure 9.19

Think of $\gamma[o](e)$ as a finite numeral in binary notation. It is immediate from the definition of limiting relative frequency that the straight rule gradually identifies the limiting relative frequency of o in any data stream in which o has a limiting relative frequency.

One might expect a Π_3^B characterization of gradual identification, in analogy with the case of gradual verification. But while this condition is evidently necessary, it is not sufficient, as the following example shows.

$$C(\varepsilon, \theta) \Leftrightarrow [\forall k, \theta_k = 1 \Leftrightarrow \forall n \, \exists m \geq n \, \varepsilon_m = k]$$
$$\Leftrightarrow \forall k \, \forall n \, \exists m \geq n, \forall n' \, \forall m' \geq n',$$
$$[\theta_k = 1 \, \& \, \varepsilon_m = k \text{ or } \theta_{k'} \neq 1 \text{ and } \varepsilon_{m'} \neq k].$$

$C \in \Pi_3^B$, but no method can eventually stabilize even to the first position in θ, since that would verify the infinite divisibility hypothesis in the limit (just take the first entry of the current conjecture to be the limiting verifier's conjecture). It must be possible to verify each finite initial segment of θ in the limit, and this requires more than that some subrelation of C be Π_3^B. The following characterization provides the correct condition. As usual, the proof may be viewed as a completeness theorem for an inductive architecture suited to gradual identification. Let $C \subseteq \mathcal{N}^2$. Define $C^* \subseteq \mathcal{N} \times \omega^*$ as follows:

$$C^*(\varepsilon, s) \Leftrightarrow \exists \theta \in \mathcal{N} \text{ such that } s \subseteq \theta \text{ and } C(\varepsilon, \theta).$$

Also, recall that $C_\varepsilon = \{\theta: C(\varepsilon, \theta)\}$. Now we have:

Proposition 9.26

Correct$_C$ hypotheses are identifiable gradually given $\mathcal{K}$
$\Leftrightarrow$ there is a $\mathcal{D} \subseteq \mathcal{N}^2$ such that

(1) *$\mathcal{D} \subseteq C$ and*

(2) *$\mathcal{K} \subseteq dom(\mathcal{D})$ and*

(3) *$\mathcal{D}$ is single valued and*

(4) *$\forall s \in \omega^*, \mathcal{D}_s^* \in \Sigma[\mathcal{K}]_2^B$.*

Proof: ($\Rightarrow$) Suppose that γ gradually identifies$_C$ correct hypotheses given $\mathcal{K}$. Define, for each $\varepsilon \in \mathcal{K}, \theta \in \mathcal{N}$:

$$\mathcal{D}(\varepsilon, \theta) \Leftrightarrow \forall k \, \exists n \, \forall m \geq n, \theta | k \subseteq \gamma(\varepsilon | m).$$

Then since γ succeeds, we have (1) and (2). Since the hypothesis gradually approached is unique, we have (3). Finally, we have

$$\forall \varepsilon \in \mathcal{K}, \, s \in \omega^*, \, \mathcal{D}^*(\varepsilon, s) \Leftrightarrow \exists n \; \forall m \geq n, \, s \subseteq \gamma(\varepsilon | m),$$

so (4) is satisfied.

($\Leftarrow$) Suppose that $\mathcal{D}$ satisfies (1–4). Let η be an infinitely repetitive enumeration of ω. Let α verify$_{\mathcal{D}*}$ ω^* in the limit given $\mathcal{K}$ by (4). Assume an unlimited supply of pointers, *pointer* [1], *pointer* [2], ... Now define:

$\gamma(e)$:
for each k from 1 to $lh(e)$ do
begin
    initialize *pointer*$[k] = 0$;
    for each k' from 1 to $lh(e)$ do
        if $\alpha((\eta_{pointer[1]}, \ldots, \eta_{pointer[k]}), e|k') \neq 1$
        then set *pointer*$[k] = pointer[k] + 1$.
end
output $(\eta_{pointer[1]}, \ldots, \eta_{pointer[lh(e)]})$.

To see that this *nested pointer architecture* works, let $\varepsilon \in \mathcal{K}$. Then for some unique θ, $\forall k \; \mathcal{D}(\varepsilon, \theta | k)$, by (2) and (3), and hence $C(\varepsilon, \theta)$ by (1). Consider *pointer*[1]. If $\eta_{pointer[1]} \neq \theta_1$, then (*) α conjectures infinitely many non-1s on ε for the hypothesis $(\eta_{pointer[1]})$, by the uniqueness claim in (2). But α eventually stabilizes to 1 on ε for θ_1, say by stage n_1. Since η is infinitely repetitive, (*) implies that there is an $n \geq n_1$ such that $\eta_{pointer[1]} = \theta_1$ after γ reads $\varepsilon | n$ and pointer[1] stays put forever after. Inductively, the same argument works for *pointer*$[k + 1]$, given that the pointers 1 through k have stabilized to the first k values of θ, respectively. ∎

Exercises

9.1. Finish the proof of proposition 9.5. (c) and (d) are straightforward. The argument for (a) and (b) involves a demon who produces an ε with finite range if α stabilizes to 1 and an ε with infinite, recursive range otherwise.

9.2. Show that the following discovery problem is solvable almost stably but not stably in the limit.

$C(\varepsilon, i) \Leftrightarrow i$ *occurs infinitely often in* ε.
$\mathcal{K} = \{\varepsilon:$ *only finitely many distinct* i *occur in* $\varepsilon\}$.

9.3. Show that the method discussed at the end of section 9.6 is indeed data-minimal.

9.4. Prove proposition 9.16.

9.5. Define $C_{lim}(\varepsilon, i) \Leftrightarrow \forall n \; \exists m \; \forall m' \geq m, \; \phi_i(n, m') = \varepsilon_n$, and let $\mathcal{K}_{lim} = dom(C_{lim})$. This is the paradigm of *limiting recursive function identification*. Derive Borel complexity bounds for C_{lim} relative to $\mathcal{K}_{lim}$. Isolate some interesting subsets of $\mathcal{K}_{lim}$ over which C_{lim} is identifiable in the limit and some other interesting subsets for which it is not.

9.6. Exact identification in the limit demands that the method stabilize to a correct hypothesis whenever one exists, and fail to stabilize to any hypothesis when no correct hypothesis exists (Osherson et al. 1986). State and prove a modified version of proposition 9.8 for this notion of reliability. (Hint: look for a complexity bound on $\mathcal{K}$). Give an example of a problem solvable in the limit in the usual sense that is not solvable in this sense.

9.7. Define:

> γ *repetitively identifies correct*$_C$ *hypotheses in the limit given* $\mathcal{K}$
> $\Leftrightarrow \forall \varepsilon \in \mathcal{K}$,
>
> (a) $\exists n \; \forall m \geq m, \; C(\varepsilon, \gamma(\varepsilon|m))$ *and*
>
> (b) $\exists h \; \forall m \; \exists m' \geq n, \; \gamma(\varepsilon|m') = h$ *and*
>
> (c) $\forall \varepsilon \in \mathcal{K} - dom(C), \; \forall h \; \exists m \; \forall m' \geq n, \; \gamma(\varepsilon|m') \neq h$.

State and prove a topological characterization.

9.8. Suppose that instead of requiring convergence to a correct hypotheses for each $\varepsilon \in \mathcal{K}$, we require this performance only when $\varepsilon \in dom(C)$. On this definition, it is not the fault of the discovery method if there is no correct hypothesis to conjecture. Call this notion of reliability *weak identification*. Show that there exist single valued correctness relations of arbitrary Borel complexity relative to $\mathcal{K}$ that admit of weak limiting verifiers.

9.9. Show proposition 9.24.

9.10. Apply the nested pointer architecture of proposition 9.27 to the problem of inferring limiting relative frequencies given that some limiting relative frequency exists. Simulate the method on a short data stream to see how it works.

9.11. Let $C \subseteq \mathcal{N}^2$. The approximation methods of numerical analysis typically provide bounds on how close the approximation is to the true value at a given time. We can define a discovery paradigm that has this character.

> γ *identifies correct*$_C$ *hypotheses by certain approximations given* $\mathcal{K} \Leftrightarrow \forall \varepsilon \in \mathcal{K}$,
> $\exists \theta \in \mathcal{N}$, *such that* $C(\varepsilon, \theta)$ *and* $\forall s \; \exists n$ *such that* $\alpha(\varepsilon|n) = \text{`![s]'}$ *and* $\forall m > n$,
> $\gamma(\varepsilon|m) \in \omega^* \Rightarrow \theta|s \subseteq \gamma(\varepsilon|m) \; \exists k \geq m$ *such that* $\gamma(\varepsilon|m) \in \omega^*$.

Provide a characterization of this notion of success parallel to that given by proposition 9.26. Show by example that there are problems solvable gradually that are not solvable by certain approximations.

9.12. What could go wrong with the method γ constructed in the proof of proposition 9.26 if the uniqueness condition (3) were dropped? Construct an example that illustrates such a failure.

10

Computerized Discovery

1 Introduction

If philosophers have been unhappy with the idea of a normative logic of discovery, they have been all the less enthusiastic about the idea of discovery *machines.*

> The same point has sometimes been formulated by saying that it is not possible to construct an inductive machine. The latter is presumably meant as a mechanical contrivance that, when fed an observational report, would furnish a suitable hypothesis, just as a computing machine when supplied with two factors furnishes their product. I am completely in agreement that an inductive machine of *this* kind is not possible.[1]

But just as in the ideal case, it is not too hard to imagine discovery problems that are solvable by computer (e.g., to identify in the limit the number that the data stream converges to when it is known in advance that it will converge to some value). Such problems may be trivial, but then the real question, as always, is precisely where the line between the effectively solvable and the effectively unsolvable discovery problems falls. That is the subject of this chapter.

2 Computable Hypothesis Enumerations

A large part of our work is already done, since the difference between ideal and computable hypothesis assessment was already characterized in chapter 6 and ideal discovery was characterized in the preceding chapter. Let us focus, then,

---

[1] Carnap (1950).

on the special wrinkles that arise in the case of computable discovery. Suppose that computable α verifies$_C$ $rng(C)$ in the limit given $\mathcal{K}$ and that $\mathcal{K} \subseteq dom(C)$, so that some hypothesis is correct for each data stream. We have already seen a recipe for turning α into an ideal discovery method γ, namely, the bumping pointer architecture of proposition 9.8. Recall that this architecture requires an infinitely repetitive enumeration η of $rng(C)$ and bumps a pointer on this enumeration whenever α returns a value other than 1 on the hypothesis currently pointed to. When all of the current input data sequence e is read, γ conjectures the hypothesis currently pointed to (*Fig. 10.1*).

All of this is clearly computable as long as the enumeration η is computable. So the only new consideration over and above computable assessment is finding a procedure for enumerating a set of hypotheses covering all of $\mathcal{K}$. This is not always trivial. Recall the problem of recursive function identification:

$$C_{cmp}(\varepsilon, i) \Leftrightarrow \varepsilon = \phi_i; \qquad \mathcal{R} = \text{the set of all (total) recursive functions.}$$

It is immediate that $dom(C_{cmp}) = \mathcal{R}$. Let Tot be the set of all total program indices. Thus $rng(C_{cmp}) = Tot$. It is also easy to see that $C_{cmp} \in \Pi[\mathcal{R}, Tot]_1^A$. To test $i \in Tot$ on data e, simply compute the required values of ϕ_i and check whether they agree with the corresponding entries in e. This is all computable since total program i never gets caught in an infinite loop.

So we would have a computable discovery procedure for recursive functions if Tot could be enumerated effectively. But it is one of the most basic facts of the theory of computability that there is no procedure for enumerating Tot, or any subset S of Tot that *covers* all of $\mathcal{R}$ in the sense that S contains indices for all and only the total recursive functions.

Proposition 10.1

$\forall S \subseteq Tot$, if $\mathcal{R} = C_{cmp}^{-1}(S)$ then $S \notin \Sigma_1^A$.

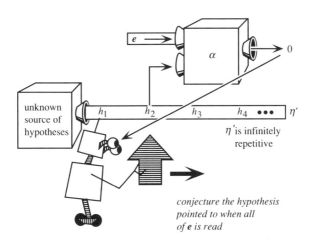

Figure 10.1

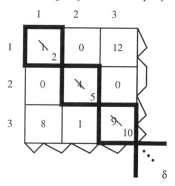

Figure 10.2

Proof: Suppose otherwise. Then some machine can list all of S on a tape. This tape determines a total recursive function ξ whose range is S. Since $S \subseteq Tot$, the function $\psi(x, y) = \phi_{\xi(x)}(y)$ is also total recursive and may be thought of as determining a recursive table such that each $\varepsilon \in \mathcal{R}$ is a row of the table (*Fig. 10.2*). Since ψ is computable, so is $\delta(x) = \psi(x, x) + 1$. δ is total recursive since ψ is, but δ clearly differs from each row of the table somewhere. Thus, $\delta \in \mathcal{R} - C_{cmp}^{-1}(S)$, contrary to hypothesis. ∎

Let us review our options. If we could recursively enumerate some subset of *Tot* covering $\mathcal{R}$, we would be done, but that is impossible. If we enumerate a *subset* of *Tot* that does not cover $\mathcal{R}$, then the bumping pointer method fails because the truth is missing from its enumeration. If we choose a recursively enumerable *superset* of *Tot*, then we add into our enumeration indices for programs that go into infinite loops, and hence the hypotheses are no longer computably refutable or even computably verifiable in the limit.

In fact, these difficulties cannot be overcome. The proof is a demonic argument, except that in this case the demon's strategy, like the scientist's, is computable (*Fig. 10.3*). The reason for this is that the problem assumes $\mathcal{R}$ as background knowledge, so the data stream produced by the demon must be a recursive sequence. Since the scientist's method is computable, if the demon is also computable, then the data stream produced is computable.

Figure 10.3

Proposition 10.2 (H. Putnam 1963, E. M. Gold 1967)

Correct$_{Ccmp}$ hypotheses are not computably identifiable in the limit given $\mathcal{R}$.

Proof: Suppose for reductio that computable γ succeeds. The computable demon proceeds as follows:

Stage 0: $e[0] = \mathbf{0}$.

Stage $n + 1$: Let $\underline{x}$ denote the infinite data stream in which only x occurs. Find some pair (i, k) such that $\gamma(e[n]*\underline{0}|i) \neq \gamma(e[n]*\underline{0}|i*\underline{1}|k)$ in the following manner. Employ an effective enumeration of the pairs (i, k). For each, simulate γ to see whether $\gamma(e[n]*\underline{0}|i) \neq \gamma(e[n]*\underline{0}|i*\underline{1}|k))$. When such a pair (i, k) is found, set $e[n + 1] = (e[n]*\underline{0}|i*\underline{1}|k)$.

Let $\varepsilon = \bigcup_{i \in \omega} e[i]$. To see that ε is total recursive, it suffices to show that the pair i, k sought by the effective demon always exists. For each $e[n]$, the infinite data stream $(e[n]*\underline{0})$ is recursive and the infinite data stream $(e[n]*\underline{1})$ is recursive. So by feeding enough 0s after $e[n]$, the effective demon can get γ to produce an index for $(e[n]*\underline{0})$, say by the time $e = (e[n]*00\ldots0)$ has been presented, else γ would fail on $(e[n]*\underline{0})$, contrary to assumption. By feeding sufficiently more 1s after this, the demon can get γ to produce an index for $(e'*\underline{1})$, which is recursive and which has an index different from the index of $(e*\underline{0})$. Observe that the effective demon does not have to know when γ's answer is correct. The fact that the pair i, k exists guarantees that the demon's effective search will find it. Since the demon's search is guaranteed to succeed, and since the demon performs effective calculations and bounded searches using total recursive γ as a subroutine, $\varepsilon \in \mathcal{R}$. Moreover, γ changes its mind at each stage, and hence fails on ε. ∎

So although a computable mechanism (the bumping pointer architecture) hooked up to a noncomputable hypothesis enumeration η can solve the problem, no entirely computable method can solve it, whether using the bumping pointer architecture or any other possible arrangement. H. Putnam saw this fact as a novel argument for the hypothetico-deductive position that testing hypotheses is a mechanical, pedestrian affair while discovering hypotheses to test requires human imagination and intuition.

> I suggest that we should take the view that science is a method or possibly a collection of methods for *selecting a hypothesis*, assuming languages to be given *and hypotheses to be proposed*. Such a view seems better to accord with the importance of the hypothetico-deductive method in science, which all investigators come to stress more and more in recent years.[2]

[2] Putnam (1963): 292, my emphasis.

You need hypotheses?
Switch this stupid thing off.
I have <u>creative intuition!</u>

Hypothesis
Generator

Scientist   Philosopher

Figure 10.4

In other words, let human creative intuition provide the hypothesis enumeration η, and leave the machines to the trivial work of testing and rejecting what has been proposed, in standard hypothetico-deductive fashion (*Fig. 10.4*).

Putnam deserves credit for seeing the applicability of the theory of computability to methodological questions and for proving a version of proposition 10.2, which might be considered the first result of formal learning theory and hence the original inspiration for all the results described in this book. But his argument for hypothetico-deductivism falls short of the mark. In order for "creative intuition" to beat all computable methods at identifying recursive functions, it must provide a hypothesis stream η for a non-r.e. subset of *Tot*. Call such a hypothesis stream *transcendent*. It is hardly obvious a priori that "creative intuition," "informal rationality," "common sense," or any other alleged source of hypotheses is transcendent in this sense. So if we are to discover that creative intuition can beat all the machines at scientific discovery, we must do so a posteriori—by induction. It won't do for Putnam to appeal to some vague notion of confirmation at this point—his whole argument is based on a logical reliabilist perspective on inquiry. For him, the question must be whether we could reliably determine whether a given hypothesis source (e.g., Uncle Fred) is transcendent. But it turns out that no possible method can do this, computable or otherwise. In fact, determining whether a hypothesis source is transcendent is intrinsically harder than the problem the source is supposed to permit us to solve, since the latter is at least ideally solvable while the former is not.

Proposition 10.3

Transcendence is not ideally verifiable in the limit given $\mathcal{N}$.

Proof: Let method α be given. Let η be a fixed, transcendent hypothesis stream. Let η' be a fixed, effective enumeration of a subset of *Tot*. The demon presents η while α conjectures a value less than 1 and starts from scratch presenting η' when α conjectures 1, ensuring that a new entry in η is presented before switching to η'. If α stabilizes to 1, the demon presents η' with a finite initial segment tacked on front, which is computable (and hence not transcendent) because η' is. Otherwise, each entry in η is presented, and since the entries from η' are all in *Tot*, the result is transcendent. Either way, α fails. ∎

Moreover, it can be shown that *no effective method* can figure out even whether the oracle produces only programs for total functions (i.e., programs that never go into an infinite loop). Incidentally, the proof of this fact affords another opportunity to use the Kleene recursion theorem to construct a "computer disguise" for the demon (cf. chapter 6). Say that a hypothesis stream η is *total* just in case $rng(\eta) \subseteq Tot$.

Proposition 10.4

Totality is not verifiable in the limit given $\mathcal{N}$ by any computable method.

Proof: For reductio, suppose that computable assessment method α verifies totality in the limit. The demon starts out with the empty hypothesis stream 0. Inductively, suppose that the demon has presented the finite sequence h of total indices to α so far. Let η be a computable, total hypothesis stream. Define:

$$\psi(x, y) = \begin{cases} 0 & \text{if } \exists n > lh(h^*x) \text{ such that } \alpha((h^*x^*\eta)|n) \neq 1 \\ \uparrow & \text{otherwise.} \end{cases}$$

This function is partial recursive (simulate α on increasing initial segments of the recursive hypothesis stream $h^*x^*\eta$ and wait for a non-1 output to appear). So by the *s-m-n* theorem (proposition 6.3), there is a total recursive s such that $\phi_{s(x)}(y) = \psi(x, y)$. Applying the Kleene recursion theorem (proposition 6.5), there is an i such that for each x, $\phi_i(x) = \psi(i, x)$. If α refuses to drop its conjecture below 1 after reading h^*i, on the data stream $h^*i^*\eta$, then ϕ_i is the everywhere undefined function and α stabilizes to 1 on $h^*i^*\eta$, which is incorrect. Since α succeeds, we may conclude that α drops its conjecture below 1 after reading h^*i on the data stream $h^*i^*\eta$. Then i is a total index. Let $h^*i^*s \subset h^*i^*\eta$ be least extension of h^*i on which α drops its conjecture below 1. h^*i^*s is a finite sequence of total indices, so we may repeat the preceding argument, replacing h with h^*i^*s. Let ε be the data stream so produced. ε satisfies totality, but α does not stabilize to 1 on ε. Contradiction. So no computable α succeeds. ∎

One can add uncertainty about the hypothesis source to the definition of inductive success so that its significance for successful prediction is explicit. Our knowledge about the hypothesis source determines a set $S \subseteq \mathcal{N}$ of infinite hypothesis streams, any one of which the mysterious hypothesis source might generate, for all we know. Then reliable discovery using the source as an oracle can be defined as follows, where γ now takes a finite, initial segment of η as well as a finite, initial segment of ε as input.

γ identifies correct$_C$ hypotheses in the limit given $\mathcal{K}$ and a hypothesis oracle in S ⇔ for each possible data stream ε in $\mathcal{K}$, for each possible hypothesis stream η in S, there is a time n such that for each later time m, $C(\varepsilon, \gamma(\varepsilon|m, \eta|m))$ and $\gamma(\varepsilon|m, \eta|m) = \gamma(\varepsilon|n, \eta|n)$.

If the oracle may produce a computable hypothesis stream for all we know, then no γ relying on the oracle can succeed where a completely computable method cannot. It would have to be known a priori that the oracle is transcendent. But no such thing is known about "creative intuition", "informal rationality", and "common sense". Of course, Putnam may hope that the actual hypothesis stream bestowed on us by the oracle will be transcendent, but then he may as well hope that the world agrees with the fixed conclusions of an unreliable discovery method to begin with, rather than insisting on reliability. In other words, reliance on external, unanalyzed hypothesis oracles leads to a version of world-dependent reliability (cf. chapter 2), whereas fully computable methods can be reliable in a world-independent and hence a priori sense.

3   Characterization

The following characterization of effective discovery looks just like the corresponding result in the ideal case (proposition 9.8) except for condition (3), which substitutes arithmetical complexity for Borel complexity and restricts the overall complexity of $\mathcal{D}$ rather than the complexities of individual hypotheses under $\mathcal{D}$.

Proposition 10.5

Correct$_C$ hypotheses are identifiable in the limit given $\mathcal{K}$ by a computable method ⇔ there is some $\mathcal{D}$ such that

(1) $\mathcal{D} \subseteq C$ *and*

(2) $\mathcal{K} \subseteq dom(\mathcal{D})$ *and*

(3) $\mathcal{D} \in \Sigma[\mathcal{K}]_2^4$.

Corollary 10.6

The proposition remains true if we add the condition:
(4) $\mathcal{D}$ is single valued.

Corollary 10.7

The proposition remains true if we replace (3) with:
(3′) for each $h \in \omega$, $\mathcal{D}_h \cap \mathcal{K} \in \Delta[\mathcal{K}]_2^4$.

Proof: ($\Rightarrow$) just as in the proof of proposition 9.8. ($\Leftarrow$) Assume that $\mathcal{D}$ satisfies (1–3). ω is recursively enumerable. Implement the bumping pointer method with an effective limiting verifier$_\mathcal{D}$ α of ω given $\mathcal{K}$ and an infinitely repetitive recursive enumeration η of ω. ∎

The attentive reader is no doubt wondering how this result accounts for the problems one can have with the recursive enumerability of hypotheses, since in the proof, we simply enumerated ω. In fact, it suffices that the hypothesis set be Σ_2^A, since we may replace condition (3) with condition

(3″) $\exists R \in \Sigma_2^A$ *such that* $rng(\mathcal{D}) \subseteq R$ *and* $\mathcal{D} \in \Sigma[\mathcal{K}, \mathcal{R}]_2^A$.

Here, the complexity bound on S is restricted to R, which may not be r.e. (recall the case of C_{cmp}), so we must add the requirement that $R \in \Sigma_2^A$. (3) clearly implies (3″), for we may choose $R = \omega$. In the other direction, let $\mathcal{D}$ satisfy (3″). Define $C(\varepsilon, h) \Leftrightarrow h \in R$ and $\mathcal{D}(\varepsilon, h)$. Since $R \in \Sigma_2^A$, C satisfies (3).

Proposition 10.5 illustrates what a strong result proposition 10.2 is in standard, recursion-theoretic terms. It shows not only that $C_{cmp} \notin \Sigma_2^A$ (the usual sort of complexity result) but also that no $\mathcal{D} \subseteq C_{cmp}$ such that $\mathcal{R} \subseteq dom(\mathcal{D})$ is in $\Sigma[\mathcal{R}]_2^A$. This is a very robust lower bound on the arithmetical complexity of C_{cmp}.

Analogous characterizations can be given for the other identication criteria introduced in chapter 9. These follow along the lines of the ideal results of the preceding chapter and are left as exercises.

4   Function Identification

Much learning-theoretic research has focused on the identification of indices for recursive functions. One problem of this sort is automated computer programming. We would like to have a computer that produces a program for keeping the company ledger after watching how the ledger is kept for a while. Another example is the scientific task of producing computer models of cognitive or physical systems.

We have already seen that this paradigm has special properties. Recall that $C_{cmp} \in \Pi_1^B$, which trivially ensures the ideal identifiability of recursive function indices in the limit given $\mathcal{R}$. Proposition 10.2, however, entails that $C_{cmp} \notin \Sigma[\mathcal{R}]_2^A$. This result cannot be improved in the arithmetical hierarchy because $C_{cmp} \in \Pi[\mathcal{R}]_2^A$. To see this, observe that

$$C_{cmp}(\varepsilon, i) \Leftrightarrow \forall n \; \phi_i(n) = \varepsilon_n \Leftrightarrow \forall n \; \exists m \; \phi_i(n) \text{ halts in } m \text{ steps with output } \varepsilon_n.$$

Since $\phi_i(n) = \varepsilon_n$ is a topologically clopen relation, we have from the first equivalence that $C_{cmp} \in \Pi_1^B$. But the relation $\phi_i(n) = \varepsilon_n$ is not recursive, due to the halting problem (cf. chapter 6). So we must add an extra existential quantifier over run times, raising the arithmetical complexity of C_{cmp} to $\Pi[\mathcal{R}]_2^A$.

It is typical for a proposition concerning computable inquiry to have one extra existential quantifier over steps of computation, as compared to the corresponding ideal result. It is also typical to use the recursion theorem to turn uncertainty about run times into inductive uncertainty after the basic pattern discussed in section 6.5. We have seen just such an example in proposition 10.4.

The following result applies the recursion theorem in a more sophisticated manner than we have seen up to now. Recall from the preceding chapter that

$$C_{cmp}^k(\varepsilon, i) \Leftrightarrow \phi_i \subseteq \varepsilon \ \textit{and} \ |\varepsilon - \phi_i| \leq k.$$

In other words, an index i for a partial recursive function is correct (to within degree k) for ε just in case all of the outputs of ϕ_i are correct and ϕ_i is undefined on no more than k arguments.

C_{cmp}^k is no easier for ideal agents than C_{cmp} is, for suppose that γ can identify correct$_{C_{cmp}^k}$ hypotheses given $\mathcal{K}$. γ^* simulates γ on the data to obtain conjecture i. γ^* can (ideally) tell where ϕ_i is undefined. If all these positions have already been observed in the data, γ^* can substitute for i an index j such that ϕ_j is total and defines all the undefined places in ϕ_i to match the data. Such a program exists because program i can be augmented with a lookup table. Eventually, γ stabilizes to a correct$_{C_{cmp}^k}$ hypothesis and all its undefined places are observed and fixed, so γ^* stabilizes to a correct$_{C_{cmp}}$ hypothesis.

The same argument does not apply to computable methods because they cannot determine from i where ϕ_i is undefined, so they do not know where to patch it. This suggests that finding theories with gaps may be easier for computable agents than finding theories with no gaps, which is in fact the case. Define:

$$S\mathcal{R}[k] = \{\varepsilon: C_{cmp}^k(\varepsilon, \varepsilon_0)\}.$$

$S\mathcal{R}[k]$ is the set of all data streams ε such that the first item occurring in ε is the index of a program for computing some data stream $\tau \subseteq \varepsilon$ such that τ is undefined in at most k places. Now we have:

Proposition 10.8 (Case and Smith)[3]

(1) *Correct*$_{C_{cmp}^1}$ *hypotheses are identifiable by stage* 1 *given* $S\mathcal{R}[1]$ *by a computable method.*

(2) *Correct*$_{C_{cmp}}$ *hypotheses are not even identifiable in the limit given* $S\mathcal{R}[1]$ *by a computable method.*

Proof: For (1), simply define $\gamma(e) = \varepsilon_0$, which works given the definition of $S\mathcal{R}[1]$. For (2), let computable γ be given. The demon must produce a

---

[3] Case and Smith (1983): theorem 2.3.

recursive data stream ε such that $\varepsilon_0 = k$ and $\phi_k \subseteq \varepsilon$ and ϕ_k is undefined in at most one place. In other words, the demon requires an almost perfect computer disguise, and we will use the recursion theorem to provide it. We will define ϕ_k in stages, so that the finite subset of ϕ_k defined by stage n is denoted by $\phi_k[n]$. There is a pointer π, whose position at stage n is denoted by $\pi[n]$. The greatest uninterrupted initial segment of $\phi_k[n]$ will be denoted $e[n]$. The procedure will be arranged so that the only gap in $\phi_k[n]$ is at the pointer position, and so that all entries following the pointer are 0s. Let $x[n]$ denote the first position beyond the greatest defined position of $\phi_k[n]$ (i.e., $max(dom(\phi_k[n])) + 1$). All of this is illustrated in *Figure 10.5*. It is possible for $\phi_k[n]$ to be an uninterrupted segment with the pointer located at $x[n]$.

At stage 0, define:

$$\phi_k[0] = \{(0, k)\}$$
$$\pi[0] = 1$$

where k is an index of the function computed by the overall procedure we are about to define. This is obtained by the recursion theorem in the usual manner (cf. proposition 10.4).

At stage $n + 1$, some places have been defined with no gaps between them except at the pointer position.

(1) If there is an e such that $e[n] \cup \{(\pi[n], 0)\} \subseteq e \subset \phi_k[n] \cup \{(\pi[n], 0)\}$ and $\gamma(e) \neq \gamma(e*0)$ then define (*Fig. 10.6*):

$$\phi_k[n + 1] = \phi_k[n] \cup \{(\pi[n], 0)\};$$
$$\pi[n + 1] = x[n].$$

(2) Else, if $\phi_{\gamma(e[n])}(\pi[n])$ halts in n steps with output y, then define:

$$\phi_k[n + 1] = \phi_k[n] \cup \{(\pi[n], y + 1)\};$$
$$\pi[n + 1] = x[n].$$

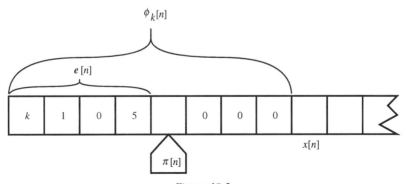

Figure 10.5

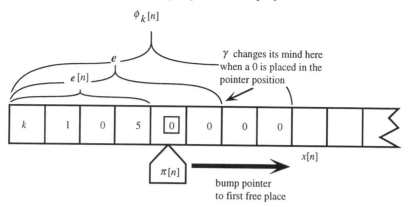

Figure 10.6

(3) Else, define (*Fig. 10.7*):

$$\phi_k[n+1] = \phi_k[n] \cup \{(x[n], 0)\};$$
$$\pi[n+1] = \pi[n].$$

There are two cases. (A) Suppose that the pointer never stops moving. Then $\phi_k \in \mathcal{SR}[0]$. If γ does not stabilize to an index, then it is immediate that γ fails, so suppose that γ stabilizes to index j on ϕ_k. Once γ stabilizes, case (1) never again applies, so the pointer must bump infinitely often because of (2). But then the index converged to is wrong about infinitely many positions in ϕ_k, so γ fails.

(B) So suppose that the pointer gets stuck at position m. Then after some time, neither (1) nor (2) is satisfied. Let $\varepsilon = \phi_k \cup \{(m, 0)\}$. $\varepsilon \in \mathcal{SR}[1]$ since $\varepsilon_0 = k$ and ϕ_k is just like ε except for being undefined at position m. Here is the important point: since we test for mind changes in condition (1) by tentatively defining the gap at the pointer position m to be 0, it follows that γ stabilizes to some index j before stage m on ε, because $\varepsilon_m = 0$ and the pointer would have bumped from position m (in light of condition (1)) had a mind change occurred on ε after position m. But since (2) never applies after the pointer reaches m, ϕ_j is undefined at m, so γ fails. ∎

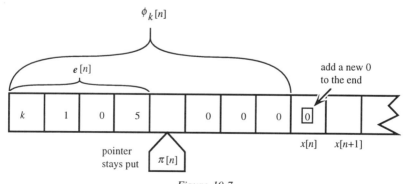

Figure 10.7

This proposition is just the first step in a series of ever more subtle applications of the recursion theorem to methodological questions.[4]

Another special property of the recursive function identification paradigm is that almost stable and stable identification are equivalent. In the ideal case this result is trivial, since there are only countably many hypotheses and each hypothesis has either a singleton or the null set as its empirical content. But in the computable case, it is impossible for a method to decide which case obtains, so the matter is not trivial. Once again, the proof illustrates how computable methods must often interleave formal problems with inductive inference.

Proposition 10.9 (Case and Smith)[5]

Correct$_{Ccmp}$ hypotheses are almost stably identifiable in the limit given $\mathcal{K} \Leftrightarrow$ they are stably identifiable given $\mathcal{K}$.

Proof: Let computable γ succeed almost stably given $\mathcal{K}$. Let $e \in \omega^*$. Define:

$$S_e = \{i\colon \exists n \leq lh(e) \text{ such that } \gamma(e|n) = i\}.$$

$$S'_e = \{i \in S_e\colon \forall x < lh(e), \phi_i(x) \text{ does not halt in } lh(e) \text{ steps or } \phi_i(x) = e_x\}.$$

Now for an arbitrary, finite S, define:

$\psi_S(x)$: *stage* n: *if* $\exists i \in S$ *such that* $\phi_i(x)$ *halts in* n *steps, let* j *be the least such* i *and output* $\phi_j(x)$. *Otherwise go to stage* $n + 1$.

Since ψ_S is partial recursive, let i_S be such that $\psi_S = \phi_{i_S}$. Define $\gamma^*(e) = i_{S'_e}$.

Since γ is total recursive, S_e can be obtained effectively by recording the outputs of γ along e. S'_e can be obtained from S_e by simulating a finite number of bounded computations and comparing the results with e. To effectively obtain $i_{S'_e}$ from S'_e, let π be an effective, 1–1 mapping from finite subsets of ω to ω. Let $\delta(\pi(S), x) = \psi_S(x)$. Applying the *s-m-n* theorem, there is a total recursive g such that $\phi_{g(\pi(S))}(x) = \psi_S(x)$. So $\gamma^*(e) = g(\pi(S'_e))$, which is total recursive.

Let $\varepsilon \in \mathcal{K}$. Since γ is almost stable, (*) $\exists n \, \forall m \geq n$, $S_{\varepsilon|m} = S_{\varepsilon|n} = \{i\colon \exists n \, \gamma(\varepsilon|n) = i\}$. Let n' be the least such n. Suppose $i \in S_{\varepsilon|n'}$ is such that $\exists x \, \phi_i(x)$ halts with a value other than ε_x. Let x_i be the least such x. Let n_i be the least n such that $\phi_i(x_i)$ halts in n steps. Define $R = \{i \in S_{\varepsilon|n'}\colon \exists x \, \phi_i(x){\downarrow} \neq \varepsilon_x\}$. Let $n^* = max(\{n_i\colon i \in R\} \cup \{n'\})$. Then $\forall m \geq n^*$, $\gamma^*(\varepsilon|m) = \gamma^*(\varepsilon|n^*)$ and $\phi_{\gamma^*(\varepsilon|m)} = \varepsilon$. So γ^* succeeds stably given $\mathcal{K}$. ∎

---

[4] Further results of this sort may be found in Case and Smith (1983).
[5] Case and Smith (1983): corollary of theorem 2.3.

5 Cognitive Science Revisited

In chapter 7 it was shown that the question whether the brain is or is not a computer is very hard for a computer to decide. But cognitive scientists don't just want to investigate a single hypothesis forever. They aspire to discover some program whose performance duplicates that of the brain. Let's consider how difficult this objective is.

No hypothesis generator can generate more than countably many distinct hypotheses when the data are discrete, as I have been supposing. If we have no background knowledge concerning the brain under study, then there are uncountably many possible data streams. Hence, the hypothesis generator cannot possibly produce a correct behavioral theory for each of them.

This difficulty can be overcome by introducing a single catchall hypothesis that says "this behavior is not computable" to cover all the noncomputable data streams. I reserve number 0 for this hypothesis and move all other code numbers one step to the right. So correctness may be defined as follows:

$$C_{cog}(\varepsilon, i) \Leftrightarrow i > 0 \text{ and } \phi_{i-1} = \varepsilon \text{ or } i = 0 \text{ and } \varepsilon \text{ is not recursive.}$$

Clearly, a computable identifier of $correct_{C_{cog}}$ hypotheses over $\mathcal{N}$ could be transformed easily into a computable, limiting decision procedure for the hypothesis that the brain is a computer. Hence, C_{cog} is not identifiable given $\mathcal{N}$, even ideally.

But cognitive scientists seem to assume at the outset that the brain's behavior is computable. So suppose they believe that the brain is a computer on the basis of physiological or metaphysical arguments. Then we can let $\mathcal{R}$ stand as a background assumption. This added knowledge still doesn't suffice for the reliable solution of the problem of finding a program to duplicate the brain's behavior. Proposition 10.2 says that the problem is unsolvable by a computable method even given $\mathcal{R}$.

On the other hand, since $\mathcal{R}$ is countable, $C_{cog} \in \Sigma[\mathcal{R}]_2^B$, for each $i \in \omega$. So once again, the cognitivist program confronts a curious irony. Suppose we know that we are computers. Then since we are computers, we cannot identify the program of the brain given our knowledge, by proposition 10.2. But given no knowledge, we still could not identify the behavior of the brain, since no possible method could.

Knowledge stronger than $\mathcal{R}$ can make the problem solvable. If we knew that the behavior of the brain is *primitive recursive* then the irony disappears. A Turing machine implementing an enumerate and test method can identify the class of primitive recursive functions since the primitive recursive functions are enumerable by index. By metering computational steps performed by this Turing machine along the lines discussed in the proof of proposition 8.10, the set of primitive recursive functions is identifiable by a primitive recursive method. Hence, given the knowledge that the brain is primitive recursive, it is possible for us to identify our own program.

Exercises

10.1. State and prove effective versions of all the characterizations given in the preceding chapter. In the case of almost stable identification, the result is:

> *Correct$_C$ hypotheses are almost stably identifiable in the limit given $\mathcal{K} \Leftrightarrow$ there is some $\mathcal{D} \subseteq C, H' \subseteq \omega$ such that*
>
> (1) *H' is recursively enumerable,*
>
> (2) *$\mathcal{K} \subseteq \mathcal{D}^{-1}(H')$,*
>
> (3) *$\mathcal{D} \in \Sigma[expand(H'), \mathcal{K}]^A_2$,*
>
> (4) *for each $\varepsilon \in \mathcal{K}$ there are at most finitely many $h \in H'$ such that $\mathcal{D}(\varepsilon, h)$.*

*10.2. State and prove the natural generalization of proposition 10.8 for C^n_{cmp} and C^{n+1}_{cmp}.[6] (Hint: use a block of $n + 1$ pointers, and whenever one of them is moved to a new location, all are moved together.)

10.3. Construct a discovery problem in which correctness is disjoint and some hypothesis is not arithmetically definable but the truth is identifiable in the limit by a computable method.

10.4. Characterize exact identification in the limit by a computable method (cf. exercise 9.6).

10.5. Define $C_{limrec}(\varepsilon, i) \Leftrightarrow \forall x \; \exists n \; \forall m \geq n, \; \phi_i(x, m) = \varepsilon_x$. Does proposition 10.9 hold for this correctness relation?

[6] Case and Smith (1983): theorem 2.6.

11

Prediction

1. Introduction

Since the time of Francis Bacon, a popular, pragmatic conception of science has been that discovery and assessment are means toward the end of predicting what will happen next. On this view, assessment is a means toward discovery, and discovery is a means for finding predictive hypotheses. It is therefore of interest to determine just how prediction relates to discovery. It turns out that the pragmatic conception of science works fine for ideal methods, but it breaks down in the computable case in the following sense: there are problems for which it is possible for a Turing machine to discover a correct, predictive theory in the limit, but for which it is nonetheless impossible for a Turing machine to eventually predict what will happen next. Hence, prediction cannot in general be the motive for discovering the truth. This chapter establishes the claims just made and also provides a pair of characterizations of predictability, both for ideal and for Turing-computable agents.

2. Ideal Extrapolation

Recall from chapter 2 that a *prediction method* is a function $\pi: \omega^* \to \omega$, where $\pi(e)$ is interpreted as π's prediction of ε_n on data $\varepsilon|n$ (*Fig. 11.1*).
Define:

> π *extrapolates* $\mathcal{K} \Leftrightarrow$ *for each* $\varepsilon \in \mathcal{K}$ *there is an* n *such that for each* $m \geq n$, $\pi(\varepsilon|m) = \varepsilon_m$.

$modulus_\pi(\varepsilon)$ = the least n such that for all $m \geq n$, $\pi(\varepsilon|m) = \varepsilon_m$.

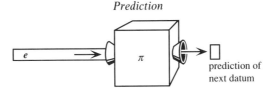

Figure 11.1

In the ideal case, the pragmatic notion that discoverability implies predictability is immediate as long as we assume that only empirically complete hypotheses are considered to be correct. Recall that C is *empirically complete* $\Leftrightarrow \forall h \in \omega$, $|C_h| \leq 1$.

Proposition 11.1

If C is empirically complete and correct$_C$ hypotheses are identifiable in the limit given $\mathcal{K}$, then $\mathcal{K}$ is extrapolable.

Proof: Let γ identify correct$_C$ hypotheses in the limit given $\mathcal{K}$. Let $\pi(e) = \varepsilon_{lh(e)}$, if $C_{\gamma(e)} = \{\varepsilon\}$, and let $\pi(e) = 0$ if $C_{\gamma(e)} = \varnothing$. ∎

Though it is not part of philosophical lore, the converse relation is also true, in a sense. The basic idea is this. If π extrapolates data stream ε, then there is some finite initial segment $e \subset \varepsilon$ such that after reading e, π is always correct about the next datum. That means that we can use π to construct ε in the following manner:[1] feed e to π. Thereafter, feed π the result of concatenating the last prediction of π onto what has been fed before (*Fig. 11.2*).

Let $\varepsilon_{\pi, e}$ denote the data stream constructed by π after being started with e in this manner. If π extrapolates ε, then if e is any initial segment of ε such that $lh(e) \geq mod_\pi(\varepsilon)$, then $\varepsilon_{\pi, e} = \varepsilon$. Thus, we may think of finite sequences in ω^* as empirically complete hypotheses according to the following correctness relation:[2]

$$C_\pi(\varepsilon, e) \Leftrightarrow \varepsilon = \varepsilon_{\pi, e}.$$

Since this relation is empirically complete, it is also Π_1^B, so correct$_{C_\pi}$ hypotheses are identifiable in the limit given $\mathcal{K}$. Thus, we have:

Proposition 11.2

If $\mathcal{K}$ is extrapolable, then there is an empirically complete C such that correct$_C$ hypotheses are identifiable in the limit given $\mathcal{K}$. ∎

---

[1] Barzdin and Freivald (1972), also reported in Blum and Blum (1975).
[2] Strictly speaking, a finite sequence is not a hypothesis, but this can be corrected by encoding finite sequences as natural numbers.

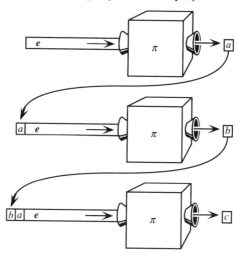

Figure 11.2

Now we have the following, extremely simple characterization of ideal extrapolability:

Proposition 11.3

   $\mathcal{K}$ *is extrapolable* $\Leftrightarrow$ $\mathcal{K}$ *is countable.*

Proof: ($\Leftarrow$) Enumerate $\mathcal{K}$ as $\varepsilon[0]$, $\varepsilon[1], \ldots$. Define $C(\varepsilon, i) \Leftrightarrow \varepsilon = \varepsilon[i]$. Apply proposition 11.1. ($\Rightarrow$) Suppose $\mathcal{K}$ is extrapolable. Apply proposition 11.2. Since there are only countably many hypotheses and C_π is empirically complete, $\mathcal{K}$ is countable. ∎

That pretty well wraps up the subject of ideal extrapolability. It is noteworthy that unlike all our other characterizations, this one is given entirely in terms of cardinality.

3.   Computable Extrapolation

The main objective of this section is to show that the computable analogue of proposition 11.2 holds but the computable analogue of proposition 11.1 fails. Thus, prediction can be harder than the discovery of empirically complete hypotheses for computable agents. This result sharpens the debate about the ultimate aims of science. There are scientific activities that make sense from the point of view of finding a true, predictive theory for its own sake that do not automatically entail an ability to predict the future.

First we consider some preliminary results that are interesting in their own right.

Proposition 11.4

If π is recursive then so is $\varepsilon_{\pi, e}$.

Proof: To compute $\varepsilon_{\pi, e}(x)$, effectively simulate $\pi(e)$ and then continue feeding π its own predictions thereafter until the xth prediction is obtained. Return the xth prediction. ∎

Thus we have:

Corollary 11.5

If $\mathcal{K}$ is effectively extrapolable, then $\mathcal{K} \subseteq \mathcal{R}$. ∎

But perhaps the first result of formal learning theory is that:

Proposition 11.6 (Putnam 1963)

$\mathcal{R}$ is not effectively extrapolable.

Proof: Let recursive π be given. The demon presents the data stream ε such that $\varepsilon_0 = \pi(0) + 1$ and $\varepsilon_{n+1} = \pi(\varepsilon|n) + 1$. ε is recursive since π is, but π is wrong on each prediction. ∎

Thus, if $\mathcal{K}$ is effectively extrapolable, then $\mathcal{K} \subset \mathcal{R}$, so the condition $\mathcal{K} \subseteq \mathcal{R}$ cannot characterize effective extrapolability. The following result provides an exact characterization (*Fig. 11.3*).

Proposition 11.7

$\mathcal{K}$ is effectively extrapolable $\Leftrightarrow$ there exists a C such that

(1) $C \subseteq C_{cmp}$ *and*

(2) $\mathcal{K} \subseteq dom(C)$ *and*

(3) $rng(C) \in \Delta_1^A$.

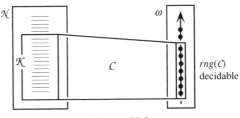

Figure 11.3

Corollary 11.8

The result remains true if we replace Δ_1^A with Σ_1^A.

Proof: ($\Rightarrow$) Let P_e be the procedure "on input x, simulate π on e, and then on the successive predictions of π, until the xth prediction is reached; output the xth prediction" P_e computes $\varepsilon_{\pi, e}$. Define:

$$C_\pi(\varepsilon, i) \Leftrightarrow i \text{ is an index for a program of form } P_e \text{ and } \forall n \ \phi_i(n) = \varepsilon_n.$$

(1) $C_\pi \subseteq C_{cmp}$, by the second conjunct of its definition. (2) $\mathcal{K} \subseteq dom(C)$ because π extrapolates $\mathcal{K}$, so for each $\varepsilon \in \mathcal{K}$, $\varepsilon = \varepsilon_{\pi, e}$, for some e and hence some program P_e computes ε. (3) Since π is total, we have that for each e, P_e computes some total function, so $rng(C_\pi) = \{i: i \text{ is an index of a program of form } P_e\}$, which is recursive (effectively decode i and perform a syntax check on the resulting program).

($\Leftarrow$) Suppose C satisfies (1–3). Let η be an effective enumeration of $rng(C)$ (by 3). Let $\gamma(e) = $ the first index in η that agrees with e. Since each index in η is total (by 1), this procedure is computable. Let $\pi(e) = \phi_{\gamma(e)}(lh(e))$. This is recursive, again since $\gamma(e)$ occurs in η and hence is total. Let $\varepsilon \in \mathcal{K}$. By (2), there is an i such that $C(\varepsilon, i)$. Let k be the first such i occurring in η. Since all preceding j in η are total and incorrect, each of these is eventually rejected by γ, so there is a time n such that for each later time m, $\gamma(\varepsilon|m) = k$. Since $C(\varepsilon, k)$, we have by (1) that $\phi_k = \varepsilon$. Thus $\phi_{\gamma(\varepsilon|m)}(m) = \varepsilon_m$.

Corollary 11.8 follows because we only required an effective enumeration of $rng(C)$.   ∎

It is interesting to compare this result with the characterization of recursive function identification in the limit. Recall that in general, limiting identification demands that there exists a $\mathcal{D}$ such that

(1′) $\mathcal{D} \subseteq C$ *and*

(2′) $\mathcal{K} \subseteq dom(\mathcal{D})$ *and*

(3′) $\mathcal{D} \in \Sigma[\mathcal{K}]_2^A$.

In the special case of C_{cmp}, we have $C_{cmp} \in \Pi_2^A$, so the condition is equivalent to requiring the existence of a $\mathcal{D}$ such that:

(1″) $\mathcal{D} \subseteq C_{cmp}$ *and*

(2″) $\mathcal{K} \subseteq dom(C)$ *and*

(3″) $\mathcal{D} \in \Delta[\mathcal{K}]_2^A$.

The only difference between this result and proposition 3.4 is that the third condition ($\mathcal{D} \in \Delta[\mathcal{K}]_2^A$) is replaced by $rng(\mathcal{D}) \in \Delta_1^A$. In fact, (3) entails (3′) in light of (1) and (2), but not conversely.

Proposition 11.9

If C satisfies (1–3) then $C \in \Pi_1^A$.

Corollary 11.10

The effective version of proposition 2.2 holds.

Proof: Suppose (1) and (2). Let $\alpha(i, e)$ start by deciding whether $i \in rng(C)$ by (3). If so, then ϕ_i is total by (1). Then α simulates i to check whether $e \subseteq \phi_i$. This computation terminates because ϕ_i is total. α refutes$_C$ ω with certainty given $\mathcal{N}$. The corollary follows from the characterization of effective identifiability in the limit, since $\Pi_1^A \subset \Sigma_2^A$. ∎

This purely recursion-theoretic relationship accounts for the entire difference in difficulty between computable extrapolation and computable identification in the limit of recursive functions. Computable extrapolation is possible just when there is a computable test on hypotheses that singles out a priori a set of total hypotheses that covers all of $\mathcal{K}$.

It remains to exhibit a concrete example of a $\mathcal{K} \subseteq \mathcal{R}$ that is effectively identifiable but not effectively extrapolable. The following, ingenious example is taken from Blum and Blum (1975). Let $\Phi_i(n)$ denote the number of computational steps required by program i to halt on input n, if $\phi_i(n)$ is defined, and let $\Phi_i(n)$ be undefined otherwise. Φ_i is called the *step counting function* for i. Step counting functions have the following remarkable property. Even though Φ_i may be undefined on some arguments, it is nonetheless true that:

Proposition 11.11

The relation $\Phi_i(n) = k$ is decidable.

Proof: To decide $\Phi_i(n) = k$, simulate program i until it halts or until $k + 1$ steps have been counted, whichever comes first. Return 1 if i halts after using just k steps. Return 0 otherwise. ∎

Let $\mathcal{TSC}$ denote the set of all *total* step counting functions. $\mathcal{TSC}$ is computably identifiable in the limit but is not computably extrapolable. Here is the basic idea. The *partial* step counting functions are recursively enumerable by index. An arbitrary such function Φ_i can be computably refuted with certainty (as in the proof of the preceding proposition) even though it may be impossible to tell what $\Phi_i(n)$ is (if $\phi_i(n)$ is undefined, the step counting will go on forever). Refutability and recursive enumerability of the step counting functions suffices for identifiability in the limit, but in the short run, the discovery method may conjecture partial step counting indices. A predictor who tries to derive the next prediction from such a conjecture will hang in an infinite loop. A predictor could get around this problem by considering only total indices, but, alas, no r.e. set of total indices covers $\mathcal{TSC}$.

Proposition 11.12

$\forall S \subseteq \omega$, if $\mathcal{TSC} \subseteq C_{cmp}^{-1}(S)$ then S is not r.e.

Proof: Suppose otherwise. Then as in proposition 10.1, we may effectively construct a table $\psi(x, y) = \phi_x(y)$, so that each $\Phi \in \mathcal{TSC}$ is a row of the table. (There may be total functions other than step counting functions in the table.) It is now possible to construct a total step counting function that is not any row of the table. Simply define $\delta(n) = \psi(n, n) + 1$. Since δ is total recursive, there is a j such that $\delta = \phi_j$. Recall (section 6.3) that our Turing machines take inputs and deliver outputs in unary notation so that to make output n, the read-write head must move n spaces to the right. Hence, $\Phi_j(n) \geq \Phi_n(n) + 1$, so Φ_j is not any row in the table. But $\Phi_j \in \mathcal{TSC}$, because Φ_j counts steps for δ, which is total. Contradiction.   ■

Thus we have the desired result:

Proposition 11.13 (Blum and Blum 1975)[3]

(1) *Correct*$_{C_{cmp}}$ *hypotheses are identifiable in the limit given* $\mathcal{TSC}$ *by a computable method, but*

(2) *no computable method extrapolates* $\mathcal{TSC}$.

Proof: (1) $\gamma(e)$ finds the first i such that $e \subseteq \Phi_i$. The relation $e \subseteq \Phi_i$ is decidable, as was mentioned above, so this search is effective. We can also recursively recover an index j such that $\Phi_i = \phi_j$. Define $\psi(i, x) =$ the least k such that $\phi_i(x)$ halts in k steps. By the *s-m-n* theorem (proposition 6.3), there is a total recursive s such that $\phi_{s(i)}(x) = \psi(i, x) = \Phi_i(x)$.

(2) Suppose $\mathcal{TSC} \subseteq dom(C) \subseteq C_{cmp}$. Then by proposition 11.12, $rng(C)$ is not r.e. So by proposition 11.7, we have (2).   ■

There is an alternative characterization of extrapolability based on the computational complexity of the functions that can be extrapolated. If $\zeta \in \mathcal{R}$, then we say that

$$\psi \text{ is } \zeta\text{-easy} \Leftrightarrow \exists i \text{ such that } \psi = \phi_i, \exists n, \forall m \geq n, \Phi_i(n) \leq \zeta(n).$$

In other words, some program for ψ runs under recursive time bound ζ for all but finitely many arguments. We say that $S \subseteq \mathcal{R}$ is ζ-*easy* just in case each $\varepsilon \in S$ is ζ-easy.

---

[3] Blum and Blum (1975): 131, example 2.

Proposition 11.14 (Barzdin and Freivald 1972)[4]

$\mathcal{K}$ *is computably extrapolable* $\Leftrightarrow$ *there is* $\zeta \in \mathcal{R}$ *such that* $\mathcal{K}$ *is* ζ-*easy.*

Proof: ($\Leftarrow$) Let $\zeta \in \mathcal{R}$ be given. Let η effectively enumerate ω^2. Define:

$\pi(e)$:
find the first pair (x, y) *in* η *such that*
   (a) $\forall k < lh(e)$, $\Phi_x(k) \leq max\{y, \zeta(k)\}$ *and*
   (b) $\forall k < lh(e)$, $\phi_x(k) = e_k$;
return $\phi_x(lh(e))$.

Let $\mathcal{K}$ be ζ-easy. Let $\varepsilon \in \mathcal{K}$. Then for some i such that $\phi_i = \varepsilon$, there is an n such that for all $m \geq n$, $\Phi_i(m) \leq \zeta(m)$. Let $a = max\{\Phi_i(b): b \leq n\}$. Then for all n, $\Phi_i(n) \leq max\{a, \zeta(n)\}$ and (b') $\forall n\ \phi_i(n) = \varepsilon_n$. Thus, the search for the pair (x, y) will succeed, and since the run time on the computation $\phi_i(lh(e))$ is bounded by $max\{a, \zeta(lh(e))\}$, it terminates with a prediction. Eventually, each incorrect such pair is refuted, and the search actually finds a pair (x, y) such that $\phi_x = \varepsilon$, after which all predictions by π are correct.

   ($\Rightarrow$) Let computable π extrapolate $\mathcal{K}$. From proposition 11.7, we have that for some $C \subseteq C_{cmp}$, $\mathcal{K} \subseteq dom(C)$ and $rng(C)$ is r.e. Let η effectively enumerate $rng(C)$. Define:

$$\zeta(x) = max\{\Phi_{\eta(i)}(x): i \leq x\}.$$

$\zeta \in \mathcal{R}$ since η is recursive, and each $\Phi_{\eta(i)}$ is recursive since η enumerates $rng(C)$. Moreover, for each i, $\Phi_{\eta(i)}$ is bounded almost everywhere by ζ. ∎

Exercises

11.1. Use proposition 11.7 to show that the primitive recursive functions are effectively extrapolable.

11.2. Draw a picture summarizing all the relations of implication between assessment, discovery, and prediction that we have seen up to now.

*11.3. Suppose that Frank and Gertrude have to pass one another in the hall every day. On the first day, Frank thinks Gertrude will move to her right, so he does the same. But Gertrude moves to her left. Frank assumes that her convention is to always move to the left, so he moves to his left. But Gertrude draws the symmetrical inference and moves to her right. Thinking that this has gone far enough, Frank moves to his right again, resolving never to move so that Gertrude can get past. But Gertrude, equally exasperated, makes the same decision! The two die of starvation in the hallway (*Fig. 11.4*).

---

[4] Also reported in Blum and Blum (1975).

By now it must be obvious to her that I will move to the right.

Surely he's tired of moving to the right by now. I guess he'll try left this time.

Figure 11.4

Think of passing in the hall as a game for two players, in which both players receive the payoff 1 if they both move right or if they both move left and receive 0 otherwise. Think of the mutual history of Frank and Gertrude as a sequence of successive attempts or trials at passing, whether consecutive attempts occur on the same day (because previous attempts on that day failed) or on successive days (because the last attempt on the preceding day succeeded). Since they will continue to have "rites of passage" for the unforseeable future, it would certainly be nice if they could eventually reach a state in which they always pass on the first attempt.

Suppose that Frank knows in advance that Gertrude will use some stategy in G and Gertrude knows in advance that Frank will use some strategy in $\mathcal{F}$. Then it would be desirable if Frank could pick a strategy in $\mathcal{F}$ that eventually always passes Gertrude on the first attempt, no matter what strategy in G Gertrude happens to be using, and similarly for Gertrude. Show that this is possible when $G = \mathcal{F} = $ the set of all primitive recursive prediction methods. Show it is not possible when $G = \mathcal{F} = $ the set of all total recursive prediction methods.

Game theorists attempt to explain social phenomena in terms of the concept of an *equilibrium*. An equilibrium for the passing game is a pair of plays (e.g., (left, left)) such that given Frank has played the first, Gertrude would not be inclined to deviate from the second, and given that Gertrude has played the second, Frank would not be inclined to deviate from the first. Hence, (left, left) and (right, right) are the equilibria of the passing game. Suppose that we always observe Gertrude and Frank pass each other in an orderly way, by both moving to their own right sides. Does the fact that (right, right) is an equilibrium explain their success?

12

Inquiry Concerning First-Order Theories

1. Introduction

In the preceding chapters, hypotheses and evidence reports were both taken to be unanalyzed units represented by natural numbers (*Fig. 12.1*). These abstractions yield general characterizations of inductive success in terms of the complexity of the relation of correctness. An interesting special case of this setting arises when we take data and hypotheses to be sentences in a first-order language, and when we take correctness to imply model-theoretic truth (*Fig. 12.2*).[1] The added logical structure imposed by this application raises more detailed methodological questions.

Abstraction can be taken in two senses. In one sense, "abstract" means "general." The topological paradigm developed in the preceding chapters is

Figure 12.1

[1] In this chapter, several model-theoretic results are assumed as lemmas. All these results are standard, however, and may be found in Chang and Keisler (1973). Readers unfamiliar with model theory may skip this chapter without compromising their understanding of what follows.

$B(a), R(a), \neg B(b), \neg R(b), B(c), \ldots$ $\forall x\, (R(x) \rightarrow B(x))$

Figure 12.2

more abstract than the logical paradigm in this sense, since it applies to any notion of empirical correctness. "Abstract" can also mean "suggestive but false for the sake of easier analysis." The logical paradigm is more abstract than the topological paradigm in this sense, since it forces us to choose some clearly defined notion of correctness for the sentences of a logical language and any such choice will be a simplification of the many concerns that regulate real scientific inquiry (*Fig. 12.3*). Still, it is worth examining the issues that arise even in an overly simplified application of the results of the preceding chapters.

2. Logical Hypothesis Assessment from Complete, True Data

The logical paradigm to be considered in this chapter is idealized in several respects. First, I suppose that hypotheses involve only *first-order quantification*. First-order quantifiers range over individual objects rather than over infinite sets or sequences of objects. Second, I assume that the evidence is perfect, in that all true data are presented and no false datum is presented. Third, I suppose that hypotheses do not involve any *theoretical terms* (i.e., nonlogical vocabulary that does not occur in the data). Such hypotheses will be referred to as *empirical generalizations*. Fourth, I assume that the evidence true of a world may arrive in any order whatever, for all the scientist knows. Fifth, I assume that all possible worlds involve at most countably many events or objects to be observed, and that each of these events or objects is eventually described in the evidence. All

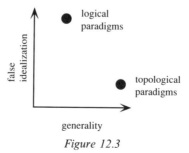

Figure 12.3

these assumptions are often, or perhaps usually, false in scientific practice, but they make the analysis easier and cause no harm as long as they are not taken too seriously. Some of them will be eased later on.

The rudiments of first-order syntax and semantics will be assumed in what follows. Let the *hypothesis language* L be a countable, first-order language. Hypotheses are sentences or theories expressed in L. Let *Const* be a countably infinite, decidable set of constants that do not occur in L. Let L_{Const} be the *expansion* of L with the constants in *Const*. In other words, L_{Const} contains all sentences that can be formed with the vocabulary elements of L together with the constants in *Const*. The *evidence language* E is some set of L_{Const} sentences. For example, E might be the set of all quantifier-free sentences of L_{Const}.

Let $\mathfrak{A}$ be a *relational structure* for L. In other words, $\mathfrak{A}$ consists of a *domain* A, an assignment of a relation $R \subseteq A^n$ to each n-ary predicate symbol of L (except for '$=$', whose interpretation is fixed), an assignment of a total function $f: A^n \to A$ for each n-ary function symbol of L, and an assignment of an element of A to each constant symbol of L. As is common, I will also use $\mathfrak{A}$ ambiguously to denote the domain A of $\mathfrak{A}$. Let δ be a map from *Const* into $\mathfrak{A}$. Then $(\mathfrak{A}, \delta)$ denotes the *expansion* of $\mathfrak{A}$ to a structure that assigns denotations to elements of *Const* according to δ. $(\mathfrak{A}, \delta)$ is therefore a structure for L_{Const} if $\mathfrak{A}$ is a structure for L.

Let $\mathfrak{A}$ be a structure for L_{Const}. Let $\vDash$ denote the model-theoretic concept of truth in a structure. The *E-diagram* of $\mathfrak{A}$ is defined as

$$D_E(\mathfrak{A}) = \{s \in E: \mathfrak{A} \vDash s\}.$$

One may think of $\mathfrak{A}$ as a "possible world" under investigation and of $D_E(\mathfrak{A})$ as the *total* evidence true of $\mathfrak{A}$. The scientist learns about world $\mathfrak{A}$ only by seeing increasing amounts of such evidence.

Now I define the set of data streams that may arise in structure $\mathfrak{A}$ for L_{Const} (*Fig. 12.4*). I assume that each ordering of $D_E(\mathfrak{A})$ is possible for all the scientist knows. The effect of this assumption is to ensure that the only information received by the scientist is recorded in the evidence sentences occurring in the data stream.[2] Without it, the data stream could, for example, signal the truth value of the hypothesis under study by presenting a true evidence sentence involving constant c first when the hypothesis is true and by presenting a true evidence sentence involving constant c' first when the hypothesis is false.

$$\mathcal{D}ata_E(\mathfrak{A}) = \{\varepsilon: rng(\varepsilon) = D_E(\mathfrak{A})\}.$$

I assume that every domain element is named by some $c \in Const$. Define the set of *everywhere named* structures for L_{Const} as follows:

$$EN = \{(\mathfrak{A}, \delta): \mathfrak{A} \text{ is a countable structure for } L \text{ and } \delta \text{ is onto } \mathfrak{A}\}.$$

---

[2] This questionable idealization is also assumed in Osherson et al. (1986, 1989, 1991), Shapiro (1981), and Lauth (1993), as well as in the voluminous literature on language identification in the limit.

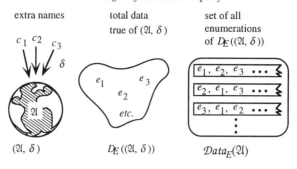

extra names   total data   set of all
               true of $(\mathfrak{A}, \delta)$ enumerations
                                  of $D_E((\mathfrak{A}, \delta))$

$(\mathfrak{A}, \delta)$ $D_E((\mathfrak{A}, \delta))$ $Data_E(\mathfrak{A})$

Figure 12.4

Let $T \subseteq L_{Const}$. The set of everywhere named *models* of T is then given as

$$EN(T) = \{\mathfrak{A} \in EN: \mathfrak{A} \vDash T\}.$$

The set of all *data streams* for a given theory may now be defined as

$$\mathcal{D}ata_E(T) = \bigcup_{\mathfrak{A} \in EN(T)} \mathcal{D}ata_E(\mathfrak{A}).$$

Now it is possible to define successful inquiry. Let K be an L-theory representing background knowledge and let s be a hypothesis under investigation.[3] Then the following definitions of limiting success are analogous to the criteria examined in previous chapters. Let $s \in L_{Const}$ and $K \subseteq L_{Const}$.

> α *verifies* s *in the limit given* K *from E-data* $\Leftrightarrow \forall \mathfrak{A} \in EN(K)$, $\forall \varepsilon \in \mathcal{D}ata_E(\mathfrak{A})$, $\mathfrak{A} \vDash s \Leftrightarrow \exists n$ such that $\forall m \geq n$, $\alpha(\varepsilon|m) = 1$.

> α *refutes* s *in the limit given* K *from E-data* $\Leftrightarrow \forall \mathfrak{A} \in EN(K)$, $\forall \varepsilon \in \mathcal{D}ata_E(\mathfrak{A})$, $\mathfrak{A} \nvDash s \Leftrightarrow \exists n$ such that $\forall m \geq n$, $\alpha(\varepsilon|m) = 0$.

> α *decides* s *in the limit given* K *from E-data* $\Leftrightarrow \alpha$ both verifies and refutes s in the limit given K from E-data.

The gradual and n mind-change cases may be defined in a similar manner.

3.   Truth and Underdetermination

The definition of verification in the limit is based on the relation $\vDash$ of truth in a structure, which is a relation between possible worlds and hypotheses rather than between data streams and hypotheses. This raises the possibility of global underdetermination (cf. chapter 2), since there may exist $\mathfrak{A}, \mathfrak{B} \in EN(K)$ such that $\mathfrak{A} \vDash s$ and $\mathfrak{B} \nvDash s$ but $\mathcal{D}ata_E(\mathfrak{A}) \cap \mathcal{D}ata_E(\mathfrak{B}) \neq \varnothing$ (*Fig. 12.5*).

---

[3] Note that the change in font from $\mathcal{K}$ to K indicates that K is a set of finite objects (sentences) rather than a set of infinite data streams, as in the preceding paradigms.

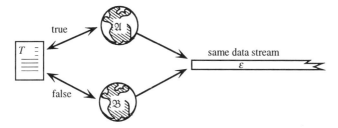

Figure 12.5

The question of global underdetermination did not arise in the topological paradigm, because hypotheses were assumed to be representable as sets of data streams. When global underdetermination is not a concern, we may think of logical theories as a special way of generating sets of data streams, just as in previous chapters. It is immediate that

Proposition 12.1

T is assessable given K [in any of the senses just defined] ⇔ T is not globally underdetermined by E-data given K and $Data_E(T)$ is assessable given $Data_E(K)$ [in the corresponding, topological sense]. ∎

So everything said before applies to the logical paradigm. But further questions specific to the logical setting remain, such as how the syntactic form of a hypothesis relates to the complexity of its set of possible data streams, which determines how difficult the hypothesis is to investigate empirically. This question is examined in detail in the following sections.

4. Quantifier Prefix Complexity

In order to find a syntactic characterization of success, we must have some notion of the syntactic complexity of a logical formula. A standard measure of formula complexity is based on quantifier alternations. A *prenex normal formula* is a formula of form $Q_1 x_1 Q_2 x_2 \cdots Q_n x_n \Psi$ such that Ψ is quantifier-free and $Q_1 x_1 Q_2 x_2 \cdots Q_n x_n$ is a sequence of quantifiers. Say that $Q_1 x_1 Q_2 x_2 \cdots Q_n$ is a *block* of quantifiers just in case $Q_1 = Q_2 = \cdots = Q_n$. A prefix that is the concatenation of at most k blocks starting with a $\forall$ block is said to be a Π_k prefix, and a prefix that is the concatenation of at most k blocks starting with an $\exists$ block is said to be a Σ_k prefix. Trivially, the empty prefix is both Π_0 and Σ_0. So, for example, $\forall x \forall y \exists z \forall w$ is a Π_3 prefix.

Let Φ be a prenex normal formula of L. Define:

$$\Phi \in \Sigma_n^q [\Pi_n^q] \Leftrightarrow \text{the prefix of } \Phi \text{ is } \Sigma_n [\Pi_n].$$

$$\Phi \in \Delta_n^q \Leftrightarrow \Phi \in \Sigma_n^q \text{ and } \Phi \in \Pi_n^q.$$

The superscript q indicates *quantifier* complexity. Note that $\Delta_0^q = \Sigma_0^q = \Pi_0^q = \Delta_1^q$. Let K be an L-theory (i.e., a set of L-sentences) representing background knowledge. Define the quantifier complexity of an arbitrary formula Φ of L_{Const} relative to K as follows:

$$\Phi \in \Sigma[K]_n^q \Leftrightarrow \exists \text{ prenex } \Psi \in L \text{ such that } K \vDash \Phi \leftrightarrow \Psi \text{ and } \Psi \in \Sigma_n^q.$$

$$\Phi \in \Pi[K]_n^q \Leftrightarrow \exists \text{ prenex } \Psi \in L \text{ such that } K \vDash \Phi \leftrightarrow \Psi \text{ and } \Psi \in \Pi_n^q.$$

$$\Phi \in \Delta[K]_n^q \Leftrightarrow \Phi \in \Sigma[K]_n^q \cap \Pi[K]_n^q.$$

For example, '$\forall x \, \exists y \, P(x, y)$' $\in \Pi_2^q$ and if $K = \{\forall x \, \exists y \, P(x, y) \leftrightarrow P(a)\}$ then '$\forall x \, \exists y \, P(x, y)$' $\in \Delta[K]_1^q$.

Quantifier complexity can be extended to data sequences and theories. Let Γ be one of the syntactic complexity classes $\Sigma[K]_n^q$, $\Pi[K]_n^q$, $\Delta[K]_n^q$. Let T be an L-theory and let e be a finite data sequence. Define:

$$e \in \Gamma \Leftrightarrow \forall i, e_i \in \Gamma.$$

$$T \in \Gamma \Leftrightarrow \exists S \subseteq \Gamma \text{ such that } S \cup K \text{ is logically equivalent to } T \cup K.$$

5. An Example

Let's return to Kant's question (cf. chapter 3) concerning the infinite divisibility of matter. We can think of the hypothesis as asserting that it is possible to cut between any two given cuts:

$$DO: \forall x \, \forall y \, (x < y \rightarrow \exists z \, (x < z \, \& \, z < y)),$$

where x, y, and z range over positions in which cuts are possible. This axiom is known as *dense order* (*DO*). The experimental design assumed for this problem in chapter 3 provides the scientist with some background knowledge. He knows, for example, that he is going to repeatedly cut a finite length of matter (say a banana) between its two endpoints, 1 and 0. So he knows the following theory, called *simple order with endpoints* (*SOE*):

$$\forall x \, \neg \, (x < x)$$

$$\forall x \, \forall y \, \forall z \, (x < y \, \& \, y < z \rightarrow x < z)$$

$$\forall x \, \forall y \, (x < y \vee y < x \vee x = y)$$

$$\forall x \, (x \neq 0 \rightarrow 0 < x \, \& \, x \neq 1 \rightarrow x < 1)$$

Then we have:

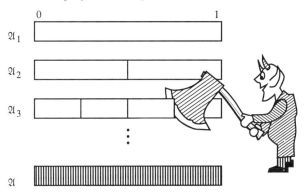

Figure 12.6

Proposition 12.2 (Osherson and Weinstein 1989)

DO is not verifiable in the limit given SOE from Δ_1^q data.

Proof: The problem is that the demon can construct the chain of countable models of SOE depicted in *Figure 12.6*, in which each relational structure is a substructure of its successor. In this chain, we start out with the physically indivisible banana $\mathfrak{A}_1$ (i.e., a banana that is a large, yellow elementary particle!) and each model $\mathfrak{A}_{n+1}$ adds a possible cut between each pair of cuts passed along from model $\mathfrak{A}_n$. This can plainly go on forever. Let $\mathfrak{A} = \bigcup \{\mathfrak{A}_i : i \in \omega\}$. Then $\mathfrak{A}$ is densely divisible. This is a situation that pleases the demon. For suppose for reductio that scientist α can verify DO in the limit given SOE from Δ_1^q data. The demon starts presenting data true of $(\mathfrak{A}, \delta)$, where δ is onto $\mathfrak{A}$, until α says that DO is true, which must eventually happen, else α fails on a data stream for $\mathfrak{A}$. However much data the demon has presented, it concerns some finite subset of $\mathfrak{A}$ (*Fig. 12.7*).

This finite subset is included in the domain of some $\mathfrak{A}_{n'}$ in the chain. The demon chooses assignment δ' onto $\mathfrak{A}_{n'}$ that preserves the assignments made by δ to constants that already occur in the data and proceeds to present data from $(\mathfrak{A}_{n'}, \delta')$ until α says that DO is false, which again must happen since $\mathfrak{A}_{n'} \nvDash$ DO. At this point, the demon chooses δ'' onto $\mathfrak{A}$ that preserves assignments of constants already presented in the data and proceeds to present data from $(\mathfrak{A}, \delta'')$, and so forth forever. α does not stabilize to 1 on the data stream ε so constructed. If the demon is careful to assign new constants at each stage in such a way that no domain elements are missed in the limit and if the demon ensures that each L_{Const} atom is presented either negated or nonnegated, then

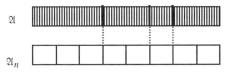

Figure 12.7

$\varepsilon \in \mathcal{D}ata_{\Delta_1^q}((\mathfrak{A}, \delta))$, where δ is onto $\mathfrak{A}$. But since $\mathfrak{A} \vDash \text{SOE} \cup \{\text{DO}\}$, so does $(\mathfrak{A}, \delta)$, so α stabilizes to 1 on ε. Contradiction.   ∎

In the next section it will be shown that for each hypothesis that is not verifiable in the limit given some background theory K, the demon can avail himself of a chain-and-union construction of this sort to fool the scientist.

On the other hand, it is easy to program a computable scientist that can refute DO in the limit given SOE.

Proposition 12.3

DO is refutable in the limit given SOE.

Proof: α maintains two queues called *Distinct* and *Cut*, which are both initially empty. Whenever a datum of form $a \neq b$ is received and the pair $\{a, b\}$ does not occur in *Cut*, $\{a, b\}$ is added to the tail of *Distinct*, where a precedes b in some fixed ordering of *Const*. When there is a c such that the current data contains both $a < c$ and $c < b$ or both $b < c$ and $c < a$, then $\{a, b\}$ is removed from the head of *Distinct* and is added to the tail of *Cut*. Whenever the head of *Distinct* does not change after a datum is read, α conjectures 0. Otherwise, α conjectures 1.   ∎

SOE $\cup$ DO is known as the theory of *dense simple order with endpoints* (*DSOE*). What happens if the scientist assumes DSOE as background knowledge? A standard fact of model theory is that each $s \in L$ is in $\Pi[\text{DSOE}]_1^q$, from which it is not hard to see that every hypothesis in the language involving just the binary predicate $<$ is refutable with certainty given DSOE. So model theory can serve as a source of results about empirical underdetermination in a formal language relative to a given background theory.

6. Data Complexity

It is commonly supposed that the evidence language E is some subset of the quantifier-free (Δ_1^q) fragment of L_{Const}. This reflects the ancient philosophical assumption that the objects of perception are *particular*.[4] Nonetheless, it is interesting to ask how far reliable inductive inference could take us if our data were to contain generalizations.

For example, in the artificial intelligence learning literature, the *closed world hypothesis* states that whenever two things are not explicitly said to be related in the data, they may safely be assumed not to be related. When one attempts

---

[4] Note that nothing in the topological paradigm determines whether the data express particular or general claims. It is completely noncommittal on this issue.

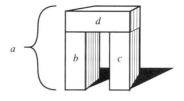

Figure 12.8

to teach a robot what an arch is by example, the robot is shown lots of examples and counterexamples of arches. The closed world hypothesis asserts that whatever objects the teacher does not explicitly specify as parts of the training instance are, in fact, not parts of the instance.[5] For example, the following description of an arch (*Fig. 12.8*)

Arch(a), *Part-of(b, a)*, *Part-of(c, a)*, *Part-of(d, a)*, *On-top(d, b)*,
On-top(d, c), ¬ *Touch(b, c)*

carries with it, according to the closed world hypothesis, the following universal claim:

$$\forall x \, [x \neq b \, \& \, x \neq c \, \& \, x \neq d \rightarrow \neg Part\text{-}of(x, a)].$$

Such universal data can be extremely helpful in assessment and discovery problems, for it puts to rest unbounded worries that objects not yet described in the data (e.g., the Andromeda galaxy) are relevant parts of an object described in the data. Such an assumption amounts to the provision of universal data, and yet it is plausible in many applications.

Once the possibility of universal data is entertained, a general question arises. Given complete, true evidence of a given quantificational complexity, how much more complex can the hypotheses be that are decidable or verifiable from this evidence in the limit (*Fig. 12.9*)? The traditional assumption that the data is quantifier-free then constitutes the base of a hierarchy of inductive paradigms corresponding to ever more complex generalizations in the data. Each level of data complexity poses a new and generalized version of the problem of induction to scientists using data of that kind.

The following result says that the arithmetical complexity of a hypothesis (viewed as a set of data streams) is at most the quantifier complexity of the hypothesis less the quantifier complexity of the data plus one. It is important that the bound is for *arithmetical* (computational) complexity rather than for *Borel* (ideal) complexity. To improve legibility in what follows, I abbreviate $\mathcal{D}ata_{\Delta_n^q}(K)$ as $\mathcal{D}ata_n(K)$.

---

[5] E.g., Winston (1975).

Hypothesis complexity

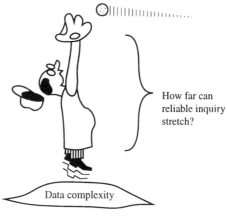

How far can
reliable inquiry
stretch?

Data complexity

Figure 12.9

Proposition 12.4

If $m \geq n$ then

(a) *If $s \in \Sigma[K]_m^q$ then $Data_n(s) \cap Data_n(K) \in \Sigma[Data_n(K)]_{(m-n)+1}^A$.*

(b) *If $s \in \Pi[K]_m^q$ then $Data_n(s) \cap Data_n(K) \in \Pi[Data_n(K)]_{(m-n)+1}^A$.*

When we plug this result into the topological characterizations of chapter 4, we obtain intuitive, syntactic, sufficient conditions for effective hypothesis assessment:

Corollary 12.5

(a) *If $s \in \Sigma[K]_n^q[\Pi[K]_n^q, \Delta[K]_n^q]$ then s is effectively verifiable [refutable, decidable] with certainty given K from Δ_n^q data.*

(b) *If $s \in \Sigma[K]_{n+1}^q[\Pi[K]_{n+1}^q, \Delta[K]_{n+1}^q]$ then s is effectively verifiable [refutable, decidable] in the limit given K from Δ_n^q data.*

Proof of proposition: The idea is just to build up a set of data streams stage by stage, using the quantifier prefix of *s* as a guide. I show (a) by induction on $(m - n) + 1$. (b) is similar. The proof will be given for open formulas rather than for sentences, in order to strengthen the induction hypothesis. Let $\Phi(\bar{x})$ be an *L*-formula open in variable vector $\bar{x}$ of length *i*. Let $\bar{c} \in Const^i$. Define the correctness relation:

$$C_{\Phi, n}(\varepsilon, \bar{c}) \Leftrightarrow \varepsilon \in Data_n(\Phi(\bar{c})).$$

I will use the following lemma:

Lemma 12.6

For each $\varepsilon \in \mathcal{D}ata_n(K)$ and $\bar{b} \in Const^i$, $C_{\neg\Phi, n}(\varepsilon, \bar{b}) \Leftrightarrow \neg C_{\Phi, n}(\varepsilon, \bar{b})$.

Proof of lemma: Suppose $\varepsilon \in \mathcal{D}ata_n(K)$ and $\bar{b} \in Const^i$. ($\Rightarrow$) Suppose $C_{\neg\Phi, n}(\varepsilon, \bar{b})$, so that $\varepsilon \in \mathcal{D}ata_n(\neg\Phi(\bar{b}))$. Then there is an $\mathfrak{A}$ such that $\mathfrak{A} \vDash K$ and $\mathfrak{A} \nvDash \Phi(\bar{b})$, and for some δ onto $\mathfrak{A}$, $\varepsilon \in \mathcal{D}ata_n((\mathfrak{A}, \delta))$. Then since $\mathfrak{A} \nvDash \Phi(\bar{b})$, $\varepsilon \notin \mathcal{D}ata_n(\Phi(\bar{b}))$, so $\neg C_{\Phi, n}(\varepsilon, \bar{b})$. ($\Leftarrow$) Let $\neg C_{\Phi, n}(\varepsilon, \bar{b})$. Then for some $\mathfrak{A}$ such that $\mathfrak{A} \vDash K$ and for some δ onto $\mathfrak{A}$, $\varepsilon \in \mathcal{D}ata_n((\mathfrak{A}, \delta))$ but $(\mathfrak{A}, \delta) \nvDash \Phi(\bar{b})$. So $\varepsilon \in \mathcal{D}ata_n(\neg\Phi(\bar{b}))$ from which we have $C_{\neg\Phi, n}(\varepsilon, \bar{b})$. ∎

I claim:

(*) If $\Phi(\bar{x}) \in \Sigma[K]_m^q$ then
$C_{\Phi, n} \cap (\mathcal{D}ata_n(K) \times Const^i) \in \Sigma[\mathcal{D}ata_n(K)]_{(m-n)+1}^A$.

(*) implies (a), for when $\Phi = s$ so that no variables occur free in Φ, then $\varepsilon \in \mathcal{D}ata_n(s) \Leftrightarrow C_{s, n}(\varepsilon, \mathbf{0})$, where $\mathbf{0}$ is the empty vector of constants. I now establish (*).

In the base case, suppose $(m - n) + 1 = 1$. Let $\Phi(\bar{x}) \in \Sigma[K]_n^q$. Let $\Psi(\bar{x}, \bar{y})$ be a Δ_n^q formula $\Psi(\bar{x}, \bar{y})$ such that $K \vDash (\Phi(\bar{x}) \leftrightarrow \exists\bar{x}\Psi(\bar{x}, \bar{y}))$. Then for each $\varepsilon \in \mathcal{D}ata_n(K)$ and for each i-tuple $\bar{b}$ of constants, we have:

$$C_{\Phi, n}(\varepsilon, \bar{b}) \Leftrightarrow \exists\bar{c} \in Const^j \text{ such that } C_{\Psi, n}(\varepsilon, \bar{b}*\bar{c}).$$

The relation $C_{\Psi, n}(\varepsilon, \bar{b}*\bar{c})$ is effectively decidable given $\mathcal{D}ata_n(K)$ by simply watching for the sentence $\Psi(\bar{b}, \bar{c})$ to occur negated or nonnegated in the Δ_n^q data ε, which must eventually occur if ε is in $\mathcal{D}ata_n(K)$. Hence, $C_{\Psi, n}(\varepsilon, \bar{b}*\bar{c}) \in \Delta[\mathcal{D}ata_n(K)]_1^A$ and so $C_{\Phi, n}(\varepsilon, \bar{b}) \in \Sigma[\mathcal{D}ata_n(K)]_1^A$, since $Const^j$ is a recursive set.

Now suppose that (*) holds for all $(m - n) + 1 \leq k$. Suppose, further, that $\Phi(\bar{x}) \in \Sigma[K]_m^q$, that $\bar{x} \in Var^i$, and that we are dealing with Δ_n^q data, where $(m - n) + 1 = k + 1$. So for some prenex normal formula $\Psi(\bar{x}) \in \Sigma[K]_{m-1}^q$, $K \vDash (\Phi(\bar{x}) \leftrightarrow \exists\bar{y}\neg\Psi(\bar{x}, \bar{y}))$, where $\bar{y} \in Var^j$. By the inductive hypothesis, $C_{\Psi, n} \cap (\mathcal{D}ata_n(K) \times Const^{i+j}) \in \Sigma[\mathcal{D}ata_n(K)]_{(m-n)}^A$. Then for each $\varepsilon \in \mathcal{D}ata_n(K)$ and for each i-tuple $\bar{b}$ of constants,

$$C_{\Phi, n}(\varepsilon, \bar{b}) \Leftrightarrow \exists\bar{c} \in Const^j \text{ such that } C_{\neg\Psi, n}(\varepsilon, \bar{b}*\bar{c}) \Leftrightarrow \exists\bar{c} \in Const^j$$
$$\text{such that } \neg C_{\Psi, n}(\varepsilon, \bar{b}*\bar{c}),$$

where the second equivalence follows from lemma 12.6. Since $Const^i$ is a recursive set, we have that $C_{\Phi, n} \cap (\mathcal{D}ata_n(K) \times Const^i) \in \Sigma[\mathcal{D}ata_n(K)]_{(m-n)+1}^A$. ∎

With some help from model theory, it is possible to obtain necessary conditions for success that meet our sufficient conditions of proposition 12.4 more than halfway. That is, it can be shown that if the syntactic sufficient conditions for *computable* decidability and verifiability are not met, then no *ideal* agent can succeed, either. So in the logical paradigm, the problems solvable by ideal agents are exactly the problems solvable by Turing machines. Putting both results together, we have proposition 12.7, which provides an exact correspondence between syntactic complexity and reliability, given the idealizing assumptions of the logical paradigm. The proof of proposition 12.7 involves the contruction of a winning strategy for the demon whenever the scientist has none. This fact stands in marked contrast to the situation in the more general, topological paradigm, in which it is impossible to show that the demon has a winning strategy whenever the scientist does not, if ZFC is consistent (corollary 5.10).

Proposition 12.7[6]

(a) s is $\begin{bmatrix} computably \\ ideally \end{bmatrix} \begin{bmatrix} verifiable \\ refutable \\ decidable \end{bmatrix}$ with certainty given K from Δ_n^q

$$data \Leftrightarrow s \in \begin{bmatrix} \Sigma[K]_n^q \\ \Pi[K]_n^q \\ \Delta[K]_n^q \end{bmatrix}.$$

(b) s is $\begin{bmatrix} computably \\ ideally \end{bmatrix} \begin{bmatrix} verifiable \\ refutable \\ decidable \end{bmatrix}$ in the limit given K from Δ_n^q

$$data \Leftrightarrow s \in \begin{bmatrix} \Sigma[K]_{n+1}^q \\ \Pi[K]_{n+1}^q \\ \Delta[K]_{n+1}^q \end{bmatrix}.$$

By proposition 4.10, it follows that:

Corollary 12.8

Let $0 \leq m - n \leq 1$. Then

(a) $s \in \Sigma[K]_m^q$

$$\Leftrightarrow \mathcal{D}ata_n(s) \cap \mathcal{D}ata_n(K) \in \begin{bmatrix} \Sigma[\mathcal{D}ata_n(K)]_{(m-n)+1}^A \\ \Sigma[\mathcal{D}ata_n(K)]_{(m-n)+1}^B \end{bmatrix};$$

(b) $s \in \Pi[K]_m^q$

$$\Leftrightarrow \mathcal{D}ata_n(s) \cap \mathcal{D}ata_n(K) \in \begin{bmatrix} \Pi[\mathcal{D}ata_n(K)]_{(m-n)+1}^A \\ \Pi[\mathcal{D}ata_n(K)]_{(m-n)+1}^B \end{bmatrix}.$$

[6] Kelly and Glymour (1990).

Traditionally, philosophers with empiricist leanings have attempted to characterize cognitive significance in terms of logical form.[7] Proposition 12.7 and corollary 12.8 show that each result in the first-order hypothesis assessment paradigm can be factored into two parts: a purely topological result concerning the complexity of sets of data streams and a purely model-theoretic result relating the syntax of a theory to the complexity of the set of data streams for that theory, relative to strong assumptions about the completeness and truth of the data.[8] Syntactic form thus bears only a *contingent* and *incidental* relationship to the intrinsic difficulty of induction, since the relation between topology and syntax is a function of our prior knowledge of the nature of the data protocol. If the data were incomplete or false, the tight correspondence between topology and logical form presented in this section could fail. Topological complexity is therefore more fundamental to underdetermination and inductive reliability than logical form is.

Proof of proposition: The ($\Leftarrow$) side of the proposition is just proposition 12.4. To prove the ($\Rightarrow$) side, we require a few concepts from model theory. Let $\mathfrak{A}$, $\mathfrak{B}$ be structures for L. Let K be an L-theory. Define:

$$\mathfrak{A} \leq_n \mathfrak{B} \Leftrightarrow \mathfrak{A} \subseteq \mathfrak{B} \text{ and } \forall \text{ formula } \Phi \in \Sigma_n^q, \forall \text{ assignment } v \text{ into } dom(\mathfrak{A}),$$
$$\mathfrak{A} \vDash \Phi[v] \Rightarrow \mathfrak{B} \vDash \Phi[v].$$

Then we say that $\mathfrak{A}$ is a Σ_n-*substructure of* $\mathfrak{B}$ and $\mathfrak{B}$ is a Σ_n-*extension of* $\mathfrak{A}$. A *countable* Σ_n *chain in* K is just an ω-sequence $\mathfrak{A}_0, \mathfrak{A}_1, \mathfrak{A}_2, \ldots, \mathfrak{A}_n, \ldots$ of countable models of K such that $\forall i \in \omega$, $\mathfrak{A}_i \leq_n \mathfrak{A}_{i+1}$ and the structure $\bigcup \{\mathfrak{A}_i : i \in \omega\}$ is also a model of K. For example, the sequence of bananas constructed by the demon in the proof of proposition 12.2 is a countable Σ_1-chain in DSOE, as the reader may verify (exercise 12.2). Now let s be a sentence of L. Define:

s *is preserved under countable* Σ_n-*substructures in* $K \Leftrightarrow \forall$ *countable* $\mathfrak{A}$, $\mathfrak{B}$, *if* $\mathfrak{A}$, $\mathfrak{B} \vDash K$ *and* $\mathfrak{A} \leq_n \mathfrak{B}$ *and* $\mathfrak{B} \vDash s$ *then* $\mathfrak{A} \vDash s$.

s *is preserved under countable* Σ_n-*extensions in* $K \Leftrightarrow \forall$ *countable* $\mathfrak{A}$, $\mathfrak{B}$, *if* $\mathfrak{A}$, $\mathfrak{B} \vDash K$ *and* $\mathfrak{B} \leq_n \mathfrak{A}$ *and* $\mathfrak{B} \vDash s$ *then* $\mathfrak{A} \vDash s$.

s *is preserved under unions of countable* Σ_n-*chains in* $K \Leftrightarrow \forall$ *countable* Σ_n-*chain* $\mathfrak{A}_1, \mathfrak{A}_2, \mathfrak{A}_3, \ldots, \mathfrak{A}_n, \ldots$ *in* K *if* $\forall i \in \omega$, $\mathfrak{A}_i \vDash s$, *then* $\bigcup \{\mathfrak{A}_i : i \in \omega\} \vDash s$.

For example, in the proof of proposition 12.2, the negation of the infinite divisibility hypothesis is not preserved under the union of the sequence of

---

[7] Cf. Hempel (1965): ch. 4.

[8] For example, Osherson and Weinstein (1991) is a consequence of proposition 12.7 (modulo some technical differences about the data protocol). One may think of proposition 4.10 as the topological core of their result and of corollary 12.8 as plugging proposition 4.10 into a model-theoretic setting.

Br r r r r r t
Br r r r r r r r r r t

evidence true   evidence true
hypothesis true   hypothesis false

Figure 12.10

finitely divisible bananas. But since the sequence is a Σ_1-chain in DSOE, both background knowledge and data are preserved.[9]

The trick to the proof is to unpack the *semantic* significance of the purely *syntactic* assumption that *s* is not equivalent to a statement with a given syntactic complexity. This will be done by means of three model-theoretic *preservation theorems*. A preservation theorem characterizes the quantifier complexity of a hypothesis in terms of some operation on relational structures that preserves its truth. Preservation theorems are just what the demon needs to fool the scientist. They show how the demon can alter the world so as to change the truth value of the hypothesis under study while preserving the truth of the (lower complexity) data he has presented to the scientist in the past (*Fig. 12.10*). Recall that this is just what goes on in the divisible banana example.

First, we require a technical lemma, which says that Σ_n chains could have been defined in terms of constant assignments instead of variable assignments.

Lemma 12.9

Let $\mathfrak{A}$, $\mathfrak{B}$ *be structures for L. Then* $\mathfrak{A} \leq_n \mathfrak{B} \Leftrightarrow \mathfrak{A} \subseteq \mathfrak{B}$ *and* $\forall s \in L_{Const}$ *such that* $s \in \Sigma_n^s$, $\forall \delta$ *into* $dom(\mathfrak{A})$, $(\mathfrak{A}, \delta) \vDash s \Rightarrow (\mathfrak{B}, \delta) \vDash s$.

Proof: Just think of elements of *Const* as variables so far as the definition of $\leq_n$ is concerned. ∎

Now we proceed to the model-theoretic preservation theorems we require.

---

[9] Remember that individuals in the banana structures are not times, but *possible cut positions*. The only predicate in the language is a spatial ordering relation over these positions.

Lemma 12.10

$s \in \Pi[K]_n^q \Leftrightarrow s$ *is preserved under countable* Σ_n-*substructures in* K.

Proof: Relativize and generalize Chang and Keisler (1973): theorem 3.2.2. Then apply the downward Lowenheim Skolem theorem at each stage in the proof in which the existence of a model is established. ∎

Lemma 12.11

$s \in \Sigma[K]_n^q \Leftrightarrow s$ *is preserved under countable* Σ_n-*extensions in* K.

Proof: Similar to the proof of lemma 12.10. ∎

Lemma 12.12

$s \in \Pi[K]_{n+1}^q \Leftrightarrow s$ *is preserved under unions of countable* Σ_n-*chains in* K.

Proof: Relativize Chang and Keisler theorem 5.2.8 to K and apply the downward Lowenheim Skolem theorem each time the existence of a model is established. The relativization and countability restrictions imposed on chains in lemma 12.11 present worries only for the right-to-left side of theorem 5.2.8. But the chain constructed in Chang and Keisler's proof of this side of the theorem happens to be of order type ω, (as required) and has the property that its union is a model of K (as required), since the union of the chain is an elementary extension of a model of K in the relativized version of the proof of 5.2.8. ∎

The following lemma says that the union of a Σ_n-chain is as high in the $\leq_n$ order as any structure in the chain.

Lemma 12.13

$\forall$ *countable* Σ_n-*chain* $\mathfrak{A}_0, \mathfrak{A}_1, \mathfrak{A}_2, \ldots, \mathfrak{A}_n, \ldots$ *in* K, $\forall i \in \omega$, $\mathfrak{A}_i \leq_n$ $\bigcup \{\mathfrak{A}_i : i \in \omega\}$.

Proof: Instance of Chang and Keisler lemma 3.1.15. ∎

Proof of proposition 12.7(a): Suppose for reductio that $s \notin \Pi[K]_n^q$ but some scientist α can refute s with certainty given K from Δ_n^q-data. Since $s \notin \Pi[K]_n^q$, we have from lemma 12.10 that there are two countable models $\mathfrak{A}, \mathfrak{B}$ of K such that $\mathfrak{A} \leq_n \mathfrak{B}$ and $\mathfrak{B} \models s$ but $\mathfrak{A} \not\models s$. The demon chooses *Const* assignment δ onto $\mathfrak{A}$ and chooses $\varepsilon \in \mathcal{D}ata_n((\mathfrak{A}, \delta))$ (*Fig. 12.11*). Since $\mathfrak{A} \not\models s$ and $\mathfrak{A}$ is a countable model of K, there is some n at which α becomes certain that h is false (i.e., $\alpha(\varepsilon|n) = $ '!' and $\alpha(\varepsilon|n + 1) = 0$). Since the data consists of Δ_n^q sentences of L_{Const} which are therefore Σ_n^q sentences of L_{Const}, we have by lemma 12.9 that

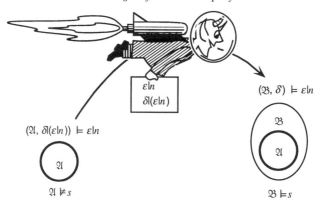

Figure 12.11

$(\mathfrak{B}, \delta|(\varepsilon|n)) \vDash \varepsilon|n$, where in general we let $\delta|e$ denote the restriction of δ to the constants occurring in finite data segment e.

Now the demon selects $\varepsilon' \in \mathcal{D}ata_n((\mathfrak{B}, \delta'))$, where δ' extends $\delta|(\varepsilon|n)$ and is onto $\mathfrak{B}$ and ε' extends $\varepsilon|n$. But since $\mathfrak{B} \vDash K$ and $\mathfrak{B}$ is countable and $\varepsilon' \in \mathcal{D}ata_n(\mathfrak{B})$, α does not refute s with certainty given K from Δ_n^q data, contrary to assumption. The $\Sigma[K]_n^q$ case is similar, using lemma 12.11 in place of lemma 12.10. The $\Delta[K]_n^q$ case follows from the $\Sigma[K]_n^q$ case and the $\Pi[K]_n^q$ case.

Proof of proposition 12.7(*b*): Suppose $s \notin \Sigma[K]_{n+1}^q$. Then $\neg s \notin \Pi[K]_{n+1}^q$. So by lemmas 12.12 and 12.13, there is a countable Σ_n-chain (in K) of countable structures $\mathfrak{A}_0, \mathfrak{A}_1, \mathfrak{A}_2, \ldots, \mathfrak{A}_n, \ldots$ such that the following conditions hold: Let $\mathfrak{A} = \bigcup \{\mathfrak{A}_i : i \in \omega\}$. Then:

(i) $\forall i \in \omega, \mathfrak{A}_i \leq_n \mathfrak{A}_{i+1}$,

(ii) $\forall_i \in \omega, \mathfrak{A}_i \vDash K$,

(iii) $\forall i \in \omega, \mathfrak{A}_i \nvDash s$,

(iv) $\mathfrak{A} \vDash K$,

(v) $\forall i \in \omega, \mathfrak{A}_i \leq_n \mathfrak{A}$,

(vi) $\mathfrak{A} \vDash s$.

Let e be a finite sequence of Δ_n^q sentences in L_{Const}. The following two lemmas describe how the demon can move e back and forth between $\mathfrak{A}$ and the chain without changing the intepretation of its constants or the truth of e under this interpretation.

Lemma 12.14

If $e \in \Sigma_n^q$ *and* $(\mathfrak{A}_i, \delta) \vDash e$ *then* $(\mathfrak{A}, \delta) \vDash e$ *(Fig. 12.12).*

Proof: By lemma 12.13, lemma 12.9, and the definition of $\leq_n$. ∎

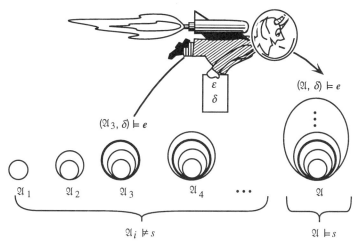

$$(\mathfrak{A}, \delta) \vDash e$$

$$(\mathfrak{A}_3, \delta) \vDash e$$

$$\mathfrak{A}_1 \quad \mathfrak{A}_2 \quad \mathfrak{A}_3 \quad \mathfrak{A}_4 \quad \cdots \quad \mathfrak{A}$$

$$\mathfrak{A}_i \nvDash s \qquad\qquad \mathfrak{A} \vDash s$$

Figure 12.12

Lemma 12.15

If $e \in \Pi_n^q$ and $(\mathfrak{A}, \delta) \vDash e$ then $\exists i$ such that $\forall k \geq i$, $(\mathfrak{A}_k, \delta|e) \vDash e$ (Fig. 12.13).

Proof: Let $(\mathfrak{A}, \delta) \vDash e$. $\mathfrak{A} = \bigcup \{\mathfrak{A}_i : i \in \omega\}$, so for some i, $rng(\delta|e) \subseteq dom(\mathfrak{A}_i)$. Since $e \in \Pi_n^q$, we have that for each $j < lh(e)$, $e_j \in \Pi_n^q$. Hence, for each $j < lh(e)$, $\neg e_j \in \Sigma_n^q$. By lemma 12.9, the fact that $\mathfrak{A}_i \leq_n \mathfrak{A}$, and the fact that $rng(\delta|e) \subseteq dom(\mathfrak{A}_i)$, we have from the definition of $\leq_n$ that (*) $(\mathfrak{A}_i, \delta|e) \vDash \neg e_j \Rightarrow (\mathfrak{A}, \delta|e) \vDash \neg e_j$. Since $(\mathfrak{A}, \delta|e) \vDash e_j$, it follows from the contrapositive of (*) that $(\mathfrak{A}_i, \delta|e) \vDash e_j$. Since this is true for each $j \leq lh(e)$, $(\mathfrak{A}_i, \delta|e) \vDash e$. ∎

Proof of proposition 12.7(b): continued: Given the preceding lemmas, we are in a position to provide a completely general version of the demonic argument

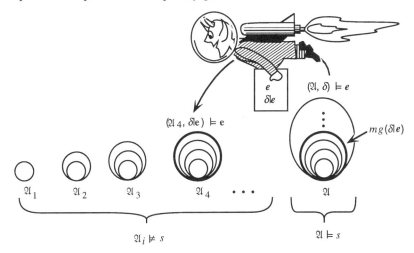

$$(\mathfrak{A}, \delta) \vDash e$$

$$(\mathfrak{A}_4, \delta e) \vDash e$$

$$mg(\delta e)$$

$$\mathfrak{A}_1 \quad \mathfrak{A}_2 \quad \mathfrak{A}_3 \quad \mathfrak{A}_4 \quad \cdots \quad \mathfrak{A}$$

$$\mathfrak{A}_i \nvDash s \qquad\qquad \mathfrak{A} \vDash s$$

Figure 12.13

of proposition 12.2. Since the chain is countable, $\mathfrak{A}$ is also countable, so since $\mathfrak{A} \vDash K$, α must succeed over the data streams in $\mathcal{D}ata_n(\mathfrak{A})$. The demon picks arbitrary *Const* assignment δ onto $dom(\mathfrak{A})$, and then proceeds to feed some $\varepsilon \in \mathcal{D}ata_n((\mathfrak{A}, \delta))$ to α. Hence, $\exists n$ such that $\alpha(\varepsilon|n) = 1$ since $\mathfrak{A} \vDash s$ and α is assumed to verify s in the limit given K from Δ_n^q data. Since Δ_n^q data is Σ_n^q data, we have by lemma 12.15 that there is some i such that for all $k \geq i$, $(\mathfrak{A}_k, \delta|(\varepsilon|n)) \vDash \varepsilon|n$. The demon chooses some δ' onto $dom(\mathfrak{A}_i)$ such that δ' extends $\delta|(\varepsilon|n)$ and then picks some $\varepsilon' \in \mathcal{D}ata_n((\mathfrak{A}_i, \delta))$ such that ε' extends ε. Hence, $\exists m > n$ such that $\alpha(\varepsilon'|m) = 0$, since $\mathfrak{A}_i \nvDash s$. Since Δ_n^q data is Σ_n^q data, we have by lemma 12.14 that $(\mathfrak{A}, \delta'|(\varepsilon'|m)) \vDash \varepsilon'|m$.

Now the demon selects the first domain element d of $\mathfrak{A}$ (under some fixed enumeration) that is not in $rng(\delta'|(\varepsilon'|m))$ and picks the first $c \in Const$ that does not occur in $\varepsilon'|m$ and the first Δ_n^q sentence s' involving only constants occurring in $\varepsilon'|m$ that does not occur either negated or nonnegated in $\varepsilon'|m$. The demon forms assignment $\phi = \delta'|(\varepsilon'|m) \cup \{(c, d)\}$. He then selects δ'' onto $dom(\mathfrak{A})$ such that δ'' extends ϕ, and then selects $\varepsilon'' \in \mathcal{D}ata_n((\mathfrak{A}, \delta''))$, such that ε'' extends $\varepsilon'|m*(\neg)s'$ where $(\neg)s'$ and occurs and $(\mathfrak{A}, \delta'') \vDash s''$ negated or nonnegated depending on whether or not $(\mathfrak{A}, \delta'') \vDash s'$. The demon proceeds to feed ε'' to α, and then waits for some m' when $\alpha(\varepsilon''|m') = 1$, where $m' \geq m + 1$ to ensure that s' occurs in $\varepsilon''|m'$ (*Fig. 12.14*).

This cycle can be repeated forever. In the limit some ε^*, δ^* are constructed. Each time the demon returns to $\mathfrak{A}$, he assigns a new domain element to the range of δ^*. Also, for each Δ_n^q sentence s, eventually all constants occurring in s remain in the domain of the demon's assignment and for all $s' \in \Delta_n^q$ prior to s in the ordering, either s' or $\neg s'$ has been added to the data. Thereafter,

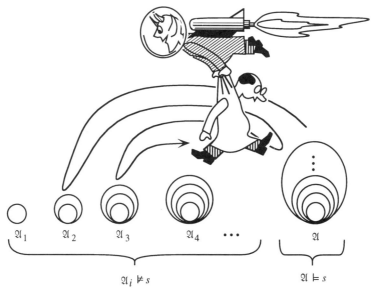

Figure 12.14

either s or $\neg s$ is added to the data. Hence δ^* is onto $dom(\mathfrak{A})$ and $rng(\varepsilon^*) = D_{\Delta_n^q}((\mathfrak{A}, \delta^*))$. So $\varepsilon^* \in Data_n((\mathfrak{A}, \delta^*))$. But α changes its mind infinitely often on ε^*, which contradicts the assumption that α verifies s in the limit given K from Δ_n^q-data, since $\mathfrak{A} \vDash s$.

The $\Pi[K]_{n+1}^q$ case is similar and the $\Delta[K]_{n+1}^q$ case follows from the $\Pi[K]_{n+1}^q$ case and the $\Sigma[K]_{n+1}^q$ case.   ∎

7. Theories and Axiomatizations

So far I have entertained only hypotheses that can be expressed as single sentences. What if the topic under investigation is a *theory* rather than an isolated hypothesis? How does the problem of the wholesale assessment of a theory differ from the piecemeal investigation of individual hypotheses? How should the assessments of individual hypotheses be assembled into the assessment of an entire theory?

From the topological perspective, theories are odd beasts. As has just been seen, the quantifier complexity of a sentence lines up perfectly with the computational complexity of the empirical content $Data(s)$ generated by the sentence under the idealizing assumptions of the logical paradigm. A theory T, on the other hand, translates into an arbitrary, countable intersection $Data(s_0) \cap Data(s_1) \cap \cdots$ of arithmetical sets of data streams. If there is no upper bound on the quantifier complexities of the sentences involved, there may be no finite upper bound on the Borel complexity of $Data(T)$. If there is a uniform bound on quantificational complexity of the axioms of T, however, then the Borel complexity of $Data(T)$ can be no worse that the result of adding one countable intersection to this bound (assuming that the language is countable). So, for example, if each $h \in T$ is in Σ_n^q, then $Data(T) \in \Pi_{n+1}^B$.

But even when S axiomatizes T and there is a uniform, arithmetical complexity bound on the axioms in S, the difficulty of deciding whether an axiom is in or out of S can make the arithmetical complexity of $Data(T)$ arbitrarily high. For example, define:

$$T_{Bad} = \{P(n): n \in Bad\},$$

where Bad is a set of arbitrarily high arithmetical complexity and P is some unary predicate. In this case, we have for each n that $Data(P(n)) \in \Delta_1^A$, but $Data(T_{Bad})$ has arithmetical complexity at least as high as Bad.

We can gain control over the arithmetical complexity of $Data(T)$ if we have some arithmetical bound on the difficulty of deciding a set of axioms of bounded quantifier complexity for T. Say that $S \in \Sigma_n^A [\Pi_n^A, \Delta_n^A]$ just in case the arithmetical complexity of S as a decision problem over a set of Gödel numbers of sentences is $\Sigma_n^A [\Pi_n^A, \Delta_n^A]$. $S \subseteq \Sigma_n^q [\Pi_n^q, \Delta_n^q]$ just in case each postulate in S is a $\Sigma_n^q [\Pi_n^q, \Delta_n^q]$ sentence of L. Let T be a theory and let K be another theory representing background knowledge. Then define:

$S \subseteq T$ is a Σ_n^A $[\Pi_n^A, \Delta_n^A]$, Σ_m^q $[\Pi_m^q, \Delta_m^q]$ *axiomatization of T given K*
$\Leftrightarrow T$ *is logically equivalent to S in K and $S \in \Sigma_n^A$ $[\Pi_n^A, \Delta_n^A]$ and S*
$\subseteq \Sigma_m^q$ $[\Pi_m^q, \Delta_m^q]$.

T *is Σ_n^A $[\Pi_n^A, \Delta_n^A]$, Σ_m^q $[\Pi_m^q, \Delta_m^q]$ axiomatizable in K*
$\Leftrightarrow \exists S \subseteq T$ *such that S is a Σ_n^A $[\Pi_n^A, \Delta_n^A]$, Σ_m^q $[\Pi_m^q, \Delta_m^q]$ axiomatization*
of T given K.

Now the following natural question arises: suppose we know that T is axiomatizable by S in background knowledge K. How does the arithmetical complexity of $\mathcal{D}ata_n(T) \cap \mathcal{D}ata_n(K)$ depend jointly on the complexity of deciding S and the maximum quantifier complexity of the postulates in S? If the only way to use an axiomatization were to find postulates and then to assess them, these complexities would have to be added. But the following result shows that the two dimensions of complexity (syntactic complexity of the axioms and computational complexity of the axiomatization) nearly collapse into one another.

Proposition 12.16

Let T be an L-theory. Let $m, n, k \geq 1$. Then

(a) *If T is Σ_m^q axiomatizable then*
$\mathcal{D}ata_n(T) \cap \mathcal{D}ata_n(K) \in \Pi[\mathcal{D}ata_n(K)]_{(m-n)+2}^B.$

(b) *If T is Π_m^q axiomatizable then*
$\mathcal{D}ata_n(T) \cap \mathcal{D}ata_n(K) \in \Pi[\mathcal{D}ata_n(K)]_{(m-n)+1}^B.$

(c) *If T is Σ_k^A, Σ_m^q axiomatizable then*
$\mathcal{D}ata_n(T) \cap \mathcal{D}ata_n(K) \in \Pi[\mathcal{D}ata_n(K)]_{max(m-n, k)+1}^A.$

(d) *If T is Σ_k^A, Π_m^q axiomatizable then*
$\mathcal{D}ata_n(T) \cap \mathcal{D}ata_n(K) \in \Pi[\mathcal{D}ata_n(K)]_{max(m-n, k)+2}^A.$

(e) *If T is Π_k^A, Σ_m^q axiomatizable then*
$\mathcal{D}ata_n(T) \cap \mathcal{D}ata_n(K) \in \Pi[\mathcal{D}ata_n(K)]_{max(m-n, k)+1}^A.$

(f) *If T is Π_k^A, Π_m^q axiomatizable then*
$\mathcal{D}ata_n(T) \cap \mathcal{D}ata_n(K) \in \Pi[\mathcal{D}ata_n(K)]_{max(m-n, k)+2}^A.$

Proof: (a) Let S be a set of Σ_m^q axioms for T in K. Let $s \in S$. Then by proposition 12.4, $\mathcal{D}ata_n(s) \cap \mathcal{D}ata_n(K) \in \Sigma[\mathcal{D}ata_n(K)]_{(m-n)+1}^A.$ Since

$$\mathcal{D}ata_n(S) \cap \mathcal{D}ata_n(K) = \bigcap_{s \in S} \mathcal{D}ata_n(s) \cap \mathcal{D}ata_n(K),$$

we have that $\mathcal{D}ata_n(s) \cap \mathcal{D}ata_n(K) \in \Pi[\mathcal{D}ata_n(K)]_{(m-n)+2}^A.$ (b) is similar. (c) Let S be a Σ_k^A set of Σ_m^q axioms for T in K. First, I show:

Lemma 12.17

Let $S \in \Sigma_k^A$ and $S \subseteq \Sigma_m^q$. Then there is $S' \in \Sigma_k^A$ such that S is logically equivalent to S' and $S' \subseteq \Sigma_m^q - \Pi_m^q$.

Proof of lemma: It is easy to construct a recursive procedure that takes a prenex normal sentence s as input and that then counts the number of alternations of blocks of quantifiers in the prefix of s. If the count falls short of m, then the procedure adds a sufficient number of dummy quantifier blocks on the outside of the prefix of s until s is properly Σ_m^q. Since the procedure is recursive, the new set S' so constructed must be Σ_k^A. The dummy quantifiers do not change meaning, so S is logically equivalent to S'. ∎

Proof of proposition 12.16(*c*) *resumed*: Apply the lemma to construct S' logically equivalent to S, such that S' is Σ_k^A and each $s \in S'$ is properly Σ_m^q. Assume a fixed effective Gödel numbering $s_0, s_1, \ldots, s_j, \ldots$ of the properly Σ_m^q sentences of L. (Remember that Σ_m^q refers entirely to the form of the sentences, so no logical relations must be decided.) The strategy of the proof is to construct a recursive relation P that can turn itself into the matrix of any such s_i when provided with i. Choose a fixed machine that produces for each k' a complete enumeration of the set of all k'-tuples of constants from *Const*. Now define the recursive predicate P in terms of the following decision procedure:

> Decision procedure for $P(\varepsilon, i, i', x_1, \ldots, x_{m-n})$:
> Begin
> Set $s = s_i$.
> For $w = 1$ to $m - n$ do   (recall, each s_i has exactly m blocks of quantifiers)
> > Begin
> > set $(Qy_1, \ldots, Qy_{k'})$ = the wth block of quantifiers occurring in s.
> > set $(c_1, \ldots, c_{k'})$ = the x_wth k'-tuple of constants from the fixed, recursive enumeration of k'-tuples of constants.
> > set $\Phi(y_1, \ldots, y_{k'})$ = the result of stripping $(Qy_1, \ldots, Qy_{k'})$ from s.
> > reset $s = \Phi(c_1, \ldots, c_{k'})$.
> > End
> If $s \in rng(\varepsilon | i')$ then return 1; else return 0.
> End.

This program recovers s_i, strips off the first n-m blocks of quantifiers from s_i, and instantiates constants into the remaining open formula as directed by $x_1, \ldots, x_{m-n}$ and the quantifier prefix of s_i. Finally, it checks whether the instance occurs in ε by stage i'. Then we have:

$$\forall \varepsilon \in \mathcal{D}ata_n(K), \varepsilon \in \mathcal{D}ata_n(s_i) \Leftrightarrow \exists i' \exists x_1 \cdots Qx_{m-n} P(\varepsilon, i, i'x_1, \ldots, x_{m-n}),$$

where each quantifier in the prefix alternates in sense from its predecessor so

$$
\begin{array}{cccccc}
1 & 2 & 3 & 4 & 5 & 6 \\
\overline{\forall i\, \forall y_1} & \overline{\exists y_2} & \overline{\forall y_3} & \overline{\exists y_4} & \overline{\forall y_5} & \\
\end{array}
$$

$$
\begin{array}{ccccc}
\overline{\exists i'\, \exists x_1} & \overline{\forall x_2} & \overline{\exists y_3} & \overline{\forall y_4} & \overline{\exists y_5}
\end{array}
$$

Figure 12.15

that Q is $\exists$ or $\forall$, depending on whether m is even or odd. Let R be the set of all Gödel numbers of elements of S. Then:

$$
\forall \varepsilon \in \mathcal{D}ata_n(K),\ \varepsilon \in \mathcal{D}ata_n(S)
$$
$$
\Leftrightarrow \forall i,\ \text{either } i \notin R \text{ or } \exists i'\, \exists x_1 \cdots Q x_{m-n} P(\varepsilon, i, i', x_1, \ldots, x_{m-n}).
$$

Since $R \in \Sigma_k^A$, we have that $\bar{R} \in \Pi_k^A$. So choose recursive M such that

$$
i \in \bar{R} \Leftrightarrow \forall y_1 \cdots Q y_k M(i, y_1, \ldots, y_k).
$$

Then $\forall \varepsilon \in \mathcal{D}ata_n(K)$,

$$
\varepsilon \in \mathcal{D}ata_n(S) \Leftrightarrow \forall i,\ \forall y_1 \cdots Q y_k,\ \exists i'\, \exists x_1 \cdots Q x_{m-n}[M(i, y_1, \ldots, y_k)
$$
$$
\vee\ P(\varepsilon, i, i', x_1, \ldots, x_{m-n})].
$$

It does not matter if we interleave variables $y_1, \ldots, y_k$, which occur only in M with the variables $x_1, \ldots, x_{m-n}$, i', which occur only in P. So $\forall \varepsilon \in \mathcal{D}ata_n(K)$,

$$
\varepsilon \in \mathcal{D}ata_n(S) \Leftrightarrow \forall i\, \forall y_1\, \exists i'\exists y_2 \exists x_1 \cdots \forall y_{k+1}\, \forall x_k \cdots
$$
$$
Q x_{m-n}\,[Q y_k\, \text{if } k > m]\,(M(i, y_1, \ldots, y_j) \vee P(\varepsilon, i, i', x_1, \ldots, x_{m-n}))).
$$

In the case in which $k = m = 5$, the blocks of quantifiers can be merged as depicted in *Figure 12.15*. In general, we can always merge blocks to obtain just $max(m - n, k) + 1$ blocks. The extra block results from the fact that the leading blocks cannot be merged.

(e) If S is Π_k^A then $max(m - n, k) + 1$ blocks again suffice (*Fig. 12.16*).

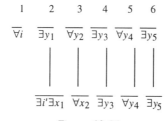

$$
\begin{array}{cccccc}
1 & 2 & 3 & 4 & 5 & 6 \\
\overline{\forall i} & \overline{\exists y_1} & \overline{\forall y_2} & \overline{\exists y_3} & \overline{\forall y_4} & \overline{\exists y_5}
\end{array}
$$

$$
\begin{array}{ccccc}
\overline{\exists i' \exists x_1} & \overline{\forall x_2} & \overline{\exists y_3} & \overline{\forall y_4} & \overline{\exists y_5}
\end{array}
$$

Figure 12.16

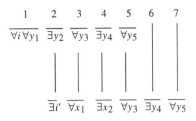

Figure 12.17

(d) If we redefine P by replacing the Gödel numbering of properly Σ_m^q sentences with a Gödel number of properly Π_m^q sentences, then everything is the same except that now the leading quantifier on the x variables is $\forall$. Since the quantifier $\exists i$ must precede the quantifier $\forall x_1$, there may be an extra block in the merged quantifier prefix (*Fig. 12.17*). In general, we require at most $max(m - n, k) + 2$ blocks in this case.

(f) In the final case, the situation is as in *Figure 12.18*. We require no more than $max(m - n, k) + 2$ blocks in this case. ∎

Perhaps no recursion theoretic result has enjoyed more attention among philosophers of science than the following proposition due to Craig. Philosophers view it as a way to "eliminate" theoretical terms without losing recursive axiomatizability.[10] From the present perspective, it says something very interesting, namely, that each Σ_n^A, Σ_m^q [Π_m^q] axiomatization can be *improved* to a Π_{n-1}^A Σ_m^q [Π_m^q] axiomatization.

Proposition 12.18 (Craig)[11]

$\forall n \geq 1$, T is Σ_n^A, Σ_m^q [Π_m^q] *axiomatizable* $\Leftrightarrow$ T is Π_{n-1}^A, Σ_m^q [Π_m^q] *axiomatizable*.

Proof: ($\Leftarrow$) trivial.

($\Rightarrow$) Suppose $S \in \Sigma_n^A$ and $S \subseteq \Sigma_m^q$ [Π_m^q]. Then for some Π_{n-1}^A relation R, $s \in S \Leftrightarrow \exists x \, R(s, x)$. Let $\&_n s = s \& s \& \cdots \& s$, where s is conjoined with itself n

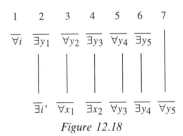

Figure 12.18

---

[10] Hempel (1965): 212.
[11] This generalizes the version presented in Boolos and Jeffrey (1980): 180.

times. Define $S' = \{\&_n s: R(s, n)\}$. S' is Π^A_{n-1}, since R is. Also, we can effectively convert each s_n into a Σ^q_m [Π^q_m] formula by renaming variables and shuffling quantifiers. Let S'' be the result of doing this to each member of S'. Then $S'' \in \Pi^A_{n-1}$ and $S'' \subseteq \Sigma^q_m$ [Π^q_m]. Let $s \in S$. Then $\exists x$ such that $R(s, x)$. Let m be the least such x. Then $\&_m s \in S'$. Hence, $S'' \vDash S$. And since for each $\&_n s \in S'$, $s \in S$ and $s \vDash \&_n s$, we have $S \vDash S''$.   ∎

So it appears as though Craig's result provides a way to give a computable scientist something for nothing! But observe that our upper bound on the arithmetical complexity of a theory (proposition 12.16) goes up one step for Π^A_m as opposed to Σ^A_m axiomatizations, thereby exactly canceling the apparent advantage of Craig's theorem for computable inquiry! So there is no free lunch after all. This helps explain the asymmetry between Π and Σ in proposition 12.16.

8. Theory Discovery

In the assessment paradigm, we could assume that correctness is the same as model-theoretic truth, since a particular theory or hypothesis is assigned to the scientist for testing. But in discovery problems, it is trivial to interpret correctness as truth, since any such discovery problem can be solved trivially by always conjecturing a fixed tautology. This triviality can be undercut if correctness specifies some lower bound on the informativeness of the theory to be discovered. But now the specified, lower bound on theory strength can add its own dimension of complexity to the problem of discovery, over and above the semantic complexity of the theory discovered or the computational complexity of its axiomatizations. This undermines the analogy between assessment and discovery in the logical paradigm, as we shall see shortly.

One way to specify a lower bound on the strength of the discovered theory is to require the scientist to discover a theory that is *complete* over some collection H of sentences. H could be a quantifier complexity class, for example. By enriching H with hypotheses of higher complexity, we place ever more stringent demands on discovery. Accordingly, let H be a collection of L-sentences. Let $H(\mathfrak{A}) = \{s \in H: \mathfrak{A} \vDash s\}$. Now define (*Fig. 12.19*):

> γ *uniformly identifies the complete H-truth in the limit given K from E-data* $\Leftrightarrow \forall \mathfrak{A} \in EN(K)$, $\forall \varepsilon \in \mathcal{D}ata_E(\mathfrak{A})$, $\exists n \; \forall m \geq n$, $\gamma(\varepsilon|m) \vDash H(\mathfrak{A})$ *and* $\mathfrak{A} \vDash \gamma(\varepsilon|m)$.

This kind of identification is called *uniform* because it requires that the complete truth be stabilized to at once. In a bit, we will examine *nonuniform* or *piecemeal* theory identification.

Let us now consider the problem of uniformly identifying the set of all CHAIN sentences true of an arbitrary, countable structure for L in the limit,

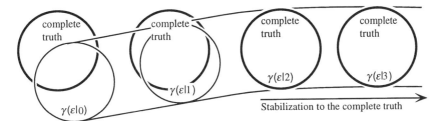

Figure 12.19

where CHAIN is the following set of sentences ordered by proper entailment from top to bottom:

$$\forall x_1, x_2(P(x_1, x_2))$$

$$\forall x_1, x_2, x_3(P(x_1, x_2) \lor P(x_2, x_3))$$

$$\forall x_1, x_2, x_3, x_4(P(x_1, x_2) \lor P(x_2, x_3) \lor P(x_3, x_4))$$

$$\vdots$$

$$\forall x_1, x_2, x_3, x_4, \ldots, x_n(P(x_1, x_2) \lor P(x_2, x_3)$$
$$\lor P(x_3, x_4) \lor \cdots \lor P(x_{n-1}, x_n))$$

$$\vdots$$

Each $s \in$ CHAIN is universal and hence is decidable with just one mind-change, starting with 1. This might lead one to conclude that the complete Π_1^q-truth is identifiable with no background knowledge. But that is not so. Either all sentences in CHAIN are false, or some finite initial segment of CHAIN is false and the rest of CHAIN is true. Now, consider a demon who proceeds as follows. He picks a structure in which the first sentence of CHAIN is true, so all successive sentences are true. After some time, the scientist concludes that the first sentence in CHAIN is in the complete, true theory. At this point, the demon picks a structure that preserves the data to this point, but that makes the first sentence false and all successive sentences true. This is possible because the entailments are proper. In the limit, the scientist receives a data stream in which all hypotheses in CHAIN are false, but the scientist has changed his mind infinitely often about which theory is complete, rather than stabilizing to the empty theory, as required.

The problem is that uniform identification depends not just on the truth of the identified theory, but on the truth of the *metahypothesis* that the theory stabilized to is the *complete H-truth* for the underlying structure. This hypothesis is expressed not by a sentence in L, but by a set of relational structures, as follows:

$$Complete_H(T) = \{\mathfrak{A}: \mathfrak{A} \in EN \text{ and } T \vDash H(\mathfrak{A}) \text{ and } \mathfrak{A} \vDash T\}.$$

That is, $Complete_H(T)$ is the proposition that T is the complete H-truth. This metahypothesis may be too complex to verify in the limit, even when the theory T is itself quite simple to decide. It is easy to establish by a demonic argument similar to the one just given that $Complete_{CHAIN}(\varnothing)$ is not verifiable in the limit. In light of the topological characterization of limiting identification (cf. chapter 9), it is the intractability of this limiting verification problem that precludes the identification of the complete CHAIN truth in the limit.

There is another complication in the problem of theory identification. For a given H, there may be uncountably many distinct H-complete theories. For example, if L has a countable infinity of closed terms and at least one predicate, then there are uncountably many logically incompatible Δ_1^q-complete theories. Since a scientist's domain is always countable, it is immediate that no scientist can succeed when he is responsible for uncountably many theories. On the other hand, there do exist cases in which there are at most countably many possible H-complete theories (e.g., when $H = $ CHAIN). These observations give rise to the following characterization of uniform theory identifiability.

Proposition 12.19

The complete H-truth is uniformly identifiable in the limit given K from E-data $\Leftrightarrow$ there are at most countably many distinct equivalence classes of H-complete theories in K and $\forall S \subseteq H$, $Data_E(Complete_H(S)) \in \Sigma[K]_2^B$.

Proof: ($\Leftarrow$) Since there are only countably many equivalence classes, we can choose countably many representatives S from all of these classes, and define the correctness relation $C(\varepsilon, S) \Leftrightarrow \varepsilon \in Data_E(Complete_H(S))$. Apply proposition 9.8.

($\Rightarrow$) If there are more than countably many such equivalence classes, the problem is unsolvable, because some of them cannot even be conjectured. By corollary 9.11, the problem is also unsolvable if for some equivalence class S, $Data_E(Complete_H(S)) \notin \Sigma[K]_2^B$, since C is *disjoint* in the sense of that corollary.

∎

The characterization of uniform theory identification suggests that discovery could be made easier if the empirical problem of determining completeness could be "spread out" in the limit or even avoided altogther. One way to soften the problem of deciding completeness is to permit nonuniform or piecemeal convergence to the complete truth. The following definition captures this idea (*Fig. 12.20*):

> γ *nonuniformly identifies the complete H-truth in the limit given K from E-data $\Leftrightarrow \forall \mathfrak{A} \in EN(K)$, $\forall \varepsilon \in Data_E(\mathfrak{A})$, $\forall s \in H$, $\exists n \, \forall m \geq n$, $\gamma(\varepsilon|m) \vDash s \Leftrightarrow \mathfrak{A} \vDash s$.*

That is, γ nonuniformly identifies the complete H-truth just in case for each possible data stream in $Data_E(K)$, γ produces a sequence of theories that eventually stops entailing s if s is false, and that eventually entails s forever

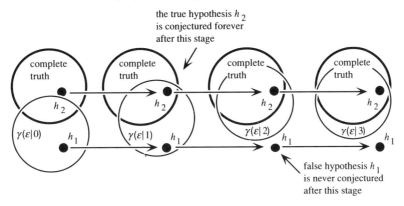

the true hypothesis h_2
is conjectured forever
after this stage

false hypothesis h_1
is never conjectured
after this stage

Figure 12.20

after if s is true. More simply put, the status of each hypothesis is eventually settled by the scientist, although there may be no time at which all sentences have their status settled at once. This ambition corresponds roughly to Peirce's image of science, in which each scientific question can be settled in the limit by the methods of science, but there may be no time at which all such questions are settled.

Nonuniform identification is a more feasible ambition for science than uniform identification for a variety of reasons. First, as we have seen, it ameliorates the difficulty of empirically deciding completeness. Second, it sidesteps the problem that there are too many theories to conjecture. Uncountably many theories can be converged to, using only countably many distinct conjectures. Third, it extends the range of computable inquiry to nonrecursively axiomatizable theories. A computable scientist can piece together a nonaxiomatizable theory out of a sequence of recursive axiomatizations. Fourth, for any particular hypothesis that can be stated in L, nonuniform convergence is just as useful in arriving at a correct answer to this question as is uniform convergence. Finally, nonuniform convergence does some justice to the fact that science actually proceeds by investigating hypotheses in light of theories, rather than by taking entire worldviews as units of inquiry.

It has been shown that the relationship between assessing individual hypotheses and uniform discovery of the complete truth is obscured by the complexity of determining completeness. Does the move to nonuniform identification eliminate this problem altogether? The following characterization shows that it does.

Proposition 12.20

The complete H-truth is nonuniformly identifiable in the limit given K from E-data $\Leftrightarrow$ H is decidable in the limit given K from E-data.

Proof:[12] ($\Rightarrow$) Suppose γ nonuniformly identifies the complete H-truth given K from E-data. Let $s \in H$. Then define α as follows:

$$\alpha(s, e) = \begin{cases} 1 & if \quad \gamma(e) \vDash s \\ 0 & otherwise. \end{cases}$$

α decides H in the limit given K from E-data.

($\Leftarrow$) Suppose that α decides H in the limit given K from E-data. We must now address the problem of assembling a theory to conjecture, by putting together the various judgments of α concerning the different hypotheses in H into a theory to conjecture on evidence e. We must guard against producing conjectures not known to be false that entail hypotheses known to be false. Define γ as follows. Let $s_1, s_2, \ldots, s_n, \ldots$ be an enumeration of H. On evidence e, form

$$Pos(e) = \{s_k : k \leq lh(e) \,\&\, \alpha(s, e) = 1\} \text{ and}$$

$$Neg(e) = \{s_k : k \leq lh(e) \,\&\, \alpha(s, e) = 0\}.$$

For each $S \subseteq H$, define $S|k = \{s_i \in S : i \leq k\}$. Set $\rho(e) = max\ k \leq lh(e)$ such that $\forall s \in Neg(e)|k$, $Pos(e)|k \nvDash s$. Note that $\rho(e)$ is total because the expression maximized is satisfied when $k = 0$. Now define $\gamma(e) = Pos(e)|\rho(e)$.

To see that γ works, let $\mathfrak{A} \in EN(K)$ and let $\varepsilon \in \mathcal{D}ata_E(\mathfrak{A})$. Let $k \in \omega$. Then $\exists n_k$ such that $\forall i \leq k$, $\forall m \geq n_k$, $\alpha(s_i, \varepsilon|m) = $ the truth value of s_i in $\mathfrak{A}$. Then (i) $\forall m \geq n_k$, $\mathfrak{A} \vDash Pos(\varepsilon|m)|k$ and $\forall s \in Neg(\varepsilon|m)|k$, $\mathfrak{A} \nvDash s$. Since truth does not entail falsehood, $\forall m \geq n_k$, $Pos(\varepsilon|m)|k \nvDash Neg(\varepsilon|m)|k$. Hence, (ii) $\forall m \geq n_k$, $\rho(\varepsilon|m) \geq k$.

Case 1. Suppose $\mathfrak{A} \vDash s_k$. By (i) and (ii), $\forall m \geq n_k$, $s_k \in Pos(\varepsilon|m)|\rho(\varepsilon|m) = \gamma(\varepsilon|m)$, so $\gamma(\varepsilon|m) \vDash s_k$.

Case 2. Suppose $\mathfrak{A} \nvDash s_k$. By (i) and (ii), $\forall m \geq n_k$, $s_k \in Neg(\varepsilon|m)|\rho(\varepsilon|m)$. By (ii), $\forall m \geq n_k$, $Pos(\varepsilon|m)|\rho(\varepsilon|m) = \gamma(\varepsilon|m) \nvDash s_k$. ∎

Proposition 12.20 yields, for example, that the complete Π_1^q theory is nonuniformly identifiable in the limit from Δ_1^q data, so the complete CHAIN truth is nonuniformly identifiable in the limit. The proposition does not cover the computable case, however, due to the possibly undecidable entailment test in the definition of ρ.

9.   Discovery and Vocabulary

Plato, Aristotle, J. S. Mill, R. Carnap, and many recent artificial intelligence programmers all share one feature in common. Their accounts of methodology assume *monadic* hypothesis languages (i.e., languages involving only unary predicates). This apparently harmless assumption makes discovery and hypo-

---

[12] Kelly and Glymour (1989), Osherson and Weinstein (1989).

thesis assessment appear much easier than they are in general and gives rise to reliable methods of inquiry that would be utter failures in slightly enriched vocabularies. Monadic predicates are only one possible such restriction. We might exclude function symbols, restrict the arity of function symbols, or eliminate the identity relation from the vocabulary of a given first-order language. In this section, we will investigate the effects of these vocabulary restrictions on the problem of discovery.

First, I introduce a compact notation for categorizing logical vocabularies. One way to categorize languages is by *maximum predicate arity*. Say that a language is P_n just in case its nonlogical predicate of greatest arity has arity n. P_0 means that the language in question has no nonlogical predicates at all. As it turns out, the only values that matter are P_0, P_1, and $P_{\geq 2}$. I do the same thing for *maximum function symbol arity*. F_0 means that there are no function symbols of arity 1 or greater, although there may be individual constants (0-ary function symbols). Once again, the only values that matter are F_0, F_1, and $F_{\geq 2}$. Finally, I categorize languages according to *presence of the identity predicate* $=$. If a language has the identity predicate, the language is I_1, and the language is I_0 otherwise. So for example, the language of sentence "$\forall x \, \forall y \, (P(f(x), y))$" is $P_2 F_1 I_0$. I will assume that the vocabularies under discussion are finite, unless it is explicitly stated otherwise.

In this notation, monadic languages are the $P_1 F_0 I_0$ languages. Such languages make discovery easy for the following reason:

Proposition 12.21

Let $L \in P_1 F_0 I_0$. Let T be a consistent, complete L-theory. Then T is logically equivalent to a Δ_2^q sentence of L.

Proof: Let x be a variable. There are at most finitely many atoms of L in which x occurs. Call the set of all such atoms At_x. Let Bas be the set of all atoms or negated atoms in which no variable occurs (and hence, in which some constant occurs). Define:

$$Ex = \{\exists x \, (\pm a_1(x) \, \& \, \pm a_2(x) \, \& \, \cdots \, \& \, \pm a_n(x)): a_i(x) \in At_x\}.$$

Let Ex' be the result of choosing a unique representative from each logical equivalence class in Ex. $Ex' \cup Bas$ is finite, since repeated basic formulas of the same sign may be deleted and repeated basic formulas of opposite sign yield tautologies. An L-sentence is in *primary normal form*[13] just in case it is a finite Boolean combination of sentences in $Ex' \cup Bas$. Each L-sentence is equivalent to a sentence in primary normal form (by pushing in quantifiers). Let a *pseudo-state-description* be a conjunction in which each consistent, nonvalid element of $Ex' \cup Bas$ occurs exactly once, either negated or nonnegated. Since $Ex' \cup Bas$ is finite, there are only finitely many distinct pseudo-state-descriptions. Let T be a consistent, complete L-theory. Let s be the (finite) disjunction of all

---

[13] Hilbert and Bernays (1934).

pseudo-state-descriptions that entail each element of T. T entails s because each assignment making T true makes some disjunct in s true (since each disjunct in s corresponds to a truth assignment on $Ex' \cup Bas$). Finally, s is equivalent to a Δ_2^q sentence, by rearrangement of quantifiers.   ■

The following consequence of this proposition shows why monadic languages are so popular in methodological studies:

Corollary 12.22

Let $L \in P_1 F_0 I_0$. Let n be the number of predicates in L and let m be the number of constants in L. Then the complete L-truth is effectively uniformly identifiable with at most $2^{mn+3^n} + 1$ mind changes starting with 0.

Proof: Let e be a finite data sequence and let s be a pseudo-state-description. Let $\alpha(s, e) = 1$ if (a) no instance of a negated existential conjunct of s occurs in e, (b) instances of each existential conjunct of s occur in e, and (c) no basic sentence in s is contradicted by a basic sentence occurring in e. $\alpha(s, e) = 0$ otherwise. γ starts with an arbitrary pseudo-state-description conjecture. Thereafter, γ conjectures the first pseudo-state-description s in a fixed enumeration such that $\alpha(s, e) = 1$, if there is one, and sticks with its preceding conjecture, otherwise. $|Ex'| = 3^n$ and $|Bas| = mn$. Hence, there are at most 2^{mn+3^n} logically distinct, consistent pseudo-state-descriptions in γ's enumeration. γ is computable, since it employs a finite enumeration and α works by simple syntactic matching between conjuncts and the data. In the worst case, γ changes its mind at most once for each pseudo-state-description. Adding 1 for the first conjecture, we obtain the bound $2^{mn+3^n} + 1$.   ■

Monadic vocabularies paint a comparatively rosy picture of the prospects for finding universal, knowledge-independent inductive methods. Uniform convergence to the complete truth with bounded mind changes is possible for computable agents who have no background knowledge. But this optimism evaporates when the vocabulary of the hypothesis language is enriched ever so slightly. For example, suppose we add a single, unary function symbol f to L, which already has some monadic predicate P. Then we can set up the following, infinite sequence of proper entailments:

$$\forall x(P(x)) \vDash \forall x(P(f(x))) \vDash \forall x(P(f(f(x)))) \vDash \cdots$$

Similarly, suppose our language has identity. Let $most(n)$ denote the pure-identity sentence

$$\forall x_1 \cdots \forall x_{n+1} \bigvee_{i=1}^{n+1} \bigvee_{j=1}^{i-1} x_i = x_j,$$

which says there are at most n things. Then we can form the sequence of proper entailments:

$$most(0) \vDash most(1) \vDash most(2) \vDash \cdots$$

In either case, a demonic argument can be given just as in the CHAIN example (cf. section 12.8) to show that the complete Π_1^q-truth in L is not uniformly identifiable in the limit. A dual argument works when the quantifiers are existential. Hence,

Proposition 12.23

If L is in one of the following classes:

$$P_1 F_1 I_0 - (P_0 \cup F_0),$$

$$P_0 F_0 I_1$$

Then neither the complete Π_1^q-truth in L nor the complete Σ_1^q-truth in L is uniformly identifiable in the limit. ∎

When we move to nonuniform identification, the situation regarding these languages is much more optimistic.

Proposition 12.24

Let L be in one of the following classes:

(a) $P_1 F_1 I_0$,

(b) $P_1 F_0 I_1$

Then the complete L-truth is nonuniformly identifiable in the limit. (Note: there is no restriction on quantifier complexity.) In case (b), the result can be made effective.

Proof: (a). By shuffling quantifiers, each sentence of L is Δ_2^q. Apply proposition 12.20. (b) Let $S_1, S_2, \ldots, S_n$ be all the state descriptions in the language. Let $S_i(n)$ be the identity sentence asserting that exactly n things satisfy S_i. On input e, γ produces some arbitrary conjecture until e entails a state description for each of the finitely many constants in L (not including the infinitely many constants in *Const*). Let c be this conjunction, which will remain fixed forever after. Let c_e' denote the conjunction of all $S_i(n)$ such that n is the greatest k for which e entails that at least k distinct individuals satisfy S_i. Then define $\gamma(e) = c \,\&\, c_e'$.

If $\mathfrak{A}$ has a finite domain of cardinality m, then eventually c is entailed and eventually c_e' stabilizes as well, since all objects satisfying each state description S_i are eventually seen to satisfy S_i and are also seen to be distinct. Let $c \,\&\, c'$ be the theory so converged to. Since all models of this theory are isomorphic, it is L-complete.

Suppose $\mathfrak{A}$ is countably infinite. Then the extension of some S_i is infinite. For each such S_i, the upper bound on cardinality is raised infinitely often by γ, so no upper bound is entailed by the theory nonuniformly converged to by γ. On the other hand, each lower bound is entailed all but finitely often for each S_i of infinite extension, so the theory nonuniformly converged to entails each lower bound for each S_i of infinite extension. Hence, the theory converged to is $\aleph_0$-categorical (i.e., its countably infinite models are all isomorphic) and so is L-complete by Vaught's test.[14]   ∎

If a bit more vocabulary is added, reliable inference becomes even harder. It is noteworthy that identity with unary function symbols is a much harder case than identity with unary predicates.

Proposition 12.25

Let L be in one of the following classes:

(a) $P_2 F_0 I_0 - P_1$

(b) $P_1 F_2 I_0 - (P_0 \cup F_1)$

(c) $P_0 F_1 I_1 - F_0$

Then the complete Σ_2^q-truth in L is not nonuniformly identifiable in the limit.

Proof: Define:

$$(h_a): \forall x \exists y\, P(x, y)$$

$$(h_b): \forall x \exists y\, P(f(x, y))$$

$$(h_c): \forall x \exists y\, f(x) = y.$$

Case (a). I show by demonic argument that h_a is not verifiable in the limit. Let α be an assessment method for h_a. Let $\mathfrak{A} = (\omega, R)$, where $R = \{(x, x): x \in \omega\}$. The demon presents the data stream $\varepsilon = P(0, 0), P(1, 1), \ldots, P(n, n)$ until α conjectures 1 for h_a. Then the demon repeats $P(n, n), P(n, n), \ldots$ until α conjectures a value less than 1. Then the demon proceeds with $P(n + 1, n + 1)$, $P(n + 2, n + 2), \ldots$ until α conjectures 1 again, and so forth. The data stream ε presented in the limit will be for $\mathfrak{A}$ if α conjectures a value other than 1 infinitely often, but $\mathfrak{A} \vDash h_a$, so α fails. If α stabilizes to 1, then ε is for a structure $\mathfrak{A}_n = (\omega, R_n)$ such that $R_n = \{(x, x): x \leq n\}$, but $\mathfrak{A}_n \nvDash h_a$ so again, α fails.

Similar demonic arguments can be given for (b) and (c), using h_b and h_c, respectively. These are left as exercises.   ∎

---

[14] Chang and Keisler (1973).

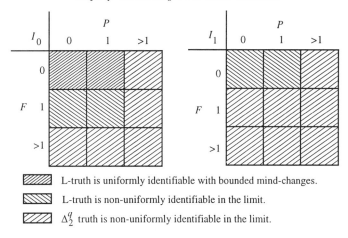

L-truth is uniformly identifiable with bounded mind-changes.

L-truth is non-uniformly identifiable in the limit.

Δ_2^q truth is non-uniformly identifiable in the limit.

Figure 12.21

The positive results of this section are summarized in *Figure 12.21*. Except for the $P_1 F_1 I_0$ case, the positive results all hold for the computable case as well. The negative results show that the bounds given in the tables cannot be improved.

Exercises

12.1. Prove proposition 12.4(b).

12.2. Show that the sequence of bananas constructed in the proof of proposition 12.2 is a countable Σ_1-chain in DSOE.

12.3. Characterize n-mind-change decidability in the logical paradigm (cf. proposition 4.16). For the hard side, use induction over the preservation theorem for Π_1^q sentences.

12.4. Jean-Paul Sartre emphasized the overflowing richness of experience. Suppose we interpret this as the thesis that L contains infinitely many predicates. What happens to the results of section 12.9 when we drop the assumption that L has only finitely many predicates, function symbols, and constants?

12.5. In light of proposition 12.7, explain the difference between uniform and nonuniform theory identification in terms of the difference between identification in the limit and gradual identification.

*12.6. Give an example of a language over which the method of proposition 12.20 succeeds, but is not consistent in the sense that each conjecture is consistent with e, K. Define a complete architecture for nonuniform theory identification that is consistent.

13

Probability and Reliability

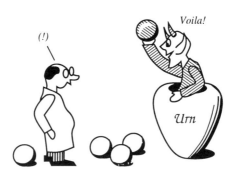

1. Introduction

The results of the preceding chapters make no reference whatever to probability. Since probability and induction have long been viewed as inseparable, it is interesting to relate the probabilistic perspective to the purely logical point of view of the preceding chapters. Of particular interest are the limiting reliability claims made for probabilistic methods.[1] For example, it is often said that the process of updating probabilities by Bayes' theorem will almost surely approach the truth in the limit:

> The person learns by experience. The purpose of the present section is to explore with a moderate degree of generality how he typically becomes almost certain of the truth, when the amount of his experience increases indefinitely. ... It is to be expected intuitively, and will soon be shown, that under general conditions the person is very sure that after making the observation he will attach a probability of nearly 1 to whichever element of the partition actually obtains.[2]

In light of the many negative results in the preceding chapters, such claims sound too good to be true. Are they? Or do they illustrate the triumph of modern, probabilistic thinking over skepticism? The aim of this chapter is to address these important epistemological questions.

---

[1] I am indebted to my colleague Teddy Seidenfeld for many useful discussions and references concerning the material in this chapter.
[2] Savage (1972): 46.

2. Conditionalization

Let *Bo* denote the closure of the open sets of $\mathcal{N}$ under complementation and countable union. Thus, *Bo* contains the union of the complexity classes Σ_n^B. Let *P* be a real-valued function taking elements of *Bo* as arguments. *P* is a *probability measure* on *Bo* (or, I will say, on $\mathcal{N}$) just in case

(1) *for each $S \in Bo$, $P(S) \geq 0$,*

(2) $P(\mathcal{N}) = 1$ *and*

(3) *If $S_0, S_1, \ldots, S_n$ is a finite sequence of pairwise disjoint elements of Bo, then* $P\left(\bigcup_{i=1}^{n} S_i\right) = \sum_{i=1}^{n} P(S_i).$

Whatever probability is, it is supposed to behave sort of like mud spread out on a table marked with areas representing subsets of $\mathcal{N}$. The first two axioms say that we start out with a unit block of mud. The third axiom says that the total mud spread over a finite number of disjoint regions can be found by summing the mud on each region. In other words, the probability of a whole region is the sum of the probabilities of the parts of the region when the region is divided into only finitely many parts. This property is called *finite additivity* (*Fig. 13.1*).

Countable additivity requires, further, that if an event is divided into a countable infinity of nonoverlapping parts, the probability of the whole is still the sum of the probabilities of its parts (*Fig. 13.2*). In other words, if $S_0, S_1, \ldots, S_i, \ldots$ is an ω-sequence of pairwise disjoint elements of *Bo*, then

$$P\left(\bigcup_{i \in \omega} S_i\right) = \sum_{i \in \omega} P(S_i).$$

finitely additive

$S_0 \qquad S_1$

S

Figure 13.1

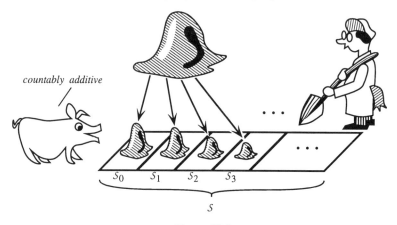

Figure 13.2

P is a *countably additive probability measure* just in case P is a probability measure that is also countably additive. When a probability measure is not countably additive, we say that it is *merely finitely additive*. Countable additivity can be expressed in a different form. Define (*Fig. 13.3*):

> P is continuous $\Leftrightarrow$ *for each downward nested sequence*
>
> $$Q_1 \subseteq Q_2 \subseteq \ldots \subseteq Q_i \subseteq \ldots \textit{ of Borel sets,}$$
>
> $$P\left(\bigcap_{i \in \omega} Q_i\right) = Lim_i P(Q_i).$$

Proposition 13.1

If P is a finitely additive probability measure on $\mathcal{N}$ then P is countably additive $\Leftrightarrow$ P is continuous.

Proof: Exercise 13.1.   ∎

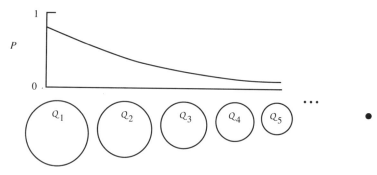

Figure 13.3

If P is a probability measure on $\mathcal{N}$, and $\mathcal{H}$, $\mathcal{E} \subseteq \mathcal{N}$ and $P(\mathcal{E}) > 0$, then the *conditional probability* of $\mathcal{H}$ given $\mathcal{E}$ is given by:

$$P(\mathcal{H}, \mathcal{E}) = \frac{P(\mathcal{H} \cap \mathcal{E})}{P(\mathcal{E})}.$$

It is an immediate consequence of this definition that:

Proposition 13.2 (Bayes' theorem)

If $P(\mathcal{E}) > 0$ then $P(\mathcal{H}, \mathcal{E}) = \dfrac{P(\mathcal{H})P(\mathcal{E}, \mathcal{H})}{P(\mathcal{E})}$ and hence

$$P(\mathcal{H} \cap \mathcal{E}) = P(\mathcal{H})P(\mathcal{E}, \mathcal{H}).$$

Proof: Exercise 13.2.   ∎

According to a popular conception of learning from experience, the scientist starts out with some initial probability measure P_0 and then updates this measure in response to new data by defining $P_n(\mathcal{H})$, the probability of $\mathcal{H}$ at time n, to be $P_0(\mathcal{H}, \mathcal{E})$, the conditional probability of $\mathcal{H}$ given the total evidence $\mathcal{E}$ encountered so far. The process of updating one's current degrees of belief by replacing them with probabilities conditional on all the evidence gathered so far is known as *temporal conditionalization*. Bayes' theorem is often used to compute $P_0(\mathcal{H}, \mathcal{E})$ because a statistical model typically provides an explicit formula for $P_0(\mathcal{E}, \mathcal{H})$ and the Bayesian statistician also concocts an explicit formula for $P(\mathcal{H})$. Thus conditionalization is sometimes referred to as *Bayesian updating*. When Bayes' theorem is used in temporal conditioning, $P(\mathcal{H}, \mathcal{E})$ is called the *posterior probability* of $\mathcal{H}$ given $\mathcal{E}$, $P(\mathcal{H})$ is called the *prior probability* of $\mathcal{H}$, and $P(\mathcal{E}, \mathcal{H})$ is called the *likelihood* of $\mathcal{H}$ given $\mathcal{E}$.

Since I have not defined the value of $P(\mathcal{H}, \mathcal{E})$ when $P(\mathcal{E}) = 0$, one might suppose that Bayesian updating goes into a coma whenever such evidence is encountered (*Fig. 13.4*). In fact, it is possible to extend conditional probability

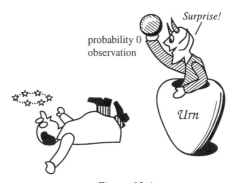

Figure 13.4

$$\text{Figure 13.5}$$

to such cases.[3] Having noted this possibility, I will sidestep the complications it raises by considering only conditionalizers that assign nonzero
prior probabilities to all relevant hypotheses and to all finite data sequences
logically consistent with background knowledge, so that $\mathcal{K}$ *entails* that no finite
data sequence of probability zero will ever be seen. Accordingly, define:

> β *is a conditionalizer for H, C, $\mathcal{K} \Leftrightarrow$ there is a probability measure P*
> *on $\mathcal{N}$ such that*

(a) $P(\mathcal{K}) = 1$,

(b) *for all $e \in \omega^*$, if $[e] \cap \mathcal{K} \neq \varnothing$ then $P(e) > 0$, and*

(c) $\beta(h, e) = P(C_h, [e])$.

Conditionalizers produce real-valued probabilities and hence are not assessment methods in the sense defined in chapter 3, since assessment methods
were defined to conjecture only rationals. Nonetheless, every conditionalization method β induces a rational-valued assessment method α_β with
the same limiting performance, as follows. First, digitize the $[0, 1]$ interval
by two rational-valued sequences that start at the middle of the interval
and converge to its end points, treating the end points as special cases
(*Fig. 13.5*):

$$\gamma(r) = \begin{cases} 2^{-i}, \text{where } i = \text{the least } n > 0 & \\ \quad \text{such that } 2^{-(n+1)} \leq r < 2^{-n} & \text{if } 0 < r < 2^{-1} \\ 1 - 2^{-i}, \text{where } i = \text{the least } n > 0 & \\ \quad \text{such that } 1 - 2^{-n} \leq r < 1 - 2^{-(n+1)} & \text{if } 2^{-1} \leq r < 1 \\ r, & \text{if } r = 0 \text{ or } r = 1. \end{cases}$$

Then $\alpha_\beta = \gamma \circ \beta$ is a rational-valued assessment method. It is easy to see

---

[3] There are applications in which it is both natural and desirable to suppose that
$P(\mathcal{H}, \mathcal{E})$ is uniquely determined, even though $P(\mathcal{E}) = 0$. For example, suppose that for
each $\theta \in R$, P_θ is a probability measure on $\mathcal{N}$. Then Bayesian statisticians usually let
$P(S, \{\theta\}) = P_\theta(S)$ even though $P(\{\theta\}) = 0$ in the typical case in which P is continuous.
The general theory of which this example is an instance is presented, for example, in
Billingsly (1986).

that:

Proposition 13.3

Let β be a conditionalization method.

If $\beta \begin{bmatrix} approaches \\ stabilizes\ to \end{bmatrix} \begin{bmatrix} 1 \\ 0 \end{bmatrix}$ *on ε then so does* α_β.

It follows immediately that:

Corollary 13.4

If h is $\begin{bmatrix} verifiable_C \\ refutable_C \\ decidable_C \end{bmatrix}$ *gradually given* $\mathcal{K}$ *by a conditionalizer then*

$$C_h \in \begin{bmatrix} \Sigma[\mathcal{K}]_3^B \\ \Pi[\mathcal{K}]_3^B \\ \Delta[\mathcal{K}]_2^B \end{bmatrix}.$$

If h is $\begin{bmatrix} verifiable_C \\ refutable_C \\ decidable_C \end{bmatrix}$ *in the limit given* $\mathcal{K}$ *by a conditionalizer then*

$$C_h \in \begin{bmatrix} \Sigma[\mathcal{K}]_2^B \\ \Pi[\mathcal{K}]_2^B \\ \Delta[\mathcal{K}]_2^B \end{bmatrix}. \quad \blacksquare$$

Conditionalization, therefore, cannot evade the negative results of the preceding chapters. Whatever conditionalization does, it cannot do the impossible.

It remains to ask whether conditionalization does what is possible. In fact, conditionalization can fail to solve inductive problems that are fairly trivial from the point of view of the preceding chapters. It follows from Bayes' theorem that if $P(C_h) = 0$, then for all evidence e such that $P(e) > 0$, $P(C_h, e) = 0$. So if the prior probability of C_h is 0, then a conditionalizer employing this measure will fail to approach the truth when C_h is true. But this sort of trivial failure can arise even when $P(C_h) > 0$, for example if $P(C_h, e) = 0$ for some e logically consistent with C_h and $\mathcal{K}$. Nobody would be surprised to see conditionalization fail when the underlying measure "closes the door" forever on a hypothesis by assigning it probability zero before it is refuted or that assigns unit probability to a hypothesis before it is logically entailed by the data and background knowledge. It would be more interesting, however, to find a probability measure

P that always "keeps the door open" such that conditionalization *still* fails to converge to the truth. Accordingly, define:

> P is an open door probability measure for $\mathcal{K}, C, H$
> $\Leftrightarrow$ for each $h \in H$, $e \in \omega^*$ such that $[e] \cap \mathcal{K} \neq \emptyset$,
>
> (i) $P(e) > 0$ and
>
> (ii) $P(C_h, e) = 0 \Leftrightarrow [e] \cap \mathcal{K} \subseteq \overline{C_h}$ and
>
> (iii) $P(C_h, e) = 1 \Leftrightarrow [e] \cap \mathcal{K} \subseteq C_h$.

But even when the measure P is assumed to be an open door measure, it is possible for a conditionalizer to remain stuck for eternity on a value less than one when the hypothesis in question is true, even when the hypothesis is trivially refutable with certainty by a finite state automaton that does not conditionalize. Indeed, the following example has the property that there are uncountably many possible data streams on which conditionalization never updates its initial probability on the hypothesis for eternity.

Proposition 13.5

There exists a $C_h \subseteq 2^\omega$ and a countably additive probability measure P on 2^ω such that

(a) *P is an open door measure for 2^ω, C, $\{h\}$,*

(b) *h is refutable$_C$ with certainty (by a five-state automaton) given 2^ω, and*

(c) *for uncountably many $\varepsilon \in C_h$, for each n, $P(C_h, \varepsilon|n) = P(C_h) = 0.5$.*

Proof: Let h be the hypothesis that there will never appear two consecutive zeros with the first zero appearing at an even position. In other words, $C_h = \{\varepsilon: \forall n, \varepsilon_{2n} = 0 \Rightarrow \varepsilon_{2n+1} \neq 0\}$. The shaded fans in *Figure 13.6* are all included in the *complement* of C_h.

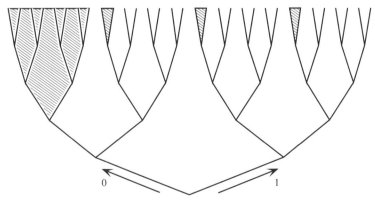

Figure 13.6

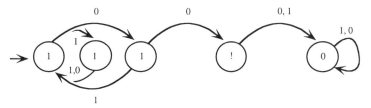

Figure 13.7

h is refutable$_C$ with certainty given 2^ω by the automaton depicted in *Figure 13.7*, which establishes (b).

Let $x \in \{0, 1\}$, $e \in 2^*$. Define $[x, i] = \{\varepsilon : \varepsilon_i = x\}$. If P is a probability measure, let us abbreviate $P([x, lh(e)], [e])$ as the more readable expression $P(x, e)$ and abbreviate $P([e])$ as $P(e)$. Now define measures P_+, P_- as follows:

$$P_+(x, e) = \begin{cases} 0 & \text{if } [e^*x] \subseteq \overline{C_h} \\ 1 & \text{if } [e^*|1 - x|] \subseteq \overline{C_h} \\ 0.5 & \text{otherwise.} \end{cases}$$

$$P_-(x, e) = 0.5.$$

The function $|1 - x|$ simply exchanges 0s and 1s. Intuitively, P_- thinks the next datum is generated by a fair coin toss, while P_+ thinks the next datum is generated by a fair coin toss if both outcomes are consistent with h; else the outcome logically excluded by h occurs with probability 0 and the other outcome occurs with probability 1. $P_+(e)$, $P_-(e)$ are extended, by induction, to each $e \in 2^*$, as follows:

$$P_+(0) = P_-(0) = 1.$$

$$P_+(e^*x) = P_+(e)P_+(x, e).$$

$$P_-(e^*x) = P_-(e)P_-(x, e).$$

Figure 13.8 illustrates the values of P_+ on data sequences of length ≤ 5.

Observe that,

$$\sum_{lh(e) = k} P_+(e) = 1,$$

and similarly for P_-. It then follows by standard extension techniques[4] that P_+ and P_- have unique, countably additive extensions to all Borel events on 2^ω, so that for each Borel set $S \subseteq 2^\omega$, $P_+(S)$ and $P_-(S)$ are defined. The following two lemmas solve for the priors assigned to C_h by P_+ and P_-, respectively.

[4] Halmos (1974): 212, theorem A.

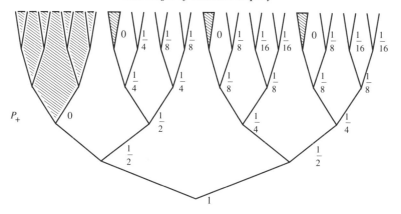

Figure 13.8

Lemma 13.6

$P_+(\overline{C_h}) = 1.$

Proof: $\overline{C_h}$ is a disjoint, countable union of fans. Since each of these fans is assigned zero probability by P_+, the sum of these probabilities is zero so $P_+(\overline{C_h}) = 0$ by countable additivity. Hence, $P_+(C_h) = 0.$ ∎

Lemma 13.7

$P_-(\overline{C_h}) = 1.$

Proof: For each $i \geq 1$, let G_i = the set of all Boolean sequences e of length $2i$ such that $[e] \subseteq \overline{C_h}$ and for no $e' \subset e$ is $[e'] \subseteq \overline{C_h}$. Let $\mathcal{G}_i = \bigcup \{[e]: e \in G_i\}$. A glance at *Fig. 13.8* reveals that $|G_i| = 3^{(i-1)}$. Also, for each $e \in G_i$, $P_-(e) = 1/2^{2i} = 1/4^i$. Since for all distinct $e, e' \in G_i$, $[e] \cap [e'] = \varnothing$, it follows by finite additivity that:

$$P_-(\mathcal{G}_i) = \sum_{e \in G_i} P_-(e) = |G_i| \frac{1}{4^i} = \frac{3^{(i-1)}}{4^i}.$$

By countable additivity and the fact that $\mathcal{G}_i \cap \mathcal{G}_{i+1} = \varnothing$, we have:

$$P_-(\overline{C_h}) = \sum_{i=1}^{\infty} P_-(\mathcal{G}_i) = \sum_{i=1}^{\infty} \frac{3^{(i-1)}}{4^i} = \frac{1}{4} \sum_{i=0}^{\infty} \frac{3^i}{4^i} = \frac{1}{4} 4 = 1.$$ ∎

For each Borel set $S \subseteq 2^\omega$, define P_0 to be the 50-50 *mixture* of P_+ and P_-:

$$P_0(S) = 0.5 P_+(S) + 0.5 P_-(S).$$

The following lemma shows that P_0 satisfies (b).

Lemma 13.8

P_0 is an open door measure for $\mathcal{K}$, C, H.

Proof: (i) $P_0(e) \geq 0.5P_-(e) = 1/2^{lh(e)+1} > 0$. (ii) Suppose $[e] - \overline{C_h} \neq \emptyset$. Then $P_+(e) > 0$. But then:

$$P_0(C_h, e) = \frac{P_0(e \,\&\, C_h)}{P_0(e)} = \frac{0.5P_+(e \,\&\, C_h) + 0.5P_-(e \,\&\, C_h)}{P_0(e)} \geq \frac{0.5P_+(e \,\&\, C_h)}{P_0(e)}$$

$$= \frac{0.5P_+(e)}{P_0(e)} > 0.$$

The last identity is by lemma 13.6. A similar argument using proposition 13.7 establishes condition (iii). ■

Let β_P be a conditionalizer who starts out with measure P. Let us now consider how β_P fails. The following lemma is very useful in studying the asymptotic performance of conditionalization:

Lemma 13.9

Let P be an arbitrary probability measure and let $S \subseteq 2^\omega$ be a Borel set.
Then $Lim_{n \to \infty} P(S, \varepsilon | n) = 1 \Leftrightarrow Lim_{n \to \infty} \dfrac{P(\varepsilon | n, S)}{P(\varepsilon | n, \overline{S})} = \infty$.

Proof: Since $P(S, \varepsilon | n) = 1 - P(\overline{S}, \varepsilon | n)$,

$$Lim_{n \to \infty} P(S, \varepsilon | n) = 1 \Leftrightarrow Lim_{n \to \infty} P(\overline{S}, \varepsilon | n) = 0$$

$$\Leftrightarrow Lim_{n \to \infty} \frac{P(S, \varepsilon | n)}{P(\overline{S}, \varepsilon | n)} = \infty$$

$$\Leftrightarrow Lim_{n \to \infty} \frac{P(S)P(\varepsilon | n\, S)}{P(\overline{S})P(\varepsilon | n, \overline{S})} = \infty \text{ (by Bayes'}$$
$$\text{theorem)}$$

$$\Leftrightarrow Lim_{n \to \infty} \frac{P(\varepsilon | n, S)}{P(\varepsilon | n, \overline{S})} = \infty \text{ (since } P(S), P(\overline{S})$$
$$\text{are positive}$$
$$\text{constants).} \quad ■$$

The ratio on the right-hand side of the lemma is called the *likelihood ratio* for S. It is also clear that if the likelihood ratio stabilizes to a fixed value, then $P_0(C_h, \varepsilon | n)$ stabilizes to a fixed value less than 1 in the limit. The following lemma solves for the likelihood ratio and priors of P_0.

Lemma 13.10

For each $e \in 2^*$,

(a) $\dfrac{P_0(e, C_h)}{P_0(e, \overline{C_h})} = \dfrac{P_+(e)}{P_-(e)}$.

(b) $P_0(C_h) = P_0(\overline{C_h}) = 0.5$

Proof of (a):

$$\frac{P_0(e, C_h)}{P_0(e, \overline{C_h})} = \frac{P_0(e \& C_h)/P_0(e)}{P_0(e \& \overline{C_h})/P_0(e)} = \frac{P_0(e \& C_h)}{P_0(e \& \overline{C_h})}$$

$$= \frac{0.5P_+(e \& C_h) + 0.5P_-(e \& C_h)}{0.5P_+(e \& \overline{C_h}) + 0.5P_-(e \& \overline{C_h})}$$

$$= \frac{0.5P_+(e \& C_h)}{0.5P_-(e \& \overline{C_h})} \quad \text{(by lemmas 13.6 and 13.7)}$$

$$= \frac{P_+(e)}{P_-(e)} \quad \text{(by lemmas 13.6 and 13.7)}.$$

(b) Follows immediately from lemmas 13.6 and 13.7. $\qquad\qquad\qquad$ □

Let us now consider where β_P fails to gradually decide$_C$ h in the limit. If $[e] \subseteq \overline{C_h}$, then $P_0(C_h, e) = 0$, so β_{P_0} is correctly certain of the falsehood of h and remains so, since $P_0(e) > 0$ whenever e is consistent with $\mathcal{K}$. So β_{P_0} can only fail by refusing to approach 1 when h is correct. To see how P_0 can fail to approach 1 when h is correct, consider the everywhere 1 data stream ζ. From lemma 13.10(a) and the definitions of P_+ and P_- we have for each n,

$$\frac{P_0(\zeta|n, C_h)}{P_0(\zeta|n, \overline{C_h})} = \frac{P_+(\zeta|n)}{P_-(\zeta|n)} = \frac{1/2^n}{1/2^n} = 1.$$

So by lemma 13.10(b), we have that for each n, $P_0(C_h, \zeta|n) = P_0(C_h) = 0.5$. So on the data stream ζ, β_{P_0} never updates its initial conjecture of 0.5 for eternity. Notice that the same phenomenon will arise on any data stream for which the likelihood ratio remains unity forever. This will occur on any data stream in the following set (*Fig. 13.9*):

$$\mathcal{V}ery \; \mathcal{B}ad = \{\varepsilon: \forall n, \{\varepsilon|n*0] \text{ is not a subset of } \overline{C_h}\}.$$

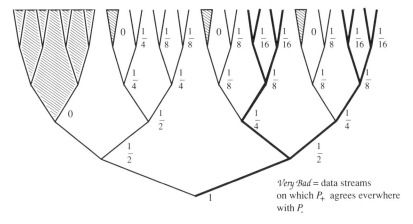

Figure 13.9

Moreover, there are data streams on which the likelihood ratio changes only finitely often before stabilizing to some value less than 1:

$$\mathcal{B}ad = \{\varepsilon: \exists n \; \forall m \geq n, \; [\varepsilon|m*0] \text{ is not a subset of } \overline{C_h}\}.$$

If $\varepsilon \in \mathcal{B}ad$, then $P_0(C_h, \varepsilon|m)$ goes up for a finite time and then remains fixed at a value less than 1. Furthermore, $\mathcal{V}ery \; \mathcal{B}ad$ and hence $\mathcal{B}ad$ are both uncountably infinite, which may be seen as follows: let $\varepsilon \in 2^\omega$. Encode 0 as 10 and 1 as 11. Then the sequence τ such that for each $i \geq 1$, $(\tau_{2i}, \tau_{2i+1}) = code(\varepsilon_i)$ is an element of $\mathcal{V}ery \; \mathcal{B}ad$ and τ uniquely codes ε. By a similar argument, there are uncountably many more data streams in $\mathcal{B}ad - \mathcal{V}ery \; \mathcal{B}ad$ on which β_{P_0} fails. This establishes (c). ∎

So no conditionalizer can do what is impossible, and some conditionalizers (even those who always "leave the door open" concerning alternative hypotheses) can fail in uncountably many possible worlds to arrive at the truth even when a trivial method is guaranteed to do so. It remains to consider whether every solvable inductive problem is solved by some conditionalizer or other. It is unreasonable to demand a strict conditionalizer to conjecture 0 or 1 unless he is certain, since a strict conditionalizer can never take back a 0 or a 1. The natural criterion of success for a conditionalizer is therefore gradual decidability. The measure defined in the preceding example does not succeed even in this sense. But the same problem can be solved in this sense by a strict conditionalizer whose initial probability measure is carefully tailored to the particular hypothesis at hand.

Proposition 13.11 (T. Seidenfeld)

Let C_h be as in example 2.5. Then there exists a countably additive probability measure P_1 on 2^ω such that β_{P_1} gradually decides$_C$ h given 2^ω.

Proof: Let $e \in 2^*$, $lh(e) = n$. Then define:

$$P_-(e) = 1/2^n.$$

$$P_+(e) = \begin{cases} 0 & \text{if } [e] \subseteq \overline{C_h} \\[2ex] \dfrac{1}{3^{(n+1)/2}} & \text{if } n \text{ is odd and } e \text{ ends with } 0 \\[2ex] \dfrac{2}{3^{(n+1)/2}} & \text{if } n \text{ is odd and } e \text{ ends with } 1 \\[2ex] \dfrac{1}{3^{n/2}} & \text{otherwise.} \end{cases}$$

P_- is just as in proposition 13.5, so once again we have that P_- induces a countably additive probability measure on 2^ω with $P_-(C_h) = 0$. As *Figure 13.10* should make clear, the values assigned by P_+ also add up to 1 over data segments of a fixed length, so just as in the proof of proposition 13.5, P_+ induces a unique, countably additive probability measure on 2^ω.

Since P_+ assigns each fan in $\overline{C_h}$ probability zero, we have by the proof of lemma 13.9 that $P_+(\overline{C_h}) = 0$, so $P_+(C_h) = 1$. For each Borel set $S \subseteq 2^\omega$, define:

$$P_1(S) = 0.5P_+(S) + 0.5P_-(S).$$

Then by lemmas 13.7 and 13.10 and an obvious analog of lemma 13.6, we have that:

$$(*) \quad \frac{P_1(e, C_h)}{P_1(e, \overline{C_h})} = \frac{P_+(e)}{P_-(e)}.$$

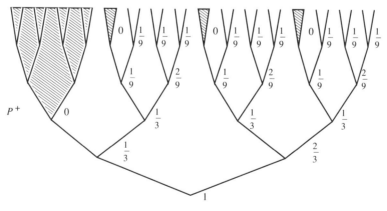

Figure 13.10

It remains to see that β_{P_1} gradually decides$_C$ h given 2^ω. Let $\varepsilon \in 2^\omega$. Suppose $\varepsilon \in \overline{C_h}$. Then there is an n such that $[\varepsilon | n] \subseteq \overline{C_h}$, since $\overline{C_h}$ is a union of fans. Then it is immediate that for each $m \geq n$, $P_1(C_h, \varepsilon | n) = 0$, so β_{P_1} stabilizes to 0 on ε, which is correct. Now suppose $\varepsilon \in C_h$. By lemma 13.9, it suffices to show that

$$Lim_{n \to \infty} \frac{P_1(\varepsilon | n, C_h)}{P_1(\varepsilon | n, \overline{C_h})} = \infty.$$

For this it suffices, in turn, to show that both the even and the odd subsequences of likelihood ratios go in infinity:

$$Lim_{n \to \infty} \frac{P_1(\varepsilon | (2n), C_h)}{P_1(\varepsilon | (2n), \overline{C_h})} = \infty \quad and \quad Lim_{n \to \infty} \frac{P_1(\varepsilon | (2n + 1), C_h)}{P_1(\varepsilon | (2n + 1), \overline{C_h})} = \infty.$$

On the odd subsequence we have:

$$\frac{P_1(\varepsilon | (2n + 1), C_h)}{P_1(\varepsilon | (2n + 1), \overline{C_h})} = \frac{1/3^{((2n + 1) + 1)/2}}{1/2^{2n + 1}} = \frac{2^{2n + 1}}{3^{n + 1}},$$

while on the even subsequence we have:

$$\frac{P_1(\varepsilon | (2n), C_h)}{P_1(\varepsilon | (2n), \overline{C_h})} = \frac{1/3^{(2n)/2}}{1/2^{2n}} = \frac{2^{2n}}{3^n}.$$

To see that both subsequences go to infinity, observe that $2^8/3^4 > 3$. Let $k \in \omega$ be given. Either ratio exceeds k by stage $4 \log_3 (k)$ and remains above k thereafter. So by lemma 13.10, $P_1(C_h, \varepsilon | n)$ correctly approaches 1 as n goes to infinity. ∎

The examples show that not all initial, joint probability measures are equal when it comes to finding the truth about a deterministic hypothesis. Even an open door measure can result in failures on uncountable sets of data streams, while choosing another measure may guarantee success no matter what. Since a familiar criticism of personalism is that one's initial probabilities are arbitrary,[5] this is a consideration that might be taken into account in constraining one's choice.[6] The logical perspective on induction therefore has

[5] This advice pertains more to purely subjective personalists than to those who think that the likelihoods are given by an objective statistical model. The latter are not free to tinker at will with the probabilities $P(\mathcal{E}|\mathcal{H})$, and these are the probabilities that drive the convergence arguments in the examples.

[6] There is some evidence of such concerns in the statistical literature: e.g., Foster (1991). Diaconis and Freedman (1986) show that for some prior probability measures, Bayesian updating is not reliable in a classical sense (it does not have a unit likelihood of converging to the truth regardless of which likelihood parameter is the true one). If likelihoods are interpreted strictly as limiting relative frequencies so that parameters pick out determinate subsets of $\mathcal{N}$, then their question is of just the sort under discussion.

relevance for philosophies of induction and confirmation that are based on updating by Bayes' theorem. In fact, an important and general question for Bayesians is whether or not conditionalization actually prevents success by ideal agents when success is possible. In other words:

Question 13.12

If h is gradually decidable$_C$ given $\mathcal{K}$, does there exist a strict conditionalizer that gradually decides$_C$ h given $\mathcal{K}$?

Regardless of the outcome of the question for arbitrary, ideal methods, conditionalization is definitely restrictive for the class of all arithmetically definable methods. Recall from chapter 6 that this class includes highly idealized methods much more complex than computable methods.

Since the conjecture of a conditionalizer is a real number, we must specify what it is for such a method to be arithmetically definable. We will represent the conjecture as an infinite decimal expansion and require that for each given *n*, the arithmetical definition of β determines the *n*th position of $\beta(h, e)$. For β to be computable, we will require that there be a program *M* such that $M[h, e, n]$ returns the *n*th decimal position of $\beta(h, e)$.

Now we have the following result:

Proposition 13.13

Let $C_h = \{\delta\}$, as in proposition 7.19. Then

(1) *h is computably refutable with certainty but*

(2) *no arithmetically definable conditionalizer can even gradually verify$_C$ or refute$_C$ h.*[7]

Proof: If $C_h \cap [e] \cap \mathcal{K} = \varnothing$, then $P(h, e) = 0$. Hence, a conditionalizing method is consistent. Apply corollary 7.24. ∎

So if an arithmetically definable agent elects to update probabilities by Bayes' rule, he may have to pay a price in terms of logical reliability.[8] Even under liberal standards of constructiveness, the respective aims of short-run coherence and long-run reliability compete rather than reinforce one another.

---

[7] In fact, no *hyper-arithmetically definable* method can succeed, either. Cf. Kelly and Schulte (1995). For a definition of the hyper-arithmetical functions, cf. Rogers (1987).

[8] For a different sort of restrictiveness result for conditionalization, cf. Osherson and Weinstein (1988). Their result concerns discovery rather than assessment, and its model of Bayesian discovery would be considered controversial by some Bayesians.

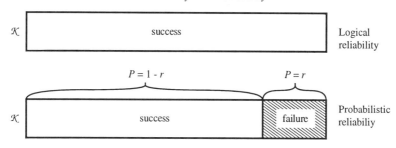

Figure 13.11

3. Probabilistic Reliability

In the preceding section, the reliability of conditionalization was analyzed from the logical point of view developed in the preceding chapters. But advocates of conditionalization as an inductive method rarely adopt the logical perspective just considered. Their sweeping convergence claims are based on *probabilistic* rather than *logical* reliability. Logical reliability demands convergence to the truth on each data stream in $\mathcal{K}$. Probabilistic reliability requires only convergence to the truth over some set of data streams that carries sufficiently high probability (*Fig. 13.11*).

Let P be a probability measure on $\mathcal{N}$.

> α *decides$_C$ H gradually with probability r in P*
> $\Leftrightarrow$ *there exists $\mathcal{K} \in$ Bo such that*

(1) $P(\mathcal{K}) \geq r$ and

(2) α *decides$_C$ H gradually given $\mathcal{K}$.*

Similar definitions can be given for the other notions of success, including the discovery case. Now we can state the sort of result that some probabilists have in mind when they say that conditionalization will arrive at the truth. The following proposition says that the conditionalization method β_P that starts out with measure P has a unit probability *according to the measure P* of approaching the truth value of an arbitrary Borel hypothesis. Observe that this result imposes no restrictions on the probability measure P other than countable additivity.

Proposition 13.14[9]

Let P be a countably additive probability measure on $\mathcal{N}$. Let $C \in$ Bo. Then $P(\{\varepsilon: \beta_P$ gradually decides$_C$ ω on $\varepsilon\}) = 1$.

Proof: Halmos (1974): section 49, theorem B, shows that β_P can identify in the limit each $h \in \omega$ with probability 1 in P. Let $\mathcal{L}_h$ be the set of probability 0

---

[9] For a detailed discussion of this similar results, cf. Schervish et al. (1990).

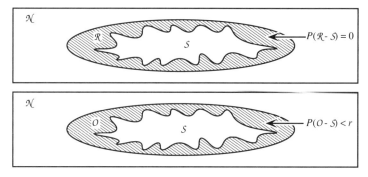

Figure 13.12

"neglected" in the case of hypothesis h. The union of all these sets still has probability 0 by countable additivity. ∎

Proposition 13.14 entails that each Borel hypothesis is decidable in the limit with probability 1. It can also be shown that if we are willing to countenance an arbitrarily small but positive probability of error, then each Borel hypothesis is decidable with certainty. These facts are summarized as follows.

Proposition 13.15

For each countably additive P, for each $C \in Bo$

(a) *for each $r > 0$, ω is decidable$_C$ with certainty with probability $1 - r$ in P;*

(b) *ω is decidable$_C$ in the limit with probability 1 in P.*

Proof: (b) follows from proposition 13.14. (a) follows from proposition 13.16 below. ∎

In light of the strong, negative results of preceding chapters, this is amazing. Problems unsolvable even with strong background knowledge in the logical sense are *all* solvable in the limit with unit probability and are decidable with certainty with arbitrarily high probability.[10] Arbitrarily low or zero probabilities of error hardly seem worth haggling over. Indeed, some probabilists refer to unit probability events as being *almost sure* or *practically certain*.

The usual proof of proposition 13.15 involves the following result as a lemma. It states that every Borel set is "almost surely" Π_2^B and is a Σ_1^B set with arbitrarily high probability. Moreover, the approximating sets can always be chosen as *supersets* (*Fig. 13.12*).

---

[10] In light of chapter 9, these results carry over to discovery problems as well.

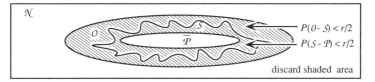

Figure 13.13

Proposition 13.16   The approximation theorem

For each countably additive P, for each $S \in Bo$

(a) *for each $r > 0$ there is an $O \in \Sigma_1^B$ such that $S \subseteq O$ and $P(O) - P(S) < r$.*

(b) *there is an $\mathcal{R} \in \Pi_2^B$ such that $S \subseteq \mathcal{R}$ and $P(\mathcal{R}) = P(S)$.*

Proof: Royden (1988): 294, proposition 7. ∎

This fact implies the following proposition, which places the approximation theorems into the context of the characterization theorems of the preceding chapters. The proof illustrates how a probabilist can neglect the ragged "periphery"[11] of a complex hypothesis while leaving most of its probability intact.

Proposition 13.17

For each countably additive P, for each $S \in Bo$,

(a) *for each $r > 0$, for each $h \in \omega$, there is $\mathcal{K} \in Bo$ such that $P(\mathcal{K}) > 1 - r$ and $C_h \in \Delta[\mathcal{K}]_1^B$;*

(b) *for each $h \in \omega$, there is $\mathcal{K} \in Bo$ such that $P(\mathcal{K}) = 1$ and $C_h \in \Delta[\mathcal{K}]_2^B$.*

Proof: (a) Let $S \in Bo$ be given. We want to find $\mathcal{K}$ such that $P(\mathcal{K}) > 1 - r$ and $S \in \Delta[\mathcal{K}]_1^B$. By proposition 13.16(a), we can choose open sets O, $\mathcal{P}$ such that $S \subseteq O$, $\bar{S} \subseteq \mathcal{P}$, $P(O) - P(S) < r/2$ and $P(\mathcal{P}) - P(\bar{S}) < r/2$ (*Fig. 13.13*). Thus, $P(S) - P(\bar{\mathcal{P}}) < r/2$, since $\mathcal{P} - \bar{S} = S - \bar{\mathcal{P}}$.

So we have a closed $\bar{\mathcal{P}} \subseteq S$ that differs in probability from S by less than $r/2$ and an open $O \subseteq S$ that differs in probability from S by less than $r/2$. By finite additivity, $P(O - \bar{\mathcal{P}}) < r$. Now we may "neglect" this difference by choosing $\mathcal{K} = O - \bar{\mathcal{P}}$. Evidently, $P(\mathcal{K}) > 1 - r$, and since $\mathcal{K} \cap S = \mathcal{K} \cap \bar{\mathcal{P}} = \mathcal{K} \cap O$, we have $S \in \Delta[\mathcal{K}]_1^B$. The argument for (b) is similar, except that we end up with a Σ_2^B approximation from within and a Π_2^B approximation from without whose difference has probability zero. ∎

[11] I did not say *boundary*, because in the measure 1 case, not all of the boundary is ignored. Otherwise, all hypotheses would be decidable with certainty with unit probability.

Probabilistic reliability is easier to achieve precisely because the probabilist entitles himself to augment his background knowledge by removing a set Z of probability zero from $\mathcal{K}$, whereas logical reliability demands success over all of $\mathcal{K}$. That the probabilist's "negligible" sets may be uncountably infinite even when the data, the hypothesis, and its negation all start out with nonzero probability is clear from propositions 13.5 and 13.7. It is a fine thing for the realist that alleged canons of inductive rationality entitle him to claim sufficient knowledge to solve all inductive problems in the limit. A competent skeptic, on the other hand, will reject this blanket entitlement to knowledge as a technically disguised form of dogmatism (*Fig. 13.14*).

We have seen in chapter 4 that local underdetermination and demonic arguments depend on missing limit points in the boundary of the hypothesis. The probabilistic convergence and approximation theorems just described imply that the boundary of a hypothesis (in the topological sense) is always a set of negligible probability. In other words, *arbitrarily high* topological complexity can be discounted in a set of *arbitrarily small* probability, and complexity higher than the Δ_2^B level can be neglected in a set of zero probability.

This discussion may shed some light on the stubborn persistence of debates between realists and skeptics. The antirealist looks at a problem and points out that it has high topological complexity and hence a high degree of under-determination, subjecting it to demonic arguments against logical reliability, as we saw with Sextus Empiricus. The realist focuses on size rather than complexity. He observes that the boundary of the hypothesis, in which all of the antirealist's complexity resides, is a set of negligible probability. Neither position contradicts the other. The difference is one of emphasis on different, objective mathematical features of the problem at hand.

If, indeed, the scientific realism debate hinges to some extend on one's attitude toward neglecting the logically "rough" peripheries of hypotheses, it is of the utmost epistemological import to understand how it is that the axioms of probability guarantee that this periphery is always neglectable. In the next section, I will focus on the crucial role of countable additivity in this regard.

Figure 13.14

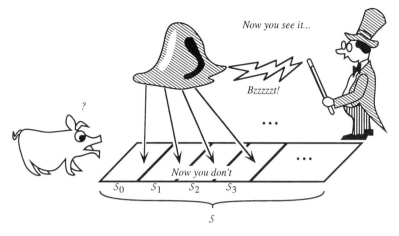

Now you see it...

Bzzzzzt!

?

Now you don't

S_0 S_1 S_2 S_3

S

Figure 13.15

4. Countable Additivity

All the results reported in the preceding section assume countable additivity. Countable additivity was introduced by Kolmogorov[12] for expedience, and most probabilists have followed suit.

> The general condition of countable additivity is a further restriction ... —a restriction without which modern probability theory could not function. It is a tenable point of view that our intuition demands infinite additivity just as much as finite additivity. At any rate, however, infinite additivity does not contradict our intuitive ideas, and the theory built on it is sufficiently far developed to assert that the assumption is justified by its success.[13]

Without countable additivity, we would be left with the apparently magical possibility that the probability of the whole could end up being more than the sum of its parts when it consists of a countable infinity of nonoverlapping parts. In particular, a countable infinity of probability zero parts could add up to a set with probability one (*Fig. 13.15*).[14] That seems strange.

On the other hand, countable additivity has the awkward consequence that probabilities on a countable partition of $\mathcal{N}$ must be "biased" in order to add

---

[12] Kolmogorov (1956).

[13] Halmos (1974): 187.

[14] This is an instance of what DeFinetti (1972: 143) calls *nonconglomerability*. Let $\Pi = \{\mathcal{H}_1, \ldots, \mathcal{H}_n, \ldots\}$ partition $\mathcal{N}$. Then P is *conglomerable* in Π just in case for all measurable events C, $P(C) = \Sigma_{i\in\omega} P(\mathcal{E}, \mathcal{H}_i)$. In the example, we have $P(S) = 1$ but for each i, $P(S, S_i)P(S_i) = P(S_i) = 0$ so $\Sigma_{i\in\omega} P(S, S_i)P(S_i) = 0$. Schervish et al. (1984) show that subject to some conditions concerning the existence of conditional probabilities, every merely finitely additive P is nonconglomerable in *some* partition (depending on P). The "strangeness" of nonconglomerability is sometimes cited as an argument for countable additivity.

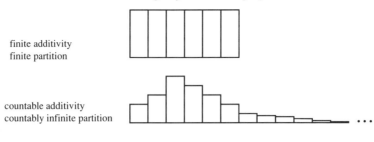

finite additivity
finite partition

countable additivity
countably infinite partition

Figure 13.16

up to 1, since if the same probability is assigned to each cell, then the sum must be either 0 or infinity (*Fig. 13.16*). DeFinetti puts the issue this way:

> Suppose we are given a countable partition into events E_i, and let us put ourselves into the subjectivistic position. An individual wishes to evaluate the $p_i = P(E_i)$: he is free to choose them as he pleases, except that, if he wants to be coherent, he must be careful not to inadvertently violate the conditions of coherence. Someone tells him that in order to be coherent he can choose the p_i in any way he likes, so long as the sum $= 1$ (it is the same thing as in the finite case, anyway!).
>
> The same thing?!!! You must be joking, the other will answer. In the finite case, this condition allowed me to choose the probabilities to be all equal, or slightly different, or very different; in short, I could express any opinion whatsoever. Here, on the other hand, the content of my judgments enter into the picture: I am allowed to express them only if they are unbalanced. ... Otherwise, even if I think they are equally probable ... I am obliged to pick "at random" a convergent series which, however I choose it, is in absolute contrast to what I think. If not, you call me incoherent! In leaving the finite domain, is it I who has ceased to understand anything, or is it you who has gone mad?[15]

In keeping with this spirit, DeFinetti and L. J. Savage[16] have proposed foundational interpretations of probability in which countable additivity is not guaranteed. For frequentists, the issue is more readily settled, since limiting relative frequencies do not always satisfy countable additivity.[17]

From the logical reliabilist perspective, there is another reason to question countable additivity. It will be seen in this section how countable additivity is invoked in probabilistic convergence and approximation theorems like

---

[15] De Finetti (1990): 123.

[16] Savage (1972).

[17] For example, we can have each natural number occur in a collective with limiting relative frequency 0 by having it occur finitely often, but the limiting relative frequency that some natural number will occur is unity, since only natural numbers occur. De Finetti chided "frequentist" practice for failure to respect this failure of countable additivity on their interpretation: "So far as I know, however, none of [the frequentists] has ever taken this observation into account, let alone disputed it; clearly it has been overlooked, although it seems to me I have repeated it on many occasions" (De Finetti 1990: 123).

propositions 13.14, 13.15, and 13.16. We will see that the objectionable bias imposed by countable additivity is involved directly in these arguments. In section 13.5, it will be shown, moreover, that countable additivity is necessary for obtaining the probabilistic convergence and approximation theorems at issue. If probabilistic convergence theorems are to serve as a philosophical antidote to the logical reliabilist's concerns about local underdetermination and inductive demons, then countable additivity is elevated from the status of a mere technical convenience to that of a central epistemological axiom favoring scientific realism. Such an axiom should be subject to the highest degree of philosophical scrutiny. Mere technical convenience cannot justify it. Neither can appeal to its "fruits," insofar as they include precisely the convergence theorems at issue.

Let us consider in a concrete example how the bias imposed by countable additivity can make universal hypotheses decidable with arbitrarily high probability, as is claimed in proposition 13.15(a). Sextus argued that no matter how many 1s have been observed, the next observation might be a 0, so "every observation will be 1" is not verifiable with certainty. The complement $\{\bar{\zeta}\}$ of this hypothesis is the union of all fans of form $[(1, 1, 1, \ldots, 0)]$ (i.e., with handles consisting of a finite sequence of 1s followed by a single (0). Let $\mathcal{F}_i$ be the fan of this form with exactly i 1s occurring in its handle, as depicted in *Figure 13.17*.

Suppose that the prior probability of the hypothesis in question is r (i.e., that $P(\{\zeta\}) = r$). Then $P(\{\bar{\zeta}\}) = 1 - r$, by finite additivity. Since the fans are disjoint, the sum of the probabilities of the individual fans is exactly $P(\{\bar{\zeta}\}) = 1 - r$, by countable additivity. Since this infinite sum is the limit of the finite initial sums of the series, it follows that for each $u > 0$, there is a position n in the series such that the probability left in the remaining fans is less than u (*Fig. 13.18*). In other words, the bias imposed by countable additivity is in this case a bias for seeing refutations of $\{\zeta\}$ sooner rather than later.

For measure u decidability, the scientist is entitled to assume that none of the fans after position n will ever be entered. This amounts to cutting the infinite tail off of Sextus's argument, so that the demon runs out of opportunities to fool the scientist. Let $C_h = \{\zeta\}$. Let $\mathcal{K} = \{\zeta\} \cup$ the union of all fans veering off

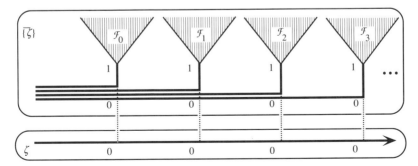

Figure 13.17

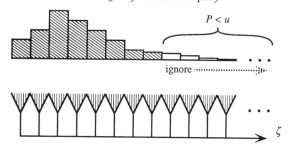

Figure 13.18

from ζ at a stage $\leq n$. Clearly, there exists an effective method α that is guaranteed to decide$_C$ h by time n given $\mathcal{K}$;

$$\alpha(h, e) = \begin{cases} 1 & \text{if } e \subseteq \zeta \\ 0 & \text{otherwise.} \end{cases}$$

Hence, if P is countably additive and $r > 0$, then h is decidable$_C$ by some fixed time n with probability $1 - r$ in P. Since the ancient skeptical argument is driven by concerns of error in the indefinite future, it is not surprising that an axiom of rationality imposing the attitude that a universal hypothesis will be refuted sooner rather than later should have antiskeptical consequences.[18] It might be claimed that such an attitude is justified, because finite beings have no interest in what happens in the long run. But be that as it may, such indifference ought to be reflected in the utilities we associate with outcomes in the indefinite future, rather than in general axioms governing rational beliefs about what will happen then.

In the example at hand, we have not only decidability with certainty (with high probability), but an a priori bound (calculated from P) on how long it will take to arrive at the right answer with a given probability, which is something far stronger than what is claimed in proposition 13.14. Once we discount "trifling" probabilities of error concerning a universal hypothesis, the only interesting question remaining is how long we have to wait until we are sufficiently sure we are right[19] and whether a computer could efficiently recognize counterexamples.[20]

---

[18] Assuming that the data are generated by independent and identically distributed (IID) trials of an experiment yields an even stronger result, namely, that the probability of refutation always decreases with time, with well-known bounds on the rate of decrease. But while no one accepts IID as a general postulate of rationality, countable additivity is often treated as such. For that reason, I focus on the convergence theorems that assume only countable additivity.

[19] This may not be true of hypotheses of higher complexity, as we shall see shortly.

[20] These questions have been drawing increased attention from computer scientists under the rubric of PAC (probably approximately correct) learning theory. At present, the results of this theory depend not just on countable additivity, but on strong independence assumptions as well.

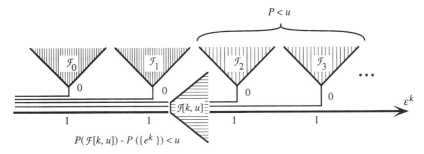

Figure 13.19

High probabilities of inductive success by a given time may evaporate depending on how the evidence comes in. For example, if the hypothesis states that heads will be observed, then the probability that the hypothesis will be verified by the tenth toss already exceeds 0.999, but the probability that it will be verified by the tenth toss given failures on the first nine tosses is just 0.5. So unlike logical reliability, which never disappears with time, a high probability of success can be an evanescent virtue.

A unit probability of success with certainty is permanent, assuming that data of probability 0 are not encountered. But universal hypotheses cannot always be verified with certainty with unit probability. For suppose that $P(\{\zeta\}) = r$ where $0 < r < 1$ and the remaining $1 - r$ probability is distributed in a countably additive way over the diverging fans, so that $P(\mathcal{F}_i) > 0$, for infinitely many i. To succeed with probability 1, the method must succeed on ζ, since $P(\{\zeta\}) = r > 0$, and must also succeed on infinitely many fans veering off from ζ, since infinitely many such fans carry positive probability. Sextus's demonic argument shows that no possible method has this property.

On the other hand, if $C_h \in Bo$, then decidability in the limit is guaranteed with unit probability when P is countably additive, by proposition 13.15. Now we consider the role of countable additivity in the argument for this claim. Let us return to the simple and familiar case of finite divisibility, introduced in chapter 3. In this example, $C_{h_{fin}}$ is the set of all infinite, Boolean-valued data streams that stabilize to 0. We know that $C_{h_{fin}} \in \Sigma_2^B - \Pi_2^B$ and that $C_{h_{fin}}$ is countable. So if h_{fin} is to be decidable$_C$ in the limit with probability 1, as proposition 13.17 says, then there must be some set $\mathcal{K}$ of probability one such that $C_{h_{fin}} \in \Pi[\mathcal{K}]_2^B$. In other words, $\bar{\mathcal{K}}$ is to be neglected.

What does $\mathcal{K}$ look like?[21] Enumerate $C_{h_{fin}}$ as $\varepsilon^1, \varepsilon^2, \ldots, \varepsilon^n, \ldots$. If we repeat the above discussion of Sextus' argument, treating $\{\varepsilon^k\}$ as a hypothesis, then we have that for each specified u, we can find a fan $\mathcal{F}[k, u]$ containing ε^k such that $P(\mathcal{F}[k, u]) - P(\{\varepsilon^k\}) < u$ (*Fig. 13.19*). This is again because countable additivity forces us to drop probability on the complement of $\{\varepsilon^k\}$ in "lumps" on the countably many disjoint fans veering off from ε^k, so that it is eventually

---

[21] The construction that follows is a minor adaptation of the standard proof that the [0, 1] interval can be partitioned into a meager set and a set of Lebesgue measure zero (Royden 1988: 161, no. 33b.)

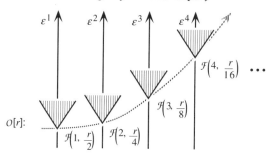

Figure 13.20

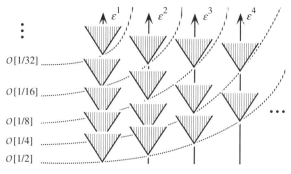

Figure 13.21

almost entirely used up (*Fig. 13.19*). For each $r \in [0, 1]$, we have:

$$\sum_{n=1}^{\infty} \frac{r}{2^n} = r.$$

Define for each $r \in [0, 1]$:[22]

$$O[r] = \bigcup_{n=1}^{\infty} \mathcal{F}\left[k, \frac{r}{2^n}\right].$$

$O[r]$ is open, $\varepsilon^k \in O[r]$ and, by construction, $P(O[r] - P(C_{h_{fin}}) \leq r$. Also, we have $O[r] \subseteq O[r']$ if $r \leq r'$ (*Fig. 13.20*). Now define:[23]

$$\mathcal{R} = \bigcap_{n=1}^{\infty} O\left[\frac{1}{2^n}\right].$$

$\mathcal{R} \in \Pi_2^B$, since $\mathcal{R}$ is a countable, downward-nested intersection of open sets, and $C_{h_{fin}} \subseteq \mathcal{R}$ since each ε^i is included in each open set in the intersection (*Fig. 13.21*). So we have a nested sequence of open set around $\mathcal{R}$ whose probabilities

---

[22] $\overline{O[r]}$ is an example of a nowhere dense, closed set.

[23] $\mathcal{R}$ is a meager set.

converge to $P(C_{h_{fin}})$. By continuity (cf. proposition 13.1), $P(\mathcal{R}) = P(C_{h_{fin}})$. But recall from proposition 13.1 that continuity is equivalent to countable additivity in light of the other axioms. So this construction of a probability 1 approximation of $C_{h_{fin}}$ appeals to countable additivity twice. The first application yields arbitrarily close, downward nested open approximations $O_1, O_2, \ldots, O_n, \ldots$ while the second shows that the probability of the intersection $\mathcal{R}$ of these sets is the limit of the probabilities of the O_i in the sequence.

5. Probabilistic Reliability without Countable Additivity

We have seen that countable additivity suffices for probabilistic reliability over all Borel hypotheses. It remains to see that probabilistic reliability is *impossible* to achieve for some merely finitely additive probability measures.

Let's return again to Sextus's argument. Let $C_h = \{\zeta\}$, where ζ is the everywhere 0 data stream. It makes life too easy for the scientist if $P(\{\zeta\}) = 0$, so let's set $P(\{\zeta\}) = 0.5$, so $P(\overline{\{\zeta\}}) = 0.5$ as well. Now let's turn to the probabilities of the fans veering off from ζ that form a countably infinite partition of $\overline{\{\zeta\}}$. Dropping countable additivity, we no longer have to concentrate almost all of the probability on $\overline{\{\zeta\}}$ over a finite number of fans veering off from ζ. But *finite* additivity still implies that we cannot place some uniform, positive probability on each fan, or some finite union of fans would carry more than unit probability. But we may place probability 0 on each fan, so that by finite additivity, every finite union of fans veering off from ζ carries probability 0. Nonetheless, the countable union of all these fans is $\overline{\{\zeta\}}$, which must carry probability 0.5. Every union of a cofinite set of fans veering off from ζ must carry probability 0.5 as well, since finite unions of these fans carry probability 0 by finite additivity. One might doubt whether these assumptions are coherent, in the sense that there really does exist a finitely additive probability measure that satisfies them. After all, contradictions need not be obvious. But it is shown in section 13.9 that:

Proposition 13.18

There is a finitely additive probability measure P on 2^ω satisfying the constraints just described (Fig. 13.22). ∎

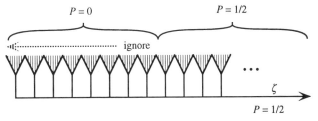

$P = 0$ $P = 1/2$

ignore

ζ

$P = 1/2$

Figure 13.22

Figure 13.22 depicts an *exact reversal* of the epistemological situation guaranteed by countable additivity. Instead of *most* of the probability mass on $\overline{\{\zeta\}}$ being exhausted after a finite amount of time, we now have that *none* of the mass on $\overline{\{\zeta\}}$ is exhausted after any finite amount of time. Whereas the limit was formerly negligible, it now carries the full weight of the probability on $\overline{\{\zeta\}}$.

What happens to a conditionalizer that starts out with such a joint measure? Consider $\zeta|n$, which is a sequence of n zeros. The fan $[\zeta|n]$ includes $\{\zeta\}$. Now consider the fan $\mathcal{F}_m = [(\zeta|m)*1]$. $\mathcal{F}_m$ has a handle consisting of m 0s followed by a 1, and hence is the mth fan veering off from ζ in Figure 13.22. For each $m \geq n$, $\mathcal{F}_m \subseteq [\zeta|n]$. Since the union of all the $\mathcal{F}_m$ has probability 0.5 and $\{\zeta\}$ also has probability 0.5, finite additivity yields $P([\zeta|n]) = 1$. That is, each finite data sequence consistent with $\{\zeta\}$ has probability 1. Since $\{\zeta\} \subseteq [\zeta|n]$, we also have $P(\{\zeta\} \cap [\zeta|n]) = P(\{\zeta\})$. Hence, $P(\{\zeta\}, [\zeta|n]) = P(\{\zeta\}) = 0.5$. Conditionalization fails to approach 1 on data stream ζ, and so has a *probability* of failure of at least 0.5, despite the fact that h is refutable with certainty over all of $\mathcal{N}$ in the logical sense. Moreover, this 0.5 probability of error is never diminished through time. This shows that the measure 1 limiting success of Bayesian method reported in proposition 13.14 depends on the biasing effect of countable additivity.

We can also see from this example that the finitely additive versions of propositions 13.15(a) and 13.16(a) fail.

Proposition 13.19

Let P be the merely finitely additive measure just defined. Let $C_h = \{\zeta\}$. Then no possible assessment method α can verify$_C$ h with certainty with a probability (according to P) greater than 0.5.

Proof: If α never outputs 1 with certainty on ζ, then α fails with probability 0.5. So suppose α declares its certainty for h on $\zeta|n$. Then α is wrong on each data stream in the union of the fans veering off from ζ whose handles extend $\zeta|n$. The probability of this (cofinite) union of fans is 0.5, so in this case, the probability that α has committed an error is again 0.5.   ∎

So when we relax countable additivity, the demons of logical reliabilism can return to haunt the probabilist. The skepticism of the example can be made to appear less extreme by mixing the finitely additive measure with a more standard, countably additive measure. Then conditionalization can "learn from experience" and yet a healthy, skeptical concern about refutation in the unbounded future will always remain, if the hypothesis is true.

It remains to show that probability 1 success may be unachievable by arbitrary methods in the limiting case when countable additivity is dropped, so that the finitely additive versions of propositions 13.15(b) and 13.16(b) also fail. The following construction accomplishes this by showing that there is a Σ_2^B hypothesis and a finitely additive probability measure P such that no possible method (conditionalization or otherwise) can refute the hypothesis in the limit with probability 1. This is the main result of the chapter.

Proposition 13.20   (with C. Juhl)

There is a merely finitely additive probability measure P on $\mathcal{N}$ such that h_{fin} is not refutable$_C$ in the limit with probability 1 in P.

Proof sketch: (a detailed proof is presented in the appendix at the end of the chapter). Let S denote $C_{h_{fin}} = \{\varepsilon: \varepsilon$ stabilizes to $0\}$. The idea is to place discrete, nonzero probabilities summing to 0.5 on the countably many elements of S and to use the latitude permitted by dropping countable additivity to add a thin cloud of "virtual probability" of total mass 0.5 just outside of S so that any Π_2^B superset of S picks up this extra mass (and hence differs in probability from S by 0.5) and any Π_2^B nonsuperset of S loses the mass on some element of S (and hence has a probability strictly less than that of S) (*Fig. 13.23*). Then we have that S has no Π_2^B approximation that differs in probability by a set of measure 0, from which the proposition follows. The bulk of the proof in section 13.9 is devoted to showing that the metaphor of the thin cloud of probability 0.5 is in fact consistent with the axioms of finitely additive probability. ∎

Note that we cannot recover from this construction any *fixed* lower bound on the difference between the probability of S and the probability of an arbitrary Π_2^B approximation to S because finite additivity alone ensures that the elements of S carry arbitrarily small probabilities, and we cannot be sure which of them will be missed by a Π_2^B nonsuperset of S.

The mysterious cloud of probability adhering to S throws a wrench into the countably additive argument (presented in section 13.4) that h_{fin} is refutable$_C$ in the limit with probability 1. It is interesting to consider where the breakdown occurs. Recall that the convergence argument in section 13.4 involves the construction of an infinite sequence of open supersets $O[1], O[1/2], O[1/4], \ldots$ of $C_{h_{fin}} = S$. We observed that the probabilities of these open sets converge to the probability of S and then invoked continuity (proposition 13.1)

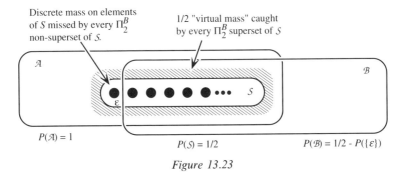

Figure 13.23

to argue that the intersection $\mathcal{R}$ of these sets has the same probability as S. But in this case, each open superset $O[r]$ of S is a fortiori a Π_2^B superset of S. Hence, each such set catches the probability cloud around S, together with all the probability on S, and therefore has probability 1. Thus, the limit is 1 rather than $P(S) = 1/2$.

The general idea is that in countably additive measures, continuity determines the probabilities of events of higher Borel complexity as the limits of probabilities of events of lower Borel complexity. The thin clouds of probability admitted by finite additivity block this determination, and thereby block the countably additive, measure 1 approximation and convergence arguments.

6. Probabilistic Mathematics and Nonprobabilistic Science

Philosphers have long been accustomed to examine mathematical method in terms of logic and to study scientific method in terms of probability. Empiricists like Hume attempted to provide an account of this distinction. Mathematics, on their account, is the mere comparison of ideas within the mind, as though one idea could be laid on top of the other and seen directly, all at once, by the mind's eye. Empirical generalizations, on the other hand, cannot be compared against the future "all at once" so Sextus's argument applies.

Nowadays, few would assent to such a picture of mathematical method. The modern theory of computability has shown us how to view formal proof systems as computable positive tests. In chapter 6, I argued that a computer is akin to an empirical scientist in that it can scan mathematical structures only by finite chunks. Recall that the halting problem was reconstructed in chapter 6 as an instance of Sextus's skeptical argument against inductive generalization. In hindsight, it is no great step from uncomputability to Gödel's celebrated incompleteness results and beyond. One interpretation of these results is that effectively checkable mathematical proofs are limited in their power by precisely the same sorts of demonic arguments that plague inductive generalization. The difference, however, is this. In discussions of proof, we take demonic arguments seriously, while in discussions of inductive method, we discard them in sets of probability zero. To underscore this difference in attitude, let us consider what the theory of computability might look like if it were approached from the probabilistic methodologist's more lenient point of view.

Computer scientists have recognized for some time that what appears intractable from a purely logical point of view can be viewed as tractable if a measure is introduced. For example, *expected complexity theory* imposes a uniform measure over the (finite) set of inputs of a given size, as though for each input size we are uncertain which inputs of that size we will encounter. The result is that some problems that seem to be intractable in the worst case are tractable in the expected case. There also has been interest in finding tractable *random algorithms* for primality testing,[24] where

---

[24] E.g., Solovay and Strassen (1977) and Adleman and Manders (1977).

a random algorithm is run by a machine that flips coins as part of its operation.

But when someone turns on a computer, one evidently does so because one is uncertain about what the machine will do on the input provided. One is not uncertain about the input one will provide to the machine (the designer of the algorithm may have been uncertain about that). Nor is it that the machine is actually equipped with dice or decaying radium atoms; it is paradigmatically discrete and deterministic. The user of a deterministic machine is, in fact, uncertain about what the output will be on the input he is interested in because the operation of the program is too complicated for him to see in his mind's eye in an instant. If it weren't for this kind of uncertainty, there would be no computer industry.

One way to try to resolve the uncertainty in question is to turn on the machine, provide the input, and run it! But here we face a difficulty: how long do we wait before concluding that nothing will ever come out? In short, the halting problem becomes an empirical problem for the user of the machine. But this is just the sort of problem that can be "solved" with arbitrarily high probability along the lines discussed in section 13.3. If this is "good enough" in the empirical case, then it should be good enough for computation, and hence for formal proof.

The reader may object at this point. In the empirical case, it is no contradiction to suppose that all ravens are black, and it is no contradiction to suppose that some raven is not black. But in the computational case, if the program we know the machine to be running halts on input n in k steps, then it is a fact of elementary arithmetic that it does so. If we place probability 1 on the axioms of elementary arithmetic, the axioms of probability theory dictate that we already have probability 1 or 0 on the outcome of the computation in question.[25]

But this objection puts the computer user in a dilemma. If he does not know the outcome of the computation in advance, he is incoherent and hence irrational. And if he does know the answer in advance, going to the trouble and expense of using the computer is again irrational.[26]

Moreover, intuitively probabilistic reasoning does occur in using a computer. When undergraduates write their first computer program and it goes into an infinite loop, their degrees of belief that it will eventually halt go down rapidly, and they eventually terminate the computation and look for the bug.

The same may be said of mathematicians looking for proofs. Many mathematicians are uncertain whether P = NP, but they are inclined to believe that it is false, in the sense that they would try to prove its negation first. Such

---

[25] I am disregarding uncertainty about the program the machine runs, the fidelity of the machine to its program, and the input provided to the machine. The kind of uncertainty one has when one turns on a computer is clearly *not* the sum of these, or computers would never be used.

[26] Note the similarity to Plato's *Meno* paradox.

opinions suggest personal degrees of belief on an undecided proposition of arithmetic.[27]

If it is conceded, at least provisionally, that degrees of belief should be entertained over mathematical propositions, then probabilistic reliability quickly removes many skeptical concerns in the philosophy of mathematics. Let $S \subseteq \omega$ be a purely computational problem that is arithmetically definable, so that for some n, $S \in \Sigma_n^A$. Then by the universal indexing theorem,[28] there is an i such that for each x,

$$(*) \quad S(x) \Leftrightarrow \exists y_1 \, \forall y_2 \ldots T(i, \langle x, y_1, \ldots, y_n \rangle, y_{n+1}).$$

where $T(i, n, k) \Leftrightarrow$ program i halts on input x in k steps. Assuming that we are uncertain about what will happen when we feed a computer a given input x, we are in fact uncertain about the extension of the Turing predicate T. In light of our uncertainty about the extension of T, the statement $(*)$ may be thought of as an *empirical hypothesis*, to be investigated by running different program indices on different inputs for different amounts to time, observing what happens. For simplicity, I adopt the convention that we receive a binary data stream such that a 1 or a 0 at position $\langle \langle x, y_1, \ldots, y_n \rangle y_{n+1} \rangle$ indicates whether $T(i, \langle x, y_1, \ldots, y_n \rangle, y_{n+1})$ or $\neg T(i, \langle x, y_1, \ldots, y_n \rangle, y_{n+1})$, respectively. In other words, the purely formal question "$x \in S$?" may be viewed as posing the following inductive problem:

$$C^S(\varepsilon, x) \Leftrightarrow \exists y_1 \, \forall y_2 \ldots \varepsilon_{\langle x, y_1, \ldots, y_n \rangle y_{n+1}} = 1.$$
$$\mathcal{K} = 2^\omega.$$

Suppose we have a computable method α that decides$_{C^S}$ ω with certainty. Let ε be the unique data stream corresponding to the true extension of T. It is immediate that ε is computable. Then we can decide S by running $\alpha(x, e)$ on greater and greater initial segments e of ε and passing along the first certain conjecture of α (i.e., the first one occurring after "!"). So a computable scientific decision procedure for the scientific problem generated by S yields an ordinary decision procedure for S. But if we follow the modern point of view, it should suffice to have a probabilistic solution to this inductive problem. Say that S is *probability r recursive* just in case there is a computable method α that decides$_{C^S}$ ω with probability r.

It is immediate that for each x, $C_x^S \in \Sigma_n^A$. Thus, for each x, $C_x^S \in Bo$. Let P be a probability measure on Bo. By proposition 13.14, we have that for each

---

[27] This discussion is closely related to ideas in Garber (1983). Garber proposes degrees of belief over entailment relations, in the spirit of the preceding discussion. He is interested in how old evidence (evidence already conditioned on) can raise the posterior probability of a new theory. His answer is that one later conditions on the formal fact that the data is entailed by the theory.

[28] Cf. proposition 7.4 and the example following proposition 7.18.

$x \in \omega$, $r > 0$ there is an $\mathcal{R} \subseteq 2^{\omega}$ such that $P(\mathcal{R}) = 1 - r$ and $C_x^S \cap \mathcal{R}$ is $\mathcal{R}$-clopen. Each $\mathcal{R}$-clopen subset of 2^{ω} is a finite union of fans (cf. exercise 4.14). Since this union can be specified by a lookup table, it follows that $C_x^S \cap \mathcal{R}$ is $\mathcal{R}$-*recursive*. So by proposition 7.8, some computable method decides ω with certainty given $\mathcal{R}$ (and hence with probability $1 - r$ given 2^{ω}). Thus, we see that by the probabilistic reliabilist's standards of success, Turing computability is no upper bound on what is effectively computable (up to "mere trifles" of uncertainty in the computer user).

The point is that uncomputability is about quantifiers over the natural numbers. Countably additive probability permits us to truncate the infinite universe of quantification up to "trifles," and thus to dismiss the demons of uncomputability along with those of induction. So there is some pressure on the traditional view that the stringent standards of logical reliabilism should be relaxed in the philosophy of science but not in the philosophy of mathematics. In either case, lowering standards flatters our abilities.

7. Probabilistic Theories

So far, the discussion has proceeded as though hypotheses always pick out a determinate subset of $\mathcal{N}$. But some scientific theories, including our most fundamental theory of matter, entail only probability statements concerning observable events. Moreover, even a thoroughly deterministic theory like classical mechanics can be viewed as making only probabilistic predictions if it is assumed that real-valued measurements are all subject to a normally distributed probability of error.

A logical reliabilist's approach toward such theories depends on how the probability statements are interpreted. A thoroughgoing personalist takes all probabilities to be someone's coherent degrees of belief. This is a fairly clear proposal and it causes no difficulty from a logical reliabilist's point of view. Recall that the personalist typically advocates a double reduction of probability to degree of belief and of degree of belief to betting behavior. Hence, the problem of inferring physical probabilities reduces, on this view, to the problem of reliably discovering the odds at which the subject will bet on a given event. The personalists themselves have proposed such inferential procedures in their foundational discussions of the meaning of probability. So in this sense there is no incompatibility between logical reliabilism and the purely personalistic account of physical probabilities. It is just that the data streams, to which the probabilities in quantum theory are logically connected, concern somebody's acceptance or rejection of various preferred bets.

It seems strange that the probabilities in quantum mechanics should literally refer to somebody's opinions. So it is common, even among advocates of personalism, to allow that the probabilities introduced in scientific theories refer to objective, physical realities. As we have seen in chapter 2, one such view is that physical probabilities either are or at least logically entail limiting relative frequencies of experimental outcomes. As was shown in chapters 3 and 9, this *logical* connection between probabilistic hypotheses and the data stream permits a nontrivial learning-theoretic analysis of the assessment and discovery of such hypotheses.

A careful frequentist cannot adopt all of the methods and results of Kolmogorov's probability theory, however, since many of those results are proved using countable additivity, and we have seen that countable additivity is not satisfied by limiting relative frequencies.[29] Moreover, for those who are used to the Kolmogorov axioms, frequentism appears to be an elementary fallacy. The strong law of large numbers, which is a consequence to the Kolmogorov axioms, implies that if P corresponds to independent trials with a fair coin, then $P(LRF_{\{0.5\}}(\text{heads})) = 1$. In other words, the probability that an infinite sequence of independent flips of a fair coin will have a limiting relative frequency of 0.5 is one. But a unit probability falls far short of logical necessity, as the discussion of probability one convergence in this chapter makes abundantly clear. From the point of view of a probability theorist who starts out with the Kolmogorov axioms, the frequentist simply confuses a measure one property of sequences with a logical definition of the probability of an outcome type in an infinite run of trials. The problem is compounded by the fact that there are stronger "measure one" properties than the strong law of large numbers that could have been chosen to define probability, and there is a lack of motivation for choosing one such law rather than another.[30]

Such reflections lead to the propensity account of objective probability. This account tells us just three things about propensities: they satisfy Kolmogorov's axioms; they are physical rather than mental; and whatever they are, they do not entail limiting relative frequencies of outcomes in the data stream. Evidently, this proposal permits free use of Kolmogorov's axioms and sidesteps the nettlesome project of forging a logical connection between probability and the data stream. But there seems to be a principle of conservation of mystery operating, for it becomes unintelligible on the propensity view (a) why propensities should be of any practical interest to anyone and (b) how we could ever find out about propensities with any reliability, since they are globally underdetermined in the sense of chapter 2.

The propensity theorist responds by tying personal degrees of belief to propensities by means of an axiom known as the *direct inference principle*. Let P_b be a probability measure representing personal degrees of belief. Let P be some arbitrary probability measure over the events thought to be governed by propensities. The hypothesis that propensities are distributed according to P may be abbreviated as h_P. Then the direct inference principle may be stated roughly[31]

---

[29] Historically, this seems to have been the decisive argument when most probability theorists dropped von Mises' theory in favor of Kolmogorov's axioms (Van Lambalgen: 1987).

[30] The *law of the iteratred logarithm* is such a theorem (Billingsly 1986). A neofrequentist could strengthen his theory by defining probability in terms of this law rather than in terms of the strong law of large numbers.

[31] A more sophisticated account is stated in Levi (1983): 255.

as follows:

$$P_b(\mathcal{E}, h_P) = P(\mathcal{E}).$$

In other words, given only that the true propensity function if P, one's degree of belief in $\mathcal{E}$ should also be the propensity of $\mathcal{E}$. Given this principle, evidence can bear on propensity hypotheses via Bayes' theorem:

$$P_b(h_P, S) = \frac{P_b(h_P) P_b(S, h_P)}{P_b(S)} \quad \text{(Bayes' theorem)}$$

$$= \frac{P_b(h_P) P(\mathcal{E})}{P_b(S)} \quad \text{(the direct inference principle)}.$$

The direct inference principle also makes propensities figure into one's personal expected utilities for various acts, and hence makes them relevant to practical deliberation. Without it, propensities are irrelevant, inaccessible, metaphysical curiosities, whether or not they exist (*Fig. 13.24*). There are some who maintain that propensities are no worse than any other theoretical entities in this regard. But I reject the analogy. Theoretical entities can be unobservable in principle and yet figure into determinate, logical predictions about observable events. For example, the light waves in Fresnel's optical theory figured into deductions of exact positions for diffraction bands. Propensities are very different, in that a propensity theory entails only propensity consequences, which in turn bear no logical connection to the data stream, even in the limit. Without the direct inference principle, propensities are entirely insulated from experience.

But now the question is: Why accept the principle? Some defend it

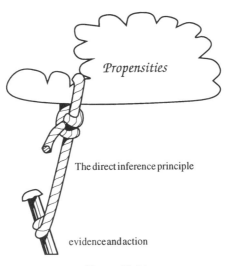

Figure 13.24

as an "incorrigible background stipulation" that requires no justification.[32] But I am not so sure. Suppose there is an omnipotent, omniscient god. Suppose this god has an infinite tape marked out with squares labeled by all the propositions expressible in some language more expressive than any we will ever use. The god also has an infinite supply of infinitely divisible mud. Then, for his own amusement, he places a mud pie on each tape square so that the masses of the pies satisfy Kolmogorov's axioms with respect to the corresponding propositions (normalizing to unit mass on the tautology). After this is done, he determines the truth values of all the sentences by zapping some universe into existence, without giving any thought to his mud pies.

For all that has been said about propensities, they could be the masses of the god's mud pies. These masses are real and they satisfy the Kolmogorov axioms. Certainly, they don't entail limiting relative frequencies for outcomes of experiments. The question is: Why should I, in accordance with the direct inference principle, contribute 2.4% of the stake on a bet that an alpha particle will be emitted from a given uranium atom because the mass of the mud pie on that proposition is 0.024? I see no reason.

In a recent text on Bayesian philosophy of science, Howson and Urbach[33] argue for the direct infererence principle by interpreting statistical probabilities as limiting relative frequencies and pointing out that those who bet in accordance with known limiting relative frequencies will minimize their limiting relative frequency of losses. This defense of the principle succeeds, but only by undercutting its importance, since the admission that propensities entail limiting relative frequencies opens propensities to empirical investigation along the lines discussed in chapter 3, with no detour through personal probabilities or direct inference. Of course, it is still possible on their approach to study, along the lines of section 2 of this chapter, whether conditionalization together with the direct inference principle is as reliable as other methods might be, both for ideal and for computable agents, but in such a study the direct inference principle is a restriction on one's choice of possible inductive strategies rather than the theoretical linchpin of statistical inference.

In summary, logical reliabilism is compatible with the foundations both of frequentism and of pure personalism, even though there might be quibbles about actual practice (e.g., with avowed frequentists who nonetheless assume countable additivity). It is harder to square the logical reliabilist approach with the increasingly popular hybrid view in which globally underdetermined propensities are connected to personal degrees of belief by the direct inference principle. That position avoids standard objections raised against its competitors, but it does so at a cost that should not be neglected. According to it, science is arbitrary (but coherent) opinion about propensities that entail nothing about what will be observed (except for more propensities, about which the same may be said), even in the limit.

---

[32] Levi (1983): 255.
[33] Howson and Urbach (1990).

I do not mean to suggest that hybrid probabilism is a mistake. I only wish to make it clear that the apparent advantages of the view (e.g., its correspondence with statistical practice and its ability to overcome global underdetermination) come at the expense of a clear, logical account of what science is about, of what its import is for observation, and of how scientific method leads to the truth. Logical reliabilism begins with a clear, logical account of precisely these issues. Accordingly, its strengths and weaknesses are somewhat complementary to those of today's hybrid probabilism. Logical reliability results are hard to apply in particular cases because it is hard to say in particular cases what the empirical import of a hypothesis actually is. But on the other hand, the relations between empirical content, under-determination, computability, methodological recommendations, and the reliability of inquiry as a means for finding the truth all stand out in bold relief.

At the very least, logical reliabilism provides a vantage point from which to raise questions that do not arise naturally within the hybrid probabilist perspective; questions such as whether updating one joint probability measure would be more reliable than updating another concerning a given hypothesis. More ambitiously, logical reliabilism is a persistent remnant of the ancient idea that scientific inquiry should have a clear logical connection with finding the truth, in an age in which both philosophy and professional methodology urge us to forget about it.

8. Logic and Probability

On the face of it, the probabilistic approach to induction seems much more practical and natural than the logical one presented in this book. My purpose in this chapter has been to clarify the relationship between the two perspectives and to urge that some of the apparent advantages of the probabilistic approach may be merely apparent. The first point was that probabilistic methods may fail in the logical sense to solve problems solvable by simple, nonprobabilistic methods. Then I examined some probabilistic convergence theorems and showed how they depend on countable additivity, a powerful epistemological axiom rejected by some personalists and inconsistent with frequentism that is often advertised as a mere technical convenience. To address the objection that logical reliabilism is a cranky, skeptical viewpoint that is never taken seriously, I appealed to the analogy between induction and computation that was developed in chapter 6. According to this analogy, the demonic arguments of logical reliabilism are routinely taken seriously in the philosophy of mathematics. Finally, I reviewed the standard interpretations of stochastic theories, arguing that the logical reliabilist perspective is compatible with pure personalism, pure frequentism, and mixtures of personalism and frequentism. The view that mixes personalism and propensity theory is founded on the direct inference principle, which is questionable exactly insofar as it is required to link propensities to evidence and to practical action.

9. Proofs of Propositions 13.18 and 13.20

Proposition 13.18

Let $\mathcal{F}_n = [\zeta | n*1]$. Then there is a finitely additive probability measure P on the power set of 2^ω such that

(i) $P(\zeta) = 0.5$,

(ii) *For each cofinite union S of fans in $\{\mathcal{F}_n : n \in \omega\}$, $P(S) = 0.5$, and*

(iii) *For each finite union S of fans in $\{\mathcal{F}_n : n \in \omega\}$, $P(S) = 0$.*

Proof: Define

Θ *is an algebra on $\mathcal{N} \Leftrightarrow \mathcal{N} \in \Theta$ and Θ is closed under finite union and complementation.*

Let Θ be an algebra on $\mathcal{N}$,

P is a finitely additive probability measure on $\Theta \Leftrightarrow$

(1) *for each $S \in \Theta$, $P(S) \geq 0$,*

(2) *$P(\mathcal{N}) = 1$ and*

(3) *If $S_0, S_1, \ldots, S_n$ is a finite sequence of pairwise disjoint elements of Θ, then $\bigcup_{i=1}^{n} S_i \in \Theta \Rightarrow P\left(\bigcup_{i=1}^{n} S_i\right) = \sum_{i=1}^{n} P(S_i)$.*

Lemma 13.21

If P is a finitely additive probability measure on an algebra Θ on $\mathcal{N}$, then there is a finitely additive P' defined on the entire power set of $\mathcal{N}$ such that for all $S \in \Theta$, $P(S) = P'(S)$. (Unlike the countably additive case, the extension is not necessarily unique.)

Proof: Consequence of the Hahn Banach theorem (Ash 1972).   ∎

In light of lemma 13.21, it suffices to prove that there is a finitely additive measure satisfying the intended constraints over some algebra of subsets of $\mathcal{N}$. Define:

$\Xi = $ *the set of all cofinite unions of fans in $\{\mathcal{F}_n : n \in \omega\}$.*

$\Theta = $ *the least algebra containing $\{\zeta\} \cup \Xi$.*

Consider two different types of elements of Θ.

$Q \in A \Leftrightarrow $ *for some $\mathcal{R} \in \Xi$, $\mathcal{R} \subseteq Q$.*

$Q \in co\text{-}A \Leftrightarrow \bar{Q} \in A$.

Lemma 13.22

$\{A, co\text{-}A\}$ *partitions* Θ.

Proof: $A \cap co\text{-}A = \varnothing$, since if Q contains a cofinite union of fans in $\{\mathcal{F}_n : n \in \omega\}$ then $\bar{Q}$ does not, and conversely. $\{\zeta\} \in co\text{-}A$ and each $\mathcal{R} \in \Xi$ is in A. Let Q_1, $Q_2 \in \Theta$. Suppose $Q_1, Q_2 \in A$. Then $Q_1 \cup Q_2 \in A$ and $\overline{Q_1} \in co\text{-}A$. If $Q_1 \in A$ and $Q_2 \in co\text{-}A$ then $Q_1 \cup Q_2 \in A$. If $Q_1, Q_2 \in co\text{-}A$ then $Q_1 \cup Q_2 \in co\text{-}A$ and $\overline{Q_1} \in A$. So by induction, each element of Θ is in $A \cup co\text{-}A$. ∎

Define for each $Q \in \Theta$:

$$P(Q) = \begin{cases} 1 & \text{if } Q \in A \text{ and } \zeta \in Q \\ 0.5 & \text{if } Q \in A \text{ and } \zeta \notin Q \\ 0.5 & \text{if } Q \in Co\text{-}A \text{ and } \zeta \in Q \\ 0 & \text{if } Q \in Co\text{-}A \text{ and } \zeta \notin Q. \end{cases}$$

In light of lemma 13.22, P is uniquely defined and total over Θ. P also has properties (i), (ii), and (iii) of the proposition.

We now verify that P is a finitely additive probability measure on Θ. By lemma 13.21, the proposition follows. Number the conditions in the definition of P from 1 to 4. We must show that finite additivity is satisfied when Q_1, Q_2 satisfy each possible combination of such conditions. The combinations are $(1, 1), (1, 2), (1, 3), (1, 4), (2, 2), (2, 3), (2, 4), (3, 3), (3, 4), (4, 4)$. If $Q_1, Q_2 \in A$ then $Q_1 \cap Q_2 \neq \varnothing$, so finite additivity is trivially satisfied. This accounts for $(1, 1)$, $(1, 2), (2, 2)$. If $\zeta \in Q_1, \zeta \in Q_2$ then $Q_1 \cap Q_2 \neq \varnothing$, so finite additivity is satisfied. This accounts for $(1, 3), (3, 3)$. In case $(1, 4)$, $P(Q_1) = 1$ and $P(Q_2) = 0$. $Q_1 \cup Q_2$ satisfies condition 1 so $P(Q_1 \cup Q_2) = 1 = P(Q_1) + P(Q_2)$. In case $(2, 3)$, $P(Q_1) = 1/2$ and $P(Q_2) = 1/2$. $Q_1 \cup Q_2$ satisfies condition 1 so $P(Q_1 \cup Q_2) = 1 = P(Q_1) + P(Q_2)$. In case $(2, 4)$, $P(Q_1) = 1/2$ and $P(Q_2) = 0$. $Q_1 \cup Q_2$ satisfies condition 2 so $P(Q_1 \cup Q_2) = 1/2 = P(Q_1) + P(Q_2)$. In case $(3, 4)$, $P(Q_1) = 1/2$ and $P(Q_2) = 0$. $Q_1 \cup Q_2$ satisfies condition 3 so $P(Q_1 \cup Q_2) = 1/2 = P(Q_1) + P(Q_2)$. In case $(4, 4)$, $P(Q_1) = 0$ and $P(Q_2) = 0$. $Q_1 \cup Q_2$ satisfies condition 4 so $P(Q_1 \cup Q_2) = 0 = P(Q_1) + P(Q_2)$. ∎

Proposition 13.20 (with C. Juhl)

There is a merely finitely additive probability measure P defined on $2^{\mathcal{N}}$ such that h_{fin} is not refutable$_C$ in the limit with probability 1 in P.

Proof: Let $S = C_{h_{fin}}$. Define:

$$\Theta_0 = \{S\} \cup \{\mathcal{P} \in \Pi_2^B : S \subseteq \mathcal{P}\} \cup \{\{\varepsilon\} : \varepsilon \in S\}.$$

Let Θ be the least algebra containing all elements of Θ_0. Let $Q \in \Theta$. Then define:

$$Q \in A \Leftrightarrow \exists \mathcal{R} \in \Pi_2^B \text{ such that } S \subseteq \mathcal{R} \text{ and } \mathcal{R} - S \subseteq Q.$$

$$Q \in B \Leftrightarrow \exists \text{ finite } \mathcal{F} \subseteq S \text{ such that } S - \mathcal{F} \subseteq Q \text{ and } \mathcal{F} \subseteq \bar{Q}.$$

$$Q \in \text{co-}B \Leftrightarrow \bar{Q} \in B.$$

Now, define four subclasses of Θ:

$$\Gamma_1 = A \cap B \ (\textit{Fig. 13.25}).$$

$$\Gamma_2 = A \cap \text{co-}B \ (\textit{Fig. 13.26}).$$

$$\Gamma_3 = \bar{A} \cap B \ (\textit{Fig. 13.27}).$$

$$\Gamma_4 = \bar{A} \cap \text{co-}B \ (\textit{Fig. 13.28}).$$

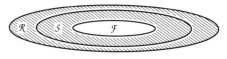

Figure 13.25

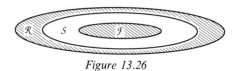

Figure 13.26

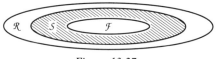

Figure 13.27

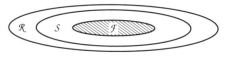

Figure 13.28

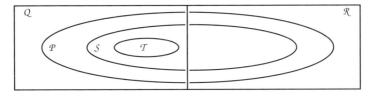

Figure 13.29

Lemma 13.23 (Closure laws)

For each Q, $\mathcal{R} \in \Theta$:

(a) *If $Q \in A$ and $\mathcal{R} \in A$ then $Q \cup \mathcal{R} \in A$.*

(b) *If $Q \in \bar{A}$ and $\mathcal{R} \in \bar{A}$ then $Q \cup \mathcal{R} \in \bar{A}$.*

(c) *If $Q \in A$ and $\mathcal{R} \in \bar{A}$ then $Q \cup \mathcal{R} \in A$.*

(d) *If $Q \in B$ and $\mathcal{R} \in B$ then $Q \cup \mathcal{R} \in B$.*

(e) *If $Q \in co\text{-}B$ and $\mathcal{R} \in co\text{-}B$ then $Q \cup \mathcal{R} \in co\text{-}B$.*

(f) *If $Q \in B$ and $\mathcal{R} \in co\text{-}B$ then $Q \cup \mathcal{R} \in B$.*

Proof: All these results are immediate except for (b). Let $co\text{-}\Theta_0$ denote the set of complements of elements of Θ_0. A *term* is a finite intersection of sets in $\Theta_0 \cup co\text{-}\Theta_0$. Each $Q \in \Theta$ can be expressed as a finite union of terms.

Suppose $Q \in \bar{A}$ and $\mathcal{R} \in \bar{A}$. Write $Q = \bigcup X$ and $\mathcal{R} = \bigcup Y$, where X and Y are finite sets of terms. In each term, we can intersect all the finite subsets[34] of S into one finite subset of S, all the complemented, finite subsets of S into one complement of a finite subset of S, all the Π_2^B supersets of S into one Π_2^B superset of S, and all the complements of Π_2^B supersets of S into complements of Π_2^B supersets of S, since the finite sets, the cofinite sets, the Π_2^B supersets of S and the complements of Π_2^B supersets of S are all closed under finite intersection. We may now assume that each term in $(X \cup Y)$ is expressed in this normal form.

Suppose for reductio that $Q \cup \mathcal{R} \in A$, so that $\bigcup (X \cup Y) \in A$ (*Fig. 13.29*). Suppose some term $\mathcal{T}$ in $X \cup Y$ involves an uncomplemented subset of S. Since $\bigcup (X \cup Y) \in A$, there is a $\mathcal{P} \in \Pi_2^B$ such that $\mathcal{P} - S \subseteq \bigcup (X \cup Y)$. But no element of $\mathcal{T}$ is in $\mathcal{P} - S$, so $\mathcal{P} - S \subseteq \bigcup ((X \cup Y) - \{\mathcal{T}\})$ and hence $\bigcup ((X \cup Y) - \{\mathcal{T}\}) \in A$.

Let K be the result of removing from $X \cup Y$ all terms in which uncomplemented subsets of S occur. Hence, $\bigcup K \in A$. The remaining terms in K are of one of two types: type (i) terms are of form $\mathcal{A} \cap \mathcal{B}$ and type (ii) terms are of form $\bar{\mathcal{A}} \cap \mathcal{B}$, where $\mathcal{A}$ is a Π_2^B superset of S and $\mathcal{B}$ is the complement of a subset of S. Since $\bar{\mathcal{A}} \subseteq \mathcal{B}$, $\bar{\mathcal{A}} \cap \mathcal{B} = \bar{\mathcal{A}}$. So type (ii) terms reduce to the form $\bar{\mathcal{A}}$, where $\mathcal{A}$ is a Π_2^B superset of S.

---

[34] These are all singletons.

Suppose for reductio that K consists of only type (ii) terms. Then $\bigcup K$ is a finite union of complements of Π_2^B supersets of S. So there are $G_0, \ldots, G_n \in \Pi_2^B$ such that for each $i \leq n$, $S \subseteq G_i$, and

$$\bigcup K = \bigcup_{i=0}^{n} \overline{G_i}.$$

Also let $\mathcal{Y}$ be an arbitrary Π_2^B superset of S. Since $S \notin \Pi_2^B$ and Π_2^B is closed under countable intersection, we have that

$$(\mathcal{Y} - S) - \bigcup K = (\mathcal{Y} - S) - \bigcup_{i=0}^{n} \overline{G_i} = \left(\mathcal{Y} \cap \bigcap_{i=0}^{n} G_i \right) - S \neq \varnothing.$$

So $(\mathcal{Y} - S)$ is not a subset of $\bigcup K$. Since $\mathcal{Y}$ is an arbitrary Π_2^B superset of S, $\bigcup K \notin A$. Hence, $\bigcup (X \cup Y) \notin A$. Contradiction. So K involves at least one type (i) term $\mathcal{A} \cap \mathcal{B}$. $\mathcal{A} \cap \mathcal{B} \in A$ since $\mathcal{A}$ is a Π_2^B superset of S and $\mathcal{A} - S \subseteq \mathcal{A} \cap \mathcal{B}$. But the term $\mathcal{A} \cap \mathcal{B}$ is either a subset of Q or of $\mathcal{R}$, so either Q or $\mathcal{R}$ is in A. Contradiction. ∎

Lemma 13.24

$\{\Gamma_1, \Gamma_2, \Gamma_3, \Gamma_4\}$ *partitions* Θ.

Proof: First it is established by exhaustion that the Γs are pairwise disjoint. Suppose $Q \in B \cap co\text{-}B$. Then $\exists$ finite $\mathcal{F}_1 \subseteq S$ such that $S - \mathcal{F}_1 \subseteq Q$ and $\mathcal{F}_1 \subseteq \overline{Q}$ and there is an $\mathcal{F}_2$ such that $S - \mathcal{F}_2 \subseteq \overline{Q}$ and $\mathcal{F}_2 \subseteq Q$. But since S is infinite and $\mathcal{F}_1, \mathcal{F}_2$ are finite, there is some $\varepsilon \in S - (\mathcal{F}_1 \cup \mathcal{F}_2)$ such that $\varepsilon \in Q$ and $\varepsilon \in \overline{Q}$, which is a contradiction. Hence $B \cap co\text{-}B = \varnothing$. Evidently, $A \cap \overline{A} = \varnothing$. Thus, the Γs are pairwise disjoint.

Now it is shown by induction that $\Theta \subseteq \Gamma_1 \cup \Gamma_2 \cup \Gamma_3 \cup \Gamma_4$. Evidently, $\Theta \subseteq A \cup \overline{A}$, so it suffices to show that $\Theta \subseteq B \cup co\text{-}B$.

Base case: For each $\varepsilon \in S$, $\{\varepsilon\} \in co\text{-}B$, choosing $\mathcal{F} = \{\varepsilon\}$. $S \in B$, choosing $\mathcal{F} = \varnothing$. Let $\mathcal{R}$ be a Π_2^B superset of S. Then $\mathcal{R} \in B$, choosing $\mathcal{F} = \varnothing$.

Induction: By definition, $Q \in B \Leftrightarrow \overline{Q} \in co\text{-}B$. Union is covered by the preceding lemma. ∎

Lemma 13.25

For each $Q \in \Theta$, there is a unique, finite $\mathcal{F} \subseteq S$ such that $S - \mathcal{F} \subseteq Q$ and $\mathcal{F} \subseteq \overline{Q}$ or $S - \mathcal{F} \subseteq \overline{Q}$ and $\mathcal{F} \subseteq Q$.

Proof: By the preceding lemma, $\{B, co\text{-}B\}$ partitions Θ. Suppose $Q \in B$. *Then* (*) $\exists \mathcal{F}$ such that $S - \mathcal{F} \subseteq Q$ and $\mathcal{F} \subseteq \overline{Q}$. Suppose distinct $\mathcal{F}, \mathcal{G}$ satisfy (*). Without loss of generality, suppose $\varepsilon \in \mathcal{F} - \mathcal{G}$. Since $\mathcal{F} \subseteq \overline{Q}$, $\varepsilon \in \overline{Q}$ and

$\varepsilon \in S$. Since $S - G \subseteq Q$ and $\varepsilon \in S - G$, $\varepsilon \in Q$. Contradiction. The same argument applied to $\overline{Q}$ works when $Q \in co\text{-}B$. ∎

If $Q \in \Theta$, then let $\mathcal{F}_Q$ denote the unique $\mathcal{F}$ guaranteed by lemma 13.25. Now I define a finitely additive probability measure P on Θ. Enumerate S as $\varepsilon[1]$, $\varepsilon[2], \dots, \varepsilon[n], \dots$. Let

$$P'(\{\varepsilon[i]\}) = 1/2^{i+1}.$$

For each finite $\mathcal{F} \subseteq S$ define:

$$P'(\mathcal{F}) = \sum_{\varepsilon \in \mathcal{F}} P'(\{\varepsilon\}).$$

Now for each $Q \in \Theta$, define:

$$P(Q) = \begin{cases} 1 - P'(\mathcal{F}_Q) & \text{if } Q \in \Gamma_1 \\ 0.5 + P'(\mathcal{F}_Q) & \text{if } Q \in \Gamma_2 \\ 0.5 - P'(\mathcal{F}_Q) & \text{if } Q \in \Gamma_3 \\ P'(\mathcal{F}_Q) & \text{if } Q \in \Gamma_4. \end{cases}$$

P is uniquely defined and total on Θ since the Γs partition Θ (lemma 13.24), and $\mathcal{F}_Q$ is uniquely defined on Θ (lemma 13.25). We need to show coherence over Θ.

Lemma 13.26

P is a finitely additive probability measure on Θ.

Proof: Let $Q, \mathcal{R} \in \Theta$. If both Q and $\mathcal{R}$ are in A or if both Q and $\mathcal{R}$ are in B, then $Q \cap \mathcal{R} \neq \varnothing$, so finite additivity is trivially satisfied. This leaves just the cases (a) $Q \in \Gamma_1$ and $\mathcal{R} \in \Gamma_4$; (b) $Q \in \Gamma_2$ and $\mathcal{R} \in \Gamma_3$; (c) $Q \in \Gamma_3$ and $\mathcal{R} \in \Gamma_4$; and finally (d) $Q \in \Gamma_4$ and $\mathcal{R} \in \Gamma_4$.

In case (a) (*Fig. 13.30*), $P(Q) = 1 - P'(\mathcal{F}_Q)$ and $P(\mathcal{R}) = P'(\mathcal{F}_\mathcal{R})$. By lemma 13.23, $Q \cup \mathcal{R} \in \Gamma_1$ so $P(Q \cup \mathcal{R}) = 1 - P'(\mathcal{F}_{Q \cup \mathcal{R}})$. Suppose $Q \cap \mathcal{R} = \varnothing$. (Note:

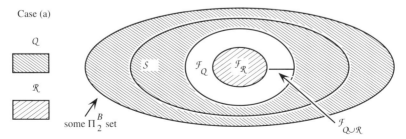

Figure 13.30

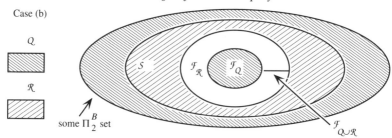

Figure 13.31

therefore Q and R cannot overlap in Figure 13.30.) Then $\mathcal{F}_R \subseteq \mathcal{F}_Q$. So $\mathcal{F}_{Q \cup R} = \mathcal{F}_Q - \mathcal{F}_R$ and hence $P'(\mathcal{F}_{Q \cup R}) = P'(\mathcal{F}_Q) - P'(\mathcal{F}_R)$. So $P(Q \cup R) = 1 - P'(\mathcal{F}_{Q \cup R}) = 1 - [P'(\mathcal{F}_Q) - P'(\mathcal{F}_R)] = P(Q) + P(R)$.

In case (b) (*Fig. 13.31*), $P(Q) = 1/2 + P'(\mathcal{F}_Q)$ and $P(R) = 1/2 - P'(\mathcal{F}_R)$. By lemma 13.23, $Q \cup R \in \Gamma_1$, so $P(Q \cup R) = 1 - P'(\mathcal{F}_{Q \cup R})$. Suppose $Q \cap R = \emptyset$. Then $\mathcal{F}_Q \subseteq \mathcal{F}_R$. So $\mathcal{F}_{Q \cup R} = \mathcal{F}_R - \mathcal{F}_Q$ and hence $P'(\mathcal{F}_{R \cup R}) = P'(\mathcal{F}_R) - P'(\mathcal{F}_Q)$. So $P(Q \cup R) = 1 - P'(\mathcal{F}_{Q \cup R}) = 1 - [P'(\mathcal{F}_R) - P'(\mathcal{F}_Q)] = 1/2 + 1/2 + P'(\mathcal{F}_Q) - P'(\mathcal{F}_R) = P(Q) + P(R)$.

In case (c) (*Fig. 13.32*), $P(Q) = 1/2 - P'(\mathcal{F}_Q)$ and $P(R) = P'(\mathcal{F}_R)$. By lemma 13.23, $Q \cup R \in \Gamma_3$ so $P(Q \cup R) = 1/2 - P'(\mathcal{F}_{Q \cup R})$. Suppose $Q \cap R = \emptyset$. Then $\mathcal{F}_R \subseteq \mathcal{F}_Q$. So $\mathcal{F}_{Q \cup R} = \mathcal{F}_Q - \mathcal{F}_R$ and hence $P'(\mathcal{F}_{Q \cup R}) = P'(\mathcal{F}_Q) - P'(\mathcal{F}_R)$. Hence, $P(Q \cup R) = 1/2 - P'(\mathcal{F}_{Q \cup R}) = 1/2 - [P'(\mathcal{F}_Q) - P'(\mathcal{F}_R)] = 1/2 - P'(\mathcal{F}_Q) + P'(\mathcal{F}_R) = P(Q) + P(R)$.

In case (d) (*Fig. 13.33*), $P(Q) = P'(\mathcal{F}_Q)$ and $P(R) = P'(\mathcal{F}_R)$. By lemma 13.23, $Q \cup R \in \Gamma_4$ so $P(Q \cup R) = P'(\mathcal{F}_{Q \cup R})$. Suppose $Q \cap R = \emptyset$. Then since $Q = \mathcal{F}_Q$ and $R = \mathcal{F}_R$, $\mathcal{F}_Q \cap \mathcal{F}_R = \emptyset$ and $\mathcal{F}_{Q \cup R} = \mathcal{F}_Q \cup \mathcal{F}_R$. Hence, $P'(\mathcal{F}_{Q \cup R}) = P'(\mathcal{F}_Q) + P'(\mathcal{F}_R) = P(Q) + P(R)$. ■

By lemma 13.26 and lemma 13.21, there exists a finitely additive probability measure P'' extending P to the power set of $\mathcal{N}$. Now, let α be an arbitrary assessment method. Let $Stab_0(\alpha) = \{\varepsilon : \alpha$ stabilizes to 0 on $\varepsilon\}$. Let $\mathcal{F}ail_{\bar{S}}(\alpha) = \overline{Stab_0(\alpha)} - S$, let $\mathcal{F}ail_S(\alpha) = Stab_0(\alpha) \cap S$, and let $\mathcal{F}ail(\alpha) = \mathcal{F}ail_{\bar{S}}(\alpha) \cup \mathcal{F}ail_S(\alpha)$. Since $C_h = S$, $\mathcal{F}ail(\alpha)$ is the set of all data streams on which α fails to refute$_C$ h in the limit, either by stabilizing to 0 on an element

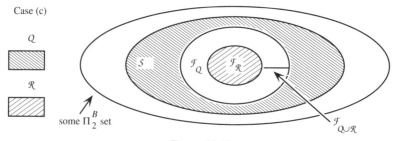

Figure 13.32

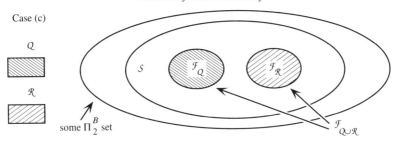

Figure 13.33

of C_h or by failing to stabilize to zero on an element of $\overline{C_h}$. Since h_{fin} is not refutable$_C$ in the limit (cf. chapter 3) we have that $\mathcal{F}ail(\alpha) \neq \varnothing$. We need to show that $P''(\mathcal{F}ail(\alpha)) > 0$. Case I: $\mathcal{F}ail_S(\alpha) \neq \varnothing$. Let $\varepsilon \in \mathcal{F}ail_S(\alpha)$. Then $\varepsilon \in S$, so for some i, $\varepsilon = \varepsilon[i]$. So $P''(\{\varepsilon\}) = P'(\{\varepsilon[i]\}) = 1/2^{i+1} > 0$. Case II: $\mathcal{F}ail_S(\alpha) = \varnothing$. Then since $\mathcal{F}ail(\alpha) \neq \varnothing$, we have $\mathcal{F}ail_{\bar{S}}(\alpha) \neq \varnothing$. Since $\mathcal{F}ail_S(\alpha) = \varnothing$, (a) $S \subseteq \overline{Stab_0(\alpha)}$. Also, (b) $\overline{Stab_0(\alpha)} \in \Pi_2^B$, since we can define:

$$\varepsilon \in \overline{Stab_0(\alpha)} \Leftrightarrow \forall n \,\exists m > n, \alpha(h_{fin}, \varepsilon|m) \neq 0.$$

Then since $\mathcal{F}ail_{\bar{S}}(\alpha) = \overline{Stab_0(\alpha)} - S$, we have that $\mathcal{F}ail_{\bar{S}}(\alpha) \in A$. Since $S \subseteq \overline{Fail_{\bar{S}}(\alpha)}$, $\mathcal{F}ail_{\bar{S}}(\alpha) \in co\text{-}B$. So $\mathcal{F}ail_{\bar{S}}(\alpha) \in \Gamma_2$. So by the definition of P'', $P''(\mathcal{F}ail_{\bar{S}}(\alpha)) = 0.5 > 0$. So no method α can refute$_C$ h_{fin} in the limit given 2^ω with probability 1 in P''. ∎

Exercises

13.1. Prove proposition 13.2.

13.2 Prove proposition 13.1. (Hint: let $Q_0, Q_1, \ldots, Q_n, \ldots$ be an ω-sequence of mutually disjoint Borel sets sets.) Use the fact that

$$\bigcup_{i=0}^{\infty} Q_i = \overline{\bigcap_{n=0}^{\infty} \left(\overline{\bigcup_{i=0}^{n} Q_i} \right)}.$$

Then observe that the intersection is over a downward nested sequence of Borel sets and apply continuity to the probability of the intersection. On the other side, let $Q_0, Q_1, \ldots, Q_n, \ldots$ be a downward nested sequence of Borel sets. Use the fact that

$$\bigcap_{i=0}^{\infty} Q_i = Q_0 - \bigcup_{i=0}^{\infty} (Q_i - Q_{i+1}).$$

Then apply countable additivity to express the probability of the union as a limit of finite sums.)

13.3. For each $r \in (0, 1)$, let P_r be the probability measure on 2^ω corresponding to independent flips of a coin that comes up 1 on each trial with probability r. Suppose that Fred's initial joint probability measure P is a mixture of finitely many P_rs. Is Fred reliable concerning the hypothesis constructed in proposition 13.5?

13.4 Show that gradual identification can be accomplished with probability 1. (Hint: apply proposition 13.17 to the degrees of approximation of each hypothesis.)

13.5. Define

> P *is a countably additive probability measure on* Δ_1^B $\Leftrightarrow$
>
> (1') $\forall S \in \Delta_1^B$, $P(S) \geq 1$,
>
> (2') $P(\mathcal{N}) = 1$, *and*
>
> (3') $\forall$ *sequence* $S_0, S_1, \ldots, S_n, \ldots$ *of pairwise disjoint* Δ_1^B *sets,*
>
> $$\bigcup_{n=0}^{\infty} S_n \in \Delta_1^B \Rightarrow P\left(\bigcup_{n=0}^{\infty} S_n\right) = \sum_{n=0}^{\infty} P(S_n).$$

Let P be a countably additive probability measure on Δ_1^B. Let $S \in Bo$. Define:

$$\Gamma(S) = \left\{ \xi \in (\Delta_1^B)^\omega : S \subseteq \bigcup_{i \in \omega} \xi_i \right\}.$$

$$P^*(S) = \inf_{\xi \in \Gamma(S)} \sum_{i \in \omega} P(\xi_i).$$

P^* is called the *outer measure* generated by P. It can be shown that[35]

> *If P is a countably additive probability measure on* Δ_1^B, *then P^* restricted to Bo is the unique,*
> *countably additive probability measure on Bo such that* $P \subseteq P^*$.

Using this result, prove proposition 13.16. (Hint: use exercise 13.1.)

[35] (Royden 1988): 295, theorem 8.

14

Experiment and Causal Inference

We'll never know until we try.

1. Introduction

Until now, I have represented the scientist as a passive observer who watches the world pass before his fixed and undirectable gaze. But in fact, an experiment is not just a question put to nature, it is an *act* that changes the state of the world under study in some way. This chapter examines active, experimental science from a logical reliabilist point of view. Since the issues that arise are more complex, the development will be correspondingly more heuristic and suggestive than in the preceding chapters. What follows may be thought of more as an outline than as a fully articulated theory.

Since Aristotle's time, empirical science has aimed at discovering necessary laws and causal mechanisms rather than merely contingent generalizations. Does scientific method measure up to this aim? Scholastic realists held the view that essences may be observed directly in virtue of a special power of the mind, and that this ability accounts for the reliable discovery of necessary truths. Nominalistic scholastics like William of Ockham undercut this theory by denying that essences could function in causal accounts of perception. Methodology was then faced with explaining how *necessary* conclusions can be drawn from *contingent* evidence if the natures grounding the necessity are not given in perception. For example, even if all ravens ever observed are black, the essence or DNA of ravens may indeed admit of other colors that *happen* not to have been realized for accidental reasons.

Francis Bacon thought that experimentation could bridge the gap between contingent data and modal conclusions. The manipulation of nature was supposed by him to somehow provide access to essences rather than to mere accidents. David Hume held, to the contrary, that necessary connections in things could never be determined from observed regularities in merely contingent data and concluded on empiricist grounds that if necessary connections are anything at all, they are habitual feelings of expectation in our own minds. From the point of view developed in preceding chapters, a more measured opinion than either of these is appropriate: the prospects for reliable causal inference, whether from passive or from experimental data, depend on what the scientist assumes a priori. This chapter will present a learning-theoretic paradigm for causal inference in which the significance of such assumptions can be assessed.

2. Systems

Scientists often speak in terms of *variables*, or *attributes* such as weight and height, and *values* of variables such as eighty pounds or six feet. Some variables are *observable* (e.g., height and weight) and others are not (intelligence, intentions). The latter are said to be *latent* or *theoretical*. Some variables can have their values altered at will by the scientist (e.g., the position of a knob). They are *manipulable*. An *assignment* maps various variables to various values. When an assignment is total (i.e., when it assigns values to all the variables) the assignment is called a *system state* (*Fig. 14.1*).

A *system* is something that is always in a unique state at each time, but that may change its state through time. As in preceding chapters, I assume that time is discrete, so that I may speak of one system state following another. I also assume that the nature of the system may prevent some states from following others. A system, then, specifies a *state transition relation S* between states. If s, r are states, then $S(s, r)$ may be read as: if the system is in state s at stage n, then the system may possibly be in state r at stage $n + 1$ (*Fig. 14.2*). The sense of possibility here is intended to be physical, causal, or metaphysical rather than epistemological. I do not assume that the state transition relation is *deterministic*, in the sense that exactly one state succeeds each given state. Even if the real world works that way (and physicists now say that it does not), a localized system of the sort we are often interested in studying (e.g., a social system) may be bumped by outside influences that are not reflected in the system variables, leading to indeterminism. I do assume, however, that the system has no memory. The possible successors of a given state are always the same, no matter how many times that state occurs. Nonetheless, we can model cases in which this assumption seems to fail by introducing latent variables whose values record the system's memories.

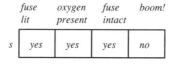

Figure 14.1

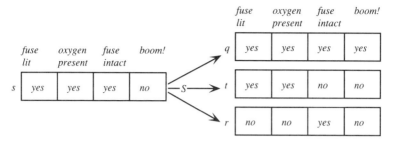

Figure 14.2

Altogether, then, a system $\mathfrak{S}$ specifies a set X of variables, a set V_x of values for each variable $x \in X$, subsets O and M of X, representing the observable and manipulable variables, respectively, and finally a state transition relation S.

The transition relation tells us which states can possibly follow other states. We can imagine chaining along from one possible successor state to the next to obtain finite or infinite possible *trajectories* of $\mathfrak{S}$ through time. When $\mathfrak{S}$ is indeterministic, these trajectories can branch off from one another toward the future. All of this is made clearer by way of a few, simple examples.

Example 14.1   An *n*-bulb marquee

Think of the usual cascading light effect once commonly observed on motion picture theaters. The effect can be produced by wiring each successive bulb to adopt at stage $k + 1$ the state of the preceding bulb at stage k (*Fig. 14.3*). The following system represents a marquee effect involving exactly n lightbulbs in a row. Let variables $\{x_1, \ldots, x_n\}$ be given, let each variable be dichotomous so that for each i from 1 to n, $V_{x_i} = \{0, 1\}$, and finally let:

$$\mathfrak{M}_n(s, r) \Leftrightarrow \forall i \text{ such that } 1 \leq i < n, s(x_i) = r(x_{i+1}).$$

The system imposes no restriction on the successive states of the first lightbulb. This can be interpreted as letting the first bulb be governed by a

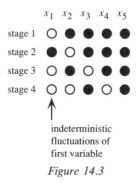

Figure 14.3

genuinely indeterministic process, or as saying that the first bulb's behavior is determined by factors outside the system. In either case, what we observe is some pattern of winking in the leftmost bulb, with each of these winks being cascaded across the other bulbs. It is possible that the pattern adopted by the first bulb is to never go on at all, in which case the marquee will appear to be broken or switched off even though it is in proper working order all the while.

Some bulbs may be painted black so that their status cannot be observed, and some bulbs may have buttons permitting the scientist to *force* them to light or to remain dark for as long as the respective button is depressed. Then O is the set of bulbs that are not painted black and M is the set of bulbs equipped with buttons.

Example 14.2   Cycles

Suppose that the marquee is wrapped around a cylinder and the first bulb is wired to the last bulb the same way the $n + 1$th bulb is wired to the nth bulb. Then the marquee is locked for eternity in some fixed, orbiting pattern, though nothing about the system itself determines what that pattern is. The following system on the same variables and values has just this character:

$$\mathfrak{C}_n(s, r) \Leftrightarrow r(x_1) = s(x_n) \text{ and } \forall i \text{ such that } 1 \leq i < n, s(x_i) = r(x_{i+1}).$$

In the special case when $n = 2$ we have the following, intriguing system (*Fig. 14.4*):

$$\mathfrak{C}_2(s, r) \Leftrightarrow r(x_1) = s(x_2) \text{ and } s(x_1) = r(x_2).$$

$\mathfrak{C}_2$ represents, for example, the commonplace situation in which two siblings must choose among two ice-cream cones and each sibling prefers the cone last preferred by the other sibling.

Example 14.3   Finite state automata

Let M be a *DFA* with input–output alphabet A, states Q, output assignment δ, and transition function τ (cf. chapter 8). Let $\mathfrak{M}_M$ be a system with variables

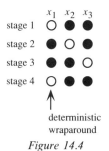

Figure 14.4

$\{q, x, o\}$, so that $V_q = Q$ and $V_o = V_x = A$ and for all s, r,

$$\mathfrak{M}_M(s, r) \Leftrightarrow r(q) = \tau(s(q), s(x)) \text{ and } r(o) = \delta(\tau(s(q), s(x))).$$

The variable q corresponds to M's current state, the variable x corresponds to M's next input, and the variable o corresponds to M's current output. $\mathfrak{M}_M$ acts through time as though M were being fed inputs from an unaccountable, indeterministic source. In the happiest situation, q, x, and o are all observable and manipulable. In a more typical situation, the scientist can manipulate only the next input to M and can observe only the current output of M because an opaque cover hides the works of M (as with a vending machine). When the workings of the machine are hidden in this way, the observable variables will appear to reflect "memories" that can surprise scientists who think they have discovered a simple repeating pattern in the observable variables. In a hybrid situation, the works of the machine sit under glass, so that the scientist can see the effects on the machine state of manipulating the input but cannot directly intervene in the gears and levers.

Example 14.4   Structural equation systems

Let w, x, y, z be variables taking real values. In economics, biology, and the social sciences, there is much interest in systems known as *linear causal models* or as *structural equation systems*. Often, such a model is presented as a system E of linear equations, such as the following:

$$x = 5y + z + 7$$
$$y = w.$$

Variables that occur only on the right-hand sides of these equations are said to be *exogenous*, and the others are said to be *endogenous*. This notation indicates that the form of the equations matters. If we were to solve the first equation for y so as to obtain the arithmetically equivalent system E',

$$y = (x - z - 7)/5 = w,$$

we would not have an equivalent structural equation model.[1] This sort of claim makes sense if the structural equations in E are really shorthand for the following *system* $\mathfrak{E}$:

$$\mathfrak{E}(s, r) \Leftrightarrow r(x) = 5s(y) + s(z) + 7 \text{ and } r(y) = s(w).$$

In system $\mathfrak{E}$, the equations define functions that constrain the values of some variables at stage $n + 1$ in terms of the values of other variables at the

[1] Simon (1953).

preceding stage. On this view, there is no difficulty interpreting the following structural equation system F:

$$x = 4y$$

$$y = 2x.$$

In arithmetic, F entails that $x = x/8$, so $x = 0$. But if these equations represent a system $\mathfrak{F}$ in the manner just described, we have the much less trivial situation in which

$$\mathfrak{F}(s, r) \Leftrightarrow r(x) = 4s(y) \text{ and } r(y) = 2s(x).$$

This tells us that the variables are involved in a cycle, in which the subsequent value of x is a function of the prior value of y, and the subsequent value of y depends on the prior value of x. This entails no constraint on possible values of x at a given time; certainly not that $x = 0$ at every stage in the evolution of $\mathfrak{F}$.

3. Causation and Manipulation

To consider the sorts of issues raised by causal inference for learning theory, we need at least a sketch of what a nonprobabilistic, learning-theoretic paradigm for causal inference might look like. For this, we require some logical model of deterministic causation that is both sequential and explicit enough to be coupled with a learning-theoretic model of reliability. The following model is based on two ideas, manipulability and J. L. Mackie's[2] proposal that a cause is a necessary element of a sufficient set of conditions.

The proposal that causality is manipulability doesn't seem very promising because we all concede that causation obtains in places we cannot reach, just as we admit that things exist that cannot be seen. But the objection can be sidestepped if we take causality to be a matter of the results of *ideal* manipulations that we may not be able to perform ourselves. If there is a small hole in a fence through which we can see a faucet, it still makes sense to say that the position of the faucet causes water to flow or not to flow even though it is in some sense impossible to get one's hand on the faucet. In this case, manipulating the faucet would be an *ideal* manipulation from the point of view of the observer beyond the fence. The causal relation, on this proposal, is grounded by ideal rather than by experimental manipulability.

Even ideal manipulability is insufficient to account for the asymmetry of causation, if one's logical model of manipulation is too simplistic. For example, consider the case of the sun's altitude causing the length of a shadow to change (*Fig. 14.5*). On a simplistic approach, a causal relation is a *fixed* functional

---

[2] Mackie (1974).

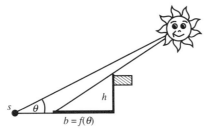

Figure 14.5

relation $f(x) = y$ between solar altitude (measured from a point s painted on the schoolyard) and shadow length and to manipulate one or another variable is merely to provide different arguments either to f or to its inverse f^{-1}. If f is 1–1 (as it is in this case) then we immediately have the paradox that the shadow's length uniquely determines the sun's elevation (modulo the functional relationship) just as the sun's altitude uniquely determines the shadow's length, so the causal relation is symmetrical, contrary to what most people think.

The solution is that the relationship between the variables x and y is itself a function of *which* variables are manipulated, so that when solar altitude is manipulated (by jacking up one side of the schoolyard to which the pole is attached) the function f from altitude to shadow length obtains, and when the shadow length is modified (by holding up a stick in just the right place to extend the shadow) no variation in solar altitude is observed so a constant function $g \neq f^{-1}$ obtains (*Fig. 14.6*). The ontology of systems just introduced is rich enough to support an asymmetrical account of manipulability of the sort just described if we add to it a precise account of what manipulation is. Consider the marquee system. Intuitively, manipulation should work like this. If we manipulate light 0 at stage n, then light i's state at stage $n + i$ is uniquely determined to be the same as the state of light 0 at stage n. If we manipulate light i at stage n, anything may happen with light 1 at stage $n + i$. So the second relation is not the inverse of the former, since the former relation is 1–1 and the second relation is one-many.

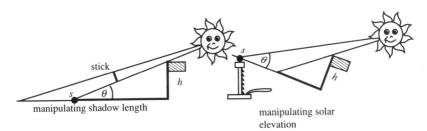

Figure 14.6

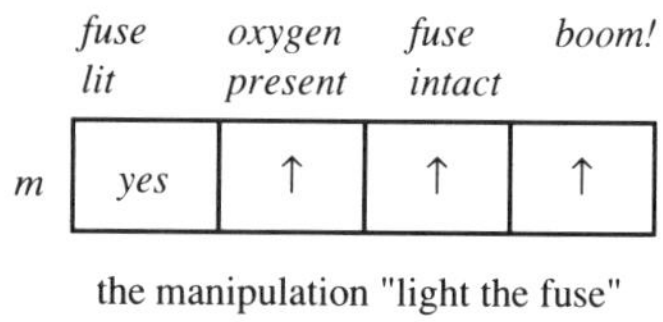

	fuse lit	oxygen present	fuse intact	boom!
m	*yes*	↑	↑	↑

the manipulation "light the fuse"

Figure 14.7

Formally, *manipulations* and *outcomes* are (possibly partial) variable assignments. The idea is that a system state specifies the values of all variables at a time, while a manipulation specifies special values for special variables that the scientist orders his laboratory to "make so" and an outcome tells the scientist which values some specified variables have at a given time (*Fig. 14.7*).

It remains to specify how the trajectory of the system is affected when the lab carries out this order. I will assume the simplest account imaginable. Suppose that ℭ is in state *s* at stage *n*, and that we perform manipulation *m* at stage *n*. The effect of this manipulation is to replace values of variables in *s* with the values indicated in *m* and then to allow ℭ to proceed in its usual way to the next state as though the modified state were its current state. In the marquee system, if the "on" button for light 3 is depressed, light 4 is on at the next stage and light 5 is on at the next stage, etc., just as though light 3 had come on naturally. I call this the *state substitution* model of manipulation (*Fig. 14.8*). It is worth being a bit more precise about how it works. Let *subst(s, m)* be the state that results when the values specified in *m* are substituted for the corresponding variables in *s*, leaving all other values unaltered. Then we may define ℭ(*s, r*|*m*) (read as: *r possibly succeeds s given manipulation m*) ⇔ ℭ(*subst(s, m), r*).

It would be shortsighted to suppose that the effects of manipulations are felt immediately. For example, an evil scientist might force a subject to listen to Wagner's *Ring der Nibelungen* for a long period, carefully observing for ill effects for some time afterward. This experiment involves both a (very) extended manipulation and an extended outcome. An *extended manipulation* or *outcome*

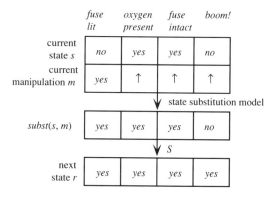

Figure 14.8

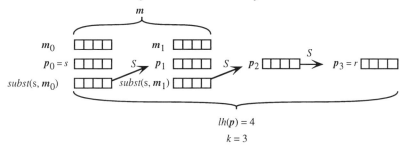

Figure 14.9

is therefore nothing but a finite sequence of manipulations or outcomes. We may now consider what happens with a given time lag after the onset of an extended manipulation m (Fig. 14.9).[3]

$\mathfrak{S}_k(s, r|m) \Leftrightarrow$ *there is a finite sequence p of states such that*

(1) $lh(p) = k + 1$,

(2) $\forall i < lh(m)$, $\mathfrak{S}(subst(p_i, m_i), p_{i+1})$,

(3) $p_k = r$, *and*

(4) $\forall i$ *such that* $lh(m) \leq i < k$, $\mathfrak{S}(p_i, p_{i+1})$.

$\mathfrak{S}_k(s, r|m)$ may be read: *r possibly follows from s with time lag k given m.* Let o be an outcome. Define $\mathfrak{S}_k(s, o|m)$ to hold just in case for some state r extending o, $\mathfrak{S}_k(s, r|m)$. If o is an extended outcome of length n, then $\mathfrak{S}_k(s, o|m)$ holds just in case for each $i < lh(o)$, $\mathfrak{S}_{k+i}(s, o_i|m)$. It may be that but for each result o' of changing the value of a variable assigned in o, $\mathfrak{S}_k(s, o|m)o$, $\mathfrak{S}_k(s, o'|m)$. Then I say that m *is causally sufficient for o with time lag k given s*. If the relationship holds regardless of s, then m *is causally sufficient for o with time lag k*, and I write $m \geq_k o$ in $\mathfrak{S}$. Use of the symbol $\geq$ suggests that causal sufficiency is transitive. In fact it is *temporally transitive*, in the following sense:

Proposition 14.5

If $m \geq_i n$ in $\mathfrak{S}$ and $n \geq_j o$ in $\mathfrak{S}$ then $m \geq_{i+j} o$ in $\mathfrak{S}$.

Proof: Exercise 14.1.　　　　　　　　　　　　　　　　　　　　■

Say that

m *expands* $n \Leftrightarrow lh(n) \leq lh(m)$ *and* $\forall i < lh(n)$, $n_i \subseteq m_i$.

---

[3] In the following definitions, it is good to remember that the first position in p is p_0, so the last position in p is one less than the length of p.

Then causal sufficiency is also *monotone*, in the sense that an unextended expansion of a causally sufficient, unextended manipulation is a causally sufficient manipulation.

Proposition 14.6

For all unextended manipulations m, n, if $m \geq_k o$ in $\mathfrak{S}$ and n expands m then $n \geq_k o$ in $\mathfrak{S}$.

Proof: Exercise 14.2.   ∎

Causal sufficiency is not necessarily monotone when extended manipulations are considered. Intuitively, it may be that the system is guaranteed to stabilize to an equilibrium under some conditions, but later manipulations can disturb this natural equilibrium.

Proposition 14.7

$\exists \mathfrak{S}$, m, n such that n extends m and $m \geq_k o$ in $\mathfrak{S}$ but $n \not\geq_k o$ in $\mathfrak{S}$.

Proof: Let $V = \{0, 1\}$, let $X = \{x, y\}$, and define system $\mathfrak{W}$ as follows (*Fig. 14.10*):

$\mathfrak{W}(s, r) \Leftrightarrow$ *if $\exists z \in X$ such that $s(z) = 1$ then $\exists z \in X$ such that $s(z) = 1$ and $r(z) = 0$ and $\forall u \in X - \{z\}, s(u) = r(u)$.*

Then the manipulation $(\varnothing)$ is causally sufficient for $x = 0$ with time lag 2, but the expanded manipulation $(\varnothing, \{(y, 1)\})$ is not causally sufficient for $x = 0$ with time lag 2.   ∎

For another example of a failure of extended monotonicity, consider an automaton with a dead state or sink in its transition diagram. Suppose that by stage *n*, we have fed inputs sufficient to send the automaton into a dead state. These inputs determine the dead state for every successive state. But if we later intervene and bump the automaton out of the dead state, the dead state may no longer be determined at the subsequent stage.

It may happen that not every aspect of an extended manipulation *m* is *necessary* for *m* to be causally sufficient for some outcome *o*, in the

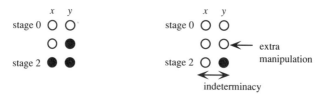

Figure 14.10

following sense. Let $(x = a)$ denote the partial assignment $\{(x, a)\}$. Then define:

> $(x = a)$ *at i is necessary for the causal sufficiency of **m** for* $(y = b)$ *with time lag k in* $\mathfrak{S} \Leftrightarrow$
>
> (1) $\mathbf{m} \geq_k (y = b)$ *in* $\mathfrak{S}$ *and*
>
> (2) $\mathbf{m}_i(x) = a$ *and*
>
> (3) *If **n** is just like **m** except that* $\mathbf{n}_i(x)$ *is undefined,*[4]
>
> *then* $\mathbf{n} \not\geq_k (y = b)$ *in* $\mathfrak{S}$.

Let x, y be variables and let a, b be values. Then define:

> $(x = a)$ *is a contributing causal factor of* $(y = b)$ *with time lag k in* $\mathfrak{S} \Leftrightarrow \exists$ *extended manipulation **m**,* $\exists i < lh(\mathbf{m})$ *such that* $(x = a)$ *at i is necessary for the causal sufficiency of **m** for* $(y = b)$ *with time lag k in* $\mathfrak{S}$.

I will abbreviate this important relation as $(x = a) \rightarrow_k (y = b)$ in $\mathfrak{S}$. In other words, a contributing causal factor is a *necessary* part of a *causally sufficient* condition. This is a manipulability version of J. L. Mackie's INUS account of causation, which states that a cause is an insufficient but necessary part of an unnecessary but sufficient condition.[5] Causal sufficiency corresponds to idealized control of *all* relevant factors. Causal contribution corresponds to the more usual sort of causal claim that is subject to *ceteris paribus* conditions, since a causal contributor is not guaranteed to yield its effect unless other contributing causes are held at appropriate values.

Causal contribution is not temporally transitive, since the course of nature may close off some values of an intermediate variable that are relevant to the value of a third variable. So even though these values may be relevant to the value of the third variable when they occur, they do not occur unless they are forced to occur by manipulation. This idea is made precise in the following proposition.

Proposition 14.8

> $\exists \mathfrak{S}$ *in which* $(x = 0) \rightarrow_1 (y = 0)$ *and* $(y = 0) \rightarrow_1 (z = 0)$
> *but not* $(x = 0) \rightarrow_2 (z = 0)$.

Proof: Let $X = \{x, y, z\}$ and let $V = \{0, 1, 2\}$. Define:

$$\mathfrak{S}(s, r) \Leftrightarrow r(z) = g(s(y)) \text{ and } r(y) = f(s(x)),$$

where $f(n) = 0$ if $n = 0$ and $f(n) = 1$ otherwise and $g(n) = 2$ if $n = 2$ and

---

[4] It is assumed that if $\mathbf{m}_i = \{(x, a)\}$ then $\mathbf{n}_i = \emptyset$, so that $\mathbf{n}$ is no shorter than $\mathbf{m}$. Otherwise, the later entries in $\mathbf{n}$ would be out of step with $\mathbf{m}$.

[5] Mackie (1974).

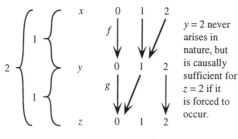

Figure 14.11

$g(n) = 0$ otherwise (*Fig. 14.11*). Then $(x = 0) \rightarrow_1 (y = 0)$ and $(y = 0) \rightarrow_1 (z = 0)$ but it is not the case that $(x = 0) \rightarrow_2 (z = 0)$ because $(z = 0)$ is determined in two steps regardless of the value of x.   ■

On the other hand, temporal transitivity *does* hold when all variables are Boolean (cf. exercise 14.4), so the example in the proof of proposition 14.8 is the simplest of its kind.

4. Variable Causation

For all that has been said, it may be that one extended manipulation determines a unique outcome with time lag k, but some other manipulation of the same variables at the same times does not. For example, manipulating the barnyard gate to the closed position determines the vicinity of the cows to within a distance of fifty meters ten hours hence, but setting the gate to the open position does not. It may also happen that every setting of a given collection of variables at appropriate times determines some value. A *schedule* is a sequence of sets of variables to be manipulated or observed. An extended manipulation or outcome *instantiates* a given schedule just in case it assigns values to all and only the specified variables at the specified times. Schedule M is *causally sufficient* for schedule O with time lag k just in case each instantiation of M is causally sufficient for some instantiation of O with time lag k. Then I write $M \geq_k O$ in $\mathfrak{S}$. If $O = (\{x\})$ then I write $M \geq_k x$ in $\mathfrak{S}$. Also define:

> x at i is necessary for the causal sufficiency of M for y with time lag k in $\mathfrak{S} \Leftrightarrow$
>
> (1) $M \geq_k y$ in $\mathfrak{S}$ and
>
> (2) $x \in M_i$ and
>
> (3) $\forall N$, if N is just like M except that $x \notin N_i$, then $N \not\geq_k y$ in $\mathfrak{S}$.
>
> $x \rightarrow_k y \Leftrightarrow \exists M \exists i < lh(M)$ such that x at i is necessary for the causal sufficiency of M for y with time lag k in $\mathfrak{S}$.

Again, the relation $M \geq_k O$ is temporally transitive but the relation $x \rightarrow_k y$ is not and $M \geq_k O$ is monotone for unextended schedules but not for extended ones. Also, we have that a variable whose value never changes except by direct manipulation has no variables as contributing causal factors, since its value does not functionally depend on the values of any set of variables, even though every schedule determines its value. In a causal contribution relationship among variables, wiggling the value of the cause has to wiggle the effect, at least for some values.

Some examples will clarify the definitions. Recall the 10-bulb marquee system:

$$\mathfrak{M}_{10}(s, r) \Leftrightarrow \forall i \text{ such that } 1 \leq i < 10, r(x_i) = s(x_{i+1}),$$

where $X(\mathfrak{M}_{10}) = \{x_1, \ldots, x_{10}\}$ and $V(\mathfrak{M}_{10}) = \{0, 1\}$. Imagine that a control room has two buttons for each lightbulb on the marquee. Depressing one button makes the light go on and pressing the other makes it go off. Pressing neither permits the signal from the preceding bulb to dictate the state of the bulb in question. An example of a manipulation schedule for this system would be to manipulate bulb 1 for three successive times: $M = (\{x_1\}, \{x_1\}, \{x_1\})$. An extended manipulation instantiating this schedule would be to hold the "on" button for bulb 1 down for three consecutive stages:

$$m = (\{(x_1 = 1)\}, \{(x_1 = 1)\}, \{(x_1 = 1)\}).$$

This manipulation would produce a white streak of length 3 that would then propagate to the right and off the face of the marquee as new noise feeds in from the first bulb (*Fig. 14.12*).

An example of an observation schedule would be to observe bulbs 7, 8, and 9 simultaneously and then to observe bulbs 8, 9, and 10 at the following stage: $O = (\{x_7, x_8, x_9\}, \{x_8, x_9, x_{10}\})$. It turns out that if we wait eight stages after the onset of the extended manipulation before making these observations, we observe two successive snapshots of the streak we generated earlier, first in positions 7, 8, 9 and then in positions 8, 9, 10. In fact, the observed instance of O is uniquely determined no matter what instance of M is tried, so we have $M \geq_8 O$. On the other hand, if we wait for nine steps rather than eight, then the indeterministic influence of the first bulb will propagate into the region of

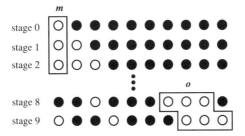

Figure 14.12

Figure 14.13

our observations so that M is not causally sufficient for O with lag 9. It is also evident from the structure of the system that for each i such that $0 \leq i \leq 10$, $x_1 \rightarrow_i x_{i+1}$. The relation $\rightarrow$ is temporally transitive in this particular system, so all of its contributing causal relations are uniquely determined by the directed graph depicted in *Figure 14.13*, in which each arc represents the relation $\rightarrow_1$.

Next, consider the 2-cycle system involving just the variables $\{x, y\}$ taking values in $\{0, 1\}$:

$$\mathfrak{C}_2(s, r) \Leftrightarrow r(x) = s(y) \text{ and } s(x) = r(y).$$

Recall the interpretation in which x and y indicate the preferences of two siblings who prefer one another's ice-cream cones. In this system, $x \rightarrow_1 y$ and $y \rightarrow_1 x$. But due to the circuit in the system, $x \rightarrow_k y$ and $y \rightarrow_k x$, for each *odd* k and $x \rightarrow_{k'} x$ and $y \rightarrow_{k'} y$ for each *even* k'. Again, the relation $\rightarrow$ is temporally transitive, so the contributing causal relations may all be read off of the cyclic graph depicted in *Figure 14.14*.

Next, recall the linear structural equation system:

$$\mathfrak{E}(s, r) \Leftrightarrow r(x) = 5s(y) + s(z) + 7 \text{ and } r(y) = s(w).$$

The relation $\rightarrow$ is temporally transitive in this system and is uniquely determined by the graph depicted in *Figure 14.15*. The exogenous variables of the system turn out to be exactly the nodes in the graph that have no arrows feeding in. The direct contributing causes to a variable turn out to be exactly the variables occurring in the right-hand sides of the structural equations having x on the left-hand side. This accords with the usual practice of coordinating graphs with structural equation models.[6]

The automaton example illustrates the difference between causation among variables and causation among values of variables. At the variable level, all one can say is that the current state and the current input are the only contributing

Figure 14.14

---

[6] Cf. Spirtes et al. (1993) for an extensive monograph on the interpretation of linear causal models. Their approach is based on postulates linking causal relations to statistical independence relations, rather than on an underlying analysis of causation as manipulability.

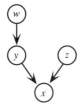

Figure 14.15

causes to the next state and the next output (*Fig. 14.16*). At the level of values, however, we see that a given value of q and a given value of s are causally sufficient for a given value of q and a given value of o at the next stage, so that the causal graph of the automaton is just the usual state transition diagram.

This account of causation is hardly the last word on the subject. First, the manipulation of linguistic conventions can determine an outcome but does not seem to cause what it determines. For example, suppose that geographers were to manipulate a reversal of the north and south poles in all their maps. This would uniquely determine that Houston is north of New York, but it is odd to say that it causes Houston to be north of New York. The causal claim seems to suggest a massive movement of tectonic plates rather than a coordinated manipulation of the world's printing presses. If the crux of the matter is that tectonic plate manipulation is a different sort of manipulation than altering linguistic conventions is, the difference is not accounted for or explained by the proposed theory of causation.

Second, I have simply assumed temporal direction in this theory of causation, whereas one of the traditional aims of the theory of causality has been to define temporal direction in terms of causal relations. A similar objection is that the primitive notion of "possible next states" of a system is already an unexplained causal relation and that what has been done is to define a few causal notions from this primitive causal notion. Both objections are legitimate if what is being sought is a reduction of time to causation or a reduction of causation to something else that is utterly noncausal. But my purpose here is different—namely, to say just enough about causation to define a learning-theoretic paradigm of reliable causal inference through time without

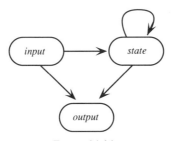

Figure 14.16

doing too much violence to intuitions. The proposed account seems to suffice for this more modest end.

Third, causation, on this approach, may depend on the variables chosen to describe a system. But intuitively, it seems that causation in a system is more than the values of an arbitrary set of variables and values chosen to describe it. One response to this objection is to assume that some (possibly infinite) set X of variables provides a complete description of every possible system that might be actual for all the scientist knows. From an operationalist point of view, X may correspond to every possible measurement procedure the scientist could possibly perform. The existence of X should be understood in an abstract sense that does not imply that the elements of X have ever been conceived of by anybody. It is then the scientist's responsibility to find causal relations among variables in X. This does not imply, however, that it is easy to determine empirically which variables to study for the purpose of finding interesting causal laws, since X may be infinite and the scientist's background knowledge may admit infinitely many possible systems whose interesting causal relations all involve different variables. Thus, we must not confuse the abstract existence of X with the epistemological problem of finding an interesting subset of X given one's background knowledge about the system under study.

Fourth and finally, the theory of causal contribution presented here is not a theory of actual causation. The two concepts are importantly different. Joe can causally contribute to Sam's death by aiming at him and pulling the trigger, but if Sam doesn't die, Joe is not an actual cause of Sam's death. This may happen either because no causally sufficient package of factors was actualized (the powder was wet, the bullet was defective, the gun barrel was crooked) or because a later manipulation intervened in the subsequent course of nature (Joe runs faster than the speeding bullet and catches it in his teeth before it hits Sam), as in proposition 14.7. Even if Sam dies, it does not follow that Joe's act is an actual cause. Sam may have died spontaneously (through a non-deterministic state transition) or Sam's death may have been overdetermined by competing, causally sufficient packages of factors, one of thich does not involve Joe's heinous act. But overdetermination alone does not preclude Joe from being an actual cause, since two bullets striking Sam simultaneously would both be causes. It is interesting to consider exactly what the conditions are that extend causal contribution to actual causation, but this project lies beyond the scope of the present chapter. For now, we may think of causal contribution as a structural condition necessary but not sufficient for actual causation.

5. Experimental Methods

With a provisional account of causal contribution in hand, it is time to return to methodology. As usual, I assume a collection H of *hypotheses*, any one of which the scientist may be assigned to investigate. I also assume for simplicity that the scientist is prepared to directly manipulate a fixed set M of manipulable

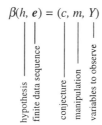

$$\beta(h, e) = (c, m, Y)$$

hypothesis — finite data sequence — conjecture — manipulation — variables to observe

Figure 14.17

variables and to directly observe a fixed set O of observable variables whose possible values are known. Other variables may be observed or manipulated only mediately, through the values of these. *Experimental manipulations* are finite manipulations that assign values only to manipulable variables, and *experimental outcomes* are finite outcomes that assign values only to observable variables. A *data sequence* is a finite sequence of experimental outcomes.

Relative to these assumptions, an *experimental assessment method* is a total function that takes a hypothesis and a finite data sequence as inputs and that outputs a triple consisting of a conjecture (a rational in the unit interval or the certainty mark "!"), a finite manipulation m, and a finite set Y of variables to observe (*Fig. 14.17*). The finitude of m and Y precludes the unrealistic possibility of β seeing or directly controlling infinitely many variables in one stage of inquiry.

6. The Course of Experimental Inquiry

The actual evolution of the system under study through time depends on the manipulations performed by the method investigating it. This is why experimental inquiry is both more complicated and more interesting than passive inquiry. Let a *possible state of inquiry* be a quintuple of form (s, e, c, m, Y), where s is a system state, e is a finite data sequence, c is a conjecture, m is a manipulation, and Y is a set of variables to be observed.

Let ρ be an infinite sequence of possible states of inquiry. Let $\rho_i = (s(\rho_i), e(\rho_i), c(\rho_i), m(\rho_i), Y(\rho_i))$. Then we say that ρ is a *possible course of inquiry* for $\mathfrak{S}, \beta, h$ just in case:

> $s(\rho_0)$ *is some arbitrary state of* $\mathfrak{S}$,
> $e(\rho_0) = \mathbf{0}$,
> $\beta(h, \mathbf{0}) = (c(\rho_0), m(\rho_0), Y(\rho_0))$,
> *for each* $i \geq 0$, $\mathfrak{S}(s(\rho_i), s(\rho_{i+1})|m')$, *where* m' *is the restriction of* $m(\rho_i)$ *to* M, $e(\rho_{i+1}) = e(\rho_i)*o$, *where* o *is the restriction of* $s(\rho_i)$ *to* $Y(\rho_i) \cap O$, *and* $\beta(h, e(\rho_{i+1})) = (c(\rho_{i+1}), m(\rho_{i+1}), Y(\rho_{i+1}))$.

Then let $Inq(\mathfrak{S}, \beta, h)$ be the set of all possible courses of inquiry for $\mathfrak{S}, \beta, h$.

A possible course of inquiry for $\mathfrak{S}$, β, h is a record or a motion picture of everything that actually happens when β is assigned to investigate hypothesis h in $\mathfrak{S}$. According to the definition, the result of attempting to manipulate a nonmanipulable variable is that nothing is done to the variable in question and the result of an attempted observation of an unobservable variable is that this variable and its value are omitted from the data stream, as though the value had not been requested. We may think of the method as sending orders to a lab that attempts to accomplish as much as possible of what is ordered. Other conventions might be considered, as when attempts to alter unmanipulable variables have side effects for other variables (cf. exercise 14.5).[7]

7. Hypothesis Correctness and Background Knowledge

A hypothesis may be entirely about the structure of $\mathfrak{S}$, entirely about the contingent course of inquiry, or about some combination of the two. Of the first sort is the hypothesis "x is a contributing cause of y with time lag 2." Of the second sort is the hypothesis "$(x = 0)$ will eventually be observed." Of the last sort is the hypothesis "$(x = a)$ at n is an actual cause of $(y = b)$ at $n + 1$," whatever this should ultimately turn out to mean. Hypotheses that depend entirely on $\mathfrak{S}$ are *structural*. Hypotheses that depend entirely on the actual course of inquiry are *material*. The rest are *hybrids*.

Hypothesis correctness should be defined to embrace all these cases at once. Accordingly, let an *experimental correctness relation* be a quaternary relation $C_{\beta}(\mathfrak{S}, \rho, h)$, where $\mathfrak{S}$ is a system, h is a hypothesis, β is a method, and $\rho \in Inq(\mathfrak{S}, \beta, h)$. $\mathfrak{S}$ represents the total structural reality and ρ represents the total contingent reality of the system under study when β investigates h. When h is understood to be structural, I write $C(\mathfrak{S}, h)$, since ρ and β are irrelevant in this case.

Of special interest are structural hypotheses such as $M \geq_k O$ and $x \rightarrow_k y$, whose correctness conditions are derived directly from the manipulability account of causation

$$C(\mathfrak{S}, M \geq_k O) \Leftrightarrow M \geq_k O \text{ in } \mathfrak{S}.$$

$$C(\mathfrak{S}, x \geq_k y) \Leftrightarrow x \geq_k y \text{ in } \mathfrak{S}.$$

[7] The definition is general enough to cover cases in which the variable whose manipulation or observation is requested is not even in the system under study. It is not so clear how to understand such a claim. Perhaps it corresponds to situations in which a measurement has a precondition (e.g. the subject must wear a helmet with a stylus for pecking answers with his head) but a given system does not meet the precondition (the helmet does not fit his head). In such a case, the result of trying to measure the variable would be to obtain no value, as the above definition requires. But in any event, this odd generality can easily be eliminated by choosing background knowledge in which every system has all the variables that β is ever disposed to measure or to manipulate. None of the following results turns in any interesting sense on this issue.

A rigorous definition of the correctness of actual causation would essentially depend on both $\mathfrak{S}$ and ρ.

Background knowledge may likewise constrain possible combinations of $\mathfrak{S}$ and ρ depending on which method β is employed and which hypothesis h is under investigation. Therefore, *experimental background knowledge* is a relation $\mathcal{K}_{\beta,h}(\mathfrak{S}, \rho)$ satisfying the constraint that $\rho \in Inq(\mathfrak{S}, \beta, h)$. $\mathcal{K}_{\beta,h}(\mathfrak{S}, \rho)$ may be read as: for all the scientist knows, the system under study may be $\mathfrak{S}$ and inquiry in $\mathfrak{S}$ may evolve according to ρ given that method β is employed to investigate h. Remember that ρ is not uniquely determined by $\mathfrak{S}, \beta, h$, because $\mathfrak{S}$ may be indeterministic.

8. Experimental Reliability

The ground has now been laid for a learning-theoretic definition of reliability. As usual, I give the definition for verification in the limit, leaving the definitions of the other convergence criteria to the reader.

> β *experimentally verifies$_C$ h in the limit given*
> $\mathcal{K} \Leftrightarrow \forall \mathfrak{S}, \forall \rho \in Inq(\mathfrak{S}, \beta, h), \text{ if } \mathcal{K}_{\beta,h}(\mathfrak{S}, \rho)$
> $\text{then } C_\beta(\mathfrak{S}, \rho, h) \Leftrightarrow \exists n \forall m \geq n, c(\rho_m) = 1.$

The definition requires that for each possible course of inquiry that might have arisen given the scientist's choice of method, the hypothesis the scientist is assigned to investigate and the knowledge the scientist starts out with, the method stabilizes to 1 just in case the hypothesis is correct (relative to the resulting course of inquiry).

The ability of the method β to operate on the system under study raises an apparent objection. Since reliability requires success in any possibility admitted by $\mathcal{K}$, a method can succeed by *making* a known contingency false, even if the contingency has nothing to do with the hypothesis under study. So for example, if the scientist knows that a fence post will never be black in the actual course of inquiry, then the scientist can reliably decide with certainty whether smoking causes lung cancer simply by choosing a method whose first experimental act is to paint the post black. That seems like theft over honest toil! But I maintain that it is the right result: if the scientist actualizes a situation he knows will not occur, then his background knowledge is false, and it has already been agreed in chapter 2 that the scientist should be exempted from error when his knowledge is false.

It has taken some doing, but we now have an explicit paradigm for experimental inquiry and an explicit account of causation. We may now consider a few of the issues that arise in this paradigm, but what follows is far from being a systematic survey.

9. Dreaming and the Principle of Plenitude

Let us take a peek into an experimental scientist's happy daydream. The scientist dreams that he has knowledge $\mathcal{K}$ with the following properties:

> *There is a variable set X and a set V of values such that*:
> *D1. X is finite.*
> *D2. V is r.e..*
> *D3. Every system $\mathfrak{S}$ occurring in $\mathcal{K}$ has variable set X and value set V.*
> *D4. In every system $\mathfrak{S}$ occurring in $\mathcal{K}$ each variable in X is observable.*
> *D5. In every system $\mathfrak{S}$ occurring in $\mathcal{K}$ each variable in X is manipulable.*

In short, the scientist knows that the system under study is manipulable, is observable, and has finite state vectors involving exactly the variables in X.

Even in such a dream, experimental inference is far from trivial. If the system under study is not known to be *deterministic*, in the sense that a unique state can follow each state, then the scientist will have to rely on luck to see some possible state transitions of the system. Since the correctness of a structural hypothesis can depend essentially on these transitions, such a hypothesis may be globally underdetermined even when *D1–D5* are met. For example, suppose that $\mathfrak{M}_2$ is the 2-bulb marquee with bulbs $\{x_1, x_2\}$ and $\mathfrak{P}$ is a completely indeterministic system on the same variables in which any state can follow any other. Sup-pose that the scientist can observe and manipulate both bulbs, but knows nothing else a priori about the course of inquiry except what follows from his choice of method and from the fact that the system under study may be either $\mathfrak{M}_2$ or $\mathfrak{P}$. If he is very unlucky, it may be that the indeterministic system just happens to restrict itself for eternity to outcomes that could also have occurred in $\mathfrak{M}_2$.

Scientists don't seem to worry much about such possibilities. One way to agree with them is to assume the *principle of plenitude*,[8] which asserts that if state s occurs infinitely often (either by nature or through manipulation) and if $\mathfrak{S}(s, r)$, then r actually follows s infinitely often.

> ρ *is plentiful for* $\mathfrak{S} \Leftrightarrow \forall s, r$ *such that* $\mathfrak{S}(s, r)$, *if there are infinitely many distinct i such that* $s = subst(s(\rho_i), m(\rho_i))$ *then there are infinitely many distinct k such that*
>
> $$s = subst(s(\rho_k), m(\rho_k))$$
>
> *and* $r = s(\rho_{k+1})$.
>
> $\mathcal{K} \vDash plenitude \Leftrightarrow \forall \mathfrak{S}, \beta, h \; \forall \rho \in Inq(\mathfrak{S}, \beta, h)$, *if* $\mathcal{K}_{\beta,h}(\mathfrak{S}, \rho)$ *then* ρ *is plentiful for* $\mathfrak{S}$.

---

[8] The plenitude principle was employed as a definition of possibility by Aristotle. It was already assumed in the language identification paradigm of chapter 9. But there we didn't have the complication that the method may have to set up the conditions for the occurrence of an observation.

If $\mathcal{K}$ entails plenitude and *D1–D5*, then the analysis of experimental inquiry about structural hypotheses reduces to the passive paradigm of the preceding chapters. For then it is possible to effectively enumerate all states over these variables and values in such a way that each state occurs infinitely often. Let ζ be such an enumeration. Then say that ζ is *infinitely repetitive* for $\mathcal{K}$. Method β *uses* ζ just in case for each $h \in H$ and for each $n \in \omega$ and for each finite data sequence e of length n, the manipulation performed by $\beta(h, e)$ is ζ_n. If β uses an infinitely repetitive ζ in this way, then by the plenitude principle, β eventually sees every transition in the system $\mathfrak{S}$ under study, so $\mathfrak{S}$ is uniquely determined by the data stream received by β in the limit.

Let $Data_{\mathcal{K},\zeta}(\mathfrak{S})$ be the set of all data streams that a method β relying on ζ might possibly see in light of $\mathcal{K}$ if the actual system under study is $\mathfrak{S}$. If h is a structural hypothesis, then let $Data_{\mathcal{K},C,\zeta}(h)$ denote the union of all $Data_{\mathcal{K},\zeta}(\mathfrak{S})$ such that $C(\mathfrak{S}, h)$. Finally, let $Data_\zeta(\mathcal{K})$ denote the union of all $Data_{\mathcal{K},\zeta}(\mathfrak{S})$, such that $\mathfrak{S}$ occurs in $\mathcal{K}$. Then the sense in which h can be reliably assessed depends in the usual way on the Borel or arithmetical complexity of $Data_{\mathcal{K},C,\zeta}(h)$ relative to $Data_\zeta(\mathcal{K})$.

Proposition 14.9

If h is structural and $\mathcal{K}$ entails plenitude and satisfies D1–D5, then

$$h \text{ is computably} \begin{bmatrix} verifiable_C \\ refutable_C \\ decidable_C \end{bmatrix} \text{ with certainty given } \mathcal{K}$$

$$\Leftrightarrow Data_{\mathcal{K},C,\zeta}(h) \in \begin{bmatrix} \Sigma[Data_\zeta(\mathcal{K})]_1^A \\ \Pi[Data_\zeta(\mathcal{K})]_1^A \\ \Delta[Data_\zeta(\mathcal{K})]_1^A \end{bmatrix}.$$

$$h \text{ is computably} \begin{bmatrix} verifiable_C \\ refutable_C \\ decidable_C \end{bmatrix} \text{ in the limit given } \mathcal{K}$$

$$\Leftrightarrow Data_{\mathcal{K},C,\zeta}(h) \in \begin{bmatrix} \Sigma[Data_\zeta(\mathcal{K})]_2^A \\ \Pi[Data_\zeta(\mathcal{K})]_2^A \\ \Delta[Data_\zeta(\mathcal{K})]_2^A \end{bmatrix}.$$

Proof: ($\Leftarrow$) Follows from the above comments and the usual bumping pointer techniques from the preceding chapters. ($\Rightarrow$) If β succeeds on h in light of $\mathcal{K}$, then a method β' using ζ can succeed as well: repeat the last conjecture of β and perform experiments according to ζ until enough information is gathered about $\mathfrak{S}$ to know what data β would have received had its last manipulation actually been performed; pass this data to β to find the next manipulation, conjecture, and observation produced by β. Since β' uses ζ, there is no global underdetermination, so we can use the success of β' to define $\mathcal{D}ata_{\mathcal{K},C,\zeta}(h)$ relative to $\mathcal{D}ata_\zeta(\mathcal{K})$ in the usual way.   ∎

Proposition 14.9 permits us to apply techniques from earlier chapters to problems of causal inference.

Proposition 14.10

(a) *If $\mathcal{K}$ satisfies plenitude and D1–D5 then "$M \geq_k O$" is computably refutable with certainty given $\mathcal{K}$.*

(b) *$\exists\ \mathcal{K}$ satisfying plenitude and D1–D5 such that "$M \geq_1 O$" is not ideally verifiable with certainty given $\mathcal{K}$.*

Proof of (a): If h is the hypothesis "state x possibly follows y," then $\mathcal{D}ata_{\mathcal{K},C,\zeta}(h) \in \Sigma[\mathcal{D}ata_\zeta(\mathcal{K})]_1^A$, since given plenitude and D1–D5, $\forall \varepsilon \in \mathcal{D}ata_\zeta(\mathcal{K}),\ \varepsilon \in \mathcal{D}ata_{\mathcal{K},C,\zeta}(h) \Leftrightarrow \exists i$ such that $\zeta_i = x$ and $\varepsilon_{i+1} = y$. Then the same bound holds for the existence of a path of a given length in the system under study, since that hypothesis is a finite conjunction of hypotheses of the form "x may follow y." $M \geq_k O$ is correct just in case there do *not* exist two paths of length $k + lh(O)$ that lead to different O outcomes, so $M \geq_k O \in \Pi[\mathcal{D}ata_\zeta(\mathcal{K})]_1^A$. Apply proposition 14.9.

Proof of (b): Let $\mathfrak{M}_2$ be the 2-bulb marquee system on variables $\{x, y\}$ assuming values $\{0, 1\}$. Let $\mathfrak{P}(s, r)$ be a system involving the same variables and values that permits any possible transition. Assume that both variables are manipulable and observable in both systems so that $M = O = \{x, y\}$. Let $M = (\{x\})$ and let $O = (\{y\})$. Then

(1) $M \geq_1 O$ [in $\mathfrak{M}_2$] but not $M \geq_1 O$ [in $\mathfrak{P}$].

Also,

(2) $\mathfrak{M}_2 \subseteq \mathfrak{P}$.

Define:

$$\mathcal{K}_{\beta,h}(\mathfrak{S}, \rho) \Leftrightarrow \mathfrak{S} \in \{\mathfrak{M}_2, \mathfrak{P}\} \text{ and } \rho \in \mathit{Inq}(\mathfrak{S}, \beta, h) \ \& \ \rho \text{ is plentiful for } \mathfrak{S}.$$

So $\mathcal{K}$ entails the plenitude principle together with D1–D5.

Let β be given. Let h denote "$M \geq_1 O$." $\mathfrak{M}_2$ and $\mathfrak{P}$ have the same possible states. For each such state s, the demon maintains an infinitely repetitive enumeration $\zeta[s]$ of the set of all states in $\{0, 1\}^{\{x, y\}}$. Each such enumeration is equipped with a pointer initialized to position 0.

At stage 0, the demon chooses $s(\rho_0)$ to be some arbitrary state s and lets $\mathfrak{S}[0] = \mathfrak{M}_2$. $e(\rho_0) = \mathbf{0}$. Then $\beta(h, e(\rho_0)) = (c(\rho_0), m(\rho_0), Y(\rho_0))$.

At stage $n + 1$, the demon has already defined $\rho_n = (s(\rho_n), e(\rho_n), c(\rho_n), m(\rho_n), Y(\rho_n))$ and $\mathfrak{S}[n]$. If $c(\rho_{n-1}) = (!)$ and $c(\rho_n) = 1$ and $\forall j < n - 1$, $c(\rho_j) \neq (!)$, then the demon sets $\mathfrak{S}[n + 1] = \mathfrak{P}$. Otherwise, the demon sets $\mathfrak{S}[n + 1] = \mathfrak{S}[n]$. In either event, the demon sets $s = subst(s(\rho_n), m(\rho_n)|M)$ and moves the pointer associated with s to the next state r occurring in $\zeta[s]$ such that $\mathfrak{S}[n](s, r)$ and sets $s(\rho_{n+1}) = r$. Then $e(\rho_{n+1})$, $c(\rho_{n+1})$, $m(\rho_{n+1})$, $Y(\rho_{n+1})$ are all uniquely determined by the definition of the course of inquiry.

Let ρ be the unique course of inquiry determined by β and by the demon just described. If β conjectures $(!)$ and the first such conjecture is preceded by a 1, then $\rho \in Inq(\mathfrak{P}, \beta, h)$ since all state transitions according to $\mathfrak{M}_2$ are also state transitions in $\mathfrak{P}$ by (2). ρ is plentiful for $\mathfrak{P}$, for suppose $\mathfrak{P}(s, r)$ and s occurs infinitely often in $s(\rho)$. Then after some time $\mathfrak{S}[n] = \mathfrak{P}$, and after that time r occurs infinitely often in $s(\rho)$ because $\zeta[s]$ is infinitely repetitive. Hence, $\mathcal{K}_{\beta,h}(\mathfrak{S}, \rho)$. But by (1), β is mistaken. Otherwise, $\rho \in Inq(\mathfrak{M}_2, \beta, h)$ and ρ is plentiful for $\mathfrak{M}_2$ (by an argument similar to the one given in the preceding case) so $\mathcal{K}_{\beta,h}(\mathfrak{M}_2, \rho)$. But by (1), β is mistaken. ∎

Causal contribution is somewhat harder to determine empirically.

Proposition 14.11

(a) If $\mathcal{K}$ satisfies plenitude and D1–D5 then "$x \rightarrow_k y$" is effectively verifiable in the limit given $\mathcal{K}$.

(b) $\exists \mathcal{K}$ satisfying plenitude and D1–D5 such that "$x \rightarrow_1 y$" is not ideally refutable in the limit given $\mathcal{K}$.

Proof of (a): $x \rightarrow_k y$ in $\mathfrak{S} \Leftrightarrow \exists M \, \exists i < lh(M)$ such that x at i is necessary for the causal sufficiency of M for y with time lag k in $\mathfrak{S}$:

$\Leftrightarrow \exists M \, \exists i < lh(M)$ such that

(i) $M \geq_k y$ in $\mathfrak{S}$ and

(ii) $x \in M_i$ and

(iii) $\forall N$, If N is just like M except that $x \notin N_i$,

then $N \not\geq_k y$ in $\mathfrak{S}$.

By proposition 14.10, $\mathcal{D}ata_{\mathcal{K},C,\zeta}(i) \in \Pi[\mathcal{D}ata_\zeta(\mathcal{K})]_1^A$. For the same reason, $\mathcal{D}ata_{\mathcal{K},C,\zeta}(iii) \in \Sigma[\mathcal{D}ata_\zeta(\mathcal{K})]_1^A$, since $N \geq_k y$ occurs negated. The universal quantifier over N is bounded since there is a unique such N. Adding the outermost existential quantifier, we have that $\mathcal{D}ata_{\mathcal{K},C,\zeta}((x \rightarrow_k y)) \in \Sigma[\mathcal{D}ata_\zeta(\mathcal{K})]_2^A$. Apply proposition 14.9.

Proof of (b): Let h denote "$x \rightarrow_1 y$." Let $X = O = M = \{x, y, z\}$, $V = \omega$. Define:

$\mathfrak{T}_n(s, r) \Leftrightarrow$

(1) $r(x) = s(x)$ *and*   (first input stays constant)

(2) $r(y) = s(y) + 1$ *and*   (increment counter)

(3) $s(y) \geq n + 1 \Rightarrow r(z) = s(x)$ (determine $z = x$ when y reaches $n + 1$)

Think of $\mathfrak{T}_n$ as a simple device that starts out with an arbitrary input x, increments a counter y until y reaches $n + 1$, and sets z to the current value of x at that time. The device is constructed so that the user can manipulate x at will and the value of x will remain fixed thereafter. Consider the schedule $M[n] = (\varnothing, \ldots, \varnothing, \{x\})$, in which $\varnothing$ occurs $n - 1$ times. Hence, $M[n] \geq_{n+1} z$ in $\mathfrak{T}_n$. Moreover, $\{x\}$ at $n - 1$ is necessary for the sufficiency of $M[n]$, since dropping $\{x\}$ from the schedule leaves x, and hence z, undetermined $n + 1$ steps after the onset of $M[n]$. Thus,

(i) *for each* n, $x \rightarrow_1 z$ *in* $\mathfrak{T}_n$.

Moreover, since conditions (1–2) are the same for each n and (3) becomes more lenient as n increases, we have:

(ii) $\forall n$, $\mathfrak{T}_n \subseteq \mathfrak{T}_{n+1}$.

Let $\mathfrak{T}_\omega$ be the system on the same variables whose transition relation is $\bigcup_n T_n$, where T_n is the transition relation of $\mathfrak{T}_n$. Then $\mathfrak{T}_\omega(s, r) \Leftrightarrow$ (1) and (2) hold of s, r, so:

(iii) *It is not the case that* $x \rightarrow_1 z$ *in* $\mathfrak{T}_\omega$.

Assume that all variables are observable and manipulable in each of the systems just defined, so $M = O = \{x, y, z\}$. Define:

$\mathcal{K}_{\beta, h}(\mathfrak{S}, \rho) \Leftrightarrow \mathfrak{S} = \mathfrak{T}_\omega$ or $(\exists n$ such that $\mathfrak{S} = \mathfrak{T}_n)$ and ρ is plentiful for $\mathfrak{S}$ and $\rho \in Inq(\mathfrak{S}, \beta, h)$.

So $\mathcal{K}$ entails plenitude and *D1–D5*.

Let method β be given. As before, for each state s, the demon maintains an infinitely repetitive enumeration $\zeta[s]$ of the set of all states in $\{0, 1\}^{(x, y, z)}$. Each such enumeration is equipped with a pointer initialized to position 0.

At stage 0, the demon chooses $s(\rho_0)$ to be some arbitrary state s and lets $\mathfrak{S}[0] = \mathfrak{T}_1$. $e(\rho_0) = 0$, and $\beta(h, e(\rho_0)) = (c(\rho_0), m(\rho_0) Y(\rho_0))$.

At stage $n + 1$, the demon has already defined $\rho_n = (s(\rho_n), e(\rho_n), c(\rho_n),$ $m(\rho_n), Y(\rho_n))$, and $\mathfrak{S}[n]$. If $c(\rho_n) = 0$, then the demon sets $\mathfrak{S}[n + 1] = \mathfrak{S}[n]$. Otherwise, the demon sets $\mathfrak{S}[n + 1] = \mathfrak{T}_{m+1}$, where $\mathfrak{S}[n] = \mathfrak{T}_m$. In either event, the demon sets $s = subst(s(\rho_n), m(\rho_n) | M)$ and moves the pointer to the next state r occurring in $\zeta[s]$ such that $\mathfrak{S}[n](s, r)$ and sets $s(\rho_n + 1) = r$. Then $e(\rho_{n+1})$, $c(\rho_{n+1})$, $m(\rho_{n+1})$, and $Y(\rho_{n+1})$ are all uniquely determined by the definition of the course of inquiry.

Let ρ be the unique course of inquiry determined by β and by the demon just described. If β stabilizes to 0, then $\mathfrak{S}[n]$ stabilizes to some $\mathfrak{T}_m$ and $\rho \in Inq(\mathfrak{T}_n, \beta, h)$ since by (ii), all state transitions in $\mathfrak{T}_k$ are also permitted by $\mathfrak{T}_m$, where $k \leq m$. Also, ρ is plentiful for $\mathfrak{T}_n$ due to the demon's use of infinitely repetitive enumerations. So $\mathcal{K}_{\beta, h}(\mathfrak{T}_n, \rho)$. But by (i), β is mistaken. So suppose that β conjectures a value other than 0 infinitely often. Then by (ii), $\rho \in Inq(\mathfrak{T}_\omega, \beta, h)$. If $\mathfrak{T}_\omega(s, r)$ and s occurs infinitely often, there is a stage n after which the demon's current system $\mathfrak{S}[n]$ permits that transition (by the definition of $\mathfrak{T}_\omega$) so since s occurs infinitely often, each possible successor state licensed by $\mathfrak{T}_\omega$ will also occur infinitely often, since $\zeta[s]$ is infinitely repetitive. So ρ is plentiful for $\mathfrak{T}_\omega$, and hence $\mathcal{K}_{\beta, h}(\mathfrak{T}_\omega, \rho)$. But by (iii), β is mistaken. ∎

Corollary 14.12

(a) If $\mathcal{K}$ satisfies plenitude and D1–D5 then "x is endogenous" is effectively verifiable in the limit given $\mathcal{K}$.

(b) $\exists \mathcal{K}$ satisfying plenitude and D1–D5 such that "x is endogenous" is not ideally refutable in the limit given $\mathcal{K}$.

Proof of (a): x is endogenous just in case for some $y, k, y \to_k x$. This hypothesis is $\Sigma[\mathcal{D}ata_\zeta(\mathcal{K})]_2^4$ by (a) of the preceding result.

Proof of (b): The construction used in the proof of (b) of the preceding result suffices because $x \to_1 z$ (so z is endogenous) in $\mathfrak{T}_k$, but there are no u, k such that $u \to_k z$ in $\mathfrak{T}_\omega$ so z is exogenous in $\mathfrak{T}_\omega$. ∎

10. Weakened Assumptions and Global Underdetermination

The positive results of the preceding section depend heavily on assumption *D1*, for when there are infinitely many variables, the scientist cannot ensure that each state is visited infinitely often. This follows immediately from the fact that the scientist may manipulate only finitely many variables at once, but even if this restriction were lifted, there would be too many states on infinitely many variables for the scientist to enumerate. Hence, plenitude no longer ensures that every transition in the system under study is eventually revealed. In light of this fact, it is easy to construct an example involving a countable infinity of variables in which causal sufficiency is globally underdetermined (cf. exercise 14.7).

Global underdetermination may also arise if we relax assumption *D4*, which guarantees that all system variables are directly manipulable. For suppose that the scientist knows that the system under study is any one of the three finite state machines illustrated in *Figure 14.18*, but whereas the input is under the control of the scientist, the machine's current state is under glass and kept out of reach. Suppose, furthermore, that the initial state is seen by the scientist to be *b*. A dead state is a state that leads back to itself on any input. *a, c* are dead in A_1, *c* is dead in A_2, and *a* is dead in A_3. Consider the hypotheses:

(i) *a is a dead state.*

(ii) *b is a dead state.*

(iii) *both* (i) *and* (ii).

(i) is decidable with certainty by feeding input 1 and then seeing whether any input leads out of a. (ii) is similarly decidable with certainty by feeding input 0. But (iii) presents a problem. If the actual system under study is A_1, then whether or not the scientist feeds an input, the automaton goes into a dead state, so that only that state will ever be seen again. Then for all the scientist will ever see in the limit, the system under study might be A_2 (if the first input is 0) or A_3 (if the first input is 1).

This example illustrates the problem of *experimental interference*, in which doing one thing (providing input 1) prevents the scientist for eternity from seeing what would have happened had he done something else instead (i.e., provide input 0). Experimental interference complicates the analysis of experimental reliability, since it leads to the violation of the closure laws for verifiability, refutability, and decidability: for example, (i), (ii) are both decidable with certainty, but (iii) = ((i) & (ii)) is globally underdetermined.

Experimental interference arises when some states of a system are inaccessible from others. Two states are *connected* in $\mathfrak{S}$ just in case finite paths in $\mathfrak{S}$ exist from each to the other. $\mathfrak{S}$ is *connected* just in case every two states of $\mathfrak{S}$ are connected. If $\mathcal{K}$ entails connectedness, plenitude, and *D1–D4*, then we have

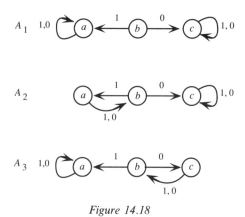

Figure 14.18

essentially the same results as when $\mathcal{K}$ entails plenitude and *D1–D5*, because the system is then guaranteed to spontaneously exercise each transition infinitely often, without the help of the scientist.

A common background assumption made in statistical causal studies[9] is that each variable has an exogenous "random error" variable as a causal contributor. The addition of such variables to a disconnected system can have the effect of connecting it, if the structure of the expanded system is such that some values of the error variable can possibly shake the reduced system out of its deterministic sinks. The randomness and independence assumptions often associated with such variables imply plenitude with respect to their states (with probability 1), so that the system is guaranteed (with probability 1) to be shaken out of sinks infinitely often. This accounts, in part, for the apparent paradox that causal inquiry can be easier in noisy systems than in deterministic ones.

It may be that connectivity is an underlying motive for positing ideal, immutable entities in physics. Natural connectivity fails, intuitively, when the system under study can be permanently altered or deformed. Things that wear out never duplicate the same state twice, so plenitude cannot underwrite reliable causal inferences among them. But ideal, immutable, things have immutable dispositions, so the disposition can be checked under various conditions in various orders with no fear of experimental interference effects. It is instructive in this connection to recall the ancient origins of the atomic theory of matter. One goal of ancient atomism was to explain all events by the principle of plenitude: i.e., that whatever happens was bound to happen sooner or later, and in fact will repeat itself infinitely often. By retreating to invisible, immutable atoms with hooks and catches that never wear out but that eventually shake apart when jostled enough, the possible states of the world may be imagined to be connected, so plenitude guarantees that every possible state transition is eventually actualized.

Unfortunately, this strategy has a price—namely, that unobservable entities reintroduce global underdetermination in another way, because they cannot be seen. It remains an interesting question why it is that in some cases global underdetermination due to failures of connectivity among observable variables is traded for global underdetermination due to unobservability of ideal entities and in other cases the trade is not considered worthwhile.

A familiar sort of global underdetermination arises when we drop both *D4*, and *D5*, so that some variables are latent and inquiry is passive, for then latent common causes can exactly duplicate the appearance of causal relations among passively observed variables. For example, consider the common cause system (*Fig. 14.19*)

$$\mathfrak{C}(s, r) \Leftrightarrow r(x) = s(z) \text{ and } r(w) = s(z) \text{ and } r(y) = s(w).$$

If we restrict the states of $\mathfrak{C}$ to the observable variables x and y, $\mathfrak{C}$ licenses

---

[9] Spirtes et al. (1993).

Figure 14.19

exactly the same transitions as the 2-bulb marquee system $\mathfrak{M}_2$: the value of x
at stage n is the value of y at stage $n + 1$, and the value of x at stage $n + 1$ is
arbitrary. Hence, each system generates only data streams possible for the other.
This fact was behind Hume's insistence that constant conjunctions do not suffice
for conclusions about the hidden springs of nature and was also exploited in
defense of the *occasionalist* thesis that God is the direct common cause of
everything, for how could passive observation tell the difference?

If we allow experimentation on x and y but drop plenitude, then it is still
possible for $\mathfrak{C}$ to duplicate experimental outcomes observed in $\mathfrak{M}_2$ for eternity,
for it is possible (by a curious and infinite run of luck) for z to anticipate
experimental conditions on x so as to force y to adopt the same value one step
after x is manipulated.

Assuming plenitude, however, $\mathfrak{M}_2$ is refutable with certainty with respect to
$\mathfrak{C}$, for suppose that the scientist manipulates x to value 1 for eternity. Plenitude
guarantees that z will assume value 0 at some stage n. Since x is always
manipulated to 1, x is manipulated to 1 at stage $n + 1$. By stage $n + 2$, the 0
value on z at stage n has propagated deterministically to y, even though x was
manipulated to 1 at stage $n + 1$. This is impossible in $\mathfrak{M}_2$. So given enough background knowledge, experimentation can lead to logically reliable conclusions
about hidden causes, which was the question with which the chapter began.[10]

Exercises

14.1. Prove proposition 14.5.

14.2. Prove proposition 14.6.

---

[10] There is a growing body of statistical literature in which it is argued on
probabilistic grounds that latent causes can be reliably inferred from passive data (Spirtes
et al. 1993). Many of the assumptions required concern statistical independence relations.
It would be interesting and useful to analyze the significance of these assumptions from
the point of view of the purely logical setting for causal inference developed in this
chapter. We have already considered the role of uncorrelated random error terms from
this point of view, for example. One could go further and try to duplicate the
distributional assumptions by material background knowledge restricting the limiting
relative frequencies of occurrences of system states and assuming the frequentist
interpretation of probability.

14.3. Say that M is *minimally sufficient* for O with lag k in $\mathfrak{S} \Leftrightarrow M \geq_k O$ in $\mathfrak{S}$ and for each N properly extended by M, it is not the case that $N \geq_k O$. Show that at most one M is minimally sufficient for O with lag k in $\mathfrak{S}$. Show that this statement is not true in general if we replace the schedules M and O with instances m, o, respectively.

14.4. (T. Richardson) Show that causal contribution is temporally transitive in systems having only Boolean variables.

*14.5. (with Oliver Schulte) Develop an alternative paradigm in which a system is an arbitrary, ternary relation $\mathfrak{S}(s, r | m)$. Say that $\mathfrak{S}$ *has side effects* just in case the result of manipulating a variable to a value it already has is different from the result of not manipulating anything. In other words, $\mathfrak{S}$ has side effects just in case there are m, n, s, r such that m extends n and $m-n$ is extended by s but not $\mathfrak{S}(s, r | m) \Leftrightarrow \mathfrak{S}(s, r | n)$. Say that $\mathfrak{S}$ *has manipulative failures* just in case the result of manipulating a variable would have been different had things already been the way the manipulation intended to set them. That is, $\mathfrak{S}$ has manipulative failures just in case there are m, q, s, r such that $s - m = q - m$ and s extends m but not $\mathfrak{S}(s, r | m) \Leftrightarrow \mathfrak{S}(q\, r | m)$. Give intuitive examples of systems with side effects or manipulative failures. Is the overwrite model equivalent to assuming no side effects and no manipulative failures? Which of these two assumptions (or both) is required to derive the temporal transitivity of causal sufficiency? How about synchronic monotonicity?

14.6. (P. Spirtes) Consider a more "grainy" experimental paradigm in which each stage of inquiry is as long as n discrete stages of evolution of the system under study and observations are received only at the end of each stage of inquiry. Show that global underdetermination can arise even when $\mathcal{K}$ entails plenitude and $D1$–$D4$. Investigate the prospects for causal inference in this paradigm.

14.7. Show that $D2$–$D5$ together with plenitude are consistent with global underdetermination of causal sufficiency.

15

Relativism and Reliability

blah blah paradigms
blah meaning variance *blah*
historical context *blah*
blah social norms *blah*
positivists *blah blah blah*   ?

1. Introduction

Consider the following two axioms governing hypothesis correctness.

> *Semantic Immutability: Hypothesis correctness is unaffected by the acts of the scientist.*

> *Semantic Eternity: Hypothesis correctness is independent of time.*

Neither principle implies the other. Correctness could change spontaneously through time in a way that the scientist cannot affect, and correctness could depend on what the scientist does in the limit without changing through time. The nonexperimental inductive setting considered in chapters 1 through 13 satisfies both axioms, since correctness is taken to be a fixed relation between data streams and hypotheses in that setting. Experimental investigation of structural hypotheses also satisfies both axioms, since structural relations in the system under study are not altered by the manipulation of variables. But there are circumstances in which both axioms can fail.

Case (a): Sometimes hypotheses are indexical sentences rather than propositions. For example, a quality control official at a factory may be interested in the indexical sentence "the *current* batch produced by machine *A* is good," where the denotation of the indexical expression "the current batch" changes with time. The truth value of the sentence will change from time to time as the current batch changes, violating semantic eternity.[1] If the quality

---

[1] In the standard, Neyman-Pearson account of hypothesis testing, the significance level is interpreted as an upper bound on the limiting relative frequency of type one error in an infinite sequence of trials in which the quality of the batch is allowed to vary, so in such cases it is the indexical sentence rather than any of the propositions

Figure 15.1

control manager also has control over the machinery of production, the example may also violate semantic immutability because the manager can tune the machinery to improve the next batch.

Case (b): Experimentation can evidently affect truth when the hypothesis under investigation is a material or a hybrid proposition (cf. chapter 14). For example, the hypothesis that no purple cow will ever be seen on top of the World Trade Center can be reliably decided with certainty by an experimentalist who finds a cow, paints it purple, and deposits it the place in question. Assuming (plausibly) that no such event would have occurred without the scientist's intervention, semantic immutability is violated. Whether or not semantic eternity is also violated depends on one's metaphysics. On one view, the hypothesis has no truth value until the scientist has decided upon a course of action. In this case, the truth value changes through time so semantic eternity is violated. On another view, the truth value is fixed according to a "God's eye view" of the universe in which the acts chosen by the scientist are part of the future even before they are actually chosen. In that case, semantic eternity is saved.[2]

Case (c): A famous economic prognosticator can cause the truth of his prediction that the market is ready to crash by announcing that prediction. Such predictions are referred to as *self-fulfilling prophecies* (*Fig. 15.1*). The very act of observing can also affect the system observed. This is always a concern in behavioral research (*Fig. 15.2*).

It seems that each of these examples can be skirted if the scientist is sufficiently careful. The first can be dispensed with by insisting that a hypothesis be a proposition rather than an indexical sentence. The second and third can be overcome by secrecy. But if modern physics is correct, the avoidance of all such truth dependencies is imposible in principle. Case (d): Einstein argued that the truth about mass and simultaneity depends unavoidably on the reference

---

that it picks out at a particular time that is under assessment. In this respect, the analysis of Neyman-Pearson hypothesis testing provided in chapter 3 was not sufficiently general, for it assumed the truth of the hypothesis under study to be fixed.

[2] William of Ockham held both theories at once to resolve the apparent contradiction between human freedom and God's omniscience.

Figure 15.2

frame of the observer. Quantum theory has been interpreted to say that the physical character of a system (wave vs. particle) depends on which experimental measurements the scientist elects to perform (*Fig. 15.3*).

The theses of semantic immutability and eternity are also called into question by the philosophy of language. Case (e): Upon being awakened from his dogmatic slumbers by Hume's underdetermination arguments, Kant responded with the view that truth depends on the manner in which humans perceive and conceive of things. On Kant's view, raw sensations are the *matter of experience*. The human faculty of perception imposes space and time as organizing principles on raw sensations, so that space and time are the *pure forms of experience*. According to Kant, the *world-in-itself* is the unknowable source of the matter of experience. Kant was adamant that scientific hypotheses are neither true nor false of the world-in-itself. They are true or false, rather, of the *world of experience*, which may be thought of as all experience that could possibly result from the imposition of geometrical (spatial) and arithmetical (temporal) structure upon the raw sensations produced in us by the world-in-itself. The imagination's active process of ordering sensations in space and time was referred to by Kant as *synthesis* (*Fig. 15.4*).

Since the world of possible experience is in part constituted by the structure of the human mind, it is conceivable that other sorts of beings with different mental structures would literally inhabit different worlds of possible experience from ours so that their truth would be different from ours. In fact, Kant explicitly entertains this possibility, but does not pursue it since he is concerned only with the scope of human knowledge.

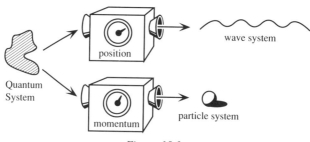

Figure 15.3

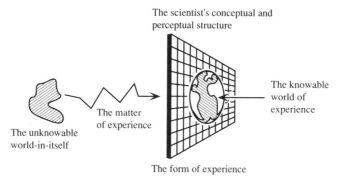

Figure 15.4

It would be absurd for us to hope that we can know more of any object than belongs to the possible experience of it or lay claim to the least knowledge of how anything not assumed to be an object of possible experience is determined according to the constitution that it has in itself. ... It would be ... a still greater absurdity if we conceded no things in themselves or declared our experience to be the only possible mode of knowing things, our intuition of them in space and in time for the only possible intuition and our discursive understanding for the archetype of every possible understanding; for this would be to wish to have the principles of the possibility of experience considered universal conditions of things in themselves.[3]

The *logical positivists* self-consciously replaced Kant's pure form of experience with *meaning postulates*, a special class of statements that are true by convention. Since the meaning postulates may be changed at will, positivism violates both semantic eternity and semantic immutability. Subsequent developments led to a widening of the scope of these dependencies. W. V. O. Quine attacked the doctrine of analyticity and concluded that meaning and truth depend on one's total belief set rather than on some privileged set of allegedly analytic beliefs, a position known as *holism*.

T. S. Kuhn went even further, arguing that truth and meaning depend on extralinguistic factors such as one's membership in a social unit called a *paradigm*. The paradigm involves such factors as one's education, one's peers, one's methods, one's metaphysical beliefs, and a store of relevant examples of solved problems to emulate in other applications. When scientific change extends to the basic elements of the paradigm, a *scientific revolution* occurs. Between scientific revolutions, inquiry is said to be *normal*.

Looking at a bubble-chamber photograph, the student sees confused and broken lines, the physicist a record of familiar subnuclear events. Only after a number of such transformations of vision does the student become an inhabitant of the scientist's world, seeing what the scientist sees and responding as the scientist does. The world that the student then enters is not fixed once

[3] Kant (1950): 99.

and for all by the nature of the environment, on the one hand, and of science on the other. Rather, *it is determined jointly by the environment and the particular normal-scientific tradition that the student has been trained to pursue.*[4]

To the extent that a scientist can alter his paradigm, whether by admitting new members, by providing new examples of solved problems, or by changing its most basic assumptions, the scientist literally has control over the structure of his world and hence over the correctness of structural hypotheses about that world, so semantic immutability and eternity both fail.

Redundancy or *minimalist* theories take truth to be nothing more than assertion.[5] A related view identifies truth with warranted assertability in one's social context.[6] These views clearly may violate semantic eternity. Semantic immutability is also violated if the data or if what counts as justification on the data is affected by the acts or attitudes of the scientist.

Some philosophers maintain that whatever truth is, it is eternal. One way to preseve eternity without insisting on semantic immutability is to characterize truth as what the scientist is disposed to believe (or is justified in believing) in the limit of inquiry. C. S. Peirce seems to have held such a view.[7] Putnam's *internal realism*[8] defines truth to be justified belief when observational circumstances are pushed to an ideal limit. Semantic mutability may still fail, if justification or data depend on the scientist.

2. Relativism, Truth, and Interpersonal Agreement

Relativism is sometimes taken to be the view that whatever I believe is true-for-me. The terminology is unfortunate, since relativity is not arbitrariness. It is the systematic dependence of truth (or, more generally, correctness) on some parameter manipulable by the scientist. The adoption of one parameter

---

[4] Kuhn (1970): 111–112, emphasis added.

[5] E.g., Horwich (1990).

[6] Dummett (1978).

[7] "The real, then, is that which, sooner or later, information and reasoning would finally result in, and which is therefore independent of the vagaries of me and you" Peirce (1958): 69. I find Peirce to be systematically ambiguous on this issue. He may mean, as I have proposed, that if the scientific community were to converge to some other view, then the other view would be true because convergence constitutes truth. It might also be that Peirce believes science to be reliable, so that its convergence can be used to find a fixed reality that does not depend upon anything science does. Then if science were to converge to some other view than the one that it (reliably) converges to, it would be wrong.

[8] "A statement is true, in my view, if it would be justified under epistemically ideal conditions ... the two key claims of such an idealization theory of truth are: (1) that truth is independent of justification here and now, but not independent of *all* possibility of justification. To claim that a statement is true is to claim that it could be justified; (2) that truth is expected to be stable, or 'convergent'; if either a statement or its negation could be justified, even if conditions were as ideal as one could hope to make them, there is no sense in thinking of the statement as *having* a truth value" (Putnam 1983: 84–85).

as opposed to another is arbitrary, but the truth relative to a given parameter is not. In general, I take *relativism* to be the view that there is a parameter associated with the local situation of the agent upon which truth for that agent depends. The *subjectivist* position that whatever I believe is true-for-me amounts to the specific proposal that truth is exhausted by or depends only on what I believe. In my usage, this is the most extreme version of relativism rather than a general characterization of the position.

Relativism is often viewed as a menace to the very idea of a normative logic of scientific method. It is prudent to step back and ask why it is so regarded. The concerns in question arose with the collapse of logical positivism. Positivists held that the meaning of evidence is fixed and unproblematic and that people can decide the truth of evidence statements reliably. Hypotheses about unobservable properties or entities were held to be problematic, however, so they were to be reduced to observation statements by meaning postulates, so that to change the postulates is to change the meaning of one's theoretical language. Moreover, it was held that these postulates are analytic or true by meaning and hence impervious to empirical assessment.

Given these assumptions, the positivist could portray the course of scientific inquiry as follows. First, one chooses meaning postulates that fix a theoretical language. Then one chooses an inductive method matching that language, and the inductive method draws conclusions about hypotheses in that language until the scientist alters the meaning postulates and selects a new method. The data from the past can be retained since only theoretical meaning depends on the meaning postulates. Since the meaning postulates eliminate global under-determination and since judgments concerning evidence are interpersonally shared, it can be hoped that inquiry will force those sharing meaning postulates to the truth (relative to the meaning postulates adopted) and hence to agreement with one another.

> The condition thus imposed upon the observational vocabulary of science is of a pragmatic character; it demands that each term included in that vocabulary be of such a kind that under suitable conditions, different observers can, by means of direct observation, arrive at a high degree of certainty whether the term applies to a given situation. ... That human beings are capable of developing observational vocabularies that satisfy the given requirement is a fortunate circumstance: without it, science as an *intersubjective* enterprise would be impossible.[9]

But convergence to agreement founders when the positivist's assumptions are relaxed. First, suppose that theoretical truth depends on the conclusions that arise in the normal operation of inductive inquiry, rather than on meaning postulates isolated from scientific inquiry by their analytic status. Then even though two scientists start out with the relevant semantic parameters set the same way, minor differences in the order in which they receive the data may lead to different inductive conclusions in the short run. These distinct

---

[9] Hempel (1965): 127, n. 10, emphasis added.

conclusions cause a divergence of meaning between the two scientists, which can lead to still further variation in conclusions as the data increases, and so forth, so that agreement in the limit is no longer to be expected. The situation is exacerbated if we also allow the truth of the data to depend on the conclusions drawn during the course of inquiry. This is often expressed by saying that the data is *theory-laden*. In that case, the data arriving to the two scientists diverges as their conclusions diverge, so divergence both of conclusions and of meaning is accelerated.

Kuhn and Quine targeted exactly the two assumptions in question. Quine rejected analyticity, concluding that all beliefs are relevant to meaning, so the operation of induction cannot help but cause meaning shifts insofar as it leads to changes in belief. Kuhn made truth relative to the scientist's paradigm and extended this thesis to the data. While Quine's attack was based on logical considerations internal to the positivistic program, Kuhn's critique arose from the examination of major episodes in scientific history, in which both the observational and the theoretical worlds of the scientist seemed to change.

This still wouldn't have been fatal to the positivist's hope for interpersonal agreement, for if the one scientist could translate the other's views at each stage and they turned out to be synonymous with his own, intersubjectivity would be preserved despite the fact that the scientists draw syntactically distinct conclusions at each stage. But Quine argued on strict behaviorist (and hence reductionist) grounds that radical translation of this sort is conceptually impossible because meaning is not definable in terms of overt, linguistic behavior. For his part, Kuhn argued on the basis of some historical examples (e.g., the difference between relativistic and classical mass) that competing paradigms are *incommensurable*, which is supposed to entail the impossibility of translations between them.

In the wake of these developments, many in the philosophy of science have taken the following advice of Kuhn to heart:

> As in political revolutions, so in paradigm choice—*there is no standard higher than the assent of the relevant community.* To discover how scientific revolutions are effected, we shall therefore have to examine not only the impact of nature and of logic, but also the techniques of persuasive argumentation effective within the quite special groups that constitute the community of scientists.[10]

Kuhn's paradigms are above rational argument, and hence may be studied only *naturalistically*, through history, rhetoric, psychology, and sociology. Quine draws a similar conclusion, insisting that the only topic remaining for epistemology is the psychological study of how it actually happens that rudimentary sensory input causes us to draw extensive theoretical conclusions. We must not confuse epistemological naturalism with a healthy interest in the history, psychology, and sociology of science. The naturalist's position is not ecumenical but exclusive: it asserts that there is nothing to epistemology *but*

---

[10] Kuhn (1970): 94, emphasis added.

psychology, history, and sociology. I will refer to that position as *methodological nihilism*.

Does methodological nihilism actually follow from the considerations leading to the downfall of logical positivism? Suppose we grant, outright, that data is theory-laden, that meaning is affected by the normal operation of inquiry through time, and that different theoretical traditions are incommensurable. We have just seen that without these assumptions, different inquirers using the same method could end up disagreeing, even in the limit. But it does not follow that the method employed is not reliable, for in light of relativism it may be that each user is guaranteed to arrive at some version of the truth even though there is no version of the truth that all users converge to. Indeed, to force the various users to agree after minor differences in the data send them in different directions might require that some of them abandon their own truths in favor of what are for them falsehoods. But since logical reliability is a normative, logical matter, the nihilist's conclusion that the philosophy of science must collapse into history, sociology, or psychology is premature.

3. Relativistic Reliabilism

The inference from relativism to methodological nihilism is blocked by the proposal that a scientific method reliably find the truth relative to what the method does, even though other methods may find other truths relative to the things they do. I will refer to this position as *relativistic reliabilism* (*Fig. 15.5*). According to it, two logically reliable scientists can stabilize in the limit to theories that appear to each scientist to contradict one another. The two scientists are not guaranteed to converge to agreement in the limit, but then why should they be expected to if their truths differ?

Figure 15.5

The idea that a normative methodologist might try to absorb relativistic objections by proposing methods that actively change the truth has already been anticipated and rejected by R. Rorty:

> The notion that it would be all right to relativize sameness of meaning, objectivity, and truth to a conceptual scheme, as long as there were some criteria for knowing when and why it was rational to adopt a new conceptual scheme, was briefly tempting. For now the philosopher, the guardian of rationality, became the man who told you when you could start meaning something different, rather than the man who told you what you meant.

I confess that this sounds a good deal like what I am proposing, as long as "rationality" may be taken in the sense of "directed by a reliable method." Rorty objects that any such proposal must *somehow* presuppose intertranslatability of conjectures by competing scientists.

> But this attempt to retain the philosopher's traditional role was doomed. All the Quinean reasons why he could not do the one were also reasons why he could not do the other. ... [As] soon as it was admitted that "empirical considerations" ... incited but did not require "conceptual change" ... the division of labor between the philosopher and the historian no longer made sense. Once one said that it was rational to abandon the Aristotelian conceptual scheme as a result of this or that discovery, then "change of meaning" or "shift in conceptual scheme" meant nothing more than "shift in especially central beliefs." The historian can make the shift from old scheme to the new intelligible. ... There is nothing the philosopher can add to what the historian has already done to show that this intelligible and plausible course is a "rational" one. Without what Feyerabend called "meaning invariance," there is no special method (meaning-analysis) which the philosopher can apply.[11]

But as a matter of fact, nothing in what follows presupposes meaning invariance or intertranslatability. In fact, it is much more freewheeling in its relativism than Rorty is in the above passage, for while Rorty seems to assume Quine's particular account of relativism in which meaning and truth are altered by changing one's beliefs, I am prepared to entertain inductive settings in which it is not known a priori how the underlying truth dependency works or even what the relevant parameters are. Moreover, Rorty is off the mark when he claims that there is nothing the philosopher can add to make shifts in meaning intelligible. Intelligibility is a notion broad enough to include logical investigations showing that one strategy for relativistic inductive inference is more reliable at finding the truth than another, or transcendental deductions for various relativistic senses of inductive success.

The popular inference from relativism to methodological nihilism has led both to a repudiation of logic in the philosophy of science and to the dismissal of relativism among logically minded methodologists. But both sides are mistaken. Logic can take account of relativistic dependencies if the logician simply takes the extra time and effort to do so.

---

[11] This and preceding quotes from Rorty (1979): 272–273.

There are perhaps two reasons why relativistic reliabilism has not enjoyed much attention. First, the goal may seem too difficult. The idea of a method for shifting among alternative conceptual schemes seems implausible. One often hears that the *interesting* problem in science is picking the right concepts, as though once the frame is set, induction proceeds mechanically from there. But this kind of talk must be received with caution. The many demonic arguments of the preceding chapters should dispel the impression that reliable induction in a fixed conceptual scheme is trivial.

Moreover, taking relativism seriously may make induction easier. This is obvious if it is assumed that the scientist's conclusions *color* the truth, so that meaning variance always narrows the gap between truth and conjecture. Also, if the scientist has any control over truth that is not linked to his conjectures, then he essentially has an extra move in the game of science; a move that he may learn to use to his advantage, just as a chess player would learn to take advantage of an extra queen on his side.

The preceding discussion may suggest the contrary objection that relativistic reliability is too easy: If truth depends on the scientist, then why doesn't the scientist just make some theory true and quit? Admittedly, if the scientist has absolute control over truth, then reliability is trivial to achieve. But we have already seen that relativism does not imply subjectivism, the view that truth depends only on the state of the investigator. If truth not only depends on the investigator but also has some aspect over which the investigator has no control, then the scientist may not know exactly *how* truth depends on what he does. For example, an archaeologist can never be entirely sure how his presence will affect the social structures he intends to study, it was not obvious to Newton how the truth about simultaneity depends on one's inertial frame, and nothing is less durable than philosophers' views about the nature of meaning and reference. Given such uncertainty about the workings of the underlying truth dependency, reliably finding even the relative truth about a given hypothesis can be difficult or even impossible, just as in the nonrelativistic case. As always, the interesting question is where the line between the solvable and the unsolvable problems falls. The question is complicated by relativism, but it does not go away.

4. Functional versus Metaphysical Relativism

Relativism demands that truth,[12] meaningfulness, and what counts as data all depend not only on the way things are, but also on something else associated with the scientist. According to a traditional manner of speaking, the part of truth that depends on the way things are is the *objective* component and the part of truth that depends in some way on the scientist is the *subjective* component. This view I refer to as *metaphysical relativism*, since it is based on

---

[12] As always, *truth* is taken as a placeholder for any semantic or global, epistemic hypothesis virtue.

the metaphysical distinctions between objectivity and subjectivity, between the mental and the physical, or between the "inner" and the "outer."

It is easy to slip into the supposition that the subjective (or mental or "inner") component of truth is more subject to *control* by the scientist than is the objective (or physical or "outer") component. But this isn't even approximately true. I have far less control over my central beliefs or over the concepts imposed by my perceptual apparatus than I have over a blob of clay on the table.

From a methodological perspective, it doesn't matter much whether a component of truth is objective or subjective. What matters is whether it is controlled during the course of inquiry by the demon or by the scientist. Accordingly, *Functional relativism*[13] analyzes the factors contributing to truth into those controlled by the scientist and those that are not.

According to these definitions, Kant was a metaphysical but not a functional relativist since he took space and time to be conceptual contributions to truth that remain fixed despite our wills. On the other hand, a self-fulfilling prophecy is functionally but not metaphysically relativistic, since what is manipulated by the economist is the objective state of the economy rather than his own subjective state. The positivists were both functionally and metaphysically relativists, as they took their meaning postulates to be a subjective component of meaning and hence of truth under the volitional control of the scientist. Followers of Wittgenstein take truth, insofar as it is anything, to be assertability warranted by the norms of the relevant community. From an individual scientist's point of view, the community's norms and the truths that depend on them are objective, "external" facts. From the functional viewpoint, the scientist's social status and political rights give him some control over these norms. So such a view is functionally, but not metaphysically, relativistic. Since I am interested in the methodological structure of convergence to the relative truth rather than in the metaphysics of objectivity and subjectivity, I will restrict my attention to functional relativism in what follows.

5. Causal versus Semantic Relativism

In functional relativism, there may be different sorts of reasons that truth depends to some degree on the choices of the scientist. In the case of the economist, the dependency is *causal*: the scientist's act causes a certain reaction in the market. So for example, experimental investigation of contingent or indexical hypotheses counts as an instance of causal relativism. This may sound like an odd way to talk, but from a purely functional/methodological point of

---

[13] The term *functional* alludes to functionalism in the philosophy of mind, in which mental entities are characterized in terms of the computational notion of control. Here, the components of truth are distinguished according to the notion of methodological control.

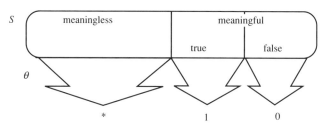

Figure 15.6

view, it indicates a strong formal analogy between the issues raised by experimentation and relativism.

In other cases, as with positivism or Kuhn's relativism, the scientist's effect on truth results from his partial control over *meaning*, in which case we have an instance of *semantic relativism*. Once again, the structure of reliable inference is indifferent to the philosophical interpretation of the dependency, so we need not dwell on this distinction. Nonetheless, the formal analogy between semantic relativism and experimental inquiry of contingent hypotheses underscores the parallel logic of the two subjects.

6. Acts, Scientists, and Worlds-in-Themselves

Let S be a set of *strings*. S is not a language or even a set of well-formed strings. Rather, it should be viewed as the syntactic raw material for all possible languages—e.g., the set of all finite strings over all characters that will ever be typed in the future. It is up to the scientist and the world-in-itself which of these strings are meaningful. Thus I do not assume a fixed language or a fixed vocabulary for inquiry. All that is fixed is the ability to typographically distinguish, say, (B) from (b).[14] I will assume, further, that S is countable, since at most a countable infinity of type fonts and characters will ever be used, and the set of all finite strings over a countable set is countable.

An *assignment* θ attaches truth values and asterisks to strings, where an asterisk denotes *meaningless*. $\mathcal{T}$ denotes the set of all possible assignments (*Fig. 15.6*). Let A be a set of possible *acts* of the scientist, on which the assignment may depend. In causal relativism, these are just ordinary physical acts. In semantic relativism, we may think of an act as the choice of one conceptual scheme, paradigm, or central belief set over another, or an act that influences the linguistic norms of one's community.

[14] There are cases in which even this assumption begs relativist questions—as when we attempt to decode alien messages received in a radio telescope. Who is to say what sorts of modulations in the intensity or the frequency of the waveform count as identical or distinct symbols? But such extreme worries have never been at stake in the real historical cases that motivate relativism in the philosophy of science.

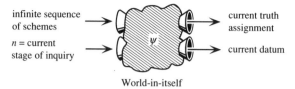

Figure 15.7

Let E be a set of *possible evidence items*. Again, I do not assume that the items in E are well formed, meaningful, true, or anything else. All of that will depend on the acts of the scientist. I assume only that exactly one such item appear in the data stream at any given time.

Relativistic assessment methods take a string and a finite sequence of evidence items as input, and produce an act-conjecture pair as output:

$$\phi: S \times E^* \rightarrow (A \times \{1, 0, *\}).$$

Whatever is required to determine the truth assignment in addition to the acts of the scientist will be referred to as the *world-in-itself*. My functional understanding of the term must always be distinguished from metaphysical usage. Those who hold that truth is nothing more than community assent, for example, would include the tendency of the scientist's colleagues to disagree with him when he wears a red necktie as part of that scientist's word-in-itself, even though these tendencies are grounded by ordinary psychological processes.

There are several ways in which truth may depend upon the acts of the scientist. In the most radical case, truth, meaningfulness, and evidence now may depend on everything the scientist will ever do, as in the Peircean view described earlier. The collection of all worlds-in-themselves is defined generally enough to embrace even such radical cases.[15] A world-in-itself takes an infinite act sequence and a time as inputs and outputs a truth assignment and a datum for the time in question. More precisely, the set of all worlds-in-themselves is defined as follows (*Fig. 15.7*):

$$\mathcal{W} = \{\psi: (A^\omega \times \omega) \rightarrow (\mathcal{T} \times E)\}.$$

Most relativists entertain only more restricted sorts of dependencies. A world-in-itself is *historical* just in case the current assignment and datum depend only on all acts up to the present.[16] If ψ is historical, then we may

---

[15] In the Peircean case, the method's conjecture is the semantically relevant act. To analyze such cases without complicating the following machinery, let the act output by the scientist always be identical to the conjecture.

[16] Of course, one could also consider cases in which truth is historical but evidence is not. Brevity precludes the consideration of every possibility here, though the reader is encouraged to pursue them at leisure.

identify ψ with the map $\psi'(e) = \psi(e, lh(e))$. It seems, for example, that Kuhn proposed no more relativism than this. In fact, it sometimes seems that he holds the even more restrictive view that the current assignment depends only on the current act. Such a world-in-itself is *immediate*. Marxists and literary critics who emphasize the inescapable influence of past oppression on truth and meaning in public discourse seem to be claiming that the world-in-itself is historical rather than immediate. Without endorsing any of these bold claims, the logical framework just presented is general enough to embrace all of them.

7. Transcendental Background Knowledge

The scientist's prior knowledge will be represented by a set $\mathcal{K}$ of possible worlds-in-themselves. This is just to say that the scientist is uncertain a priori about how truth depends on his chosen sequence of acts. Even though truth depends in some way on what he does, the scientist may not know exactly how.

Since $\mathcal{K}$ entails constraints on the structure of the world-in-itself, $\mathcal{K}$ is *transcendental* and hence unknowable according to Kant. These days, transcendental metaphysics goes under the sanitized rubric of *theory of reference* and is no longer considered to lie beyond our ken. Here are just a few examples. Truth does not depend on a privileged set of analytic meaning postulates (Quine). No chosen conceptual scheme can be very different from our own (Davidson). Truth does depend on the social milieu, education, and problem-solving techniques of the scientist (Kuhn). Evidence depends on the same factors (Kuhn, Hanson, Goodman). Truth is warranted assertability relative to the norms of the relevant community (Dummett). Truth is an ideal limit of warranted assertability (Putnam). Even the proposal that there are nontrivial truth dependencies (as opposed to raising the bare possibility) represents a claim about the nature of the actual, underlying truth dependency. As always, my methodological stance is neither to accept nor to reject the scientist's assumptions, but to ask whether reliable induction is possible relative to them; even if they are transcendental.

Earlier, I mentioned the objection that relativistic inquiry is too easy. This objection stems from *subjectivism*, the view that the scientist's conjectures are correct when he makes them *because* he makes them. This extreme position makes truth depend entirely on the acts of the scientist. At the other extreme is *Platonic realism*, in which truth depends entirely on the world-in-itself and is independent of the acts of the scientist. The interesting relativisms are the ones that lie between these extremes, and these interesting cases allow for the possibility of uncertainty about what the nature of the actual truth dependency is.

8. The Course of Relativistic Inquiry

A *state* s of relativistic inquiry is a quadruple (c, a, θ, e), where c is a conjecture, $a \in A$, θ is an assignment, and $e \in E$. A *possible course of relativistic inquiry* is an infinite sequence ρ of such states. Let $\rho_i = c(\rho_i), (a(\rho_i), \theta(\rho_i), e(\rho_i))$ and let

$a(\rho) = (a(\rho_0), a(\rho_1), \ldots, a(\rho_n), \ldots)$ and $e(\rho) = (e(\rho_0), e(\rho_1), \ldots, e(\rho_n), \ldots)$. ρ is a *possible course of inquiry for* ϕ, ψ, s just in case for each $n \in \omega$,

(1) $(\theta(\rho_n), e(\rho_n)) = \psi(a(\rho), n)$ and

(2) $(a(\rho_n), c(\rho_n)) = \phi(s, e(\rho)|n)$.[17]

Let $Inq(\psi, \phi, s)$ be the set of all possible courses of inquiry for ψ, ϕ, s. The definition is general enough to include cases in which the world-in-itself can "see" once for all everything that ϕ will actually do.[18] The ability of the world-in-itself to see the future acts of the scientist implies that $Inq(\psi, \phi, s)$ may contain more than one element. For example, let ϕ perform act 0 so long as no 1 occurs in the data and perform act 1 forever after the first 1 appears. Let ψ clairvoyantly produce as data at stage n whatever act ϕ performs at stage n after seeing $e(\rho)|n$, which includes all the data presented up to stage $n - 1$. The sequence ρ, in which for each i, $e(\rho_i) = 0$ and $a(\rho_i) = 0$, is in $Inq(\psi, \phi, s)$. But so is each sequence in which $e(\rho_i) = 0$ and $a(\rho_i) = 0$ until some point n such that for all $j \geq n$, $e(\rho_j) = 1$ and $a(\rho_j) = 1$.

$Inq(\psi, \phi, h)$ may also be empty. For now let ϕ choose as its act at stage n the reversal of the datum at stage $n - 1$ (1 if 0, 0 if 1), and let ψ produce as a datum at stage $n - 1$ the act performed by ϕ at stage n. This example is a simple formalization in terms of the worlds-in-themselves of the temporal paradox of a rocket that sends a probe into the past just in case it does not detect the return of the probe from the past.[19]

These subtleties disappear if we assume that ψ is historical. In that case, each successive datum and act is uniquely determined, respectively, by the acts and data presented in the past. In this case, we may let $\rho[\phi, \psi, s]$ denote the unique element of $Inq(\psi, \phi, s)$.

9. Relativistic Hypothesis Assessment

Now it remains to define relativistic reliability. The dependency of truth on the scientist's acts opens up a range of new possibilities. One intuitive proposal is that the scientist must first eventually stop fiddling with semantics so that there is a fixed truth value to find.

ϕ *truth-stably decides* s *in the limit given* $\mathcal{K} \Leftrightarrow \forall \psi \in \mathcal{K}$, $\forall \rho \in Inq(\psi, \phi, s)$, $\exists n \, \forall m \geq n$,

(1) $c(\rho_m) = \theta(\rho_m)(s)$ and

(2) $\theta(\rho_m)(s) = \theta(\rho_n)(s)$.

---

[17] Recall that $e(\rho)|0 = \mathbf{0}$, so $(a(\rho_0), c(\rho_0))$ is the blind output made by ϕ on the empty data sequence $\mathbf{0}$ and $(a(\rho_1), c(\rho_1))$ is the output of ϕ on the data sequence $e(\rho)|1$, etc.

[18] Thus, the world-in-itself stands to the scientist in much the same way that the omniscient deity of scholastic theology stands to his creatures.

[19] Earman (1972).

In the case of semantically immediate worlds, truth can be stabilized by stabilizing to a fixed, semantically relevant act or conceptual scheme.

> ϕ *scheme-stably decides* s *in the limit given* $\mathcal{K} \Leftrightarrow \forall \psi \in \mathcal{K}$,
> $\forall \rho \in Inq(\psi, \phi, s), \exists n \, \forall m \geq n$,
>
> (1) $c(\rho_m) = \theta(\rho_m)(s)$ *and*
>
> (2) $a(\rho_m) = a(\rho_n)$.

Even in the historical case, stabilizing to a particular act may not suffice to stabilize truth, so scheme stability does not imply truth stability.

One might suppose that convergent reliability cannot be defined unless stabilization to truth or some sort of translatability between conceptual schemes is assumed. But, in fact, we can require convergence to the state of being correct about the ever changing truth value of h, rather than convergence to the unique truth value of s (which does not exist independently of time). Thus, convergence to the truth is possible even when meaning shifts never stop occurring.

> ϕ *unstably decides* s *in the limit given* $\mathcal{K} \Leftrightarrow \forall \psi \in \mathcal{K}$,
> $\forall \rho \in Inq(\psi, \phi, s), \exists n \, \forall m \geq n, c(\rho_m) = \theta(\rho_m)(s)$.

Insistence on stabilizing the truth value of a hypothesis may prevent success when it would have been possible to track the (changing) truth value for eternity. For a trivial example, suppose that $\mathcal{K} = \{\psi\}$ and the truth of $s \in S$ changes forever in ψ independently of whatever the scientist does. It is impossible to stabilize the truth value of s in ψ, even in the limit, but a scientist who knows a priori the fixed sequence of truth values assumed by s in ψ decides h unstably with certainty given $\mathcal{K}$.

More interesting examples can be constructed in which truth can be stabilized, and the truth can be found, but not by any scientist who stabilizes it. The idea is that the scientist must perform "semantic experiments" in order to explore the nature of the underlying truth dependency and the experiments must eventually stop if truth is to be stabilized.[20] For example, let $A = E = \{0, 1\}$. Let $\zeta: \omega \to \{0, 1\}$, and let $\#n(\mathbf{a})$ be the number of occurrences of n in $\mathbf{a} \in \{0, 1\}^*$. Now define:

$$\theta_1^{\mathbf{a}}(s) = \begin{cases} 1 & \textit{if } last(\mathbf{a}) = 1 \\ 0 & \textit{otherwise.} \end{cases}$$

---

[20] Relativists never propose doing such experiments to my knowledge, but I do not see anything in their view that precludes the possibility. One might object that what was taken to be observed in previous schemes cannot remembered in later ones. But historicists like Kuhn routinely tell us what was taken as evidence for what in a given paradigm, so it would seem that while the meaning of the data does not survive paradigm shifts, the enscriptions recording the data do.

$$\theta_2^a(s) = \begin{cases} 0 & if\ last(a) = 1 \\ 1 & otherwise. \end{cases}$$

$$\psi_1(a) = (\theta_1^a, 0)$$

$$\psi_2^\zeta(a) = \begin{cases} (\theta_2^a, 1) & if\ \zeta(\#1(a)) = 0\ and\ last(a) = 1 \\ (\theta_2^a, 0) & otherwise. \end{cases}$$

$$\psi_3^\zeta(a) = \begin{cases} (\theta_2^a, 1) & if\ \zeta(\#0(a)) = 0\ and\ last(a) = 0 \\ (\theta_2^a, 0) & otherwise. \end{cases}$$

Let $\mathcal{K}_0 = \{\psi_1\} \cup \{\psi_2^\zeta, \psi_3^\zeta: \zeta^{-1}(0)$ is infinite$\}$. The dilemma posed by $\mathcal{K}$ is that if the scientist ϕ is actually in the world-in-itself ψ_1 and stabilizes the truth value of s to 1, then ϕ stabilizes to act 1. The data will consist of all 0s. But then the demon may choose ζ so that $\zeta^{-1}(0)$ is infinite but ψ_3^ζ also produces only 0s as data in response to the same acts: let n be the number of 0s enacted by ϕ prior to convergence to act 1, and let $\zeta(k) = 1$ for all $k \leq n$. So ϕ fails in ψ_3^ζ. By a similar argument, ϕ fails in ψ_2^ζ if ϕ stabilizes the truth value of s to 0 in ψ_1. So s is not truth-stably decidable in the limit given $\mathcal{K}_0$.

But s is unstably decidable in the limit given $\mathcal{K}_0$ using the following method.

$$\phi(s, e) = \begin{cases} (1, 1) & if\ 1 \notin rng(e)\ \&\ lh(e)\ is\ even \\ (0, 0) & if\ 1 \notin rng(e)\ \&\ lh(e)\ is\ odd \\ (1, 0) & otherwise. \end{cases}$$

In ψ_1, 1 is never observed so ϕ alternates forever between acts 0 and 1. Hence, the truth of s vacillates at each stage, but ϕ's conjecture is always correct. In ψ_2^ζ, eventually datum 1 appears since 1 repeated infinitely often by ψ_2^ζ if ϕ performs act 1 infinitely often. Then ϕ stabilizes to act 1 and conjecture 0, which is correct for ψ_2^ζ. By a similar argument, ϕ eventually sees a 1 in ψ_3^ζ, and hence stabilizes to act 1 and to conjecture 0, which is correct for ψ_3^ζ.

10. Relativistic Hypothesis Assessment as Nonrelativistic Discovery

From a purely logical point of view, relativistic hypothesis assessment in immediate worlds-in-themselves is a special case of nonrelativistic discovery. The key to the reduction is to view the scientist's act or conceptual scheme as a "hypothesis" of the form "s is correct in the underlying world-in-itself relative to a." Scheme-stable decidability in the limit then corresponds to stable identification in the limit and unstable decision in the limit corresponds to unstable identification in the limit. The reduction suggests yet another relativistic assessment criterion—almost stable decision in the limit—that reduces to almost stable identifiability in the same manner. The stable and almost stable cases therefore inherit characterization theorems from the corresponding discovery problems, and the unstable case inherits the difficulties attending a complexity-theoretic characterization of unstable identification.[21]

When we move to historical worlds-in-themselves, the proposed analogy is complicated by the possiblity that the world may "remember" past acts. This corresponds to a discovery problem in which the correctness of a hypothesis depends upon what was conjectured in the past. These historical encumbances lead to violations of the usual closure laws for reliably assessible hypotheses (cf. section 14.11), so that a simple, nontrivial characterization of success is difficult to provide.

11. Relativistic Theory Discovery

So far, the scientist's conceptual scheme or semantically relevant act has been treated as a parameter independent of the scientist's conjecture. But if anything seems to be relevant to meaning and truth, it is the scientist's current theory of the world, which is altered to some extent by his inductive activities. Hence, it is perhaps more natural to conceive of inquiry along the lines of the piecemeal or nonuniform theory identification paradigm of chapter 12, in which the aim of the scientist is to add and to weed out hypotheses so that in the limit he stabilizes to some version of the complete truth. But in this case, we must add the complication that both entailment and truth depend on the theory conjectured at a given stage, so that the world-in-itself is a function $\psi(T) = (\theta, e)$, where T is a theory, θ is a truth assignment on the language in which the theory is stated, and e is a datum.

Let us assume for simplicity that truth and evidence depend immediately on the set R of strings currently conjectured by the scientist. Let R, T be sets of strings. Then define:

$$\mathcal{K}, R \vDash s \text{ relative to } T$$
$$\Leftrightarrow \forall \psi \in \mathcal{K}, \forall e, \text{ if } \psi(T) = (\theta, e) \text{ and } \forall r \in R, \theta(r) = 1 \text{ then } \theta(s) = 1.$$

This definition has the virtue that actual truths cannot entail actual gibberish relative to T (though a more curious consequence is that actual gibberish entails everything, including all gibberish, relative to T). It also has the desirable consequence that as T varies, the structure of entailment may change radically over R, which should quell fears that interpersonal logical laws have been smuggled into the scientist's background knowledge. We might hope that for each string s, there is a time after which s is entailed (with respect to the sense of entailment induced by the current conjecture) if and only if s is true

---

[21] A nontrivial characterization theorem for unstable decidability in the limit is given in Kelly and Glymour (1992). In that result, worlds-in-themselves are assumed to satisfy a plenitude principle (cf. chapter 14), so it applies only to a special case of the framework developed in this chapter.

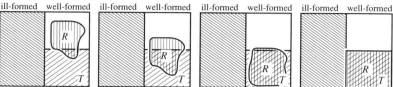

Figure 15.8

(with respect to the sense of truth induced by the current conjecture). Let method γ conjecture a set of strings when provided with a finite sequence e of observations. Let $\varepsilon[\psi, \gamma]$ be the unique data stream determined by the interaction of ψ and γ, since ψ is immediate, and let $\psi(R) = (\psi(R)_1, \psi(R)_2)$. Then define:

> γ *nonuniformly identifies the complete truth given* $\mathcal{K}$ $\Leftrightarrow$
> $\forall \psi \in \mathcal{K}, \forall s \in S, \exists n \, \forall m \geq n, \, [\psi(\gamma(\varepsilon[\psi, \gamma]|m))_1(s) = 1$
> $\Leftrightarrow \mathcal{K}, \gamma(\varepsilon[\psi, \gamma]|m) \vDash s \text{ relative to } \gamma(\varepsilon[\psi, \gamma]|m)].$

In realist settings, truth and well-formedness are naively fixed and truth stays put while science tries its best to home in on it in light of increasing data, as in the nonrelativistic paradigm examined in detail in chapter 12. In *Figure 15.8*, T is the set of all true hypotheses, *wf* is the set of all well-formed strings, and R is the set of strings entailed by γ's current conjecture. In the case of positivism, we must add to the story the set C of all conventionally selected meaning postulates that tie down the language. Assuming with the positivists that inductive methods do not alter analytic truths, the picture is the same, except that it is now guaranteed a priori that the meaning postulates are well formed and true (*Fig. 15.9*). If the meaning postulates C are changed, however, then truth and well-formedness can change. Positivists didn't entertain the possibility of convergent success through changing conventions, and this is what left them vulnerable to the objections of Kuhn and Quine. But the above definition of relativistic discovery does allow for convergence through revolutions.

Since the time of Kant, philosophers have been enchanted with the idea that relativistic truth might meet us halfway. Kuhn and Hanson, for example, spoke of theory-ladenness, as though the theories we entertain are goggles that

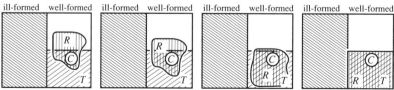

Figure 15.9

the joy of coherentism

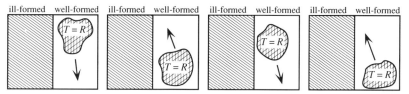

Figure 15.10

color both truth and the data to suit themselves. Radical coherentists go further and assume that every coherent theory is true, so that coherent conjectures necessarily track the truth. The effect, in our setting, is the same as assuming that the truth unflaggingly adapts itself to whatever self-consistent conjecture the scientist produces (*Fig. 15.10*). But it is also transcendentally possible for truth to run away from us, in the sense that our conjectured theories are always false *because* we conjecture them. Thus, a theory could remain true as the scientist homes in on it, only to melt spitefully into falsehood (or even worse, into nonsense) the minute he comes to believe it. Such worlds-in-themselves might well be called *Sysiphian* to underscore the futility of inquiry within them. In such a world-in-itself, uniform convergence to the complete truth is impossible, even if the scientist's transcendental background knowledge is perfect. It is interesting to observe that nonuniform convergence to the complete truth may still be possible, however, so long as the scientist can find a way to conjecture theories that are increasingly true with respect to themselves (*Fig. 15.11*). Sisyphian relativism is not an empty, theoretical possibility. If truth is nothing more than the relevant community's assent to one's beliefs, as some contemporary philosophers would have it, then the situation just described occurs whenever one loses the trust of that community. Thereafter, the community always manages to find some objection to what the pariah says (perhaps by modifying the community's standards of evidence) just because the pariah says it. Sisyphian relativism also explains the undisputed fact that every scientific theory accepted prior to our current ones has proved, upon close inspection, to be false. This is to be expected if whatever we believe is false (in some respect) because we believe it.

Coherentism, the philosopher's ultimate refuge from skepticism, is not immune from these difficulties. Putnam has correctly remarked that

sisyphian relativism

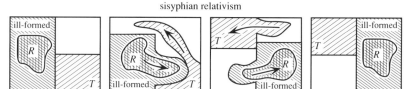

Figure 15.11

Figure 15.12

coherentism is a dangerous position for a relativist, for it is vacuous if coherence is nothing at all and if coherence is the same for everybody then it is naively objectivistic.[22] But if coherentism steers a moderate relativist course between these two extremes, so that coherence, itself, depends to some extent on the acts of the scientist, then sisyphian skepticism looms once again, for it may happen that what we believe is *incoherent* because we believe it.[23]

It is an ironic footnote on the history of philosophy that sisyphian skepticism is much worse than the inductive skepticism that relativism (in its Kantian and positivistic incarnations) was summoned to defeat (*Fig. 15.12*). Inductive skepticism tells us that belief might happen to be false, for all we know. Relativistic skepticism tells us that belief might be self-falsifying, for all we know.

12. Whiggish Relativism

Some relativists are adamant that truth in one scheme is no better than truth in any other, and this is the sort of relativism that I have explored so far. The proposed definitions of relativistic reliability do not impose any constraints whatsoever on which schemes the scientist tries out, so long as the scientist is eventually correct about the truth value under study, just as physics refuses to distinguish inertial reference frames. But is seems that most would-be relativists find it hard to reconcile themselves to this absolute symmetry for long. Some Marxists and literary theorists teach that truth is ineluctably bound to ideology, but it is abundantly clear on their view that possession of capitalistic truth is not as good as possession of Marxist truth. I refer to the position that some truths are better, if no truer, than other truths as *Whiggish relativism.*

[22] Putnam (1990): 123.

[23] This may be understood in a precise way if we define relative satisfiability along the lines of our definition of relativistic entailment. For example, say that h is satisfiable relative to γ at time n just in case h is correct relative to γ at n in some possible world-in-itself.

If some schemes are better than others, then the scientist ought to find the truth in a good one. This imposes a side constraint on the kinds of schemes the scientist can visit in the limit and makes relativistic inference correspondingly more difficult. To pursue this proposal in more detail, one must eventually come up with some concrete ideas about what sorts of schemes make good ones. One way that a theory that is complete and true with respect to itself can fail to be desirable is that it is empty. For example, a chicken uniformly identifies the complete truth because, presumably, the chicken's worldview is empty and it is plausible to suppose that an empty worldview makes all strings meaningless. So in the limit, the chicken's worldview excludes all nonsense and includes all truth with respect to itself! A Whiggish relativist would no doubt insist that a true, nonempty worldview would be better.

But it does not suffice merely to prefer more truths, for the truths might all say the same thing. One would like more truths that collectively say more. If a theory makes every string true in every possible world of experience (with respect to itself), then all of these truths are equivalent and vacuous. The problem is that such a theory fails to separate possible worlds of experience with respect to itself. In general, the proposition expressed by *s* relative to *T* is the set of all possible worlds of experience for which *s* is well formed and true with respect to *T*. Then what we would prefer is a theory *T* that is true with respect to itself and also informative with respect to itself.

But mere expressiveness may not satisfy us, either, particularly when policy is at stake. Then we want a scheme that gives rise to a tidy causal structure, so that cheap and effective manipulations of the world-in-itself can be made. A suggestive, Whiggish paradigm of this sort might be constructed from concepts introduced in chapters 12, 14, and 15.

Exercises

15.1. Prove the claims in section 15.10.

15.2. Investigate some particular problems in the paradigms discussed in sections 15.11 and 15.12.

*15.3. Remember the example of Frank and Gertrude (exercise 11.3). In such a paradigm, there is no reality except the totality of the conjectures of a population of *n* agents, which the *n* agents simultaneously investigate and construct by investigating it. How might this example be expanded into a relativistic model of learning to communicate? (cf. Lewis 1969). Consider how the task of language learning changes in character when we move from one infant (in a population of millions of adults) to two infants growing up together in the woods. Also speculate on how such a paradigm might be used to model financial markets, in which market value is nothing but the result of everyone trying to discover from past evidence what the market value is.

16

Closing Conversation

Yak! *On the contrary.* *Let's get back to the lab.*
Yak yak yak!

Philo: I've skimmed through this book on learning theory. I found it quite odd.

Learnio: I read it a little while ago and found it interesting. Why don't you try your objections out on me? I'm sure I would learn something from them.

Philo: Excellent. To begin with, isn't the goal of converging to the truth trivial? Whatever hypothesis is true, there is always some method that converges to just that hypothesis, no matter what.

Learnio: Actually, the whole point of the book is to rule out such examples. A logically reliable method is guaranteed by its structure to converge to the truth on each possible data stream that might arise for all we know in advance. If we do not know in advance that a hypothesis is true, then the method that always conjectures that hypothesis is far from being logically reliable.

Philo: Oh, I see. Here is another concern. Isn't it naive to assume that the data is simply given by nature? The scientist must use his creative intuition to think of hypotheses, which in turn guide experiments from which the data is derived.

Learnio: In chapter 14 there is a paradigm for causal inference from experimental data that has exactly this character.

Philo: Here is another objection I hear all the time. You assume that science is the search for Truth with a capital T. But there is no such thing, so the proposed aim of science is specious.

Learnio: The results of this book apply not only to truth but also to verisimilitude, empirical adequacy, and any mixture of these attributes with such side constraints as simplicity or lower bounds on content and explanatory power. And even when truth is intended, the term "truth" can be understood in a minimal sense.[1] For example, decidability in the limit could be defined

---

[1] Horwich (1990).

as follows: $\mathcal{K}$ entails that α stabilizes to 1 if h and α stabilizes to 0 if $\neg h$. This definition makes no reference to relations of correspondence between worlds and hypotheses. It is just a matter of entailment of a pair of material conditionals by $\mathcal{K}$.

Philo: Well, I had in mind a more sophisticated objection. Every philosopher of science knows that meaning and truth depend on the concepts and beliefs of the scientist. In a scientific revolution, meanings are altered so that it is impossible to translate the data and the hypotheses of the past into the language of the present. When this happens, we say that a *scientific revolution* had occurred, and it is hopeless to suppose that scientific convergence or progress can be defined across such revolutions. Perhaps normal science can proceed mechanically, in the manner that learning theorists seem to require, but the *interesting* part of science is the revolutionary part, and there learning theory has nothing to say, since any interesting sort of convergence must be disrupted during each scientific revolution.

Learnio: First of all, a major theme of the book is that inquiry is not trivial when all the concepts are fixed, a theory is given to test, and the data simply pours in. In fact, one can systematically characterize which inductive problems are solvable and which are not. It turns out that reliable methods exist only for topologically simple hypotheses, and reliable, computable methods exist only for computationally simple hypotheses.

Second, chapter 15 extends learning-theoretic analysis to a setting in which the truth of the hypothesis and the data received both depend on various acts of the scientist (and possibly on what the scientist conjectures at a given stage). And it is shown in that chapter that from a purely methodological point of view, relativistic dependencies can make inquiry easier rather than harder.

Philo: But, as I said, you have to suppose intertranslatability of theories in order to define convergence when meaning changes. And that is just what the philosophers deny. This is the celebrated thesis that theories are *incommensurable* across different traditions or paradigms.

Learnio: Not really. If truth changes in response to what the scientist does, then all the scientist should be expected to do is to eventually conjecture the correct truth value relative to what he does. Nothing in this definition entails intelligibility across scientific revolutions. Indeed, a hypothesis true at one stage may be meaningless at the next.

Philo: You are talking about assessing a given hypothesis. But if one wants to discover the complete truth, one must compare successive theories to ensure that they include more and more truth. And that is just where incommensurability breaks the back of your proposal.

Learnio: That isn't true, either. The book requires simply that for each string, eventually it is entailed by the current conjecture if it is currently true with respect to the theory conjectured and is not entailed when it is false or meaningless with respect to the theory conjectured. Nothing about this requires translations across theories.

Philo: You have smuggled in objectivity in the notion of entailment. But of course, logical relations can change when theories change, as we see in the case of quantum logic. And Quine teaches that logical relations are not immune from empirical revision, but are simply more central.

Learnio: You are wrong again. In chapter 15 of the book, entailment is defined as truth preservation over all possible worlds-in-themselves. Since truth depends on the tradition of the scientist, so does entailment, so the relation of entailment over strings of symbols changes across scientific revolutions.

Philo: *Something* sneaky has to be going on. I have heard for years that scientific progress requires intertranslatability of data and hypotheses. What about scientific consensus? You have just described an image of science in which everyone believes as he pleases and ignores everyone else: a veritable tower of Babel. Surely that is not a sufficiently dignified picture of inquiry.

Learnio: If truth really depends on what we do and on what we believe (as you insist), then why should we expect everyone to agree? Requiring agreement might force some of the parties to abandon their own truths, and on your view, there is no truth higher or better than one's own. As for believing what one pleases, it does not follow from meaning variance that whatever we believe is true because we believe it. That is a very special form of relativism that we may call radical subjectivism. If truth depends on something other than our acts and beliefs, then finding the truth can still be nontrivial or even impossible, as shown in chapter 15.

Philo: You seem to be assuming a private language for the scientist. But Wittgenstein taught us that there can be no such thing.

Learnio: If meaning depends on the community, then the scientist's input to meaning and truth is diminished, and we have the case in which truth changes spontaneously, in a manner that the scientist cannot completely control. This may preclude truth-stable convergence, but the prospects of unstable convergence to the truth depend, as always, on precisely what is known in advance about how truth might change.

Philo: Now I know what's bothering me. I bet the book's proofs about reliabililty across conceptual revolutions make free use of classical logic. So the conceptual scheme of classical logic is really being imposed on all the other schemes, even though its inferences may fail in some of the schemes in question.

Learnio: According to you, every proof is given in some conceptual scheme because there is no such thing as truth or logic above conceptual schemes. So I don't see why the book should apologize to you for selecting the one shared by most prospective readers. The important point is that classical logic is flexible enough to represent what would happen if entailment were to change in some arbitrary way across scientific revolutions, as I have already explained.

Philo: Maybe convergence to the truth is a more flexible concept than I imagined. But science is not about convergence to the truth. Looking at real scientific practice (something this idealized book seems far from doing) reveals that science is about following some community norms, maintaining internal coherence, finding explanations, justifying belief in hypotheses that may be false, manufacturing worldviews, increasing journal publications, or some other aims that I haven't thought of yet.

Learnio: Learning theory is frankly addressed to those who view science as a proposed means for finding the truth. I suspect that outside of philosophy departments, this is the majority view, but if you suspect otherwise, we should run a proper poll. For now, I propose the following policy. Those scientists who do not see it as their business to find the truth in a reliable way should be required to state that fact clearly on the covers of their research papers, so that taxpayers and potential users of their results will be fairly warned about what they are supporting. And the science programs on public television should recruit children to scientific careers without subterfuge. Instead of promoting science as a method for unlocking the true secrets of nature, as they currently do, they should frankly explain that while there is no truth for scientists to find, the children can participate in the grand adventure of maintaining arbitrary, coherent degrees of belief, of obeying social norms, or of "justifying" beliefs in a manner that has no clear connection to finding the truth about anything.

Philo: You scoff, but I welcome the suggestion. We may as well present a realistic picture of science to future generations, rather than enthralling them with an idealized fiction of the sort you are proposing. And while we are posting warnings for the public, perhaps you should remind everyone that the sun may explode long before your methods arrive at the truths they are guaranteed to "find." Aside from a few devotees of messianic cults, you will find few people attracted to your methods when they are fairly advertised.

Learnio: First of all, the negative results of learning theory are relevant to the short run, for if you can't find the truth in the limit, you can't find it in the short run, either. But there is more to it than that. If you ask if you can get to Flagstaff in fifteen minutes and I simply answer no, without bothering to mention that you have to cross the Grand Canyon on foot, there is a mistaken (and dangerous) conversational implicature that getting there might not take much more than fifteen minutes. I ought to tell you what I know about the yawning chasm between you and your goal, unless I intend to play a trick on you. Again, it would be considered incompetent for a computer scientist to publish that a problem cannot be solved in linear time if in fact it is easy to show that the problem is not even decidable. In a similar manner, even if you are interested only in getting to the truth in fifteen minutes, it would be incomplete and misleading to tell you only that it can't be had in fifteen minutes if in fact the hypothesis is not even verifiable in the limit.

But perhaps you intended only to question the relevance of the positive results regarding limiting reliability. Of course, we would all like to be guaranteed to find the truth right away. But a little thought about demons reveals that almost no interesting questions can be answered in that sense. A wider range of problems is solvable without relinquishing a clear, logical connection between method and truth if we weaken the operative notion of convergence. Moreover, we can sometimes prove that no method converges always as fast as a given method and sometimes faster. Then we say that the given method is data-minimal. For example, every problem verifiable, refutable, or decidable in the limit is solved in the corresponding sense by a data-minimal method (proposition 4.13). If what is demanded is a method that gets to the truth at least as fast as a data-minimal method and sometimes faster, then this demand cannot possibly be met. There may indeed be methods that achieve other goals faster than a data-minimal method can find the truth, but learning theory, as I have said, is steadfastly dedicated to the aim of finding the truth.

Philo: Of course you can't get the truth in the short run. What you get in the short run is *justified* belief. Justification is part of what separates merely true belief from knowledge. A properly philosophical perspective views justification as an abstract relation holding between theory and evidence. It is the proper job of inductive methodology to discover the nature of this relation.

That reminds me of a concern I had about the way the book mixes inductive methodology with computability. Implementing the relation of inductive justification on computers is for engineers and studying how the relation is wired into human cognition is for empirical psychologists. Viewed either way, computational considerations are irrelevant to inductive methodology, since they add nothing to the underlying object of study, the relation of inductive justification.

Learnio: I am highly suspicious of your alleged notion of justified belief. Either this justification is categorical or it is hypothetical and derived from some other aim. The usual categorical approach is to propose some relation of justification and then to show that it is illustrated in historical practice by famous scientists. But I do not see how *was* implies *ought*. Another approach is to set up "intuitive conditions of adequacy" and then to show that they are satisified by the proposed relation. But what are these intuitions other than reflections of our own psychological biases? Either way, the allegedly categorical, pure logic of induction collapses into sociology or psychology.

Then there are those who view inductive justification as a hypothetical imperative. Science can be a means for many things: convincing others, avoiding lawsuits when bridges fall, avoiding sure-loss bets with your bookie, making a living as a scientist, gathering rewards and respect, or finding the truth. But I suspect that the prestige, rhetorical force, and legal efficacy of science derive from its popular image as an enterprise that submerges ancillary interests to the quest for truth, rather than vice versa. Dutch book arguments for Bayesian conditioning are interesting, and when coherence does not interfere with reliability, they are worthy of consideration. But when it can be shown that avoiding Dutch book precludes reliability for agents of a given class, as is done in the book even for the arithmetically definable methods, it seems odd to say that conditioning confers inductive justification. Rather, it would seem to confer suspicion.

In general, I am suspicious of any proposed notion of inductive justification that fails to advance or even hinders the reliability of inquiry. Learning-theoretic analysis begins and ends with the reliable quest for truth. It is genuinely logical and free of any psychological or social bias. Philosophers of the inductive support stripe may complain that the results appear abstract and alien. But that is precisely because the results are logically grounded in the aim of reliably finding the truth, rather than being mere reflections of our social or psychological habits.

Now let us turn to your objection to the relevance of computability to inductive methodology. One of the major themes of the book is that the problem of induction is very similar to the problem of uncomputability. Indeed, from a certain perspective the two can be viewed as different applications of the very same topological structure. Moreover, both problems arise from similar human limitations (i.e., the bounded nature of perception in space and time, on the one hand, and our bounded access to infinite mathematical objects, on the other). Hence, it seems questionable practice to provide an intricate treatment of the one limitation while ignoring the other entirely. One of the appealing features of learning theory is that its treatment of formal and empirical problems is entirely parallel, since its approach to induction is inspired by the theory of computability. This smooth analogy between induction and deduction faciltates the study of the interaction between formal and empirical methods. For example, it is shown (proposition 7.19) that there is a hypothesis whose predictions are not definable in arithmetic that is nonetheless reliably refutable with certainty by a computer.

Philo: Are you claiming that human inductive capacities are computable?

Learnio: Not at all. Indeed, learning-theoretic analysis shows how hard it would be to settle the question reliably (example 3.5). I am simply saying that computability and induction arise out of parallel limitations (bounded external perception and bounded internal perception). Humans may be capable of insights that transcend computability, for all I know. They may also be capable of occult visions that transcend conventional views about sense perception. I am just saying that the motivations and consequences of such limitations are similar and are naturally studied together.

But regardless of the arcane abilities humans can muster in extraordinary circumstances, methodology deals with methods. Sufficiently explicit and effective methods are algorithms, and Church's thesis states that anything such a method can do, a Turing machine can do, so it is especially natural for a methodologist to look at Turing-computable methods.

Come to think of it, even uncomputable methods are subject to recursion-theoretic analysis. If a method is arithmetically definable, it will have a determinate arithmetical complexity and its abilities will be bounded by that complexity. Computable methods are just the first step in a hierarchy of results. The proof of this complexity-relativized characterization theorem is entirely parallel to the proof in the computable case, so merely maintaining that humans have uncomputable abilities does not allow one to escape from computational considerations in one's methodological analysis.

Philo: You can't make interest in inductive justification go away with just a few flimsy arguments and analogies. But let's move on to another difficulty with the book. The demonic skeptical arguments bothered me. Science isn't a game against a malicious demon. It is an interaction with nature, which isn't trying to fool us. So learning theory might have applications to cryptography, war strategy, or espionage, but not to science.

Learnio: From a learning-theoretic point of view, nature is just the actual world. For all the scientist knows at the outset, the actual world might be any one of many. The demon is merely a technical artifice for proving that there exists no method that finds the truth in each world that might be actual for all the scientist knows. Notice that the demon is a personification of the scientist's *ignorance*, rather than of the *actual system* that the scientist studies. So while I agree that nature is not a demon devoted to fooling us, it is a mistake to conclude that demonic arguments are irrelevant to science.

Philo: I have another problem with your demonic arguments. The Bayesians can show that updating by conditionalization almost surely converges to the truth. So how can the demonic arguments be sound?

Learnio: That is because "almost surely" means "with probability 1." Learning-theoretic results require success in every possible circumstance consistent with the scientist's background knowledge, whereas measure 1 results countenance failure on a set of data streams of measure 0.

Philo: Aha! You concede that Bayesian updating is guaranteed to succeed with probability 1?

Learnio: One can show that conditioning is guaranteed to gradually decide each Borel hypothesis over some set of data streams of measure 1 under the initial, joint measure with which the Bayesian starts out, assuming countable additivity.

Philo: Well there you go. If you just adopt a modern notion of reliability, all inductive problems are solvable. So who cares about these worst-case demons and goblins of a bygone era that the book goes on and on about?

Learnio: It is shown (propositions 13.18 and 13.20) that the almost sure convergence theorem for conditionalization can fail without countable additivity, an assumption that is simply false on the frequentist interpretation and that is rejected as a general axiom by some prominent personalists. Once the blanket, almost-sure convergence theorem fails, demonic arguments can also have significance for probabilistic reliability (e.g., proposition 13.18). Until countable additivity finds a philosophical home, perhaps we should not be too dogmatic about consequences that depend on it.

Philo: Well, I hear that probability theory gets pretty strange when you drop countable additivity. But leaving that aside, nothing prevents a Bayesian from starting out with a countably additive measure, and those Bayesians are all covered by the measure 1 convergence theorem. So why should *they* care about demons?

Learnio: Other things being equal, more reliability is preferable to less. If probability 1 success can be improved to necessary success, why not improve it? And if it cannot be, why not be aware of that fact?

Philo: Why bother to improve a method, if it succeeds with probability 1?

Learnio: Suppose that there were two methods. One of them succeeds everywhere and the other succeeds with probability 1 and yet fails on an uncountable set of data streams. So far as cardinality is concerned, considerable improvement is possible.

Philo: Can that really happen, or are you just posing hypothetical conditions?

Learnio: There exists a hypothesis *h* that is computably refutable with certainty, but some countably additive probability measure fails to update its prior probability on *h* over an uncountable set of possible data streams (proposition 13.5).

Philo: Oh, I see. Everybody knows that if you put zero prior probability on a hypothesis, conditioning won't necessarily converge to its truth value. You have to require that the measure keep the door open with respect to each hypothesis by placing nonzero prior probability on it.

Learnio: But in the example, the hypothesis is assigned prior probability 1/2 and is never assigned probability zero thereafter unless it is logically refuted by the data.

Philo: Oh really? So the adage that we should leave the door open concerning the hypothesis is not sufficient to guarantee convergence to the truth?

Learnio: Not if "guarantee" means "on all but a countable number of possible data streams".

Philo: Would conditioning according to some other method be guaranteed to lead to the truth?

Learnio: Yes (proposition 13.11). But there is another example (proposition 13.13) of a hypothesis that is computably refutable with certainty such that no arithmetically definable conditioning method can even gradually decide it. So for a highly idealized class of agents, Bayesian updating can be a severe impediment to reliability.

Philo: What is the trick to the example?

Learnio: The example arises from another major theme of the book—the smooth analogy in learning theory between formal and empirical reasoning. The problem with Bayesianism is that it forces a method to notice immediately when a hypothesis is refuted by the data, but the relationship of consistency with the data can be so intractable that it cannot even be defined in arithmetic. The successful, computable method uses future empirical data to help it determine formally whether the current data refutes the hypothesis. Hence, it cannot notice refutation as soon as the refuting data is received. I think this is a nice illustration of how formal and empirical matters meld together in the learning-theoretic approach.

Philo: Well, I have heard of a clever way for Bayesian updaters to avoid putting probability 0 on refuted hypotheses immediately.[2] The idea is to make the Bayesian agent coherent not over the object language of interest, but over a metalanguage involving logical relations among statements in the object language. Then one may place nonzero probability on a hypothesis refuted by the current data as long as one has not yet conditioned on the logical fact that the data refutes the hypothesis.

Learnio: The proposal is intriguing, and the book discusses it or a related one (section 13.6), but there is a major difference between this attenuated Bayesianism and the learning-theoretic perspective. Probabilism is nothing

[2] Garber (1983).

without logical omniscience over some algebra. In the scheme you just described, the algebra over which omniscience must be maintained is the finitary Boolean closure of atomic sentences asserting entailment among quoted strings in an object language. Other proposals are conceivable. In section 13.6, it is proposed that a computationally uncertain Bayesian be omniscient over the set theoretic relations among Borel sets of possible extensions of the Turing normal form predicate.

Learning-theoretic analysis, on the other hand, is free from measure theory and hence need not impose logical ominiscience over *any* algebra of propositions or sets. Every formal task can therefore be spread out through time as new data are read. Every consideration, including deciding logical relations, is subordinated to the overall goal of reliable convergence to the truth.

Philo: Even if I agreed that learning theory has some relevance, I am afraid that its recommendations are irrational. A rational agent is indifferent among acts with identical expected utilities. But acts (choices of methods) that differ in performance on a set of measure zero have identical expected values. Hence a rational agent cannot care about improvements in methods that succeed with probability 1, since those improvements occur in a set of measure 0.

Learnio: First, your argument rides heavily on the assumption that degrees of belief must be real numbers. Real numbers are good enough when the probability space is countable. But on an uncountable space like the Baire space, real numbers are lumpy and leave gaps when one tries to spread them out over a continuous space. In particular, suppose our learning-theoretical preferences extend the weak dominance order with respect to reliability (i.e., α is as preferable as $\beta \Leftrightarrow \alpha$ is as reliable as β). Then it is evident from the "almost sure" convergence theorem that there is no probability measure that represents our preferences with respect to this utility. But if we allow infinitesimal probabilities, the weak dominance ordering can be represented, so it no longer follows that a Bayesian must be indifferent to improvability of methods that succeed with probability 1.[3]

Philo: This reminds me of another objection to learning theory that I have read recently. Granted that reliability is a relevant methodological desideratum, it is not sufficient. We need guidance about what to believe in the here and now, and limiting reliability does not provide it. Something like Bayesian updating still seems to be required,[4] whether it is reliable or not.

Learnio: All the methods studied by learning theory provide just that sort of guidance to their users. They determine conjectures for each finite data sequence you might observe.

Philo: But learning theory doesn't tell you which such method to use. A method correct in the limit can conjecture any nonsense in the short run.

Learnio: I think you will find that nonsense is constrained if we also insist on data-minimality (chapter 4). And when it comes to data-minimal methods, I am indeed tempted to say that any further restrictions on conjectures

---

[3] Fishburn (1974), De Finetti (1990).
[4] Earman (1992).

in the short run are epistemologically arbitrary. When no data-minimal method exists, we do not cast good sense to the winds either. Rather, more good sense and effort lead to less time to convergence.

Philo: It is still foolish to favor a conjecture that is unjustified by the data when some other hypothesis is justified. I don't see how data-minimality can prevent that from happening.

Learnio: Now it is clear that your notion of justification contributes nothing to reliably finding the truth as soon as possible, since you appeal to it to discriminate among data-minimal, reliable methods. It is precisely that notion of epistemic justification that I find dubious. Perhaps we can at least agree that it is a good idea to know when "justification" helps, hinders, or is irrelevant to reliability.

Philo: Here is another objection. Learning theory seems to apply only to theories that make determinate claims about the character of the data stream. In practice, however, even a deterministic theory must be augmented with a model of measurement error, so it entails only a probability distribution over possible measurements. I don't see how to apply learning-theoretic analysis in such cases.

Learnio: One possible response is to translate the probabilities into claims about limiting relative frequencies. Then a probabilistic hypothesis determines a subset of the data stream space and can be subjected to learning-theoretic analysis (cf. chapter 3). Indeed, conflicting probability claims then have non-overlapping empirical contents, so that they are not globally underdetermined.

Philo: Isn't that unrealistic? Limiting relative frequencies do not satisfy countable additivity, the strong law of large numbers, or the law of the iterated logarithm. How do you expect statisticians to get along without such helpful theorems?

Learnio: The book does not claim, as far as I recall, to make life easier for statisticians. There are a few suggestive results in the book, such as that limiting relative frequencies are refutable in the limit given that they exist (proposition 3.9), but are only gradually verifiable given no background knowledge (propositions 3.7, 3.8, and 3.14) and that unbiased statistical testability is equivalent to limiting verifiability or refutability, depending on the topology of the rejection zone (proposition 3.11). But a great deal of work would be required to develop a comprehensive, learning-theoretic statistics. In particular, no analysis of background knowledge entailing randomness is provided in the book—a question of the utmost importance to such a project.

Philo: Who takes frequentism seriously any more? I am a personalist.

Learnio: Then all probabilistic hypotheses are propositions about someone's degrees of belief, and according to a standard account, a degree of belief can be gradually identified (when it exists) by offering the subject a sequence of bets whose odds narrow in on it. Some personalists may disagree with some of the assumptions behind this procedure, but whether or not the identification of degrees of belief is possible or impossible, it is subject to learning-theoretic analysis precisely because personalism, like frequentism, provides an empiricist reduction of the concept of probability.

Philo: Oh, I should have mentioned. When probabilities are postulated by a scientific theory, it is silly to suppose that the theory is talking about anyone's degrees of belief. The postulated probabilities are propensities, which are in the world, but which do not entail limiting relative frequencies of outcomes in repeated trials. So what can learning theory say about propensities?

Learnio: Learning theoretic analysis does not apply until one has a good idea about what a hypothesis logically entails about the nature of the data stream. Frequentism and personalism are both quite explicit in this regard, so I told you how the learning-theoretic analysis would go. But propensity statements allegedly entail no constraints on the data stream for eternity, so learning-theoretic analysis says only that they are globally underdetermined and thus are inaccessible to reliable empirical inquiry.

Philo: Isn't that a *reductio ad absurdum* of learning theory? Scientists discover facts about propensities as a matter of course.

Learnio: Scientists draw conclusions about probabilities. It is only your contention that those probabilities are propensities. But granting that, how do scientists investigate propensities?

Philo: Well, if a hypothesis says that an observation has a high propensity and then it does not occur, the hypothesis is disconfirmed.

Learnio: By disconfirmation, do you mean that your degree of belief in the hypothesis goes down, conditional on such evidence?

Philo: Something like that.

Learnio: But your personal degree of belief in the observation given the hypothesis is entirely up to you. I don't see how personal coherence would be violated if your degree of belief in the observation given the hypothesis were to deviate from the propensity postulated by the hypothesis.

Philo: Oh, you have forgotten the *direct inference principle*: if you know the physical probability, quite naturally, you adjust your degree of belief to agree with it. That's the easy side of statistical inference. The controversial part is *inverse inference*, or finding the probability of a propensity hypothesis given an observation.

Learnio: I disagree. From the learning-theoretic perspective, the deeper mystery is posed by the direct inference principle. That is precisely because to prove it, one would have to know something about the empirical significance of propensities. But instead of proving the principle, the propensity theorist uses it. The direct inference principle is what permits the propensity theorist to speak of confirming and disconfirming propensities without ever saying what propensities entail about what will happen. Without it, there could be a complete disagreement as to whether a given observation confirms or disconfirms a given propensity hypothesis, and the learning theorist's conclusion that propensities lie beyond the scope of inquiry starts to look pretty intuitive.

Philo: Do you realize what you are saying? Just for the sake of a fictive idealization of induction, you are calling the entire edifice of theoretical physics into question! If you are so smart, find a theory better than quantum mechanics.

Learnio: What I question is your philosophical reconstruction of the physicist's reasoning via propensities. The propensity view's apparent advantage over learning-theoretic analysis is that it underwrites short-run, objective confirmation levels for globally underdetermined hypotheses concerning hidden realities. That is just what the scientific realist wants to say we can have. But this realist advantage is bought at a steep methodological price: namely, adherence to an arbitrary axiom that ensures we behave in concert as though propensities had some empirical or practical significance, even though it is left entirely unspecified what this significance might be. Frequentism and personalism, in contrast, require no such arbitrary axiom, because they carefully specify logical relations between probabilistic hypotheses and the data stream. Learning theory is not wedded to either of these proposals. Maybe some better account is waiting to be found. But learning theory does demand that hypotheses, probabilistic or otherwise, entail some logical constraint on the form of the infinite data stream if reliable inference is to be possible.

Philo: It would be nice if the learning theorists had any real statistical results to report so that one could see how much would be lost in the rigid sort of frequentism you are proposing to replace the standard, propensity view with.

But I am growing weary of all this technicality. Here is a genuinely philosophical concern. Learning theory draws a sharp distinction between background knowledge and conjectures. Background knowledge is unquestioned and unalterable, whereas conjectures fluctuate through time. But isn't the role of the scientist to modify our knowledge? What is the point of doing science if your conclusions are never taken seriously in the way that your initial assumptions are?

Learnio: Augmenting the initial knowledge base presents no special problems. Suppose that γ is a discovery method. Add the theory conjectured by γ at a given stage to the knowledge operative at that stage. If γ is reliable with respect to the original knowledge, γ will remain reliable with respect to the augmented knowledge.

Philo: But now I don't see why we should stick with γ through all the stages. Suppose γ conjectures a complete theory h at stage n. Thereafter, the method that repeats h forever, regardless of the data, is reliable relative to the knowledge operative at each later stage (namely, h). And no doubt, this fixed method is much easier to compute than γ is.

Learnio: It seems you have discovered that science is quite easy, after all. Why needlessly delay having the complete truth? Just conjecture h from the beginning.

Philo: But what if h is refuted by the data?

Learnio: Then on your proposal a contradiction is *known*, assuming that the data are also known, so background knowledge entails that every method is reliable and hence that the method that always conjectures h is. But if we now insist that background knowledge be consistent, it suffices for reliability to always extend the current data to a maximally consistent theory at each stage of inquiry. That is still pretty easy, as long as we are talking about ideal methods that can decide the consistency problem. I'm glad you taught me to take conjectures as seriously as background knowledge, or I might have missed this elegant solution to the problem of induction.

Philo: You are sneering, but I recall that Isaac Levi (1983) has an ingenious response to that sort of objection. William James taught us that seeking truth and avoiding error are two competing aims. Either can be trivially satisifed alone, but the right balance between the two is a matter of taste. Suppose that our tastes regarding truth and error are clearly specified as a utility function and that we have personal degrees of belief. The scientist adds to background knowledge that hypothesis whose belief maximizes expected utility (with respect to the given utilities and probabilities). Now recall the ridiculous conclusion that it is reliable to add an arbitrary, complete theory to background knowledge on the basis of little or no data. Given any sort of sensible utilities and probabilities, the complete theory will have too great a risk of error to warrant the decision to believe. On the other side, one's interest in finding more truth can outweigh one's concern to avoid error, so that it can still be rational to accept a stronger hypothesis rather than a weaker one, to the chagrin of the skeptic.

Learnio: That is interesting, but I don't understand how there can be any risk of error in adding a hypothesis to background knowledge on the view you have proposed. Once a conclusion is added, there is no serious possibility that it is false. So knowing this, how can we run the risk of adding a false hypothesis to our background knowledge? If King Midas knows that whatever he touches turns to gold, does he run any risk of touching what is not gold?

Philo: He doesn't risk touching iron while he *touches* it. But he runs the risk of touching what is iron while he *decides* to touch it. Similarly, one runs the risk of deciding to add to background knowledge what is false while one is deliberating.

Learnio: So would you also say I made an error when I ordered the roast chicken because the chicken was raw in the kitchen when I decided to order it? Or that I made an error when I decided to arrange to meet you downtown tomorrow morning, even though you were home in bed when I made the decision?

Philo: Of course not. Enough of your sophisms.

Learnio: Then why is it an error to decide to believe what is false when I decide to believe it, even though I know for sure that it will be true when I believe it?

Philo: Maybe we don't know at t that h will be true at $t + 1$ if we accept h at t.

Learnio: Why not? We can't understand in our own case precisely what we have just been assuming must apply to everyone else?

Philo: I can't think of an answer now. But at least Levi takes seriously the idea that science contributes to knowledge.

Learnio: I agree. There are three possible views. According to the first, there is no unquestioned knowledge at all. According to the second, we start out with unquestioned knowledge but continue to question the subsequent conclusions of science. According to the third, we question neither the initial knowledge nor the successive conclusions of science once they are drawn. The first view makes science impossible. The third view makes science trivially easy, despite Levi's heroics. The middle way raises questions about the difference in status between background knowledge and the intermediate conclusions of science, but it does provide a nontrivial backdrop for the investigation of reliability, and for that reason I provisionally swallow its difficulties.

Philo: I prefer to ignore risk of error altogether and simply talk about which beliefs are justified. Strong beliefs are unjustified, but nontrivial beliefs are justified and that is all there is to it. But you prefer to put up with endless difficulties because you insist on proving or second-guessing fundamental principles of inductive inference using deductive logic.

I have many more objections in mind, but we can discuss them some other time. I do have a final objection, though. The results I looked at in the book are all so abstract. People need to see more concrete examples from science or it will never catch on.

Learnio: I agree. Learning theory is an application of the theory of computability, and the parent's features are reflected in the child. The theory of computability is like a wonderful, infinite castle whose walls and hallways have been carefully mapped but whose tenants are still largely a mystery. Similarly, the results in this book provide general conditions for separating solvable from unsolvable inductive problems, but to determine whether the conditions hold of a given problem can be quite difficult. First of all, it can be extremely difficult to find tight bounds on the complexity of a clearly specified, mathematical object. Furthermore, when we move to empirical problems, it is rarely even clear what the background assumptions are or even what the theory implies about the structure of the data stream. So there is a tendency to discover and name new halls and chambers rather than to stop to find out who lives in the familiar ones. Recent work in recursive analysis has shown that the wave equation can have uncomputable solutions.[5] This work suggests a promising avenue for bringing learning-theoretic analysis somewhat closer to real work in physics, and I, for one, would be interested to see some of the results of the book apply to such examples.

But after all of your telling objections, Philo, let's not lose sight of how fruitful the approach is at suggesting novel methodological questions and finding surprising answers to them; answers that correct a number of traditional dogmas in the philosophy of science. For example, reliable testability need not (and sometimes should not) proceed by deriving successive predictions from the theory and checking them against the data. Reliable discovery need not (and sometimes should not) proceed by generating bold conjectures and testing them against the data. Indeed, there are cases in which sequential generation and test is reliable only if the test is not reliable. Discovery is easier rather than harder than assessment and prediction is harder rather than easier than discovery. Uncomputability is not simply relevant to epistemological discussions; it shares the same topological structure with the problem of

---

[5] Pour-el and Richards (1980).

induction. Bayesian updating can significantly impede the reliability of even highly idealized agents. The reliability of Bayesian updating can depend on one's joint distribution even if the probability of the hypothesis never goes to zero unless it is refuted.

In addition, there are structural characterizations of inductive problem solvability for ideal agents, Turing machines, and finite state automata. There are general results about the availability or nonexistence of maximally reliable methods and data-minimal methods. There are rigorous learning-theoretic analyses of limiting relative frequencies and unbiased testability. It is shown that the existence of a demon for each unsolvable problem outruns the resources of classical mathematics. Architectures for discovery, assessment, and prediction are defined and shown to be complete. The signficance of probabilistic convergence is clarified. And it is shown how to extend the approach to causal inference and to cases in which data and truth depend in an arbitrary way on the concepts and beliefs of the scientist. I agree that much more needs to be done, but I think the book has at least shown the approach to be a systematic, powerful, and intriguing perspective on the aims and prospects of scientific inquiry.

References

Addison, J. (1955). "Analogies in the Borel, Lusin, and Kleene Hierarchies," *Bulletin of the American Mathematics Society* 61: 171–172.

Adleman, L., and K. Manders (1977). "Reducibility, Randomness, and Intractability," in *Proceedings of the 9th Annual ACM Symposium on Theory of Computing.* New York: Association for Computing Machinery.

Anderson, J. R. (1976). *Language, Memory, and Thought.* Hillsdale, N.J.: Erlbaum.

Angluin, D. (1978). "On the Complexity of Minimum Inference of Regular Sets," *Information and Control* 39: 337–350.

Angluin, D. (1980). "Inductive Inference of Formal Languages from Positive Data," *Information and Control* 49: 117–135.

Angluin, D. (1981). "A Note on the Number of Queries Needed to Identify Regular Languages," *Information and Control* 51: 76–87.

Angluin, D., and C. Smith (1982). *A Survey of Inductive Inference Methods*, Technical Report 250, New Haven: Yale University.

Aristotle (1941). *The Basic Works of Aristotle*, ed. R. McKeon. New York: Random House.

Ash, R. B. (1972). *Real Analysis and Probability.* New York: Academic Press.

Ayer, A. J. (1958). *Language, Truth and Logic.* New York: Dover.

Barzdin, J. M., and R. V. Freivald (1972). "On the Prediction of General Recursive Functions," *Soviet Math. Dokl.* 12: 1224–1228.

Berkeley, G. (1960). *Berkeley's Philosophical Writings*, ed. D. Armstrong. London: Collier.

Billingsly, P. (1986). *Probability and Measure.* New York: Wiley.

Blum, M., and L. Blum (1975). "Toward a Mathematical Theory of Inductive Inference," *Information and Control* 28: 125–155.

Boolos, G., and R. Jeffrey (1980). *Computability and Logic.* Cambridge: Cambridge University Press.

Bridgman, P. (1936). *The Nature of Physical Theory.* London: Dover.

Brown, R., and C. Hanlon (1970). "Derivational Complexity and the Order of

Acquisition of Child Speech," *Cognition and the Development of Language*, ed. J. Hayes. New York: Wiley.

Büchi, J. (1960). "Weak Second-Order Arithmetic and Finite Automata," *2. Math. Logik Grundlagen Mathematika* 6: 66–92.

Bulmer, M. G. (1979). *Principles of Statistics*. New York: Dover.

Carnap, R. (1950). *The Logical Foundations of Probability*. Chicago: University of Chicago Press.

Carnap, R. (1966). *The Philosophy of Science*. New York: Harper.

Carnap, R. (1974). *Der logische Aufbau der Welt*. Wien: Ullstein.

Case, J., and C. Smith (1983). "Comparison of Identification Criteria for Machine Inductive Inference," *Theoretical Computer Science* 25: 193–220.

Chang, C., and H. Keisler (1973). *Model Theory*. New York: North Holland.

Chomsky, N. (1965). *Aspects of the Theory of Syntax*. Cambridge: MIT Press.

Cutland, N. J. (1986). *Computability: An Introduction to Recursive Function Theory*. Cambridge: Cambridge University Press.

Daley, R. P., and C. H. Smith (1984). "On the Complexity of Inductive Inference." Manuscript presented at the Mathematical Foundations of Computer Science Conference, Prague, Czechoslovakia.

DeFinetti, B. (1972). *Probability, Induction and Statistics*. New York: Wiley.

DeFinetti, B. (1990). *Theory of Probability*, 2 vols. New York: Wiley.

Descartes, R. (1981). *A Discourse on Method, Meditations and Principles*, trans J. Veitch, London: Dent.

Diaconis, P., and D. Freedman (1986). "On the Consistency of Bayes Estimates," *Annals of Statistics* 14: 1–26.

Dreyfus, H. (1979). *What Computers Can't Do*. New York: Harper and Row.

Dummett, M. (1978). *Truth and Other Enigmas*. Oxford: Clarendon Press.

Earman, J. (1972). "Implications of Causal Propagation outside the Null Cone," *Australiasian Journal of Philosophy* 50: 223–237.

Faye, J. (1991). *Niels Bohr: His Heritage and Legacy*. Dordrecht: Kluwer.

Feldman, R. (1985). "Reliability and Justification," *Monist* 68: 159–174.

Feyerabend, P. K. (1979). *Against Method*. London: Verso.

Fishburn, P. C. (1974). "Lexicographic Orders, Utilities and Decision Rules: A Survey," *Management Science* 20: 1442–1471.

Fishburn, P. C. (1981). "Subjective Expected Utility: A Review of Normative Theories," *Theory and Decision* 13: 139–199.

Fishburn, P. C. (1983). "The Axioms of Subjective Probability," *Statistical Science* 1: 335–358.

Foster, D. (1991). "Prediction in the Worst Case," *Annals of Statistics* 19: 1084–1090.

Freund, J. E., and R. E. Walpole (1980). *Mathematical Statistics*. Englewood Cliffs, N.J.: Prentice-Hall.

Gaifman, H., and M. Snir (1982). "Probabilities over Rich Languages, Testing and Randomness," *Journal of Symbolic Logic* 47: 495–548.

Gale, D., and F. Stewart (1953). "Infinite Games of Perfect Information," *Annals of Mathematics Studies* 28: 245–266.

Gandy, R. (1980). "Church's Thesis and Principles for Mechanisms," in *The Kleene Symposium*, ed. J. Barwise, J. J. Keisler, and K. Kunen. Amsterdam: North Holland.

Garber, D. (1983). "Old Evidence and Logical Omniscience in Bayesian Confirmation Theory," in *Testing Scientific Theories: Minnesota Studies in the Philosophy of Science*, vol. 10, ed. J. Earman. Minneapolis: University of Minnesota Press.

Garey, M., and D. Johnson (1979). *Computers and Intractability*. New York: Freeman.

Ginet, C. (1985). "Contra Reliabilism," *Monist* 68: 175–187.

Glymour, C. (1977). "Indistinguishable Space-Times and the Fundamental Group," in *Foundations of Space-Time Theories: Minnesota Studies in the Philosophy of Science*, vol. 8., ed. J. Earman, C. Glymour, and J. Stachel. Minneapolis: University of Minnesota Press.

Glymour, C. (1980). *Theory and Evidence*. Princeton: Princeton University Press.

Glymour, C., R. Scheines, P. Spirtes, and K. Kelly (1987). *Discovering Causal Structure*. New York: Academic Press.

Gold, E. M. (1965). "Limiting Recursion," *Journal of Symbolic Logic* 30: 27–48.

Gold, E. M. (1967). "Language Identification in the Limit," *Information and Control* 10: 447–474.

Gold, E. M. (1978). "Complexity of Automaton Identification from Given Data," *Information and Control* 27: 302–320.

Goldman, A. I. (1986). *Epistemology and Cognition*. Cambridge: Harvard University Press.

Goodman, N. (1983). *Fact, Fiction and Forecast*, 4th ed. Cambridge: Harvard University Press.

Hacking, I. (1965). *Logic of Statistical Inference*. London: Cambridge University Press.

Hàjek, P. (1978). "Experimental Logics and Π_3^0 Theories," *Journal of Symbolic Logic* 42: 515–522.

Halmos, P. R. (1974). *Measure Theory*. New York: Springer.

Hanson, N. R. (1958). *Patterns of Discovery*. Cambridge: Harvard University Press.

Haussler, D. (1989). "Generalizing the PAC Model: Sample Size Bounds from Metric Dimension-based Uniform Convergence Results," in *Proceedings of the 2nd Annual Workshop on Computational Learning Theory*, ed. R. Rivest, D. Haussler, and M. Warmuth. San Mateo, Cal.: Morgan Kaufmann.

Hempel, C. G. (1965). *Aspects of Scientific Explanation*. New York: Macmillan.

Hempel, C. G. (1966). *Philosophy of Natural Science*. New York: Prentice-Hall.

Hilbert, D., and P. Bernays (1934). *Grundlagen der Mathematik*. Berlin: Springer.

Hinman, P. G. (1978). *Recursion-Theoretic Hierarchies*. New York: Springer.

Hopcroft, J., and J. Ullman (1979). *Introduction to Automata Theory, Languages, and Computation*. Reading, Mass.: Addison-Wesley.

Horwich, P. (1990). *Truth*. London: Basil Blackwell.

Howson, C., and P. Urbach (1990). *Scientific Reasoning: The Bayesian Approach*. LaSalle, Ill.: Open Court.

Hume, D. (1984). *An Inquiry Concerning Human Understanding*, ed. C. Hendell. New York: Bobbs-Merrill.

Hyman, A., and J. Walsh (1982). *Philosophy in the Middle Ages*. Indianapolis: Hackett.

James, W. (1948). "The Will to Believe," in *Essays in Pragmatism*, ed. A. Castell. New York: Collier Macmillan.

Juhl, C. (1991). "Topics in the Metatheory of Inductive Methods." Ph.D. thesis, Department of History and Philosophy of Science, University of Pittsburgh.

Kadane, J., M. Schervish, and T. Seidenfeld (1986). "Statistical Implications of Finitely Additive Probability," in *Bayesian Inference and Decision Techniques*, ed. P. Goel and A. Zellner. Amsterdam: Elsevier.

Kant, I. (1950). *Prolegomena to Any Future Metaphysics*, trans. L. Beck. Indianapolis: Bobbs-Merrill.

Kelly, K. (1987). "The Logic of Discovery," *Philosophy of Science* 54: 435–452.

Kelly, K. (1988). "Theory Discovery and the Hypothesis Language," *Proceedings of the 5th International Conference on Machine Learning*, ed. J. Laird. San Mateo, Cal.: Morgan Kaufmann.

Kelly, K. (1989). "Induction from the General to the More General," in *Proceedings of the 2nd Annual Workshop on Computational Learning Theory*, ed. R. Rivest, D. Haussler, and M. Warmuth. San Mateo, Cal.: Morgan Kaufmann.

Kelly, K. (1991). "Reichenbach, Induction, and Discovery," *Erkenntnis* 35: 1–3.

Kelly, K. (1992). "Learning Theory and Descriptive Set Theory," *Logic and Computation* 3: 27–45.

Kelly, K. (1994). "Reliable Methods," in *Logic, Methodology and Philosophy of Science*, vol. 9, ed. D. Prawitz, B. Skyrms, and D. Westerstahl. Amsterdam: Elsevier.

Kelly, K., and C. Glymour (1989). "Convergence to the Truth and Nothing but the Truth," *Philosophy of Science* 56: 185–220.

Kelly, K., and C. Glymour (1990). "Theory Discovery from Data with Mixed Quantifiers," *Journal of Philosophical Logic* 19: 1–33.

Kelly, K., and C. Glymour (1992). "Inductive Inference from Theory-Laden Data," *Journal of Philosophical Logic* 21: 391–444.

Kelly, K., and C. Juhl (1994). "Realism, Convergence, and Additivity," in *Proceedings of the 1994 Biennial Meeting of the Philosophy of Science Association*, ed. D. Hull, M. Forbes, and R. Burian. East Lansing, Mich.: Philosophy of Science Association.

Kelly, K., C. Juhl, and C. Glymour (1994). "Reliability, Realism, and Relativism," in *Reading Putnam*, ed. P. Clark. London: Blackwell.

Kelly, K., and O. Schulte (Forthcoming). "The Computable Testability of Theories with Uncomputable Predictions," *Erkenntnis*.

Kemeny, J. (1953). "The Use of Simplicity in Induction," *Philosophical Review* 62: 391–408.

Kleene, S. (1956). "Representation of Events in Nerve Nets and Finite Automata," In *Automata Studies*, ed. C. Shannon. Princeton: Princeton University Press.

Kolmogorov, A. N. (1956). *Foundations of the Theory of Probability*. New York: Chelsea.

Kugel, P. (1977). "Induction, Pure and Simple," *Information and Control* 33: 276–336.

Kuhn, T. (1970). *The Structure of Scientific Revolutions*. Chicago: University of Chicago Press.

Kunen, K. (1980). *Set Theory: An Introduction to Independence Proofs*. Amsterdam: North Holland.

Kuratowski, K. (1966). *Topology*, vol. 1. New York: Academic Press.

Laudan, L. (1980). "Why Abandon the Logic of Discovery?" in *Scientific Discovery, Logic, and Rationality*, ed. T. Nickles. Boston: D. Reidel.

Lauth, B. (1993). "Inductive Inference in the Limit for First-Order Sentences," *Studia Logica* 52: 491–517.

Levi, I. (1967). *Gambling with Truth*. Cambridge: MIT Press.

Levi, I. (1983). *The Enterprise of Knowledge*. Cambridge: MIT Press.

Levi, I. (1990). "Rationality Unbound," in *Acting and Reflecting*, ed. W. Sieg. Dordrecht: Kluwer.

Lewis, D. (1973). *Counterfactuals*. Cambridge: Harvard University Press.

Lewis, D. (1981). "A Subjectivist's Guide to Objective Chance." in *Studies in Inductive Logic and Probability*, ed. R. Jeffrey. Berkeley: University of California Press.

Littlewood, J. E. (1944). *Lectures on the Theory of Functions*. Oxford: Oxford University Press.

Lucas, J. R. (1961). "Minds, Machines, and Gödel," *Philosophy* 36: 120–124.

Lycan, W. (1988). *Judgement and Justification.* New York: Cambridge University Press.

Mackie, J. (1974). *The Cement of the Universe.* New York: Oxford University Press.

Malament, D. (1977). "Observationally Indistinguishable Spacetimes," in *Foundations of Space-Time Theories: Minnesota Studies in the Philosophy of Science,* vol. 8, ed. J. Earman, C. Glymour, and J. Stachel. Minneapolis: University of Minnesota Press.

Martin, D. A. (1975). "Borel Determinacy," *Annals of Mathematics* 102: 364–371.

McNaughton, R. (1966). "Testing and Generating Infinite Sequences by a Finite Automaton," *Information and Control* 9: 521–530.

Moschavakis, Y. (1980). *Descriptive Set Theory.* Amsterdam: North Holland.

Newall, A. and H. Simon (1976). "Computer Science as Empirical Inquiry: Symbols and Search," *Communications of the ACM* 19: 113–126.

Neyman, J., and E. Pearson (1933). "On the Problem of the Most Efficient Tests of Statistical Hypotheses," *Philosophical Transactions of the Royal Society* 231A: 289–337.

Nozick, R. (1981). *Philosophical Explanations.* Cambridge: Harvard University Press.

Oakes, M. (1986). *Statistical Inference: A Commentary for the Social and Behavioral Sciences.* New York: Wiley.

Osherson, D., M. Stob, and S. Weinstein (1986). *Systems That Learn.* Cambridge: MIT Press.

Osherson, D., and S. Weinstein (1986). "Identification of the Limit of First Order Structures," *Journal of Philosophical Logic* 15: 55–81.

Osherson, D., and S. Weinstein (1988). "Mechanical Learners Pay a Price for Bayesianism," *Journal of Symbolic Logic* 53: 1245–1252.

Osherson, D., and S. Weinstein (1989). "Paradigms of Truth Detection," *Journal of Philosophical Logic* 18: 1–41.

Osherson, D., and S. Weinstein (1991). "A Universal Inductive Inference Machine," *Journal of Symbolic Logic* 56: 661–672.

Peirce, C. S. (1958). *Charles S. Peirce: Selected Writings,* ed. P. Wiener. New York: Dover.

Penrose, R. (1989). *The Emperor's New Mind.* New York: Oxford University Press.

Plato (1931). *Theaetetus, in The Works of Plato,* ed. I. Edman. New York: Tudor.

Plato (1949). *Meno,* trans. B. Jowett. Indianapolis: Bobbs-Merrill.

Popper, K. (1968). *The Logic of Scientific Discovery.* New York: Harper.

Pour-el, M., and J. Richards (1980). *Computability in Analysis and Physics.* New York: Springer.

Putnam, H. (1963). "'Degree of Confirmation' and Inductive Logic," In *The Philosophy of Rudolph Carnap,* ed. A. Schilpp. LaSalle, Ill.: Open Court.

Putnam, H. (1965). "Trial and Error Predicates and a Solution to a Problem of Mostowski," *Journal of Symbolic Logic* 30: 49–57.

Putnam, H. (1978). *Meaning and the Moral Sciences.* London: Routledge and Kegan Paul.

Putnam, H. (1983). "Reference and Truth," in *Realism and Reason.* Cambridge: Cambridge University Press.

Putnam, H. (1990). *Reason, Truth and History.* Cambridge: Cambridge University Press.

Quine, W. (1951). "Two Dogmas of Empiricism," *Philosophical Review* 60: 20–43.

Quine, W. (1960). *Word and Object.* Cambridge: MIT Press.

Quine, W. (1990). *Pursuit of Truth.* Cambridge: Harvard University Press.

Reichenbach, H. (1938). *Experience and Prediction.* Chicago: University of Chicago Press.

Reichenbach, H. (1949). *The Theory of Probability.* London: Cambridge University Press.

Reichenbach, H. (1956). *The Rise of Scientific Philosophy*. Berkeley: University of California Press.

Rogers, H. (1987). *The Theory of Recursive Functions and Effective Computability*. Cambridge: MIT Press.

Rorty, R. (1979). *Philosophy and the Mirror of Nature*. Cambridge: Princeton University Press.

Royden, H. L. (1988). *Real Analysis*. New York: Macmillan.

Rubin, D. (1978). "Bayesian Inference for Causal Effects: The Role of Randomizations," *Annals of Statistics* 6: 34–58.

Russell, B. (1972). *Our Knowledge of the External World*. London: Unwin.

Salmon, W. (1967). *The Foundations of Scientific Inference*. Pittsburgh: University of Pittsburgh Press.

Savage, L. (1967). "Implications of Personal Probability for Induction," *Journal of Philosophy* 44: 593–607.

Savage, L. (1972). *The Foundations of Statistics*. New York: Dover.

Schervish, M., T. Seidenfeld, and J. Kadane (1984). "The Extent of Non-Conglomerability of Finitely Additive Probabilities," *Zeitschrift für Wahrscheinlichkeitstheorie und verwandte Gebiete* 66: 206–226.

Schervish, M., T. Seidenfeld, and J. Kadane (1990). "An Approach to Consensus and Certainty with Increasing Evidence," *Journal of Statistical Planning and Inference* 25: 401–414.

Schlick, M. (1936). "Meaning and Verification," *Philosophical Review* 45: 339–369.

Seidenfeld, T. (1988). "Decision Theory without 'Independence' or without 'Ordering,'" *Economics and Philosophy* 4: 267–290.

Sextus Empiricus (1985). *Selections from the Major Writings on Scepticism, Man and God*, ed. P. Hallie, trans. S. Etheridge. Indianapolis: Hackett.

Shapiro, E. (1981). *Inductive Inference of Theories from Facts*, Report YLU 192. New Haven: Department of Computer Science, Yale University.

Sieg, W. (1994). "Mechanical Procedures and Mathematical Experience," in *Mathematics and Mind*, ed. A. George. Oxford: Oxford University Press.

Simon, H. (1953). "Causal Ordering and Identifiability," in *Studies in Econometric Methods*, ed. W. Hood. New York: Wiley.

Simon, H. (1973). "Does Scientific Discovery Have a Logic?" *Philosophy of Science* 40: 471–480.

Solovay, R., and V. Strassen (1977). "A Fast Monte Carlo Test for Primality," *SIAM Journal of Computation* 6: 84–85.

Spirtes, P., C. Glymour, and R. Scheines (1993). *Causality, Search and Statistics*. New York: Springer.

Stalnaker, R. (1968). "A Theory of Conditionals," in *Studies in Logical Theory*, ed. N. Rescher. Oxford: Blackwell.

Turing, A. (1936). "On Computable Numbers, with an Application to the Entscheidungsproblem," *London Mathematics Society* 42: 230–265.

Van Fraassen, B. (1980). *The Scientific Image*. Oxford: Clarendon Press.

Van Lambalgen, M. (1987). "Random Sequences." Ph.D. thesis, University of Amsterdam.

Vision, G. (1987). *Modern Anti-Realism and Manufactured Truth*. London: Routledge.

Von Mises, R. (1981). *Probability, Statistics, and Truth*. New York: Dover.

Winston, P. H. (1975). *The Psychology of Computer Vision*. New York: McGraw-Hill.

Index

Abstraction, 269, 411. *See also*
    Idealization
Acceptance
    by finite state automata. *See* Finite
      state automata
    of a hypothesis, 61
Actions, 12–41, 40, 347
Addison, J., 89
Additivity. *See also* Probability
    countable, 8, 10, 33, 304, 317, 321–30,
      337, 404, 407
      bias imposed by, 321–27
    finite, 303, 327–30
Admissibility, 98
Agents. *See also* Methods; Scientist
    arithmetically definable, 316
    cognitive powers of, 13
    computable, 6, 116, 183–86, 186
    ideal, 6, 116, 138, 158–60, 183–86
Agreement, interpersonal, 4, 31, 380–85,
    400
Algebra, 338
Algorithm, 4
    random, 330
Analytic, 19, 381
Approach, 29, 66
Approximation
    degrees of, 66, 241
Approximation theorem, 319
Architectures
    bumping pointer. *See* Bumping pointer
      architecture
    complete, 3, 5, 36

for almost stable identification,
    238–40
for decision by n, 84
for decision with n mind changes,
    106, 110–11
for extrapolation, 262, 264
for gradual identification. *See*
    Nested pointer architecture
for gradual verification, 113–15
for identification in the limit. *See*
    Bumping pointer architecture
for nonuniform theory identification,
    296
for uniform theory identification,
    294
for verification with certainty, 85–86
for verification in the limit, 171–72,
    200–202
conjectures and refutations. *See*
    Conjectures and refutations
consecutive ones. *See* Consecutive ones
    architecture
data-minimal
    for decision in the limit, 99–100
    for verification in the limit, 100–102
of discovery, 5, 7, 101, 217. *See also*
    Enumerate and test architecture;
    Nested pointer architecture; Quasi
    enumerate and test architecture
Aristotle, 7, 296, 347, 366n
Arithmetical hierarchy theorem, 167.
    See also Hierarchies, arithmetical
Arithmetical indexing theorem,

419

Index of Symbols

Listed in order of appearance